IN GOOD TIMES PREPARE FOR CRISIS

In
GOOD TIMES
PREPARE
for
CRISIS

—

*From the Great Depression to
the Great Recession:
Sovereign Debt Crises
and Their Resolution*

IRA W. LIEBERMAN

BROOKINGS INSTITUTION PRESS
Washington, D.C.

The Brookings Institution is a private nonprofit organization devoted to research, education, and publication on important issues of domestic and foreign policy. Its principal purpose is to bring the highest quality independent research and analysis to bear on current and emerging policy problems. Interpretations or conclusions in Brookings publications should be understood to be solely those of the authors.

Library of Congress Cataloging-in-Publication data are available.

ISBN 978-0-8157-3534-2 (pbk. : alk. paper)
ISBN 978-0-8157-3546-5 (ebook)

9 8 7 6 5 4 3 2 1

Typeset in Granjon and Avenir Next

Composition by Westchester Publishing Services

To my wife, Phyllis
my children, Aaron, Jessica, and Michael
and my grandchildren, Maggie, Ethan, and Jared

Contents

Part III

Globalization, Financial Sector Liberalization, and Emerging Market Crises, 1990–2005

Part IV

The Great Recession and Crises in the Advanced Economies, 2007–15

Acknowledgments

This book began a long time ago as part of a doctoral (D. Phil.) thesis at Oxford University, an institution I attended from 1982 to 1985. The 1980s sovereign debt crisis was in full bloom, and I decided to explore the history of sovereign debt crises from both an economic and an international relations perspective, beginning with the British export of capital to the periphery after London became the financial capital of the world in 1815 as a result of the Napoleonic Wars. The four chapters in my thesis on the nineteenth-century export of capital, sovereign defaults, and the renegotiation and resolution of debt service disruption have now been encapsulated into one chapter that provides the background for the rest of the book. Other sections of the thesis on sovereign debt crises during the Great Depression in the interwar period (1919–37) and after World War II, in particular the sovereign debt crises of the 1980s, constitute the core of Parts I and II of this book.

During my two stints at the World Bank, from 1985 to 1987 and again from 1992 to 2004, I had the opportunity to work during or in the aftermath of crises. In studying the 1985–87 crisis in Mexico, I focused on crisis recovery, while during and after the East Asian crises I examined the effects on the economy in Korea in 1998–2001, in Turkey in 2001–02, and in Argentina 2002. My experience observing these crises on the ground during the "fog of war," leading teams to devise a recovery strategy for the industry sector in Mexico, to design and implement the restructuring of corporate debt between distressed companies and their banks in Korea and Turkey, and simply to evaluate the depth of the crisis in Argentina, recognizing that little could be done as governments failed in rapid succession, contributed to Part III of this book.

Finally, brief stints advising the IMF and the "Troika"—the IMF, the European Commission, and the European Central Bank—in Portugal in 2013 and 2014 and in Spain in 2015 as corporations renegotiated debt to meet the crisis gave me some sense of the depth and complexity of the eurozone crisis.

It has taken much time and effort to integrate these diverse experiences into an account that seeks to provide a coherent story about debt crises and their resolution. I have found the journey fascinating and hope the reader will come away from the book with a greater understanding of this important aspect of finance and globalization in developing countries.

During the course of working on crises and subsequently writing this book, I have had a great deal of support, which I acknowledge with gratitude: Hedley Bull and Loukas Tsoukalis as my thesis advisers at Oxford University; Magdi Iskander, Hoon Mok Chung, Zia Quereshi, Bill Mako, and Eunok Lee during my work on Korea and East Asia; Paul Siegelbaum, Kemal Derviş, Ajay Chibber, Zekeriya Yildrim, and Mario Gobbo on Turkey; Cesare Calari for his guidance; and Jose Ruisanchez and Faustino Garza for their insights and collaboration on Argentina. Through the U.S. Treasury I was introduced to George Soros, who was advising the first democratically elected president of Korea, Kim Dae Jung, on the crisis. Soros also became my adviser during the Korean crisis, and I later went to work for him as his senior economic adviser. I am thankful to him for his sage advice on the Korean crisis and his support during the time I worked for him.

My son, Michael Lieberman, worked with me throughout in preparing the tables and figures, which form an integral part of the book. I am deeply grateful for his excellent work and constant support. Alana Heath worked with me throughout as my research associate and manuscript guru. She worked hard and with dedication; my deep thanks to her as well. J. D. Mack was available from the start to assist on a variety of IT issues. He has always provided outstanding support, and I extend my sincere thanks to him.

A number of people agreed to be readers during various draft stages of the manuscript. For their time, helpful comments, and insights I thank Iris and Mike Lav, Aaron Lieberman, Bill Mako, and Jose Ruisanchez. Of course, any errors in the work are mine.

Bruce Ross-Larson, my previous editor at the World Bank, was of great assistance in structuring the book, suggesting how to reduce it in size and scope so that it would be more readable. I thank Bruce for his knowledgeable input and the time he afforded me.

The editorial team, led by Angela Piliouras of Westchester Publishing Services, did an outstanding job in editing the manuscript and also in catching my mistakes. It was a pleasure to work with them throughout the editing process. My deepest thanks to them. Again, any mistakes are mine.

I also thank the team at Brookings Institution Press, led by Bill Finan, Janet Walker, Marjorie Pannell, and Elliott Beard, for providing their input and expertise in reviewing the book, making helpful and insightful suggestions, and getting the book ready for publication. I cannot thank them sufficiently.

My most important thanks go to my wife, Phyllis, who patiently watched me craft this book over many years, beginning from its early incarnation as a doctoral thesis, with full support, encouragement, and love; to my children, Aaron, Jessica, and Michael; and to my grandchildren, Maggie, Ethan, and Jared, all of whom provided support and love. I cherish you all.

Ira W. Lieberman

Introduction

International relations theorists use a Latin phrase—*si vis pacem, para bellum*, or, in peace prepare for war. I would borrow from that and say, in good economic times prepare for crisis. Economic crises are frequent and costly both in financial terms and in the pain they inflict on the population of countries undergoing the crises.

Charles P. Kindleberger, an economic historian known for his work on the Great Depression and financial crises more broadly, wrote, "Speculative excess, referred to concisely as a mania, and revulsion from such excess in the form of a crisis or crash, or panic can be shown to be, if not inevitable, at least historically common."[1]

A more recent book examining 800 years of economic crises, *This Time Is Different: Eight Centuries of Financial Folly*, by Kenneth Rogoff and Carmen Reinhart, notes that the lack of memory or understanding of prior crises leads policymakers to ignore the signs of a bubble or impending crisis.[2] I would emphasize the words *crisis of confidence* and add to that *contagion* as a crisis moves from country to country, often based on psychological issues, such as a loss of confidence. Once it has started, a crisis has the tendency to move to other countries in a region, as foreign investors quickly withdraw funds from the local market in what is known as a flight to quality or safety. In the East Asia crisis, which began in 1997 in Thailand, the crisis quickly moved from country to country in the region and adversely affected Korea, Indonesia, and Malaysia. In the recent crisis that began in 2007, with its epicenter in the United States, there was a flight to quality to German *bunds* (bonds) and Swiss francs in Europe, and even to the U.S. dollar, despite America's economic problems and large public debt.

Sovereign debt burdens, beyond what is prudent, take away a country's ability to act to prevent a crisis or during a crisis to resolve the crisis. My own analysis and conclusion in this book, and of Rogoff and Reinhart in *This Time Is Different*, is that the impact or effects of a financial or sovereign debt crisis can be felt for an extended period of time and manifest themselves, among other ways, in a debt overhang that, if not resolved in one crisis, weighs in during a subsequent crisis. I observed this in 1994 and again in 2001 while working for the World Bank in Turkey, initially on privatization and then during the 2001–02 financial crisis. Turkey experienced a series of crises—in 1994, 1999 (largely due to two massive earthquakes), 2000, and 2001. During the previous crises policymakers failed to resolve Turkey's core economic issues and left the economy vulnerable to the major crisis that struck in 2001.

Major Issues

This book examines the incidence of crisis leading to debt service disruption, to crisis resolution, and to the restructuring of external sovereign debt with a view to answering some key questions:

- What are the causes of debt service disruption, and how do debtors reach the point where their only apparent alternative is to break contractual service on their external debts and default?[3]

- What have been the responses of creditors and debtors to the problems associated with debt service disruption?

- Have they developed generally accepted practices for restructuring debt?

- Are these practices effective?

The inability of debtors to resolve their problems of overindebtedness has persisted over time, such as (i) throughout the nineteenth century, with the long-running defaults of the new republics in Latin America and Greece; (ii) in the interwar years, marked by defaults during the Great Depression from 1931 to 1933 and the attempt to resolve war debts, reparations, and debts of succession; (iii) in the early 1980s, when a few socialist economies such as Poland and Yugoslavia and many developing and emerging market countries were forced to default on their syndicated bank loans. Owing to the initial defaults on syndicated bank loans in the early 1980s, when bankers' committees were reluctant to agree to long-term rescheduling or restructuring on concessionary terms, or to provide fresh funds, debtors and creditors engaged in repeated debt restructurings throughout the 1980s and early 1990s under the Baker and Brady Plans. The bank creditor committees focused on the major cases of Mexico, Argentina, and Brazil, but most of the countries in Latin America were forced to restructure their loans, as well as many African countries and others such as Morocco and the Philippines; (iv) during the emerging market crises of the mid-1990s to early 2000s, when important emerging market countries and one major transition country experienced crisis—Mexico (1994), East Asia (1997), Russia (1998), Turkey (2001), and Argentina (2001). Argentina, perhaps the prime example of a defaulting debtor, went into crisis in 2001 and defaulted in 2003; it reached one settlement of its debts in 2004 at great cost to the bondholder (the creditors), another in 2010, and a final settlement with holdout bondholders in 2016; and (v) during the eurozone crisis (beginning in 2009), when Greece, Portugal, Ireland, and Cyprus required bailouts, and Spain required a large loan to provide liquidity to its banks in difficulty. Greece required three bailouts from 2010 to 2015 with no resolution of Greece's debt problems currently in sight.

These cases raise three primary issues to consider with respect to sovereign debts—the capacity to pay, the willingness to pay, and the role of an international lender of last resort. The issue of the capacity to pay or the ability to service sovereign debts is at the heart of all negotiations over sovereign loans. It is a very complex issue involving the projection of a future stream of revenues over an extended time horizon and the ability to project a fiscal surplus for the entire economy. In the case of external sovereign debt there is also the need to generate surplus foreign exchange to pay back foreign creditors. Witness the constant recalibration of the Greek "bailout" package by the so-called Troika—the European Central Bank (ECB), the European Commission (EC), and the International Monetary Fund (IMF).[4] Capacity goes beyond financial capacity; it also implies institutional and technical capacity to address a crisis, which some governments have had—the United States, the United Kingdom, and Korea are examples—and others such as Greece and Argentina lacked at the time of their most recent crises. Surprisingly, the eurozone lacked any institutional mechanism to address its members' crises starting in 2009. The eurozone countries were, in fact, slow to adopt necessary crisis measures, relying instead on policy measures focused on austerity, which only deepened the crisis in some member countries.

Not all of the crises discussed in this book were external sovereign debt crises. Several of the emerging market crises in the 1990s and early 2000s started as currency crises and morphed into financial crises; and most countries, with the exception of Argentina, were not in danger of defaulting on their sovereign debt. Yet most of them required external financial and technical assistance from the IMF, World Bank, and regional development banks, supported by the Group of 7 (G-7) as necessary to resolve their crises.

Because most developing, emerging market, and transition countries lack robust capital markets, they and their private sector banks and corporations have been forced to borrow from external capital markets such as London or New York or from major money center banks, in foreign currency.[5] The euro is unique in this respect since the member countries in the eurozone cannot affect monetary policy; the euro operates like a foreign currency for each of the eurozone countries, presenting a significant issue for debt resolution by Greece, Portugal, Ireland, and Cyprus, which needed to be bailed out. The euro also presented a problem for the major banks in the region, which held significant amounts of member countries' eurobonds, without adequate reserves, because they assumed that eurozone countries could not or would not be allowed to default.

A second primary issue, the will to pay, goes to two concepts governing all loans to sovereign states—the sanctity of contracts, *pacta sunt servanda*, the basis of all contract law; and the vital interest of states, *clausula rebus sic stantibus,* under changing conditions. In cases where states see debts as threatening their existence, there is a strong tendency for them to default. This is especially true when the possibility of new loans no longer exists or when the debt service on existing loans exceeds the revenue from new loans.

A third primary issue is the necessary role of a lender of last resort in a crisis. Walter Bagehot first identified this issue in the nineteenth century with respect to the role of the Bank of England.[6] Kindleberger wrote with respect to the Great Depression, "I reached the conclusion that the 1929 depression was so wide, so deep, and so prolonged because there was no lender of last resort."[7] Looking at historical crises and at the link to the present crises, I draw on Kindleberger again. In his classic work on crises, *Manias, Panics, and Crashes*, he wrote:

> The issues to be probed are several. Are markets so rational that manias— irrational by definition—cannot occur? If, on the other hand, such manias do occur, should they be allowed to run their course without government or other authoritative interference? Or, is there a salutary role to be played by a "lender of last resort," who comes to the rescue and provides the public good of stability that the private market is unable to produce for itself? And if the services of a lender of last resort are provided nationally by a government or

such official institutions as a central bank, what agency or agencies can furnish stability to the international system, for which no government exists?[8]

This was one of the critical issues in the recent crises in the advanced economies—the role of the U.S. Federal Reserve Bank (the Fed), the European Central Bank, and the Japanese Central Bank, serving primarily as national lenders of last resort.[9] The multilateral financial institutions, primarily the IMF, supported by the World Bank, regional development banks, and the G-7 as appropriate, have served de facto if not de jure as international lenders of last resort for developing, emerging market, and transition countries.

The active interventionist role as a lender of last resort by the Fed with the U.S. Treasury and the Federal Deposit Insurance Corporation (FDIC) in the financial/economic crisis that began in the United States in 2007 was widely debated by policymakers.[10] This issue has been even more widely debated within Europe, with the German government and the Bundesbank (the German central bank) against allowing the European Central Bank to play the role of lender of last resort in the eurozone crisis. The charter of the ECB prohibited it from participating in bailouts and purchasing sovereign bonds directly. With a change in ECB governors at the end of 2011 and the arrival of Mario Draghi as governor, promising to do whatever he had to do to stem the crisis, the ECB became the de facto lender of last resort to the European banking system, but not directly to eurozone countries; however, the ECB was able to mitigate the threat of a liquidity crisis.

The IMF played a role in each of the four bailouts in the eurozone—Greece, Ireland, Portugal, and Cyprus—as part of the troika together with the European Commission and the European Central Bank.

Debt Crises in Perspective

The debt crisis—2007–09 in the United States and 2009–15 in the eurozone—has been viewed by most analysts and participating institutions such as the commercial banks as sui generis, arising from a confluence of unique economic circumstances without precedent. This view ignores a history of debt crises and subsequent crisis resolutions. Moreover, the debt overhang of one historical period has often contributed to the next crisis, as restructurings have typically been palliative in nature, failing to strike at the root of the problem.

This book focuses on what has been termed the pathology of debt,[11] or the causes of debt service disruption, crisis resolution, and the process of renegotiation between debtor and creditor leading to debt restructuring. An essential premise of this book is that disruption of debt service has been a recurring theme in international relations.[12] The most common approach to debt resolution between a debtor and its creditors has been negotiations between a sovereign debtor and its creditors case by case, with the objective of restoring the debtor's creditworthiness at the earliest possible moment. As Edwin Borchard notes, "The method best suited for settling a default situation to the mutual benefit of all parties involved remains the exchange of views by discussion and negotiation, and experience shows that it has actually been followed in the great majority of all cases."[13]

There have been notable exceptions, such as the Russian repudiation in 1917 during the Bolshevik Revolution; the extended fight between the Argentine government and its bondholders over many years starting in 2003, which finally reached a settlement during the first quarter of 2016; and the Greek impasse in the crisis of the early 2000s. The benefit to the debtor of such a solution is clear: the quid pro quo for resuming debt service has invariably been access to credit markets and additional loans. The benefit to the creditor is equally clear: negotiations restore the principal value of the loan and, assuming no further disruption of debt service, allow payments of the interest and principal to continue, although invariably under modified conditions. The sanction is the denial of further credit to the debtor until the restructuring is achieved.[14]

The difficulty inherent in using renegotiation and restructuring of external sovereign debt as the primary solution to debt service disruption is that this approach rarely addresses the heart of the problem—that is, the underlying cause of debt service disruption. Typically, the process has left a large "overhang" of debt that has been subject to disruption in subsequent generalized international, regional, or country-specific financial or sovereign crises.[15]

The review of external sovereign debt presented in this book, over an extended period, demonstrates clearly that debt service disruption has been a common occurrence and that, despite differences in debt instruments and institutional mechanisms to facilitate restructuring, shows a great deal of commonality. Moreover, the response of creditors has been consistent over time, with the primary solution being renegotiation and restructuring. This book assesses the spiral of disruption and crisis sequencing starting with an initial spark such as a real estate bust or a stock market crash, a currency crisis, a financial crisis, a sovereign debt crisis, or a default, and ending eventually with negotiations and the restructuring of external sovereign debt. This sequence has varied from crisis to crisis. Since major crises are complex, a country in crisis often faces combinations of crises that need to be resolved simultaneously. Crisis resolution is difficult and often requires the support of a lender of last resort to financially assist and augment the country's technical capacity to address it. This discussion of crisis, crisis resolution, sovereign debt defaults, and renegotiation over several distinct time periods is the major contribution of the book.

Creditors' losses due to sovereign crises have been substantial. The assumptions by many analysts that the losses of creditors have been modest are valid only if the analysis is stopped at the convenient frontiers where historians often choose to end their analysis—for example, World War I, the point that virtually all analysts of the nineteenth-century export of capital have chosen as a convenient breaking point. In contrast, the defaults and repudiations during World War I and the interwar period from the earlier nineteenth-century debt overhang were considerable. Similarly, those defaults that occurred during the Great Depression in the period 1931–33 remained largely unresolved owing to the depth and length of the Great Depression and the outbreak of World War II. Again, most interwar analysis of external debt has stopped at the convenient frontier of World War II. In fact, the resolution of the defaults that happened from 1931 to 1933 was still in process during the 1980s debt crises. The 1982–83 Annual Report of the Council of Foreign Bondholders provides detailed information on the continued service of both nineteenth-century and interwar defaults that resulted in debt restructurings, as well as on loans that have remained in default.[16] Thomas Piketty observes that Britain and France, the major exporters of capital during the nineteenth century, lost virtually their entire portfolios of foreign bond holdings as a result of World War I and in the interwar years including the Great Depression and World War II, equal to approximately two times their GDP, leaving them with net foreign asset holdings near zero.[17]

The book addresses creditor losses in the primary crisis cases presented herein. The book also discusses both the process and the costs of crisis resolution—for example, for Korea during the East Asia crisis, for Ireland during the eurozone crisis because of the government's guarantee of all banking liabilities, and for the United States owing to the costs of bailing out key banking and shadow banking institutions and propping up financial markets. The ultimate losses due to a crisis are hard to measure because restructurings may extend for a considerable time and be fully resolved, if at all, many years later.

What rational economist or EU official really believes that the three Greek bailouts from 2010 to 2015 have resolved Greece's crisis? Ultimately it seems clear, almost certain, that a large amount of the outstanding debt will need to be written down at a cost to the creditors in order for the Greek economy to stabilize in the longer term. That cost is unknown and may remain unknown for some time if that debt is rescheduled over a long period of time and interest in arrears, if any, is recapitalized.

Another feature of crises is the pain they inflict on their population. Crises invariably deepen poverty, exacerbate inequality, lead to high unemployment, and lead to high levels of business failure, especially for small and medium-sized enterprises (SMEs) that are often "family businesses" and the main source of support for the family unit for food, health care, shelter, and education. SMEs are usually cut off from financing during and in the immediate aftermath of crises.

Several East Asian economies regressed with respect to poverty during the East Asian crisis that began in Thailand in 1997, and with respect to GDP per capita after years of steady, export-led growth. Indonesia, for example, saw GDP per capita fall by some $1,000, back to levels observed twenty years before the crisis that began in 1997. Poverty spread broadly and deeply throughout East Asia.[18]

The eurozone experienced double-digit unemployment of 10 to 11 percent from the beginning of its crisis in 2009 through 2015, with Spain's unemployment at some 25 percent and youth unemployment at 50 percent for an extended period during the crisis. The United States saw a large-scale increase in poverty, as many poorer families lost their most valuable asset, their homes, during the crisis. Also, inequality in the United States, as measured by the Gini coefficient, rose dramatically during the crisis. The economic and poverty impact of these crises is addressed in several of the cases discussed in the book.

The political economy and international relations perspective of this book is another major contribution to understanding the responses to debt crises. Rather than focusing solely on economic issues, the analysis herein is also directed toward the political economy and international relations during global financial crises. Specifically, the book examines the following issues:

1. The relationship between the power of states and capital export;

2. The links between sovereign loans and the strategic interests of creditor states;

3. The importance of trade and trade relations and external sovereign debt;

4. The relationship between debt military expenditures, war, revolutions, and reparations and indemnities that result from wars;

5. International law governing state succession and debts;

6. The reasons for direct intervention by states on behalf of their creditors in the affairs of sovereign debtors;

7. International law concerning intervention by creditor states as a result of defaults and repudiations by debtors; and

8. The role of multilateral financial institutions, in particular the IMF, but also the World Bank and historically the Bank for International Settlements (BIS) during the interwar years, in helping sovereign debtors in difficulty to resolve debt service disruption.

Underlying the analysis of these specific issues of political economy and international relations and external sovereign debt crises is an overriding issue always present in the relationship between a sovereign debtor and its creditors. There is a fine line between the sanctity of contracts, *pacta sunt servanda,* the basis of all contract law, and the vital interests of states under changing conditions, *clausula rebus sic stantibus*.[19] In cases where debt service has been perceived as a threat to their existence or stability, states saw it in their self-interest to default. John Maynard Keynes perhaps expressed it most clearly, indicating that there was a strong tendency for states to default on the occasion of wars and revolutions, and whenever the prospects for new loans failed to exceed the debt service on other loans. He concluded that defaults were worldwide and frequent and that the investor had no remedy against such practices. He and other analysts, such as Dragoslav Avramovic, spoke of the "will" of the debtor to repay its loans under adversity.[20] There is a clear link, therefore, between sovereign debt and international relations and the political economy of sovereign debt crises. A major contribution of this book is to detail this link.

ONE

Historical Context

The Export of Capital and Sovereign
Debt Crises, 1815–1914

Starting about 1815, when the Napoleonic Wars ended and the Concert of Europe, or Pax Britannica, was established, the newly industrialized European states began exporting capital to the periphery.[1] Great Britain, the most advanced industrialized country, led the way but was soon joined by France, Germany, Switzerland, and the Low Countries.[2] By the end of the nineteenth century the United States, until then the largest borrowing country, also began to export capital, primarily to the Far East and Latin America.[3] The process continued throughout the nineteenth century and the beginning of the twentieth century up to World War I, despite numerous intervening debt defaults by borrowing states, the failure of important financial institutions, and periodic financial crises. Capital was exported through the capital markets of the advanced economies largely to sovereign states in the periphery (at present known as developing or emerging market countries, depending on their economic status).

Loans also went to great powers, empires, and former empires—Russia, the Ottoman Empire, the Austro-Hungarian Empire, China, Spain, and Portugal, as examples—who were often in financial distress. As the century progressed, Great

TABLE 1-1.   British Overseas Investments in Publicly Issued Securities, 1913

Region or area	Millions of British pounds	Percent
Total British Empire	1,780.0	47.3
Total Latin America	756.6	20.1
Total Europe	218.6	5.8
All foreign countries	1,983.3	52.7
Total	3,763.3	100.00

Source: Herbert Feis, *Europe: The World's Banker, 1870–1914* (London: Frank Cass, 1936), p. 27.

TABLE 1-2.   British Overseas Investments in Publicly Issued Securities, December 1913, by Category

Class of security	Millions of £	Percent
Government and municipal	1,125.0	29.9
Railways	1,531.0	40.6
Other public utilities	185.1	5.0
Commerce and industry	208.5	5.5
Raw materials	388.5	10.3
Bank and finance	317.1	8.4
Total	3,763.3	100.0

Source: Feis, *Europe: The World's Banker*, p. 27.

Britain began to concentrate its loans in the areas of recent settlement—Canada, New Zealand, Australia, and the United States—where the human capital was able to productively absorb the financial capital. Finally, Britain exported capital to its colonies, above all India (see tables 1-1 and 1-2). Most of these loans were private, raised in the London capital market or the European bourses in the form of long-term debt, usually fifty-year bonds. At times, when countries were in deep distress and the bond markets unavailable to them, they borrowed via floating debt or short-term loans arranged by the issue houses, later known as merchant banks.[4]

During the nineteenth century, defaults on sovereign loans were frequent, particularly to newly independent republics in Latin America or to Greece and the older empires. Some sovereign debtors defaulted for an extended time period. Many of these same debtors were at the heart of sovereign debt crises in the interwar years and the Great Depression (discussed in Part I of this book). Also, several of these debtors featured prominently in the debt crises of the early 1980s or the emerging market crises of the 1990s and early 2000s (Parts II and III of this book), and some featured prominently in the rescue packages or "bailouts" during the crisis of the early 2000s in the euro-zone (Part IV of the book). Some countries were serial defaulters who lacked either the capacity or the will, or both, to service their sovereign debts. Greece, Mexico, Argentina, and Turkey (the Ottoman Republic) are prominent examples, but they are no means alone among frequent defaulters.

The approach to negotiating debt service disruption soon was well established—creditor committees in the various countries representing the bondholders negotiated restructuring of their loans on a case-by-case basis, with the creditors often consolidating all loans, reducing interest or principal due, or extending the amortization period. The fundamental principle was that a debtor in default could not return to the capital market for fresh capital until its debts were recomposed (today we would say resolved or restructured) and the debtor was servicing its debts. The approach to resolving debt service disruption set a precedent for the sovereign crises discussed in subsequent parts of this book. This chapter provides background for the chapters that follow.

Capital export took place through the intermediation of capital market issues on the stock exchange in London and various European bourses, which became the centers for issues of international shares and debentures. These investments were held largely by private investors, as were the two earliest forms of debt securities issued to the public via the market, consols and *rentes*.[5] As the nineteenth century progressed, merchant banks, sometimes referred to as issue houses, which arranged the initial stock exchange listings for debentures or share issues, took on an underwriting role. They were followed by joint-stock banks (which made direct loans or directly assumed investments), by trusts, and by other investment institutions, all of which achieved a more prominent position in international investing as the century progressed.[6] While the capital markets in each of the primary creditor countries—Great Britain, France, Germany, and the United States—developed in different ways, the main actors throughout this period were in the private sector.[7] Government loans and government guarantees were rare.[8]

Two types of conclusions may be drawn from the history of capital export during the period 1815–1914 with respect to the primary focus of this book, sovereign debt crises and their resolution from the Great Depression to the Great Recession. The first set of conclusions is economic in nature. The second set concerns capital export and the political economy and international relations during sovereign crises.

Economic Conclusions

Loans were initially provided by the London capital market and as the century progressed by France and Germany and a number of the traditional European creditors through their bourses in Amsterdam, Frankfurt, and Zurich (see tables 1-3, 1-4, and 1-5).

Hard-Core Creditors and Their Capital Markets

During this era, 1815 to 1914, a small, "hard-core" group of creditor countries and capital markets emerged as the primary sources of capital export. Financial instruments were primarily long-term bonds floated on the London market and various European bourses and subscribed to by private investors. Export capital was intermediated in London, Paris, Frankfurt, Zurich, and Amsterdam primarily by the merchant banks, which were also deeply involved in trade finance. Later in the century the German "great banks" played a strong role in international finance as Germany increasingly emerged as a great power and competed with Great Britain and France in trade, in railway development, and for colonies (see tables 1-4 and 1-6). Capital export went to countries without their own or with weak capital markets.[9]

Toward the end of the century up to World War I, New York emerged as a source of credit to the periphery, particularly Latin America,[10] and the New York investment banks rivaled their competitors in London. In the interwar years New York assumed the mantle as the leading world capital market. Thereafter the bond markets in New York and London, to a lesser extent the other European bourses, and eventually Toronto, Tokyo, Hong Kong, and offshore convenience centers such as the Cayman Islands constituted the major source of capital export to the rest of the world in the post–World War II era and the emerging markets crises of the 1990s.[11]

The issue houses of this period, the private banking concerns that evolved into merchant and investment banks during the nineteenth century, are the key players in the current eurobond market. Moreover, the money center banks, the successors to the Credit Mobilier movement in France, the German great banks, and the concentration of banking in Europe after 1870 resulted in the formation of the large joint-stock banks,[12] which are now, with the addition of the major U.S. money center banks, the market makers in the eurocurrency market. These banks were responsible for most of the syndicated lending to the developing and emerging market countries during the 1970s and 1980s in the leadup to the 1980s debt crisis.

The recent crisis, known as the Great Recession (from 2007 to 2010 in the United States and from 2009 to 2015 in the eurozone), is anomalous in the post–World War II

TABLE 1-3.   French Foreign Investment, as of 1914

Country or region	Thousands of millions of francs	Percent
Russia	11.3	25.1
Turkey	3.3	7.3
Spain and Portugal	3.9	3.7
Austria-Hungary	2.2	4.3
Balkan states	2.5	5.5
Rest of Europe	1.5	3.4
Europe total	27.5	61.1
French colonies	4.0	8.9
Egypt, Suez, and South Africa	3.3	7.3
United States and Canada	2.0	4.4
Latin America	6.0	13.3
Asia	2.2	5.0
World total	45.0	100.0

Source: Feis, *Europe: The World's Banker*, p. 51.

TABLE 1-4.   German Foreign Investment, as of 1914

Country or region	Billions of marks	Percent
Austria-Hungary	8.0	29.3
Russia	1.8	6.6
Balkan countries	1.7	6.2
Turkey (including Asiatic Turkey)	1.8	6.6
France and Great Britain	1.3	4.8
Spain and Portugal	1.7	6.2
Europe total	16.3	59.7
Africa (including German colonies)	2.0	7.3
Asia (including German colonies)	1.0	3.7
United States and Canada	3.7	13.6
Latin America	3.8	13.9
Other areas	0.5	1.8
Outside of Europe total	11.0	40.3
Total	27.3	100.0

Source: Feis, *Europe: The World's Banker*, p. 74.

TABLE 1-5. German Foreign Investments, as of 1908, by Category

Class of security	Millions of 1914 marks	Percent
Provincial and municipal	700	2.4
Mortgage bonds	1,087	3.8
Bank shares and debentures	384	1.3
Railway shares	2,681	9.2
Rail debentures	3,929	13.6
Industrial shares and debentures	281	1.0
Total	28,958	100.0

Source: J. Riesser, The German Great Banks and Their Concentration in Connection with the Economic Development of Germany, 3rd ed. (Washington: Government Printing Office, 1911), pp. 392–93, citing Statisches Jahrbuch fur das Deutsche Reich, Vol. 29 (1908), p. 228. Translated for Hearings of the United States Congress, National Monetary Commission, 61st Congress, 2nd session, Document No. 593. First published as Die deutschen Grossbanken und ihre Konzentration (1908).

Note: Included in this nominal amount of approximately 29 billion marks is 8.2 billion marks of conversion issues, of which 6.6 billion represent conversion on state loans.

TABLE 1-6. Main Creditor and Debtor Countries, as of 1913

Gross creditors	Billions of US$	Percent	Gross debtors	Billions of US$	Percent
United Kingdom	18.0	40.9	Europe	12.0	27.3
France	9.0	20.4	Latin America	8.5	19.3
Germany	5.8	13.2	United States	6.8	15.5
Belgium, Netherlands, and	5.5	12.5	Canada	3.7	8.4
Switzerland			Asia	6.0	13.6
United States	3.5	8.0	Africa	4.7	10.7
Other countries	2.2	5.0	Oceania	2.3	5.2
Total	44.0	100.0		44.0	100.0

Source: United Nations, International Capital Movements during the Inter-War Period (Lake Success, N.Y.: United Nations Department of Economic Affairs, 1984), p. 2.

era as a throwback to the Great Depression of the 1930s. The crisis was primarily centered on the large money center banks and the financial markets, the historically traditional sources of capital to the rest of the world. The economic crises that have followed the financial crises were centered largely in the advanced industrial economies starting in Japan in the 1990s, followed by the United States in 2007, then Japan again and the eurozone whose respective economies were characterized by low growth and low to near deflationary conditions. Japan and the United States, two of the major creditor states, are now substantial sovereign debtors, as is China.[13]

Hard-Core Debtors and Their Reliance on External Capital

Joining the hard-core group of creditors was a hard-core group of debtor states in the periphery. Some, particularly those in the areas of recent settlement—the United States, Canada, Australia, and New Zealand—emerged as creditors toward the end of the era or as a result of World War I. These states were generally unencumbered by rigid political and social systems, while benefiting from a transfer of human capital attributable to immigration.[14] However, relatively few states absorbed their external debt well, and, after a series of cycles of default and renegotiation, they emerged as hard-core debtors. This pattern was most pronounced in the Latin American states, the Ottoman Empire (Turkey), Egypt, Greece, Spain, Portugal, Russia, and the Balkan states[15] (see table 1-6 above). At present, several of these or their successor states rank among the major debtor nations, with Mexico, Argentina, Russia, and Turkey needing to be bailed out during the emerging market crises in the 1990s and early 2000s and Greece and Portugal needing to be bailed out during the eurozone crisis.

During the nineteenth century, the peripheral states, with their weak domestic capital markets and undeveloped banking systems, were reliant on external loans for industrialization, particularly capital-intensive infrastructure investments such as railways and utilities.[16] In addition, states borrowed to cover persistent budget deficits. Often their rulers failed to distinguish between their own purse and that of the state. With their narrow fiscal bases, external capital markets were tapped to provide additional resources for governments. This reliance has not changed markedly today.[17]

Expensive Loans to Peripheral States Reflected Perceived Credit Risks

Bonds floated on the bourses of Europe usually had long amortization periods, which matched the capital intensiveness or "lumpiness" of the investments made in railways and other infrastructure projects. However, these loans were expensive. Real rates of interest were high: the nominal interest rates of 5 percent and 6 percent for the peripheral states were doubled through the deep discounting of bonds, a deduction of one to two years of debt service in advance, and heavy commissions paid to the issue houses. In addition, railway concessions often required state-guaranteed returns or revenue per mile of track laid, as well as land grants, all of which added to the expense of these loans (see table 1-7).[18]

TABLE 1-7.   Realized Rates of Return on Capital Export, 1870–1913

Percent

Category	1870–76	1877–86	1887–96	1897–1909	1910–13
Consols	3.59	3.76	4.13	0.93	−0.37
French *rentes*	4.79	5.41	5.55	2.73	2.34
Colonial and provincial governments	6.08	4.72	4.95	2.78	1.77
Indian railways	4.63	4.70	6.01	0.74	2.36
U.S. railways	7.84	7.69	4.63	6.13	2.08
Latin American railways	5.96	7.04	6.77	4.09	1.73
Social overhead investment	0.00	0.00	5.20	3.70	2.55

Source: Michael Edelstein, *Overseas Investment in the Age of High Imperialism: The United Kingdom, 1850–1914* (London: Methuen, 1982), pp. 153–54, table 6.30.

Excessive Short-Term Borrowing (Floating Debt) Signaled Debt Crisis

When states were unable to float bonds during cyclical downturns in the market or when their creditworthiness had declined, they resorted to short-term borrowing in excess of trade requirements. This floating debt was a sure sign that a debt crisis or default was at hand.[19]

High real rates of interest on variable rate commercial bank loans and a concentrated buildup of short-term loans in excess of reserves was characteristic of the 1980s debt crisis and the emerging market crises of the 1990s. The short-term borrowing and very high leverage of the shadow banks leading to the U.S. crisis (2007–10) also triggered financial economic crises in the United States and Europe, particularly in the eurozone.

Defaults, Recurring and Sustained

The relatively frequent defaults during this period were concentrated among the hard-core debtors—Greece, Mexico, Argentina, the Ottoman Empire (Turkey), and Austria, as examples. During the Bolshevik Revolution, Russia was the primary case of sovereign repudiation, on ideological grounds. During the U.S. Civil War the southern U.S. states, financed by British merchants against cotton exports, also defaulted on their debts and the federal government thereafter refused to recognize those debts. Defaults tended to recur and at times were longlasting. At the heart of defaults, subsequent debt negotiations, and resolution are two primary issues: the capacity of states to pay versus their will to pay. John Maynard Keynes, in a commentary on capital export and defaults, voiced a general distrust of foreign lending based on the experience of the nineteenth century:

> Indeed, it is probable that loans to foreign governments have turned out badly on balance—especially at the low rates of interest current before the War. The investor has no remedy, none whatever against default. There is, on the part of most foreign countries, a strong tendency to default on the occasion of wars, revolutions and whenever the expectation of further loans no longer exceeds in amount the interest payable on the old ones. Defaults are world-wide and frequent.[20]

At times during the nineteenth century the negotiations extended over many years. In the interwar years many countries defaulted from 1931 to 1933 during the Great Depression and remained in default until after World War II, with debts still being settled twenty or so years after the end of World War II. Similarly, after the 1980s debt crisis the major debtors—Mexico, Argentina, Brazil, and others—renegotiated repeatedly with their bank creditors from 1982 to 1994.

During the emerging markets crisis of the mid-1990s and early 2000s, Argentina was in crisis and defaulted in 2002. Argentina then negotiated its debts with bondholders over an extended period of time; it agreed to a punitive and partial settlement with the bondholders, bordering on repudiation, in 2004 and again in 2010. Argentina's default was finally settled after extensive litigation with minority creditors in the first quarter of 2016. Greece went into default in 2010 and has since experienced three bailouts and a major political crisis. The bailouts have not solved the problem of its overindebtedness or restored Greece to a sustainable growth path.[21]

Renegotiation between a Debtor and Its Creditors

Relatively few defaults ended in repudiation, as it was in the interest of both debtors and creditors to renegotiate. Creditors sought to preserve their principal and eventually see full debt service restored, while debtors sought to regain their creditworthiness and access to the external capital markets of Europe. Renegotiation reflected a delicate balance of power between creditor and debtor: the former denied loans to debtors in default via closure of their capital markets and other forms of pressure, including diplomatic representation, while the latter maintained moratoriums on their debt service until a satisfactory restructuring was achieved. Renegotiations and restructurings were thus common throughout the period.[22]

All restructurings in the nineteenth century were handled case by case. Creditors initially negotiated with a sovereign debtor through separate bondholder committees formed to handle a default on a single loan. Over time, country committees were formed and eventually incorporated as the Corporation of Foreign Bondholders in England and its continental equivalents. In England the Council of the Corporation coordinated the efforts of the individual committees and brought the weight of the City of London to bear on a sovereign debtor in default, as well as encouraging diplomatic representation from the foreign office in difficult cases. This practice was emulated in Europe, with the various national bondholder committees cooperating to avoid competitive settlements and to maintain maximum leverage over the debtor.[23]

During the 1980s debt crisis, bank creditor committees, chaired by the major money center banks, negotiated restructurings case by case, a clear parallel with the nineteenth-century experience. This practice of case-by-case restructuring continued during the sovereign crises in the 1990s, such as in Mexico (1994–95), East Asia (1997–2003), Russia (1998), Turkey (2001–02), and Argentina (2001–03). However, restructuring support was provided by the IMF, World Bank, and G-7 acting as international lenders of last resort during the crises in the 1990s and early 2000s. In the eurozone crisis individual country bailouts were handled on a case-by-case basis in Greece (beginning in 2010 through 2015), Ireland (2010–14), Portugal (2010–14), and Cyprus (2013) under the auspices of the troika of the European Investment Bank (ECB), the European Commission (EC) and the IMF, which served as lenders of last resort and also provided oversight over crisis reforms.

In the major financial and economic crises in Japan, the United States, and Europe, where sovereign bailouts were not required, the primary central banks—the Bank of Japan, the U.S. Federal Reserve Bank (the Fed) supported by the Treasury and Federal Deposit Insurance Corporation (FDIC), the Bank of England, and the ECB—served as domestic lenders of last resort but also cooperated with each other, as well as with other central banks throughout the world, to prevent a wider banking and financial markets crisis. The U.S. Fed extended currency swap lines to the major central banks noted above, as well as to the central banks of Switzerland, Mexico, Brazil, South Korea, and Singapore. In total the Fed had swap arrangements with some fourteen central banks around the world.[24]

A Flexible Approach to Restructuring

During the nineteenth century there was flexibility in resolving the debt crises. For example, debt service arrears were frequently capitalized and subject to low escalating rates of interest over time; interest rates on the original principal were reduced if the prevailing market rates were lower than the bond coupon rate; debt was consolidated and unified into relatively few classes; debt service was tied to a percentage of import and/or export duties, to earnings from an important export crop such as coffee or rubber, or to state monopolies over tobacco or spirits; and bonds were converted to stocks or equity in newly formed railway concessions. Creditors recognized that there was a cost to default that would be borne by both debtor and creditor, and solutions had to reflect the debtors' capacity to pay in order to be at all workable. Nevertheless, even with those more pragmatic approaches to restructuring, recurring defaults were not avoided.[25] The large external debt overhang that remained throughout World War I and the interwar period was subject to massive defaults in the Depression beginning in 1931. Most of these defaults were renegotiated and settled following World War II.

In the 1980s crisis, after extensive and difficult negotiations between a sovereign debtor and its banks as creditors, the U.S. government stepped in, initially to ensure that its major money center banks with heavily concentrated exposure to Latin American debt were protected, but also to resolve protracted sovereign debt crises through the Baker and Brady Plans (named for U.S. secretaries of the Treasury James Baker and Nicholas Brady); the latter emphasized partial debt forgiveness for debtors that resolved their defaults. Each of these resolutions was handled on a case-by-case basis. Calls for generalized, rather than case-by-case, solutions for debt forgiveness or market buyback of debt on a discounted basis were usually rejected by the creditors and their governments and went nowhere.[26]

The IMF and the World Bank played important roles as lenders of last resort in the 1990s emerging market crises. The IMF served as the primary lender of last resort supported by the World Bank, regional development banks such as the Asian Development Bank for Korea, and the G-7 countries. The idea was to develop sufficiently large packages on a case-by-case basis so that they were credible in international financial markets.

In the crisis that began in 2007, sovereign debtors in difficulty in the eurozone were supported by the troika—the ECB, the European Commission, and the IMF. For the first time in a crisis in the advanced industrial countries, the IMF was called in to play a major role in crisis resolution. Each of the bailout packages was negotiated and monitored individually. Each one required unanimous approval by the other eurozone countries.

Losses from Defaults

The losses from defaults during the period under discussion (1815–1914) are difficult to evaluate. However, a conservative estimate based on repudiations, conversion of interest to lower rates on arrears and original principal, and conversion to scrip from hard currency debt on British bond holdings up to 1914 generated losses estimated at one third of the cumulative defaults during the period, but only 7 percent of the foreign bonds issued on the London Stock Exchange during this same period.

French losses were much higher owing to the Russian repudiation in 1917 during the Bolshevik Revolution. Since most bonds issued between 1815 and 1914 were fifty-year bonds (amortized over fifty years), the real losses far exceeded the historical estimates made at the convenient stopping point used by most analysts of the period, World War I. The overhang of nineteenth-century debt to the interwar years through the Great Depression and World War II led to losses far greater than the nineteenth-century estimates. As a result of the two World Wars and the Great Depression, Great Britain and France lost most of their portfolios. Germany of course was saddled with reparations after World War I and became a debtor state; and the United States, now the major creditor country, took losses on commercial loans to Latin America and on inter-Allied war loans. Thomas Piketty notes that British and French portfolio losses after the Great Depression, the two World Wars, and the loss of colonies were very substantial: "In the wake of the cumulative shock of two world wars, the Great Depression and de-colonialization these vast stocks of foreign assets would eventually evaporate. In the 1950s, both France and Great Britain found themselves with net foreign asset holdings close to zero."[27]

In more recent times, the large money center banks reached settlements with their major debtors and took partial writedowns of their loans. Argentine bondholders were forced to live with significantly discounted returns from negotiated settlements in 2004 and 2010. In 1998 and 1999 the major Russian banks defaulted on and even repudiated some of their loans from their Western creditors. Creditors absorbed initial losses from the Greek bailouts, but ultimately it is unknown what the losses will be on Greece's substantial sovereign debt outstanding. It is a reasonable assumption, given the state of the Greek economy and its proven difficulty mobilizing tax receipts and effecting structural reforms such as privatization, that the eventual writedown of Greek debt will be very large. In the bailout of Cyprus even deposit holders (largely Russians who had parked money offshore) were "bailed in" and forced to suffer losses (discussed in greater detail in parts III and IV herein).

Finally, there are Japanese government bonds and U.S. Treasuries with gross sovereign debt at 240 percent and 100 percent of GDP, respectively. Since virtually all of the Japanese debt is held by individual Japanese investors and individuals, there appears to be no immediate threat of a sovereign default. U.S. debt is mostly held by U.S. investors and institutions, though other governments such as the Chinese and other East Asian exporters holding large reserves in dollars make the United States somewhat more vulnerable, in principle, than Japan. However, the U.S. dollar remains the world's major trade and reserve currency, and it strengthened against the euro and yen during the Great Recession. To date, when there has been a flight to quality from emerging market countries, it has been primarily to the U.S. dollar. However, because both Japan and the United States have elevated sovereign debt, both are vulnerable to a future shock and/or a change in sentiment or loss of confidence in their respective currencies, and their debt trajectories are not sustainable (see Part IV).

International Relations Aspects of Capital Export

Although the economic aspects of capital export during the nineteenth century have received substantial attention, the link between external debt and international relations is for the most part not adequately addressed.

Capital Export and State Power

From the viewpoint of the creditor states, capital export has to be seen as a projection of state power in its broadest sense: "The export of capital has in recent times been a familiar practice of powerful states. The political supremacy of Great Britain throughout the nineteenth century was closely associated with London's position as the financial center of the world."[28]

Not only did Great Britain project its power via capital export to the periphery, so did France in loans to its continental allies, most notably to Russia as a way to counter the growing power of Germany, and in loans to Tunisia and Morocco as a way to extend its sphere of influence in North Africa. Germany backed its primary ally on the continent, Austria-Hungary, and sought to project itself as a major power, following unification in 1870, in a number of peripheral states. The German great banks, guided by the chancellor, were the vehicle for Germany's growing industrial power and increased penetration of overseas trading markets, largely in competition with Great Britain.

Even Russia, a major debtor, sought to extend its influence in Persia and China via loans. In the beginning of the twentieth century, the United States, still a major debtor, demonstrated its role as a growing power by supporting capital export to several Central American and Caribbean states. All the powers contested with each other for political and economic spheres of influence in China via loans, until the creditors curtailed this competition.

Creditor states such as France and Germany maintained direct control over their capital markets, while the British government maintained close but unofficial ties to the financial community in the City. Moreover, in Great Britain, legislation was used to channel loans to India after 1857.

State Intervention and Debt

When the powers sought to maintain the balance of power or the independence of newly created states, they intervened directly via loan guarantees, as in Turkey, Greece, and Egypt. Some authors on imperialism, such as Hobson, Hilferding, and Lenin, argued that the creditors—that is, capitalist states—were pushed into imperialism by finance or monopoly capital.[29] This view does not appear to be supported by the facts. These states acted in what they perceived as their higher political and strategic interest and often clouded their actions in a veil of financial maneuverings.

Direct intervention by the creditor states over defaults was relatively rare. However, where strategic interests were involved, defaults served as a convenient pretext for intervention, as, for example, by Britain in Egypt, France in Morocco, or the United States in the Dominican Republic or Panama. More frequently, the creditor states tried indirect intervention, such as international control commissions, banking consortiums, or customs authorities. These institutions, which amounted to enclaves of creditor control, were used in Greece, Turkey, Egypt, China, the Dominican Republic, Haiti, and Nicaragua to assist the debtor states in reorganizing their external debt, to maintain control over sources of revenues dedicated to debt service, and to report extensively on the economic and political status of the debtor.

In the case of post–World War II defaults on public credits such as trade credits insured by bilateral export finance institutions, sovereign debtors are required to renegotiate their debts with their creditors through the Paris Club, with the IMF in attendance to report on the debtors' economic prospects. During the 1970s and 1980s, Paris Club negotiations were frequent and recurring, as many of the poorer developing countries found it difficult to service their debts. During the 1980s debt crisis, sovereign debtors frequently renegotiated their Paris Club debts in parallel with their commercial bank loans.

In recent debt crises the creditor states have used the multilateral financial institutions—the Bank for International Settlements (BIS), the International Monetary Fund (IMF, the International Bank for Reconstruction and Development (World Bank), and regional development banks such as the Asian Development Bank, supported by backup facilities from the G-7 countries, to support countries in crisis—for example, during the East Asian crisis. The objective was to keep debt restructurings and negotiations politically "neutral." During the the eurozone crisis as noted, the troika provided most of the support in the so-called bailouts of Greece, Ireland, Portugal, and Cyprus. However, the bailout of Greece took the low politics of debt to high politics as the newly elected government from the socialist party Syriza threatened default and exit from the eurozone, while Greece's creditors, notably Germany and other northern tier countries, took a hard line on the writedown of debt and at some point threatened or seemed to favor a Greek exit from the eurozone.

During the nineteenth century, in cases of default where strategic interests were not involved, creditors often sought the assistance of local consuls in making diplomatic representations to debtor governments. These representations, often made jointly by all the creditor powers, were perceived as direct interventions by the weaker states of the periphery. In addition, governments would intervene when violations of international law occurred, such as default on a loan guaranteed by the creditor government, alienation of the collateral hypothecated to one loan, or servicing of domestic debt in preference to external debt. A default per se was not a violation of international law.

International Law and Debt Intervention

The Calvo Doctrine maintained that the powers discriminated against the weaker states in their interventions and rarely exhausted their remedies under national law before intervening. The Drago Doctrine, pronounced in the wake of the Venezuelan intervention, viewed all interventions over pecuniary claims as immoral and illegal under international law. The Latin American states, often the objects of intervention, sought to define "American international law" on debt interventions, eventually bringing this issue to the second Hague Convention of 1907. The convention expressed a preference for nonintervention and for arbitration over armed intervention. However, the powers refused to rule out intervention in cases of arbitrary and discriminatory treatment of their nationals as creditors. Overall, however, from the turn of the century until World War I, attitudes and customary practices in international law related to defaults evolved away from intervention.

Many developing country debtors, however, view the IMF or the combination of the IMF and World Bank as anything but politically neutral, since loans from these institutions are often conditional on economic reforms to be undertaken by the borrowers. In the late 1980s and 1990s the view was that globalization, including financial sector liberalization, was based on the Washington Consensus promoted by the United States, Great Britain, and other European countries, the major shareholders of the IMF and World Bank, and strongly endorsed by the management and staff of the IMF and World Bank. Joseph Stiglitz, among others, sees the push toward rapid globalization, especially the support of financial sector liberalization by the IMF and World Bank, as an important contributor to the emerging market crises of the 1990s and early 2000s (as discussed in Part III of this book).[30]

Trade and Capital Export

Another important component of capital export was trade and commercial relations. Trade, an important element of economic policy, was intimately tied to the export of capital, as the powers competed via loans to gain concessions in the peripheral states seeking to industrialize, and to supply them with capital equipment and other finished goods and services. Britain's initial recognition of the Latin American republics was embodied in a series of commercial treaties. Competition over the Baghdad Railway project and other concessions in Turkey opened that country to loans and probably accelerated the demise of the Ottoman Empire. All the powers vied for concessions and trade with China, using loans as a means of securing trading enclaves and spheres of influence.[31]

External Loans as a Basis for State Sovereignty

Viewed from the perspective of the borrowing states, external loans provided the resources for action. Initially, many smaller countries such as Greece, the Balkan states, and the Latin American republics sought loans to secure and maintain their independence. Newly established states then needed to pay off the external debt they inherited, as was the clearly established practice in the international law of state succession. The successor states to the Ottoman Empire, the Austro-Hungarian Empire, the Central American Republic, and Colombia all acquired external debt in this way.[32] In recent times, Russia and the other states of the former Soviet Union negotiated over debts of succession and the retention of assets by these countries, such as Aeroflot's fleet and factories of large Russian enterprises located in the former states of the Soviet Union.[33]

Debts Arising from Wars, Indemnities, and Pecuniary Claims

States borrowed to finance wars. The Balkan states, Turkey, Russia, and China all borrowed extensively to prepare for, engage in, or pay indemnities resulting from war. If, as Raymond Aron writes, peace is the other side of war, or if the dictum "in peace prepare for war" is accepted, then it follows that a substantial amount of debt was acquired to prepare for or engage in war.[34] At present, a hidden component of the external indebtedness of many states is expenditures for armaments.

In the current era the United States fought two wars—Afghanistan and Iraq— that were not formally in the budget approved by Congress; and the country spends more on defense annually than the next eight countries collectively. The wars and continuously heavy spending on defense have added significantly to the United States' sovereign debt problem.

Civil wars and internal strife in the peripheral states also created a demand for loans, as well as pecuniary claims resulting from damage to the property and lives of citizens of the major powers. The Southern states of the United States, individually and collectively the Confederate states, repudiated their debt acquired before and during the American Civil War. The Mexican intervention was occasioned in part by the pecuniary claims of the powers and resulted in Mexico's repudiation of the Maximilian Debt following the French occupation. The Venezuelan intervention was largely over pecuniary claims arising from civil strife and revolution. China was forced to borrow to pay indemnities arising from the Boxer Rebellion. Perhaps the classic case of borrowing to pay indemnities claimed by citizens of the European powers under extraterritorial privilege was Egypt.[35]

Developmental versus Revenue Borrowing

Although states in the periphery were potentially able to absorb external loans for major investments, such as railways, their borrowing for nonproductive purposes such as wars or to cover budget deficits inevitably led to defaults. The states in the periphery, with weak capital markets and narrow fiscal bases, often saw their economies buffeted by political events. The Ottoman Empire, the Austro-Hungarian Empire, Spain, Portugal, China, and most of those in the Caribbean were untouched by meaningful social and political change and were unable to absorb capital productively. It could be argued that borrowing forced a certain amount of opening up in these empires that accelerated their disintegration. Japan, in contrast, a non-Western society, was able, following the Meiji Reformation, to utilize external capital effectively and industrialize rapidly. Japan later borrowed extensively through the intermediation of

the New York investment banks and the New York bond market to support imperial expansion in Manchuria.

The Vital Interests of States versus the Sanctity of Contracts

In the nineteenth century, governments of the peripheral states faced a difficult balance between the sanctity of contracts, *pacta sunt servanda*, the basis of all contract
law, and the vital interests of their states under changing conditions, or *clausula rebus
sic stantibus*. In extreme crisis, states chose to default. Many hard-core debtor states
during this period found themselves locked into a vicious cycle of default, renegotiation and restructuring, and subsequent default that elevated finance from low to high
politics. External debt was inevitably linked to other international issues. Argentina,
Mexico, and Greece are examples of such states in the current era.

Part I

EXTERNAL FINANCING DURING THE INTERWAR PERIOD AND THE GREAT DEPRESSION, 1919–39

TWO

Private Market Lending

World War I had a profound impact on the status of the major European creditors. During the course of the war, Great Britain, through a program of voluntary exchange of foreign-held securities by its citizens, liquidated almost $4,000 million of foreign investment; France did the same with $700 million of externally held investments. Further, investors in both countries took losses on their external investments as a result of the fighting in Central Europe, the Near East, and Russia. The British lost approximately $600 million and the French approximately $4,000 million, or around half their external investments as of 1914; the Russian debt repudiation accounted for a substantial portion of this amount.[1] Germany, like France, had invested heavily in Central Europe and Turkey and also suffered substantial losses there. Moreover, German investments in Allied countries were liquidated, expropriated, and sequestered, and by 1919 Germany had lost almost all its external assets. Sizable losses were also sustained by Switzerland, Belgium, and Sweden (in Russia).[2]

The United States moved from its earlier status as major debtor to the second largest creditor. Its citizens not only repatriated much of their prewar debt to European creditors but also invested in British and French securities in an estimated amount of $1,500 million.[3] Britain remained, however, the largest creditor nation as a result of its stock, or portfolio, of external investments built up over the course of a century, which remained relatively untouched by the war. Britain's propensity to invest outside Europe—in the dominions and the Empire, the United States, and Latin America—proved fortunate in comparison with Germany and France.[4]

Initial private market loans after World War I, during the period 1919–23, went principally to refund, or extend, the terms on private market loans granted by investors in the United States to Europe in the early war years.[5] As a result of the war and the problems of postwar recovery, the world economy remained unstable and uncertain, and substantial lending through the capital markets during the early reconstruction period was not attractive to investors.[6] Out of all external private market loans from the United States ($2 billion) to public entities in 1920–23, 65 percent went to Western Europe and 30 percent to Canada, with little left for the rest of the world.[7]

It should be noted that the statistics on international debt in the interwar period are difficult to interpret and even more difficult to compare from year to year or country to country because of inflation, which was rampant at times, such as in Germany, and frequent exchange devaluations, among other problems. Complicating the matter was the varying inclusion or exclusion of reparations, prewar succession debts, Russian debts following the repudiation, and inter-Allied war debts. Exchange rates were artificially controlled by the devaluations of the mark and various Eastern European currencies in the early postwar years, the delayed stabilization of the French franc, the devaluation of sterling and the U.S. dollar during the Great Depression, and a wave of competitive devaluations. Those issues, combined with the termination of the gold exchange standard in most countries, complicate the problem of measuring external sovereign debt on a comparative basis during this period.

The Creditor States

Both Great Britain and France tried to continue capital exports after the war, but their capital was constrained. Britain focused on support for its colonies and also owed war debts to the United States. France was focused on extracting reparations from the Germans. In time, it also provided loans to its allies on the Continent as a potential bulwark against the Germans.

The United States

Although the year 1924 is considered pivotal for new external loans, it is important to note that private market loans from the United States to foreign countries had expanded continuously from 1900, rising from an estimated $500 million in that year to $2 billion in 1909 and $2.5 billion in 1913. By 1923, U.S. foreign investments were

FIGURE 2-1. U.S. Foreign Capital Issues by Geographic Area, 1920s

Percent

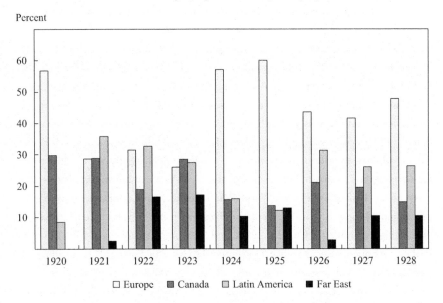

□ Europe   ■ Canada   □ Latin America   ■ Far East

Source: National Industrial Conference Board, *The International Financial Position of the United States* (New York, 1929), p. 58.

approximately $7.7 billion; direct investment by large corporations and loans to corporations accounted for over half the total, while loans to sovereign nations and to state and municipal governments equaled $2.6 billion.[8] The dominant share of these loans and investments went to areas adjacent to the United States—Canada and Central and South America.[9] Until World War I the United States was a net debtor. However, as a result of the war and the immediate postwar years, it reduced its debts by $3 billion and became a net creditor to the extent of $4 billion (see figure 2-1).[10]

The spark that reawakened the private capital markets and led to a boom in private lending was the Dawes Loan in 1924. In the amount of 800 million gold marks, it was the catalyst for the boom in international lending. The loan was floated on various international capital markets, secured by German railway securities. In its role as a confidence builder for the capital markets, this loan is comparable to those underwritten by Barings, Hope and Company and the *hautes banques* to assist France in paying the allied indemnity following the Napoleonic Wars, or the loans raised on the world capital markets to aid France in paying the indemnity of 5,000 million francs following the Franco-Prussian War.[11] Charles Kindleberger described the situation: "The Dawes Loan played a fateful role. One hundred and ten million dollars of it was sold in New York, underwritten by Morgan's. It was oversubscribed ten times. More than anything else, this was the spark that ignited foreign lending from New York, first to Germany and shortly thereafter to Latin America and much of the rest of Europe."[12]

New York banks and private investment firms—J. P. Morgan & Co., Kuhn Loeb, Dillon Read, and Kidder Peabody—pursued the role played by Barings, Rothschilds, and other London merchant banks during the earlier prewar period, organizing syndicates through which most foreign loans were sold. The House of Morgan, in syndicates or consortiums with other banks, arranged the flotation of $6 billion of bonds and securities during this period, of which $2 billion was foreign.[13] These banks had come to prominence in international lending primarily as a result of their intermediation of loans for the Allies in the New York capital market before the entry of the United States into World War I. International connections were also important: Morgan retained interlocking ownership in Drexel & Co. of Philadelphia, Morgan Grenfell & Co. of London, and Morgan et Cie. of Paris, while Kidder Peabody retained close ties with Hottinguer et Cie. and Barings.[14] In addition to these so-called Yankee investment banks, there were the investment banks of German Jewish immigrants such as Kuhn Loeb and Warburg, which also had important continental ties.[15]

The decisive role of New York as a financial center cannot be exaggerated and seemed to parallel that of London during the nineteenth century. One reason for its prominence was that branch banking was prevented throughout the United States by regulation. Another was that New York had extensive experience in finance and other financial services and was the domestic epicenter for financial services, insurance, commodity trade, trade finance, shipping and trans-shipping. The New York Stock Exchange was the primary public equity exchange in the country.[16] Within this framework the New York deposit banks and their affiliated investment banks were of major importance as a source and as intermediators of capital market funds. During the interwar period the concentration in banking continued.

One difference between the New York investment banks and affiliates of the joint-stock banks and their London counterparts proved critical toward the end of the 1920s: the relative importance of international lending to their overall activity. During the interwar period, foreign issues were normally only a small percentage of the total capital issues of U.S. banks (see figure 2-2). As such, the flotation of foreign bonds was not critical to the growth of the New York market. A direct reflection of the domestic orientation was the sharp decline in foreign lending in the United States in the latter part of 1928 as the stock market boomed.

This shift was also illustrative of the cyclical fluctuations in foreign lending seen in the nineteenth century; the process was not smooth and ever-increasing, but rather

FIGURE 2-2.   U.S. Foreign Capital Issues, 1920–29

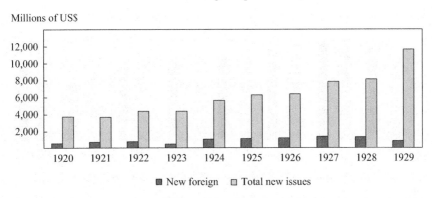

Millions of US$

■ New foreign   ☐ Total new issues

Source: Vincent P. Carosso, *Investment Banking in America—A History* (Harvard University Press, 1970), p. 231.

proceeded in waves.[17] Charles C. Abbott presents a detailed quarter-by-quarter analysis of bond issues from 1919 to 1930 by classification of bonds that clearly demonstrates the cyclical nature of foreign lending in this period. Foreign government bonds represented as little as 2 to 4 percent of the total market in the second half of 1922 and the first half of 1923, and well over 30 percent during the second through fourth quarters of 1924.[18]

The long-term capital exported from the United States abroad during the period 1919–35 was estimated at a nominal $12,671 million, of which $2,334 million involved refunding issues and new nominal issues $10,337 million. Loans to governments and government-guaranteed loans represented the largest portion of the total.[19]

Foreign loans from New York during the period 1924 to 1930 can be compared to those from London in the nineteenth century in yet another respect. They were profitable to the issue houses involved because of the commissions, underwriting fees, foreign exchange dealings, administrative fees for handling syndications, and control of the operating balances for the interest and sinking fund payments (see figure 2-3). Conversely, bonds were relatively expensive to the peripheral states. Canada, a preferred borrower, raised funds at a reasonable premium over the cost of funds to a triple A–rated lender in the United States, but a Latin American borrower paid a substantial premium.[20] However, after 1924, when the boom in foreign lending took off, aggressive salesmanship to both the public and potential borrowing states expanded the market's acceptance of foreign bonds issued in New York. As Mintz observed, "Lower grade, high yielding bonds drove higher quality lower yielding bonds from the market."[21]

FIGURE 2-3.   Foreign Bond Yields on U.S. Issues, Averages 1922–29

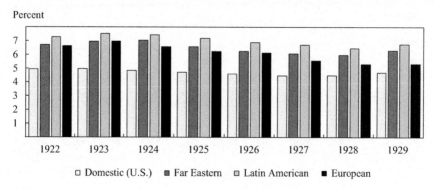

Percent

1922   1923   1924   1925   1926   1927   1928   1929

□ Domestic (U.S.)   ■ Far Eastern   □ Latin American   ■ European

Source: Hal B. Lary, *The United States in the World Economy* (Washington: U.S. Government Printing Office, 1943), pp. 97–98.

Syndicates were used extensively to sell the foreign bond issues. Using the experience gained floating the Liberty bonds (U.S. war bonds), the New York investment banks, trust banks, and investment affiliates of the large joint-stock banks developed a sophisticated network of syndicates to underwrite and participate in the sale of bond issues to the public. As many as three different types of syndicates could be formed to float a large issue, each taking a profit percentage or share of the loan issue.[22] The downside of this situation is noted by Hal B. Lary: "The flotation of one loan frequently came to be regarded as adequate justification for further issues to the same borrower or the same country without adequate regard to the growing burden of indebtedness."[23]

The boom in external lending was also fueled by the absence of defaults on sovereign loans issued during the interwar period from 1920 to 1930, a situation that created a false sense of market confidence in all foreign bonds. Finally, the distance from the last severe depression led people to forget the historical incidence of default. Throughout the 1920s, the restraining force of risk receded, as investors and investment banks strove to maximize their profits.[24]

Foreign bonds during the 1920s generally followed the market for yields on domestic medium-grade issues. From 1923 to 1928, the average yield on foreign bonds declined from 6.77 percent to 5.64 percent, a decline of 16.7 percent. The drop occurred despite the increased risk embodied in the heavier debt service burdens of sovereign borrowers.[25] However, the yield differential on foreign bonds versus high-quality, triple A–rated domestic bonds remained substantial throughout the period. The average from 1920 to 1929 was 33 percent, ranging from a low of 24 percent in 1929 to a high of 41 percent in 1926.[26]

Over the period in question, the geographic emphasis of government loans shifted dramatically. In the early postwar years, Western Europe was the major taker of U.S. external capital investments as Europe sought to recover from the war. By 1925, however, the emphasis was on loans to Germany, Eastern and Central Europe, and Latin America. Historically, loans to Latin America and Eastern Europe (excluding Germany) had proved far more risky than other areas of the world, and they would prove so again when the Depression struck. Short-term loans were also substantial by 1929, but were heavily concentrated between the New York and German banks.

As of 1929 the United States was a net creditor to the extent of $8.1 billion, a startling reversal from its pre–World War I debtor status.[27] Moreover, throughout the decade the United States maintained a substantial surplus on its trade account in its international balance of payments with the rest of the world. By virtue of the consistent trade surpluses, the interest and dividend payments on loans and investments, and remittances on war debts and reparations, the United States built up a large pool of capital that much of the world needed desperately for war reconstruction, trade, overall economic development, and retirement of prior debt. There was a "dollar gap" with the world during this period that sovereign borrowing and direct investments only partially offset.[28]

Great Britain

Great Britain entered World War I as the largest creditor nation. With external portfolio investments of approximately £3,500 million on a nominal basis and an extra £500 million in direct equity investments, Britain's cumulative external investments were twice those of the next largest creditor, France. As of 1919, Great Britain still had a large stock of accumulated foreign investments, which provided substantial interest and dividends.

During the period 1919 to 1923, capital export from Great Britain to the rest of the world was £416 million, partially achieved as a result of borrowing on a short-term basis from the United States.[29] The main recipients were the Empire and the Commonwealth, accounting for 60 percent of British loans in the interwar period up to 1931. Britain also moved increasingly toward direct external investments in public utilities, mining, petroleum, and finance.[30] As an exception to this pattern, it made substantial short-term loans to Germany; they went primarily from British banks to German banks and industry. Britain participated in the Dawes and Young Loans, as well as in a number of long-term market loans to German states, municipalities, and industry.[31] Great Britain also took an active role in organizing and financing the League Loans to Eastern and Central Europe. As of 1929, Britain's direct investment overseas was a nominal £3,438 million, excluding private investments held abroad and not registered on any exchange or bourse and foreign investments held by foreigners in Great Britain. Since many of Britain's loans and investments dated to the nineteenth and early twentieth centuries, there were substantial repayments and amortizations of principal throughout the interwar period.[32]

British loans were increasingly directed to the Empire, in part because of the Trustee Acts and the Colonial Stock Act of 1900, which brought almost all loans to governments and municipalities within the Empire under the scope of authorized trust investments.

This geographic pattern of British overseas investments in the interwar period continued the trend started toward the last quarter of the nineteenth century and beginning of the twentieth century up to World War I. The exception was Latin America, which received 20.2 percent of external investments, equal to £643 million, primarily direct private investment.[33] It should be noted that Britain still held large investments in railways in the Empire and South America, much of which had government-guaranteed returns associated with them.[34]

As to yields, those computed by Kindersley on nominal capital do not reflect market yields. The investor naturally demanded more substantial yields on investments perceived as risk-laden; Latin American, Eastern European, and other bonds therefore traded at a discount to Commonwealth and colonial banks, all of which provided a premium over consoles (British Treasury bills).[35]

Britain's balance of payments remained persistently negative on the trade or merchandise account during the interwar period. Offsetting this condition were earnings from shipping, which, however, declined substantially during the Depression, and income from overseas investments. However, by 1931 the receipts from overseas investments had fallen dramatically, while the merchandise account as a result of the Depression grew increasingly negative, a shift that put severe pressure on Britain's balance of payments.[36]

During this period John Maynard Keynes repeatedly expressed his concern over British policy, which he asserted "forced" capital abroad. He wrote in 1924:

> In the future the motives towards repudiation partial or complete may become much stronger. At present many of our debtors, especially in the Dominions, borrow afresh each year more than the interest on previous loans. But in the long run, partially from mere operation of compound interest, partially perhaps from our not having so large a surplus to lend abroad, this will cease. Our difficulties on a grand scale will then begin.[37]

Keynes returned to this theme in 1925 and advocated some tests or qualifications for loans to foreign and colonial governments, stressing the need to differentiate productive foreign investment from government loans: "It is, therefore, mainly loans to foreign and colonial governments which must be examined with a critical eye and be called upon to justify themselves on every ground."[38] Keynes's theoretical objections to external loans for governments were that they neither provided employment for the home market equivalent to an equal amount of home investment nor necessarily generated exports. In fact, Keynes believed that in the interwar period Britain was under pressure to export to provide earnings sufficient to cover external investment commitments.[39]

As before the war, Britain was devoting a substantial portion of its national savings to overseas investments. Unlike the New York market, these external investments continued to play a major role in London's capital market.[40] According to a detailed study of international investments by the Royal Institute of International Affairs: "There is, therefore, prima facie evidence for the assertion that Britain was overlending in those years in that new overseas issues greatly exceeded in amount the foreign exchange made available by current transactions, and that the balance was completed by imports of short-term funds."[41]

Britain's external lending was concentrated in London, whose role as a world financial center, including insurance, foreign exchange transactions, shipping and ship brokering, commodity trade, banking, and investment banking, was extremely important to Britain's position as a trading nation. Still, London's position was being challenged by New York.[42] Paul Einzig noted the rise of "financial diplomacy" in the interwar period: "Since the war a system of financial diplomacy has arisen, the importance of which has risen steadily. In these days economic and financial capabilities tend more and more to influence sympathies and antipathies in foreign policy."[43]

This competition produced changes. Britain's clearing or large joint-stock banks now began to play a major role in international finance, a position formerly occupied by the merchant banks. The "Big Five"—Barclays Bank, Midland Bank, Westminster Bank, Lloyds Bank, and the National Provincial Banks—had emerged as a result of a trend toward concentration in 1917–18 that continued with their merger and acquisition programs of the postwar era (see table 2-1).[44]

On the eve of World War I, France, the second largest creditor nation in the world, had external investments of approximately 45,000 milliard francs. During the war, however, it sold approximately $700 million in external investments to help finance that effort and lost another $4,000 million owing to defaults and repudiations on prewar investments and war loans to Russia. The defaults and repudiations represented

TABLE 2-1.   Geographic Distribution of British External Investments
by Category, as of 1931

Millions of £

Country or region	Government and municipal	Railway	Utilities	Mines	Misc.[a]	Total	Percent
Australia	432	2	9	9	42	494	15.7
New Zealand	110	0	0	0	13	123	3.9
Canada	97	213	32	2	102	446	14.0
South Africa	118	20	3	50	33	224	7.0
India and Ceylon	261	90	12	14	81	458	14.4
Malaya	4	0	4	8	92	108	3.4
Other British territories	65	29	3	9	28	134	4.0
Total Empire	1,087	354	63	92	391	1,987	62.4
Europe	120	30	18	6	71	245	7.7
South America	134	353	54	6	96	643	20.2
China and Japan	83	0	5	1	14	103	3.2
United States, Mexico, and Central America	2	49	29	10	41	131	4.1
Others	14	2	3	3	55	77	2.4
Total foreign	353	434	109	26	277	1,199	37.6
Total world	1,440	788	172	118	668	3,186	100.0

Source: Sir Robert Kindersley, "British Overseas Investments in 1931," *Economic Journal* 43 (1933): 201, table IX.

a. Miscellaneous investments were industrial investments, finance and banking, land, etc. The total nominal capital of 3,186 £ had to be augmented by British private capital held abroad and not registered and diminished by foreigners holding external investments in London.

approximately one half of France's total external investments as of the beginning of World War I.[45] The Russian debt repudiation accounted for a substantial proportion of these losses, but Austria-Hungary, Turkey, the Balkans (Bulgaria, Romania, and Greece), and Germany also contributed (see table 2-2). To Keynes, France offered clear evidence of the imprudence of loans to sovereign states: "No investments have ever been so foolish and so disastrous as the loans of France to Russia, and on a lesser scale to the Balkans, Austria, Mexico and Brazil, between 1900 and 1914. They represented a great proportion of the national wealth of the country, and nearly all has been lost."[46]

In addition to these investment losses, France also had to borrow substantially from the private markets in Britain and the United States to sustain its war effort. Because of the investment losses and private market and inter-Allied debt, France became a substantial external debtor by 1919. Some 38 milliard francs (1914 gold value)

TABLE 2-2.   French Investment Losses, as of 1919

Region/Country	Milliard French francs
Losses	
Russia	20,000
Austria-Hungary	3,000
Turkey	2,000
Germany	1,000
Balkans (Bulgaria, Romania, Greece)	1,000–2,000
	27,000–28,000
Severely depreciated investments	
Italy, Turkey, Serbia, Bulgaria, Romania, Greece	3,000
Total	30,000–31,000

Source: Royal Institute of International Affairs, *The Problem of International Investment* (Oxford University Press, 1937), p. 131.

of foreign holdings were wiped out and replaced by a net indebtedness to foreigners of about 22.3 milliard francs (1919 paper value).[47]

During the early postwar years, France relied on German reparations for reconstruction and development. When these failed to materialize within the time frame and on the scale anticipated, France ran substantial deficits on the current account in its international balance of payments and had to borrow heavily, both internally and externally.[48] Substantial short-term loans were obtained from New York during 1919 to 1920, estimated at $1,350 million.[49] To offset this borrowing, considerable external French capital was repatriated from Spain, the Netherlands, Switzerland, and Scandinavia from 1921 to 1924.[50]

The accumulated budget deficits and large trade imbalance resulted in heavy inflation in France and a strong depreciation of the franc. These factors, plus uncertainty over reparations, resulted in capital flight, which became severe in 1924.[51] The devaluations of the franc, as with the mark, resulted in a substantial reduction in the value of the public French franc debt from the war and early postwar years. To stabilize the franc, France arranged private market loans from New York banks organized by J. P. Morgan in cooperation with Lazard Brothers. The loans were conditional on the French government's adopting a conservative fiscal program. Kindleberger observed that J. P. Morgan served as a lender of last resort to the French government when Great Britain and the United States refused support because of French resistance to negotiating the war debt settlements.[52] In 1925–26, after another flight from the franc, the administration of Prime Minister Raymond Nicholas

Landry Poincaré imposed tough fiscal and economic reforms. This action restored stability, and France returned to the gold standard.[53]

It is not surprising that throughout the interwar period, political considerations aside, France clung tenaciously to the hope of receiving large-scale reparations as a way to restore its financial integrity. In their absence, France was forced to maintain tight control over capital exports during the interwar years until the stabilization of the franc. A law of April 3, 1918, forbade all forms of capital export, although it was frequently evaded in the early interwar period.[54]

After 1926 a sizable portion of French assets abroad was invested on a short-term basis in London and New York in the form of foreign exchange reserves. In the early 1930s, France was in a semi-monopolistic position as a provider of credit for foreign loans, and it attempted to reassert the position of Paris as a great financial center.[55] French long-term lending and investments, when they resumed, were largely tied to France's strategic concerns over Germany. Einzig noted the important political dimension to French lending: "In spite of the depreciation of the franc, and of bad financial conditions, the French government, industrial and financial interests pursued an ambitious policy of expansion which had a strong political flavor. They endeavored to establish themselves in countries which were in the French political sphere of influence such as Poland, Rumania, and Yugoslavia."[56]

Small (individual) French investors were no longer willing to invest as before the war; however, because of the Russian repudiation, the absorptive capacity of the French market had declined.[57] The reluctance of small investors to buy foreign bonds led some French banks to take a direct role in foreign investment and the French government to extend loans directly or to provide guarantees where political interests dictated a need. On the whole, however, the major French banks largely withdrew from foreign finance during this period, and increasingly the *banques d'affaires* (investment banks) assumed that role throughout the world. Their principal shareholders in turn were the firms of the *hautes banques*.[58]

In the early 1930s, following the stabilization of the franc and the increase in political tensions within Europe, the French government also began to make or guarantee largely politically directed loans (see figure 2-4).[59] The French government made loans to Poland, Hungary, and Yugoslavia in 1931 and to Czechoslovakia in 1932, despite a law of parliament prohibiting lending to foreign states without explicit parliamentary approval. Parliament debated and ultimately approved the loan to Czechoslovakia in 1932, with the French Treasury guaranteeing 8 percent interest and principal of 600 million francs. Similarly, in 1932 the French government guaranteed a loan to Austria of AS100 million (Austrian schillings), in conjunction with the

FIGURE 2-4. Foreign Loans Floated in Paris, 1919–33, by Country

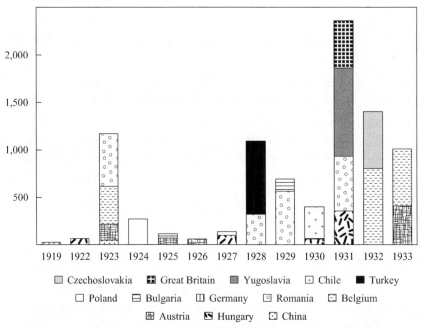

Millions of French francs

Czechoslovakia   Great Britain   Yugoslavia   Chile   Turkey

Poland   Bulgaria   Germany   Romania   Belgium

Austria   Hungary   China

Source: Marget C. Myers, *Paris as a Financial Centre* (Londong: P. S. King, 1936), p. 142, table XIX. Author cites *Le Temps*, March 2, 1932, and *La France Economique*.
Grand total: 7,765 million French francs (approx. 80 French francs to 1 pound sterling and 19 French francs to 1 U.S. dollar at 1923–24 exchange rates).

Bank for International Settlements (BIS) and other creditor governments, as well as an Austrian conversion loan in 1934.[60]

Excluding the French Treasury loan of 2.5 milliard francs to prop up the pound sterling in 1931, a large percentage of French loans, 61.4 percent, went to Central and Eastern Europe because of France's concern over security at Germany's eastern frontier. A great proportion of the rest went to Belgium and Turkey; the latter's loans were issued to consolidate the pre–World War I loans to the Ottoman Empire. Several of the loans to Eastern and Central Europe were offered under the auspices of the League of Nations, but those in 1931 to 1933 primarily came directly from the French Treasury or were government-guaranteed loans (see figure 2-4).

Another area of investment of French external capital in the interwar period was the French colonies. However, most of it involved refunding issues from prewar loans.[61] In conclusion, France offered little to the world in general in the way of development capital in the interwar period, and Paris was hardly a primary capital center, despite its potential. Most of France's external loans were politically directed.

Other Creditor States: The "Neutrals"

Only three other states remained creditors to the rest of the world during the interwar period: Switzerland, the Netherlands, and Sweden. Termed the "neutrals," they had a long tradition of trade and trade-related finance. During the early interwar years, 1919–20, they imported capital largely through the liquidation of foreign investment and the repatriation of short-term deposits held abroad. Argentina also loaned some funds to Europe in support of its trade in agricultural products and foodstuffs.[62]

The Debtor States

During the interwar period the debtor states fell into several different groupings, classified for convenience as: the British Empire; Germany; Central and Eastern Europe; Latin America; and China and Japan (see table 2-3). Borrowing during this period by the dominion states, particularly Australia, New Zealand, and Canada, largely represented a continuation of the loans from London to areas of recent settlement begun in the prewar period and requires no further discussion here. The other classifications are discussed briefly in the following sections.

Germany

Germany lost a considerable portion of its prewar external investments in the Ottoman Empire, Russia, and Austria-Hungary. In addition, external investments in Italy, the United States, and Belgium were sequestered. The only remaining external assets of Germany following the war were in Switzerland, Scandinavia, principally Sweden, and Latin America. Of approximately £1 billion of external investments as of 1914, £585 million were seized, £150 million were sold in the United States before its entry into the war, and some £200–300 million were lost or severely depreciated. Some £100–200 million remained unaffected at the end of the war, or 10–20 percent of the original capital invested.[63]

During the early postwar years, from 1919 to 1922, Germany ran a large current account deficit of $2,400 million in its balance of payments, largely offset by specula-

TABLE 2-3. Foreign Capital Issues by Category of Debtor

Annual average, millions of US$

Issues for the account of	United States	United Kingdom
Creditor countries		
Belgium	38	16
France	37	2
Netherlands	9	4
Sweden	16	7
Switzerland	9	–
Others	12	4
Total	121	33
Debtor countries (developed or semi-developed)		
Argentina	81	19
Australia and New Zealand	45	171
Canada	185	25
Denmark	17	0
Germany	224	34
Italy	69	4
Japan	59	16
Norway	26	0
Union of South Africa	0	30
Others	45	10
Total	751	309
Less-developed countries		
Latin American countries (except Argentina)	197	52
Asian countries (except Japan)	8	53
European less-developed countries	62	37
African countries (except Union of South Africa)	0	54
Others	2	0
Total	269	196
International corporations and unspecified	1	48
Total all issues	1,142	586

Source: United Nations, *International Capital Movements during the Inter-War Period* (Lake Success, N.Y.: Department of Economic Affairs, 1949), p. 26.

FIGURE 2-5.   Geographic Distribution of Long-Term Loans to Germany, 1925–30

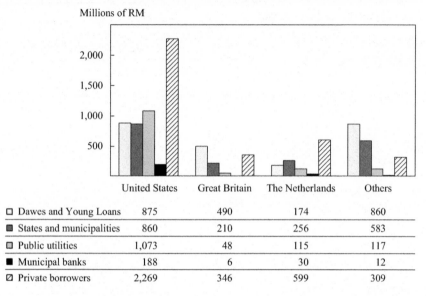

	United States	Great Britain	The Netherlands	Others
☐ Dawes and Young Loans	875	490	174	860
◼ States and municipalities	860	210	256	583
☐ Public utilities	1,073	48	115	117
◼ Municipal banks	188	6	30	12
☑ Private borrowers	2,269	346	599	309

Source: "The Credit Situation of Germany," *The Economist—Supplement*, August 21, 1931, Appendix II.

tive purchases of marks and mark-denominated assets by foreigners expecting the German economy and mark to stabilize.[64] *The Economist* estimated the sale of marks and mark-denominated assets to foreigners at 11,000 million gold marks between 1919 and 1923. Ironically, during this same period there was also flight from the mark, related largely to the anticipated heavy reparations burden.[65] Not only did rampant inflation and rapid devaluation of the mark wipe out Germany's internal public debt and the savings of the German people from mid-1921 through 1923, but it also effectively annulled these short-term speculative claims on its balance of payments.[66]

The Dawes Loan assisted Germany in stabilizing its currency and renewed confidence in the economy. Thereafter, during the period 1924–30, international private market loans began to pour into Germany in ever-increasing amounts (see figure 2-5). They went to the federal government, states and municipalities, industry, and major German banks. Not only was private capital attracted by the apparent German stability, but the shortage of external capital forced Germany to raise interest rates. As Derek Aldcroft notes: "The main attraction for investors was the high rates of interest consequent upon the scarcity of capital. Lenders poured capital into Germany without a thought as to how the loans were to be serviced."[67]

The Wiggins Committee that investigated the credit situation in Germany during August 1931 concluded that its gross indebtedness had grown by Reichmarks (RM) 25.5 milliard from 1924 to 1931,[68] with net foreign indebtedness at RM15.8 milliard. C. R. S. Harris, however, concluded that the Wiggins report underestimated Germany's total indebtedness,[69] and *The Economist* pointed out that the report omitted some RM6 milliard of direct external investments in Germany.[70]

The transfer burden was largely ignored by the market as long as Germany could continue borrowing to roll over its debt service. Keynes repeatedly called attention to this transfer burden, culminating in his article in 1929 and the debate that ensued between him and Bertil Ohlin and Jacques Rueff.[71] Toward the end of the decade, the pressure resulting from the short-term borrowing of German banks from international banks on acceptances that were then re-lent on a long-term basis within Germany became substantial (see table 2-4).[72] There is no question, however, that external financing assisted Germany in rebuilding its infrastructure and industrial plant during the interwar period. German industry either borrowed abroad directly or received loans from the German great banks, which had borrowed abroad to finance a broad spectrum of large-scale German industry.[73]

After World War I there was also a continuation of the trend toward concentration in the banking industry. Parallel with the banking mergers was the formation of large concerns and trusts in heavy industry. However, the condition of the major German banks deteriorated significantly after 1914 during the interwar period. They had lost significant overseas assets during World War I, and the inflation in the 1921–23 period severely eroded their capital base. By 1929, foreign deposits and loans amounted to some 42.5 percent of the banks' overall liabilities. The maturity of these loans and deposits had also shortened dramatically since the prewar period.

As early as November 1924, the German federal government could, through the Foreign Loans Advisory Council, reject foreign loans for municipal and state governments. The council actually refused $121.5 million of the $411 million in loan projects submitted. However, the will to continue refusing loans in the midst of apparent prosperity and what might be termed a credit "mania" soon dissolved, and little was done to stem the tide as the decade progressed.[74]

Germany built up large-scale external indebtedness in the period 1924 to 1928, much of it sovereign debt. When the reparations burden is added to that of private market loans, it is open to question whether Germany could have continued absorbing external debt at the same pace for much longer, even if an economic crisis had not by 1931 abruptly stemmed its borrowing. Germany's economic alternatives were limited: an attempt to balance its external balance of payments would have required a severe deflation, and the alternative of inflating out of the crisis by ignoring a balanced

TABLE 2-4. German Short-Term Debts, as of September 30, 1932

Millions of Reichmarks

Debtors	Banks	Reichsbank and Golddiskont Bank	Industry, Commerce, Transport, and Agriculture	Other debtors	Government municipalities	Total
Total short-term debts	3,861	814	3,745	305	622	9,347
Creditors						
Banks	3,342	814	1,656	95	535	6,442
Financial houses	118	0	355	47	4	524
Commercial and industrial companies	109	0	1,405	47	2	1,563
Other creditors	292	–	329	116	81	818
Creditor countries						
United States	1,592	190	640	33	443	2,898
Great Britain	661	0	423	25	62	1,171
France	239	0	134	8	18	399
Netherlands	373	0	1,081	78	27	1,559
Switzerland	613	0	859	84	55	1,611
Belgium	34	0	89	4	1	128
Italy	17	0	39	6	2	64
Czechoslovakia	54	0	68	5	2	129
Denmark	18	0	27	5	0	50
Sweden	35	0	48	7	12	102
Other countries	225	0	337	50	0	612
Bank for International Settlements	–	624	0	0	0	624

Source: C. R. S. Harris, *Germany's Foreign Indebtedness*, published under the auspices of The Royal Institute of International Affairs (Oxford University Press, 1935), p. 21.

budget and going off the gold standard was largely precluded because of the earlier experience with hyperinflation. (Germany's response to the financial crisis of 1931 and the subsequent Depression is discussed in the ensuing chapters.)

The Central and Eastern European States

The Paris peace treaties left a legacy of sovereign debt and reparations for the Eastern and Central European states, primarily the new ones emerging from the dissolution of the Austro-Hungarian Empire; these debts were known as debts of succession.[75]

TABLE 2-5.   League of Nations Loans (League Loans)

Millions of £

| | | Issuing countries | | | |
Loan	Amount of issue	Great Britain	United States	France	Others
Austrian (6%) Gold Loan, 1923	32.0	14.0	5.1	1.4	11.5
Hungarian (7½%) state loan, 1924	14.1	7.9	1.5	n.a.[a]	4.7
Greek (7%) refugee loan, 1924	12.3	7.5	2.3	n.a.	2.5
Bulgarian (7%) settlement loan, 1926	3.2	1.7	0.9	n.a.	0.6
Estonian bank and currency reform loan (7%), 1927	1.5	0.5	0.8	n.a.	0.2
Danzig 6½% (tobacco monopoly) state loan, 1927	1.9	1.5	0	n.a.	0.4
Greek stabilization and refugee loan (6%), 1928	7.6	3.4	3.1	n.a.	1.1
Bulgarian stabilization loan (7½%), 1928	6.2	1.5	1.8	1.0	1.9
Total League Loans	78.8	38.0	15.5	2.4	22.9

Source: The Economist, November 19, 1932, pp. 938–39.

a. Not applicable.

Their debt burdens coexisted with the need of these states to establish stable currencies, feed their populations in the midst of war-ravaged economies, rebuild those economies, and establish an administrative infrastructure for their governments.

Initial aid for relief and reconstruction was supplied primarily by the United States and Great Britain, as private capital was not attracted to the region's fragile economies.[76] In addition, there were the League Loans. The overall objective of these loans was to establish a basic economic independence for these states, without which political independence would not have been meaningful.[77] More specifically, the loans were designed to provide exchange reserves with which to establish central banks, following the liquidation of the Austro-Hungarian Bank, as well as to fund short-term debt, incurred mostly to finance imports. They were also provided to support the vast resettlement of refugees that resulted from the breakup of the Empire.

Between 1923 and 1928, eight loans for £79 million in capital were floated in the private capital market of the creditor countries under the auspices of the League of Nations (see table 2-5).[78] Only the first of these loans to Austria was guaranteed by creditor governments, while the rest were floated freely as private market loans.

However, all the loans were issued under schemes recommended by the financial committee of the League of Nations and approved by the Foreign Loans Advisory Council. In some cases, a definite system of League control or conditionality was included to monitor the economies of these states with respect to amortization. In effect, the League served as an intermediary, supervising the loans through a financial committee that reviewed the economies and financial requirements of these states. A League commission oversaw the service of the loans, which were usually secured by a first charge on particular state revenues or real assets.[79]

The issuance of the League Loans was handled by a consortium or syndicate of merchant and joint-stock banks in London, Vienna, New York, Berlin, Stockholm, and Milan. They effectively revived the nineteenth-century practice of syndicating sovereign loans in several international capital markets as part of one loan package. In this case the purpose was to spread the loans geographically to avoid the potential political pressure on these states that might arise were the loans to be concentrated in one market.

To raise these loans in the various financial markets, the Reparations Commission had to agree temporarily to suspend reparations and to release some of the assets securing the reparations as security for the League Loans. This measure was accomplished starting with the Austrian loan. In many respects, this initial League Loan was comparable to the Dawes Loan, as thereafter it was possible to raise all further loans to the region through the private market. As noted, some were issued under League auspices. As V. N. Bandera observed, "The loans under the auspices of the League of Nations are especially interesting since they were the first experiments in arranging concrete economic action by a worldwide community of nations."[80]

Foreign capital formed the bulk of the commercial liabilities of the Baltic states, as well as of Hungary, where the influence of private external bank capital was the most pronounced. Only Czechoslovakia remained the exception: it was a small creditor state throughout the interwar period, following initial stabilization.[81]

Bandera notes the overwhelming problem of the ever-mounting debt service from some states as the decade progressed: "By 1928, a 'normal' pre-Depression year, out payments on account of capital service were 40 percent of the net capital inflows for Hungary, 28 percent for Poland, and 70 percent for Estonia. Little wonder that at the outset of the international financial crisis the rigid capital services demand rose rapidly, swiftly above the abruptly reduced capital inflows."[82]

Only the Baltic states escaped crisis. They borrowed selectively for immediately productive purposes, allocating the foreign funds meticulously to projects with the highest priority. Thus the potential service difficulties were mitigated by the generally high productivity of borrowed capital.[83] Virtually all of the Eastern and Central

European states, with the exception of Czechoslovakia and the Baltic states, were capital importers on an increasing scale, until their financing was abruptly cut off in the Depression. Their dependency on external capital was clear.[84]

Latin America

Investments in Latin America in the interwar period have to be viewed in two distinct geographic areas. The first is the Caribbean and Central America, in which the United States continued to invest for strategic reasons and because of the general economic and political instability in those areas. Despite a qualified acceptance of the principles of the Calvo Doctrine and the approval of the Hague Convention on Pecuniary Claims of 1907, the United States maintained "economic protectorates" in Nicaragua, the Dominican Republic, Haiti, and Panama intermittently from 1912 on through much of the interwar period.[85]

The second area was South America. From 1924 to 1930, external loans to South America were revived after a period of relative financial isolation due to World War I and the immediate postwar recovery years. Latin America was one of the major borrowing regions in the 1920s, as it had been during much of the nineteenth century. However, the United States replaced Great Britain as the region's major source of capital, with Latin America absorbing 24 percent of the new external capital issued in New York between 1924 and 1928. In addition, direct investment from the United States, primarily in public utilities, extractive industries, and agricultural commodities, moved in parallel with the loans, accounting for 44 percent of new direct external investment from the United States abroad.[86]

Most of the loans were publicly floated bonds for Latin American governments and municipalities, with an average yield of over 7 percent, substantially higher than the yield on U.S. domestic bonds. Frequently, this capital was used to cover obligations on prior loans to British, French, and German bondholders. In addition, loans were acquired to finance domestic budget deficits. When these deficits persisted toward the end of the decade, the debt service became difficult to sustain. The transfer problem was also acute because of a secular decline in commodity prices throughout the latter part of the decade. By the end of the 1920s, Latin America was paying some $600 million abroad in debt service annually, a sum substantially larger than the capital inflow.[87]

Initially, most of the loans and investments to expand agricultural commodity production during the war and interwar period increased the region's export earnings. However, some of the borrowing—Brazil's coffee loans, for example, acquired to build a buffer stock to prop up the export price of coffee—proved unsupportable once the Depression set in,[88] and the progressive decline in commodity prices in the late 1920s led to a drop in export earnings. A further problem was that the demand for these products proved relatively unstable and actually fell during the Depression.

The difficulty Latin American states had in meeting their debt service after the fall in commodity prices was not unique; the Central and Eastern European states, Canada, Australia, New Zealand, and India, among others, all experienced it.[89] However, other countries were not as reliant on single commodity exports; nor had they borrowed outside as heavily during the interwar period. By the early 1930s all the Latin American states had a debt service problem except Venezuela, an exporter of petroleum, which was able to retire its external debt during this time. Argentina, a relatively developed country, exported a diversity of products and was not as severely affected by the drop in commodity prices.[90]

Instead of adopting economic adjustment measures, the Latin American states responded to the severe transfer problems toward the end of the 1920s and in the early 1930s by acquiring a continuous stream of external loans, primarily from the United States, to cover their debt service. The substantial unamortized debt that had accumulated in the prewar period added to the total burden. Even had loans not suddenly been cut off, the debt service problem of these states would have been difficult to resolve because most of the Latin American states failed to adopt adjustment policies. As it was, the combination of poor fiscal administration, budget deficits, falling commodity export earnings, and a sharp cutback in external loans led to pervasive defaults through the region, as detailed in chapter 3.

It is striking to note that the cumulative British and French investment in Latin America, built up over a period of almost a century, was surpassed by U.S. investments in just a thirty-year period, from 1900 to 1930, with the large majority of those loans and investments occurring in just five years, from 1924 to 1928.[91] The scale of those loans and investments in such a few years would prove costly when the speculative bubble burst during the Depression.

Japan and China

During the period just before World War I, Japan had become a regular borrower in the European capital market. Despite tight control over external financing and a strong industrial and banking base, Saburo Okita and Takeo Miki maintain that Japan would have faced difficulties in servicing its external debts had the war not arrived.[92] As it was, exports to Europe as a result of the war allowed Japan to become a creditor nation.

The end of the war brought a sharp recession, and Japan limited its borrowing to three purposes: (i) national and local government loans, primarily related to the Yokohama earthquake disaster; (ii) a substantial increase in corporate loans, particularly for electric utilities; and (iii) support for colonial expansion, particularly in Taiwan, Korea, Manchuria, and later, northern China.[93] In addition to government borrowing, a large number of loans were secured by the Oriental Development Company, the South Manchuria Railway Company, and the Taiwan Electric Power Company in order to promote economic development in Japan's spheres of influence.[94] The expansion into Manchuria and northern China conflicted with U.S. foreign policy, which sought an open door for all powers within China, as well as respect for Chinese sovereignty. The State Department sought to deny loans to Japan explicitly destined for use in China or other spheres of Japanese influence.[95]

Great Britain and the United States were Japan's principal creditors, with the former's investment at £63 million and the latter's at $445 million ($383 million of which were loans or portfolio investments).[96]

In China, on the other hand, the prewar pattern in which direct investments were more important than sovereign loans persisted. Direct investment by foreigners in China doubled between 1902 and 1914 and then doubled again from 1914 to 1931 (see table 2-6). Foreign investments in China in 1931 ran $3,000–$3,500 million, while external debt obligations were $711 million, of which $428 million had been borrowed for general purposes by the Chinese government and $248.5 million were government-guaranteed railway obligations.[97]

The increase in Japanese economic penetration of China in contrast to that of the other powers between 1914 and 1931 is striking.[98] The most important loans of this period to China were the so-called Nishihara loans of 1918, which virtually doubled China's obligations to Japan overnight. These loans were extended via negotiations between Japan and China headed by K. Nishihara, the representative in China of Premier Count Terauchi of Japan. They took place outside the framework of the "old consortium." The loans were offered in exchange for an agreement in principle by China to recognize Japan's interests and claims in Manchuria. This violation of the consortium arrangement was protested unsuccessfully by the member banks, even the Yokohama Specie Bank of Japan, and by the powers.

In the interwar period, as in the prewar period, China remained open to the economic exploitation of the powers. Increasingly, however, Japan replaced all other creditors, as it attempted to extend its sphere of influence. As the period progressed, the relationship between Japan and China, and between Japan and the other powers, grew increasingly strained over Japan's establishment of Manchuko, a puppet state

TABLE 2-6.   Investments in China, as of 1931

Country	Investment amount (US$)	Percent
Great Britain	1,189,000,000	34
Japan	1,137,000,000	32
Russia	273,000,000	8
United States	197,000,000	6

Source: C. F. Remer, *Foreign Investments in China* (New York: Macmillan, 1933), p. 133.

Note: Britain and Japan held the majority of government debt. Geographically, investments remained confined to spheres of influence.

in Manchuria, and its militaristic adventures in northern China. Moreover, China faced a growing internal threat from the Communists.[99] The financial aid and loans that flowed to China went increasingly for armaments; by 1931–32, half the expenditures of the Chinese government were for military purposes.[100]

Like other underdeveloped borrowing states, China bore a heavy burden of external debt from the prewar period. In China's case it was primarily the result of the large reorganization loan provided by a consortium of lenders in 1913.

Why Did Creditors Provide External Finance in the Interwar Period?

It must be asked why private capital market lending resumed on such a large scale after the war, particularly in light of the Russian debt repudiation and other losses in the Ottoman Empire, Central and Eastern Europe, Central America, and Mexico. One answer was certainly the renewed faith in the international economy following the Dawes Loan, Britain's return to the gold standard, with sterling at its prewar exchange rate against the dollar, and the widespread return of economic prosperity. In the United States and Great Britain, the two major creditor states, there was a resurgence of the spirit of laissez-faire in international capital movement, spurred by the assumption that the economic harmony of interests that had prevailed during the nineteenth century was again present in the interwar period.[101]

The increased concentration in banking in all the major creditor states during this era allowed large joint-stock banks to extend their influence in international finance, continuing a trend started in the last quarter of the nineteenth century. The flotation of foreign issues was profitable for the fees, commissions, foreign exchange business, and operating balances it offered. Syndicates of the now powerful New York investment and joint-stock banks marketed loans aggressively throughout the world, just as the British and continental merchant bankers had during their heyday.

The investing public purchased external loans because they offered a high return or yield. In the United States, foreign loans averaging 7 percent interest and selling at a discount meant yields substantially above those offered by triple A–rated domestic bonds. In Great Britain, the Trust Acts and Colonial Stock Act channeled investments into the British Empire, even though the yields were not substantially greater than domestic alternatives. However, foreign loans outside the Empire did provide substantial "spreads" or yields above those in the domestic market.

The United States retained a substantial surplus on the trade account in its international balance of payments with the rest of the world during the entire interwar period. The only way this trend could be sustained and the "dollar gap" narrowed was by relending capital to the world, just as Great Britain had in the nineteenth century. However, the United States also remained a strongly protectionist nation during this period, a trade policy that was inconsistent with its position as the world's economic power.

Private market loans were supported by creditor governments where political and strategic interests were at stake. Britain encouraged loans to the Empire, particularly India, and to the dominions, which were considered essential to Britain's ability to maintain its position as a great power. The Empire was also becoming increasingly costly to sustain, and private market loans relieved part of the burden. The United States, in its shift from a major debtor state before the war to a major creditor state, now increasingly projected its economic power via the international capital market and large-scale direct investments by multinational corporations in areas of political and economic interest. The government encouraged private bank loans, under paternal supervision, to help the Central American and Caribbean states achieve financial stability.

The creditor states had supported the Dawes and Young Loans to Germany and the League Loans to Central and Eastern Europe, raised through the private capital markets, in an attempt to provide economic and political stability in Europe. In addition, the U.S. government wanted payment of the inter-Allied war debts, while the Allies wanted the reparations to continue, both of which could only be achieved by supplying Germany with alternative sources of funds.

Later in the decade France supported loans to the Little Entente and Poland in renewed strategic concern over Germany. Direct loans and loan guarantees from the French government were in principle a departure from its nineteenth-century practice and much of the interwar practice. However, for the most part, higher political and strategic concerns prevailed over those of the creditworthiness of Eastern Europe.

In a similar vein, loans were denied to states whose political and strategic interests were deemed adverse to creditor states. The capital markets never opened up for loans to Russia, in large part because it had repudiated its debt and in part because of opposing ideological viewpoints. The United States denied loans to Japan that were specifically earmarked for Manchuria. Other reasons for denying loans related to purchases of armaments and support for monopolies or cartels.[102]

Why Did States Borrow in the Interwar Period?

After the war, states borrowed initially to reconstruct their economies. Germany, the largest debtor in the interwar period, also needed to pay the reparations and rid itself of the onerous French-Belgian occupation of the Ruhr; it expected that the reparations would end the occupation of the Rhineland. Germany also borrowed to stabilize its currency following the rampant inflation and currency devaluation of 1922 to 1923.

The Eastern European states used the League Loans primarily for currency stabilization and to establish central banking, as well as to pay the debts they inherited from the Austro-Hungarian Empire. They also owed reparations, or some of the burden of "liberation costs." To a great extent, private market loans were inextricably linked to the legacy of the war and the peace treaties.

Many states, aside from the successor states, bore a substantial burden of unamortized prewar private market loans, and they contracted new loans to re-fund or repay these old ones. In Latin America, for example, older British and French loans were often retired by fresh borrowing from the United States.

After 1924, Latin America and the Commonwealth states used loans to support agricultural and other commodity production. Direct investment also flowed into these and other areas for ventures in mining and oil exploration and development. Toward the end of the 1920s, some states borrowed increasingly in an attempt to prop up commodity prices by building buffer stocks, the classic example being the Sao Paulo Coffee Realization Loan of 1930.

States also borrowed, as in the nineteenth century, in emulation of the industrial creditor states. In Eastern Europe, industrialization was attempted through state capitalism, in Poland and Czechoslovakia, for example. Mexico incurred debt as a result of the nationalization of its railways, a precursor to the 1938 oil and agricultural land expropriations.

Many states borrowed for social overhead projects which were unlikely to produce any financial returns, particularly the German states and municipalities after the 1924 Dawes Loan. This trend caused Hjalmar Schacht, Germany's currency commissioner in the Finance Ministry, as well as Parker Gilbert, the agent general for

FIGURE 2-6.   External Public Indebtedness of Selected Countries, 1930

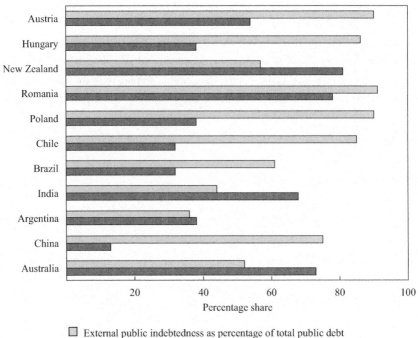

Source: The Royal Institute of International Affairs, *The Problem of International Investment* (Oxford University Press, 1937), p. 225.

reparations, , to question whether Germany's external borrowing could ever produce a productive stream of earnings to resolve the transfer problem.

Countries also borrowed to postpone adjustment. States with weak fiscal systems and great social demands for infrastructure and social welfare found external borrowing to be politically easier than reorganizing their economies. Many used loans to cover persistent trade deficits and balance of payments disequilibriums.[103] Finally, the debtor states, lacking financial centers of their own, were forced to revert to the few creditor states and their banks and capital markets.

The developing nations attracted only a small percentage of the external capital (see figure 2-6). The major debtors—Germany, Canada, Australia, New Zealand, Argentina, and Japan—were considered to be developed or semi-developed countries. On an annual basis from 1924 to 1928, external capital issues to other creditor countries, both developed and semi-developed countries, averaged $1,314 million, while external capital issues for underdeveloped countries averaged $513 million annually. Loans from the smaller creditors, the Netherlands and Switzerland, went primarily to other creditors or to their colonies. On the basis of the proportion of external public indebtedness to total foreign capital employed, New Zealand, Japan, and Australia were clearly the major sovereign debtors. However, on the basis of external public indebtedness to total public debt (external and domestic), Romania, Austria, Poland, Hungary, Chile, China, Peru, and Colombia were the major debtor states, a fact that illustrates their dependence on external capital for public revenues.

THREE

Debt Service Disruptions

At the onset of World War I, Mexico defaulted on its external debt obligations, largely as a result of the Mexican Revolution. In the midst of World War I, Russia repudiated its debt as a result of the Bolshevik Revolution. There were, however, no substantial defaults in the interwar period until the Depression. Then, starting in 1931, there was a wave of defaults, moratoriums, and standstill agreements that peaked in 1933. What were viewed initially as temporary debt service disruptions hardened during the depths of the Depression. During the interwar period, the capital markets remained closed to states in permanent and semi-permanent default, with many substantive debt settlements occurring only after World War II and the establishment of the Bretton Woods institutions, the International Monetary Fund (IMF) and the International Bank for Reconstruction and Development (the World Bank).

Pre-Depression Defaults

There were a few notable defaults before the Depression in Mexico owing largely to the Mexican Revolution and the major debt repudiation by the Bolsheviks in 1917.

Mexico

After many years of defaults, conversions, reconversions, and defaults during the nineteenth century, following an initial default in 1825, Mexico resumed borrowing in the capital markets of Europe and the United States in 1886, after the consolidation of its external debt.[1] Thereafter, Mexico was a regular and large-scale external borrower, primarily for railway construction and subventions, and payment of guarantees to railway concessionaires.[2] In 1914, however, in the midst of the anarchy of the Mexican Revolution, Mexico again defaulted on its external debt and also nationalized the railways.[3]

In 1922, following extensive negotiations with the International Committee of Bankers established to renegotiate Mexico's debt service obligations, creditors assumed that an agreement had been reached,[4] and an arrangement for payment of the Mexican debt was declared operative at the end of 1923. However, after making an initial payment, Mexico made no further ones and instead reverted to the earlier default.[5]

In 1925 the International Committee of Bankers again believed they had reached an agreement with Mexico, with the resumption of debt service payments to be secured by national oil exports and oil production taxes. Moreover, the railways were to be turned over to private management and the railway loans secured by mortgages on the system and on revenues.[6] In 1926, Mexico revised the settlement relating to the national external debt, although not the railways. Then, in 1927, because of internal political difficulties, Mexico failed to effect even the transfer on the railway loans.[7] To keep the renegotiated agreement of 1925 intact, the International Committee of Bankers provided Mexico with two "involuntary" loans, one of which—for $2 million—was used to pay the service on the external debt for the current period. These loans were issued without security on the good faith of the Mexican government.[8]

Plagued by internal political disorder, including the assassination of President Alvaro Obregon, Mexico terminated the agreement with the bondholders on January 1, 1928, and negotiations between the bankers and the Mexican government began again.[9] In 1930, Mexico reached an ad referendum agreement with the Bankers Committee to convert the external debt into two series of conversion bonds, A and B, at a unified rate of 5 percent interest, to be secured by all the customs revenue. The national railway debt was also to be converted under a separate scheme. In recognition of Mexico's capacity to pay—or lack thereof—the committee agreed to a rescheduling of Mexico's debt over forty-five years. It also agreed to a reorganization of the insolvent national railway into a new system, with payments also rescheduled over forty-five years and an improvement loan of $25 million to be arranged by the bankers.[10] Added to the external debt were claims resulting from the Mexican Revolution that had not been included in the settlement.[11]

In 1931, after Mexico failed to respect the 1930 agreement because of the Depression, the bankers made a fresh arrangement calling for a postponement or a moratorium until January 4, 1934.[12] At the Pan-American Conference in Montevideo in 1933, Mexico proposed a six-year moratorium on all of Latin America's external debt, but the other countries declined to participate in this proposal for a "debtors' cartel."[13] In addition, in 1932–33 Mexico reached agreement with three leading foreign oil companies—Aguila, Huasteca, and Pierce—whereby they agreed to advance a loan of $7 million in anticipation of oil tax receipts.[14]

By 1934, as the Depression extended, Mexico was in a full default that continued until a 1942 agreement was reached on direct external debt that was not enemy owned or controlled. The agreement provided for a repurchase of the external debt by the Bank of Mexico at a steep discount on the outstanding bonds.[15] Moreover, the national railway debt was excluded from the arrangement, and a separate agreement on it was not concluded until 1948.[16] The Mexican Oil Expropriation of 1938 was subject to separate negotiations; an agreement for payment concluded on August 29, 1947, was thereafter respected by the government.[17]

Thus Mexico's default, which had begun in 1914 and continued owing largely to the Mexican Revolution, went through several interim agreements and was finally renegotiated in stages in 1942 and 1948. The negotiations were exceedingly difficult, given that the revolution had at its roots a profound rejection of all things foreign, the length and depth of the worldwide Depression, and the symbolic actions and assertions of economic sovereignty embodied in the nationalization of the railways and expropriation of the foreign-owned oil companies. The ultimate agreements came at great cost to bondholders but did uphold the principle of negotiation to resolve external debt in default. The International Committee of Bankers on Mexico, representing the major international banks of New York, the Continent, and Great Britain, was powerless to enforce an agreement without support or diplomatic representation from the creditor governments. On the other hand, Mexico did default repeatedly and failed to respect several negotiated arrangements, but ultimately did not repudiate despite the revolution.

The Russian Debt Repudiation

It is estimated that at the outbreak of World War I the Russian government owed external creditors approximately ₽5.5 billion (Russian rubles) in the form of direct

TABLE 3-1.   Foreign Investment in Russia, 1914

Millions of US$

Creditor	Government municipal and railway bonds	Percent	Commercial investments	Percent	Maximum total	Percent
France	2,720	62.9	323–377	22.5	3,097	51.6
Great Britain	333	7.7	261	15.6	594	9.9
Belgium	205	4.7	165–470	28.0	675	11.3
Germany	554	12.8	227–446	26.6	1,000	16.7
United States	10	0.3	58	3.5	68	1.1
Other countries	503	11.6	63	3.8	566	9.4
Total	4,325	100.0	1,097 to 1,675	100.0	6,000	100.0

Source: Harvey E. Fisk, *Inter-Ally Debts: An Analysis of War and Post-War Finance* (New York: Bankers Trust Publications, 1924), p. 302

Note: Percentages added based on highest figure provided.

government debts, railway guarantees, and municipal loans (see table 3-1). Moreover, private loans by banks, industry, and commerce totaled an additional ₽2 billion.[18] These loans were extended by the primary capital markets of Europe, with French investors accounting for approximately 63 percent of the total and the rest spread among German (13 percent), British (8 percent), Belgian (5 percent), and other investors (11 percent).[19] In addition to the pre-1914 investments up to the moment of the Bolshevik Revolution, Russia received substantial loans from the Allies, equal to approximately ₽7.7 billion, a virtual doubling of the external debt. If credit is given for an estimated ₽1 billion of gold shipped by Russia to Great Britain as partial security for the Allied loans, the total net external debt is estimated at ₽13.8 billion, or approximately $6.9 billion.[20]

The socialist revolutionaries Lenin, Nikolai Bukharin, and Rosa Luxemburg focused on finance capital as the "highest stage of capitalism," which they believed was the major cause of imperialism. The exploitation of the world by a handful of capitalist powers and their banks—referred to as monopoly capital—would lead inevitably to competition and conflict among the powers and the destruction of capitalism.[21] These ideas were not only expressed as ideological beliefs; they also formed the basis for the policies of debt repudiation and bank nationalization instituted when the Bolsheviks came to power. As E. H. Carr observed: "The financial policy of the Bolsheviks before the October revolution had been summed up by two demands repeatedly and emphatically expressed, the nationalization of the banks and the annulment of the financial obligations of previous Russian governments."[22]

The principle of nonrecognition of the debts of the Tsarist regime was first pro-
claimed in the Viborg Manifesto, which the Petrograd Soviet issued in December 1905
to discredit the government's attempts to raise loans abroad following the war with
Japan.[23]

The Bolsheviks, particularly Lenin, perceived World War I as presenting new
and unique opportunities for socialist revolution, a stance that led to a split with the
Second International. International socialists somewhat naively believed that a general strike would quickly end the war once it had begun, and the International Congress of 1907 made it the duty of socialists to lead a general strike in the event of war.[24]
However, the war, as Lenin wrote from his Swiss exile early in 1917, was "a mighty
accelerator of events and its social, political and economic results were even more lasting than the immense physical damage which it inflicted on Europe."[25] Lenin concluded that the inability of capitalism to preserve international order, as reflected by
the war, afforded socialism great strategic opportunities. He stated that: (i) the task
of the socialist revolutionary was to wage a constant revolutionary struggle and take
advantage of the propensity of capitalists to wage war—that is, to turn the proletar-
iat against the ruling class and the state; and (ii) the stages of economic development
crucial to Marx's theory must be relegated to second place in view of the unique opportunity offered by the war. Russia therefore offered a unique opportunity for the
Bolshevik Revolution to be followed, it was assumed, by a general proletarian revolution, to begin in Germany as a result of disillusionment with the war and capitalist
leadership.[26]

One of the first steps taken by the new Soviet government following the revolution was to enact what became two planks of their program: annulment of the foreign debt and nationalization of the banks. On February 8, 1918, a decree was printed
in Pravda annulling the public loans. The decree, adopted by the Central Executive
Committee of the Soviet, read as follows: "All State loans concluded by the Governments of the Russian landlords and Russian bourgeoisie, enumerated in a special
list, are hereby repudiated as from December 14, 1917. In the same way are all the
guarantees repudiated which the said Governments gave to loans of various concerns and bodies. All foreign loans, without exception, are absolutely repudiated."[27]

As Carr noted, the annulment of the debt caused little reaction within Russia itself, where the inability as well as the unwillingness of the Soviet government to
discharge its obligations for foreign loans were taken for granted. However, the
repudiation provoked violent official and unofficial protests in the Allied countries.
The representatives of the principal creditor governments delivered a note to the
Soviet government declaring the annulment "without value" as far as they were
concerned.[28]

In addition to the debt repudiation, the government nationalized the banks, many of which were foreign owned. As Carr observed, this action "was the simplest and most concrete item in the Bolshevik financial program."[29] Lenin turned to the vital issue of nationalizing the banks in the course of 1917. "A group of banks," he wrote shortly after his return to Russia, "is feathering its nest out of the war and holds the whole world in its hands." He described the banks as "chief nerve centers of the whole capitalist system of national economy. Without nationalizing the big banks, socialism would be unrealizable."[30]

The debt repudiation became the focus of international contention. The Bolsheviks declared that the debts of the imperial (Tsarist) and provisional governments were not authorized by the people of Russia and that those governments were not representative of the people. Consequently, they said, the Soviet government was not liable for the debts.[31] Britain, France, and the other creditor governments claimed, on the other hand, that under international law the sanctity of a contract and generally accepted principles of government succession applied to the Soviet government and that therefore it was liable for these debts. As Moulton and Pasvolsky observed: "In this manner the Russian Government regime uprooted, as far as Russia was concerned, the whole economic system based on private contract and, by rejecting the very foundations upon which international credit and commercial intercourse among civilized nations is built, isolated Russia from the rest of the world."[32]

The Great Depression, Debt, and Defaults

The worldwide Depression that started in 1929 and lasted in many parts of the world through the mid-1930s had a profound impact on the external sovereign debt acquired by debtor states during the 1920s. That same debt also played a formidable role in causing the Depression and its severity. Irving Fisher, in his classic thesis, noted the following with respect to debt: "Disturbances in these two factors, debt and the purchasing power of the monetary unit, will set up serious disturbances in all, or nearly all, other economic variables. The depression out of which we are now (I trust) emerging is an example of the debt-deflation depression of the most serious sort. The debts of 1929 were the greatest known, both nominally and really up to that time."[33]

A more contemporary analysis of the Depression by Charles Kindleberger likewise notes the contribution of the sudden decline in international lending to the crisis.[34] The debt deflation theory presented by Fisher reared its ugly head again in reality during the 1990s in Japan and most recently during the euro crisis of the early 2000s as the eurozone overall faced deflationary pressures and countries such as Greece, Ireland, Portugal, and Spain found it difficult to escape their debt traps.[35]

The Depression was not just an economic event. It also had a strong influence on international relations in the 1930s. Politicians turned inward to address the crises in their own economies, particularly unemployment and bank failures. International economic cooperation largely went out the window in a *sauve qui peut* environment. In the United States, one hypothesis about the cause of the Depression was that America had caught some contagious economic disease from Europe as a result of the country's involvement in World War I. "This latter view that the Depression stemmed from Wilsonian internationalism was not an intelligent view but it offered a scapegoat for economic distress. . . . The Great Depression underlay the determination of American foreign relations during the years 1929–33."[36] A. J. P. Taylor describes the relationship of the Depression to international relations as follows: "International stability was first shaken by the collapse of economic stability in the Great Depression which began in October 1929. In most countries the Depression led to a runningaway from international affairs."[37]

Several aspects of the Depression and its relationship to external sovereign debt are explored here in greater detail: (i) the contribution of the decline in lending to debt defaults; (ii) the impact of defaults on the stock of, and yield on, external loans; and (iii) the specific defaults and negotiations leading to debt restructuring.

The Decline in International Lending

The surge of international lending from the United States to the rest of the world in the period 1924 to 1928 declined dramatically in 1929, as money was initially drawn from the bond market to the booming stock market. Thereafter, following the stock market crash and the growing economic depression, the capital markets remained generally moribund. The situation of debtor states as a group deteriorated sharply between 1928 and 1929 owing to the decline in capital and rise in debt service demand. By 1929 the debtors were paying $675 million a year more in interest, dividends, and amortization than they were receiving in net new long-term investments.[38]

Foreign bond issues in the United States had reached new peaks in the fourth quarter of 1927 and first half of 1928.[39] The decline in foreign lending actually began in the second half of 1928, particularly for German and other European issues, and Canadian borrowing also dropped sharply in the third quarter of 1928. Although it seemed that lending surged in 1930, the figures are distorted by the Young Loan and a large Canadian issue.[40] In addition to the inward flow of funds for debt amortization, once the Depression gathered momentum a flight of capital occurred from many debtor states to creditor states. Capital, in a reversal of its normal flow, moved from high-interest to low-interest centers and "flight to quality" that presumably offered maximum security.[41]

Debt Service Disruption during the Depression

While the Mexican default and the Russian debt repudiation were the major service disruptions during World War I and the interwar period, the substantial legacy of debt problems left by the war should have alerted overly enthusiastic investors to the dangers of external lending in the interwar period. In 1923 the Council of Foreign Bondholders reported the continued arrears on interest of Colombia, Costa Rica, Nicaragua, the Dominican Republic, Venezuela, and Guatemala from the war period, despite current service of their external debts. Paraguay was in default on its external debt, and China was in partial default.[42] The prewar external debts of the Austro-Hungarian Empire were the subject of a proposed arrangement, the Innsbruck Convention, negotiated with the successor and cessionary states.[43] Turkey had rejected the Treaty of Serves, which provided explicit protection for bondholders. The Treaty of Lausanne that replaced it gave explicit assurances for the debt service of the prewar Ottoman debt only in the territories under British and French control—Palestine, Mesopotamia, and Syria. The remainder was subject to future negotiations with Turkey, Greece, and other Balkan states that were assigned a portion of the Ottoman debt, debts of succession.[44]

As the period progressed, defaults on Chinese loans increased because of internal conflict, and by 1930 bondholders had failed to reach an accord with Turkey, despite years of negotiation. Greece, Bulgaria, Yugoslavia, and Albania continued to resist settlements as well.[45] The prewar debts of Austria-Hungary, the most complicated of the succession problems, were still subject to continuous negotiations with successor and cessionary states.[46] In Latin America, however, Ecuador and Mexico remained the only republics in default. Payments by Colombia, Costa Rica, Nicaragua, and other smaller Latin American debtors "created an aura of confidence perhaps unjustified by past performance."[47] By 1928 all the Latin American republics except Mexico and Ecuador were servicing their debts in a satisfactory manner.[48]

The picture changed dramatically in 1931 with the deepening of the Depression and the inability of major debtor states to raise loans in the primary capital markets. A wave of debt moratoriums, initially viewed as temporary measures, began in Latin America in the last quarter of 1931 and moved thereafter to Eastern Europe throughout 1932 and 1933. These moratoriums were accompanied by a number of other

TABLE 3-2. Defaults on Foreign Dollar Bonds, as of December 1935

Millions of US$

Region or country	Amount outstanding (1)	Interest in default (2)	Percent of interest in default (2/1)
Europe of which:	2,376	1,223	51.5
Germany	887	884	99.9
Latin America of which:	1,886	1,501	80.5
Argentina	351	88	25.3
Brazil	349	325	93.2
Chile	308	308	100.0
Colombia	156	156	100.0
Mexico	296	296	100.0
Total (all countries)	7,490	2,810	37.5

Source: Royal Institute of International Affairs, *The Problem of International Investment*, p. 307.

measures, such as exchange controls, abandonment of the gold standard, import quotas, and licensing schemes to prevent a loss of exchange.[49]

As of December 31, 1933, Winkler calculated that twenty-six countries were in default on federal, state, and municipal external debts equal to $22.3 billion in principal and $12.4 billion in interest, inclusive of the Russian repudiation and the southern states of the United States, still long in default, but exclusive of the reparations and war debts. Excluding those latter two defaults, $5.3 billion in principal and $1.5 billion in interest payments were in arrears.[50] The major incidence of default fell upon investors in the United States, as indicated in table 3-2. Some municipalities also defaulted, as did China for $81.7 million.[51]

Excluding Russia's war debt repudiations, defaults to British investors were negligible before 1930. As R. M. Kindersley observed, the only foreign loans outside the Empire after 1930 were "involuntary export of capital" or involuntary conversion of unremitted interest into capital in Latin America, Central and Eastern Europe, and Germany.[52] In comparison with the United States, Britain emerged relatively unscathed because of the concentration of investments in the Commonwealth states, which serviced their debts through great exercise of political and economic will, as well as conversions of internal and external debt. In addition, Britain's loans outside the Empire were primarily older prewar ones in productive assets that suffered a diminution in returns but not necessarily outright default.[53]

By the mid-1930s most loans in default were still that way, as the capital markets remained closed. Although the annual reports of the Bank for International Settlements (BIS) throughout these years anticipated the eventual reopening of the capital markets to international lending, it never happened.[54] As long as the capital markets remained closed, debtors had little interest in renegotiating their debts, and despite improvements in business conditions starting in 1934, most payments on bonds did not resume.[55]

As an article in the *Financial Times* notes, "Defaults in the 1930s invariably proved much deeper, larger and more subtle than anybody had expected."[56] Interestingly, the debtors proved most intractable as their economies improved. While no state in Latin America explicitly repudiated its debt, as was also true in the nineteenth century, neither did any state make a great effort to service it. Whereas in 1913 only 7.5 percent of the sterling securities in Latin America were in default, by 1938 the figure was 58 percent, and the average rate of return on nominal capital declined from 4.6 percent to 1.6 percent over the same period (see figure 3-1).[57] In eight Central and Eastern European countries (Austria, Bulgaria, Germany, Greece, Hungary, Poland, Romania, and Yugoslavia), the interest paid represented only 26 percent of that due.[58] By the end of 1932 the various League Loans were in different states of default, and their market value had declined over 50 percent from their original nominal value.[59] Cleona Lewis estimated that, by 1938, of approximately £11.3 billion in British investments in South America, 70 percent were in default, with the yield on these bonds declining from 4.6 percent to 1.6 percent.[60]

By 1940 the annual report of the Foreign Bondholders Protective Council (the American counterpart to the British Foreign Bondholders Corporation, established in 1933) indicated that the situation had not improved in Latin America. Only Argentina, the Dominican Republic, and Haiti showed no defaults, whereas of the total of public and publicly guaranteed bonds outstanding of $1,570 million, $1,168 million was in default with respect to interest and $44 million in fund payments. Thus 77.2 percent of the Latin American bonds outstanding were still in default (see figure 3-2).[61] The Latin American situation was exacerbated by political turmoil. As *The Economist* observed in January 1931: "The market felt the shock of political and economic upheavals in the leading South American republics. . . . When successive revolutions began to sweep through South America last year the cumulative effect on bondholders was naturally severe."[62]

The Liquidity Crisis in Austria and Germany:
Bank Failures and the Standstill Agreements

In 1930 the German banks that had borrowed short and lent long in the latter half of the 1920s were now faced with foreign deposit withdrawals and liquidation of external demand loans.[63] From August through October 1930 the major German

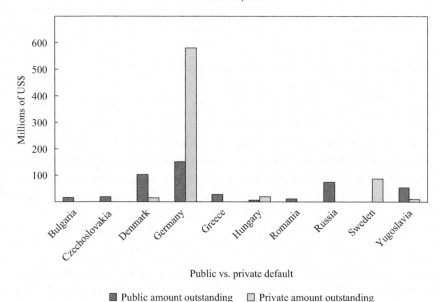

FIGURE 3-1. Interest Defaults on Foreign Dollar Bonds, Europe, December 31, 1935

Public vs. private default

■ Public amount outstanding ▫ Private amount outstanding

Source: Royal Institute of International Affairs, *The Problem of International Invesment* (Oxford University Press, 1937), p. 307.

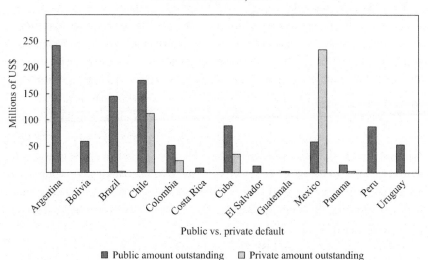

FIGURE 3-2. Interest Defaults on Foreign Dollar Bonds, Latin America, as of December 31, 1935

Public vs. private default

■ Public amount outstanding ▫ Private amount outstanding

Source: Royal Institute of International Affairs, *The Problem of International Investment*, p. 307.

banks lost RM700 million in foreign deposits and the Reichsbank RM1,000 million in gold. In the first four months of 1931 substantial additional interbank withdrawals occurred through banks located in the United States, Britain, the Netherlands, and Switzerland, all of which faced the deepening Depression.[64]

Events in Austria contributed to and accelerated the pace of the German banking crisis. The run on the Credit Anstalt and the failure of the rescue effort by the National Bank of Austria and the House of Rothschild required external help. An arrangement was negotiated through the BIS for a loan of AS100 million (Austrian schillings, or $14 million) to prop up the Credit Anstalt. It was a test case for the BIS as a lender of last resort. Given the fourteen days it took to arrange the loan through its member central banks, from May 14 to 31, and the relatively small amount raised, it is clear that the BIS was not adequate to the task.[65]

By June 5, Austria needed additional funds, which the BIS arranged by June 14, contingent on Austria's raising a two- to three-year loan of AS180 million. The French, as a condition for the proposed loan, insisted that the Zollverein (customs union) with Germany be abandoned, which Austria refused to do. The Bank of England then stepped in with a one-week loan that was thereafter rolled over for two months. When the League of Nations provided a loan of AS250 million in August 1931, the Bank of England was repaid. As Kindleberger observed, "It marked the beginning of the end of Great Britain's role as an international lender of last resort."[66]

The Credit Anstalt crisis was a pivotal event in the banking and liquidity crisis of the Depression. It proved the BIS was inadequately structured to serve as an international lender of last resort and that the major powers and their national banks were pulling against each other in the crisis, as the French politicized their demands. It also demonstrated Great Britain's inability to go it alone as a lender of last resort. The Austrian crisis led to widespread runs on banks in Central and Eastern Europe, as a lack of confidence in the financial system spread throughout the region.

The Austrian crisis also affected the German banks, causing a flight from the mark of RM3.5 milliard in 1931. Part of the withdrawals reflected the increasing difficulty of New York banks, which were exposed as a result of having made excessive short-term loans to German banks.[67] In turn, the German banking crisis provoked a widespread domestic liquidity crisis. By June 19, 1931, the Reichsbank found itself with just RM100 million in foreign exchange and gold cover above the legal minimum as stipulated by the Young Plan.[68]

On the night of June 20, 1931, Herbert Hoover, president of the United States, proposed a one-year moratorium on all international political debts, reparations as well as inter-Allied debts. This move was designed to prevent the collapse of the major

American banks, which were overexposed.[69] The French were incensed at the protection of commercial debt over reparations, which in their view had a prior claim on the credit of Germany, and delayed approval of the moratorium, since France stood to lose £100 million in unconditional reparations payments.

On June 27, 1931, the run on the German banks resumed. The Bank of England, the United States Federal Reserve Bank, and the Bank of France provided a joint credit of $100 million to stem the tide,[70] an amount that proved inadequate, and the crisis continued. The French approved the Hoover moratorium on July 6, but it was too late. On July 13, with the German banking crisis at a peak, the government called a bank holiday, and on July 16 the German banks joined in a "community of liabilities" under the leadership of a newly created institution, the Goldiskont (Gold Discount) Bank, a subsidiary of the Reichsbank, which opened to allow discounting of notes at the Reichsbank.[71]

It was obvious that Germany needed more external help. France, with its large gold reserves still relatively untouched by the Depression, was a logical candidate. However, the French continued to attach political conditions on their assistance to the German government under Chancellor Heinrich Brüning. They now insisted on: (1) an end to military demonstrations by the National Socialists; (2) the breakup of plans for the Zollverein with Austria; (3) an end to naval construction; and (4) following the Hoover moratorium, an end to Germany's objection to reparations.[72] France and Germany disagreed on the terms of the loan as well.[73]

A special group of financial experts, the Wiggins Committee, met under the auspices of the BIS and formulated the idea of the German standstill agreements. The committee recommended that existing short-term foreign credits to Germany be maintained and that the short-term loans previously withdrawn be replaced and converted into long-term ones.[74] Eventually a series of standstill agreements were negotiated between a committee representing the creditor banks and the major German banks. However, the latter two recommendations of the Wiggins Committee were never implemented.[75]

The liquidity crises that struck Austria, Central and Eastern Europe, and Germany in 1931 were indicative of the destabilizing influence of the short-term capital transfers during the interwar period. According to Hal Lary, no other development was more crucial to the deterioration and eventual collapse of the international financial system.[76]

The Response of Debtors and Creditors to Defaults in the Great Depression

The wave of defaults on private market debt during the Depression, the Hoover moratorium on inter-Allied debts, and the Lausanne Conference that effectively canceled the reparations highlighted the problem that all countries had in servicing their external debt in the midst of the Depression. In the nineteenth century, commonly accepted practices had evolved for renegotiating debt service disruptions or defaults; they presupposed that the capital markets would open to a sovereign debtor once its external debts were renegotiated. The 1930s changed the established pattern. With the capital markets moribund, the economic nationalism that asserted itself with vigor during the Depression resulted in a plethora of controls over international capital movements that had not been present from 1815 to 1914. Governments tried to reassert the assumed "community of common interest" that the doctrine of laissez faire implied for a short while after World War I—during the 1924–28 period—but it disintegrated before the forces of economic nationalism. Eventually autarky took control.[77]

Short-Term Debt

Faced with problems in securing long-term bond financing toward the end of the 1920s, Germany and the Central and Eastern European states, particularly Austria and Hungary, had begun to acquire significant short-term debt. To a large extent, these debts, based on acceptance financing from banks in the United States, were not backed by trade transactions and took on the characteristics of floating debt.[78] The German standstill agreements, which were debt moratoriums on these short-term loans, were concluded in 1931 and renewed thereafter until the German debt default in 1933–34.[79] Similar standstill arrangements were also concluded in Austria and Hungary to resolve the problem of short-term interbank debt.[80]

Ideological Defaults and Repudiations

The defaults and repudiations that had an ideological basis in this period were a new phenomenon. The Russian debt repudiation was the first major instance of a sovereign state denying its responsibility for the debts of a predecessor government for ideological reasons. The German debt defaults in 1933 and 1934, while not outright repudiation, were also cloaked in ideology, as the National Socialists wrapped all debts in the same nationalistic propaganda as reparations.[81] The Allies likewise objected to paying war debts when their citizens had liberally shed their blood in what was viewed as a common cause in defense of democracy.[82]

The defaults in Latin America were certainly politicized as a rash of new regimes came to power during the Depression, invariably overthrowing their debts or perpetuating existing defaults. The Mexican Revolution led Mexico to default on its direct external debt, a stance it held to throughout the Depression despite the series of negotiated agreements. It also resulted in the nationalization of the debt-laden railway system and the 1938 oil expropriation, as Mexico asserted its right to control its own resources and in general rejected foreign influence over its economy.

The repudiation and defaults in the interwar period clearly established not only that weak states would act "immorally," but also that the powers would default if it was in their perceived self-interest to do so. The focal issue I introduced in the introduction to this book with respect to sovereign defaults is best illustrated by these defaults—debtors needed to balance the sanctity of the contract, *pacta sunt servanda,* against the vital interest of states, *clausula rebus sic stantibus.*

Controls over Debt Repayment

The Depression saw the end of free capital movements. The major creditor states as well as the states of Latin America, Central and Eastern Europe, and Germany sought unlinked, autonomous solutions to protect their economies. These included, inter alia, abandonment of the gold standard, higher tariffs, preferential tariff arrangements, clearing agreements, exchange controls, quotas, blocked currency accounts, and a plethora of other devices.

The objective of the debtor states was in part to stop the flight of capital and to conserve foreign exchange by halting the payments of interest and dividends and the amortization of principal.[83] For example, under a law promulgated in Germany in June 1933, all payments on foreign debts were subject to control by a Konversionskasse (debt conversion office). Except for loans made by the Reichsbank, payments were no longer transferred in full, and even the partial payments were affected, paid partly in foreign exchange and partly in "scrip" discountable at various rates at the Goldiskont Bank. In addition, three categories of "blocked marks" were established: (i) registered marks arising out of repayments on the 1933 standstill agreements; (ii) credit marks, derived from credits not covered by the standstill agreements; and (iii) security marks, originating from the sale of securities. These three different types of marks were sold at various rates, from 15 to 50 percent of par value, and were subject to diverse restrictions. Their overall purpose was to cheapen their foreign exchange value while maintaining their domestic parity.[84] As a United Nations study on capital movements in the interwar years notes, "To a considerable extent, both long and short-term capital movements were blocked by exchange controls introduced in the majority of debtor countries at the time of the financial crisis of 1931, or in the course of the next few years."[85]

Open Market Repurchase of Debts

The exchange controls and defaults interacted to depress the bond market, so it was easier for debtor states to divert funds meant for debt service to the repurchase of bonds in the depressed capital markets.[86] In June 1934 the Reichsbank, under Hjalmar Schacht's direction, decided to suspend cash transfers on all medium- and long-term debt, including the Dawes and Young Loans.[87] Despite the protests of Britain and other creditor governments, particularly with respect to the Dawes and Young Loans, which were fully guaranteed by the German government, Germany turned toward the capital markets to repurchase its bonds at deep discount.[88]

Between 1930 and 1934, U.S. long-term investments abroad declined by over $2,000 million. The purchase of bonds on the open market accounted for approximately $566 million, or one quarter of the value of the decline. Germany alone repatriated RM781 million, of which RM549 million was used to stimulate exports. Argentina, Australia, and Japan all bought blocks of their bonds at depressed prices to reduce their external debt.[89]

Most analysts of the period considered repurchase of bonds in the open market immoral. As Edwin Borchard observed, "Repatriation, however, becomes tainted with bad faith and objectionable to bondholders if it is carried out by a debtor in default on its bonds."[90] H. C. Wallich had another viewpoint with respect to an overall solution to the problem of defaults and Latin American debtor states. He recognized that while countries benefited from their own defaults, repurchase still offered a potential solution to the debt problem because: (i) it was a one-time act that could be accomplished by drawing down foreign exchange reserves and gold and did not represent a perpetual drain, unlike debt service; (ii) repurchase would drive up the market price of the bonds and in the long run give as good a return to bondholders as any other solution; (iii) it would facilitate an overall debt settlement; and (iv) repurchase would improve the debt standing of the Latin American countries.[91]

Clearing Agreements

Another alternative to the direct payment of debts was bilateral clearing agreements. They rewarded vital trade partners but discriminated against nontrade partners in the settlement of external debts. Germany employed such agreements extensively during the 1930s, and by September 1934 it had established clearing agreements with the major creditor nations except the United States. As H. W. Arndt observed, "The possibilities of exchange rate manipulation and the accumulation of clearing debts together turned the clearing system into a powerful weapon of which the Nazi Government made full use in its foreign trade policy."[92] Creditors also employed clearing agreements to secure payments of external debts. Between 1933 and 1938, Great Britain concluded clearing agreements with a number of debtor countries to facilitate debt settlements.[93]

Negotiation

The 1920s saw continued negotiation of debts. The objective of sovereign debtors was to improve the terms of debt service and if possible lower the amount of principal outstanding. The classic negotiations were over inter-Allied debts; they stretched from 1922 to 1926 and resulted in both significant reductions in the principal and interest rates and extended payout periods. The quid pro quo for settlement was access to capital markets in the United States for new loans, which were denied to Allied states that refused to reach agreement on their debts, most specifically France.[94] Reparations followed the same path and were reduced repeatedly through the various international conferences leading up to the final decision of the Reparations Commission. Thereafter, German reparations were renegotiated via the Dawes Plan, the Young Plan, and the Lausanne Conference.[95]

The linkage between inter-Allied war debts and reparations was always explicit, although the Americans refused to acknowledge it. At the Lausanne Conference, the so-called Gentleman's Agreement tied the reduction of reparations to the war debt moratorium initiated by Hoover. "The effect of this agreement was to end the debt reparations complex by mutual, though not immediate, cancellation of debts and reparations by the European nations. The debtors in effect had combined against their major creditor, the United States."[96]

Following the German defaults in 1933 and 1934, the League Loans were renegotiated with the various Central and Eastern European states under a special protective committee brought together at the initiative of the Bank of England, in light of Britain's prominent role in organizing the loans. This council coordinated its activities with the various bondholder associations.[97] As V. N. Bandera observed: "Only after flagrant defiance of external obligations by the Nazi regime and lesser misdemeanors of the debtors were acknowledged as inevitable did the creditor nations agree to renegotiate the public debt of the Eastern European countries."[98]

The negotiation of private market debt defaults was severely inhibited by the closure of the capital markets and the unilateral actions of debtors to prevent transfers of foreign exchange. Nevertheless, there were substantial renegotiations of contractual debt terms throughout the 1930s through the mediation of the bondholder councils established in Europe before World War I and through the United States Bondholders Protective Council. One of the earliest agreements was the arrangement between bondholders and Brazil negotiated by Sir Otto Niemeyer. It established a funding agreement that was similar in some respects to the agreement with Argentina in the 1890s. The Niemeyer Plan classified Brazil's external debt into seven grades, with the debt serviced in proportion to its grade.[99]

Debt agreements during this period tended to be interim and partial, confined to a period of three years or so, with expectations by the parties that the Depression would end and the capital markets reopen.[100] However, as the Depression continued, partial defaults rolled into full defaults and negotiations tended to break down.[101] In 1936 the successor states of the Ottoman Empire reached agreement with the Council of the Repartitioned Debt and the French government to service their debts in a variety of local currencies, blocked marks, and French francs, based on trade agreements with France. The agreement was for a five-year period, 1936 to 1940.[102] In contrast, the successor states to the Austro-Hungarian loans stopped making payments to the Caisse de la Dette and remained in full default. Poland resisted default until 1936, when it finally succumbed.[103] At the end of the Funding Plan, following a coup d'état, Brazil unilaterally suspended debt service in 1937.[104]

World War II disrupted virtually all debt negotiations, and it was only near or at the end of the war that most substantive agreements on interwar defaults were reached. These agreements again generally provided for a substantial scaling down of principal, interest, and arrears, with payments rescheduled over an extended period.[105] The settlements with Austria, Germany, and Japan were dependent on the peace treaties, and negotiations usually took place within the framework of the more encompassing political settlements.[106] In addition, the establishment of the Bretton Woods institutions after the war, particularly the World Bank, brought several countries to the negotiating table to settle their debts in order to enjoy the benefits of receiving World Bank loans.[107]

Approximately twenty years after the initial wave of defaults during the Depression, most private market debt had been renegotiated at great cost to bondholders.

The extended payment terms that resulted from the reschedulings meant that, even as late as 1983, substantial payments were still being made on interwar debt settlements. Moreover, the Russian debt repudiation, the defaults of a number of Eastern European states within the Russian sphere of influence, and the default by China as a result of the Communist revolution stayed in force.[108]

FOUR

International Relations and Interwar External Sovereign Debts

International relations during the relatively short interwar era were exceedingly complex. Economic recovery from World War I had barely occurred before the Great Depression set in. Soon thereafter, the powers were preparing for another great war. However, no account of the era can fail to discuss the significant role played by external sovereign debt in international relations during these years. Six aspects are most important:

1. War debts and reparations and their links to private market loans;

2. Prewar debts and reparations payable by the successor and cessionary states, to the Austro-Hungarian and Ottoman Empires;

3. Russian debt repudiation;

4. U.S. policy and Latin American debt;

5. Japanese penetration of China; and

6. International cooperation following the World Economic Conference of 1933.

The Great Depression cast a shadow over these issues as the Depression made it virtually impossible for the Allies to service war debts and for Germany to pay reparations; as a result the entire process of debt service among the parties effectively wound down.

War Debts and Reparations—A Prelude to Private Market Loans

A full discussion of inter-Allied war debts and reparations is beyond the scope of this book. However, the links between the war debts and reparations, private market loans, and international relations during the interwar period is crucial to understanding the era, and the following summarizes these critical issues.

War Debts

The war and its great mobilization of material and human resources on a hitherto unprecedented scale required enormous internal and external financing. The cost of the war in gold has been estimated at $80 billion. By comparison, Great Britain's total national wealth in 1914 was estimated at $70 billion.[1]

During the first three years of the war, Britain, and to a lesser extent France, became the bankers to their Allies, which in Britain's case included financing the dominions and the Empire as well. When their own resources were exhausted, they used their creditworthiness to become intermediators of funds from New York and other capital markets.[2] Germany, on the other hand, was forced to support the Central Powers largely from its own internal resources, which it did by raising large-scale public loans and by tapping the resources of the large deposit banks, which made over half their assets available to the Reich in exchange for short-term Treasury bills.[3]

It was the United States' entry into the war, however, that tipped the financial and resource scales. Through a series of loans under the Liberty Loan Act, the United States supplied some $9.8 billion to the Allies, primarily to purchase essential goods within the United States. In addition, immediately after the war, the United States provided war relief and reconstruction loans in the amount of $2 billion to some eighteen countries.[4]

At the time of the armistice, net inter-Allied indebtedness was $16 billion after adjustment for gold shipments, or $12.4 billion if the loans to Russia are not counted.[5] Total inter-Allied war debts, if cross claims are not netted out, amounted to some $26.5 billion, or $23 billion without the Russian loans.[6] It is not surprising, therefore, that the payment of inter-Allied war debts became an important political issue of the interwar era.

Private market loans during the war were not an issue with the exception of the loans to Russia, as the former were largely refunded after the war and serviced regularly thereafter.[7] The potential burden of these external loans on the war-weary populations of Europe and their wartorn economies was enormous. As Derek Aldcroft noted, "War debts and reparations were on a scale so vast that the problem of their solution occupied the entire decade; this caused much international friction."[8] In an early proposal aimed at resolving the issue, John Maynard Keynes suggested that the war debts be canceled entirely; alternatively, both the war debts and reparations should be scaled down and funded by raising a large bond issue floated on the private capital markets and guaranteed by the Allied governments. The bond issue would also be a means of injecting fresh capital into European countries to restore their economies.[9] The idea of resolving the problem of war debts and reparations by commercializing or privatizing them was a recurring theme in the interwar period.

Early attempts by British and French diplomats to resolve the problem of inter-Allied debt both before and during the Versailles peace treaty negotiations were generally disregarded by their American counterparts. The British chancellor of the Exchequer and the British prime minister, Lloyd George, wrote in August 1920 to their American counterparts suggesting either cancellation or, alternatively, a comprehensive settlement of inter-Allied debts.[10] The British government also linked its negotiations with France to a favorable response from the United States. On November 3, President Woodrow Wilson replied to Lloyd George that neither Congress nor public opinion in the United States "would consent to cancellation or reduction in the debts of any of the Allied Governments as an inducement towards a practical settlement of the reparations claims."[11]

U.S. policy toward the settlement of the inter-Allied debt was clearly defined by an act of Congress on February 9, 1922, which established the World War Foreign Debt Commission and set forth the terms under which it should negotiate with the Allies. The establishment of the commission was followed by a request from the U.S. government that all its debtors take steps to fund their debts.[12] Congress took the stance that the war debts were contractual obligations like any other and had to be paid. In response to U.S. policy, Britain issued its own policy statement. Lord Balfour, secretary of state for foreign affairs, transmitted the following series of notes to Britain's Allies on August 1, 1922:

> His Majesty's Government cannot treat the repayment of the Anglo-American loan as if it were an isolated incident in which only the United States of America and Great Britain had any concern. . . . The policy favored by H.M.'s Government is that of surrendering their share of German reparations, and

writing off, through one great transaction, the whole body of inter-allied indebtedness. . . . In no circumstances do we propose to ask more from our debtors than is necessary to pay our creditors.[13]

The U.S. government maintained pressure on its allies to reach an accord on
World War I debt, starting in 1921 with an informal request to investment banks
asking for prior notification of contemplated foreign government loans. This move
was confirmed in a letter of June 6, 1921, from J. P. Morgan and Company to the
president.[14] Herbert Feis observed, "Of all uses made of official influence, the most
consistent was for the purpose of collecting war debts."[15]

War debt and relief loan settlements were finally negotiated by the United States
and its former allies, as well as the recipients of reconstruction loans, starting with
the British settlement on June 19, 1923, and ending with a settlement with Greece in
1929 and Austria in 1930.[16] Negotiations were conducted on a bilateral basis, with
each case evaluated by the United States Debt Commission based on its perception
of the debtor's capacity to pay. Overall, the principal amount of the debt was scaled
down to approximately half the United States' claims.[17] Despite the reduction in payments, the burden was substantial. Keynes noted how substantial it was even for a
nation such as Great Britain: "It scarcely requires illustrations to bring home the magnitude of this burden. We shall be paying to the United States each year for sixty-
two years a sum equivalent to two times the cost of our Navy, nearly equal to the
State expenditure on education, more than the total burden of our pre-war debt, more
than the total profits of our mercantile marine and the whole of our mines together."[18]

Of the major Allied debtors, France was the most difficult in negotiations, resisting a settlement for almost five years. The U.S. government used its ability to deny
France access to its capital markets by refusing to approve a loan from J. P. Morgan
in November 1922. France was able, however, to borrow from neutral intermediaries such as Switzerland, the Netherlands, and Sweden, even from Ivar Kreuger's
Swedish Match Company, all of which were free to borrow in the U.S. markets.[19] In
negotiation with the United States, France raised the issue of its capacity to pay and
sought a safeguard clause linking debt payments to reparations under a memorandum to the World War Foreign Debt Commission, "France's Capacity to Pay."[20]
Joseph Caillaux, the French finance minister, strove to tie France's settlement of war
debts with Britain to reparation payments as established by the Dawes Plan. Britain
refused, as did the United States, but provided for a mechanism to credit France in
the event Britain paid less than was scheduled to the United States. Finally, on July 29,
1926, France ratified the war debt settlement with the United States in a policy decision

ostensibly unrelated to economic pressure but rather to the Kellogg-Briand Pact.[21] However, at the same time France sought to postpone payment on $400 million due for surplus war materials.[22]

In January 1930, France concluded agreements with five of its sovereign debtors— Romania, Yugoslavia, Greece, Poland, and Czechoslovakia—Belgium's debt having previously been transferred to Germany by the Treaty of Versailles. The French agreements were generally liberal, with low interest payments.[23]

Inter-Allied war debt settlements were invariably linked with the ability of the Allied governments to float private market loans in the United States. Keynes calculated that in addition to $2 billion a year in loans necessary for Europe to balance its trade deficit with the United States, an additional $600 million annually was necessary to sustain the funding on the war debts. He warned against the advisability of loans from the United States to Europe: "The practice of foreign investment as we know it now is a very modern contrivance, a very unstable one and only suited to peculiar circumstances. . . . The interest will be furnished out of new loans, so long as these are obtainable and the financial structure will mount always higher, until it is not worthwhile to maintain any longer the illusion that it has foundations."[24]

The inter-Allied debt settlements involved protracted negotiations by creditors and debtor states from 1922 to 1930. Although the United States never accepted the link to reparations, it was implicit throughout this period.[25]

The settlements had hardly been concluded when the world economic Depression started. Even so, the administration of President Herbert Hoover, Congress, and the American public were strongly in favor of a firm line on the payments.[26] Hoover was faced, however, with the collapse of Austria's Credit Anstalt and the pending collapse of the German economy because of the sustained flight from the mark.[27] On June 20, 1931, he announced the Hoover moratorium, which was acclaimed in the United States as an act of statesmanship.[28] The moratorium provided for a one-year suspension on all intergovernmental payments, including reparations. France, with which the U.S. government had failed to consult, initially refused to accept the moratorium, particularly the unconditional portion of reparations provided for by the Young Plan. According to Charles Kindleberger, the French had a strong moral and economic point because of the potential loss of approximately £100 million, while commercial debts, which the French insisted were not to be treated on an equal footing with reparations, were preserved. U.S. commercial interests, at least for the moment, were protected.[29]

The moratorium was not intended to terminate the payments on war debt. In approving Hoover's executive action, the U.S. Congress, in a joint resolution on December 18, 1931, added the following clause: "It is hereby expressly declared to be against the policy of Congress that any of the indebtedness of foreign countries to the United States should be in any manner cancelled or reduced."[30]

Faced with a demand by Congress for a renewal of payments in June 1932, which was eventually postponed to December 1932, the question of how the European Allies should respond was raised. The Lausanne Conference, from June 16 to July 9, 1932, reached a new agreement on reparations reduction with Germany, but explicitly tied them to the war debt moratorium via the so-called Gentleman's Agreement. Thereafter, renewed pressure on the Allies to pay the war debts would trigger renewed pressure on Germany to pay reparations.[31]

Supporting the political decision were economic considerations, such as the devaluation of sterling, which increased the cost to Great Britain of servicing its external debts; increased U.S. trade protectionism in the form of the Smoot-Hawley Tariff Act; and the general economic malaise caused by the Depression, which was putting great pressure on the budgetary systems of the European states that were faced with mass unemployment and reduced fiscal receipts. The condition of the German economy also effectively ruled out a continuation of the reparations payments in the near future.[32]

The issue of a continued moratorium or outright cancellation of war debts arose during the transition from the Hoover to the Roosevelt administration. President Franklin Roosevelt, ever the consummate politician, in a country faced with mass unemployment and severe economic conditions, was reluctant to become entrapped in what he viewed as a Republican problem. He therefore remained noncommittal on the inter-Allied debt problem during the transition.[33]

With Congress pressing for payment on December 15, 1932, Keynes contemplated Britain's alternatives: to not pay; to pay quietly; to pay firmly, demanding a final settlement; or to pay gloriously, canceling its own Allied debts. In a December 12, 1932, article in the *Daily Mail*, he advanced reasons why Britain should not pay, noting the connection between sovereign debt and international law.

> The sanctity of contract, the preservation of which is a matter of serious importance to a country with the financial organization of the United States just as it is Great Britain, cannot be preserved except by the reasonableness of the creditor. Internationally a contract has nothing to support it except the self-respect and self-interest of the debtor. A loan, the claims of which are supported by neither, will not be paid for long.[34]

In an editorial of November 26, 1932, entitled "Mr. Hoover and the Debts," *The Economist* couched its arguments in similar terms—the sanctity of contracts against the enlightened self-interest of debtors and creditors.[35]

Britain paid the December 1932 installment in full—$95 million in gold—accompanied by a note from the British government indicating that it was not a resumption of normal payment but a request for a clear commitment for renegotiation, settlement, or cancellation. Italy also paid. Poland and France defaulted, and the Greek government deposited its payment in a blocked account.[36]

Faced with the same problem in June 1933, just before the World Economic Conference of 1933, Britain made a token payment. President Roosevelt, who had chosen not to address the issue directly, considered the British in conformity with their obligations. According to Congress, however, they were not. Britain made no more payments, a step that effectively ended the inter-Allied war debt payments as far as America's major Allied debtors were concerned.[37] Congress passed the Johnson Act of 1934 to deny loans to foreign governments in default on their war debts. The act was broadly construed, however, and allowed loan adjustments. Moreover, it was not rigorously observed.[38]

From 1918 to 1931, the United States received approximately $2.6 billion in payments from the Allies, a fraction of the almost $12 billion due. Britain, a creditor, remained in deficit on inter-Allied war debts and reparations, paying more than it received.[39]

Reparations and the Capacity to Pay

War reparations, the Versailles Treaty, and treaties following the Versailles Treaty to set the amount of reparations due are an important and complex part of the political economy and international relations of the interwar period. However, reparations and war are a distraction from our primary discussion of the export of capital, sovereign loan defaults, and crises—above all the Great Depression—during this period. There is an enormous literature on reparations, including Keynes's well-known polemic *Economic Consequences of the Peace*, and Temperley's detailed account of reparations in *A History of the Peace Conference of Paris*.[40]

The economic issue that ran throughout all the negotiations on reparations was the evaluation of Germany's capacity to pay. Keynes maintained that the Versailles Peace Treaty never adequately addressed this issue. Reparations, he believed, were based on France's Carthaginian demands aimed at destroying Germany's future economic capacity and hence its potential as a European power.[41]

The issue of capacity to pay, or the ability to service external debts, goes to the heart of all negotiations on sovereign debts between creditor and debtor. It is an extremely complex issue involving the projection of a future stream of earnings over an extended time horizon and the ability to project a budget surplus for an economy. In the case of a sovereign debtor, a surplus means an excess of governmental revenues over governmental expenditures and an ability to project a foreign exchange surplus from trade and services, so that the external debt service may be transferred abroad to meet the debtor's foreign exchange obligations over the period of debt amortization. These two issues, usually spoken of as the "budgetary" and "transfer" problems, were central to the debate on reparations and lay at the heart of all evaluations of the debt service capacity of a sovereign debtor.

Hjalmar Schacht devoted considerable effort to explaining the transfer problem, which he considered the pivotal issue of reparations. He concluded that external loans had entirely masked the problem to the world: "It is thus with loans made not only to the German National Government, but to the Federal States, the cities, groups of cities and innumerable public and private corporations; and it is thus that the transfer of reparation is made possible."[42]

Keynes reverted to this theme time and again throughout the period of reparations.[43] Others, however, notably Bertil Ohlin and Jacques Rueff, criticized his economic theories through theoretical evaluations of Germany's transfer problem.[44] A more sweeping indictment of Keynes's views from both a political and an economic perspective was presented by Etienne Mantoux, who attributed the failure of the United States to ratify the treaty to Keynes's *Economic Consequences of the Peace,* as well as the revisionist stance by Great Britain,[45] and finally to the myopic view that failed to see the potential of a "Napoleonic revival" by Germany.[46]

Some contemporary views, with the advantage of hindsight, largely support Mantoux's economic assertions that: (i) Germany's taxation burdens were less than those of other European nations and could have been increased to cover the reparations; (ii) Germany ran large budgetary deficits during the entire period of the Dawes Plan that could have been constrained; and (iii) Germany imported capital via short- and long-term loans on an unprecedented scale, relatively little of which went to build an export capability or to cover reparations. In fact, large-scale borrowing had the perverse effect of raising Germany's propensity to import and thereby aggravated the transfer problem.[47]

Perhaps of greatest relevance, therefore, was not the economic issue but the political argument. Germany clearly did not perceive that it was in its self-interest to continue paying reparations well into the future. Here, Keynes's views of German attitudes toward servicing the reparations were entirely accurate.

Two plans and loans derived from those plans tried to resolve the issue of reparations—the Dawes Plan and the Dawes Loans and the Young Plan and Young Loans—both loans raised in the capital markets of Europe and the United States to supplant public funding with private funding, a reversion to the nineteenth-century approach to resolving debt defaults. Under the Dawes Plan, concern grew that Germany could not expect to continue borrowing to pay reparations on a scale equivalent to that of the previous years, 1924–28. In addition, no final figure or settlement amount on the reparations had ever been worked out. In September 1928 a new committee of experts, including German representatives, was announced under the chairmanship of Owen D. Young, a member of the Dawes Commission.[48] Economic capacity was not the primary determinant of the Young Plan. Rather, a political solution was imposed, with the upper limits defined by the Dawes Plan and the lower limits set by the inter-Allied war debt commitments.[49]

The Young Plan, as the Dawes Plan had been, was accompanied by a private market loan, the "German Government 5 1/2 Percent Loan 1930" (the "Young Plan Loan")[50] of 300 million marks, one third of which went to creditor governments.[51] The Young Plan loan partially replaced a reparations obligation to the Allied governments with a debt obligation of the German government to private creditors, part of a continuous effort by the Allies to "commercialize" the reparations. The Young Loan, however, reflected the growing apprehension of the capital markets over sovereign loans: "The Young Loan was in sharp contrast to the Dawes Loan and was a measure of the degree to which economic confidence had collapsed. The United States tranche of $100 million went to discount soon after it was issued, as opposed to the Dawes Loan which was oversubscribed ten times."[52]

The unique feature of the Young Plan was the establishment of the Bank for International Settlements (BIS) as responsible, as a trustee, for the acceptance of annuities and a guarantee fund deposited by France to make sure the creditor governments received the amounts due them in the event of postponement.[53] Eventually, the BIS took responsibility for controlling the annuities on the Young Loan, the Dawes Loan, and a loan granted to Austria in 1930 under its auspices, for the payment of these annuities to the various creditors, and for the placement of annuity funds.[54]

The Depression soon overtook the Young Plan. Germany, hit hard by the sudden cutback in international lending as well as the withdrawal of large-scale foreign deposits from its banks, was soon in economic difficulty. The link throughout the interwar era between war debts, reparations, and commercial debts was clear. Keynes had warned of the fragility of loans to sovereign states, and he proved prophetic.[55] A more contemporary analysis of the complex interrelationship is provided by Kindleberger:

Or postulate a network of reparations, war debts and commercial loans. . . .
In this circumstance, Germany is more ready to cancel reparations than to default on commercial debt, since it owns commercial assets abroad and is

interested in maintaining its credit. Britain is willing to cancel reparations but only if war debts are excused. France insists on receiving reparations, wants war debts cancelled and is relatively indifferent to commercial loans. The United States can see no connection between war debts and reparations, is prepared in extreme to accept a moratorium on reparations and war debts, but seeks to safeguard the sanctity of commercial debts and wants to revive war-debt payments after the year's moratorium is over. No equitable solution is possible. Inevitably the system runs down to wipe the slate clean of reparations, debts and service on commercial lending.[56]

Prewar Debt Allocation to the Successor and Cessionary States

The economic and political literature has focused primarily on German reparations because of the prominence of this issue in interwar political and economic negotiations. Moreover, the issue of reparations is associated with the rise to power of the National Socialists and Hitler in Germany. As such, World War II is attributed in part to the reparations.[57] However, in consideration of external sovereign debt, the other treaties of peace with the successor and cessionary states of the Austro-Hungarian and Ottoman Empires are also of substantial interest.

World War I marked the end of two great empires, the Austro-Hungarian and the Ottoman. Their dissolution raised vital questions during the treaty discussions with respect to reparations payments and debt apportionment. What part of the reparations would Austria, Hungary, Bulgaria, and Turkey bear as allies of Germany? Would the successor states that had fought for all or part of the war alongside Germany and were not considered friendly to the Allies be asked to pay reparations? What would happen to the prewar external debts of the Austro-Hungarian Empire, given its dissolution in October 1918? What would happen to the external investments held by citizens of Austria-Hungary, now citizens of the new states?[58] These same questions also applied to the Ottoman Empire, tempered, however, by the assumption of mandates by Great Britain and France in the Arab territories and Palestine.[59]

The Reparations Commission was left to work out the details of these questions, a task that was completed sometime after Germany's obligations were determined. Only Bulgaria's reparations were definitively assessed at the time of the treaty negotiations—at 2,250 million francs gold.[60] After long and delicate negotiations, Romania, Czechoslovakia, Yugoslavia, and Poland were not asked to pay reparations as such; instead, they agreed to pay a fixed sum toward their "cost of liberation" of 1,500 million francs gold, to be apportioned among them. They would issue bonds in 1926 to secure the payments, which were to begin January 1, 1931, and run for twenty-five annual installments. Italy also agreed to make a contribution toward "liberation costs," based on its assumption of a portion of the former territory of the Austro-Hungarian Empire.[61]

The financial clauses of the Paris peace treaties were exceedingly complex, involving issues of currency protection, the assets of the Austro-Hungarian Bank (the primary bank of issue of the former Empire), the recognition of contracts, and the ownership of public and private property with respect to asset ownership in the "new" states and to externally held assets. The assumption that an empire could be liquidated and its liabilities and assets passed on to an array of successor states proved a very complex undertaking in practice, although its principles, according to Temperley, were based on well-established doctrines of international law.[62]

In practice, these states assumed the pre–World War external debts of the Austro-Hungarian Empire, as well as the war debts, up to the point the Empire was dissolved. To the extent that these debts could be internalized, they were. However, a substantial burden of external sovereign debt remained that became bonded debt of the new states.[63] That the successor states could pay neither reparations nor the prewar debts of Austria and Hungary was reflected in the decision by the creditor states under the auspices of the League of Nations to arrange for the League Loans.

Following a parallel path, Poland agreed in principle to resume responsibility for a portion of the Russian public debt, as assigned under a special convention between Poland and the Allied and associated powers or, in the absence of agreement, via arbitration through the League of Nations.[64]

The Turkish Peace Treaty was signed well after the Paris treaties, as the Turkish nationalists rejected the initial provisions and resisted the Allies under Mustapha Kemal Ataturk (considered the father of modern Turkey). The Lausanne Treaty of 1923 eliminated all provisions for reparations and penalties but did assign some portion of the prewar external debt of the Ottoman Empire to the new secular state.[65] After protracted negotiations, the figure was set at £184.5 million per agreement in June 1928, with ratification by the Turkish National Assembly occurring as late as November 1930.[66]

The agreement with Turkey provided for a new debt council, called the Council of the Repartitioned Public Debt of the Former Ottoman Empire. However, as the council was obliged to shift its seat to Paris, it proved unable effectively to administer the revenues to service the debt. In 1940 the Turkish government took over control of the council, and in 1944 Turkey redeemed the remainder of its share of the old Ottoman debt.[67]

The other states that were assigned a share in the prewar Ottoman debt, other than the mandatory states under British or French control, largely avoided their responsibilities by forcing protracted negotiations over the terms of payment. The Depression then effectively terminated any real dialogue over the issue.

The Russian Debt Repudiation

The Russian debt repudiation came in the midst of World War I, at a time when the Allies were desperate to keep Russia in the war against Germany. The new Soviet government sought to bring an immediate end to World War I by appealing over the heads of the Allied and Central Powers (Germany, Austria-Hungary, Bulgaria, and the Ottoman Empire) directly to the people. Their thesis was one of strong nations versus weak ones.[68] However, the peace of Brest-Litovsk left Russia in a hopeless military position, on terms dictated by Germany, and brought unilateral intervention by the Allies within Russia.[69] The intervention was aimed first and foremost at keeping the war effort and the resistance against Germany alive there and, second, to show Allied revulsion at the debt repudiation. "The French were perhaps the most resolutely anti-Bolshevik . . . partly because one of the first acts of the revolutionary regime in Russia had been to repudiate the debts incurred by the Tsarist government, so that very many Frenchmen who had invested in Russian bonds were suddenly faced with serious losses, and formed themselves into a politically influential pressure group."[70]

The Allied intervention in Russia was an almost complete failure, but in the midst of it the Soviet foreign minister, Georgy Chicherin, offered to settle with the West. However, the Allies apparently were not ready to do business with the Bolshevik regime,[71] and although they lifted their blockade in 1920 they still refused to recognize the Soviet government.

With the period termed by E. H. Carr as "War Communism" at an end,[72] Lenin made a pragmatic attempt at rapprochement with the West to try and restore the revolution and war-torn Soviet economy. Lenin's New Economic Policy (NEP) sought loans and technology from the West in return for concessions to private investors. He also believed that investment would reduce the chance of future intervention.[73] The NEP was not very successful in attracting private market loans. The capital markets would not open to Russia because of the debt repudiation.[74]

A major dilemma for the governments of Western Europe trying to recover from World War I was how to resume financial and trade relations with Russia and its failure to respect its contractual debt commitments. Several countries responded by trying to tie the resolution of the debt problem to trade pacts and diplomatic recognition via bilateral negotiations.

The Anglo-Soviet trade pact of 1921 was an attempt by Russia to break out of isolation; it was in effect de facto recognition of the Soviet Union. The Labour government offered de jure recognition in 1924, but this approach was rejected by the newly elected Conservative government that ascended to power as Labour fell, with the question of recognition and the Russian debt repudiations major issues in the election.[75] In the preliminary negotiations during 1924 that preceded the proposal of recognition by the Labour government, representatives of the Russian government and bondholders met in London. The Russian negotiators offered to settle the external debts and accrued interest at 15 percent of the nominal value of the bonds. The draft treaty of recognition, submitted to Parliament, proposed settlement of the old debts through a new loan to Russia, to be guaranteed by Great Britain, if such a loan could be raised in the capital markets.[76] Although the Bolsheviks had repudiated their debts for ideological reasons, they were not above reverting to the long-established practice of renegotiating their debts if a proper deal could be struck.

Italy recognized the Soviet Union in 1925, France and Japan in 1926. Only the United States among the great powers refused to do so until 1933. It did not, however, refuse to allow trade or the extension of trade credits to Russia. Nevertheless, on the matter of loans for Russia, the State Department discouraged all proposals. Its rejection was as much ideological as it was to support the principle of the sanctity of contract.[77] On December 9, 1923, President Calvin Coolidge, in a message to Congress, stated, "Our government does not propose, however, to enter into relations with another regime which refuses to recognize the sanctity of international obligations."[78] In February 1928, the State Department clearly reiterated its policy once again, "The Department does not view with favor financial arrangements designed to facilitate in any way the sale of Soviet bonds in the United States."[79]

The Genoa Conference in 1922 was the major international effort by the Allied powers to negotiate a resolution of the debt repudiation by Russia in a multilateral forum. As it entered the conference, Russia feared isolation and a concentrated effort by the Allies to force it to recognize prewar and Allied war debt. Germany, also invited to the conference, feared Russian insistence on reparations and a demand from the Allies for increased reparations.

The proposal the Allied powers submitted at Genoa for the settlement of the repudiated loans offered Russia a quid pro quo in the form of loans for the purposes of finance, reconstruction, and development within Russia. The British representatives at the conference were authorized to offer credits for trade, while France, Italy, and Japan proposed substantial financial, technical, and agricultural assistance.[80] The

Allied proposal included several clauses to settle the Soviet repudiation, including the following: (i) the recognition by Russia of all public debts and obligations contracted for or guaranteed by the imperial Russian government, the Russian provisional government, or the Soviet government itself toward foreign powers; (ii) recognition by the Soviet government of the principle of debt succession; (iii) willingness of the Soviet government to recognize or have recognized the financial engagements of all the provincial and local governments and public utilities; and (iv) an agreement by the Soviet government, to be concluded within twelve months from the date the proposal came into force, to reach an agreement with foreign bondholders, irrespective of their nationality, on the arrangement on Russia's external debt. The Allies in turn proposed to ask their respective parliaments to reduce the amount of Allied loans owed and accrued interest thereon, once the issue of inter-Allied war debts was addressed in line with Russia's economic and financial capacity. Notably, the first clause of the proposal also requested that the Soviet government refrain from subversive propaganda against the Allies.[81]

Russia came to the Genoa Conference with a whole series of plans and proposals concerning the credits and loans it required, as well as a list of industrial, mining, and agricultural concessions it was willing to offer foreign investors.[82] The Allies consistently refused to entertain the Soviet proposals, however, until agreement was reached on the recognition of existing debt. The failure of the Genoa Conference and the resulting Treaty of Rapallo between Germany and Russia gave both parties a diplomatic gain in the end. The Russians were able to ensure that the capitalists were split and would not encircle them, and Germany was effectively neutralized. Germany, on the other hand, had an opening against the Treaty of Versailles.[83]

By 1928, with Stalin in firm control of the Soviet leadership following Lenin's death and after an initial struggle for power, the concept of "socialism in one country" building the strength of Mother Russia as the priority was initiated with the first Five-Year Plan.[84] The NEP was at an end, and so was the idea of offering concessions to attract Western capital.

Latin American Debt and International Law Governing Intervention over Sovereign Loans

Although Europe during this period was the focus of concern with respect to external sovereign debt and international relations, U.S. foreign policy in Latin America was still very much centered on the issue of intervention and external debt. The United States fell into a quagmire over the Roosevelt Corollary.[85] Despite the qualified adherences to the 1907 Hague Convention on Pecuniary Claims, it was still enmeshed in organizing the financial affairs of several Central American and Caribbean states during World War I and the 1920s. It maintained "economic protectorates" in Nicaragua, the Dominican Republic, Haiti, and Panama intermittently from 1912 throughout the war and much of the interwar period, and also intervened to monitor or block loans in the case of several other states in the region.[86] The presumption widely held in Latin America that the United States intervened in support of private financial interests would appear to be incorrect. The interventions during World War I and the interwar period were primarily a continuation of the United States' concern over strategic interests.

The Wilson administration supported the Roosevelt Corollary and, with typical Wilsonian zeal, proposed to save the people of the region from bad government. Secretary of State William Jennings Bryan, the great populist, proposed that the United States use its own credit standing to help reorganize Latin America's debts. Not surprisingly, his proposals gathered little support within the administration.[87]

Instead, the policy of nonintervention on behalf of creditors slowly prevailed during the interwar period. In 1923, President Warren G. Harding's secretary of state, Charles Evans Hughes, initiated negotiations on a series of pacts with various Central American and Caribbean states that were aimed at abolishing the financial protectorates established by the United States in the prewar and war years.[88] Part of the reason for Hughes's request that American investment banks review and approve foreign loans was to avoid the continuance or exacerbation of problems relating to debt in Central America and the Caribbean. The Hoover administration reversed the Roosevelt Corollary, citing the illegality of the policy.[89]

When the Mexican Revolution led Mexico to both default and nationalization, the U.S. and various European governments decided not to intervene, instead allowing their bondholders to make their own representations. And when the Mexican government failed to fulfill a succession of agreements, the creditor states also did not intervene.[90] Although American policy was deemed beneficent, few of the states on the receiving end thought so. U.S. intervention provoked distrust and extreme nationalistic and anti-American feelings in the region that were to outlast the tangible results of financial stewardship.[91]

The debtor states of Latin America attempted to counter American intervention and what they perceived as increasing political and financial penetration of Latin America by supporting the principles of international law as expressed in the Calvo Doctrine. That doctrine now took the form of the Calvo Clause. The Calvo Doctrine, which, when interpreted in its absolute or broadest terms, proscribed intervention absolutely, was rejected by the powers because it precluded action in the event of arbitrary treatment or discrimination against creditors who were their citizens. During the interwar period, the Latin American states sought to implement the Calvo Doctrine in treaties, contracts, and agreements and via constitutional provisions in the form of the Calvo Clause.[92] The United States consistently objected to the clause because it abolished the right to intervene diplomatically on behalf of its citizens and would potentially subject them to standards of justice that were not even minimally acceptable.[93]

Throughout the interwar period the Latin American states also sought to "codify" the Calvo Clause in international law through the League of Nations, the First Conference for the Codification of International Law at The Hague, March 13, 1930, and various pan-American conferences. In Montevideo in 1933, Mexico sought a moratorium on all foreign obligations for a period of six to ten years, the formation of an international judiciary agency to negotiate agreements on debts to eliminate the pressure of intervention by bankers' credit committees, and more effective guarantees for debtors as well as bondholders. Argentina rejected this attempt to legitimize continued bankruptcy.[94]

In general, the powers, and specifically the United States, resisted these attempts to establish the Calvo Clause in international law.[95] However, as the interwar period progressed, the United States modified its policy on intervention, moving from the paternal interventionism of the Wilson administration toward the Clark Memorandum, which denied the Roosevelt Corollary, and finally to support for the principle of absolute nonintervention under the administration of Franklin Delano Roosevelt. That administration implemented its policy by divesting itself of treaty rights to intervene in the Caribbean "protectorates"—Cuba, Panama, Haiti, and the Dominican Republic—starting with the annulment of the Platt Amendment in Cuba in 1934. The Convention for the Maintenance, Preservation and Reestablishment of Peace of December 23, 1936, denied the right of intervention, its third article simply saying with respect to debts, "Forcible collection of pecuniary debts is illegal."[96]

Japanese Penetration of China

During the interwar period Japan borrowed extensively, particularly from the New York capital market, to extend its sphere of influence in Asia. As noted, this policy conflicted with the United States' goal of an open door for all powers and respect for Chinese sovereignty. To back its stance, the government used its right to approve loans to sovereign states. As Feis noted, "The scrutiny over loans to Japan took the American Government into a sensitized field of foreign policy, touching our relations with both Japan and China and the struggle between them."[97]

In 1922 the Oriental Development Company arranged a $20 million loan guaranteed by the Japanese government through the National City Company. The State Department would not approve it, despite considerable pressure by the Japanese government and National City Company. In 1923 the bank revised the prospectus to confine the proceeds to Korea, and the loan was passed. Attempts by the South Manchuria Railway to borrow through National City Company in 1923 proved futile. In 1927 the South Manchuria Railway again sought a loan, with the proposal being submitted jointly by National City Company and J. P. Morgan and Company. The proposal was brought to President Coolidge for review, with Morgan pressing the State Department for approval. China officially protested the prospective loan on December 4.

The State Department informed the bankers that the adverse publicity would surely hurt the market for the loan and requested that they inform the Japanese government of the difficulties of marketing it. The Japanese government persisted, however, and in September 1928 the Oriental Development Company issued another bond without objection, as did the Japanese imperial government in 1930.[98]

In general, U.S. policy toward Japanese loans remained inconsistent, ineffective, and ambiguous. Clearly, if Japan could borrow from the United States, it could downstream these loans to whatever area of influence it desired, and usually did so. The fungibility of money absolutely thwarted U.S. policy. The State Department obviously understood this fact, but in principle still sought to prevent the appearance of explicitly sanctioning loans for Manchuria or northern China during the interwar period.

Japan increased its proportion of public loans to China relative to the other powers during the interwar period, with its share of Chinese external sovereign debt rising from approximately 10 percent in 1914 to 38 percent in 1931.[99] The most politically influential of the loans were the Nishihara loans discussed previously. Of even greater importance were Japan's direct investments in China, particularly in Manchuria, where Japan sought to consolidate its sphere of influence. Japan's loans to China reached almost 500 million yen as of 1931, while direct investments amounted to 1.8 billion yen (approximately $1.1 billion overall).[100] As the period progressed, both the United Kingdom and the United States sought to deny Japan recognition of its sphere of influence in China, particularly with respect to Manchuria and the establishment of Manchuko, a puppet state. However, Anglo-American relations were strained over other matters, and the withdrawal of the United States into increasing isolationism starting with the Depression precluded effective cooperation with Great Britain in this matter.[101]

International Cooperation after the World
Economic Conference of 1933

The American banking crisis, which manifested itself as early as 1930, deepened throughout the course of the Depression. The declaration of an eight-day, statewide banking moratorium by the governor of Michigan was the initial alarm, and it rapidly extended from region to region, state to state. By March 4, 1933, following President Roosevelt's inauguration, virtually every state in America had declared a banking holiday.[102] One of Roosevelt's earliest acts was to declare a national banking holiday for eight days by invoking the only legislation he could find that gave him the power to do so: ironically, the 1914 Trading with the Enemy Act.[103] After this action, Congress passed legislation giving the president wide powers to reorganize the American banking system.[104]

The banking holiday in America came on the eve of the 1933 World Economic Conference. In his inaugural speech, President Roosevelt clearly signaled his intention to focus on national economic reconstruction rather than international solutions to the world crisis—"Our international relations, though vastly important, are in point of time and necessity secondary to the establishment of a sound national economy."[105] While Ramsey MacDonald, chancellor of the Exchequer, was en route to Washington to discuss the World Economic Conference, the United States effectively left the gold standard.

With the devaluation of the dollar, the focus of the conference shifted from war debts, reparations, and world indebtedness to exchange rate stabilization.[106] Roosevelt rejected all the proposed multilateral agreements, referring to America's poor experience with international lending. He even rejected a British proposal to establish an international fund, a potential precursor to the IMF, to lend money to central banks in return for the end of exchange controls and the removal of tariff barriers.[107] Roosevelt was content to let the dollar float against the sterling and other major currencies, as he focused his attention on domestic problems.[108]

The Monetary and Financial Subcommission of the conference did address the problem of external sovereign debts in Annex I of its report to the conference. The commission noted five points:

1. External debts are an important component of the balance of payments of the debtor states that can only be dealt with when sufficient resources are available to do so.

2. The conditions in the debtor countries vary considerably, and it is not possible to lay down a uniform treatment applicable in all cases. Moreover, it is indis-

pensable, for the restoration of credit, that contracts should be respected in the absence of modifications agreed between the parties concerned.

3. When adjustments to contracts need to be made this should be accomplished via direct negotiation between debtor and creditor. As regards state loans, it is in the interest of the creditors themselves to conclude arrangements of such a nature as will permit the adoption at the same time of a program of economic and financial restoration by the debtor countries and its effective application.

4. It is desirable that in each of the countries concerned there should be organizations established to represent the several classes of creditors on both short-term and long-term loans, and these creditor organizations should remain in communication with one another.

5. The question of intergovernmental debts lies outside the field of discussion of the conference (at the insistence of the U.S. government as a condition precedent to agreeing to the conference).[109]

The conference retained the traditional approach to solving debt problems by insisting on a case-by-case review of each debtor's problems and by rejecting an overall or comprehensive solution to sovereign indebtedness. The World Economic Conference ended any international economic cooperation over debts, finance, or trade for the duration of the Depression.[110]

After the conference, the countries in the British Empire met formally to set up the sterling area or bloc. This step was an extension of the agreement reached by the Commonwealth countries at Ottawa in 1932, where trade preferences, commonly called "Imperial Preferences," were established.[111] These countries attached great importance to lower interest rates and the opening of the London capital market for overseas loans.[112] The "gold bloc" countries—Belgium, France, the Netherlands, Italy, Poland, and Switzerland—had preceded the announcement of the "sterling area" with one of their own just following the World Economic Conference, in which they maintained their adherence to the gold standard.[113]

By 1934 the world had begun to recover from the Depression, but unevenly and in blocs and autarkic economic units. The sterling area ultimately included the Empire countries, the Scandinavian countries, Portugal, and the South American states, whose currencies were "pegged" to sterling. The United States operated on its own, with Canada split somewhere between sterling and the dollar. The "gold bloc" consisted formally of the six named states, as well as several of the Eastern European and Central European states that were aligned closely with France and the other gold bloc economies.

The "have not" states—such as Italy, where fascism was well entrenched; Germany under the National Socialist regime; and Japan, which was in the midst of rising militarism—moved increasingly in an autarkic direction. As the decade progressed, Hitler pursued as a solution to Germany's problems the economic and political absorption of *mittel* (central) Europe, in a demand for *lebensraum* (living space).[114] Italy sought colonies in Abyssinia and North Africa for its population expansion. Japan sought a "coprosperity zone" in Asia.[115] Russia had already opted for autarky under Stalin, or "socialism in one country," through the adoption of the first Five-Year Plan in 1928 and then forced collectivization of agriculture and emphasis on heavy industry.

Russia's push toward autarky was justified internally by the potential threat of encirclement by the capitalist powers, a threat the show trials and purges were intended to prove.[116] However, Russia also was alert to the dangers of Nazi Germany in Europe and Japan in Asia and aware of its potential internal weaknesses as a result of the army purges and large-scale liquidations of population. It therefore began to move its foreign policy in the direction of accommodation with the Western powers.[117]

Carr maintains that autarky in Germany was derived from the lessons of World War I and the blockade by the Allies, a lesson reinforced by the economic sanctions of the League of Nations in 1935 against Italy following the invasion of Abyssinia: "Autarky is, however, not only a social necessity, but an instrument of political power. It is primarily a form of preparedness for war."[118] Carr contrasts the policy of autarky with the extension of power first by Great Britain and France in the nineteenth century through the export of capital and subsequently by the United States in the interwar period:

> The export of capital has in recent times been a familiar practice of powerful states. The political supremacy of Great Britain throughout the nineteenth century was closely associated with London's position as the financial centre of the world. . . . The rise of the United States to political power in the present century was largely due to their appearance in the market as a large-scale lender, first of all to Latin America, and since 1914, to Europe.[119]

During the Depression, the United States failed to learn the lessons provided by Britain in the nineteenth century. Its capital markets remained largely closed to the world's financial needs, and it failed to cooperate in matters of financial and trade policy, preferring a unilateral approach for the former and reciprocal bilateral trade agreements for the latter. With the world pulling apart economically and politically, the United States grew increasingly isolationist and offered little in the way of world leadership.

Perhaps the most important sign of isolation with respect to debt was the amendment of the Neutrality Acts in 1936. The amendment emerged out of a growing conviction in the United States that loans to the Allies in World War I had dragged the United States into the war.[120] The Senate special investigation of the munitions industry in 1936 recommended: "Legislation which would forbid the floating of loans by belligerents, their political sub-divisions, central banks, or the floating of loans of any person if the proceeds of such loans are made available to a belligerent should be enacted as permanent legislation."[121] In 1936 a provision was included against loans to belligerent governments in the amendment to the neutrality laws.[122]

Although the Soviet Union may have been very concerned about the threat posed by Germany and Japan, no power wanted to associate too closely with the Bolsheviks, who had repudiated their debts in 1917 and now were conducting purges and show trials that were slowly but surely coming to light in the West.

With the widespread closure of the private capital markets during the Depression, creditor governments responded with loans and export credits to promote bilateral trade or support strategic objectives. In Great Britain trade was being promoted by the Export Credit Guarantee Department, and many loans were tied to its activities because it assumed the risk on insolvency, exchange depreciation, and transfer difficulties.[123] In the late 1930s, loans from Great Britain were designed to support potential allies, with lending in 1938 and 1939 going to Turkey and China. The link between political and economic power was no longer subtle and indirect; it was clearly directed toward the growing conflict with Germany.

The Export-Import Bank was established to promote trade; its lending served the same purpose as that of its British equivalent.[124] The first Export-Import Bank was established by Congress to grant trade credits to Russia following its recognition by the United States. However, the quid pro quo was an anticipated renegotiation of the debts, which never materialized. Therefore the bank was never used for this purpose. Although the second Export-Import Bank was established to assist Cuba, its charter was extended to all other nations except Russia.[125]

From 1934 onward, loans from the United States to Latin America were governmental owing to the continued default by most Latin American states and the expropriations or nationalization of foreign properties, starting with the Bolivian and Mexican oil expropriations.[126]

With the world political situation growing increasingly more difficult in the late 1930s, the U.S. Treasury reached agreements with the Treasuries of Brazil (July 16,

1937), Argentina (December 27, 1940), and Mexico (November 19, 1940), through which it set aside $150 million from its stabilization fund to assist the fiscal situation of these states.[127] The Inter-American Bank was established as a result of a meeting of the ministers of foreign affairs in Panama on May 10, 1940. The bank was to promote inter-American credit and the interchange of capital and to collaborate in the reconstruction of national monetary systems.[128]

In general, as World War II approached, governments replaced the private capital markets as the primary lenders in pursuit of their own strategic objectives. Institutional solutions that sought to promote exports as well as tied loans were to carry over after World War II in the movement of capital from creditor to debtor states through export credit agencies.

Part II

EXTERNAL SOVEREIGN DEBT, SYNDICATED BANK LOANS, AND SOVEREIGN DEBT CRISES IN DEVELOPING COUNTRIES, 1955–94

FIVE

Flow of External Capital to the Developing World after World War II

1955–73

Loans to sovereign states in the period immediately following World War II were conditioned to a large extent by prewar factors—namely, the Great Depression, the large losses of investors in sovereign bonds, and the establishment by creditor nations of export credit promotion and insurance schemes to encourage trade in the wake of the Great Depression.

Despite the latter efforts, the capital markets failed to open to developing states,[1] and creditor governments, particularly in Europe, increasingly had to resort to the export credit promotion institutions to rebuild their trade with the rest of the world.[2] In addition, the Eastern European states, now within the sphere of influence of the Soviet Union, with the exception of Yugoslavia, did not participate in the international economy of the immediate postwar era.

This institutional reliance was reinforced with the creation of the Bretton Woods system and the twin pillars of the international financial system, the International Monetary Fund (IMF) and the International Bank for Reconstruction and Development (World Bank), the former to support balance of payments stabilization and the latter recovery from the war and eventually economic development.[3] The third pillar of the postwar economic system, the General Agreement on Tariffs and Trade

(GATT), emerged out of the failure to establish a proposed international trade organization. The GATT quickly became the instrument by which postwar trade was liberalized and the competitive tariffs of the Depression were averted.[4]

In addition, the decision by the United States to assist in rebuilding Western Europe—for a variety of humanitarian, economic, and politico-strategic reasons embodied in the Marshall Plan[5] and the Truman Doctrine[6]—provided another spur to governmental involvement in economic reconstruction and development. The Truman Doctrine, in seeking to contain the spread of Communism, quickly provided the rationale for the large-scale U.S. aid programs in the postwar period. America, more alert to its responsibilities than in the interwar period as the premier power in the world, began to export to a number of developing countries its own vision for the postwar world in the form of financial aid, food support programs, technical support, and military armaments.[7] In addition, its transnational enterprises began to invest directly on a large scale throughout the world.[8] Inevitably, their bankers followed and soon became important multinational enterprises in their own right. They sought business not only with their traditional customers but eventually with sovereign and private borrowers within the developing world.[9]

In the developing countries, many that had achieved their independence in the postwar period began to realize that political sovereignty was difficult to maintain without economic independence: "Development was often seen in new nations as the economic continuation of the political struggle for independence, as an important means of creating a national identity or of breaking old and restrictive ties."[10] In addition, many of the older independent states that had been cut off from external capital as a result of World War II, in particular the Latin American states, began to open their economies to external capital, with a stress on industrialization and import substitution-oriented development.[11] These states were seeking the external resources to promote economic development, with the growing theoretical conviction that the limit to economic growth in the third world was a scarcity of foreign exchange for vital imports of such items as capital goods and technology.[12] The United Nations, a forum for third world expression, declared the 1960s the "Development Decade," emphasizing the need for external capital from the advanced industrial economies or creditor states.[13]

The problems associated with external borrowing soon became evident in 1956 when Argentina, and then several other developing states, were forced to reschedule their official debts.[14] These states borrowed initially from export credit agencies on terms inconsistent with their development needs. As the era progressed, official reschedulings through the Paris Club became increasingly common.[15]

Large numbers of private market loans to the developing countries did not materialize until the growth of the eurocurrency market and the oil crisis of 1973–74 required petrodollar recycling. This recycling through the second oil crisis was abruptly curtailed during the debt crisis of 1981–83, when petrodollar recycling gave way to debt recycling. The restructurings and rescheduling in this period were a mix of official rescheduling and private commercial bank restructurings, with the latter of far larger consequence in terms of the amounts, impact on debtor states, and potential threat of defaults or extended debt moratoriums represented to the international financial system.

During the postwar era, the link between capital exports and international relations was not as obvious as it was, for example, in the interwar era. Nevertheless, many of the same issues were present throughout.

First, the hard core of creditor states remained the same, and their capital markets, integrated into a worldwide financial market with the misnomer of the eurocurrency market, were still an essential component of capital export to developing countries.

Second, a hard core of debtor states persisted, primarily Latin American and Eastern European, but also joined by many of the newly emerged African countries.

Third, capital export in the postwar era was clearly a projection of state power. In many developing countries, the United States, the primary creditor state during the era, rivaled the Soviet Union in offering aid, agricultural trade, and military credits to developing nations where perceived strategic interests were at stake. Moreover, the major Western creditor states competed with each other in the developing countries by the extension of export credits.

Fourth, while explicit military interventions over debt did not occur, official debt rescheduling via the Paris Club and other creditor forums favored certain regimes or countries over others for strategic considerations; for example, Ghana, Indonesia, Jamaica, Turkey, and Poland all were supported through Paris Club reschedulings.

Fifth, although repudiations were infrequent and small-scale, ideologically based repudiations or extended moratoriums by Vietnam, Cuba, and Nicaragua occurred.

Sixth, in private multilateral restructurings between the commercial banks and certain debtor states, creditor governments assisted where their vital interests were perceived to be at stake; Mexico, Brazil, Chile, Yugoslavia, Hungary, and the Philippines are examples.

Seventh, the use of multilateral financial institutions, above all the IMF, in support of private debt restructurings and to monitor the adjustment programs of the debtor states, was consistent with the nineteenth-century practices of international

debt commissions and the League of Nations commission. From the creditors' perspective, these institutions provide supposedly apolitical forums for resolving debt crises and avoid the potential for elevating debt restructurings to high politics.

Eighth, from the viewpoint of debtor countries, the creditor states consistently
tried to avoid elevating the problems of debt rescheduling to a higher political level
of debt considerations. Through the United Nations Conference on Trade and Development (UNCTAD) and ad hoc committees of experts on debt rescheduling, the
developing countries sought more flexible terms for official rescheduling and consideration of debt forgiveness as aid. In the meetings on the New International Economic Order in Paris following the first oil crisis, several developing countries sought
to negotiate via a debtors' cartel. The Cartagena meeting of the Latin American states
raised similar issues. For their part, the debtor states consistently tried to elevate the
level of political attention to the social, political, and economic problems that their
heavy debt burdens fostered. They sought alternative, more flexible solutions to the
debt crisis that realistically reflected their capacity to pay and to restore their creditworthiness. In the renegotiations of external sovereign debt, the essential underlying
issues of the sanctity of contracts, *pacta sunt servanda*, rather than the vital interests
of states, *clausula rebus sic stantibus*, remained relevant.

The post–World War II era remained largely crisis free until the oil crisis of the
mid-1970s and the need for developing countries to borrow from the major money
center banks and affiliated banks in banking syndicates to support their energy
imports.

The Flow of External Capital for Development, 1946–73

The concern at the beginning of the era was to encourage the private capital markets in industrial countries once again to provide capital to developing countries. In
Resolution 622 C (VII) of December 21, 1952, the General Assembly of the United
Nations noted the importance of stimulating international flows of private capital
for economic progress in underdeveloped countries, but pointed out that despite the
efforts being made, those flows were still insufficient.[16] One reason, the United Nations observed, was the experience of the 1930s, which continued to be a formidable
barrier to portfolio investments in the developing world, except where close political,
commercial, and monetary ties existed. Moreover, the continued disequilibrium in
almost all developing countries, combined with exchange controls in both these and
several capital-exporting states, were additional obstacles to floating international
loans in the private capital markets.[17]

By the end of the decade the situation had not altered materially. A substantial number of foreign bonds from the interwar period remained in default to creditors in the United States. Moreover, although the Johnson Act no longer prohibited bond flotations by countries in default on U.S. government loans once they became members of the IMF and World Bank, many individual states passed legislation to preclude institutions such as insurance companies and pension funds from investing more than a limited percentage of their portfolios in foreign bonds except Canadian and World Bank bonds.[18]

Financiers in the United States, the major source of private capital to the world, switched from the portfolio investments of the interwar period to direct private investment, primarily through the transnational companies.[19] European countries, still dependent during this period on U.S. capital flows, served essentially as intermediators of capital abroad. The United Kingdom also made portfolio loans, which went almost exclusively to the Commonwealth, with the Capital Issue Committee carefully scrutinizing all external loans. French lending, which was relatively small-scale, went primarily to colonies and affiliated territories, as did Dutch loans (to Indonesia and Surinam) and Belgian loans (to the Congo).[20]

Private Lending

By the end of the 1950s the only substantial form of private lending to the developing countries was trade-related, usually tied, export credits. The various government-supported export credit institutions provided mostly short- and medium-term loans for the purchase of capital goods by developing nations from producers within the creditor country.[21] In reality, these credits were quasi-private in nature, as they were usually provided by commercial banks or suppliers themselves, often with guarantees by the governmental export credit agency. In the event that the sovereign borrower was unable to pay the bank or supplier, the credit was rolled over into an official credit, and payment or restructuring of the credit was then negotiated by the creditor government, a process that became known as official rescheduling.[22]

These trade or export credits carried mostly hard terms,[23] and the increasing difficulty developing countries had in absorbing these loans became apparent early in the postwar era. The problem persisted, with net export credits increasing by 75 percent between 1961 and 1967, from $697 million to $1,220 million, with three- to seven-year tenures predominating.[24] Several of the developing countries experienced debt servicing difficulties during this period. As one analyst noted: "The national export credit agencies are set on a course that will lead either to a progressive mixing of increased flows of export credits and development finance to ease the burden on the debt servicing capacity of the poor countries, or to progressively greater risks of default in more and more countries."[25] The Pearson Commission reported that "excessive extension of export credit to developing countries has in some cases given rise to acute debt crises."[26]

Toward the end of the period, medium- and long-term credit from commercial banks began to emerge as a meaningful source of external flows to a select number of developing countries, with the volume reaching $2.3 billion in 1972 and $4.5 billion in 1973, representing 26 percent of total commercial bank lending to all countries in 1972 and 22 percent in 1974.[27] Among the developing countries, Argentina, Brazil, Colombia, Mexico, Peru, the Philippines, the Republic of Korea (South Korea), Yugoslavia, and Zaire (formerly the Belgian Congo) were already relatively consistent borrowers from banks. Algeria, Indonesia, Iran, and Venezuela, primarily oil-exporting countries, borrowed a substantial portion of the $1.2 billion and $2.8 billion lent in 1972 and 1973, respectively, while, among the Eastern European COMECON borrowers Poland, Hungary, and Bulgaria absorbed the bulk of the $285 million and $645 million lent to these countries in 1972 and 1973, respectively.[28] In effect, the trend of borrowing from the commercial banks was already established for the major debtor countries before the first oil shock.

In overall terms "the 1960s were remarkable for the consistency, diversity and stability in the flow of funds to the developing countries."[29] Moreover, official creditors and multilateral financial agencies provided capital in amounts over and above that projected as necessary to meet self-sustaining growth.[30] This pattern was not self-sustaining as aid flows began to stagnate toward the end of the 1960s.

Foreign Direct Investment

The movement by developing countries in the 1960s and 1970s to nationalize utilities, public transport, and natural resources, particularly metals and oil, led to a narrowing of opportunities and greater uncertainty for private investment in developing countries. In any event, the climate toward direct investment in the developing world by transnational companies had grown increasingly hostile as the period progressed.[31] Moreover, many developing countries increasingly reserved certain subsectors of their economy for state-owned enterprises, such as steel, petrochemicals, fertilizers, and telecommunications, a practice that further narrowed the opportunities available to private capital—both domestic and foreign.[32]

The Debt Problems of Developing Countries

The growing debt problems of developing countries became a concern as early as 1958, when the first of a series of studies by Dragoslav Avramovic of the World Bank focused attention on the issue.[33] The UN studies on long-term capital flows also addressed it, as did early UNCTAD publications and the Pearson Commission.[34] Although there was no specific financial crisis causing a sudden wave of defaults, by 1973 developing countries had made twenty-five requests to creditor countries for debt restructurings, involving $5.5 billion in principal, with several states restructuring repeatedly during this period. Moreover, a number of the official restructurings that occurred after the first oil crisis were attributable to problems in this earlier period.[35] Even by the end of the 1960s there had been a persistent call in several different development forums for debt relief as a form of aid for developing countries.[36] Despite the worldwide economic expansion and large-scale flows of external capital from the industrial countries, which provided a generally satisfactory mix of capital, many economists pointed to serious problems with respect to debt absorption, achievement of widely acceptable levels of borrowing for development, the debt service burden, the difficulty of debt management, and the flight of capital.[37] Moreover, the developing countries sharply questioned the principles of debt rescheduling embodied in the Paris Club process.[38] The Paris Club was the venue for the rescheduling of official debts in negotiations between representatives of the creditor states and debtors, with the IMF in attendance.

Beginning from a relatively low level of indebtedness, with the external debt from the 1920s having been severely written down after the war, the developing countries increased their external public debt and debt service significantly in the first postwar decade, 1946–55. In twenty-four developing countries, aggregate public debt service trebled, while debt outstanding rose 50 percent. The rise in debt service was largely related to a resumption of interwar debt payments, rising interest rates over the decade, and an increase in medium-term debt that required an accelerated rate of amortization.[39]

The problems of accumulating external debt and growth in debt service began to surface after the end of the Korean War, which brought with it the first postwar slowdown in industrial country expansion, and the Suez Canal crisis, which disrupted the pattern of world trade. In 1958 external public debt service rose to a peak in twenty-two out of thirty-two developing countries sampled.[40] The major difficulty with debt servicing involved several Latin American countries, which were relying on medium-term export credits for the import of capital goods.[41] Whereas the average debt maturity in Latin America at the beginning of the decade was twenty-eight years, by the end it had declined to eleven years.[42] The level of external debt increased rapidly throughout the 1960s—at an average rate of 14 percent a year—while debt service payment increased by 17 percent on average.[43]

With the governments of the developing countries assuming the primary role in development either directly or through state-owned enterprises (SOEs), it is not surprising that, of the $40 billion of recorded external public debt outstanding at the beginning of 1968, about three-quarters of the debt was direct government borrowing either from other governments (56 percent of the total) or from international financial institutions (19 percent of the total). The other quarter represented public borrowing from private lenders or private borrowing with government guarantees.[44]

Indebtedness and debt service payments were relatively concentrated in a small number of debtor countries; thirteen developing nations accounted for 80 percent of the debt service payments.[45] There was substantial geographic variation in the incidence of debt service burden. In Latin America, debt service requirements during the period 1965–67 consumed 87 percent of new loans and in Africa 73 percent, but in South Asia only 52 percent. Argentina, Brazil, Chile, and Mexico in Latin America accounted for 80 percent of the debt service; in the Middle East, one-third of the payments came from the United Arab Republic; and in Asia, two-thirds were from India and Pakistan. Colombia, Peru, Iran, and Israel completed the list of primary debtor states. Afghanistan, India, Indonesia, and Pakistan, among the countries with the lowest per capita income, had the highest indebtedness relative to exports.

By 1970 the economic situation in many developing countries had deteriorated, in part because of the stagnation in aid, heavy external debt accumulation, relatively frequent debt reschedulings, and the need for severe adjustments. In a wider context, the foundations of the international financial and trade system were under considerable stress. Confidence in an ever-expanding international economic environment had begun to fade.

U.S. policy was another problem. In the wake of the Vietnam War and with growing structural problems in its economy, the United States found it increasingly difficult to maintain its position as the center of the international monetary system. As the concern over dollar shortages in the immediate postwar decade shifted to concern over a dollar glut, President Richard M. Nixon announced his New Economic Policy in 1971. It unilaterally removed the structural support for the world monetary system as conceived at Bretton Woods by ending the fixed parity of the U.S. dollar and its convertibility to gold and the system of fixed exchange rates. Instead, the dollar was left to float.[46] The Smithsonian Agreement that followed the United States' announcement tentatively confirmed this decision and initiated a regime of pegged exchange rates, which evolved during the decade into a floating exchange rate regime, as specified in the Jamaica accord.[47]

The floating exchange rates added more uncertainty to the international economic environment, particularly for developing countries that aligned their currencies in an array of solutions around the world's reserve currencies.[48] The demands from the developing countries for reform of the monetary system, such as automatic linking of standard drawing rights (SDRs) to economic growth and greater representation in the decision making of the international financial institutions, particularly the IMF, which was effectively managed and controlled by the Group of Ten (G-10),[49] were basically shunted aside. The work on monetary reform through the Committee of Twenty came to a standstill.[50]

Trade liberalization, negotiated in accordance with the principles laid down by the GATT, reached its peak in the 1967 Kennedy Round of trade negotiations.[51] Thereafter, the industrial nations bogged down over intractable differences such as agricultural preferences, industrial subsidies, and nontariff trade barriers. The development and growth of the European Economic Community (EEC) and Japan as powerful trade competitors with the United States exacerbated the differences within the GATT. In addition, the developing countries were demanding unilateral trade concessions, a major problem for GATT's structure.[52] These countries also sought to eliminate the trade restrictions introduced outside the GATT framework, such as voluntary export restraints and orderly market agreements. The Multi-Fiber Agreement was seen as the outstanding example of restrictions on developing country exports to advanced industrial countries.[53] The difficult issue of these nontariff trade barriers was the focus of the Tokyo Round, which formally opened on September 14, 1973. It ended in April 1979, having achieved relatively little success.[54] The critical issue for the developing countries relative to their debt problem was their ability to export to the advanced economies with as little restraint as possible in order to earn foreign exchange to service their external debts.

Another key issue to emerge was oil. The rapid industrialization throughout the world was increasingly based on oil as the energy source, particularly imported oil from the Middle East Gulf states and North Africa.[55] The formation of the Organization of Petroleum Exporting Countries (OPEC) in 1960 and its increasing radicalization in the late 1960s and early 1970s, with demands for a higher share of oil revenues and threats of nationalization, increasingly exposed the vulnerability of industrial countries to an interruption or reduction in the supply of oil.[56] Fears were heightened when the Arab-Israeli War of 1973 culminated in a temporary oil boycott by the Organization of Arab Petroleum Exporting Countries (OAPEC) against the United States and the Netherlands and a unilateral decision by OPEC to increase the price of oil to $5.12 a barrel. Then, on December 23, 1973, OPEC raised the price of Persian Gulf oil to $11.65 a barrel as of January 1974.[57] The era of petrodollar recycling began.[58]

SIX

From Petrodollar Recycling to Debt Recycling, Syndicated Bank Loans and Sovereign Debt Crises

1974–83

The concept of petrodollar recycling emerged because of the inability of a number of oil-exporting states to absorb the sudden surge in revenue resulting from the higher price of crude oil. Government revenues from oil in the principal Organization of Petroleum Exporting Countries (OPEC) states rose from $22.5 billion in 1973 to $90.5 billion in 1974 and $93.3 billion in 1975. These increases were reflected in the trade and current account surpluses of the OPEC states. The trade surpluses reflected the low elasticities of the demand for crude oil in the short run, a situation that meant oil prices would remain high, since consumers could not readily switch to alternative energy sources. Further, there were no major oil suppliers outside OPEC at the onset of this period that could or would supply crude oil at substantially lower prices.[1] The primary oil exporters were unable in the short run to raise imports by an amount approaching the increase in their export earnings.[2]

Petrodollar Recycling, 1974–78

In short, the OPEC countries had to find ways to invest their surplus. At the same time, the oil-importing countries needed funds to finance their oil bills, now reflected in correspondingly large balance of payments deficits. The advanced industrial countries also felt the impact of the oil price increases. Together, the oil-importing countries ran trade and current account deficits that were largely the converse of the OPEC surpluses.

The question in petrodollar recycling was one of distribution and intermediation: How would the OPEC surpluses be distributed to countries in deficit, and what vehicle would be used to intermediate these funds? Recycling embodied two concepts that are normally combined. The first was the investment of the OPEC current account surpluses, and the second was the switching of these invested surpluses to countries that required the funds to finance their balance of payments deficits.[3]

Within OPEC itself, there were large differences in capacity to absorb the petrodollars. Defined broadly, the "high-absorbing" OPEC states had relatively large populations that could be expected to consume their surpluses relatively quickly via imports for economic development, while the "low-absorbing" states had relatively small populations that, it was presumed, would take a much longer time to use their surplus funds.[4] Moreover, over the period 1975 to 1978, several of the high absorbers became substantial sovereign debtors, and it is these states that primarily explain the declining current account balances for OPEC during the period.[5] In addition, the low-absorbing Gulf states used their surpluses far more quickly than anticipated in the pursuit of economic development, large-scale capital-intensive projects, luxury imports, the purchase of sophisticated armaments from the West, and aid, primarily to the Arab "front-line" states.[6]

At the same time, the low absorbers accounted for an increasing proportion of OPEC's surplus investments as the period progressed.[7] The investment of these surpluses was centered primarily in the capital markets of the industrial countries, with a large share of the funds deposited on a short-term basis in the eurocurrency market. Of $161.8 billion in total new investment, $56.4 billion (35 percent) was deposited in the eurocurrency market, with the remainder spread among investments in government securities in the United Kingdom and the United States, bilateral aid and loans primarily to non-oil-producing Arab states, loans to international agencies such as the International Monetary Fund (IMF) for its oil facility and to various regional development banks, and investments in properties and equities in the United States.

The eurocurrency market had begun in the 1950s mainly as a source of deposits for the "hard currency" reserves of Eastern bloc countries seeking anonymity and a return on their funds.[8] The market grew steadily thereafter as a result of deposits by developing countries of their hard currency reserves, by central banks, and by major transnational companies with surplus funds, particularly American companies whose cash surpluses from overseas earnings would have been subject to taxation if repatriated to the United States.[9] The market also developed substantial interbank activity, as large money center banks sought to balance the maturity distribution of their loans through lending and borrowing in the eurocurrency market.[10] To a great extent, U.S. monetary policy, which was directed toward regulating and controlling the flow of dollars from the United States abroad, unwittingly encouraged the development of the market.[11]

By 1974 the Euromarket was well established. The year-end 1973 figures estimated its size to be $295 billion on a gross basis and $170 billion net. At the end of 1978, with the injection of the petrodollar funds as well as other sources of liquidity, the market had grown to an estimated $903 billion gross and $540 billion net.[12]

Activity in the eurocurrency market was largely controlled by a small number of international money center banks. They constituted an inner circle of approximately twenty-five, based in the OECD countries. Their large deposit base allowed them to translate domestic currency deposits into eurocurrency deposits and eventually eurocredits.[13] For American and Japanese banks, interoffice transfers across national boundaries were an important segment of their lending capability in the eurocurrency market. The major international banks had a sufficiently strong worldwide network to attract deposits from the major international depositors—central banks, OPEC countries, transnational corporations, and other banks—for which they acted as correspondents.[14] They normally had the capacity to be simultaneously the main participants in Euromarket credits and the main suppliers, through their interbank operations, of funds to other banks in the Euromarket.

There was also a second level or tier of banks participating in the eurocurrency market, numbering approximately 3,000, located throughout the world. They fell into three principal categories—regional banks, consortium banks, and principal commercial banks from advanced developing countries.[15] Borrowing throughout this period was typically balanced between private enterprise, public entities, and sovereign borrowers (the outer circle in the market) and deposits between nonbanks, banks, and central monetary authorities.[16]

The transfer of investment funds from those facilities favored by OPEC depositors to the oil-consuming nations most in need of funds was essentially not distinguishable in the total mix of the eurocurrency market. The switching was carried out through financial intermediation primarily by the major international banks. In lending directly to external sovereign borrowers, they usually acted through syndicates and the tying in of second-level banks. As Chairman Paul Volcker of the U.S. Federal Reserve System observed: "International lending has traditionally been pretty much the province of the largest banking institutions with a long history of experience with international business, extensive information networks through foreign branches, and a resource base capable of sustaining potential losses. During more recent years, more and more essentially domestic banks were drawn into international lending."[17] Therefore, when switching took place, the original source of the funds that went in aggregate to Brazil, Mexico, Argentina, and other sovereign borrowers was not usually transparent.[18]

Eurocurrencies were created whenever a national currency was deposited in a bank outside its country of origin.[19] Typically they were deposited for specified periods of three months to one year and had a stated yield or interest rate. Banks took in eurocurrency deposits with the intention of relending them at a profit, the essential factor in the petrodollar recycling process. Thus, with the OPEC deposits, the banks fulfilled their normal function as intermediators of credit and transformed the maturity distribution of the deposits. Syndicates of banks brought together on a temporary basis for a particular loan package lent the money as "eurocredits" at variable interest rates, with the spread (profit margin) normally priced at some level over the London Interbank Offered Rate (LIBOR).[20] During the 1970s, 85 percent of publicized eurocredits were provided at terms of five to eight years. Eurocredits were technically renewed every six months, when the banks theoretically reverted to the eurocurrency market to renew their deposits and thereby reprice the loan. In addition to the LIBOR spread, various other fees were charged to borrowers, such as management, participation, and commitment fees, which were usually paid up front or discounted from the loan proceeds in advance. The fees varied with the quality of the borrower, the size of the loan package, and the number of participating banks. Fees were most often part of the negotiation and involved tradeoffs with the spread.

A decision to loan funds to a sovereign borrower was in theory based on each bank's assessment, called sovereign risk analysis, of the credit risk involved. While the large international banks quickly developed seemingly sophisticated models for analyzing credit to different countries, sovereign risk analysis focused primarily on two points. One was the question asked by any bank of a borrower: Does the borrower have the capacity to repay? This analysis involved a macroeconomic assessment of the country, complicated in the case of sovereign loans by the potential for foreign exchange shortages, known as transfer risk. The second was the political risk that, when the time came to repay the loan, the borrower would, for any one of a myriad of political reasons, choose not to repay, with the banks powerless to collect. As one analyst of sovereign risk observed: "Private banks have seen the expanding role of government as borrowers or as guarantors of international borrowing by entities in their countries. To the extent that governments assume these roles, the banks face credit assessment needs which are no longer simply analyses of individual projects and their projected cash flow. The needs are rather synonymous with an assessment of the country itself."[21]

In practice, sovereign risk analysis, because of the dynamics of the market and the lack of timely information on total credits extended to any given country or sovereign entity, ended up as de facto credit rationing, given that the bank loans went largely to a select number of seemingly safer non-oil-producing developing countries, mainly the newly industrialized countries (NICs); oil-exporting states, mainly the OPEC "high-absorbing" ones; and some select Eastern bloc countries.[22] The low-income developing countries were widely perceived as poor credit risks and could not borrow any significant amounts from the Euromarket. They were therefore dependent on official sources for external credits to finance their balance of payments deficits.[23]

Another aspect of the Euromarket during this period was the strong revival of financing through international bond issues. Eurobonds were floated in several offshore markets simultaneously by international banking groups for international borrowers, including major transnational corporations, multilateral financial agencies such as the World Bank, and sovereign borrowers.[24] However, unlike in the nineteenth century and the interwar period, the bond market was restricted to a small number of sovereign borrowers, largely the major industrial countries, and to prime transnational companies. As one analyst observed, "The Euro-bond market has become one of the world's more exclusive clubs, conferring prestige on banks and borrowers alike."[25] During the period 1974 through 1978, only Brazil, Mexico, and the Philippines among the developing countries were able to draw on this market, along with Algeria and Venezuela among the OPEC states and Hungary among the centrally planned economies. Together these countries borrowed approximately $10.6 billion of the total for sovereign and institutional borrowing of $127 billion, or approximately 8 percent of the total. International organizations, primarily the World Bank, raised $23 billion, or 18 percent of the total market,[26] during this same period. To the extent that the World Bank and regional development banks provided loans to sovereign borrowers in the third world, these countries in fact enjoyed a larger participation in the bond market, albeit indirectly, than is credited.

Developing country borrowers during this period assumed debt largely for the same reasons they did in the initial postwar period: to finance balance of payments deficits and, as the period progressed, the oil deficits, which blurred with other reasons

FIGURE 6-1.   Medium- and Long-Term Eurocredits to Developing and
Eastern European Countries, 1975–78

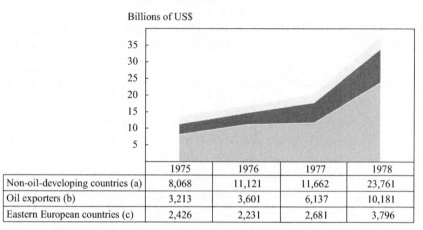

Billions of US$

	1975	1976	1977	1978
Non-oil-developing countries (a)	8,068	11,121	11,662	23,761
Oil exporters (b)	3,213	3,601	6,137	10,181
Eastern European countries (c)	2,426	2,231	2,681	3,796

☐ Non-oil-developing countries (a)   ■ Oil exporters (b)   ☐ Eastern European countries (c)

Source: Organization for Economic Cooperation and Development, *Financial Market Trends* (Paris, March 1984), pp. 149–51.
a. Includes Portugal, Greece, and Turkey, classified normally as OECD states.
b. OPEC "high absorbers" only: Algeria, Ecuador, Indonesia, Iran, Nigeria, Venezuela.
c. Excludes Yugoslavia, which is included under non-oil-developing countries; excludes USSR.

for these deficits; for economic growth and development; to spend on armaments and building military capacity; and to build monetary reserves.[27] However, the mix or proportion of borrowing for various purposes was different than in the earlier period, specifically the share of resources absorbed by oil importers. Despite initial concerns that the Euromarket would quickly reach the limit of its capability to intermediate sufficient funds for developing countries, the IMF concluded that it was operating efficiently enough to meet those needs.[28]

By 1975 the non-oil-producing developing countries had become major borrowers in the eurocurrency market, accounting for 39 percent of the market.[29] They remained major participants in the market thereafter. They were joined eventually by the oil-exporting states, specifically the "high absorbers," as their surpluses diminished.[30] Several Eastern European countries also became borrowers as a result of détente, which permitted them to increase their trade finance and access to eurocredits from Western commercial banks.[31]

The developing African countries were conspicuously absent from the list of private market borrowers, as were the major states of South Asia—India, Pakistan, and China. On the other hand, several Latin American states remained major debtors

TABLE 6-1.   Bank Debt of Twenty Non-OECD Countries Most Indebted to BIS Reporting Banks, Year End 1982

Billions of US$

| Location of banks | BIS Reporting Banks | | | | Debt service as a percentage of export of goods and services, 1983 |
	United States	United Kingdom	Elsewhere	All BIS[d]	
Mexico[a]	29.7	13.2	19.0	61.9	59
Brazil[a]	21.2	11.4	19.7	52.3	67
Argentina[a]	11.0	3.7	8.2	22.9	88
Venezuela[a]	9.2	4.4	8.9	22.5	25
South Korea	7.2	4.0	5.4	16.6	17
USSR	0.3	4.1	10.2	14.6	n.a.[e]
Poland[a]	0.6	3.1	9.5	13.2	n.a.
Chile[a]	5.3	2.1	3.2	10.6	54
Yugoslavia[a]	1.3	2.9	5.0	9.2	n.a.
German Democratic Republic	8.2	3.0	5.5	8.7	n.a.
Philippines[a]	2.6	2.2	3.2	8.0	33
Hungary	0.8	1.8	3.9	6.5	n.a.
Algeria	n.a.	1.5	n.a.	6.5	30
Taiwan[b]					
Israel[c]	1.9	1.8	2.1	5.8	n.a.
Nigeria[a]	n.a.	2.4	n.a.	5.4	14
Peru[a]	2.0	0.7	2.4	5.1	47
Colombia	2.6	0.7	1.6	4.9	38
Indonesia	0.3	0.7	3.9	4.9	14
Egypt	0.4	1.6	2.7	4.7	16

Source: Great Britain House of Commons, *International Monetary Arrangements, International Lending by Banks, Fourth Report from the Treasury Service Committee Session 1982–83,* Vol. 1 (March 15, 1983), p. x.

a. Eventual debt service disruption, 1982–84.
b. Net creditor: assets with BIS banks of $6.1 billion.
c. Net creditor: assets with BIS banks of $9.1 billion.
d. Total net bank debt: $290.5 billion.
e. Not applicable.

throughout the period, accounting for a large proportion of the total bank loans to developing countries over the period. Twenty major sovereign borrowers received an estimated $75 billion, or 83 percent of the total bank borrowing by developing and Eastern European states. Just eight countries—Brazil, Mexico, the Philippines, South

TABLE 6-2.   Developing Countries: Trend of Debt Service Payments
as a Percentage of Export Earnings, 1973–83

	1973[a]	1977	1980	1983
All developing countries[b]	n.a.[d]	15.3	17.1	22.5
Major borrowers[c]	n.a.	19.1	21.5	29.9
Non-oil-exporting developing countries	15.9	14.8	17.2	21.6
Low-income countries	14.6	12.1	10.3	13.3
Excluding India and China	n.a.	13.2	14.3	22.4
By region:				
Africa	8.8	11.9	17.4	25.1
Asia	9.6	7.9	8.4	10.8
Western Hemisphere	29.3	28.2	34.1	44.0

Source: IMF, World Economic Outlook, 1983 (Washington, 1983) and IMF, World Economic Outlook, 1984 (Washington, 1984), presented in Report by a Commonwealth Group of Experts, "The Debt Crisis," p. 21, table 1.2.

a. Figures for 1973 include China and are therefore not comparable to prior years.
b. Excluding eight oil-exporting countries: Iran, Iraq, Kuwait, Libya, Oman, Qatar, Saudi Arabia, and the United Arab Emirates.
c. The twenty-five developing countries with the largest external debt at the end of 1982.
d. Not applicable.

Korea, Algeria, Indonesia, Iran, and Venezuela—accounted for 60 percent of total bank borrowing during this period, with the oil exporters, if Mexico is included, accounting for more than half the total (see figure 6-1 and table 6-1).

Borrowing from the eurocurrency market and commercial banking syndicates was only part of the story during this period. Developing countries continued to obtain loans from official bilateral and multilateral sources, along with grants-in-aid and direct foreign investment. Although official flows virtually stagnated in real terms, the amounts were still significant and important in the total capital mix.[32]

During the period 1974–78, the public and publicly guaranteed external debt, including undisbursed, of all developing countries rose from an estimated $115.5 billion at the end of 1973 to $346 billion at the end of 1978; disbursed debt rose from $84 billion to $246 billion. Private nonguaranteed external debt increased as well, from $25.5 billion in 1973 to $54 billion at the end of 1978.[33]

The increase in debt was paralleled by a rise in the total debt service from $10 billion to $34 billion during this same period (see table 6-2). Of greatest relevance was the increase in debt service on financial market debt, which went from $5 billion at the end of 1973 to $19 billion at the end of 1978 and represented 50 percent of all debt service. All the indicators of indebtedness rose during this period.[34]

Debt Recycling, 1979–80

Many analysts saw the adjustment by developing countries to the first oil crisis as having proceeded relatively smoothly, but others did not agree.[35] A number of problems existed. First, the significant level of external sovereign debt acquired by the developing countries during this period left them vulnerable to any future adverse changes in economic conditions. Second, the debt mix or composition of debt had changed dramatically. In addition to medium-term export credits, the major borrowers, as well as other developing countries, had accumulated significant medium-term loans at variable interest rates from commercial banks. The rate on these bank loans averaged 9 percent during this period; the rate from official creditors was only 5 percent. The average maturity on bank loans was approximately 8.5 years, whereas maturities for official credits averaged 25 years, with grace periods of 3.3 years and 6.8 years, respectively. All these measures show an adverse change in debt composition.[36]

On the positive side of the ledger, because of stagflation (a combination of low economic growth and high inflation) in the industrial countries,[37] commercial bank loans were being obtained at negative, near zero, or only slightly positive real rates of interest as the period progressed. Inflation had the effect of rapidly amortizing these obligations. Thus, by the end of 1978, the nominal external debt of $208 billion of eighty-seven non-oil-producing developing countries, when deflated by export unit values, was only $95.5 billion, or $86.8 billion in import unit value.[38] In addition, as the demand for loans in the industrial countries softened because of the depressed economic conditions, the major borrowing states were able to obtain funds at relatively low spreads over LIBOR. Toward the end of the period there was a tendency to refinance loans, a practice that would later produce "bunching" of maturities.[39] Finally, owing to the changes in debt composition or mix, the developing countries were mismatching the terms of their borrowings with their development requirements. This led to a dependency by these countries to continuously roll over their credits.[40]

With the greater availability of credit, many developing countries were postponing necessary economic adjustments, a trend that eventually necessitated severe adjustment programs that restricted the prospects for economic growth.[41] However, on balance, the middle- and upper-income developing countries did manage to sustain growth during this period at a level almost comparable to that of the 1960s.[42]

The continued financing of deficits by developing countries over a prolonged period posed a potential threat to the international monetary system: if sovereign debtors proved unable to service their debts, banks that had become overcommitted to individual debtors could possibly fail.[43]

Developing countries largely avoided the one institution that might have required adjustment—the IMF (the Fund).[44] At this time the IMF was providing only modest increments to existing capital, levels that usually were not sufficient to persuade the developing countries to seek out the Fund. Not seeking IMF support allowed developing countries to avoid or postpone the politically unpalatable constraint on economic policy, IMF conditionality, that invariably accompanied IMF adjustment programs.[45]

By the end of the period the banks found themselves unable to establish any form of control over the policies of states, such as Peru and Zaire, to which they had advanced substantial funds and which were now in need of debt restructurings. The banks turned more often to the IMF in these cases, and an informal or implicit partnership developed, where the banks would provide additional financing or refinancing only if the borrower agreed to an IMF standby arrangement and certain policy preconditions. As Fabio Basagni pointed out, "In effect through these and similar experiences the Fund has gradually become a *de facto* certifier of a debtor's international creditworthiness."[46]

The World Bank, the second pillar of the Bretton Woods system, also provided relatively little additional support to developing countries during this period. Disbursements on approved loans by the Bank through its normal funding window came to $1.9 billion in 1975 and $2.8 billion by 1978. For International Development Association (IDA) loans to the poorest countries,[47] the figures were $1.0 billion in 1975, $1.3 billion in 1976 and 1977, and $1.0 billion in 1978.[48]

A problem of equity emerged. With most low-income developing countries unable to borrow in the capital markets, the gap between them and high- and middle-income developing countries grew. For the most part, the low-income countries had to accept the IMF financial support and adjustment programs. In general, their economies stagnated during this period, particularly the low-income African states.[49] In response, the IMF, World Bank, and various other institutions urged industrial countries to provide more concessional financing for countries classified by the United Nations as the "most seriously affected."[50]

There was no specific acute financial crisis during this period, as many analysts had feared would result from the oil crisis, but the increasing debt service burden forced developing states to restructure their debts with increasing frequency as the period progressed. The initial restructurings were primarily related to debt from the earlier period and involved the rescheduling of official debt through the Paris Club or the aid consortiums. However, in the later years of the period, a need emerged for parallel commercial bank restructuring.[51]

A number of countries had to negotiate repeated restructurings. The number is actually greater than it appears, since several bank restructurings were not formally labeled as such. Initially, the banks preferred refinancing to rescheduling in order to maintain the cosmetic appearance of a continuous rollover of credits so as to avoid having to reclassify these assets on their balance sheets. The major restructurings involving commercial bank creditors as the period drew to a close involved Peru, Turkey, and Zaire.[52]

The increase in commercial bank renegotiations raised concern over the mutual vulnerabilities and dependence of debtors and creditors. "Through time an escalation of commitments may develop, increasing the mutual dependence and vulnerability of both borrower and lender. . . . All the 'passengers' know that if a large debtor repudiates its debts or a large bank wants to interrupt this escalation and call in its claim, a 'domino effect' might be triggered that would set in motion worrisome forces throughout the international system."[53]

The second phase of the sovereign debt problem was sparked by oil and petrochemical shortages and a rapid rise in prices of crude oil on the spot market. This trend was followed by formal OPEC price increases and supply constraints that together boosted the official price of "marker" crude by 150 percent to $34 a barrel and the spot market price as high as $38 a barrel over the second half of 1979 and the first quarter of 1980.[54]

The second phase of petrodollar recycling had begun. During 1980 and 1981, the oil-exporting countries achieved trade surpluses of $171 billion and $122 billion and overall current account balances of $110 billion and $65 billion, respectively.[55] The non-oil-producing developing countries, on the other hand, developed aggregate trade deficits of $69.3 billion in 1980 and $70.5 billion in 1981.[56]

The response of the advanced industrial countries to the second oil crisis was different from their response to the first. By 1981, conservation measures in the West and the development of alternative sources of crude oil such as Mexico and the North Sea meant that OPEC was no longer able to dictate oil prices to the rest of the world.[57] Oil consumption during the period 1979 to 1983 declined from 51 million barrels a day to 41 million barrels a day, with OPEC's share moving from 63 percent of the world's export market to 33 percent of total consumption.[58] Inevitably, oil prices began to erode, as OPEC "high absorbers," under pressure to increase oil revenues, began to discount the official price to large consumers. From 1981 to 1983, the official price declined from approximately $35 a barrel to $29 a barrel, with the market price $4 to $5 a barrel lower.[59] As evidence of the decline in demand, this price erosion occurred during the Iraq-Iran War, which reduced world oil supplies by approximately 5 percent and threatened access to the Gulf.[60] Several high-absorbing oil exporters that continued substantial external borrowing throughout this period joined the list of problem debtors, despite their surpluses during 1979 and 1980.[61]

The industrial countries also responded with a sharp deflationary effort aimed at containing the problem of stagflation that had emerged during the first period of recycling. These efforts were led by the United States under the stewardship of Chairman Volcker of the Federal Reserve system but were pursued by the other major industrial countries as well.[62] These deflationary efforts had three primary effects on external indebtedness:

1. Real interest rates rose dramatically throughout the period, elevating the cost of debt service.[63]

2. The demand by industrial economies for the primary products and commodities of developing countries contracted, a trend that led to a substantial decline in the prices for their products and eroded their terms of trade.

3. The value of the U.S. dollar, the currency in which the greater portion of all external debt was denominated, rose substantially during this period against all other primary reserve currencies. The strength of the dollar also increased the debt service burden of developing countries, as they sold their products into world markets against a basket of currencies at world market prices.

The increase in real interest rates, coupled with relatively low inflation in the major industrial states, was the reverse of the situation that pertained in the first recycling period. The stock of external sovereign debt of developing countries, much of which was now priced at variable interest rates, became substantially more expensive, as eurocredits were rolled over and repriced.[64] The debt service burden for all developing countries on private market debt rose from $25.6 billion at the end of 1978 to $47.2 billion at the end of 1982, or 84 percent. Average interest rates increased from 9.7 percent to 14.6 percent at the end of 1981. The grant element on private market credits, reflecting the rise in real interest rates, moved from 7.1 percent at the end of 1977 to a negative −19.6 percent. Thus there was an adverse swing in the average debt terms for developing countries over this period of almost 27 percent.[65]

The high real interest rates on the U.S. dollar were sustained by federal budgetary deficits, which made the U.S. government the largest borrower in the international capital markets and necessitated the higher interest rates so as to attract sufficient capital. As Volcker observed, "I cannot resist suggesting that further efforts in resolving our budget deficits would be the single most important contribution that the Congress could make to an easing of international debt problems."[66] By the end of this period the United States was moving from major creditor to the largest external sovereign debtor, exclusive of direct private investment abroad.[67]

The decline in demand for primary products and commodities emanating from the deflationary efforts in the industrial countries, combined with the long-term technological shifts in consumption for many of these products, led to a reduced volume of trade, a sharp decrease in the prices of these products, and a deterioration in the terms of trade for developing countries. Commodity prices expressed in U.S. dollars were lower in 1982 than at any time since World War II. Food prices fell by 30 percent (in nominal terms) from 1980 to 1982, nonfood agricultural commodities by 24 percent, metals and mineral prices by 17 percent.[68] Several of the substantial debtor countries had relied on higher export earnings to provide them with sufficient foreign exchange to service their external debt. The sharp decline in these revenues was visible in higher debt service ratios.[69]

In the face of growing U.S. trade deficits, depressed economic conditions in Europe, and a decline in the terms of trade for many developing countries, apprehension increased that trade protectionism would further prevent heavily indebted states from generating sufficient exports to service their debts. This concern led to numerous comparisons with the downward spiral of world trade in the 1930s during the Great Depression and the effect protectionism had on the ability of developing countries to meet their obligations.[70] According to William Cline's estimates, these external shocks cost the developing countries $400 billion and were the major factors in the growth of external sovereign debt.[71]

External factors were not, however, the only reason for the increase in external sovereign debt and debt servicing difficulties. The economic strategies and policy decisions pursued within the developing and Eastern bloc countries also had a profound impact. For the most part, the internal strategy and policy issues were a continuation of problems that had arisen in the postwar era up to 1973.[72] However, the greater uncertainty in the international economic environment after 1974 made policy decisions more difficult and strategies more critical to economic performance.

In an overall sense, the first critical strategic decision was whether to borrow or adjust. Countries that continued to borrow after the second oil crisis, and that postponed adjustment, were forced to adopt more stringent reform policies that resulted in severe dislocations to their domestic economies and exacerbated the problem of debt service.[73]

A second initial policy decision was whether to promote exports or import substitution. Countries that emphasized their export sectors were able to earn sufficient foreign exchange to continue debt service, despite high levels of external borrowing. It was clear that countries with open economies that promoted exports, such as the newly industrialized Asian states—Hong Kong, Taiwan, Singapore, and Korea as examples—performed significantly better during this period than did, for example, the Latin American states that pursued policies of import substitution and lost export competitiveness.[74]

Most of the East Asian countries, with the exception of the Philippines, were able to avoid debt service difficulties during this period. The low-income South Asian countries (Pakistan, India, and Bangladesh) largely eschewed private market debt, instead relying on official external sources of credit to the extent that they borrowed at all. Moreover, most adopted adjustment policies early in the second oil crisis.[75] Although the newly industrialized East Asian countries did borrow heavily in this period, their exports were sufficient that they avoided debt service difficulties.[76]

Many developing countries faced further combinations of excessive domestic inflation and overvalued exchange rates that eroded their export competitiveness and implicitly encouraged capital flight into hard currencies. By the end of 1983, capital flight from developing countries, particularly Latin America, was estimated to be in excess of $50 billion.[77]

Another problem was that as the low or negative real interest rates in the 1970s suddenly converted to high real rates of interest, investment projects that seemed attractive at the margin suddenly became unprofitable. Moreover, it appears that many investments were disguised forms of public consumption, while still others relied on market distortions that concealed low social rates of return.[78]

A high rate of expenditure on armaments during this period was a substantial, normally hidden, component of the debt problem. The Stockholm International Peace Research Institute estimated that up to 25 percent of external credits could have been avoided had there been no imports of military technology and hardware during this period.[79]

An aspect of these economic strategy and policy decisions that is often obscured by discussions of the debt crisis is that developing countries with relatively fragile economies under the best of circumstances had little room for error. The difficult international economic environment during the decade of the oil crises narrowed that already thin margin considerably. Those countries that made correct decisions managed to ride out the crises. Those that failed to do so were forced to disrupt their debt service and adopt painful austerity programs when bank loans were abruptly cut off.

The last major factor contributing to the difficulties of adjustment following the 1979–80 oil crisis was the position of the major suppliers of credit, the banks. During the course of the decade, they had emerged as the major suppliers of credit to developing countries for the first time in the postwar era (see tables 6-3 and 6-4). Their balance sheets were initially relatively clean with respect to medium- and long-term loans to these countries, and the issue of country risk exposure only became highly relevant toward the end of the period. By 1979 it was clear, however, that several of

TABLE 6-3. Exposure of U.S. Banks in Eastern Europe and
Non-Oil-Producing Developing Countries, Relative to Capital, 1979–82

Percent

Nine largest banks	1979	1980	1981	1982	Value 1982 (millions of US$)
Eastern Europe	23.9	21.8	19.5	13.9	4,045
Non-oil-producing less-developed countries	182.1	199.3	220.6	221.2	64,149
Total	206	221.1	240.1	235.2	68,194

Source: William R. Cline, *International Debt Reexamined* (Washington: Institute for International Economics, 1995), p. 22, table 2.1.

TABLE 6-4. Exposure of Major U.S. Banks to Major Latin American Borrowers,
as a Percentage of Capital, 1982

Bank	Argentina	Brazil	Mexico	Venezuela	Chile	Total	Capital (millions of US$)
Bank of America	18.2	73.5	54.6	18.2	10.0	174.5	5,989
Chase Manhattan	10.2	47.9	52.1	41.7	6.3	158.2	4,799
Morgan Guaranty	21.3	56.9	40.0	24.0	11.8	154.0	4,221
Manufacturers Hanover	47.5	77.7	66.7	42.4	28.4	262.8	2,592
Chemical	14.9	52.0	60.0	28.0	14.8	169.7	2,439
Continental Illinois	17.8	22.9	32.4	21.6	12.8	107.5	2,143
Bankers Trust	13.2	46.2	46.2	25.1	10.6	141.2	1,895
First National Chicago	14.5	40.6	50.1	17.4	11.6	134.2	1,725
Crocker National	38.1	57.3	51.2	22.8	26.5	196.0	1,151

Source: Cline, *International Debt Reexamined*, p. 24, table 2.2.

the money center banks had potentially too much exposure to specific developing country debtors.[80] Not only had they lent substantially to sovereign borrowers, but in many cases they had extended loans to large private debtors in these countries as well.[81] During 1979 and 1980, although the commercial banks cut back their medium- and long-term credit to sovereign borrowers, that shift was more than compensated for by the growth in short-term borrowing[82] and the use by banks in developing countries, such as Brazil and Mexico, of the interbank market to provide funds to sovereign lenders at longer-term maturities.[83] The movement toward short-term borrowing and the mismatching of maturities by banks in the developing countries was a strong signal that a crisis was pending. In 1981 there was another burst of medium-term lending, primarily as a result of additional lending by European and Japanese banks, whereas American bankers withdrew from new commitments to some extent.[84]

The exposure of the major international banks was not isolated to sovereign debtors. The international recession brought in its wake a wave of bankruptcies in the advanced economies that included Penn Square Bank and Drysdale Securities in the United States and Banco Ambrosiano in Italy. It also created problem debtors among major corporate customers such as AEG Telefunken, International Harvester, and Dome Petroleum.[85] In developing countries, the problems of large private borrowers such as the Alpha Group in Mexico and land losses in Hong Kong added to the difficulties of international banks.[86] In addition, as the demand for crude oil declined, substantial loans for oil tanker construction made during the first oil crisis turned bad, as much of the world's tanker fleet was laid up or had become uneconomical to operate.[87] The potential problems of the money center banks in the United States in particular became widely known, primarily because reporting requirements there revealed their exposure to major third world and Eastern European borrowers.[88] The concentrated exposure of these banks to several major Latin American borrowers was of great concern. As Volcker noted, "For the nine largest banks, claims on all developing countries had grown to about twice their capital by last June (1982), and about half the claims of those banks were on Argentina, Brazil and Mexico."[89] Nor was the problem confined to the major American banks—many regional U.S. banks were drawn into the market without significant international banking experience and were also at risk, as were major European and Japanese banks.[90]

The petrodollar recycling process, which had served the interest of all parties in its initial phase, was clearly not sustainable under the economic conditions prevailing in the 1980s. Instead, the banks, which had supported this business for many reasons—its profitability, the natural expansion of their international base of activities, the highly competitive environment of the Euromarket, and the assumption that developing countries would be consistent borrowers in the future—were forced into debt recycling—that is, the provision of new loans to cover old ones. This process could continue only so long as market confidence existed and lack of confidence did not close off eurocredits to needy debtors.[91]

The scene was set for the 1981–83 financial crisis, which brought with it debt moratoriums, substantial arrears in interest and principal payments, and renegotiations and restructurings of the debt of a large number of sovereign borrowers throughout the remainder of the 1980s and into the early 1990s.

SEVEN

Debt Service Disruption and Bank Debt Restructurings

1955–94

As in earlier periods, the problems associated with the accumulation of external sovereign debt and the increasing debt service burden of developing and Eastern bloc countries became evident soon after the second oil crisis in the form of a series of debt moratoriums and requests for restructuring by sovereign debtors. These requests were made to both official and commercial bank creditors. However, commercial bank restructurings quickly took precedence because of the magnitude of this debt, the sharp increase in debt service attributable to the use of variable interest rate loans, and the threat that extended debt moratoriums, defaults, or at the extreme, repudiations posed to the solvency of the major international banks. Indeed, there was concern over the fragility of the international financial system itself.[1]

In 1983, at the height of the debt crisis, over twenty restructurings were completed, involving $60 billion in restructured principal, and additional renegotiations were in process, most of which were concluded in early 1984.[2] By mid-1984, thirty-five developing and Eastern European countries had interrupted full debt service on about $120 billion of external debt. Disruption of service on official debt was estimated at $12.7 billion, or 10.6 percent of the total. The disruption in commercial bank debt represented nearly 60 percent of the net foreign banking liabilities of the countries involved in rescheduling. Approximately 90 percent of the amount subject to restructuring was owed by eleven countries—Mexico, Brazil, Argentina, Venezuela, Chile, Peru, Ecuador, the Philippines, Poland, Romania, and Yugoslavia.[3] At the end of 1983 the countries that had restructured their external debt owed approximately $241 billion to commercial banks and $55 billion in guaranteed bank debt, most of which consisted of export credits guaranteed by export credit agencies. In comparison, the total debt of 154 borrowing countries was $523 billion and $135 billion, respectively.[4]

This chapter examines sovereign debt restructuring first in terms of debt renegotiation and restructuring with official creditors from 1956 to 1973, and then the restructuring from 1974 to 1980, the transition period from official to predominantly commercial bank restructurings. The chapter then analyzes the initial commercial bank restructurings: (i) 1981 to 1984, primarily short-term balance of payments support; (ii) 1986 to 1988, a second round of restructurings under the Baker Plan focused on longer-term structural reforms; and finally (iii) from 1989 to 1994, a third round of restructurings focused on debt reduction under the Brady Plan. Based on that review, the practices governing restructuring through the Paris Club and the bank advisory committees are discussed and compared.

Debt Restructuring, 1956–73

Given the growth of external sovereign debt during this period and its concentration among a relatively few countries, it is not surprising that developing countries experienced crises and sought restructuring of their debts from their official creditors. The initial restructurings, termed official, primarily involved countries experiencing problems servicing their export credits. However, it soon became apparent that the debt problem was more generalized. As one analyst of this era observed, "By the mid-1960s, there had been enough debt crises and near crises for some sort of pattern to be perceived and for discussion to be started on the general issue of debt rather than just on the problems of particular countries in difficulty with their international debts."[5]

The advanced industrial countries, as creditors, typically agreed to debt restructuring only when a debtor was in clear difficulty with the servicing and a crisis was imminent.[6] They sought to maintain the force of contractual debt obligations by discouraging debtors from turning to restructuring as a normal practice.[7] Several other principles guided the approach of official creditors. They would agree to the minimum relief necessary to allow the earliest possible resumption of debt service.[8] In addition, the debtor was to bear the costs to the creditors of reschedulings or refinancings through interest rates at or close to commercial terms. Once rescheduled, debts were considered ineligible for further rescheduling.[9] The debt problems of developing countries were to be evaluated not in the aggregate, but rather case by case, usually in a multilateral forum of the creditors' choosing. The initial debt renegotiations took place in a variety of ad hoc creditor forums—the Hague Club, the London Club, and the Paris Club—initially structured to pool nonconvertible currencies during the duration to provide a lasting solution.[10] The expressed objective of developing countries was to seek debt relief consistent with economic growth. Conceptually, the United Nations Conference for Trade and Development (UNCTAD) asserted, debtors and creditors should look beyond the issue of debt crises and the creditworthiness of debtors to the broader context of debt and development. A "debt crisis or debt service problem can be said to exist when minimum economic and social objectives are impaired."[11] Over the course of the 1960s and early 1970s, a series of ideas, proposals, and recommendations on reform of official debt restructuring consistent with this viewpoint were presented.[12]

Not everyone agreed with the idea of debt relief as a form of aid. P. T. Bauer warned that it would create a "moral hazard" among developing debtors. That is, it would only encourage those debtors that saw debt relief as a way out of their contractual obligations. These debtors, he maintained, correlated closely with those countries that would not use the funds productively in the first place.[13]

In any event, the major creditors showed little interest in providing additional resources for debt relief. In fact, of the numerous debt restructurings undertaken in the postwar period up to 1973, only a few addressed the issue of development and provided basic, longer-term debt relief. India and Pakistan's reschedulings, organized under World Bank auspices, were unusual in that they explicitly recognized debt relief in the context of development.

In the case of Turkey, which received external debt relief following the end of the Korean War under the umbrella of the Organization for European Economic Cooperation (OEEC), the agreement was unusual in that it reorganized debts of $423 million, which included extensive commercial obligations, and provided more generous terms than were normally associated with creditor clubs. Moreover, with Turkey facing continued external debt problems, in 1965 the Organization for Economic Cooperation and Development (OECD) rescheduled some of the previously rescheduled debts from 1959, a break from past practice, and some member states provided additional balance of payments loans in place of debt relief, another change from usual club practices.[14]

Within the context of the creditor club format, however, only Indonesia's rescheduling in 1970, after several short-term relief efforts following the overthrow of the Sukarno regime, provided substantial debt relief. The debt was rescheduled into thirty equal annual installments at 0 percent interest. Also provided was a "bisque clause" that allowed deferment of repayment under certain conditions. In addition, the contractual interest on prior Paris Club reschedulings was deferred and made payable through fifteen annual installments at 4 percent interest. The Indonesian agreement was unusual not only in its generosity but because the Eastern bloc creditors agreed to reschedule under similar terms.[15]

The experience of these early postwar experiences should have cast significant doubt on the merits of the official debt restructuring process undertaken in the majority of cases. It did not address the fundamental problems that had given rise to the debt problems, and it was, therefore, reasonable to expect they would arise again.[16] Instead, the time-honored practices of renegotiation were widely observed, according to which the guiding principle was the earliest possible restoration of a debtor's creditworthiness to allow debt service payments to recommence. Future development was ignored. The underlying problems were left for the next crisis.

Debt Restructuring, 1974–80

From 1974 through 1979, there were twenty-seven individual restructuring arrangements involving approximately $10–11 billion in principle; in comparsion, there were twenty-five such arrangements amounting to $5.5 billion in the initial postwar era.[17] The initial restructurings were primarily the result of debt service problems from the earlier period and largely involved developing countries and official creditors. However, toward the end of the period a series of restructurings occurred with commercial banks that at the time seemed sui generis. They involved Zaire, Peru, and Turkey. In retrospect, these three cases portended future developments and an all too familiar pattern of liquidity crisis, negotiations up to the brink of default, and ad hoc rescue efforts involving the International Monetary Fund (IMF), commercial banks, and Western governments. Despite the fact that these early cases paled in comparison with the later problems presented by Poland, Mexico, Brazil, and Argentina, for example, at the time they caused deep concern in the international financial community.[18]

The Turkish debt renegotiations in 1979, 1980, and 1981 involved protracted efforts to arrive at a complex set of agreements with commercial banks and other trade creditors. Included in the June 1979 agreement was new bank financing for trade-related purposes and rescheduling of bank credit. In August 1979, commercial banks agreed to reschedule convertible Turkish lira deposits in a principal amount of $2.27 billion.[19] In July 1980, Turkey also restructured its official loans and suppliers' credits in the amount of $1.5 billion, representing a consolidation of three years of debt service arrears from 1978 through 1980.[20] As an IMF study observed, "Turkey faced a highly critical debt situation that required massive debt rescheduling by official creditors and commercial banks, emergency aid by OECD countries and successive adjustment programmes."[21]

Zaire's debt restructurings in 1980 and 1981 also involved a continuous set of negotiations with official and bank creditors. As a result of successive reschedulings, a commercial banking agreement reached in 1980 rescheduled the arrears in principal of $87 million, with a ten-year maturity and a five-year grace period.[22] Zaire also rescheduled $500 million with official creditors in July 1981.[23] Peru likewise rescheduled on several occasions—June 1978, December 1978, and January 1980. The 1980 agreement, which covered the short-term reschedulings of 1978 and 1979, as well as the principal falling due in 1980, was handled on a medium-term basis.[24] In 1978, suppliers' credits falling due in 1979 and 1980 were renegotiated through an official restructuring.[25]

These initial restructurings established an early pattern to the practice of commercial renegotiations with sovereign debtors despite their apparent ad hoc approach. For one, the banks proved reluctant to move away from the short-term restructuring practices of official creditors. They therefore also became enmeshed in repeated reschedulings. In addition, they hesitated to renegotiate interest arrears and insisted that these be paid before the rescheduling agreements were completed.

The bank reschedulingss soon took precedence over official reschedulings, which were, however, concluded in all these cases roughly in parallel with the commercial bank agreements.

Debt Restructuring, 1981–83

Rescheduling and restructuring of syndicated bank loans to Eastern European and developing countries, primarily in Latin America, began in 1981 in Eastern Europe and escalated significantly as the major defaults of Argentina, Brazil, and Mexico followed.

The Eastern Bloc

The Polish debt moratorium occurred on March 27, 1981, in the context of Poland's overall economic problems and the dissent by the Solidarity Party, both of which brought Poland's economy to a virtual halt. This moratorium focused the attention

of the Euromarket and the larger economic world on the risk of sovereign lending. As
one analyst of the period observed, "Poland marked a quantum leap in the debt crisis.
The amount of debt at stake was much larger at $24 billion than the amounts at risk in
Peru, Zaire, or Turkey. The familiar supports were gone. No allowances, no hege-
mony, no International Monetary Fund were there to stand behind the bankers."[26]

Two primary issues were involved in the Polish restructuring. The first was the
broader one of a large buildup of Eastern bloc commercial bank debt via the Euromarkets, as well as the export and suppliers' credits involved in the sale of Western
technology, capital goods, and the emergence of large-scale East-West trade over the
period of détente, most of which was financed by Western credit.[27] At the end of 1981,
net commercial bank claims on the centrally planned economies were $50.1 billion,
with the short-term debt estimated at $21.6 billion of the total.[28] Overall Eastern bloc
indebtedness to the West inclusive of official credits was estimated at $80.4 billion at
the end of 1981. Debt service ratios rose substantially, as the Eastern bloc economies
slowed perceptibly, with current account deficits in 1981 estimated at $8.1 billion.[29]

The Polish debt moratorium, the first by a Council for Mutual Economic Assistance (COMECON) country, effectively pierced the veil of what many bankers considered an implicit "credit umbrella" over these countries by the Soviet Union.[30] The
moratorium raised a wave of sentiment against loans to the Eastern bloc, an attitude
that was reflected in a substantial increase in spreads, a decrease in loan commitments,
and reductions in interbank lines for Eastern European banks operating in the Euromarket. Even the impeccable credit record established by the Soviet Union after
World War II and its inherent economic strength did not prevent an erosion of its
credit standing in the market.[31] Intermediate and long-term bank credits in the Euromarket for Eastern European countries declined from an average of $500 million
per quarter in the first half of 1981 to $170 million in the second half and a negligible
$24 million in the fourth quarter of 1982.[32] With the end of détente, there was grow-
ing concern about the increased leverage of Eastern bloc debtors on Western creditors and the possibility of repudiation.[33] Moreover, there were fears that the wave of
sentiment against Eastern bloc debt would rebound to the developing countries.[34]

The Polish negotiations were protracted and difficult. They involved $2.2 billion of
official debt rescheduled in December 1981,[35] and an agreement in April 1982 with
over 500 commercial banks to restructure $2.3 billion in principal.[36] Implementation
of the agreement was delayed significantly when Poland proved hesitant to repay all
the interest arrears of approximately $500 million by the date of signing.[37] The creditor
group also differed over the terms of the agreement, with the German banks, the
primary lenders to Poland, and the American banks dissenting.[38] In this respect,
Poland became a watershed in commercial bank restructuring: "What makes the

Polish exercise of special note was the acrimony it generated among bankers and the subsequent decision by senior management at leading banks to professionalize such operations."[39]

Poland's need for continued refinancing was evident before the ink was dry on the first restructuring. In 1982 commercial bankers were compelled to negotiate continued debt service arrears, as well as additional loans to support Poland's trade requirements. The result was a series of annual restructuring agreements.[40] Moreover, Western creditors resisted official rescheduling of approximately $10–11 billion of official loans outstanding when Poland imposed martial law and cracked down on Solidarity, at the same time letting its debt service arrears accumulate.[41]

The wave of sentiment against bank loans to Eastern Europe created by the initial Polish restructuring presented problems for other Eastern bloc debtors. When the IMF agreed to help Romania, an IMF (Fund) member, with a $1.4 billion standby credit, the banks saw this move as a sign of weakness rather than as a positive step to preempt a debt service crisis. The increase in debt service arrears on Romania's external debt by the fall of 1981 led the market to anticipate a Romanian restructuring.[42] By March 1982 its debt arrears had grown to $1.1 billion, and it declared a moratorium on all debt repayment until a debt restructuring was agreed upon,[43] a procedure that would be followed in most major restructurings. A Romanian restructuring agreed to on December 7, 1982, was soon followed by another.[44] Commercial bank renegotiations were conducted roughly in parallel with the official renegotiations in July 1982; they covered $400 million due to Western creditors.[45]

Despite its impeccable debt service record, Hungary was tarred with the same brush as Poland and Romania. It quickly lost interbank deposits estimated at $1.1 billion and was forced to adopt a voluntary adjustment program, styled after similar IMF ones. In addition, the BIS provided bridging loans to the National Bank of Hungary to avert a debt moratorium.[46] In December 1982 the IMF arranged a standby credit of $600 million, following Hungary's accession to the Fund, and a group of money center banks led by Deutsche Bank formed a syndicate of 200 banks to provide $200 million in eurocredits.[47] The action of the BIS, the central banks, the IMF, and the commercial banks in seeking to prevent a deeper crisis in Hungary, following the problems in Poland and Romania, anticipated on a smaller scale their collective efforts as international lenders of last resort in Mexico, Brazil, and Argentina.

Yugoslavia, a non-COMECON member state of Eastern Europe, presented a different problem for the commercial banks. With the support of Western governments, Yugoslavia sought to avoid the taint of other Eastern European borrowers. However, a $400 million credit under negotiation in the middle of the 1981 crisis failed to materialize, and by 1982 Yugoslavia was able to raise only $200 million, with a maturity of just eighteen months, through a syndicate of U.S. and Japanese banks, the former with the support of the State Department.[48] Yugoslavia's decentralized borrowing by regional central banks meant that neither borrowing nor repayments were coordinated via its Treasury or any central banking authority. With external hard currency debt of $19 billion, Yugoslavia was the most indebted country per capita in Eastern Europe.[49]

By January 1983, Yugoslavia had fallen behind in some of its debt service payments and was forced to make the rounds of financial institutions such as the BIS, creditor governments, and agencies such as the U.S. Department of Agriculture to arrange emergency food credits. To avoid a general restructuring, Western creditors put together $1.5 billion in the form of export credit guarantees.[50] Further, the agreement covering the official credits required commercial banks to provide support as well. The Swiss government and the Swiss Bank Corporation, as "neutral" creditors, took the lead in arranging the official creditor package, as well as the lead among creditor banks in establishing an advisory committee that agreed to a ninety-day "standstill" on repayments of principal. The IMF added its support with a three-year standby credit, previously negotiated, whose third tranche amounted to $600 million. In an unusual step, the IMF chaired the negotiations with Yugoslavia, which also involved a bankers' advisory committee.[51] The BIS eventually provided bridging support of $500 million in a series of tranches. Thus this ad hoc grouping served as international lender of last resort in the Yugoslavian rescue as well. After substantial negotiating delays, a restructuring package was agreed upon in September 1983.[52]

The initial Eastern bloc renegotiations with the commercial banks, particularly the Polish restructuring, established the structure for subsequent negotiations, including the major debt restructurings of Mexico, Brazil, and Argentina, between banks and sovereign debtors. They also established the principle of a collective lender of last resort.

Mexico, Brazil, and Argentina

The mid-Atlantic war, known variously as the Falklands or Malvinas dispute, diverted attention from the problems of Eastern European debt to the heavily concentrated exposure of commercial banks in the three principal sovereign debtors of Latin America—Argentina, Brazil, and Mexico—as well as to the overall external indebtedness of Latin America as a region. Despite a commitment to meet its debt service obligations, the liquidity problems caused by the Falklands War led Argentina to suspend payments on principal in July 1982, a move that sent a ripple effect through the Euromarkets against lending to other Latin American states.[53] As the BIS observed,

"Other Latin American countries saw their access to international bank credit becoming more difficult and more expensive."[54]

Argentina's debt service difficulties were soon matched by Mexico's. As Mexico's external debt mounted—from an estimated $80 billion at the end of 1981, of which approximately $50 billion was public and $30 billion private—intermediate and long-term credit became more difficult to obtain. Commercial banks repeatedly rolled over or refinanced credit to Mexico on a short-term basis and at increasingly higher spreads.[55] Petroleos Mexicanos (Pemex), the state-owned oil company, with external debts estimated at $18–20 billion, began anticipating (financing in advance) its oil revenues. In a declining oil market, Pemex received approximately $3.1 billion in advance payments on oil in the five months preceding the debt service disruption. It also obtained $4 billion from the Bank of America on a 180-day acceptance facility as a part of its external debt supported by oil receipts.[56] In addition, Mexico's private debtors found it increasingly difficult to amortize dollar-denominated loans following a 40 percent devaluation of the peso against the dollar. By April 1982, economists were estimating that Mexico would require $30 billion in external financing for 1982, 50 percent of which would be used to service existing obligations.[57]

Virtually all commentators on the 1982–83 debt crisis cite the decision by Mexico to suspend payments of principal to its commercial banks on its external debt as of August 20, 1982, as the critical event sparking the 1982–83 debt crisis.[58] As the BIS noted, "The final blow to the morale and the smooth working of the international credit market came in the late summer of 1982, with the outbreak of Mexico's external payments and debt crisis, triggered by a 'massive flight of capital' to the United States."[59]

On August 20, at a meeting of commercial bank representatives in New York, Mexico requested a ninety-day moratorium or standstill on payments of principal and a commitment by the banks to work out, via an advisory committee, the rescheduling of some portion of the country's external sovereign debt due the commercial banks.[60] In fact, the arrangement for a moratorium, rescheduling, and emergency assistance by a lender of last resort had been agreed to in principle the weekend before in an emergency meeting in Washington, D.C., between the Mexican government, the managing director of the IMF, the chairman of the United States Federal Reserve Bank, and officials from the United States Treasury Department. In this case, the international lender of last resort included the United States Federal Reserve Bank, the United States Treasury, which coordinated support from a number of federal agencies, the BIS, and the central banks of the Group of Ten and Switzerland. The agreement was backed by a commitment from Mexico and the IMF that they would reach agreement on a three-year credit and an economic adjustment program.[61]

The terms of the rescue included concerted or "involuntary lending" by commercial banks under pressure from the Fund, supported by various national monetary authorities. New commercial bank loans for Mexico of $5 billion amounted to a pro rata assessment of 7 percent of existing bank exposure to Mexico for commercial banks involved in Mexican credits.[62]

Mexico's commercial bank restructuring was far from easy. It involved $20 billion in commercial debt, due to be repaid in 1982 and 1983, from some 1,400 banks that had provided a vast variety of credits to the federal government, a number of state agencies, and state-owned (and guaranteed) enterprises (SOEs). Difficult questions had to be addressed, such as whether external bonds should be serviced or restructured with commercial bank loans, whether interbank lines should extend through six Mexican banks active in the Euromarket, and what the terms and conditions for the $5 billion in new loans and for rescheduled amounts would be. Eventually, the renegotiation of Mexico's external debt, which required an additional moratorium of 180 days, was signed with the commercial banks on August 27, 1983,[63] a year after the initial debt service disruption.

Subsequent negotiations provided new commercial bank loans of $3.8 billion in April 1984, and in June of that year the bank advisory committee, urged by the managing director of the IMF, agreed to a multiyear restructuring of Mexico's debt, with a view to providing longer-term relief.[64] In all respects the approach to the Mexican rescheduling was the most comprehensive of the reschedulings and was usually cited as a model of success by commercial bankers.[65]

This three-pronged package of support for Mexico—the IMF at the center of the renegotiations, support from various national monetary authorities and the BIS, and "involuntary lending" by commercial banks—was the approach followed in subsequent major restructurings, including those of Brazil, Argentina, and Yugoslavia, as previously discussed.[66] The objective was to allow orderly adjustment and to avoid the extremes of a default or a repudiation and their potential consequences for the international monetary system.[67] As the Fund observed: "In particular it was made clear that large amounts of Fund credit could not be supplied in substitution for private credit, but could support orderly adjustment processes only in supplementation of adequate continuing flows of private credit."[68]

Despite the expectations within Brazil and the capital markets that Brazil would be the next major sovereign debtor to restructure, the government and its powerful minister of planning, Antonio Delfim Netto, sought to distance themselves from Mexico's debt renegotiations.[69] However, with the Euromarket virtually closed to Latin American borrowing, Brazil found it exceedingly difficult to arrange the refinancing necessary to maintain its debt service payments.

As the last quarter of 1982 progressed, it became obvious that Brazil was facing a severe "liquidity squeeze." Brazilian officials canvassed the money markets, creditor governments, and multilateral financial institutions for ad hoc emergency support and undertook confidence-building measures to accelerate commercial bank lending. However, they resisted any basic restructuring. Support measures included, inter alia, an emergency $600 million short-term loan from major money center banks in the United States; negotiations with the IMF for a three-year standby facility; a bridging loan of $1.23 billion from the United States, announced during President Ronald Reagan's visit to Brazil; and a proposed loan from various European states and Japan of up to $1.5 billion.[70]

By mid-December, with its external debt at $84 billion, Brazil could no longer sustain its high-wire act.[71] An emergency rescue of the state-owned Banco do Brazil, Brazil's largest, by New York banks, which provided $300 million in overnight money to allow it to meet its interbank commitments, signaled the end of postponement.[72] Brazil was assisted by a bridging loan from the BIS of $1.2 billion until a support package from the Fund could be arranged.[73] On January 3, 1983, Brazil declared a moratorium on debt repayment so as to push banks into early acceptance of its plan.[74]

The Brazilian plan came under significant pressure, as the commercial banks resisted restoring the interbank lines that had been withdrawn while Brazil sought to avoid an overall rescheduling. The banks also squabbled over whether short-term debt exposure should be included when calculating the rata share of new financing. The managing director of the IMF sought to pressure the banks by threatening to withhold its own loan package until the interbank lines were restored.[75] By February 25, despite significant difficulties, a commercial bank restructuring agreement was signed that was largely in line with Brazil's four-part plan, but with the interbank lines at a lower, negotiated level.[76]

Whereas Mexico's restructuring plan proceeded well, the Brazilian plan ran into constant difficulty because of its structure, a failure to comply with the IMF adjustment program, and nonrepayment of the BIS bridging loan.[77] By January 1984, Brazil and the commercial banks faced a second restructuring effort for the medium- and long-term debt due in 1984.[78]

Argentina was the third-ranking Latin American debtor, with total external debt estimated at $39 billion. As a result of the Falklands War, Argentina was soon in arrears on its payments, and by July 1982 an IMF mission reportedly doubted its ability to pay, given the $600 million in debt arrears and low level of reserves as a result of the war.[79]

The Falklands hostilities and continued diplomatic rupture between the United Kingdom and Argentina exacerbated the latter's economic problems. Britain froze

Argentina's deposits in Great Britain, and Argentina stopped debt service payments to British banks, which were among its major lenders.[80] While the Argentinians, as had the Brazilians, sought to disassociate themselves from Mexico's debt problems, by the fall of 1982, faced with renewal of a significant amount of short-term borrowing estimated at $14 billion and a fragile political consensus, it was clear that Argentina would need restructuring as well as institutional support.[81]

By January 1, 1983, all the props for a support package and an agreement in principle were in place. They comprised a bridging loan from the BIS of $500 million, an IMF credit of $2.2 billion, and an arrangement for commercial bank rescheduling, as well as a new $1.5 billion bridge loan from the banks that was to allow Argentina to make up the interest arrears of $1.1 billion.[82] This agreement in principle soon had to be renegotiated with the new military junta ruling Argentina following the Falklands War and subsequently with the successor government, led by the democratically elected Raúl Alfonsín.[83] A period of protracted negotiations ensued, with the Alfonsín regime resisting an IMF adjustment package, while practicing brinksmanship with its bankers as the debt service arrears mounted.[84]

By April 1984 the United States and four Latin American governments (Mexico, Brazil, Venezuela, and Colombia), anxious to avoid a confrontation over Argentina's debts and an unraveling of the renegotiation process, worked out a bridging arrangement of $500 million in loans to cover the interest arrears to commercial banks. This arrangement was contingent upon Argentina's reaching an agreement with the IMF on an adjustment program.[85] The banks, on the other hand, to prevent any form of cartel-type arrangement among Argentina, Mexico, Brazil, and the other Latin American debtors, agreed to a multiyear restructuring of Mexico's debts. "For the bankers it has also proved a useful way of isolating countries such as Argentina, which whether because of intransigence or internal political problems, have delayed in reaching agreement with the Fund."[86] By the end of 1984, after eighteen months of financial brinksmanship, the problem had still not been resolved.[87]

The Rest of Latin America

While the commercial banks and the international financial system appeared to concentrate their attention and resources on the three major Latin American debtors, the region as a whole went through financial upheaval, as bank lending to Latin America was generally suspended.[88] The bond market was also closed except to those developing country borrowers considered the "best" credit risks—namely, Asian ones.[89]

During 1982 and 1983, virtually every Latin American country rescheduled or was in the process of rescheduling its external debt with commercial banks. Fifteen debt renegotiations amounting to $35 billion falling due in 1983 were renegotiated.[90] As a lead article in *Euromoney* noted: "It is the region where the domino theory became reality, where one rescheduling announcement seems, almost inevitably, to follow another. Yet only a year ago, a rescheduling of the debt of Mexico, Brazil and Argentina was all but unthinkable. Yet the main question on bankers' minds—who's next?"[91]

The majority of Latin American debtors had no way out of the crisis except restructuring via renegotiation, with what they perceived as painful austerity programs under IMF auspices as a precondition to the negotiations.[92] In addition to the three major renegotiations cited, Ecuador, Chile, and Peru faced major restructurings in 1982 and 1983. Of these, only Chile, whose banking system was near collapse, received additional financial assistance.[93] Smaller-scale reschedulings were negotiated with Uruguay, Costa Rica, the Dominican Republic, and Honduras.[94] Venezuela failed to reach an agreement with the banks because of its unwillingness to negotiate an adjustment program with the IMF.[95] Cuba, on the other hand, initiated parallel restructuring negotiations with bank and official creditors.[96] During the course of 1983, several other Latin American countries sought to renegotiate debts of $7 billion in principal. The primary official restructurings involved Mexico and Brazil.[97]

Sub-Saharan Africa

While the concerns of Western governments, their central banks, and the commercial banks was clearly centered on Latin America, the sub-Saharan African countries had an acute reaction to the debt crisis.[98] Highly dependent on commodity exports, most found themselves unable to service their debts, despite the relatively soft terms of their largely official borrowing. As of December 31, 1982, of $47.5 billion of external public debt in sub-Saharan Africa—commercial bank debt represented $16 billion, or 34 percent, while official bilateral loans provided $17.5 billion, or 37 percent, and the multilateral financial agencies lent $11.5 billion, or 23 percent of the total.[99]

Because of their inability to raise more medium- and long-term capital, net disbursements of external finance fell from a peak of $3.9 billion in 1980 to $1.7 billion in 1982.[100] With the sharp decline in commodity exports and terms of trade, many African countries fell into deep arrears, relied heavily on short-term debt, and eventually fell into arrears in paying suppliers. As a result, trade credit gradually dried up, so that essential imports of such items as food and oil were more difficult to obtain.[101]

During 1980 and 1983 many sub-Saharan African states sought to renegotiate their debt with both official and bank creditors. There were twenty-six separate official reschedulings under the Paris Club forum and thirteen commercial bank reschedulings; they involved principal of approximately $6.7 billion and $4.3 billion, respectively.[102] As in the previous postwar period, several African states were forced to reschedule repeatedly.[103]

Virtually all these exercises provided strictly short-term relief, with Zaire the exception. After several rescheduling efforts, Zaire was granted eleven years maturity on rescheduled official loans, with a five-year grace period to repay 75–85 percent of $1–1.5 billion falling due in 1983.[104]

Even Nigeria, with significant oil exports, fell prey to the need to renegotiate, as oil revenues dipped suddenly, while large capital investment projects, imports of luxury items, and flight of capital were not restrained. In July and September 1983, Nigeria restructured $1.35 billion of principal falling due, representing 100 percent of the arrears on letters of credits owed by private sector debtors. In April 1984, Nigeria agreed in principle with its uninsured trade creditors to restructure approximately $3.0 billion in trade arrears over six years.[105]

Many African countries were highly reliant on IMF and World Bank resources during this period. The World Bank, through a special accelerated assistance effort, structural adjustment loans, and an effort to develop cofinancing in the low-income countries, sought to focus attention on the needs of sub-Saharan Africa.[106] In virtually all the rescheduling efforts for sub-Saharan Africa, the IMF provided support via its Supplementary Financing Facility, Stand-by Arrangements, or Compensatory Financing Facility, the latter reflecting the decline in the terms of trade in the export of primary products, minerals, and ores from Africa.[107] Nigeria resisted a major debt rescheduling with its official and commercial bank creditors, as it refused to adopt an IMF adjustment program. Nigeria preferred instead to rely on its oil revenues and a self-imposed austerity program following the overthrow of President Shehu Shagari by the military.[108]

Other Restructurings

The two other major reschedulings of consequence in this period were Morocco and the Philippines. Morocco faced an official rescheduling in November 1983 of $1.5 billion and agreed in principle to a commercial bank rescheduling in April 1984 of $1.3 billion. Both negotiations followed the normal terms of the Paris Club and commercial bank rescheduling process.[109]

The Philippine crisis, although it had been widely predicted by the international financial community, was long in coming.[110] With external debts of $16 billion at the end of 1982 and approximately 25 percent of them maturing in 1983, the Philippines was dependent on a rollover or renewal of commercial banking credits during the course of 1983. While loans to Asia remained generally unaffected by the debt crisis in the rest of the world, the Philippines proved the exception.[111]

In the end, an internal political crisis—the assassination of former senator Benigno S. Aquino Jr.—finally led to an erosion of market confidence in the regime of Ferdinand Marcos, and the government was forced to renegotiate with its official creditors as well as commercial bank ones. On October 17, 1983, the Philippine government declared a moratorium on all debt due to banks until July 12, 1984. It then proposed a rescheduling of the arrears of principal due between October 17 and the end of December 1983 and all principal falling due in 1984 and 1985, estimated at $1.2 billion. In addition, the government sought new financing of $1,650 million with a ten-year maturity.[112]

The crisis at the end of 1983 was expected to be the last in a long list of sovereign debt restructurings in 1983. However, because of problems with the IMF over the reliability of the Philippine central bank's statistics and differences with the banks over the terms of the restructuring, the signing was delayed until 1984. The U.S. government did support the Philippine government, a long-term, strategically important ally, with a bridge loan of $500 million during the negotiations.[113]

The Baker Plan—Restructurings, 1985–88

Following the second oil crisis, the substantial accumulation of external sovereign debt and increased level of debt service brought with it a wave of debt restructurings comparable in scope to the 1931–33 debt moratorium standstills and defaults. By 1983 some of the major restructurings had entered a second round of negotiations and by 1984 a third round. By mid-1985 there was no evidence that the process was at an end, although the pace and scope had abated substantially since 1983.

The Baker Plan announced at an annual meeting of the IMF and World Bank in Seoul, South Korea, was a plan to reinforce the coordinated lending strategy that had persisted since the first round of restructurings in 1981, but to shift the emphasis from short-term balance of payments packages toward longer-term structural reforms. The plan was indicative, but set lending targets of some $20 billion in new money for fifteen highly indebted countries, primarily the Latin American debtors, but also including the Philippines, Cote d'Ivoire, Nigeria, and Morocco.[114]

Total bank claims on these countries amounted to $250 billion. During this same period the multilateral development banks, the World Bank and the Inter-American

Development Bank, were asked to provide some $10 billion in net new lending to these same countries. The understanding was that the multilateral development institutions would replace IMF funding during this period.[115]

Mexico's 1986 restructuring negotiated during the second half of 1986, following the precipitous fall in world oil prices, appears to have laid the groundwork for a new, longer-term approach to restructuring. Despite the Baker Plan, the commercial banks claimed that the Mexican case was unique, although countries such as Argentina and Brazil viewed this restructuring as the basis for renegotiating their own situation.

The Mexican restructuring, the first restructuring under the Baker Plan, was tied to an economic growth program for the country. In place of an agreement on a short-term adjustment program with the IMF, the commercial banks agreed in principle to tie the provision of new funds to the World Bank's lending program, which was to focus on medium- and long-term structural adjustment issues, a departure from past practice.[116] The World Bank committed to provide $2.3 billion in net disbursements in 1986 and 1987, requiring some $2 billion a year in loans to offset repayments due on prior loans.[117] For example, World Bank–initiated industrial restructuring programs and loans for restructuring of several of Mexico's major parastatal (state-owned) enterprises—Fertilizantes Mexicanos S.A., the fertilizer monopoly; and Siderurgica Mexicano, the national steel company—were the basis for specified levels of commercial bank credits. Restructuring programs and loans for various industrial subsectors—textiles, auto parts and agro-industry—provided the basis for yet other commercial bank credits. Finally, World Bank policy-based loans for trade liberalization and an agricultural sector loan served as the basis for still other bank loans.[118] In addition, the U.S. government through the Commodity Credit Corporation agreed to provide credits for basic grains and dried milk powder to support Mexico's economically disadvantaged population, adversely affected by the economic austerity measures undertaken following the first debt restructuring. The government of Japan agreed to provide $1.0 billion in credits directed toward improvements in basic infrastructure, such as the ports, to support economic growth in Mexico. The IMF, playing a supplementary role in this case, agreed to provide $1.7 billion in short-term credits in response to the decline in Mexico's export revenues from oil.[119] (Table 7-1 summarizes the terms and components of the 1986 restructuring for Mexico.)

The Baker Plan was essentially a mid-course correction due to the fact that it was taking the banks longer than expected to renew voluntary lending. The Baker Plan sought to reinforce the concerted lending strategy tied to efforts to introduce systemic structural reforms such as privatization, discussed in Part IV, chapter 10, of this book. The overall perception of analysts was that the Baker Plan did little to change the

TABLE 7-1. Mexico: Summary of Terms and Amounts of 1986–87 Financial
Package by Major Creditor Group

Type of flow/source	Amount (billions of US$)	Terms Maturity/grace (years)	Interest rate (%)
New money	12.0		
Commercial banks	6.0[a]		
(Parallel new money facility)	(5.0)[b]	12/5	LIBOR + 13/16
(Cofinancing new money facility)	(1.0)[c]	15/9	LIBOR + 13/16
Multilateral development banks	2.7		
(International Bank for Reconstruction and Development, IBRD)	(2.3)[d]		
(Inter-American Development Bank, IDB)	(0.4)		
IMF standby	1.7[e]		
Japan	1.0[f]		
CCC	0.6		
Contingent money	2.3		
Commercial banks	1.7		
(Investment support facility)	(1.2)	8/4	LIBOR + 13/16
(Growth cofinancing facility)	(0.5)[g]	12/7	LIBOR + 13/16
IMF oil contingency mechanism	0.6[h]		
Debt restructuring	70.5		
Commercial banks	68.7		
(Pre-1983 debt)	(43.7)	20/7	LIBOR + 13/16
(1983–84 debt)	(8.6)	14/5	LIBOR + 13/16
(Private FICORCA debt)	(11.2)	Terms comparable to those covering public debt to be negotiated	
(Interbank credit lines)	(5.2)	Level to be maintained until June 30, 1989	
Paris Club	1.8[i]	10/5	Appropriate market rates

Source: IBRD staff estimates.

a. Disbursements contingent on compliance with IMF standby and implementation of specific World Bank loans. Of the total, US$3.5 billion would be released in December 1986, with the remaining US$2.5 billion being disbursed in five quarterly tranches starting on January 1, 1981.

b. Sum to be reduced by the amount Mexico saves as a result of the shift from a prime rate to a LIBOR reference rate and lower spreads on restructured debt during 1987. This savings is estimated at around US$300 million.

c. B-loan cofinancing with World Bank transport sector loans. A nonaccelerable World Bank loan guarantee for US$500 million is also provided.

(continued)

TABLE 7-1.   (continued)

d. Includes present value of two World Bank guarantees totaling US$750 million, whose present value is estimated at US$200 million.

e. The IMF standby will provide SDR1.4 billion over the period of October 1, 1986, to March 31, 1988. At current SDR-US$ conversion rates, this would amount to approximately US$1.7 billion.

f. Includes cofinancing of US$250 million with the World Bank Second Export Development Policy Loan, US$250 million for steel projects, and US$500 million for the Pacific Petroleum Project.

g. Covered by a US$250 million nonaccelerable loan guarantee of the World Bank.

h. The IMF commitment is for the lesser of SDR600 million or US$600 million.

i. Rescheduling of 100 percent of the principal and 60 percent of the interest falling due on debt outstanding as of the end of 1985 during the period from October 1, 1986, to March 31, 1988.

approach to debt restructurings. Despite an improvement in the terms of restructuring with respect to spread and tenor, the principal features remained the same for the period 1986–88 as in the immediate postcrisis restructurings detailed herein. The commercial banks offered little in debt concessions or additional voluntary capital. The fundamental case-by-case approach to restructuring remained intact. The banks and their governments steadfastly resisted global solutions. William Cline takes a different view. From 1985 to 1988 new lending from the banks reached $18.1 billion and covered ten of the seventeen countries. In addition, debt-equity conversions and debt buyback schemes further reduced debt levels of given countries. The banks delivered on some two-thirds of the Baker Plan target. Ironically the public sector institutions, the World Bank and the Inter-American Development Bank, were less effective in delivering the indicative amounts laid out in the Baker Plan.[120]

The large restructurings for Mexico, Argentina, and Brazil did not take place until 1987 and 1988—Mexico in March 1987, Argentina in August 1987, and Brazil in November 1988 (see table 7-2). Argentina was delayed because it was out of compliance with its IMF program, and Brazil by design decided to go into arrears on its interest payments, seeking to put negotiating pressure on the banks. Brazil completed negotiations for its restructuring outside the IMF framework but also without World Bank involvement. Under the restructuring plan, Brazil ended a moratorium on payment of commercial bank debt and agreed to bring substantial arrears in interest payment current. In return, the banks agreed to provide $5.8 billion in new loans. There were increasing arrears of interest in a number of countries in Latin America in addition to Brazil, as discussed later in this chapter.

The Baker Plan restructurings also opened up new debt instruments such as exit bonds for banks that did not want to increase their exposure to a country. Exit bonds were first used in Argentina. Debt-equity swaps were used extensively in Chile. The Brazilian restructuring was the most complex of all.[121] The mid-1986 collapse in oil

TABLE 7-2.   **Summary of Sovereign Debt Restructurings with Commercial Banks, 1980–89**

Year	Number of restructurings[a]	Principal amount (billions of US$)
1980	5	1,101
1981	6	1,210
1982	7	6,386
1983	21	105,578
1984	28	138,842
1985	15	77,471
1986	11	80,791
1987	15	259,946
1988	4	10,869
1989	4	14,316
Total	116	696,510

Sources: E. Brau and others, "Recent Multilateral Debt Restructurings with Official and Bank Creditors," Occasional Paper 25 (Washington: IMF, 1983), pp. 35–42, p. 23; Maxwell Watson, Peter Keller, Donald Mathieson, "International Capital Markets: Developments and Prospects," Occasional Paper 31 (Washington, IMF, 1984), pp. 64–76; IMF, "Recent Developments in External Debt Restructuring," Occasional Paper 40 (Washington, 1985), pp. 48–62; Commonwealth Group of Experts, *The Debt Crisis and the World Economy* (London: Commonwealth Secretariat, 1984), pp. 86–96; World Bank, Debt Management and Financial Advisory Services Department, "Commercial Banks' Debt Restructuring and New Money Facilities," November 13, 1987; World Bank, *Global Development Finance* (Washington, 1998), pp. 93–102, table A 3.9.

a. Excluded from the restructuring count are requests to restructure not concluded in the year and unilateral moves by countries to impose debt payment ceilings or payment moratoriums while debt negotiations were in progress. See Appendix B for the details of restructurings by year.

prices[122] and the increased provisioning of the banks for their loans to the Baker Plan countries eventually derailed the Baker Plan, and by 1988 it was clear that a new approach was needed.[123]

The Brady Plan—Restructurings, 1988–94

The collapse of oil prices in 1986, interest arrears for several countries whose macroeconomic adjustment programs with the Fund were in disarray, and a steep drop in the secondary market in the price of the bonds of countries that had restructured their debt, in the range of thirty to forty cents on the dollar, provided the basis for reconsideration of restructuring practices. The last few large restructurings under the Baker Plan set the tone for new instruments and added complexity attuned to the issues faced by the individual debtors. These transactions also provided options for groups of banks, such as the smaller banks, that were willing to exit a credit at a deep discount. Some analysts felt that the secondary market, reflecting the market valuation of the value of the debt, should be the price at which loans were settled. Clearly the banks found this hard to swallow, and with some justification. The secondary debt markets were very thin, and a country seeking to reduce its sovereign debt burden by a significant buyback program at deep discount would quickly drive up market prices closer to par.

In March 10, 1989, Secretary of the Treasury Nicholas J. Brady announced a new plan for international debt that would shift the strategy from coordinated, involuntary lending to debt reduction or partial forgiveness of the debts.[124] The Brady Plan was presented as a voluntary plan, as the U.S. government had no way to compel debt reduction for U.S. banks, and especially not for European or Japanese banks. The key new ingredient to this plan was public sector funding to collateralize conversion bonds. In presenting the plan to Congress, Under Secretary of the Treasury David Mulford, the architect of the plan, suggested that the plan would target $70 billion in debt reduction in thirty-nine countries with some $340 billion in debt. By mid-1989 some $34 billion in collateral enhancements had been designated comprising $12 billion each for the IMF and World Bank and $10 billion from the Japanese Export-Import Bank. The stick in the process was that a bank-agreed restructuring would no longer be required for IMF lending. The IMF could now lend into country arrears with the commercial banks.[125]

It took four months of difficult negotiations from the time of the Brady Plan announcement until a 1989 debt reduction restructuring with Mexico was announced. The key issue was the amount of debt reduction. The Mexicans clearly wanted the market price for secondary bonds to prevail, a 55 percent debt forgiveness. The banks offered 15 percent initially. The deal eventually struck was for 35 percent debt reduction on $48.5 billion of long-term bank debt, while maintaining a market rate of interest at LIBOR (the London Interbank Offered Rate) plus 13/16ths. The menu also offered a par bond but at a lower, fixed interest rate of 6¼ percent. A third option was to maintain the full value of the debt, but to offer new money up to 25 percent of the outstanding long-term bank debt. The ultimate agreement was very complex. The conversion bonds had thirty-year maturities. There was a total of $7.1 billion in enhancements—$2 billion from the World Bank, $1.3 billion from the IMF, $1.4 billion from the Export-Import Bank of Japan, and $1.4 billion from Mexico's own reserves. The conversion bonds provided for a claw-back depending on the price of oil, after seven years, with 30 percent of any increase in the price of oil exports from Mexico above $14 a barrel going to the bondholders. Conversely, if the price of oil sank below $10 a barrel, the banks and official lenders would provide another $800 million in loans to Mexico. The Mexican Brady deal set the pattern for a dozen or so deals that followed.[126]

By May 1994, five years after the announcement of the Brady Plan, deals had been completed or announced for eighteen countries, accounting for $191 billion in original bank claims. The set of countries overlapped substantially with the original Baker Plan list of seventeen highly indebted countries. All the Latin American countries on the Baker list had benefited from the Brady Plan except Chile, Colombia, and Jamaica, which did not require debt reductions. Peru had not benefited, but negotiations were far along with Peru. The menu of options for these transactions largely followed the menu set for the Mexican transaction. Brazil reached agreement on $50 billion of external debt. The Brazilian deal was the most complex, with six options.[127] Argentina also reached a deal, following the Brazilian and Mexican agreements, to restructure $29.6 billion of its external debt, including $7.9 billion of accrued and unpaid interest. The Argentine deal, like the Brazilian and Mexican transactions, provided for a range of creditor options, including discount bonds, par bonds, and PDI bonds (past-due interest bonds, dealing with interest in arrears). For each of these options there were variations in the debt exchange ratio, maturity (amortization), annual interest rate coupon, collateral/ interest rate guarantees, and eligible debt.

Several low-income countries were able to buy back their debt, at a deep discount, with the help of the special $100 million Debt Reduction Facility established under the World Bank's International Development Association (IDA) window for financing the low-income countries.[128]

The striking feature of the eighteen Brady deals was how little new money was provided, some 2 percent of exposure (see table 7-3). Forgiveness, however, was pervasive and deep. The typical face-value reduction in the discount bond was 30 to 35 percent. Rigidities in the Brady Plan biased outcomes in favor of debt reduction as opposed to new money. Enhancements from the IMF and the World Bank required that the debtor have a macroeconomic adjustment plan in place with the IMF, typically in the form of an IMF stabilization agreement. Brazil broke with these requirements by obtaining a bank waiver and implementing the plan without the IMF or World Bank.[129]

The Brady Plan effectively ushered in a period during much of the 1990s when the commercial banks had largely retreated from sovereign lending.[130] Emerging market countries raised external funding in a variety of ways during the 1990s—through sales to bondholders; through extensive privatization, particularly in Mexico, Brazil, and Argentina; through foreign direct investment (FDI); and through emerging market investment funds. Significant flows went to the private sector—commercial banks in the larger emerging market countries and large corporate

TABLE 7-3.   Commercial Bank Restructurings under the Brady Plan, 1990–94[a]

Country	Date	Eligible debt (billions of US$)	Forgiveness (billions of US$)[b]	Forgiveness (percent)	Depth of reduction[c]	New money (billions of US$)	Buyback price (percent)
Mexico	1989, 1990	47.17	14.15	30.0	35	1.03	n.a.
Philippines	1989, 1992	6.80	2.38	36.1	n.a.[f]	0.83	50
Costa Rica	1989, 1990	1.61	0.98	60.9	n.a.		16
Venezuela	1990	19.01	3.76	19.8	30		45
Uruguay	1990, 1991	1.60	0.50	31.3	n.a.	0.09	56
Niger[d]	1991	0.11	0.09	82.0			18
Mozambique[d]	1991	0.19	0.11	57.6	n.a.		10
Nigeria	1992	5.34	2.60	48.7	n.a.		40
Guyana	1992	0.07	0.06	86.0	n.a.		14
Argentina	1992, 1993	29.34	8.43	28.7	35		n.a.
Brazil	1992, 1994	50.00	14.00	28.0	35	0.50	n.a.
Uganda[d]	1993	0.17	0.13	78.3	n.a.		12
Dominican Republic[e]	1993	0.80	0.40	50.0	35		25
Bolivia	1993	0.18	0.14	79.0	n.a.		16
Jordan[e]	1993	0.80	0.26	35.0	35		39
Bulgaria[e]	1993	6.80	3.40	50.0	50		
Poland[e]	1994	14.00	6.30	45.0	45		
Ecuador[e]	1994	7.60	3.42	45.0	45		
Total		191.40	61.12	31.9		3.62	

Sources: William R. Cline, *International Debt Reexamined* (Washington: Institute for International Economics, 1985), pp. 234–35; World Bank, *Global Development Finance* (Washington, 1998), pp. 93–102, table A 3.9. This table provides footnotes to all of the Brady Plan agreements spelling out in some detail the various restructuring agreements affected by the Brady agreement, other options to reduce debt, and official enhancements from the IMF, World Bank, and bilateral governments—principally the United States and Japan.

a. Regular debt restructurings/reschedulings continued throughout the early 1990s albeit at a lower level than the 1980s; this table focuses on the agreements under the Brady Plan.

b. Sum of reduction on face value of original debt and reduction in present-value terms of interest reductions, less amount spent on buybacks.

c. Based on bond discount.

d. World Bank, IDA debt reduction facility.

e. Pending final agreement in 1993.

f. Not applicable.

groups. The flow of resources to emerging market countries is discussed extensively in Part III of this book.

The debt restructurings under the Brady Plan had established sufficient market confidence such that other forms of capital freely flowed to these markets. That was true until a series of crises hit emerging market countries, starting with Mexico in the latter part of 1994, followed in succession by a number of East Asian countries and Thailand in 1997, Russia in 1998, Turkey in 2001, and Argentina in 2001 (also discussed in Part III). Another measure of success of the Brady Plan initiative was the rise in secondary market prices on debt, once a Brady Plan agreement had been reached. Using fourth-quarter 1989 prices as the base, fourth-quarter 1993 secondary market prices had risen 128 percent for Mexico, 65 percent for the Philippines, 408 percent for Argentina, and 109 percent for Brazil.[131]

The Modalities of Restructuring

As the postwar period progressed, the approach to sovereign debt restructuring became increasingly concentrated in two forums, both of which provided for multilateral renegotiation of a country's external debt. The Paris Club, a noninstitutionalized consortium of official creditors, primarily representing the member states of the OECD, evolved as the principal forum for official debt restructurings.[132] The London Club was also a noninstitutional forum for commercial bank restructurings. Commercial bank restructurings were negotiated by bank advisory or steering committees controlled by the major money center banks that were the largest creditors to the developing and Eastern bloc countries.[133] Over time, both of these forums developed clearly established approaches and practices. At the same time, an implicit link developed between the two during the 1981–83 restructuring period.

The Paris Club

The philosophy behind debt restructuring under the auspices of the Paris Club was to develop a noninstitutionalized framework for multilateral debt restructuring that allowed only debtor states in distress to restructure. As noted, this approach was initially conceived of as a way to discourage debtor states from using restructuring as a means of escaping the burden of debt service.[134] Creditor governments also insisted on a case-by-case ad hoc approach without formally defined procedures, rules, or criteria in the belief that it offered the most pragmatic and flexible way to deal with the varying debt problems of individual debtor states.[135] However, it also provided creditor states with maximum leverage to see that the disruption in debt service was addressed as rapidly as possible and that the debt relief provided was followed by the prompt resumption of debt service. This method, referred to as the "short-leash" approach, emphasized short-term debt relief. At the same time, creditors sought to develop a common approach to avoid individual and potentially competitive responses to restructuring.[136] Thus, from the beginning, official creditors usually insisted that, as a precondition to negotiations, debtor states agree to implement an IMF adjustment program. In practice, rescheduling was based on conditionality. When the rescheduling country was not an IMF member, the creditor countries established a committee to monitor economic adjustment programs, but this approach was difficult to implement in countries such as Poland or Cuba.[137]

The Paris Club meetings were held under the auspices of the French Treasury. They constituted a discrete diplomatic process of negotiation whereby a consensus was reached between the major creditors at risk and the sovereign debtor.[138] A rescheduling was initiated by a request from the debtor state to the French Treasury. The major creditors agreed to assemble only when it was evident there was a "real" problem, defined as a buildup of debt service arrears and other signs of economic distress, such as a running down of reserves within the debtor's economy.[139]

Renegotiation involved representatives of the primary creditors, along with the IMF and the World Bank as observers and presenters of an economic assessment of the debtor, UNCTAD as a "friend in court" to the debtor, other multilateral institutions as appropriate, and the debtor.[140] The negotiations usually involved a series of meetings. At the preliminary one the debtor presented its case, and the IMF, and perhaps other institutions, provided an assessment of the debtor's economic situation. Subsequent meetings resulted in a negotiated agreement in principle, as documented in the minutes. The negotiated agreement was finalized and attained legal status in the form of bilateral agreements between the sovereign debtor and individual creditor states.[141]

Initially, the scope of debt relief under official restructurings was confined to export credits and export credit guarantees provided by the export agencies of OECD states. They then evolved to include medium- and long-term bilateral loans from governments and government agencies and, at times, nonguaranteed private debt, where it was an important component of debt service disruption.[142] In principle, the Paris Club was reluctant to reschedule short-term debt in order to avoid interference with the normal mechanism of trade finance. In addition, there was traditionally great reluctance to renegotiate debt previously rescheduled. In practice, however, as debtors' problems increased over the period 1974 to 1983, official creditors were often forced to relent on both points. In no instance were loans from multilateral financial institutions part of a Paris Club rescheduling.

Collateral issues such as the terms of negotiations with other creditors and consideration of future restructurings by creditors under certain terms and conditions were also addressed, as appropriate. The former took the form of a "most favored creditor" clause, the latter a "good will" clause.[143]

The specific terms of debt restructurings traditionally covered a number of detailed items relating to the contractual terms of the rescheduled loans. They included the following principal points: (i) the type of debt to be rescheduled or refinanced, (ii) the length of the consolidation period, (iii) the grace period, (iv) the repayment period, (v) the proportion of principal and interest covered by the renegotiation, and (vi) the rate of interest to be applied to restructured loans.[144]

Commercial Bank Restructurings

The link between commercial bank restructurings and Paris Club reschedulings remained implicit and was specified only through the "most favored creditor" clause. Despite the potential systemic risk, creditor governments chose not to involve themselves directly in the negotiations between commercial banks and debtor states, except in those cases where they became involved as part of the collective lender-of-last-resort efforts in a few major restructurings.

Bank restructurings from 1981 to 1983 broke new ground in the absence of broadly accepted practices for the organization and terms or conditions for restructuring external sovereign debt post–World War II.[145] Up to 1981 banks had sought to avoid formal restructurings, relying instead on a rollover approach. However, the earlier restructurings of Peru, Zaire, and Turkey established a precedent of responding before the onset of a full-scale debt crisis, while the complex and difficult Polish restructurings provided the stimulus for banks to professionalize their efforts.[146] Not surprisingly, the banks, particularly the major money center ones from the United States, drew on their experience in rescheduling domestic credits in which they had a common interest to arrive at a case-by-case approach to debt renegotiations.[147]

The bank advisory or steering committee was the vehicle through which banks usually organized restructurings. The committee normally consisted of several major money center banks, in practice those with the greatest exposure in a particular country. The committee had several functions, the primary ones being: (1) to negotiate the terms of the restructuring with the debtor; (2) to communicate these terms to the large number of creditor banks that were involved in the sovereign lending through syndication; and (3) to maintain market discipline by ensuring equitable, normally proportional, representation of creditor banks in the restructuring.[148] The need to avoid the "free-rider" problem—that is, individual banks reducing their exposure to a sovereign debtor at the expense of other banks[149]—was normally enforced by the leverage that the major money center banks exerted over the second-tier banks through a range of tied relationships and by cross-default provisions in the loan agreements.

According to a cross-default provision, a bank that initiated a default against a sovereign debtor could in principle trigger a domino effect of similar defaults by other banks seeking to retain a *pari passu*, or equivalent, position in a credit.[150] This issue became crucial as "involuntary lending" was imposed on banks, starting with the Mexican restructuring. The question of equity was particularly complex because of the different forms of bank exposure in a particular country.[151]

A fourth function of the advisory committee was to coordinate the banks' restructuring efforts with the IMF, national supervisory agencies, central banks, and various creditor governments represented through the Paris Club forum.[152]

From a historical perspective, the role of the bank steering committee was similar to that of the bondholder committees that functioned under the auspices of the Council of Foreign Bondholders or its French, Dutch, Belgian, and American equivalents in the nineteenth century or the international committee of bankers formed to renegotiate Mexico's default in the interwar period.

The modalities of sovereign debt restructuring by commercial banks were similar to official ones. However, some substantial differences emerged. The commercial banks often faced a more difficult task than official creditors did in evaluating eligible debt. Clearly, medium- and long-term loans to government and government agencies, as well as government-guaranteed loans, were the principal object of restructuring. However, the banks were also faced with difficult decisions on restructuring or rolling over short-term debt in excess of trade requirements, interbank lines, loans to state-owned enterprises that had implicit state guarantees, and private nonguaranteed loans. They also had to decide whether supplier credits and bond financing should be included in the scope of restructuring negotiations.[153] In principle, restructuring excluded refinancing export credits guaranteed by creditor governments. As these debts matured and a debtor was unable to service them, they were renegotiated within the framework of the Paris Club.[154] In most cases nonguaranteed private debt was excluded. In several instances where private loans were substantial, however, the banks negotiated arrangements with the sovereign debtor so that they could be serviced in local currency, with the foreign exchange or transfer problem then becoming the obligation of the debtor's central bank toward the commercial banks.[155]

Short-term debts were included in a substantial number of restructurings, although doing so was exceedingly difficult because of the number of banks involved, the divergence of exposure and interest in a particular country, and the number of different financing instruments involved, such as letters of credit, acceptances, and short-term credit lines. Often when short-term debt was not formally restructured an informal understanding, or "gentleman's agreement," was established to roll over these credits, with interest spreads adjusted, amounting to a de facto conversion from short-term to medium-term debt.[156] More than $20 billion in short-term debt was consolidated in this way during the period 1982–83.[157]

The consensus of the banks was to exclude interbank lines from the reschedulings because they wanted to maintain confidence in that market as a source of short-term maturity matching for banks. However, this policy proved difficult to achieve, particularly in the Brazilian agreement, of which maintenance of interbank lines was a fundamental part. Ultimately, the Brazilian agreement had to be renegotiated because the amount of these lines specified fell short of the target.[158] Bonds and similar instruments such as floating rate notes were also excluded, except for commercial bank holdings of these instruments.[159] Suppliers' credits in principle were not included, although the Turkish rescheduling agreements of 1979–81 and the Nigerian agreement of April 1984 dealt with trade arrears, the latter exclusively so.[160]

Another substantial problem for the banks was the accumulated arrears of both interest and principal as a result of the moratoriums declared by many of the debtor states during the negotiation process. In principle, the banks were prepared to reschedule the arrears on amortization of principal, but usually insisted that the interest arrears be paid before a restructuring was finalized.[161] The Argentine restructuring effort proved extremely contentious on this point. The American banks were faced with potential supervisory guidelines on the reclassification of loans with interest arrears of over ninety days, and they negotiated with Argentina to the brink on this point on various occasions.[162] In several cases the banks had to provide additional financing or refinancing so that debtors could pay the accumulated interest arrears.[163]

The major difference between commercial bank restructuring and the Paris Club approach was the banks' insistence on high spreads and substantial fees. They argued that these incentives were needed to bring the large number of banks involved into the fold and to compensate for the high risk involved in restructuring. The terms were therefore universally hard.[164] Subsequent renegotiations, however, were at reduced spreads, as in the case of Peru (February 1984), Mexico (January 1984 and 1986), and Brazil (January 1984),[165] although still not as low as those of creditworthy borrowers such as those in Asia.[166]

As noted, initially commercial banks favored rollover credits to formal restructuring. Thereafter they preferred refinancing to rescheduling to avoid having to reclassify the loans and thereby comply with the loss provisioning required by their banking supervisors.[167] From 1981 to 1983, however, this preference gave way to the reality that complex restructuring was required.[168] With the introduction of "involuntary lending," the supervisory authorities had to agree to allow banks to increase their exposure to problematic debtors in order to encourage orderly adjustment.[169]

Following initial efforts to establish control over problem debtors in Peru and Zaire, the commercial banks and the Paris Club tied their restructuring efforts to IMF-approved adjustment programs.[170] The IMF therefore emerged as the central force and in turn was able to use its leverage to ensure orderly adjustment by insisting on "involuntary" or "concerted" loans from banks.[171] During 1983, of the $27 billion in eurocredits extended by the commercial banks to developing countries, $14 billion represented "involuntary" loans.[172] In earlier restructurings, commercial banks normally had not made additional financing available. Now the IMF sought to ensure the continuation of these loans until spontaneous lending by banks resumed.[173]

Conclusions on Restructuring in the Postwar Period

The multilateral, case-by-case approach to sovereign debt restructuring by official and commercial bank creditors evolved substantially over the postwar period to the point where the customary practices of the Paris Club and the bank steering committees became well established within relatively narrow limits. The emphasis of both official and bank creditors was on a negotiated agreement with the sovereign debtor that restores the creditworthiness and debt servicing capacity at the earliest possible moment. Whereas up to 1980 the Paris Club clearly played a lead role in restructuring, during the 1981–83 debt crisis the focus shifted to commercial bank restructuring with sovereign debtors because of the demand, the magnitude of the debt, the potential threat to the solvency of the major money center banks, and the risk to the financial system as a whole. It is clear, as in past debt crises, that restructuring is a long-term effort that, by the end of 1983, had only gone through its initial phase. Subsequent renegotiations from 1984 to 1988 and 1989 to 1994 with major debtors such as Mexico, Brazil, and Argentina, referred to as rounds two, three, and so forth, only reinforced the process and recalled the long-term nature of the problem.

During the restructuring crisis of 1981 to 1983, a great many potential solutions were proposed to resolve the debt problem and improve the restructuring process. Most were technical and ignored political realities. Chapter 8 discusses the 1981–89 debt crises from the international relations viewpoint. It also examines alternative prescriptions for resolving the debt crisis, allowing for the established practice of a case-by-case renegotiation to restructure external sovereign debt once disruption of debt service has occurred.

EIGHT

Debt Restructuring and International Relations

1955–94

This chapter focuses on the international relations aspects of the debt problem by examining the roles of: (i) creditor and debtor governments in the 1981–83 debt crisis, specifically with respect to the renegotiation and restructuring of debt; (ii) an international lender of last resort; (iii) multilateral financial institutions; (iv) strategic interests and debt; and finally (v) proposed alternative solutions to the debt crisis in view of the thesis that there is an obligation of states to honor their contracts, *pacta sunt servanda*, ahead of the vital interests of states, *clausula rebus sic stantibus*.

Official Debt Restructuring

In the three decades following World War II until the first oil crisis of 1973–74, the majority of external credits to developing countries were secured through bilateral arrangements that supported trade or the strategic goals of the member states of the Organization for Economic Cooperation and Development (OECD). During this period, generalized debt crises were avoided, and those restructurings that did occur were primarily handled in ways that closely resembled prior practices. That is, debtor states were addressed case by case. Instead of national bondholder committees handling the negotiations for creditors, because the debt was primarily officially held, multilateral forums arose, such as the Hague, London, and Paris Clubs. In special circumstances reschedulings were handled through aid consortiums representing the creditors' interests. In the absence of defined norms, objective standards, and a neutral institutional structure for official debt restructuring, as advocated by the United Nations Conference for Trade and Development (UNCTAD), official restructurings were criticized as being biased toward the political and strategic concerns of the creditor states. Creditors loaned their funds on the basis of what they perceived to be their own national advantages, and they applied the same approach to debt restructuring. As evidence, sovereign debtors point to the willingness of creditors through the OECD consortium to restructure Turkey's loans on favorable terms; the generous conditions provided to Indonesia after the overthrow of the Sukarno regime; the ability of Ghana eventually to reach improved rescheduling terms after the departure of its president, Kwame Nkrumah; and the favorable support provided to the regime of Edward Seaga in Jamaica. In each case the creditor governments saw those steps both as strengthening anti-Communist positions and governments favoring democratic capitalism. In contrast, the United States was unwilling to reschedule with the government of Salvador Allende in Chile. This political orientation to official debt negotiations and restructurings was evident, despite the largely technical mechanisms applied by the Paris Club.[1]

The approach to official debt restructuring was criticized in several other respects. The short-term ad hoc nature of restructuring resulted in a need for repeated reschedulings by sovereign debtors, usually with a small group of OECD creditor states.[2] Creditor governments showed little inclination to provide additional financing during rescheduling. The role of the International Monetary Fund (IMF) as catalyst, evident in the commercial bank restructurings, was largely absent.[3] Despite repeated requests by UNCTAD and other forums such as the North-South meetings in Paris, known as the Conference on International Economic Cooperation (CIEC), that creditor governments provide long-term relief and forgiveness to the lower-income or "most affected" countries, relatively little was achieved: agreements with a selected number of creditor governments yielded only $5.7 billion in one-time efforts at debt relief, of which $3.3 billion represented debt cancellation.[4] Moreover, the relief provided in the majority of cases was short-lived and at relatively low cost to the creditors.[5]

The refusal of creditor governments to provide additional financing as part of official debt restructurings and the poor aid record of the major OECD donors during the 1970s were viewed as attenuating factors contributing to the difficulties of low-income countries in servicing their debts.[6] In short, the balance of power in official restructurings was clearly tilted toward the creditor states, a situation that left little room for negotiated solutions to debtors' problems, except in those few countries, such as Turkey and Indonesia, where strategic interests clearly prevailed over the issue of debt.

International Lender of Last Resort

During the debt crisis, beginning in 1981, creditor governments played a secondary role as lender of last resort through their central banks and other multilateral agencies such as the Bank for International Settlements (BIS). They were effective in containing what was widely perceived as a threat to the international financial system as a whole and the solvency of the major money center banks.[7] The consequences of not containing such a crisis are not clearly calculable, but they can be guessed at, based on experience during the Depression, when an adequate lender of last resort failed to stem the tide and many banks in Austria, Germany, and the United States failed.[8]

At the same time, the role played by the major central banks in the 1981 debt crisis went beyond the classical view of the central bank operating within a national banking system, as defined by Walter Bagehot and subsequently refined by numerous central banks around the world.[9] Instead, the central banks sought to preempt a wider crisis by providing temporary bridging loans in support of orderly adjustment. Critics of this effort argued, however, that had there been a more clearly defined arrangement for an international lender of last resort in advance of the major debt service disruptions, the crisis-like environment under which the ad hoc arrangements were ultimately negotiated would have been avoided. "This 'interference with the market,' indeed, has come, in practice, not from carefully conceived ILLR (international lender of last resort) supervision loan packages, but from the hasty cobbling together of rescheduling and new loan packages to specific countries, half-forced on numerous reluctant banks since late 1982 precisely because ILLR was and is inadequate."[10]

The governors of the central banks of the major creditor states carefully avoided making commitments in advance to serve as lenders of last resort to their commercial banks lending "offshore" through the unregulated Euromarket. They preferred vague assurances that the means were available for that purpose if necessary.[11] The overriding objection of central bankers was that a clear advance plan defining their role as international lenders of last resort would have given way to "moral hazard." That is, certainty on the part of banks and sovereign borrowers that they would be rescued by central monetary authorities would have encouraged imprudence.[12] Some analysts have also rejected the idea of formal plans, rules, and regulations as inappropriate, given that crises emerge from a variety of unanticipated circumstances.

Instead, they urged flexibility and case-by-case responses.[13] In addition, there seems to have been little political support among the creditor countries and multilateral financial organizations for institutionalizing the role of an international lender of last resort, despite growing awareness of a greater need created by the expansion of international lending via the Euromarket.[14] Nevertheless, the debt crisis established that the monetary authorities would come to the rescue of their major banks.

At one point the BIS became the focal institution for organizing short-term bridging arrangements. By coordinating the activities and mobilizing the resources of its major central bank members, the BIS was able to provide bridge loans until the negotiated, IMF-supported adjustment programs could be put in place. These BIS bridge loans, provided in conjunction with other central banks, along with other measures, proved effective in containing the immediate crisis. In effect, the BIS, the IMF, and various creditor governments served as a collective international lender of last resort to preempt a larger crisis. By the middle of 1983, with the initial debt crisis contained, the BIS announced it would no longer provide bridging loans during restructuring negotiations, leaving only the IMF and the World Bank to be involved.[15]

The Role of Multilateral Financial Institutions

The third role of creditor governments in the debt restructuring effort was support for multilateral financial institutions, with the IMF initially the central actor in the debt crisis. Despite the Reagan administration's initial objection to an increased role for the IMF, at the urging of the Federal Reserve the IMF found itself in a rearguard action supporting that role in the face of congressional opposition.[16]

The Role of the IMF

From the point of view of the creditor governments, perhaps the most valuable role the IMF played in the restructuring effort was that of a buffer. It allowed debt restructuring to proceed largely as a technical matter, without bilateral or multilateral diplomatic negotiations among states. In the short term, by supporting the central role of the IMF in debt restructuring, the creditor governments obscured the links between the debt crisis and other foreign and economic policy issues.

The IMF, which played a varied role, was one of the keys to the potential success of sovereign debt renegotiation and restructuring. It served as a catalyst to attract and retain commercial bank financing. It initiated the "involuntary" financing included in the major restructurings. Not least, it was at the center of efforts to negotiate adjustment programs with developing countries that restructured their sovereign debt.

From the beginning, the Fund was involved in official restructuring negotiations through the Paris Club. In fact, official creditors would only negotiate a rescheduling when a sovereign debtor reached agreement with the Fund on a standby arrangement with conditionality at its core. In addition, after the commercial banks tried unsuccessfully to apply their own conditionality in Peru and Zaire, they came to consider the IMF as crucial to any agreement on debt restructuring. In all cases in 1982–83, restructuring was considered only after the Fund approved a standby or extended arrangement involving upper credit tranche conditionality with the debtor country concerned.[17] The Fund also had responsibility for monitoring the economic adjustment efforts by member countries.

The IMF was also an important source of balance of payments financing. An increasing number of countries drew on its resources during the debt crisis and after the sudden closure of the private capital markets. In 1980 purchases from the Fund in the upper credit tranches and under special facilities totaled Special Drawing Rights (SDR) 2.20 billion. By 1982 the level had reached approximately SDR7 billion, and in 1983 and 1984 it was in excess of SDR10 billion.[18] In addition to these credit purchases, member countries, many of which were restructuring debtors, concluded extended or standby arrangements with the Fund. In line with these loans, the Fund agreed to extend its policy on larger quotas.[19]

In addition to a quota increase, the Fund made various arrangements to increase its liquidity and its ability to act as an international safety net in the event of further deterioration in the international monetary and economic situation. Nevertheless, some analysts questioned whether the IMF's resources were adequate to the task in light of the uncertain economic conditions.[20] The large-scale increase in IMF credits to deeply indebted developing countries brought with it fears that the IMF itself would become illiquid or be locked in to credits that would alter its role as a supplier of short-term stabilization funds to countries with balance of payments problems. Moreover, in principle the IMF was precluded from debt restructuring by its articles of agreement. In the event of a default by one of its member governments, the IMF would have to stop lending to the defaulter or, as a last resort, expel it. When Sudan and Vietnam, for example, fell far behind on their credit repayments to the IMF, the IMF declared Vietnam ineligible for more loans. The situation in many African nations looked equally serious: at the end of 1984, all of Africa except Nigeria owed the IMF SDR7.2 billion, more than one-fifth of its outstanding loans.[21] The IMF was potentially faced with credit renegotiations of its own with member countries.

The Fund's primary contribution to debt restructuring was not the supply of its own funds, but rather its role as catalyst for other sources of external funds. It served this role by providing assurance to creditors that sovereign debtors were carrying out suitable economic adjustment policies.[22] It is beyond the scope of this book to analyze the long-standing debate over the suitability of the Fund's policy prescriptions for adjustment.[23] However, two aspects of its adjustment policies merit comment. One was the resistance of many countries to negotiating an economic adjustment program with the IMF, to the point where they postponed adjustment policies, a step that exacerbated the social, political, and economic problems associated with adjustment. This situation pertained particularly to loans from commercial banks that provided nonconditional external financing as an alternative to adjustment.[24]

The IMF's policy prescriptions were rarely neutral in a distributive sense, a fact that engendered political opposition. Numerous country studies have pointed to the political nature of IMF negotiations with developing countries.[25] The objection of the Alfonsín regime to IMF involvement in Argentina is an outstanding example of the political resistance to the IMF that hampered debt renegotiation.[26]

A second principal concern was that a substantial number of the IMF's adjustment programs could unravel and thus undermine the Fund's credibility with both commercial banks and creditor governments as the central institution in restructuring.[27] The most obvious example was Brazil. The IMF suspended funding in 1985 under a long-term debt restructuring agreement, which called in principle for an automatic halt to debt renegotiations with the bankers if Brazil did not meet the inflation targets, as it failed to do.[28]

These two factors—political resistance to the Fund and the potential for a significant number of Fund-negotiated adjustment programs to fail—led some analysts to doubt the ability of the IMF to remain at the center of debt renegotiations in the long term.[29]

The Baker Plan

The reluctance of major debtors such as Argentina, Brazil, and Mexico to continue negotiating adjustment programs with the IMF, as well as the perceived need to support restructuring arrangements with the infusion of fresh funds, led to the announcement of the Baker Plan in October 1985. The Baker Plan sought US$29 billion in voluntary commercial bank loans for major debtors over three years and $9 billion from multinational financial institutions, primarily the World Bank, over the same period.

The Role of the World Bank

One primary feature of the Baker Plan was its intention to substitute the World Bank, which had played a largely passive role in the debt crisis to that point, for the IMF as the primary multilateral institution in the debt crisis. The objective was to move from the relatively short-term, crisis-oriented focus of the Fund to the longer-term policy and structural adjustment programs of the Bank.[30]

Unfortunately, despite the push from the Baker Plan, the World Bank, constrained by a number of factors, failed to become an effective countercyclical lender of long-term funds to highly indebted countries. First, the Bank's conservative gearing (leverage) ratio of 1:1 on its capital precluded it from becoming a large-scale lender to developing countries without a major capital increase from the creditor countries, its shareholders.[31]

Second, the Bank borrowed a substantial portion of its funds from the long-term bond markets in a diverse range of currencies. The cost of its funds, hence its lending rate, based on this pool of borrowed capital, rose sharply with the devaluation of the U.S. dollar in relation to other major currencies during this time period. Therefore the Bank became an expensive source of capital to debtor countries, even though it was one of the few suppliers of long-term funds for development.[32]

Third, the Bank's "soft" funds, provided through the International Development Association (IDA) to low-income countries, were dependent on capital contributions by member countries.[33] Negotiations for a capital increase for IDA traditionally took several years to complete. For example, the $12 billion capital increment sought by the Bank in 1983 (through the International Development Association, the highly concessional lending window of the World Bank to the least-developed or poorest countries), IDA-7 replenishment, became the subject of dispute among the major creditor countries. The Reagan administration opposed this increase on ideological grounds, as perforce the United States would have become the major contributor.[34]

Fourth, the Bank's traditional lending orientation was to specific long-term development projects. During the period under review, a time when Bank member countries faced acute balance of payments difficulties, the World Bank was confronted with the dilemma of effectively linking its project commitments to the wider issues of policy and effective adjustment programs. In this context, the World Bank launched its structural adjustment lending (SAL) program during 1980. The SAL was the Bank's first attempt at a regular commitment to lending for policy and institutional reform.[35] Up to 1984, however, the SAL loan commitments were still small, amounting to $1.5 billion in 1983. Moreover, policy-based loans were initially limited to

10 percent of the Bank's capital and 30 percent of a country's total borrowing from the Bank in any fiscal year.

Fifth, despite the commitment to increase its lending, the Bank's net transfers to highly indebted countries were limited. In 1983, at the height of the debt crisis, net transfers were $4.5 billion, and they were negative in low-income Africa.[36] For the period 1982–85, the World Bank's net transfers to fourteen Baker Plan countries averaged slightly over $1 billion per year.[37]

Finally, until later in the decade the World Bank had failed to develop a comprehensive strategy for assisting highly indebted countries that was distinct from its normal country lending program. A strategy paper addressing the needs of seventeen highly indebted middle-income countries, presented to the Bank's executive directors on March 9, 1988, stressed the catalytic role of the Bank in trying to resolve the debt problem: "The primary aspect of the Bank's catalytic role is its policy dialogue and substantial direct lending in support of countries' adjustment programs."[38]

Even with a commitment to increase policy-based lending as a defined strategy to deal with the external debt problem of its member countries, most analysts conclude that the Bank would remain marginal to any major solution to the debt crisis. Its own bureaucratic inertia and inherent conservatism precluded it from operating in tandem with the commercial banks or from offering more dynamic solutions to the external debt problem.

The Brady Plan

In 1989, Secretary of the Treasury Nicholas Brady introduced the Brady Plan. The objective of the Brady Plan was to support a $70 billion debt reduction in thirty-nine countries with some $340 billion in debt. Mutual exhaustion of the banks in renegotiating round after round of reschedulings, a drop in the secondary market in the price of debt, and accruing interest arrears in a number of the debtors, especially larger debtors such as Argentina and Brazil, necessitated a change in strategy that offered flexibility—a range of options to creditors who had differing objectives with respect to future participation in emerging market debt. The plan had to offer fresh money because bank sovereign lending had essentially dried up. Finally, the plan had to offer debt reductions at levels acceptable to the banks and also to debtors and analysts who were eyeing the secondary market price at thirty-five to forty cents on the dollar as the appropriate discount level. The Brady Plan also sought enhancements for these reductions from bilateral agencies such as Japan's Import-Export Bank, the Inter-American Development Bank, the World Bank, and the IMF. From 1989 to 1994 the Brady Plan led to a number of debt reduction agreements, including some large, highly complex agreements with Mexico, Brazil, and Argentina. There was little new money on the table, but the plan did create sufficient market confidence to usher in new resources to emerging markets from a variety of sources in line with globalization, the liberalization of financial markets, and implementation of structural adjustment programs under the Washington Consensus by a number of emerging market countries, as discussed in chapter 9.

Strategic Interests and External Debt

Despite the attempt by creditor governments to manage the debt crisis at a largely technical level, external sovereign debt, debt renegotiations, and restructurings were invariably linked to larger strategic issues, as was true in the earlier periods discussed in this book.

As noted, during the 1970s the interaction between creditor and debtor states was largely confined to official debt restructuring negotiations. The debt service disruptions that began in 1981 changed this pattern dramatically. Subsequent negotiations to restructure commercial bank loans to sovereign debtors, as well as official loans, often in parallel, involved sovereign creditors and sovereign debtors in a complex set of negotiations highlighting the critical nature of the debt problem and moving these issues from a technocratic level to that of higher political concern. Some examples are in order.

First, the long-run economic interests of the West were in part tied to successful trade with developing and Eastern European countries. The adjustment process following the initial debt crisis required a severe compression of imports by the major debtor states so as to create a trade surplus to service their debt.[39] To the extent that these countries were forced to continue deflationary adjustment policies, exports from the advanced industrial states were constrained, as was export-related employment.[40]

On the debtors' side, trade relations were also of critical importance. Perhaps the only way for heavily indebted countries to grow out of their debt burdens was by increasing direct exports. Therefore free access to world markets and resistance to increasing protectionism in the OECD countries were important features of international relations and external debt.[41] As Harold Lever and Christopher Huhne have observed, "Perhaps most contentious of all the assumptions of the debt projection studies . . . is the notion that protectionism in the developed world will not tighten, and hence will not erode the hitherto strong links between industrial-country growth and export buoyancy in the Third World. The reality is that barriers to debtor-country exports continue to mount."[42]

Second, a number of heavily indebted developing countries were of political and strategic importance to the West. The continued support by the OECD aid consortiums for Turkey's debt restructuring was certainly influenced by that country's importance to NATO.[43]

After the Falklands War, Great Britain faced the difficult dilemma of whether to allow its commercial banks to support restructuring in Argentina, in that new loans might be used to purchase weapons. It did allow its banks to take part in restructuring negotiations, despite public opinion to the contrary, because of the heavy exposure of some banks and the need to be seen as consistent in its support for debt renegotiations between commercial banks and sovereign debtors.[44]

The United States' support for Mexico's debt restructuring reflected not only the financial threat of a default, but a host of other considerations as well, including potential large-scale labor emigration into the United States, concern over political stability at the edge of Central America, the long common border, and the strategic importance of Mexico as a supplier of oil and gas.[45]

There was also the problem of the Philippines, a long-term American ally of strategic importance in the Far East. The major debt restructuring problems of the Philippines could not be delinked from internal political problems, the threat of a Communist insurgency, and the failure of the Ferdinand Marcos regime to address its most urgent social and economic problems.[46]

Third, the debt restructuring problem was linked to a number of East-West issues. During the debt moratoriums of 1981 and 1982, there was concern that the Eastern bloc was ideologically prone to repudiate its Western debt.[47] In addition, restructuring negotiations on Polish debt were affected by that government's suppression of Solidarity and the refusal of Western creditors to consider official restructuring until it took steps toward political liberalization.[48] Restructuring support was provided for Yugoslavia, a non-COMECON Eastern European state that the West wanted to keep independent of the Soviet orbit.[49] Given West Germany's strong national interest in maintaining ties with East Germany, West Germany extended substantial credits to East Germany, presumably to further its policy of Ostpolitik.[50]

The largely successful efforts of Eastern European nations to restore their creditworthiness through harsh austerity measures appeared by 1985 to be establishing the preconditions for a revival of Western-financed trade.[51] Exclusive of Poland, which remained in poor financial shape, the combined net external bank debt of the major Eastern European debtors dropped 40 percent, from $32.5 billion to $19.3 billion, from 1981 to the end of 1984, although a substantial part of the reduction was attributable to a rollover of guaranteed bank credits to official debt held by export credit agencies.[52]

Fourth, the debt problems of the low-income countries, specifically those of sub-Saharan Africa, severely tested the notion that the debt problem largely represented a temporary liquidity problem that could be resolved by short-term restructuring. These countries, mostly because of poor agricultural policies and prolonged drought, found themselves unable to feed their populations without massive food aid.[53]

The links among the problems faced by sub-Saharan Africa in servicing its external debt to official and commercial bank creditors, the increasing requirement of many African states for official development assistance, and the growing dependence on multilateral financial institutions are clear.[54] The oil crises and related debt crisis potentially put sub-Saharan Africa into a "fourth world" status, as during the 1970s and 1980s these countries moved further away from bridging the economic gap between North and South and achieving true independence.[55]

Following the initial debt crisis of 1981–83, the external debt situation in sub-Saharan Africa deteriorated considerably because of the secular decline in exports from the region. External commercial and debt service arrears grew sharply, and debt service payments were restructured regularly. During 1986–87, twenty-four sub-Saharan African countries obtained a restructuring of debt service obligations to official and commercial creditors totaling $32 billion.[56] As of May 1988, five of these countries (Liberia, Sierra Leone, Somalia, Sudan, and Zambia) were declared ineligible to use IMF resources because of their overdue obligations to the Fund.[57] During 1980–87, only twelve of forty-four sub-Saharan African countries, accounting for 13 percent of debt outstanding, were able to service their debt regularly without requiring routine debt restructurings or incurring arrears in payments.[58]

Africa's problems highlighted the difficulties inherent in the rescheduling process from the perspective of economic development. Reschedulings deterred development: they absorbed the scarce human resources of policymakers, and they created a climate of economic uncertainty that slowed necessary investment. Arrears halted new loan commitments, while arrears to multilateral creditors slowed the progress of economic adjustment programs, a situation that in turn blocked debt relief from private and bilateral creditors. Foreign suppliers, taking account of the increased risk, raised their prices accordingly.[59]

If ever a solution to the problems of servicing external debt were called for, it was in sub-Saharan Africa. Yet the composition of this debt varied markedly by country. As an IMF survey on sub-Saharan Africa noted, "Significant differences in the economic performance and debt position of individual countries have underlined the need to maintain the case-by-case approach to debt problems."[60]

In other words, other than specific measures such as greater debt relief on official debt, increases in the grant elements of new loans, a willingness to continue rescheduling, and emphasis on the need for greater concessional resources, the creditor countries and the Bretton Woods institutions—the IMF and the World Bank—lacked any real strategy for addressing Africa's external debt problems, despite almost universal pessimism that these countries could grow out of their debt burdens on their own.[61] Moreover, Africa was viewed as being of minimal strategic interest to the major creditor states. Therefore, the region's ability to negotiate improved terms and conditions was based purely on moral suasion.

A primary focus of international politics and debt restructuring was Latin America. Because of the presence of three large debtors, Argentina, Brazil, and Mexico, and a number of other countries with substantial external debt, analysts speculated openly on the advantages of repudiation or partial default over continued adherence to restructuring plans and the austerity they impose.[62] Concern mounted among a number of international analysts that the economic adjustment programs would severely retard economic growth and exacerbate the political divisions within many Latin American societies.[63] Moreover, there were fears that the trend toward democratic government, as evidenced by the end of military rule in Argentina and Brazil and the installation of democratically elected administrations, would prove fragile in the face of the overwhelming economic difficulties. As one commentator observed, "Democracy and debt were a macabre *pas de deux* in South America during 1983."[64]

It was with the major debtors of Latin America that the balance of power in debt restructurings remained in a delicate state of equilibrium. The extended moratorium of Brazil in 1987 forced commercial banks in the United States to make large loan loss provisions. Yet these banks and their governments continued to insist on case-by-case negotiations and the adequacy of the existing approach to the problem, despite the evident failure of the Baker Plan to generate voluntary loans to the major debtors.

Alternative Solutions to the Debt Crisis

There were many proposed solutions to the 1980s debt crisis. These alternatives ranged at the extremes from repudiation by the debtors to total forgiveness by the creditors.[65] Proposed solutions had to be measured in light of established international practices for renegotiating external sovereign debt—rescheduling or restructuring—once debt service disruption had occurred. They also had to allow for the political will and self-interest of both debtors and creditors. The principle that *pacta sunt servanda* (contracts are sacred) applies to the extent that the vital interests of states (*clausula rebus sic stantibus*) are not in jeopardy. This section of the chapter examines alternative prescriptions to the 1980s debt crisis and compares these with the historical experience to date.

Debt Repudiation

Some analysts suggest that the longer the debt crisis went on without an appropriate response from creditors—namely, an extension of fresh credits to the debtor states—the more likely the proclivity for longlasting defaults or repudiation of external debt. Historically, the incentive for sovereign debtors to renegotiate defaults has been the promise of new credits and future access to credit markets. If it seemed that the market would remain closed to most of them in the long run, the banks might find negotiations far more difficult, and the potential for extended debt service moratoriums or implicit defaults would be enhanced.[66]

Historically, few countries have seen it in their self-interest to repudiate their debts. Those that have done so largely for ideological reasons—Russia (during World War I), the People's Democratic Republic of Korea (North Korea), North Vietnam, and Nicaragua—have found themselves isolated from world credit markets and assistance from the multilateral financial institutions.

Historically and in the 1980s crisis, countries engaged in extended moratoriums in order to exert leverage on creditors to renegotiate and offer new credits. The extended moratorium by Brazil in 1987 was an example of such a tactic.[67] Repeated debt service disruptions and extended moratoriums, such as those that occurred in 1931 during the Depression and during the period 1984–87 among the African states, can lead to a widespread state of default without any repudiation having occurred. Some analysts thought that the situation in the 1980s offered such potential. As Lever and Huhne observed, "Though in our view it will not be in the interest of any major debtor to repudiate its obligations outright, a steady and often unilateral erosion of the large negative transfers expected by the IMF and the banks will inevitably produce a widespread perception of default."[68]

In short, there was a real danger that unless policymakers in creditor countries altered their debt strategy, a form of creeping, widespread default would occur among the debtor states. Some analysts suggested that as long as the commercial banks were willing to continue restructuring exercises with the major debtors, it was not in the debtor countries' interest to default and face a long-term loss of creditworthiness.[69] Because repudiation is a lose-lose strategy—that is, both debtors and creditors have little to gain—it was unlikely that this option would be widely adopted.

Debt Forgiveness

A number of analysts suggested that creditor governments should have recognized the realities of the situation and agreed to widespread forgiveness of debt.[70] Aside from the technical hurdles to these approaches, strong political opposition would surely have arisen from those opposed, on grounds of moral hazard, to "bailing out" both the debtor states that had defaulted and the commercial banks, where the issues were seen as privatizing the gains and socializing the losses.

The potential advantages of debt relief were, however, not without merit. Some analysts pointed, by way of example, to the Marshall Plan, in which debt forgiveness was perceived by the debtor states as an act of farsighted statesmanship.[71] It would also have lifted the sword of Damocles from over the heads of the international financial system and the major money center banks. Debt relief would have paralleled the bankruptcy proceedings in most countries, which initially provided debt relief to struggling debtors.[72] It would most likely have served as a stimulus to world trade and would have lifted the widespread economic recession in much of the developing world. In the strategic interests of the creditor states, debt relief would have provided welcome support for fledgling democracies such as those of Argentina, Brazil, and the Philippines.

The arguments against such support, with the case of the African states separated from those of the middle-income debtors, are perhaps even more compelling. Debt forgiveness would forestall into the indefinite future the restoration of creditworthiness to the debtor states. The incentives to pursue sound, outward-looking economic policies as in Chile or South Korea might also be removed.[73] Noting the frustrations inherent in the process, one analyst noted, "Thus it is tempting to call for grandiose schemes positing the large-scale availability of official money, but such schemes can only raise expectations that are sure to go unmet. Equally unhelpful are proposals for debt forgiveness and the partly or fully automatic capitalization of interest, let alone more drastic unilateral steps on the part of the debtors."[74]

Because debt forgiveness was viewed as a zero-sum game or win-lose strategy favoring the debtors, entailing substantial writedowns by commercial banks and almost certain demands from these banks for support from their governments, it is unlikely creditor governments would have pursued debt forgiveness as a strategy.

Improving the Existing Approach

Although the practice of negotiating debt restructurings evolved from and is based on earlier approaches to this problem, the relative rigidity of both official and commercial bank creditors in responding to the financial and economic situation of the debtors led to very short-lived and repetitive rescheduling agreements and frustration on the part of both debtor and creditor alike. The "short-leash" approach, based on the premise that the debt problem was a short-term one that debtors would grow out of in three to five years, has clearly not proved reasonable.[75]

What, then, were some of the options for improving this strategy that would be acceptable to both debtors and creditors? Based on experience, particularly in the nineteenth century, as well as some initiatives proposed during the crisis, many of which resemble historical practices, the key appears to be flexibility of response, based on a debtor's specific financial and economic situation. Debt restructuring needed to be perceived as a non-zero-sum game or win-win strategy. Several options are discussed in the next section.

Differentiation of the Problem: Official Support for Low-Income Debtors

It is clear that the approach to the debt problems faced by low-income countries such as those in Africa had to be differentiated from that to the major middle-income debtors such as Yugoslavia, the Philippines, or those in Latin America.

In the case of the former, where the debt is primarily officially held, the objective should have been to maximize the social welfare of the debtor while insisting on long-term adjustment programs to improve their economic performance. As *The Economist* observes, "Many African debtors really are bankrupt. In absolute terms, however, they owe little, and mostly to rich countries not banks. Aid by another name (preferably with policy strings attached) is feasible. Rich-country governments are moving, if too slowly, in this direction."[76] Some of the areas for potential improvement addressed during this period were:

Increasing the term, grace period, and consolidation period covered by rescheduling so that annual rescheduling did not become mandatory and intermediate term policy programs are given a chance to work. This effectively happened for several highly indebted countries under the Brady Plan.

Removing the restrictions on renegotiating the debt service due to multilateral institutions. In the case of Africa, debt to the IMF and World Bank formed a significant part of the debt service requirements.[77] Restrictions were removed later through the HIPC Initiative adopted by the donor countries for debts due by the poorest countries to the IMF and World Bank.

Lifting the restrictions on rescheduling other types of preferred credit such as suppliers' credits and debts previously rescheduled. De facto, this measure was applied for a number of countries—Zaire (1979, 1983), Sudan (1983, 1984), Togo (1983), Sierra Leone (1984), and Madagascar (1984).

Increasing the concessional terms of debt, in the recognition that in most African states the problem is largely a long-haul one and, in some cases, required a return to basic solvency. Again, this happened with the HIPC initiative tied to these countries meeting the goals of their economic development programs as agreed with the World Bank and/or the Fund.

Linking debt service to a percentage of the exports of specific commodities. Africa was particularly hard hit by the secular decline in the prices of basic commodities and raw materials, which severely affected export earnings. Linking debt service requirements to a percentage of export earnings for key commodities such as coffee, cocoa, tea, or copper, depending on the country, would have provided a flexible upside response to debt service requirements, as it would have reflected the reality of those countries' economic potential to service their debts.

Providing more external resources to low-income debtors. With both the World Bank and IMF, net transfers to the affected countries were barely positive and in some cases negative, voluntary commercial bank loans not available and the outlook for direct foreign investment bleak, a critical issue was the mobilization of external resources for the development of low-income countries. In recognition of this problem, the IMF strengthened its structural adjustment facility, while the World Bank and official development agencies enhanced their cofinancing programs, and there was a fifth replenishment of the African Development Fund. These steps mobilized approximately $18 billion in favor of the poorest and most indebted countries undertaking structural adjustment efforts during the three-year period 1988–90. Of this total, $15 billion was to be channeled to sub-Saharan African countries.[78]

A More Flexible Response to Major Debtors

For debt restructuring to succeed in the long term, both creditors and debtors needed to adopt a more flexible response to resolving the debt problem. A series of initiatives, some unilateral and some mutually agreed to by debtors and creditors, led to a more diversified and flexible approach to the debt problem. Several of these options are discussed here in line with the view that a pragmatic, case-by-case approach is the only one with sufficient political support to succeed in at least containing the problem.

Improving the Terms of Debt Restructurings

Since the initial round of debt restructurings in 1982–83, there was a noticeable softening of the terms for commercial bank restructurings with respect to tenure, interest rate, grace period, and fees payable. These softer terms implicitly recognized the long-term nature of the problem. Moreover, although there was not a widespread return to voluntary commercial bank credits, in the major restructurings there was a mix of new money supplied by banks, multilateral institutions, and creditor governments.[79] These restructurings provided a certain amount of credit relief, time for these countries to adopt sound economic policy programs, and sufficient new funds to maintain the debtors' interest in restructuring.

Debt Reduction Plans and Debt-Equity Swaps

After 1983 an increasing number of countries looked to debt reduction plans primarily in the form of debt-equity swaps to lower the amount of their external obligations. The swap basically consists of a buyer purchasing external debt on the open market, normally at a substantial discount.[80] (A portfolio of loans to Latin America's four largest debtors—Brazil, Argentina, Mexico, and Venezuela—traded at sixty-six U.S. cents on the dollar in February 1987 and fifty-eight cents in July; Brazil's suspension of payments then led to a decline in the trading value.)[81] This debt is then converted into the national currency of the debtor country, such as Mexican pesos, for equity in a productive investment.

By the end of 1987 it is estimated that Chile, Mexico, and the Philippines, the most active participants, had completed $6 billion in such swaps.[82] In addition, Bolivia, in agreement with commercial banks, got permission to buy back its debt on the open market, with assistance from creditor governments via a fiduciary fund supervised by the IMF.[83] Debt repurchase and reduction schemes were an important option in the 1930s debt crisis during the Great Depression, as debtor countries repurchased their bonds in default, which were trading at deep discount on the open market.[84] While investment bankers viewed such actions with deep distaste as an evasion of contractual debt service obligations, analysts such as H. C. Wallich viewed repurchase as a market-based solution to the external debt problem.[85] The advantages of such schemes, particularly debt-equity swaps, are numerous: they lower overall indebtedness and debt service; they encourage direct foreign investment; they promote capital repatriation; and they involve open market purchases in meaningful amounts that create a realistic or market price for the external debt of developing countries and perhaps a useful secondary market for such debt.[86]

Capital Repatriation

Capital flight, estimated to be as high as $80–100 billion for Latin America alone after 1984, is an important indicator of distorted economic policies in debtor countries.[87] Moreover, it is largely within the debtors' capacity to encourage capital repatriation through the pursuit of sound macroeconomic and industrial policy in key areas such as interest rates, fiscal policy, realistic exchange rates, liberalization of sectors previously preserved for state-owned enterprises, and privatization programs aimed at encouraging private sector initiatives. Continuing democratic reforms, particularly in the major Latin American states and other debtors such as the Philippines, would also have encouraged such repatriation. It was unrealistic to assume that commercial bank funds or direct foreign investment would materialize on any reasonable scale until flight capital began to be repatriated.[88] As Morgan Guaranty notes, "The acid test for stabilization in the debtor countries is to stem this drain and at least create a climate that encourages the repatriation of funds held abroad by their own residents."[89]

Economic Opening and Trade Protectionism

A critical constraint on debt service is the ability of debtors to export. In the case of several developing countries, such as Mexico, Brazil, Argentina, and Turkey, debtors imposed this constraint on themselves by following closed development strategies, largely based on import substitution, that discouraged exports. The experience of the Asian newly industrialized countries (NICs), trade liberalization, and non-oil export development by Mexico, following the 1980s crisis, demonstrated that outward, export-oriented strategies can be successful.[90] Export growth, however, also requires takers (importers). Perhaps no factor was more important to resolving the debt problem than maintaining OECD economic growth and broadening the base of importers for the products of deeply indebted countries, particularly in light of the urgent necessity for the United States to reduce its own trade deficit. This shift also required "Japan and Europe to put aside their deep-seated mercantilist instincts in favor of importing more and rooting out barriers to trade."[91]

Debt Service Tied to Trade

In the nineteenth century, debt service following default was often tied to import duties on specific goods—for example, tobacco or spirits as a form of "sin" tax, or the export of key commodities such as coffee or guano. In the 1980s debt crisis, there were proposals for debt restructurings with debt service based on the debtor's capacity to pay, tied, for example, to a percentage of exports.[92] For countries particularly reliant on single commodity exports such as oil or basic metals—Mexico, Indonesia, Nigeria, Zambia, Zaire, and Peru—export-linked payments would have had to realistically reflect their economic prospects and their ability to service their debt.

Alternative Financial Instruments

The use of more flexible, creative financial instruments could have reduced the risk of higher debt service costs to debtors that arose in the 1980s crisis through a rise in variable interest rate loans tied to the London Interbank Offered Rate (LIBOR) or the U.S. prime rate. Capitalizing the interest in arrears, variable maturity loans and payment smoothing using a reimbursable interest-averaging cap, or specifying a ceiling for interest payments would have reduced the uncertainty associated with servicing the commercial banks' variable rate loans and would have prevented the need for sharp compression of imports in debtor countries whenever interest rates rose. The Brady Plan introduced a number of such alternatives in a menu-driven approach to debt restructuring.[93]

Additional Resources

In all past debt crises, defaulting debtors have been enticed to restructure their debts by a commitment from creditors to provide fresh resources or to open capital markets that have been closed. In the major restructurings in the 1980s, the debtors clearly did not obtain what they were seeking. Nevertheless, fresh resources were made available from a mix of sources—commercial banks, creditor governments, the IMF, and the World Bank. These funds also combined long-term, intermediate-term, and trade credit lines, an approach more in keeping with the debtors' needs for a hetero-geneous mix of funds.[94] (See chapter 7, table 7-2.)

It is clear, however, that relatively few debtors obtained new financing, as the banks continued to see their problems as part of a small numbers game. Voluntary lending from commercial banks came to a virtual standstill in the 1990s, except in support of a Brady Plan agreement, and even in these cases the numbers were small. The East Asian economies not affected by the debt crisis were able to obtain signifi-cant bank funding, particularly from banks and large corporate groups, because financial sectors and capital markets in these countries were liberalized.

The United States, the world's principal financial power since World War II, was not able to take the lead on this issue because of its own growing external indebted-ness and its internal difficulties with cutting its budget deficit. The one financial power able to take leadership in the 1980s was Japan. At the annual meeting of the IMF on September 27, 1988, Japan tabled a new proposal on debt that would essen-tially have set aside the Baker Plan. The proposal was to convert a portion of com-mercial bank debt to long-term bonds. The plan was rejected by the U.S. secretary of the Treasury, Nicholas F. Brady.[95] What is interesting, however, was Japan's de-parture from its previous reluctance to take a leadership role in world economic or financial policy outside the G-7. Clearly the Brady initiative was an effort by the United States to replace the Baker Plan with an initiative that maintained the pro-cess of creditors and debtors negotiating on a case-by-case basis, with enhancements offered by the multilateral institutions—the IMF and World Bank—and bilateral institutions such as Japan's Export-Import Bank.

Creditor governments have largely resisted efforts to raise the restructuring ne-gotiations to the level of multilateral diplomatic negotiations between creditor and debtor governments, maintaining their preference for a case-by-case approach. The range of international relations issues that the debt problem raised implied that the issue of debt restructuring was likely to remain on the international agenda for the foreseeable future.[96]

Keynes once questioned whether it was serious politics to expect Germany to pay a large percentage of its export earnings year after year in the form of reparations. He also questioned the wisdom of the United States and Great Britain demanding repayment by their former Allies for inter-Allied war debts, which he and others termed political debts.[97] That question, which was raised as a result of difficult eco-nomic recovery and reconstruction in the interwar years, was no less valid in the 1980s.

Part III

GLOBALIZATION, FINANCIAL SECTOR LIBERALIZATION, AND EMERGING MARKET CRISES, 1990–2005

NINE

The Flow of Capital to Emerging Markets

1990–2005

For many emerging market countries,[1] the 1990s began with the debt overhang from the 1980s debt crisis and the adoption of the Brady Plan (1989) focused on debt reduction and forgiveness.[2] By the mid-1990s many of these highly indebted countries, after multiple debt restructurings and debt reduction agreements, were now able to manage their debt service. Lending moved from primarily syndicated commercial bank loans in the 1980s to primarily sovereign bond issues. Syndicated loans were at some 20–30 percent of total sovereign lending.[3] As the decade progressed, bank loans in Mexico and a number of East Asian countries were increasingly to the private sector, to banks or larger corporations, and short-term in nature. Short-term debts for several of these countries were in excess of foreign exchange reserves, making these countries more vulnerable to crisis.[4]

The major story of this period is globalization. Although liberalizing trade and reducing trade barriers is an important aspect of globalization, the primary emphasis of this chapter is on financial sector liberalization and the movement of private capital in a variety of ways to developing, emerging market, and transition countries. During this period the highly indebted Latin American countries undertook substantial structural reforms, including privatization, which led to the restructuring of large loss-making state-owned enterprises (SOEs) to increase their competitiveness and to reduce their external debt, which these enterprises had acquired and was guaranteed by their respective governments.[5]

This period also witnessed the opening up of countries in Central and Eastern Europe (CEE) and the former Soviet Union (FSU) and, at a later date, after the conflict was over starting in around 2001, the countries of the former Yugoslavia in southeastern Europe (SEE) and their transition to market economies. The focus of the transition to market economies was on liberalization, stabilization, and structural reforms such as privatization. Liberalization included the freeing of prices and opening of markets such as the "greenfield" establishment of hundreds of thousands of small and medium-sized enterprises in these countries that were stimulating job creation and growth. Liberalization also saw the opening of the financial sector and the creation of capital markets. Liberalization was supported by structural reforms such as laws governing private property—the laws governing contracts, corporate or company law, securities laws, bankruptcy and antimonopoly laws, and the privatization of industry and the banking sector.[6]

Toward the middle of the 1990s and continuing for the rest of this period, ten of the Central and Eastern European countries negotiated association agreements followed by accession treaties with the European Union, with reforms and economic support continuing under the oversight of the European Commission.[7]

After an intensive push focused on market reforms beginning in 1992, the reform efforts in the Russian Federation (Russia) collapsed toward the last quarter of 1995, with loans-for-shares transactions corrupting the privatization program and emergence of the financial/economic crisis in 1998. The appointment of Vladimir Putin to replace Boris Yeltsin as president on December 31, 1999, sealed the fate of promarket reforms. Under Putin, Russia has selectively renationalized former state-owned firms, primarily in the energy sector, and shut down whatever reform program remained.[8]

This period also saw the emergence of China as a transition economy following its own model of state-led capitalism. China's dynamic growth as a controlled market economy focused on export-led growth in the style of the earlier East Asian countries such as Japan, Hong Kong, Taiwan, Singapore, Malaysia, and Korea, and continued unabated during this era, making it one of the world's largest economies and a pivotal player both politically and economically.[9] China's approach to transition was quite different from that of the CEE, where political reform led the process of economic transition. The CEE countries were embraced by the Western democracies and moved rapidly to Western-style capitalism as they broke away from the FSU. Chinese reforms were also substantially different from those of Russia. Russia under Yeltsin moved toward democracy and capitalism, but Russia was breaking away from the political and economic system to which it had given birth. With concerns that the communists would reassert their power, a small, tight circle of reformers, led by Anatoli Chubais, moved aggressively to privatize as quickly as possible to make the reform process irreversible. In contrast, China moved cautiously, emphasizing control of the political system by the Communist Party and a highly centralized leadership. By the end of the era China had attracted some 13 percent of all external capital flows to emerging markets, much of it from the Chinese diaspora in Asia, had become the largest exporter and the largest manufacturing economy in the world, and had accumulated foreign exchange reserves in excess of a trillion dollars.[10]

A Diverse Source of Funds to the Emerging and Transition Economies

During this decade there was a large and diverse stream of capital to emerging market and transition economies (see tables 9-1, 9-2, 9-3, and 9-4). This capital flowed primarily to the private sector—financial institutions and industrial corporations as well as real estate and construction in the form of foreign direct investment (FDI), much of it initially tied to privatization and follow-on investments to modernize newly acquired SOEs. Privatization through initial public offerings (IPOs) or mixed privatizations including tenders and a tranche of shares offered to the public in selected sectors such as telecommunications (telecom) also attracted foreign investors. Substantial capital also flowed to capital markets in emerging markets and newly created capital markets in transition economies, largely through recently created emerging market investment funds. Much of this capital from emerging market investment funds was short-term in nature and eventually presented a problem to countries that experienced economic difficulties. When confidence eroded this capital moved quickly in a "flight to quality" to more developed markets. Larger companies in emerging market economies were also able to raise capital in the form of American depository receipts (ADRs) and global depository receipts (GDRs) primarily in the New York markets—the New York Stock Exchange and NASDAQ—and in London.[11]

In total from 1990 through 1995, some $1,640 billion, most of it private, flowed from the advanced industrial economies and their capital markets to the developing and transition economies. Latin America and the Caribbean captured 26 percent of those flows, East Asia (excluding China) 21 percent, China on its own 13 percent, the CEE and FSU 15 percent, the Middle East and North Africa 9 percent, sub-Saharan Africa 9 percent, and South Asia 9 percent.[12]

TABLE 9-1.   Net Long-Term Resource Flows to Developing Countries, 1990–97

Billions of US$

Type of flow	1990	1991	1992	1993	1994	1995	1996	1997[a]
All developing countries	98.3	116.3	143.9	208.1	206.2	243.1	281.6	300.3
Official development finance	56.4	62.7	53.8	53.6	45.5	54.0	34.7	44.2
Total private flows	41.9	53.6	90.1	154.6	160.6	189.1	246.9	256.0
Debt flows	15.0	13.5	33.8	44.0	41.1	55.1	82.2	103.2
Commercial bank loans	3.8	3.4	13.1	2.8	8.9	29.3	34.3	41.1
Bonds	0.1	7.4	8.3	31.8	27.5	23.8	45.7	53.8
Other	11.1	2.7	12.4	9.4	4.7	2.0	2.3	8.3
Foreign direct investment	23.7	32.9	45.3	65.6	86.9	101.5	119.0	120.4
Portfolio equity flows	3.2	7.2	11.0	45.0	32.6	32.5	45.8	32.5

Source: World Bank Debtor Reporting System database; *World Bank Global Development Finance 1998* (Washington: World Bank, 1998), p. 9.

a. Preliminary.

TABLE 9-2.   Foreign Direct Investment (FDI) Flows to the Top Ten Recipient Developing Countries, 1991, 1994, and 1997

Billions of US$

Country	1991	Country	1994	Country	1997[a]
Mexico	4.7	China	33.8	China	37.0
China	4.3	Mexico	11.0	Brazil	15.8
Malaysia	4.0	Malaysia	4.3	Mexico	8.1
Argentina	2.4	Peru	3.1	Indonesia	5.8
Thailand	2.0	Brazil	3.1	Poland	4.5
Venezuela	1.9	Argentina	3.1	Malaysia	4.1
Indonesia	1.5	Indonesia	2.1	Argentina	3.8
Hungary	1.5	Nigeria	1.9	Chile	3.5
Brazil	1.1	Poland	1.9	India	3.1
Turkey	0.8	Chile	1.8	Venezuela	2.9
Top ten share in FDI to all developing countries (percent)	74.2		76.1		72.3

Source: World Bank data and staff estimates; *World Bank Global Development Finance 1998*, p. 20.

a. Preliminary.

TABLE 9-3. Developing Countries' Short-Term Debt Stocks, 1994–97

Billions of US$

Region	1994	1995	1996	1997[a]
All developing countries	286.2	324.0	345.8	360.9
East Asia and the Pacific	79.9	104.2	116.6	123.9
Europe and Central Asia	30.8	36.2	43.1	41.2
Latin America and the Caribbean	105.2	110.9	111.7	120.4
Middle East and North Africa	48.6	46.1	44.9	45.5
South Asia	7.0	9.0	10.2	10.0
Sub-Saharan Africa	14.8	17.5	19.3	20.8

Source: World Bank and Bank for International Settlements; *World Bank Global Development Finance 1998*, p. 9; excludes interest arrears on short-term debt.

a. As of June 1997.

TABLE 9-4. Privatization Revenues by Region and Sector, 1990–96

	Amount (billions of US$)	Percent
Region		
East Asia and the Pacific	27.1	17
Europe and Central Asia	30.5	20
Latin America and the Caribbean	82.4	53
Middle East and North Africa	3.5	2
Sub-Saharan Africa	3.8	3
South Asia	8.0	5
Total	147.3	100
Sector		
Agriculture and mining	65	42
Financial services	37	24
Industry	26	17
Infrastructure	22	14
Other services	5	3
Total	155	100

Source: Ira Lieberman and Christopher D. Kirkness, eds., *Privatization and Emerging Equity Markets* (Washington D.C.: World Bank and Flemings, 1998).

Privatization and Other Structural Reforms in Developing and Transitional Economies

Following the debt crises in the 1980s (as discussed in Part II of this book), many developing, emerging market, and transition countries began serious reforms under what is known as the Washington Consensus. A significant portion of these reforms were structural, and privatization—the sale or divestment of state-owned enterprises (SOEs) by governments was the major such reform.

Background—Why Privatization Was So Important

In 1993 I called privatization the development theme of the 1990s.[13] This may or may not be true for the developing or emerging market economies, but it was certainly true for the transition economies of Central and Eastern Europe and the former Soviet Union. The most common explanation for the importance of privatization and related structural reforms for many of the developing countries during this period was the debt crisis in the early 1980s and the years of debt restructuring thereafter. The sovereign debt burdens in these countries led them through a decade of low to negative growth, macroeconomic instability, and a series of forced structural adjustments. Developing countries were simply unable to continue supporting the fiscal burden of large loss-making SOEs. Although the sovereign debt crises of the 1980s should not be minimized, other factors and issues emerged that required the adoption of privatization programs as a critical feature of economic policy.[14]

The first key factor was the highly successful economic performance of Japan and the East Asian newly industrialized countries (NICs)—Korea, Singapore, Taiwan, Hong Kong, Malaysia, and Thailand. Despite significant differences in their domestic economies and industrial structures, they all followed a model for growth characterized by intense competition, an outward orientation that emphasized exports, and a primary role for the private sector. During the 1980s none of these countries experienced an economic crisis. Developing countries in Latin America and international financial institutions such as the International Monetary Fund (IMF) and World Bank took note of their performance.[15]

Second, at the same time that the economic model followed by Japan and the Asian NICS was proving so successful, other models of development, such as an emphasis on import substitution in Latin America and the command economies in the CEE and FSU, had outlived their usefulness and needed to be reformed. In many countries such in Latin America, in Turkey and Egypt, and in Africa large SOEs in basic sectors of the economy such as telecommunications, electricity, water and sanitation, mining, steel, cement, oil and gas, petrochemicals, fertilizers, ports and airports, and banking dominated the economy.

A particular weakness of these inward, highly protective economic models was the inversion of the "infant industry" argument. It implied that developing countries once having developed "strategic" or "priority" sectors, such as those cited above, most often through state-owned monopolies and almost always with substantial subsidies, had to continue protecting them because they were too fragile and too uncompetitive to compete in the domestic or international markets. The anti-export bias of these regimes and the numerous trade restrictions companies faced meant that most companies—private or SOEs—were unable to compete in export markets. Moreover, if these primary sectors were uncompetitive, it was almost impossible for downstream private producers in these markets to be competitive.

In the transition economies of the CEE and FSU some 90 percent or more of industrial production was owned and operated by SOEs, before privatization. The emphasis on heavy industry crowded out the development of a service sector. Even small and medium-sized enterprises (SMEs) in retailing and the service sector, to the extent that they existed, were state owned.[16]

A third factor that emerged in the 1980s and accelerated the need for reforms was what some analysts called the fourth industrial revolution. Driven by information-based technologies, these nonsmokestack industries such as telecommunications, computers, fiber optics, robotics, biotechnology, and advanced composite materials were largely absent in the developing and transition economies. An important aspect of this revolution were newly adopted managerial practices, some developed in Japan, such as just-in-time manufacturing systems, the extensive use of computer-aided design and computer-aided manufacturing (CAD/CAM), computer-integrated manufacturing systems (CIM) in design and fabrication, and total quality control had a profound impact on productivity and efficiency. These techniques were also largely absent in developing and transition economies that were inwardly oriented. The pace of change in the world economy and a necessary commitment to research and development to stay competitive made it impossible for these SOEs to remain under state control or within a command economy—where decisions were invariably politicized and reaction to market signals sluggish—and compete in the world economy.[17]

As a fourth factor, SOEs in many of these closed or inward-looking countries were characterized by: (i) highly politicized and centralized economies; (ii) overstaffing due to political patronage; (iii) exclusion of competitive imports (focus on import substitution); (iv) corrupt practices; and, (iv) vehicles for capital flight. In addition, in the transition economies, large SOEs were responsible for operating social assets such as canteens that fed the workers and often their families, health clinics, kindergartens, vacation spas, sports teams, and often transportation and utilities when the SOE was the sole or dominant employer in a "one company town."

In the mid-1980s and early 1990s in response to the debt crisis, many of the emerging market countries such as Mexico, Turkey, and Argentina sought to restructure their large SOEs. The bureaucrats who had been incapable of managing these firms in the first place clearly lacked the skills to restructure them. Moreover, many of the countries lacked the fiscal resources or debt capacity to continue feeding them until they turned around.[18]

A fifth factor influencing privatization in the developing and transition countries is that in the 1980s advanced industrial countries, such as the United Kingdom during the Thatcher administration and the United States during the Reagan administration, began to express strong ideological commitments to private enterprise. Prime Minister Margret Thatcher sought to revive Britain's flagging industrial and economic performance, by introducing an extensive privatization program. The creation of millions of small-scale share owners through preferential share ownership programs during the privatization of firms such as British Telecoms and British Gas, also led to a deepening of the stock market and political support for the program, the cornerstone of the Thatcher administration's political and economic agenda. In 1986, New Zealand, under the direction of Finance Minister Rodger Douglas, began sweeping reforms of the SOE sector, including privatization. The success of the U.K. and New Zealand privatization programs led to an intellectual discussion and debate on this subject throughout the world.[19] The international financial institutions such as the World Bank swiftly moved their focus from support for restructuring of SOEs to privatization. The World Bank and IMF, without doubt spurred on by their major shareholders such as the United States and the United Kingdom, began to push a reform agenda known as the "Washington Consensus,"[20] which focused on liberalization, stabilization, and structural reforms, in which privatization played a major role.[21]

Sixth was the opening of the CEE and the FSU starting in 1989 with the fall of the Berlin Wall; in 1991 the breakup of the FSU gave added impetus to privatization. As the transition economies moved from socialism (command economies) toward market economies, privatization was at the center of these reforms. It soon became clear to all of the reform governments in the region that you could not have a private market economy without a critical mass of private companies. By 1995 virtually all of the transition countries in the CEE had privatized more than 50 percent of SOEs, including SMEs, and more than 50 percent of employment was in the private sector.

TABLE 9-5. Privatization Revenues, 1990–96

Region	Amount (billions of US$)	Percent
East Asia and the Pacific		
China	7.9	29
Indonesia	5.0	19
Malaysia	9.3	34
Philippines	3.4	12
Thailand	1.2	5
Other	0.3	1
Europe and Central Asia		
Czech Republic	2.2	7
Hungary	10.2	33
Poland	3.6	12
Russia	2.4	8
Slovak Republic	2.0	6
Turkey	3.1	10
Other	7.0	23
Latin America and the Caribbean		
Argentina	23.5	29
Brazil	15.6	19
Colombia	2.6	3
Mexico	26.0	32
Peru	6.2	8
Venezuela	4.5	5
Other	4.0	5
Middle East and North Africa		
Egypt	1.9	55
Morocco	1.1	32
Tunisia	0.1	4
Other	0.3	9

Source: Lieberman and Kirkness, eds., *Privatization and Emerging Equity Markets.*

Privatization Revenue Flows

Starting in 1990 and peaking in 1996 at $25 billion, privatization revenue flows reached $155 billion in developing and transition countries by 1996 (see table 9-5). Privatization in Latin America peaked by 1996, but privatization continued into the 2000s as the countries of the former Yugoslavia, after the conflict and period of isolation was over, began their own reforms, including privatization.

TABLE 9-6.   Foreign Exchange Raised through Privatization in
Emerging Markets, 1990–96

Millions of US$

Region	1990	1991	1992	1993	1994	1995	1996	Total
Latin America and the Caribbean	6,358	7,384	4,037	3,765	5,058	2,206	6,302	35,111
Europe and Central Asia	586	1,892	3,069	2,932	1,588	4,778	1,880	16,726
East Asia and the Pacific	1	102	1,556	4,156	4,036	2,026	1,990	13,865
Sub-Saharan Africa	38	5	66	566	453	275	299	1,702
South Asia	11	4	44	16	997	38	528	1,638
Middle East and North Africa	0	3	19	183	246	16	126	594
Total	6,994	9,390	8,791	11,619	12,378	9,338	11,125	69,636

Source: Lieberman and Kirkness, eds., *Privatization and Emerging Equity Markets.*

Mexico and Argentina, for example, mounted aggressive privatization programs in response to the issues cited above—fiscal deficits, specifically the drain on the budget of large SOEs, debt overhang from the 1980s crisis, and lack of competitiveness due to the SOEs' domination of upstream manufacturing sectors such as steel, oil and petrochemicals, and utilities—telecommunications and electricity. By 1996, Latin America had generated some $82.4 billion in privatization revenue (53 percent of privatization revenues), the CEE and FSU (Europe and Central Asia) $30 billion (20 percent), East Asia and the Pacific $27.1 billion (17 percent), South Asia $8.0 billion (5 percent), sub-Saharan Africa $3.8 billion (3 percent), and the Middle East and North Africa $3.5 billion (2 percent)

Infrastructure privatization—of telecom and electricity, for example—was the most important sector and attracted significant FDI to emerging and transition economies. Infrastructure privatization attracted $65 billion (42 percent of revenues); natural resource companies—oil and gas, agriculture, and mining $26 billion (17 percent); industry—mainly steel, chemicals, and construction materials (cement), $37 billion (24 percent); financial services, primarily banking $22 billion (14 percent); and other services $5 billion (3 percent).

During the 1990s virtually all foreign (external) privatization revenues entered these countries through direct investments, but portfolio investments were substantial as well. From 1990 to 1996 portfolio investments amounted to $26.5 billion, and FDI was $43.2 billion. Total foreign exchange raised through privatization during this period was $69.6 billion, almost half of it by Latin America (see tables 9-6 and 9-7).[22]

TABLE 9-7. Portfolio Investment and Foreign Direct Investment
in Privatization, 1990–96

Millions of US$

Type	1990	1991	1992	1993	1994	1995	1996	Total
Portfolio investment	106	3,873	2,752	5,190	5,965	2,959	5,627	26,472
Foreign direct investment	6,888	5,517	6,039	6,429	6,414	6,380	5,498	43,164
Total	6,994	9,390	8,791	11,619	12,378	9,338	11,125	69,636

Lieberman and Kirkness, eds., *Privatization and Emerging Equity Markets.*

Emerging Capital (Equity) Markets

Equity markets play an important role in private market economies by allocating capital to firms that require it and where it can be put to best use. Equity markets are also important politically in support of economic reforms, especially privatization, providing the citizens of the country a stake in the economy and the opportunity to participate in the benefits of economic growth and development. Many governments supported employee ownership in firms as part of the privatization process, and also the participation of the average citizen, to soften the resistance to privatization.

At the start of the 1990s most capital markets in emerging market countries were moribund, crowded out by government bond issues needed by governments to raise funds to cover fiscal deficits. Capital markets in the transition countries did not exist and were linked closely to the privatization programs and major efforts at legal reform in the region. Privatization required a privatization law and supplementing regulations governing the privatization process. These laws and regulations were invariably supplemented by the drafting of a modern company law and securities laws. Newly created capital markets also required the presence of a securities and exchange commission and regulations and systems governing operations of these markets. In addition, many of the countries developed bankruptcy and antimonopoly regimes backed by new laws governing these areas.[23]

Emerging Market Equity Market Growth and Development

During the early 1990s there was strong growth in the capitalization of emerging equity markets. An improved outlook for emerging market growth attracted funds from foreign investors, often through emerging market equity funds, and pushed valuations upward. In 1993 alone, the capitalization of emerging markets grew by

80 percent. Although growth in emerging markets slowed in 1994–95 because of the Mexican crisis, growth recovered in 1996–97 and declined again toward the end of 1997 because of the East Asia crisis. Market values declined sharply in several East Asian economies: Indonesia, Korea, and Thailand. These crises and others at the end of the 1990s demonstrated the vulnerability of emerging markets to crises of confidence.[24]

As capital markets in emerging market and transition countries grew and deepened—there were more listed companies with greater stock market liquidity, and listed companies had a higher percentage of their shares trading actively—external portfolio investors were attracted to these markets. Markets needed to achieve a critical mass of large companies in order to attract external investors, and daily higher trading volumes in order to support the liquidity and diversification required by investors. Markets also had to be large enough and have enough trading volume to create the necessary infrastructure to support automated trading and information systems, brokers and analysts, advisers, and regulators. As noted, a liquid and well-regulated market was of particular importance to foreign investors.

In the CEE and FSU virtually every country established a national capital market. For the most part they remained weak, with little liquidity and not enough depth to absorb IPOs or other listings. They attracted few external portfolio investors. Poland and to some extent the Czech Republic were different. The Russian capital market also attracted capital from external portfolio investors and dedicated investment funds for a limited period of time following its mass privatization (voucher) program, the establishment of a securities and exchange commission, and an electronic trading system linking some 400 broker-dealers throughout Russia.[25] Russian companies were also able to raise capital through American depository receipts—the value of Russian ADRs rose from $28 million in 1996 to $8 billion by May 1997.[26] However, the turning away from economic reforms and the lack of transparent large-scale privatization transaction, in particular IPOs, following the loans-for-shares transactions in late 1995 removed the needed supply of companies from the market and also dampened enthusiasm of investors for what had been previously viewed as a successful and largely transparent privatization program. The financial/economic crisis in 1998, Putin's assumption of power, and the renationalization of some of the energy companies largely killed external investor interest in the market.

In the emerging market countries equity markets were initially catalyzed by the IPOs of major SOEs, above all telecom companies. The privatization of telecom companies took center stage in privatization programs worldwide; of the $123 billion invested in emerging market privatization programs worldwide, $30 billion, or

24 percent, was invested in telecom companies from 1990 to 1996 and a long list of national companies was slated to be privatized thereafter.[27] As Phumchai Kambhato of Flemings noted:

> Telecom privatization offerings in emerging markets usually: (i) is a country's first major privatization issue and largest capital raising of any nature; (ii) is one of the largest companies on the domestic stock exchange substantially increasing market capitalization and trading volume; (iii) attracts significant foreign portfolio investment into the domestic market for the first time; (iv) increases the size and sophistication of the domestic institutional investor base; (v) broadens the domestic retail investor base attracting first-time equity investors; and, (vi) sets a precedent for marketing and execution of future privatizations.[28]

The Role of Emerging Market Investment Funds

Emerging market investment funds (EMFs) played a crucial role in intermediating funds for emerging capital markets during this period (transition country markets are also included under emerging markets).[29] These funds were usually structured as mutual funds in the United States or investment funds or trust funds in the United Kingdom. Their primary function was to intermediate capital to emerging markets from primary sources of capital such as pension funds and insurance companies. Their basic investment rationale was that emerging markets were growing rapidly, they offered investment diversification, and their performance was often not correlated to markets in the advanced economies. Most often these funds were part of a family of EMFs, and in turn many of the EMFs were tied to much larger mutual fund groups. EMFs were structured variously as global funds investing throughout the developing and transition markets. Regional funds focused on Latin America, East Asia, or Central and Eastern Europe; or country-specific funds might focus on China or Brazil. There were also bond funds and specialized equity funds focused on privatization IPOs or infrastructure.[30]

The first global fund, the Emerging Markets Growth Fund, was created in 1986 with some $50 million in capital. In less than ten years its capital had reached $5.5 billion. By the mid-1990s some one thousand EMFs were managing more than $100 billion in capital. Despite the market turbulence created by the Mexican crisis (1994–95), more than half the U.S. pension funds had assets invested in emerging markets by the end of 1996. Also, by 1996 the Global Composite Index of the International

Finance Corporation (part of the World Bank Group) was tracking 1,650 stocks in its Investable Composite Index and twenty-seven emerging markets in the Global Composite Index. At $2 trillion, emerging markets were ten times their size at the end of 1996 than they had been ten years earlier.[31]

American and Global Depository Receipts

In addition to mobilizing funds from domestic capital markets, larger firms in emerging market countries were able to attract capital through depository receipts (DRs): ADRs raised primarily in the New York capital market or GDRs raised mostly in the London capital market. DRs did not represent direct share ownership in these offshore companies, but instead were proxies, negotiable certificates, that provided evidence of ownership in these companies. These certificates are created by a depository in a custodian bank that holds the counterpart shares of the company being financed. As such, the DRs could be issued and listed in New York, London, or Luxembourg with various degrees of disclosure and regulatory rigor depending on who was able to purchase the DR—institutional investors or the investing public. The market in DRs was typically more liquid and more easily traded than the emerging country capital markets and as such met the needs of large, sophisticated, international institutional investors. These issues supported the development of these companies and nascent capital markets in emerging market countries by diversifying and deepening or broadening the capital offering—for example, in the Mexican telecom privatization or in a variety of Argentine offerings. They also set higher standards of reporting and disclosure than did many of the emerging markets, as well as cross-border valuations of these companies. Depository receipts are held in dollars, and dividends from the companies are converted in the spot foreign exchange market and paid out in dollars. Investors still bear the country and foreign exchange risk of the underlying share issuer. Clearing and settlement was handled by the Depository Trust Company in the United States and by Euroclear or Cedel in Europe, so clearing and settlement were more efficient than in domestic markets.[32]

Since their inception in 1983, and despite setbacks such as the Mexican peso crisis, the number of participating companies and amounts issued grew exponentially by 1986. Most of the growth began after 1991 and the resolution of the 1980s debt crisis. By the end of 1986 some 1,300 companies had accessed depository receipts from sixty-three countries. Some 736 issues raised almost $95 billion of new capital. Of this amount, 27 percent came from Asia and the Pacific, 53 percent from Europe and Africa, and 21 percent from Latin America. Depository receipts played a role in virtually every large-scale privatization transaction, and many of these were telecom privatizations.[33]

As it has emerged, the market for ADRs and GDRs has allowed a diversified set of larger emerging market companies to raise more equity than their own nascent markets could absorb. The market supported large-scale privatizations through IPOs or mixed sales with a partial IPO, as well as issues by large private and state-owned companies that partially privatized, such as Gazprom in Russia.

Financial and Banking Sector Deregulation and Cross-Border Flows

The liberalization of constraints on the capital accounts of many of the developing, emerging market, and transition economies, combined with the liberalization of the financial sector, especially the banking sector, supported an enormous inflow of FDI into these countries. Much of this FDI was derived from privatization revenues and portfolio flows. In addition, as the decade progressed, many countries experienced substantial external short-term banking flows, largely to the private sector either through commercial banks or other financial vehicles for intermediation or directly to corporate borrowers. Steven Radelet and Jeffrey Sachs note:

> International capital market liberalization in the industrial countries facilitated a greater flow of funds to emerging markets around the globe. New bond and equity mutual funds, new bank syndicates, increased Eurobond lending, and other innovation allowed capital to flow across borders quickly and easily. In addition, low interest rates in the U.S. and Japan favoured increased outward investment from these countries to Southeast Asia and other emerging markets.[34]

Radelet and Sachs cite five primary reasons for these capital flows, in particular to the East Asian economies but more broadly applicable to other emerging market economies:

1. The continuing, and at the time high, level of economic growth gave confidence to investors.

2. Wide-ranging financial de-regulation made it much easier for banks and corporations in emerging economies to tap into external capital markets to finance domestic investments.

3. Financial sector de-regulation was not supported by strengthened supervision in most cases so that risks rose un-checked by regulators/supervisors.

4. Nominal exchange rates were effectively pegged to the dollar for many of the countries so foreign exchange risks were perceived as minimal; and

5. Some governments provided incentives to encourage external capital inflows.[35]

While foreign direct investment was viewed as a desirable outcome of the Washington Consensus, bringing with it investors who had access to technology, good managerial practices, and capital and markets,[36] the same was not necessarily true for short-term capital flows to emerging country capital markets or for loans, especially short-term loans. As noted in earlier sections of this book, short-term loans in excess of trade requirements, with trade finance considered self-liquidating, often presaged or signaled a crisis. A measure of a country's ability to absorb short-term capital flows was its ratio of short-term debt to reserves. Foreign currency reserves in principle allow a country to react to a change in sentiment and the reverse of flows in what is often referred to as a "flight to quality."

In the 1990s few countries built the reserves necessary to mitigate a potential reversal. Moreover, short-term flows often led to maturity mismatches, especially investments that led to speculative bubbles in real estate. Reserves are also expensive for countries to maintain; there is an opportunity cost to leaving these reserves sitting idle, earning little, instead of deploying the foreign currency in productive investments. The East Asia crisis that began in Thailand in 1997 and moved rapidly to Korea, Malaysia, and Indonesia, and the Russian crisis in 1998, saw the buildup of short-term debts relative to reserves in each of these countries except Malaysia, which avoided a rescue package. Malaysia established controls over short-term capital flows, as did Chile. Malaysia's policy decision to establish capital controls was initially highly criticized by the IMF and an array of free market economists. Following the East Asia crisis this decision was reassessed and credited with contributing to moderating a potentially deeper crisis as experienced by, for example, Thailand, Indonesia, and Korea. Mexico also saw a buildup of short-term debts before its crisis.[37]

By the mid-1990s, taking five East Asian countries as an example, with data from the Bank for International Settlements (BIS), total obligations of the five countries grew from $210 billion to $260 billion in 1996 alone. Obligations by their domestic banking sector increased from $91 billion to $115 billion in that same year, and short-term debts owed to banks by these countries reached $147 billion in 1996. The actual level of liabilities was in fact higher because BIS data did not track offshore lending and borrowing through the issue of commercial paper by corporations.[38]

Discussing the East Asian crisis and its impact on other emerging market countries, Joseph Stiglitz, who at the time of the crisis was chief economist of the World

Bank, wrote: "The fact that such a large number of countries have been affected by this crisis and required large official bailouts suggests some fundamental systemic weakness. In order to deal with the risks posed by large capital flows, especially significant when financial systems are weak, the report suggests that reforms must be comprehensive."[39]

Conclusions: The Impact of Private Capital Flows in Emerging and Transition Economies

The diversity and level of financial flows to emerging market and transition economies were in principle an important outcome of the structural reforms these countries undertook during the 1990s. Large-scale privatization revenues should in principle have led to large external debt reductions. Significant levels of FDI should have supported restructuring, modernization, and greater productivity and efficiency in the private economy and in support of infrastructure. It soon became clear that such flows, particularly short-term portfolio flows and short-term loans, with inadequate regulation and supervision of weak banking systems and nascent capital markets, increased vulnerability to crises and exacerbated it during this period, especially as confidence eroded in emerging markets and contagion spread. In several countries asset bubbles formed, particularly in real estate. Each crisis reflected a different set of country circumstances and level of external flows relative to GDP and other measures, as we will see in the chapters that follow.

Countries in sub-Saharan Africa and other very poor developing countries were typically not part of this massive flow of capital to emerging markets. A number of developing countries, particularly the poorest ones, benefited from debt forgiveness programs supported by the World Bank and IMF under the HIPC Initiative.[40]

TEN

Emerging Market Crises and the Mexican Crisis

1994–97

Despite the structural reforms that took place in many of the emerging market economies during the latter part of the 1980s and through the mid-1990s, the process of transition in Central and Eastern Europe and the former Soviet Union, supported by the substantial flow of external funding to these economies, several important emerging market economies experienced crises: Mexico (1994), East Asia (1997), Turkey (2001), and Argentina (2001); also Russia (1998), a major transition economy; and some of the advanced industrial countries—Sweden, Norway, Finland, and Japan. Some analysts have categorized these crises as currency or financial crises, depending on the country in question. Several of them morphed into sovereign debt crises as market confidence eroded and a flight of capital, a "flight to quality," occurred from the crisis economies as the decade progressed. A number of these countries saw their foreign exchange reserves drained to meet repatriation demands of short-term foreign investors in their nascent capital markets and short-term lenders to the private sector—both banks and corporate entities. In most cases governments implicitly guaranteed the foreign loans owed by their banks.

This chapter discusses the Mexican crisis of 1994–97. Argentina and Brazil were also adversely affected by this crisis as contagion spread to emerging capital markets in the region. The Japanese crisis that has occupied much of the 1990s and the 2000s to date, and to a limited extent the Nordic crisis, are discussed in Part IV of the book, with the crises in other advanced industrial countries.

The Mexican Crisis, 1994–97

In 1994, Mexico experienced a currency crisis that triggered a banking crisis that deeply affected the entire economy. The Tequila Crisis, as it was known to many, had spillover or contagion effects on emerging markets, especially in Argentina.[1] The Mexican crisis was triggered by a major devaluation of the peso by the newly installed president of the republic, Ernesto Zedillo Ponce de León, in December 1994; the initial devaluation of 14 percent eventually reached 35 percent by early January 1995. The peso was also left to float.[2]

Macroeconomic Situation before the 1994 Crisis

During the 1980s, as Mexico recovered from the debt crisis, its macroeconomic situation reflected the difficult adjustment process as the government carried out a significant fiscal adjustment equal to 16 percent of GDP.[3] During this period the government undertook a series of economic reforms consistent with the Washington Consensus, including: (i) trade liberalization that sought to diversify exports away from concentration on and economic dependence away from oil; (ii) price liberalization, except for foods that were at the core of the Mexican diet—corn, tortillas, and frijoles (black beans); (iii) deregulation to support business startups and encourage the growth of existing businesses; (iv) structural reforms including demonopolizing and restructuring a number of large state-owned enterprises (SOEs) in fertilizers, steel, agribusiness, and telecommunications, as well as the banks, which were nationalized at the beginning of the crisis in 1982; and (v) eventually privatizing many of these SOEs to generate revenues and attract foreign direct investment (FDI).[4]

These measures took time to implement, and from 1982 to 1988 Mexico's growth averaged near zero. Inflation remained intermittently high during much of the 1980s, reaching 160 percent in 1987. By 1989 growth was restored, averaging 3.5 percent from 1989 to 1992, and inflation had declined (largely owing to the Solidarity Pact with the unions calling for wage restraint), though it remained too high, at 15–25 percent annually; it had fallen to 8 percent by 1993. The country ran large current account deficits, starting in 1989 at 4 percent and climbing 22.8 percent to 6.8 percent of GDP in 1992, largely because of trade liberalization and a surge of imports. Large portfolio and short-term debt inflows also contributed to the deficit.[5]

During the 1980s Mexico was also adversely affected by two external shocks—the large earthquake in 1985 that did enormous damage in Mexico City and the downward spike in oil prices in 1986 that made the adjustment process all the more difficult. In short, Mexico's economic reforms in the 1980s and early 1990s were a work in progress. Much still needed to be done to make the economy competitive and to orient the economy away from dependence on oil.

External Debt and Capital Flows

Total external debt rose substantially from $95 billion in 1989 to $142 billion in 1994; private sector debt grew from $19 billion to $57 billion over the same period. Direct foreign investment and portfolio investment rose substantially in the 1990s, largely reflecting privatization revenues and investor confidence in Mexican reforms, averaging $15.8 billion a year respectively from 1990 to 1993. Both FDI and foreign lending to Mexico dropped precipitously in 1994, reflecting investor loss of confidence in the economy. Foreign exchange reserves also declined in 1994, from $24.5 billion at the end of 1993 to $6 billion by the end of 1994.[6] Mexico was left with little alternative but to devalue, since its reserves were quickly drawn down.

Mexico's short-term debt obligations increased substantially during the 1990s leading up to the crisis, largely owing to government issue of some $17 billion in tesobonos, dollar-denominated treasury bonds, and private market debt issued by large corporate groups and the recently privatized banking system. Much of this debt was short term in nature. Short-term debt exceeded reserves by 1994, and Mexico became vulnerable to a crisis. Mexico's debt due to foreign banks was $64.6 billion at the end of 1994, of which $16.7 billion (26 percent) was held by Mexican banks, $24.9 (38.5 percent) was public sector debt, and $22.8 (35.3 percent) was nonbank private debt. Short-term debt was $33.2 billion greater than 50 percent of the total bank debt due, and reserves were $6.4 billion; so short-term debt was 5.2 times greater than reserves.[7]

The Political Situation

Politics in Mexico exacerbated the country's economic problems. During the runup to the presidential election in August 1994, with President Carlos Salinas nearing the end of his six-year term (the *sexeino*), his government was reluctant to take the economic measures necessary to deal with the looming crisis and devalue the peso. Also, President Salinas's candidate to succeed him for the PRI (Institutional Revolutionary Party),[8] Luis Donaldo Colosio, was assassinated while running for election, and a lesser-known candidate, Ernesto Zedillo, replaced him. After the PRI's victory in

August, in September the secretary general of the PRI, José Francisco Ruiz-Massieu, also was assassinated, and investors took this as a further sign of instability; portfolio investors and others began to withdraw their funds from Mexico.[9]

Spillover Effects

The crisis also had a strong adverse effect on international emerging markets, in particular Brazil and Argentina, with the latter seemingly most at risk because of its currency board. This was an early test of how emerging markets would react to a sovereign crisis where the primary debt holders were not a consortium of international banks, but rather individual and institutional bond holders. Stock prices fell some 7 percent in Brazil and Argentina within days after the devaluation, but more telling returns on the $130 billion Brady bond market turned negative at −29 percent for Mexican Brady bonds, −30 percent for Venezuela, and −13 percent for Argentina. The "Tequila Crisis" spread in the middle of January to emerging markets more broadly.[10]

The Banking Crisis

Internally the devaluation sparked a banking crisis. "The crisis that resulted from the 1994 peso devaluation caused serious deterioration of an already weak banking system."[11] The eighteen newly privatized banks were privatized primarily as bank holding companies, which allowed them to own a variety of financial service providers such as insurance companies and brokerage firms. The sale of the banks in 1991–92 represented a reversal of actions taken by the government in the 1980s debt crisis. As one of his last acts in office, President José López Portillo nationalized the banks in 1982 and reserved banking under state ownership and management. A constitutional amendment supported by President Salinas and presented to the Congress in May 1990, permitted private ownership of the banking system once again. Between 1991 and 1992 the government realized over $12 billion in privatization revenues for the government and a number of new capital market listings. Little of it represented external capital or FDI; all of the core owners of the banks were Mexican groups.[12] That would change after the crisis of 1994–95.

The purchasers were larger Mexican groups (*grupos financieros*), conglomerates, and financial service firms, but not experienced bankers. Conglomerate banking opened up the system to a number of risks that were not adequately addressed by regulation and supervision. There were no prudential norms at the conglomerate level, and conglomerates were not required to consolidate their financial statements. A large borrower, potentially a borrower within the group, could put the group at risk by borrowing from each of the entities, and that would not necessarily be recognized by financial sector supervisors. Conglomerate banking led to a concentration of financial services in Mexico and a concentration in risk.[13]

Bank management and operations were perceived as relatively weak after more than a decade of state ownership. Purchase price for the banks had normally been a multiple of book value, and in order for the investors to see a return on their investments, they began to lend aggressively and also offer other financial products such as credit cards and mortgages. Lending expanded very rapidly in a recently deregulated environment with loan growth averaging a real rate of 24 percent a year (8 times the growth of GDP) between1991 and 1994,[14] and reaching a peak of $117.8 billion in 1994.[15] Unable to fund this loan growth by domestic deposits, the banks began to raise funds in the international interbank market, from foreign banks. Starting at N$23 billion (new pesos) in 1991, loans from the interbank market, lines of credit from foreign banks, rose to N$124 billion in 1994, of which USD$17.3 billion was denominated in foreign currency.[16]

Government supervision of the banks under state ownership was also perceived as weak. With the privatization of the banks and the rapid growth of what had been a moribund capital market, the government sought to unify supervision of the banks, insurance firms, and the capital markets under a unified agency, the National Banking and Securities Commission (Comision Nacional Bancaria y de Valores, or CNBV). But when the crisis occurred, this unified agency was seen as lacking the capacity to deal with the crisis.

The immediate problem faced by the banks was to cover short and derivative positions against the dollar, to cover losses from the impairment of their portfolio of fixed investments, and to augment their liquidity to cover short-term external borrowing from international banks (primarily U.S. dollar certificates of deposit). The most immediate adverse impact on the banks was a serious deterioration in their liquidity position due to foreign exchange losses. The rapid deterioration of their loan portfolios had the most adverse effect on the banks. Since a large share of lending in Mexico was at floating (variable) interest rates, adjusted monthly, the spike in interest rates immediately after the devaluation quickly impaired the ability of debtors to service their loans. Interest rates on mortgages, consumer debt, and commercial loans rose above 80 percent, on a nominal basis, in the months immediately following the devaluation.[17]

The Impact of the Crisis

The devaluation, the banking crisis, and its impact on the real sector had a signifi-cant negative effect on the overall economy; formal employment declined by some 20 percent owing to output declines, gross fixed capital formation fell by 31 percent, imports fell by 28 percent, and exports increased by 28 percent in large part because of the devaluation of the peso. GDP contracted by −8 percent in 1995, a large down-ward spike, but by 1996 growth rebounded to some 3.7 percent and was projected at 4 percent for 1997. The peso was broadly stable and appreciating. Interest rates on the benchmark twenty-eight-day *cetes* dropped 26 basis points to reach 29 percent. Externally, the Mexican government and its agencies continued to attract international capital, raising some $16 billion by November 1996.[18] Spreads on the Mexican Brady par bond and Mexico's uncollateralized thirty-year dollar global bond also declined.[19] Mexico generated a trade surplus of $5.8 billion for the first ten months of 1996 and a fiscal surplus of N$19.6 billion (US$2.5 billion) (at N$7.90 to $1) or 1.1 percent of GDP for three quarters of 1996.[20]

An important outcome from the reforms—deregulation, industrial restructur-ing, the privatization of SOEs when combined with the devaluation—was a significant shift in Mexico's export base from dependence on oil to the export of agricultural products and manufacturing goods. The former consisted primarily of fruits and vegetables, to compete with Florida and Chile for the "winter market" in the United States, and the latter of auto exports, based on a substantial investment by European and U.S. producers to compete with Japanese exports to the United States. Total merchandise exports increased by 31 percent, manufacturing exports increased by 47 percent, and "maquiladora exports" by 18 percent in 1995, and export growth continued through the first half of 1996.[21]

The currency crisis proved to be V-shaped, and the economy recovered relatively quickly. However, the crisis was deep and demonstrated the weakness of the Mexi-can economy and institutions, especially their inability to absorb large capital flows by a financial sector that had been privatized and liberalized but was insufficiently prudent and inadequately supervised.[22]

The cost of the crisis was steep. The blanket guarantee of liabilities by the gov-ernment most likely prevented a deposit run, but at significant contingent costs. As of the end of June 1996, depending on the collection of loans financed by the Fondo Bancario para Protección de Ahorro (FOBAPROA, the Bank Fund for Protection of Savings, the asset management agency), World Bank banking analysts estimated that the cost of the bank support program would run as high as N$160.5 billion ($20.3 billion), or 8.1 percent of 1996 GDP) (see table 10-1).

TABLE 10-1. Mexico: Estimated Fiscal Cost of Bank Support Programs, as of June 1996

Support program	Subsidy aspect	Estimated fiscal cost (in present value terms)	
		Billions of N$	Percent of 1996 GDP
FOBAPROA[a] programs			
PROCAPTE temporary[b] recapitalization program[c]	Does not involve significant fiscal costs.		
Foreign currency credit 2	Does not involve significant fiscal costs.		
Assistance to intervened banks	Amount of subsidy depends on the performance of the intervened-in banks.	48.4	2.4
Purchase of loan portfolios (two for one)[d]	Amount of subsidy depends on the performance and collateral of purchased loan portfolio. As of June 1996, net loans sold to FOBAPROA totaled NS$119 billion.	28.5	1.2
UDI programs (mortage assistance)			
Expanded basic program	Loans totaling N$178 billion have been restructured so far under this program. Program was expanded in 1996 to include additional mortgage holders.	48.6	2.5
Assistance to highway concessionaires		14.1	0.7
Agricultural sector support		12.5	0.6
ADE program	Cost of subsidy depends on difference between market interest and rates charged to borrower.	13.4	0.7
Total		160.5	8.1

Source: World Bank, "Mexico Financial Sector Strategy," draft (Washington, July 22, 1996); calculations based on CNBV estimates and a projected GDP of N$1,982.4 billion for 1996.

a. Fondo Bancario para Protección de Ahorro.
b. Under this program, FOBAPROA purchases subordinate debt from banks to raise capitalization level to 9 percent. Proceeds are placed in a special account of Banco de Mexico at an interest rate equal to that on the subordinated debt.
c. Provides liquidity assistance to the banks that were intervened in and covers their operating losses.
d. Program involves the purchase by FOBAPROA of bank loans in an amount equal to twice the additional capital infusions by bank stockholders. The loans' transfer price is their book value less provisions. (FOBAPROA may not buy loans in the highest risk category.) FOBAPROA pays for the loans with ten-year maturity bonds carrying a twenty-eight-day *cetes* interest rate paid at maturity. Banks must share 25 percent of the ultimate costs in the event of a default.

As the crisis began to resolve itself in 1996, the government was left with many unresolved issues with respect to the banking system and between the banks and their debtors: (i) a system that was undercapitalized with a large contingent bad loan problem; (ii) regulatory forbearance that allowed restructured loans to be accepted as performing; (iii) accounting standards that failed to disclose the extent of losses in the system; (iv) difficulty for FOBAPROA, acting as an asset management agency, in packaging and reselling bank loans it had acquired; (v) potential conflict for CNBV as the banking supervisor and also crisis manager; permissible conflicts in lending from the banks to members of their group and the protection of concentrated deposits by group members; (vi) debtors that refrained from servicing or resolving their debts because they expected the government to offer subsidized terms and financial support. The resulting moral hazard contributed to rising nonperforming loans (NPLs) in the system; and (vii) a weak bankruptcy system that failed to provide a "stick" in the process of resolving bad debts. Debtors were able to use the system to their advantage to stretch out their inability or unwillingness to pay their debts.

Mexico's Crisis Resolution Program

With the crisis projected to cost Mexico some 8 percent of GDP, and the need to restructure its banking system as well as major corporations in difficulty, it soon became clear that Mexico required external support.

External Support

The crisis quickly drew external resources of $18 billion in support of Peso stabilization, with a consortium of countries and institutions effectively acting collectively as an international lender of last resort: $9 billion from the United States, $1 billion from Canada, $5 billion from the Bank for International Settlements (BIS), and $3 billion from large international banks led by Citibank and Morgan Guaranty. The IMF and World Bank also provided financial and technical support. On January 13, 1995, the Clinton administration announced a support package of up to $40 billion in loan guarantees,[23] which eventually was reduced to some $20 billion when the U.S. Congress resisted the size of the package. Mexico drew some $13.5 billion dollars under this facility. With the economy improving in 1996, the government prepaid $7 billion of the $9 billion since the support program was put in place and had made interest payments of $1.36 billion. The currency swaps and loans from the U.S. government were fully collateralized by Mexican crude oil, oil products, and petrochemical exports.[24]

The relevant question at the time, when the Mexican government was developing a policy response and international governments, institutions, and banks were providing external balance of payments support, was whether this was a repeat of or similar to the 1982 debt crisis. Were Mexico's efforts to stabilize and to undertake deep structural reforms somehow for naught? Cline's response was the following: "The answer was almost certainly in the negative. All of the debt indicators for Mexico were much more favorable by 1992–1994 than they had been on the eve of the debt crisis in 1981–1982. This time Mexico's economic structure was much more flexibly attuned to market forces rather than hindered by regulation, import protection and an excessive roll of state firms."[25]

Mexico's immediate problem was meeting its short-term liquidity demands, which arose largely from the Treasury bonds and portfolio redemptions. Mexico's external public debt was just 40 percent of GDP. However, the large short-term inflow of resources presented an internal transfer problem, a matter of fiscal space, as well as an external transfer problem, as discussed in chapter 9. The peso crisis was a currency crisis and not a debt crisis.[26] However, it did have a substantial impact on both the Mexican financial sector and the real sector, which needed to be resolved.

Government Support

The government responded with a series of policy and institutional measures soon after the crisis emerged. These included liquidity support to the banks, assistance in recapitalizing the banks, debtor relief, relaxation of foreign investment regulations, enhanced regulation, and supervision of banks and bank intervention. These interventions prevented a deposit run on the banks.[27]

Liquidity Support

In January 1995, the government established a window at the Bank Fund for Savings Protection (FOBAPROA), the official bank liability protection fund, to provide dollar liquidity to the banks at 25 percent interest. The central bank, Banco de Mexico, set up a liquidity window to provide pesos to the banks. As the immediate crisis passed, the banks were able to revert to private markets to replace funding from these two official institutions.[28]

Capitalization, PROCAPTE, FOBAPROA

Banking supervisors mandated that all banks increase provisions against bad loans and other losses and maintain a minimum net capital of 8 percent. Through the temporary bank capitalization program Programa de Capitalización Temporal

(PROCAPTE), FOBAPROA purchased convertible debentures from the banks to raise their net capital to 9 percent of risk-weighted assets, with the banks depositing the proceeds with the Banco de Mexico. This allowed undercapitalized but solvent banks to continue operating.[29]

FOBAPROA Loan Purchases

In response to a rapidly deteriorating portfolio and the erosion of the newly injected capital, CNBV devised a program in 1995 to have FOBAPROA purchase a portion of the banks' loan portfolios, based on a commitment from the banks' shareholders that they would inject new capital into their banks in an amount roughly equal to half of the loan purchases. The banks' owners were committed to injecting some $6.4 billion, or some 88 percent of the equity of "nonintervened" banks. The banks were to continue servicing the loans and would share in some 20–30 percent of the loan losses. This was initially seen as a program for the weaker nonintervened banks, but eventually most of the newly privatized banks were forced to go through two rounds of loan sales to FOBAPROA.[30]

Intervened Banks

Over the course of the crisis, the banking regulator-supervisor, CNBV, was forced to intervene in eight troubled banks of the eighteen privatized banks. It soon became apparent that the intervened banks had serious problems, including corrupt transactions and nonperforming loans. Loan losses began to rise rapidly in the intervened banks. There was a limit to the CNBV's capacity to manage and restructure intervened banks, hence the pressure to attract foreign banks to invest in the system.[31] (See table 10-2 on the structure of the banking system following intervention.)

Results of Bank Support: Portfolio Quality, Capitalization, and Bank Profitability

As of March 1996 the Mexican banking system remained weakly capitalized because of the large negative capital in the intervened banks: equity was $3.6 billion) (at N$7.2 [new pesos] to the dollar) and the equity of the intervened banks was a negative −$5.6 billion. Overall profits for the system were a negative −$2.2 billion). Most problematic were NPLs at 18 percent if measured under Mexican GAAP (Generally Accepted Accounting Principles), but as high as 26–32 percent if the stricter U.S. GAAP were applied. FOBAPROA's support was critical; it represented 30 percent of the total loan portfolio of the system as of March 1996. Even if only the nonintervened banks were considered, the system remained fragile.[32]

TABLE 10-2. Structure of the Mexican Commercial Banking System, as of End of September 1996

Millions of N$

Group	Number of banks	Assets	Gross loans[a]	Direct funding[b]	Equity	Net profit or loss
Intervened banks	10	154,242	143,240	109,475	−23,703	−34,308
Privatized banks[c]	12	971,631	645,548	557,256	62,588	−4,531
New local banks	14	44,109	20,428	15,632	6,606	1,077
Subsidiaries of foreign banks	17	60,891	8,930	11,458	6,061	903
Banking system	53	1,230,873	818,146	693,821	51,552	−36,859

Source: CNBV; Sri-Ram Aiyer, "Anatomy of Mexico's Banking System following the Peso Crisis," Latin American and Caribbean Technical Department Report 45 (Washington: World Bank, December 1996), p. 13.

a. Including discount loans.
b. Including deposits, bankers' acceptances, and money market repo agreements.
c. Group does not include privatized foreign-owned banks such as Inveriat and Probursa.

Foreign Investment in the Banking Sector

As the banking crisis continued and NPLs continued to rise, it became apparent that the support required from the government for both intervened and nonintervened banks would potentially be very high. Mexico's banking legislation allowed for foreign bank ownership, but limited the role of foreign banks to 1.5 percent of the capital of the Mexican banking system as a whole. The North American Free Trade Agreement (NAFTA) allowed for a gradual relaxation of these limits. As the crisis continued, the pressure increased on the government to attract foreign capital into the system. The government passed legislation in February 1995 to allow greater foreign ownership of the bank holding companies, up to 49 percent. In addition, investors could now own a majority in any bank that held less than 6 percent of the total assets of the banking system. These new laws prevented a takeover of Mexico's three major banks—Banamex, Bancomer, and Serfin.[33]

Over time a series of deals was struck with foreign banks for the intervened banks, and nonintervened bank owners also moved to bring in foreign capital in the aftermath of the crisis. Starting in 1996: (i) the Bank of Montreal agreed to purchase a 15 percent stake in Bancomer; (ii) in June 1996 Banco Vizcaya Bilbao, the Spanish bank that was the controlling shareholder in Probursa, signed a letter of intent to purchase Banca Cremi and Banco Oriente, one of the intervened banks; (iii) Banco Serfin, one of the three largest banks, retained J. P. Morgan as an adviser to find an investor for the bank; and (iv)[34] by the end of this process, even Mexico's largest bank, Banamex, had been purchased by Citibank, which until then had had a small but long-term presence in Mexico.

Weak Bankruptcy System

The weak, debtor-friendly bankruptcy system made it difficult for banks to collect on their loans. The Mexican bankruptcy law, perceived by virtually all analysts of Mexico's financial system as very weak even before the crisis, was clearly an ineffective instrument for orderly workout or liquidation of troubled companies.[35] It permitted many debtors to stave off creditors' claims almost indefinitely; during the Tequila Crisis, debtors used bankruptcy as a threat or a weapon more often than creditors did. The law did not provide for consolidated bankruptcy, so a company with many subsidiaries and affiliates could have many separate bankruptcy cases under separate judges. Any company that was insolvent (its liabilities exceeded its assets) was likely to be put into *quiebra* (liquidation) by a motion of its creditors and would not be reorganized.[36] Bankruptcy systems, however strong, get overwhelmed in a crisis, and governments have invariably sought other mechanisms to resolve nonperforming loans with the corporate sector. This was to prove true during the 1990s and early 2000s as discussed in this and subsequent chapters with respect to the emerging market crises.

Addressing the Real Sector: Government Support for Debtors

Owing to the spike in interest rates and the alarming rise in the number of nonperforming loans, debtors were either unwilling or unable to service their debts, so the government set up a series of support mechanisms to assist debtors. These were known as ADE (Acuerdo de Apoyo Inmediato a Deudores de la Banca) and UCABE (Unidad Coordinadora para el Acuerdo Bancario Empresarial). The ADE program was designed to accelerate the restructuring of nonperforming loans and was a short-term bridging mechanism between what borrowers were willing to pay and what they were obligated to pay their banks over a one-year period Additional relief was then announced in May 1996 as a subsidy for residential mortgage holders, programs for agricultural land holders, and small and medium-sized enterprises (SMEs).[37]

Given the shortcomings of the bankruptcy law, the Mexican government created an institutional structure known as UCABE during the crisis to orchestrate the voluntary restructuring of thirty to forty of the largest debtors. The Mexican Banking Commission and FOBAPROA also helped organize the banks so they could deal with their large problem cases using a unified approach.[38]

The Mexican government and the Mexican Banking Association (AMB) had also concluded that "satisfactory progress in large corporate debt restructuring was not being made by the workout groups in the individual banks, and that the relationships between debtors and creditors had deteriorated to such a degree that productive negotiations had become severely impeded."[39] In response, UCABE was established on December 13, 1995, largely through the initiative of Mexico's president, Ernesto Zedillo, in an attempt to bring stalled debt negotiations between the banks and major debtors to a rapid conclusion. UCABE could be traced back to President Zedillo's direct experience in the external debt crisis of the 1980s, in which agreements on corporate workouts were negotiated years after the crisis began in 1982.

As a "unit" of the joint commission between the National Banking Commission (CNBV) and the Mexican Banking Association (AMB), UCABE was responsible for coordinating agreements between banks and enterprises. Four senior executives ran UCABE on a voluntary basis at the direct request of the president of the republic. This meant that they had considerable clout or suasion to force solutions.

UCABE was a mediator in large corporate restructuring cases, targeting companies with $150–500 million of bank debt. Holding a total of some $8 billion in debt, these companies represented approximately 8 percent of total outstanding loans in the Mexican banking system as of the end of 1995. UCABE sought to preserve the viability of these firms, sustain employment, and promote economic recovery. It worked out potentially viable companies, defined as those having a positive cash flow, a significant base of employment, a leader or an important player in its market niche, and a competitive cost structure.

Banks operating within the UCABE framework needed to compensate for the weaknesses in the legal framework, namely the absence of a viable bankruptcy system and any formal framework for workouts. Thus they agreed to follow specific rules of conduct regarding the selection of a lead negotiator bank and decision-making by majority rule.[40] In addition, standstill agreements were adopted and seniority of secured creditors was recognized. Provisions were made for the preferential treatment of new voluntary loans together with the subordination of existing guarantees. And, once a sustainable amount of debt had been identified, the banks were allowed to enter into debt swaps among themselves and to use debt capitalization and other financial engineering techniques to reduce the overall debt burden and facilitate exit from the credit. Shareholders and debtor companies also followed rules for the provision of new capital, dilution of ownership rights, and the strengthening or replacement of company management in order to facilitate reaching a final agreement.

The advantages of the scheme appear clear: a flexible and agile voluntary process to meet the needs of the debtor and the creditors, top-level government commitment

TABLE 10-3.   Mexico: Economic Statistics for Selected Years, 1995–2010

Millions of US$ unless otherwise indicated

	1995	2000	2005	2006	2007	2008	2009	2010
Summary of external/debt data								
External debt stocks	165,379	150,901	165,841	161,192	178,611	187,137	171,485	200,081
Long-term external debt	112,250	131,969	143,640	134,934	151,249	158,732	143,895	161,068
Public and publicly guaranteed	93,902	81,488	108,482	96,029	105,376	113,950	99,374	111,467
Private non-guaranteed	18,348	50,481	35,158	38,905	45,872	44,782	44,521	49,600
Use of IMF credit	15,828	0	0	0	0	0	0	0
Short-term external debt	37,300	18,932	22,201	26,258	27,362	28,405	27,590	39,013
Interest arrears on long-term	0	0	0	0	0	0	0	0
Memorandum items								
Principal arrears on long-term	0	0	0	0	0	0	0	0
Long-term public sector debt	93,471	81,210	108,448	96,022	105,374	113,950	99,374	11,467
Long-term private sector debt	18,779	50,758	35,192	38,912	45,875	44,782	44,521	49,600
Public and public guaranteed commitments	24,610	10,828	14,933	14,974	16,663	24,384	23,318	28,741

Ratios (percent)								
External debt stocks to exports	177.8	81.2	70.4	59.2	60.1	59.0	68.7	62.7
External debt stocks to gross national income	60.5	26.6	19.9	17.3	17.6	17.3	19.8	19.5
Debt service to exports	28.1	31.5	15.2	19.7	12.3	10.4	12.3	9.8
Short-term to external debt stocks	22.6	12.5	13.4	16.3	15.3	15.2	16.1	19.5
Multilateral to external debt stocks	11.3	11.4	9.9	5.1	5.1	5.7	10.0	10.6
Reserves to external debt stocks	10.3	23.6	44.7	47.4	48.8	50.9	58.2	60.3
Reserves to imports (months)	2.1	2.0	3.4	3.0	3.1	3.2	4.3	4.2
Debt restructurings								
Total amount rescheduled	0	0	0	0	0	0	0	0
Total amount forgiven	293	478	0	0	0	0	0	0
Debt buyback	13	6,644	0	0	0	0	0	1,746

Source: World Bank, Global Development Finance 2012 (Washington, 2012).

through the office of the presidency, and provision of new financial resources. The disadvantages were that the process was discretionary and ad hoc; it lacked published guidelines, did not address the fundamental weaknesses of the Mexican bankruptcy system, and was an extralegal system that could be subject to court challenge.

Voluntary restructurings, or workouts, during a crisis are discussed extensively later in this book with respect to the East Asian and Turkish crises (and the Korean crisis in particular). Given the number of companies involved in these workout programs and the pressures of the crisis, the emphasis was on buying time until the immediate crisis had passed. The workouts focused on financial engineering—rescheduling, capitalization of interest in arrears, interest rate reduction, and some new money to meet working capital needs. In Korea, for example, in the second and third rounds of workouts, for a select set of companies and with the immediate crisis threat over, there was more substantive corporate restructuring and in some cases liquidation of a company.

The Mexican crisis involved the government, the banks, and the corporate sectors as debtors that were largely dependent on short-term loans, substantially in excess of reserves. Crisis resolution required substantial support from U.S. and international institutions coordinating their efforts as an international lender of last resort. It also required the government to substantially increase institutional capacity in several areas to resolve the bank crisis and eventually oversee the sale of several banks to foreign investors and to assist debtors, especially large corporate debtors, though a workout process that supplanted the weak bankruptcy system. The crisis that arrived during the change in presidents at the end of the six-year presidential cycle, involving two political assassinations and a challenge to the PRI, the party that had ruled Mexico for many years, further complicated the process of crisis resolution. The other crises discussed in the subsequent chapters in this part of the book address similar difficult and complex resolution issues.

Following its resolution of the crisis, the Mexican economy performed well during the period through the crisis of the early 2000s, the Great Recession (see table 10-3); external debt ratios such as debt stocks to exports, external debt stocks to gross national income (GNI), and debt service to exports all declined substantially. Mexico built substantial foreign exchange reserves and generally weathered the early twenty-first-century crisis well.

ELEVEN

The East Asian Crisis

1997–2003

The East Asian crisis was triggered by a real estate bubble and a related financial sector/banking crisis in Thailand in July 1997. A lack of confidence and contagion saw the crisis spread rapidly to Indonesia, Malaysia, and South Korea. The Philippines and Hong Kong were also adversely affected by the crisis, but to a lesser extent than the other countries. Hong Kong experienced a stock market crash, but not a broad financial/economic crisis. China was forced to address the nonperforming loans (NPLs) in its banking sector and did so by establishing four asset management companies into which the NPLs of the major banks were offloaded. China also avoided a full-blown crisis.

Few, if any, analysts anticipated the crisis. East Asia was seen as the poster child or demonstration case for the economies in Latin America or other emerging market countries such as Turkey, which were deeply affected by the debt crisis of the early 1980s. The largely open, outward-oriented East Asian economies were not affected by the debt crisis of the 1980s; they continued to grow strongly throughout much of the 1990s and were in macroeconomic balance—with low inflation, small fiscal deficits, and high savings rates—and most ran trade surpluses. Jason Furman and Joseph Stiglitz write that the miracle was real. Between 1966 and 1996 per capita incomes grew at an average rate of 4.7 percent in Indonesia, 7.4 percent in Korea,

4.4 percent in Malaysia, and 5.2 percent in Thailand. Poverty rates in the region dropped substantially from an overall poverty rate of six out of ten East Asians in 1975 to two out of ten in 1995. Indonesia's achievement was particularly impressive, moving from 64 percent of the population living below the poverty line in 1975 to 7 percent in 1997.[1]

Why then were these countries so adversely affected by the crisis, and why was the crisis so virulent? As Paul Krugman noted:

> It seems safe to say that nobody anticipated anything like the current crisis in Asia. . . . But even pessimists expected something along the lines of a conventional currency crisis followed by a modest downturn and we expected the long-term slowdown in growth to emerge only gradually. What we have actually seen is something more complex and more drastic: collapses in domestic asset markets, widespread bank failures, bankruptcies on the part of many firms, and what looks likely to be a much more severe real downturn than even the most negative minded anticipated.[2]

Steven Radelet and Jeffrey Sachs observed that "the East Asian financial crisis is remarkable in several ways. The crisis hit the most rapidly growing economies in the world and prompted the largest financial bailouts in history. It is the least anticipated financial crisis in years."[3] Furman and Stiglitz also observed: "Yet in many ways the East Asian crisis is especially notable. It occurred in the fastest growing region of the world. . . . The magnitude of the East Asian experience requires us to take a fresh look at some old debates, like the causes of currency and financial crises, the appropriate macro-economic responses to them and the costs and benefits of global financial integration."[4]

The individual country crises in East Asia were not sovereign debt crises as they were during the Great Depression; nor were they syndicated loan crises like those in developing countries in the 1980s; and they were not like the eurocurrency crisis (discussed in Part IV of this book). The East Asian crises were largely triggered by private sector debt in both the banking and corporate sectors. In the case of Thailand, the crisis started with a real estate bust. First the Thai financial sector, particularly the finance companies, and thereafter the corporate sector, were in deep distress, particularly small and medium-sized enterprises (SMEs); credits were frozen to all but the most creditworthy companies. In Korea the crisis was largely focused on the large corporate groups, the *chaebols*, which were highly diversified conglomerates. With the bankruptcy of several large groups such as Kia, the commercial banks and merchant banks were also badly affected and required interventions. Indonesia and Malaysia were likewise affected, though Malaysia much less so than Indonesia. The financial and corporate crises then morphed into economic crises throughout the region and also sovereign crises, as governments were forced to intervene heavily in the banking system and recapitalize their banks.

In the end, although most of the East Asian economies managed their macro-situation well and were not deeply indebted upon entering the crisis, the extent and depth of the crisis forced these governments, like Mexico, Turkey, and Argentina, to seek external assistance. Support packages were intermediated by the International Monetary Fund (IMF), with the World Bank and Asian Development Bank also providing support, and the G-7, largely the United States and Japan, as backup. The idea was to make the packages large enough and sufficiently credible to calm markets.[5]

Causes of the Crisis

In all such crises there is rarely a single cause. And in this case the causes in each of the four primary crisis countries—Thailand, Indonesia, Malaysia, and Korea—were somewhat different. I first look at the causes common to the East Asian countries and then focus on Korea as an example of crisis resolution (in chapter 12). First and foremost, analysts seem to agree that the accumulation of short-term debt, in excess of trade finance requirements,[6] was the primary catalyst for the crisis. This was true to some extent in the Mexican crisis, as the government issued dollar-denominated tesobonos (Treasury bonds) to finance itself. Excessive short-term debt, or floating debt as it was termed in the nineteenth century, was invariably a trigger for crises in other periods discussed in this book.

In East Asia it was primarily private sector banks and other financial institutions and nonbank private companies that borrowed primarily on a short-term basis, mostly in U.S. dollars and to some extent in Japanese yen, and often through offshore convenience centers (see Tables 11-1, 11-2, and 11-3). The borrowing was primarily an arbitrage between higher domestic rates and lower dollar interest rates. With currencies pegged to the dollar and presumably stable, these institutions perceived little risk in borrowing short term in dollars.

The globalization of capital markets, the expansion of large international money center banks, the creation of banking syndicates for large loan packages, where smaller banks "piggybacked" on the due diligence of the larger banks, and the liberalization of financial markets and capital accounts in the East Asian economies all facilitated the ability of East Asian financial institutions and corporations to borrow externally.[7]

TABLE 11-1.   Credit to Private Sector, Selected Years, 1975–96

Percent of GDP

Country	1975	1982	1990	1994	1995	1996
Indonesia	20	14	47	52	54	56
Republic of Korea	42	55	65	69	69	75
Malaysia	33	47	71	115	130	142
Philippines	32	46	22	36	45	54
Thailand	28	46	83	128	139	100
Argentina	16	34	16	18	18	19
Brazil	55	44	38	51	35	31
Chile	9	84	47	51	53	55
Mexico	27	16	21	47	36	22
Venezuela	34	55	25	13	12	10

Source: World Bank, World Economic Prospects 1998/99 (Washington, 1999), p. 64.

Radelet and Sachs cite several reasons why institutions in these countries were able to borrow so easily: (i) continuing and in some cases high growth gave confidence to foreign investors and lenders; (ii) widespread financial deregulation made it much easier for domestic banks and corporations to borrow abroad, while weak banking supervision failed to control excessive short-term leverage; (iii) nominal exchange rates were effectively pegged to the U.S. dollar either with limited variations (Thailand, Malaysia, Korea, and the Philippines) or perceived as very predictable exchange rate regime (Indonesia); and, (iv) governments provided special incentives that encouraged foreign borrowing, even as concerns arose about "hot money" flows in the 1990s. For example, banks operating in the Bangkok International Banking Facility, which was established exclusively to mobilize offshore funding, received special tax breaks. Philippine banks faced no reserve requirements for foreign currency deposits, while for domestic deposits the reserve requirement was 15 percent in 1996.[8]

The IMF clearly supported financial liberalization and capital account opening as part of the Washington Consensus, while noting weaknesses in Indonesia's banking system the IMF board noted: "The Directors agreed with the authorities' emphasis on maintaining an open capital account . . . during Board discussions on Korea in November 1996, they [the directors] also welcomed the recent acceleration of capital account liberalization, though some directors agreed with the authorities' gradual approach to capital market liberalization, a number of directors considered that rapid and complete liberalization offered many benefits at Korea's stage of development." And about Thailand in a board discussion, "Directors strongly praised Thailand's remarkable economic performance and the authorities' consistent record of

TABLE 11-2. International Claims Held by Foreign Banks, Distribution by Maturity and Sector

Billions of US$

			Obligations by sector				
	Total outstanding	*Banks*	*Public sector*	*Nonbank private*	*Short term*	*Reserves*	*Short term/ reserves*
End of 1995							
Indonesia	44.5	8.9	6.7	28.8	27.6	14.7	1.9
Malaysia	16.8	4.4	2.1	10.1		23.9	0.3
Philippines	8.3	2.2		3.4	4.1	7.8	0.5
Thailand	62.8	25.8	2.3		43.6	37.0	1.2
Korea		50.0	6.2	21.4		32.7	1.7
Total	209.9	91.3	20.0	98.4	137.5		
End of 1996							
Indonesia		11.7		36.8	34.2	19.3	1.8
Malaysia	22.2	6.5	2.0	13.7	11.2	27.1	0.4
Philippines	13.3		2.7	5.3	7.7	11.7	
Thailand	70.2	25.9	2.3	41.9	45.7	38.7	1.2
Korea	100.0	65.9		28.3	67.5	34.1	2.0
Total	261.2	115.2	19.6	126.0	166.3		
Mid-1997							
Indonesia	58.7	12.4	6.5	39.7		20.3	1.7
Malaysia	28.8	10.5	1.9	16.5	16.3	26.6	0.6
Philippines	14.1	5.5	1.9	6.8	8.3	9.8	0.8
Thailand	69.4	26.1	2.0	41.3	45.6	31.4	1.5
Korea	103.4	67.3	4.4	31.7	70.2	34.1	2.1
Total	274.4	121.8	16.7	136.0	175.1		
Memo item:							
Mexico							
End of 1994	64.6	16.7	24.9	22.8	33.2	6.4	5.2
End of 1995	57.3	11.5	23.5	22.3	26.0	17.1	1.5

Source: Bank for International Settlements data, cited in Jeffrey Sachs, *The Onset of the East Asian Financial Crises* (Cambridge, Mass.: Harvard Institute for Economic Development, March 30, 1998).

sound macroeconomic fundamentals. . . . On the other hand, the level of short-term capital flows and short-term debt were somewhat high."[9]

While citing the growth of short-term debt, Furman and Stiglitz focus on the "evidence that financial liberalization increases the vulnerabilities to crisis is over-whelming," especially when unaccompanied by a significant strengthening of banking

TABLE 11-3.   Foreign Exposure of Banks and Finance Companies, 1990–96

Percent

	Ratio of foreign liabilities to M2[a]			Ratio of foreign liabilities to assets		
	1990	1994	1996	1990	1992–96	1996
Indonesia	1.2	7.0	3.2	108	193	143
Republic of Korea	4.4	8.3	14.1	140	149	174
Thailand	6.1	25.1	32.8	265	519	775
Argentina	33.7	10.1	9.5	313	197	158
Brazil	20.6	10.0	17.3	207	177	282
Mexico	55.3	66.8	44.7	901	750	498

Source: IMF, International Financial Statistics; World Bank, World Economic Prospects 1998/99, p. 62.
a. Money supply, cash and coins in circulation and in non-interest bearing accounts.

and financial sector supervision and regulation. Moreover, the problem was compounded for economies with fixed exchange rates.[10] Net private long-term capital flows to the four Southeast Asian economies increased from 3.3 percent of GDP in 1990 to 8.3 percent of GDP by 1996, part of a wave of capital flows to developing countries in the 1990s.[11] The essential problem, Furman and Stiglitz observe, is that small open economies are small relative to the global pool of foreign capital, regardless of the reasons for their entry. These countries can find capital rushing in very rapidly, and it can rush out just as rapidly, or even more so if market sentiment changes and there is a desired flight to safety.[12]

Addressing causation in summary fashion, Krugman observes:

Let me propose the following story. The problem began with financial intermediates—institutions whose liabilities were perceived as having an implicit government guarantee, but were essentially unregulated and therefore subject to severe moral hazard problems. The excessive risky lending of these institutions created inflation—not of goods but of asset prices. The overpricing of assets was sustained in part by a sort of circular process, in which the proliferation of risky lending drove up the price of risky assets, making the financial condition of the intermediaries seem sounder than it was.

And then the bubble burst. The mechanism of crisis, I suggest, involved the same circular reasoning process in reverse: falling asset prices made the insolvency of intermediaries visible, forcing them to cease operations, leading to further asset deflation. This circularity, in turn, can explain both the remarkable severity of the crisis and the apparent vulnerability of the Asian economies to self-fulfilling crisis—which in turn helps us to understand the phenomenon of contagion between economies with few visible links.[13]

While Furman and Stiglitz, Radelet and Sachs, and Krugman all focus on the financial sector and failures of the banking system, that is just part of the story. In much of East Asia the corporate sector was excessively leveraged. In Korea, as an example, the real sector, particularly the chaebols, large complex conglomerates with listed companies among their most important holdings, relied on debt to grow and expand, as the family units that controlled them tried to maintain control with as little as 10–20 percent equity ownership. The Korean merchant banks, owned by the large chaebols, arranged foreign loans for the chaebols, often from offshore convenience centers. Also, the largest commercial banks were essentially "house banks" for the largest chaebols, even though not formally owned by them. The excessively high leverage of the large corporations in Korea and their potential bankruptcy threatened the stability of the Korean economy, particularly as interest rates rose during the crisis, and this invariably put the large commercial banks into trouble as nonperforming loans rose.

In Thailand the finance companies, or nonbank financial corporations, funded real estate investments until a speculative bubble was created and the crisis ensued. In Thailand both finance houses and banks were often part of large corporate groups with the bank at its core. The problems of the real sector embodied the problems of unemployment, the social fabric of the country, and the possibilities to restore growth. In addition, if the chaebols were virtually all technically bankrupt in Korea, as were large corporate groups in other East Asian countries, then SMEs, many of which were satellites of the larger firms, were also vulnerable and began initially to shed any labor, other than family, they employed. Thereafter SMEs began to fail on a large scale. Addressing the problems of the real sector—outside the formal bankruptcy systems, which were unsuitable for the most part to address crisis conditions—and the nexus between the banks and the real sector as reflected in rising NPLs, became a major issue in Korea and the other countries.[14]

Resolution Strategies

Generally speaking, the approaches to crisis resolution had a common framework and institutional support, which was applied somewhat differently in each country based on the capacity of the country's government and institutions, the depth of the crisis it faced, and the structure of its economy. In chapter 12 I focus in more detail on the Korean resolution strategy, largely because it was highly successful and also because I worked directly on Korea over a two-year period to assist the government, specifically the banking supervisor, on crisis resolution. My team and I focused on a systemic approach to out-of-court workouts for the chaebols and other large independent (nonconglomerate) companies in Korea.

IMF and G-7 Support

Each of these countries was supported by the IMF with the World Bank and Asian Development Bank also in support, backed by the G-7, principally the United States and Japan. Total support, including backup from the G-7, was $95 billion, not all of it drawn down by the crisis countries.[15] In this respect you could call the IMF, backed by the G-7, the international lender of last resort, as it was in other crises discussed in this book. Both the IMF and the World Bank initially provided financing tied to conditionality in such areas as banking regulation and supervision, bankruptcy reform, the adoption of workout programs between the banks and the corporate sector, and the adoption of international accounting standards. Some of these measures had direct relevance to crisis resolution and others to perceived weaknesses to be addressed in order to improve economic performance postcrisis.[16]

The IMF and the World Bank also offered technical assistance, some of which was provided by their own staff and other by expert consultants. The IMF sought to guide macropolicy adjustments during the crisis (at times highly criticized by Stiglitz, among others). Both the IMF and the World Bank supported efforts to restructure the banks. The World Bank led the effort on out-of-court corporate workouts, and both the IMF and World Bank supported improvements in the insolvency (bankruptcy) regime. The Asian Development Bank, for example, assisted the Korean government in financing the small-business sector to reduce bankruptcies among SMEs.

Banking Bailouts

The common response to a crisis such as the one in Mexico, the East Asian countries, and subsequently Turkey and Argentina was for governments to focus attention and substantial resources (typically and pejoratively called "bailouts") on the banking sector and to a lesser extent on nonbank financial institutions. For the most part these bailouts were expensive and, according to some analysts, ran the risk of creating moral hazard. That is, some analysts and policymakers believe that bailouts encourage risk-laden behavior such as excessive leveraging that can lead to a subsequent crisis.[17] The reasons for banking support seem clear: concern over potential depositor runs; the need to inject credit into the economy to renew growth, especially during a crisis; and the perceived need to maintain the stability of the banking system as essential institutions in a market-oriented economy.

As NPLs grew during the crisis, the banks typically froze credits to all but the most creditworthy clients. This invariably had an adverse effect on the small-business sector (SMEs). Bank bailout programs were very costly, and government capital injections in some cases led to quasi-nationalization of the banking system for an interim period during the crisis. Governments then invariably had to open what had previously been closed banking sectors to foreign capital.

Another less obvious reason for emphasis on the banks is that the lenders of last resort—national central banks, the Bank for International Settlements (BIS), and the IMF—understand the role and importance of the banking system best and have oversight or direct supervisory authority over the banking system. These institutions had few staff with experience in the real economy and did not understand very well what it would take to address the real economy (manufacturing and services) during a crisis. Put another way, there is excessive emphasis on the sanctity of the banking system during a crisis and too little on addressing the problems faced by sectors whose firms are the primary employers and drivers of growth. Faced with thousands of small firms, many mid-sized firms, and some large firms in trouble during a crisis, they simply have not known how to address the real sector. This issue will arise again when I discuss the crisis of the early 2000s in the more advanced economies such as Spain and Portugal.[18]

Bank interventions were supported by policy measures to improve regulatory and supervisory capacity, to strengthen financial disclosure through the adoption of international accounting standards, and to address other issues depending on the country.

Bankruptcy (Insolvency) Systems

To the extent that governments and these oversight agencies—IMF, national central banks, BIS, and so forth—have focused on the real sector, they traditionally and initially addressed the formal bankruptcy (insolvency) system and its role in a crisis. However, in several of the East Asian crisis countries the formal bankruptcy systems were weak, were usually debtor friendly, lacked dedicated bankruptcy courts, and had few trained bankruptcy judges. Korea was a minor exception, only because its bankruptcy system functioned somewhat better than those of the other countries. Moreover, during a crisis the bankruptcy systems of these countries were quickly overwhelmed, and most bankruptcy cases led to liquidation because it took so long to resolve cases through the courts.[19] IMF and World Bank policy conditionality sought to improve the formal bankruptcy system in all of the crisis countries, but given the time needed to adopt these policies and train judges, these changes were not relevant during the immediate crisis. The lack of a sound bankruptcy system made it more difficult to resolve corporate workouts on a voluntary basis. The ability to move a debtor toward liquidation provided the "stick" in the process. The bankruptcy of thirteen large groups in Korea, early in the crisis, gave other groups an incentive to accept the voluntary workout process through the large commercial banks, rather than be forced into liquidation.

Asset Management Agencies

Most crisis countries have chosen to establish at least one asset management company (AMC). The AMC's purpose is to remove assets from the books of the banks, usually assets that cannot be realized without special efforts because the loans are nonperforming. AMCs are usually publicly owned entities; however, their management may be contracted out to the private sector. Alternatively, private asset management companies may be formed and assets sold to them at a deep discount. All of the East Asian crisis countries used public AMCs to remove large chunks of bad assets from the books of the banks, in particular intervened and insolvent banks, but also banks in the process of recapitalization and restructuring, and in the case of Thailand also banks being privatized. Some Thai banks such as Farmer's Bank set up bank-operated AMCs, in this case to deal with its failed finance company. By April 1999, government-owned AMCs in Indonesia, Malaysia, Korea, and Thailand had taken over assets whose face value was equivalent to 20, 17, 10, and 4 percent of GDP, respectively (tables 11-4 and 11-5).[20]

China, not one of the crisis countries, nevertheless had very high levels of NPLs in its banking system. The government established four AMCs to absorb NPLs from the banking system to clean up and to recapitalize the banks, starting in April 1999 with CINDA AMC to take over the NPLs of China Construction Bank.[21] It also used the AMCs to absorb noncore assets from twenty-five or so of its large SOEs, which were being restructured to be floated through an initial public offering (IPO),

TABLE 11-4.   Nonperforming Loans in Asset Management
Companies (AMCs), 1997–2000

Percent of total loans

	December 1997	December 1998	June 1999	December 1999	June 2000	Latest
Indonesia (including IBRA)[a]	n.a.	n.a.	n.a.	64.0	63.5	56.1 March 2001
Indonesia (excluding IBRA)	7.2	48.6	39.0	32.9	30.0	21.1 March 2001
Korea (including KAMCO/KDIC)[b]	8.0	16.1	16.4	15.8	18.9	17.9 September 2000
Korea (excluding KAMCO/KDIC)	5.9	10.4	11.3	10.9	13.6	12.3 September 2000
Malaysia (including Danaharta)[c]	6.0	22.6	23.4	23.6	23.2	n.a.
Malaysia (excluding Danaharta)	n.a.	18.9	18.1	16.7	16.2	16.1 December 2000
Thailand (including AMCs)[d]	n.a.	45.0	47.4	41.5	34.8	26.5 June 2001
Thailand (excluding AMCs)	n.a.	45.0	47.4	38.9	32.0	13.0 June 2001

Source: W. P. Mako, "Corporate Restructuring and Reform: Lessons from East Asian," Senior Policy Forum on Economic Crisis and Structural Adjustment in Seoul, Korea, November 5–9, 2001.

a. Indonesian Bank Restructuring Agency
b. Korean Asset Management Corporation / Korean Deposit Insurance Corporation
c. Includes commercial banks, finance companies, merchant banks, and Danaharta.
d. Includes commercial banks, finance companies, and transfers to wholly owned private AMCs.

initially on the Shanghai Exchange, then in Hong Kong, and thereafter in New York or London.

The AMC has to categorize these assets by type—performing or nonperforming, supporting collateral (cars and trucks, real estate, furniture and fixtures, etc.)—and then package them for sale either as individual assets or in pools of assets. The idea is to move these assets as quickly as possible back to the market through a transparent sales process—bulk sale of pools of assets, an auction process, or securitization—so the government can recover some of the costs of bank recapitalization and liquidation. Ideally, this should happen as quickly as possible during a crisis as the assets tend to lose value rapidly. Large international financial institutions, known commonly as "bottom fishers," bid for these bundles or pools of assets,

TABLE 11-5.   Share of Nonperforming Loans, Including Shares of Debt
Transferred to Asset Management Companies, in Eight Countries, 1998–2003

Percent

Year	Indonesia	Republic of Korea	Malaysia	Thailand	Czech Republic	Turkey	Mexico	Brazil
1998	48.6	n.a.[a]	n.a.	n.a.	20.7	6.7	11.3	5.3
1999	32.9	19.7	15.0	40.5	21.9	9.7	8.9	n.a.
2000	56.3	13.9	10.6	26.8	19.9	11.0	5.8	8.4
2001	49.8	9.9	10.7	22.3	13.7	29.0	5.1	n.a.
2002	42.0	n.a.	9.6	n.a.	9.6	17.0	4.8	6.1
2003[b]	n.a.	n.a.	n.a.	15.7	7.6	15.0	n.a.	n.a.

Source: Country sources (a complete list is available from the author); Michael Pomerleano and William Shaw, eds., *Corporate Restructuring: Lessons from Experience* (Washington: World Bank, 2005), p. 42.
a. Not available.
b. March 2003 for countries outside of East Asia.

rehabilitate or restructure them as needed, and sell them over time into a recovering market. Daniela Klingebiel, who examined the role of AMCs in other banking crises—in the United States, Sweden, and Mexico, for example—concluded that AMCs work best if their purpose is narrowly defined. She viewed the AMCs as not very workable for corporate restructuring purposes.[22] My own direct experience with corporate workouts during crises supports this view.

Since AMCs were not ideally structured to deal with corporate restructuring and the formal bankruptcy system also was not ideal, the governments needed to find an alternative approach to corporate restructuring.

Corporate Workouts

Each of the crisis countries developed an approach to out-of-court corporate workouts. The Korean workout program was critical since virtually all of the large chaebols and many other large companies (nonconglomerates) were technically bankrupt owing to the combination of very high leverage and the spike of interest rates during the crisis. Governments in crisis countries had little in the way of case history from the 1980s crises to address the real sector.

A major exception to the lack of case histories to draw on was the experience of the United Kingdom in the 1970s and 1980s. The Bank of England recognized that several large corporations needed to be restructured and resolve their indebtedness. The Bank of England established the London Approach, or London Rules, as a way

TABLE 11-6. Corporate Distress, Past and Projected, 1995–2002

Percentage of firms unable to meet current debt repayments

Country	1995 Total	1996 Total	1997 Total	1998 Total	1999 Total	1999(Q2) Manufacturing	Services	Real estate	2000–2002[a] Total	2000–2002[b] Total
Indonesia	12.6	17.9	40.3	58.2	63.8	41.8	66.8	86.9	52.9	60.8
Republic of Korea	8.5	11.2	24.3	33.8	26.7	19.6	28.1	43.9	17.2	22.6
Malaysia[c]	3.4	5.6	17.1	34.3	26.3	39.3	33.3	52.8	13.8	17.4
Thailand	6.7	10.4	32.6	30.4	28.2	21.8	29.4	46.9	22.3	27.1

Source: Stijn Claessens, Simeon Djankov, and Daniela Klingebiel, "Financial Restructuring in East Asia: Halfway There?" Financial Sector Discussion Paper No. 3 (Washington: World Bank, September, 1999); sectoral estimates provided by Claessens, Djankov, and Klingebiel in World Bank, *Global Economic Prospects 2000* (Washington, 2000), p. 77.

Note: Growth rates assumed through 2002 are based on IMF projections in 1998.

a. Estimate, based on the assumption that interest rates stay at their current level throughout the period.

b. Estimate, based on the assumption that interest rates regain their 1990–95 averages.

c. Malaysian firms in agriculture and utilities bring down the average for all firms in 1999.

TABLE 11-7.   Restructuring: Out-of-Court and In-Court Progress, August 1999

	Indonesia	Malaysia	Republic of Korea	Thailand
Out-of-court procedures				
All or the majority of financial institutions signed on to accord	No	Yes	Yes	Yes
Formal process of arbitration exists, with deadlines	No	Yes	Yes	Yes
Provision of penalties for noncompliance	No	No	Yes	Yes[a]
Out-of-court restructurings				
Number of registered cases	234	53	92	825
Number of cases started	157	27	83	430
Number of restructured cases	22	10	46	167
Restructured debt as a percentage of total debt	13	32	40	22
In-court restructurings				
Number of registered cases	88	52	48	30
Number of cases started	78	34	27	22
Number of restructured cases	8	12	19	8
Restructured debt as a percentage of total debt	4	n.a.[b]	8	7

Source: Claessens, Djankov, and Klingebiel, "Financial Restructuring in East Asia"; World Bank, Global Economic Prospects 2000, p. 91.
a. In Thailand, penalties for noncompliance were introduced in August 1999 for creditors who had signed intercreditor agreements.
b. Not available.

of proceeding with out-of-court voluntary workouts between the banks and a debtor. These workouts were under the guidance or suasion of the Bank of England, but it did not interfere. The London Rules were applied on a case-by-case basis and not in a crisis situation. However, when adapted to the crisis the London Rules soon became the basis for developing a workout regime in Korea, in other East Asian countries, and in Turkey (tables 11-6 and 11-7).[23]

To deal with a crisis, the major changes in the London Rules were designed to make the workout process time bound. In Korea the process was supposed to be completed in 120 days, with another thirty days for review by a special commission in the event the parties could not come to agreement after 120 days. Some of the workout programs also provided for arbitration. In Korea the arbitration panel could be used at any point in the process to resolve any issue, such as the interest rate to be applied to debt rescheduling. After 120 days the arbitration panel would provide a solution to which all of the parties were expected to adhere. With these changes in the London Rules, each crisis country was able to provide crisis resolution for a large number of "mid-cap" companies. These were mostly focused on financial engineering—rescheduling, debt equity conversions, recapitalization of interest in arrears, and new money for working capital and trade finance.

The largest cases, such as Daewoo, were normally handled on a case-by-case basis with financial advisers. SMEs could not usually be handled through workouts because there were so many of them. Thailand tried to bring SMEs into its process, and the process became jammed with cases to be resolved. Korea, as an example, injected liquidity into the SME sector through its partial risk guarantee programs with the banks.

Korea was the largest of the East Asian economies to experience the crisis. Though not having experienced an economic downturn for some twenty years, Korean policymakers addressed the crisis aggressively and with significant success. The IMF, World Bank, Asian Development Bank, and G-7 put together a large support package for Korea. Perhaps most important, the IMF and World Bank provided the government with a significant amount of technical assistance from their own staff and outside experts on both bank and corporate restructuring.

The Impact of the East Asian Crisis

Much has been written about the failure to anticipate the East Asian crisis. Not only was the crisis not predicted by the IMF, World Bank, and leading international economists, but once the crisis had struck Thailand and moved rapidly to other East Asian countries, perhaps equally problematic was the failure of leading institutions to recognize its depth and severity.

Macroeconomic Effects

In January 1998, World Bank staff focused on the macroeconomic consequences of the crisis. They were able to capture the direction of change in the key crisis countries for 1998, but badly underestimated the severity of the crisis in a number of dimensions (see box 11-1).[24] A breakdown or decomposition of GDP by these effects—the Japanese crisis, intraregional impact, and decline in trade—illustrates the interactive nature of such a crisis when it moves through the process of contagion from country to country in an unanticipated way (see tables 11-8 and 11-9).

BOX 11-1.   Macroeconomic Consequences of the East Asian Crisis

- Drop in domestic demand, especially the decline in investment
- Severe compression in imports
- Sharp decline in exports and export process
- Large current account surpluses
- Profound effect of the credit squeeze and rising interest rates on corporate distress
- Spillover effects from Thailand to the other countries, as well as the Japanese crisis
- Implications of the regional downturn among countries that were important trading partners

TABLE 11-8.   Analysis of Forecasting Errors on the Depth of the Crisis for 1998, East Asia-5

	Estimate	Actual	Difference
GDP growth (percent)	−0.2	−7.7	−7.5
Domestic demand (percent)	−0.6	−15.0	−9.0
Total investment (percent)	−13.5	−31.3	−17.8
Exports, GNFS volume[a] (percent)	18.0	10.6	−7.4
Imports, GNFS volume (percent)	−0.8	−18.0	−17.2
Current account balance (billions of US$)	7.3	66.2	58.9
Percent of GDP	0.8	10.8	10.0
Merchandise exports (billions of US$)	392.5	329.6	−62.9
Merchandise imports (billions of US$)	362.8	268.8	−94.0
Balance of trade (billions of US$)	29.7	60.8	31.1
Export price in US$ (percent)	−5.9	−15.8	−9.9
Import price in US$ (percent)	1.2	−8.2	−9.4
Terms of trade (percent)	−7.0	−8.3	−1.3

Source: World Bank staff estimates; World Bank, World Economic Prospects 2000, p. 38.
a. GNFS: goods and nonfactor services.

Fiscal Costs

The fiscal costs of the crisis were significant for all of the crisis countries, particularly Indonesia, owing to the costs of recapitalizing its financial sector. The focus was on recapitalizing and restructuring the banks in each country. Moreover, each country

TABLE 11-9. A Heuristic Decomposition of GDP Growth Forecast Errors, 1998

Percent

	Thailand	Malaysia	Republic of Korea	Indonesia	Philippines
GDP growth forecast error	−4.5	−10.4	−6.0	−12.3	−3.6
Effects of Japanese recession	−0.8	−1.5	−0.5	−0.8	−1.0
Effects of regional downturn	−1.0	−2.8	−0.5	−0.8	−2.2
Terms of trade (percent of GDP)	−0.7	−0.5	−1.0	−0.5	−0.1
Residual effects	−2.0	−5.6	−4.0	−10.2	−0.3
Memo items					
Proportion explained by Japan, regional downturn, and terms of trade	55	45	33	17	90
Proportion attributable to balance sheet and further contagion effects	45	55	66	83	10

Source: World Bank, *World Economic Prospects 2000*, p. 39.

established institutional arrangements to absorb bad assets through an asset management agency to implement corporate workouts in view of their weak and overwhelmed bankruptcy systems. Each of the crisis countries had to develop unique institutional arrangements for corporate and financial restructuring and to support structural changes in the financial system (see tables 11-10, 11-11, and 11-12).

Poverty Impact

The poverty impact of the crisis was perhaps the most shocking. Each country had grown for decades with no or few economic downturns, skating past the 1980s debt crises with relatively little impact. As Stiglitz noted:

> Whether one calls it a miracle or not is beside the point: the increases in incomes and the reductions in poverty in East Asia over the last three decades

**TABLE 11-10.   Estimated Recapitalization Costs for Commercial Banks,
mid-October 1999**

	Estimated costs	Local currency	US Dollars	Percentage of GDP	Remaining fiscal costs as percentage of GDP
Indonesia	550 trillion rupiah	100 trillion	14 billion	11	48
Republic of Korea	72 trillion won	56 trillion	47 billion	13	4
Malaysia[a]	31 billion ringgit	13 billion	3.4 billion	4	6
Thailand[b]	1,121 billion baht	751 billion	11 billion	16	8

Source: Central bank data; World Bank, *World Economic Prospects 2000*, p. 87.

Note: These are illustrative numbers based on varying assumptions of recovery of nonperforming loans, as discussed in the text.

a. Estimated costs include those to be incurred by Danaharta for purchasing nonperforming loans (15 billion ringgit) and recapitalization funds injected by Danamodal (16 billion ringgit).

b. Amount disbursed includes significant private sector funding of recapitalization, as discussed in the text.

**TABLE 11-11.   Institutional Arrangements for Corporate and
Financial Restructuring**

Country	Voluntary corporate workout	Asset resolution company	Agency for bank recapitalization
Indonesia	Jakarta Initiative Task Force	Indonesian Bank Restructuring Authority	Indonesian Bank Restructuring Authority
Republic of Korea	Corporate Restructuring Coordination Committee	Korea Asset Management Corporation (KAMCO)	Korea Deposit Insurance Corporation (KDIC)
Malaysia	Corporate Debt Restructuring Committee	Danaharta	Danamodal
Thailand	Corporate Debt Restructuring Advisory Committee	Financial Sector Restructuring Authority and Asset Management Corporation (for nonbank finance companies)	Financial Restructuring Advisory Committee (funded by the Financial Institutions Development Fund)

Source: World Bank, *World Economic Prospects 2000* (Washington, 2000), p. 85.

TABLE 11-12. Structural Changes in the Financial System

Country	Closures	State takeovers	Mergers
Indonesia	64 banks (18 percent)[a]	12 commercial banks (20 percent)	4 of 7 state banks to be merged into a single bank (54 percent)
Republic of Korea	5 commercial banks, 17 merchant banks, and more than 100 nonbank financial institutions (15 percent)	4 commercial banks (25 percent)	9 banks and 2 merchant banks to create 4 new commercial banks (15 percent)
Malaysia	None	1 commercial bank, 1 merchant bank, and 3 financial companies under central bank control (12 percent)	6 mergers of finance companies and commercial banks (2 percent)
Thailand	57 finance companies (11 percent) and 1 commercial bank (2 percent)	7 commercial banks (13–15 percent) and 12 finance companies (2.2 percent)	5 commercial banks and 13 finance companies into 3 banks (20 percent)

Source: World Bank, *Global Economic Prospects 2000*, p. 85.
a. Figures in parentheses refer to percentage of assets in the financial sector.

have been unprecedented. No one visiting these countries can fail to marvel at the developmental transformation, the changes not only in the economy but also in society. . . . The combination of high savings rates, government investment in education, and government directed industrial policy served to make the region an economic powerhouse. Growth rates were phenomenal for decades. And the standard of living rose enormously for tens of millions of people.[25]

To support Stiglitz's assertion, in the mid-1970s six of every ten people in East Asia lived on less than $1 a day. Over a period of twenty years, per capita income growth averaged 5.5 percent a year. By the mid-1990s, growth had led to faster and larger reduction of poverty in East Asia than in any other region. With a policy focus on widespread and relatively equal distribution of these gains, labor market flexibility, rural development, and basic education for all the East Asian economies experienced a high rate of employment creation and wage growth, the latter supported by significant productivity gains.[26]

Unemployment grew rapidly in the crisis countries from some 5.3 million people in 1996 to an estimated 18 million people at the end of 1998, 13 million of whom were located in Indonesia. In Thailand and Indonesia, which had large rural, agricultural populations, the impact of the crisis was exacerbated by drought. In Thailand by the end of 1997, 70 percent of the unemployed were poor rural workers in the northeast. World Bank estimates for 1998 using $1 a day as the poverty line in Indonesia and the Philippines, and $2 a day for Malaysia and Thailand, poverty was projected to increase by some 17 million more people in Indonesia, bringing the total number of poor to 56.5 million. In other countries the numbers were projected to be smaller, but still significant—2.3 million in Thailand, 665,000 in the Philippines, and some 500,000 or less in Malaysia where the crisis was less severe and more quickly contained by government policy.[27] The experience in Latin America supports the findings in East Asia. During the 1980s crises, poverty increased in fifty-five of fifty-eight recessions in Latin America and decreased or remained stable in twenty-five of thirty-two recoveries.[28]

Conclusions

By 2000, the East Asian countries had largely returned to growth. However, restructuring of the financial and corporate sector took years beyond the initial crisis recovery. Policy changes induced or catalyzed by the crisis, such as the adoption of international accounting standards, reform of bankruptcy systems, improvements in corporate governance, and improved standards of banking regulation and supervision, also took years to adopt and to implement. The experience from prior periods is that debt overhang can leave countries vulnerable to future crisis. This was not so much the issue in East Asia, where most of the countries were not highly indebted. The other lesson is that crises have a long tail and leave much in their wake to get done in order to fully recover and avoid future crises.

TWELVE

Crisis Resolution in Korea

1997–2003

The crisis that started in Thailand quickly moved to Korea over the course of 1997. Although the Korean financial sector, especially its banks, was in deep difficulty, it was the large industrial sector, dominated by *chaebols*—large complex conglomerates that were highly leveraged—that made the situation so challenging. Korea had not experienced an economic downturn for some twenty years, macroeconomic management was viewed as strong, GDP growth had averaged 7–8 percent per year for a number of years, unemployment was at 2–2.5 percent, and inflation was below 5 percent.[1]

However, Korea's economy grew very rapidly following the Korean War through a complex triangular interaction between the government, the banking sector, and the export-focused industrial sector, led by the chaebols.[2] This growth moved Korea from one of the poorest countries in the world after the war into the ranks of the OECD countries with per capita income at US$11,000 before the crisis.[3] Growth of the chaebols and other large corporations (nonconglomerates) was based on high leverage, well above the OECD average for industrial companies, which worked well as long as the economy was growing and interest rates were relatively low and stable. When interest rates shot up to 30 percent per annum, as a result of tight monetary policy adopted at the onset of the crisis, virtually all of Korea's chaebols, especially the second-tier chaebols designated by size from six to sixty-four, were technically bankrupt.

Starting in August 25, 2007, the government announced a series of measures to try and prevent the crisis from deepening. In the face of market nervousness it announced that it would provide financial support to the commercial and merchant banks and ensure payment of foreign debt. All financial institutions would need to present restructuring plans to be implemented over the next three to five years. The markets remained nervous, especially when the National Assembly failed to approve necessary economic and financial reforms. On November 19 the government introduced additional prevention mechanisms, including: (i) expanded funding for the Korea Asset Management Corporation (KAMCO) to lift bad assets off the books of the banks; (ii) incentives to promote mergers and acquisitions among financial sector institutions; (iii) mandatory restructuring measures for financial institutions and exit of nonviable institutions; (iv) increased funding for the Korea Deposit Insurance Corporation (KDIC); (v) liberalization of capital account transactions; and (vi) a wider band on the exchange rate. These measures also failed to satisfy the markets, and the won went into a free fall, reaching 2,000 won to the U.S. dollar, from 805 in 1996 and 951 earlier in 1997.[4]

The macroeconomic stabilization program that the government embarked on supported by an IMF standby framework was focused initially on restoring exchange rate stability, rebuilding reserves, and containing potentially inflationary pressures resulting from the crisis. Sharp tightening of monetary policy led to a spike in interest rates from 12 percent in late 1997 to 30 percent at year end.[5] The rise in interest rates resulted in a sharp deterioration of the financial performance of the corporate sector, which in turn led to pressure on the banking sector, which in turn led to a freeze on new loans for all but the most creditworthy clients, the calling of loans (in particular short-term lines of credit) and rising nonperforming loans (NPLs) in the banking system.[6] For an open economy such as Korea's, the inability of the corporate sector to obtain export financing on a timely basis meant that the engine that drove growth for so many years would inevitably stall. In fact, economic growth declined to a negative −6.7 percent in 1998 from a positive 6.8 percent in 1996 and a negative −5.0 percent in 1997.[7]

In December 2007, Korea approached the IMF and arranged a three-year standby facility, which resulted in record access to the IMF's resources of $20 billion, backed by $8 billion from the World Bank and $2 billion from the Asian Development Bank (ADB) as first-in-line lenders and some $27 billion as a backup or contingency facility from the G-7 countries. Together these institutions acted as a collective international lender of last resort. The IMF focused on macroeconomic policy and banking supervision, the World Bank on bank and corporate restructuring and related microeconomic policy advice, and the ADB on lending for small and medium-sized enterprises (SMEs).[8]

Korea had not had an economic downturn for some twenty years or more. There was no one in government who had faced a crisis. Perhaps just as important as the funding was the advice provided by IMF and World Bank staff and the consultants they retained to assist the government. For example, the bank restructuring team retained the firms McKinsey and Arthur Andersen to prepare financial models of the major banks and project what the banking system should look like five and ten years after the crisis so that the government did not merge and liquidate banks in an ad hoc manner without a roadmap.

The corporate restructuring/workout advisory team from the World Bank assisted the Financial Supervisory Commission (FSC) in designing a corporate workout strategy with input from an expert formerly at the Bank of England. The corporate advisory team of the World Bank also worked with the FSC and the major commercial banks to retain international experts to help the banks create workout units where none existed and to implement the initial workouts through a technical support facility of $33 million provided by the World Bank to the government for that purpose.[9]

Over the course of 1998, the government of Korea adopted a very aggressive reform program to simultaneously address macroeconomic issues, financial sector restructuring and reforms, corporate restructuring/workouts, and policy reforms. In a document outlining its reform measures, "The Korean Economy under New Leadership," the government of newly elected president Kim Dae-Jung sought to impose its mark on the reform process. The government announced: "Comprehensive economic reform requires a strong and democratic leadership with an unyielding commitment to go beyond the simple correction of past mistakes.... Kim Dae-Jung's vision for the nation's future ... embraces the principles of democracy and a free market economy. Indeed, the principles of market competition, transparency, and openness are already superseding anachronous views in the traditional business mindset."[10]

As of September 1998 the government had: (i) built reserves to $43 million; (ii) stabilized the won at 1,350–1,400 won to the U.S. dollar; and (iii) improved the maturity on external liabilities by reducing short-term debt from 44 percent at the end of 1997 to 25 percent of total external debt (just prior to the crisis short-term debt, primarily private trade credit, normally self-liquidating by the trades associated with it, was being rolled over at around 90 percent); (iv) net offshore borrowings, not included in IMF statistics, were reduced by some $4 billion and were also rolled over as mostly trade financing; and (v) cash flow projections were updated to ensure that the government would have no problem servicing its debts.

The Government's Reform Strategy

The cost of economic restructuring was being met primarily by the institutions themselves to minimize the risk of moral hazard. Government support was conditioned on strong rehabilitation measures. The government negotiated a social pact to ensure social cohesion and stability needed to pursue the reform program. The tripartite agreement among labor, management, and government represented a social pact that sought equitable burden sharing. Government's role initially was to establish the legal framework and policy incentives to promote reform and to mobilize the fiscal resources in support of necessary financial and corporate restructuring.[11]

Financial Sector Reforms

The government sought to restructure the financial sector, liberalize the capital markets, and strengthen prudential regulation and supervision. In an unconventional but, as it turned out, very successful approach, the government established the independent Financial Supervisory Commission, which reported directly to the president's office for the duration of the crisis, giving the FSC the necessary leverage to implement both banking and corporate restructuring and reforms. The government closed a number of financial institutions, including sixteen of thirty merchant banks, largely owned by the large chaebols and used by them to intermediate offshore financing. It also closed two securities companies and one investment trust company. In total, ninety-four financial institutions had their operations suspended or closed by the end of September 1998.

Banking Sector Reforms

As of the end of 1997, thirteen banks satisfied the BIS's required capital adequacy ratios, and twelve did not. After reviewing the banks' rehabilitation programs, the FSC liquidated five commercial banks and merged them into sound banks (BIS capital adequacy ratios of 10 percent or higher). The Korean Deposit Insurance Corporation was responsible for covering any shortfalls in net worth in the merged banks. KAMCO was responsible for absorbing NPLs. Two major banks, Korea

First and Seoul Bank, were to be sold in an open auction. The sound banks were asked by the FSC to adopt a restructuring program that would strengthen them further.

Other Financial Sector Companies

Insurance companies, securities companies, investment trusts, credit unions, and leasing companies all were evaluated and treated in efforts parallel to those of the banks.

Fiscal Support

The National Assembly approved 64 trillion won (US$45 billion) in support of the restructuring/rehabilitation program.[12] The government provided additional fiscal resources to KAMCO (32.5 trillion won [US$23.2 billion] to purchase NPLs to assist in the cleanup of the banking system. KAMCO in turn structured the assets into packages with the assistance of investment banking groups and sold the assets to bidding firms in bundles or packages. Many of these firms were international financial institutions, so-called bottom fishers, who purchased the assets at a deep discount and later sold them into the market. The government also provided fiscal support of 31.5 trillion won (US$22.5 billion) for the deposit insurance agency to protect depositors. Finally, it provided resources to recapitalize the banks. Bank support, to avoid moral hazard, came after restructuring was implemented, including replacement of management as necessary, and shareholders absorbed the first losses in these institutions. As of the end of June 1998, precautionary loans were estimated at 72.5 trillion won (US$51.9 billion) and NPLs were estimated at 63.5 billion won (US$45.4 billion). NPLs were 10.2 percent of the total loans of 624 trillion won (US$445.7 billion). However, the government projected that, because of aging and tighter classification, many substandard loans would become NPLs and that NPLs would reach 100–120 trillion won (US$71.4–85.7 billion). (See comparison between NPLs in Korea and other East Asian countries in chapter 11.)[13]

Fiscal resources were raised by the government largely in the form of bonds. The Korea Asset Management Fund and the Korea Deposit Insurance Corporation were the issuers. The government guaranteed the bonds and bore the interest costs. The government expected to recoup most of the costs through the sale of intervened banks and the liquidation of KAMCO-held assets.[14]

In addition to government and government agency support for the financial sector rehabilitation, the banks were encouraged to raise their own capital and to invite

---

BOX 12-1.   Korea: Capital Market Liberalization Measures, 1998

- Lifted the ceiling on foreign equity ownership, May 1998
- Allowed foreigners to invest in local bonds and short-term money market instruments without any restrictions
- Liberalized foreign exchange transactions to be phased in starting in April 1998
- Allowed hostile takeovers (merger and acquisition transactions) by May 1998
- Opened, by May 1998, 21 sectors to foreign direct investment (FDI), leaving only 31 out of 1,148 sectors closed to FDI
- Streamlined all laws related to FDI and incorporated them into a new Foreign Investment Promotion Act, August 1998. The Korean Trade and Investment Agency (KOTRA) was assigned responsibility for one-stop service for potential foreign investors
- Provided various tax and other incentives to foreign investors, particularly in high-tech sectors

---

foreign investment in what had previously been a closed sector. As in Mexico, Argentina, and Turkey, the crisis opened up financial sectors that were previously largely closed to foreign direct investment (FDI).[15]

Capital Market Liberalization

The government recognized the need to raise substantial capital for restructuring and recapitalization of the financial sector. It prioritized the liberalization, increased efficiency, and expanded its capital markets through a series of bold policy measures to open what had been a largely closed or restrictive economy to FDI.[16] (See box 12-1.)

Banking Regulation and Prudential Supervision

In addition to recapitalizing and restructuring the financial sector, the FSC was charged with significantly upgrading prudential regulation and supervising the banking system. This included placing restrictions on credit exposure, managing liquidity (maturity structures of assets and liabilities), valuing and classifying portfolios accurately and conservatively, and a setting up a consolidated risk management system.

Among the major changes in this direction were new rules requiring banks to adopt international accounting standards and mark-to-market rules for asset valuation.[17]

Corporate Sector Restructuring

In Korea and in the other East Asian crisis countries it became clear that problems in the real sector would need to be addressed.[18] First, if the banks were to be cleaned up and the NPLs fully resolved, it was necessary to address the corporate sector. The government and its agencies simply lacked the fiscal resources to absorb these losses if corporate sector distress was not addressed.

At the beginning of the crisis in Korea the banks provided a series of emergency loans to their clients to stave off bankruptcy (see table 12-1). This process could not continue if the banks were to be restructured and stabilized.[19]

Chaebol Distress and Bankruptcy

The industrial sector and its outward-oriented export orientation was at the heart of Korea's economic success. With virtually all of the major corporations in deep distress because of excessive leverage and high interest rates that peaked at 30 percent, the government simply could not ignore the problem. Virtually all of these companies were technically in bankruptcy as their debt service coverage ratio sank below 1 (see tables 12-2 and 12-3).[20]

Early in 1997 five large chaebols and other corporate groups employing 107,000 workers and with 27.6 trillion won in assets (US$19.7 billion) petitioned for bankruptcy. Major groups such as Kia, Hanbo Steel, and Halla were among those filing for bankruptcy. In total, thirteen chaebols failed by the end of 1997 with assets of 47 trillion won (US$33.6 billion) and debt of 28 trillion won (US$20 billion) (see table 12-4). As the situation deteriorated further in 1998, several more groups outside of the five largest chaebols (the "top five")—eighteen of the top thirty chaebols employing some 225,000 workers with 103.4 trillion in assets (US$73.9 billion)[21]—seemed likely to follow into bankruptcy.[22]

Cross Guarantees

Contributing to the bankruptcies was a system of cross guarantees among the affiliates of a chaebol. Since corporate holding groups were not allowed under Korean corporate law, and the office of the chairman of the large groups existed de facto but not

TABLE 12-1.   Korea: Bankruptcy Avoidance Loans to Large Industrial Groups

Industrial group	Debt-equity, year end 1997 (percent)	Emergency loans (billions of won)	Date
Haitai	1,501	130	October 14, 1997
New Core	1,786	55	October 20, 1997
Jindo	n.a.[a]	106	November 19, 1997
Shinho	661	80	November 27, 1997
Hanwha	1,008	300	December 17, 1997
Hanil	n.a.	50	December 31, 1997
Dong-ah Construction	585	330	January 10, 1998
Kohap	511	300	January 30, 1998
Hanwha	1,008	442	February 10, 1998
Woobang Construction	n.a.	110	March 3, 1998
Dong-ah Construction	585	30	May 7, 1998
Total		1,933	

Source: Ira Lieberman and William Mako, "Korea—Corporate Restructuring Strategy" (mimeo) (Washington: World Bank, August 17, 1998), p. 3.

a. Not available.

de jure, the corporate parent could not provide bank guarantees for a subsidiary's loans. Instead the affiliates guaranteed one another in a spider web of cross guarantees. So, in 1997 and 1998 when large groups were in deep distress, both good and bad assets were failing—going into bankruptcy. For example, deeply distressed Kia Steel and Kia Trading were bringing down Kia Auto.[23]

The Special Case of Small-Business Owners

Finally, thousands of SMEs were in difficulty—some 2,000 to 3,000 a month were failing. SMEs, almost all of which were family owned, began to lay off all nonfamily employees. Also, many of the SMEs operating as satellites of the chaebols were adversely affected by the problems facing their major customers. Payments were normally through notes discounted at the banks, but during the crisis the notes were extended 90 and 180 days, squeezing the cash flow of the SMEs. In addition, there was a credit freeze due to the distress of the banking system that affected SMEs most severely. By the end of 1998 some 20,000 SMEs had failed.[24] The bankruptcy or near bankruptcy of SMEs caused deep social distress in Korea. The loss of face in not being able to provide for their families led many Korean men to wander off into the mountains, congregate in local parks, and even jump off bridges. It was clear that the government needed to act.

TABLE 12-2. Korea: Debt-Equity Ratios of Largest Thirty Chaebols, Year End 1996 and 1997

Percent

	1996[a]	1997[a]
Hyundai	437	579
Samsung	267	371
LG	347	506
Daewoo	338	472
SK	384	468
Ssangyong	409	400
Kia	517	n.a.[b]
Hanlin	557	908
Hanwha	751	1,215
Lotte	192	217
Kumho	478	944
Halla	2,066	−1,600
Dong-ah	355	360
Doosan	688	590
Daelim	423	514
Hansol	292	400
Hyosung	370	465
Dongkuk	219	324
Jinro	3,765	−894
Kolon	318	434
Kohap	591	472
Dongbu	262	338
Tongyang	307	404
Haltal	659	1,501
New Core	1,226	1,784
Anam	479	1,499
Hanil	577	n.a.
Keopyung	348	439
Miwon	417	n.a.[b]
Shinho	491	677
Average	363	519

Source: Fair Trade Commission, Korea; Lieberman and Mako, "Korea—Corporate Restructuring Strategy," p. 1.

a. Without financial affiliates.
b. Not available.

TABLE 12-3. Korea: Increases in Bank Debt of the Thirty Largest Chaebols

Billions of won

Chaebol	Year end 1996	Year end 1997	Increase	Increase (percent)
Hyundai	11,920	19,026	7,106	60
Samsung	12,329	17,326	4,997	41
Daewoo	9,524	15,105	5,581	59
LG	8,542	10,957	2,415	28
Hanjin	3,853	5,509	1,656	43
SK	3,758	4,061	303	8
Ssang yong	3,274	4,021	744	23
Han-wha	3,054	3,923	869	28
Daelim	1,798	2,894	1,096	61
Kumho	1,845	2,598	753	41
Kohap	1,464	2,422	958	65
Doosan	1,554	2,003	449	29
Dong-ah	1,335	1,889	554	41
Hyosung	1,203	1,882	679	56
Anam	1,106	1,651	545	49
Dongkuk	1,026	1,628	602	59
Hansol	840	1,540	700	83
Hanil	1,170	1,311	141	12
Kolon	768	1,219	451	59
Shinho	890	1,192	302	34
Haitai	944	1,114	170	18
Lotte	828	1,060	232	28
Kabul	528	984	456	86
Saehan	574	974	400	70
Tongkook	713	899	186	26
Keopyung	516	892	376	73
Dongbu	659	828	169	26
Samyang	621	793	172	28
Tongii	814	793	(21)	−3
Dongyang	371	783	412	111
Total	77,821	111,277	33,456	43

Source: Bank Supervisory Board via Fair Trade Commission; Lieberman and Mako, "Korea—Corporate Restructuring Strategy," p. 2.

Note: Balance sheet data for chaebol financial affiliates were not readily accessible for 1996. Data on overseas borrowing by overseas affiliates are reported separately to the Bank of Korea. As for accounting practices, local accountants note that: writeoffs for doubtful accounts are typically limited to the 1 percent that can be deducted for tax purposes; obsolescent inventory may be shipped to overseas affiliates and reported as sales revenue rather than written down or written off; fixed assets have regularly been revalued upward in recent years, despite low inflation; and companies are aggressive in capitalizing research and development (R&D) and securities issuance costs.

TABLE 12-4. Korean Chaebols under Court Supervision, 1997–99

Group	Date	Leverage (percent)	Net borrowings (billions of won)	Status
Hanbo	January 23, 1997	1,896	4,091	Court receivership; sale under way
Sammi	March 19, 1997	−3,324	875	Court receivership
Jinro	April 28, 1997	4,231	1,917	Composition; sale being finalized
Daenong	May 28, 1997	−2,806	1,172	Court receivership
Hanshin Construction	June 2, 1997	649	502	Court receivership
Kia	July 15, 1997	411	6,624	Sold to Hyundai
Ssangbangwool	October 15, 1997	711	595	Court receivership
Taeil Media	October 24, 1997	334	588	Composition
Haitai	November 1, 1997	658	3,046	Court receivership; sale under way
New Core	November 4, 1997	1,222	1,215	Applied for court receivership
Soosan Heavy	November 26, 1997	476	639	Court receivership
Halla	December 5, 1997	2,066	6,453	Court receivership
Chunggu	December 27, 1997	484	728	Court receivership
Sungwon	April 12, 1999	n.a.[a]	545	Composition
Samsung Motors	June 30, 1999	n.a.	4,170	Court receivership
Total		822	33,160	

Source: Financial Supervisory Committee; Masahiro Kawai, Ira Lieberman, and William Mako, "Financial Stabilization and Initial Restructuring of East Asian Corporations: Approaches, Results and Lessons," in *Emerging Markets in the New Financial System: Managing Financial and Corporate Distress* (Brookings, 2005), p. 79.

a. Not available.

The Corporate Workout Program

Recognizing the problem of corporate distress, the government under the FSC designed and implemented a corporate workout process that segmented the corporate restructuring problem among the top five chaebols which were asked to develop and implement their own restructuring program to reduce their leverage to 2:1, still a high leverage rate by OECD standards, within two years. Numbers six to sixty-four on the list of chaebols and other large independent corporations would "voluntarily" agree to participate in a time-bound corporate workout process with their major creditor banks under the auspices of the FSC and a Corporate Restructuring Commission (CRC) established for this process. Finally, SMEs would be supported by the government and funding from the Asian Development Bank through the banks and various ways to inject liquidity into the sector.[25]

Restructuring the Top Five Chaebols

The top five chaebols—Hyundai, Samsung, Daewoo, SK, and LG—were very large, complex conglomerates that operated in a wide variety of productive sectors and competed fiercely with each other for domestic market share. They also were highly export oriented. The top five, each of which had several publicly listed affiliates, were largely controlled by family groups. In many respects their structure and mode of operation was similar to that of the Japanese *keiretsu*.[26] These firms were clearly "too big to fail." They were also very powerful politically and difficult for the newly elected administration of Kim Dae-Jung to handle. Clearly the top five had to be addressed on a case-by-case basis. The goal set by the government was to reduce their leverage to 200 percent by the end of 1999. Each chaebol had to submit plans to the major banks, which were overseen by the FSC.

Performance under the plans was monitored closely by the FSC and by the president's office through monthly meetings with the chairmen of the top five. The top five differed greatly in their approaches to restructuring. In meetings I had with a colleague and the chairmen of the top five early in 1998, Samsung's acting chairman indicated that the company had retained Goldman Sachs to advise it on its larger companies and the International Finance Corporation, a World Bank affiliate, for its smaller companies. Samsung intended to improve on the government's target of 200 percent and come into line with other major corporations internationally, or closer to 1:1 debt to equity ratio.

During our meeting with Daewoo's chairman, in contrast, he denied that Daewoo needed to restructure and indicated that he did not believe Western advisers had sufficient knowledge of Korean business and did not trust them to maintain the confidentiality of their advice. Daewoo had been bailed out previously and clearly expected to be bailed out again.[27]

Hyundai soon became a favorite of the government because of its support for the new president's opening to North Korea, the so-called Sunshine Policy. Hyundai, despite its need to deleverage, was able to purchase Kia automotive operations in a

TABLE 12-5. Korea: Capital Structure Improvement Plan
Implementation of Top Five Chaebols

Trillions of won unless otherwise indicated

	1999 annual (A)	Plan 1999, Q1–Q3	Implementation 1999, Q1–Q3 (B)	1999 progress rate (B/A) (percent)
Capital raising	33.6	22.2	26.8	79.8
Asset sales	13.7	8.8	10.9	80.0
Equity capital	19.9	13.4	15.9	79.7
Foreign capital (billions of $)	7.19	50.9	61.6	85.6
Cross guarantee resolved	2.7	1.6	2.7	99.2
Spinoffs (number)	173	131	427	246.8
Corporate governance (No. of persons)	136	136	143	105.1
Disposition of affiliates	84	55	61	72.6

Source: Financial Supervisory Commission, Daewoo group excluded; Masahiro Kawai, Ira W. Lieberman, and William Mako, "Assessing Corporate Restructuring in Asia: Korea's Corporate Restructuring Program," Conference on Emerging Markets and Financial Development, Seattle, March 30–April 1, 2000.

bankruptcy auction and also acquire a large independent microchip producer through merger as a result of the government's asset swap program.

As of the end of April 1999, the top five chaebols were able to reduce their leverage in a variety of ways, but not in line with the target. They raised 22.1 trillion won (US$15.8 billion) in new capital, 81 percent of the target through asset sales and new capital. They also unwound cross-debt guarantees. Attraction of FDI largely through spinoff of joint venture holdings was substantial, at US$9.9 billion, but achieved just 40 percent of the target. The top five revalued their assets substantially so that their financial statements showed a significant reduction in debt-equity ratios. The Financial Supervisory Commission (which later changed its name to Financial Supervisory Service, FSS) reversed these valuations. Results varied greatly among the top five chaebols. For example, Daewoo increased its indebtedness from 1997 through 1998 by 17.1 trillion won (US$12.2 billion). Daewoo and Hyundai remained with debt-equity ratios of 526 percent and 449 percent, respectively. Samsung, LG, and SK reduced their debts by 4.9 trillion, 6.5 trillion, and 1.4 trillion won, respectively, while their debt-equity ratio fell to 275.7 percent, 341 percent, and 354.9 percent, respectively (see Tables 12-5 and 12-6). In general, the banks were too weak and unable to adequately

TABLE 12-6.   Korea: Changes in Leverage of Top Five Chaebols

Group	Debt (trillions of won)				Liabilities/equity (percent)[a]			
	1997	1998	99:IH[b]	1999 target	1997	1998	99:IH	1999 target
Hyundai[c]	61	69	65	45	572	449	341	199
Samsung	50	45	39	37	366	276	193	194
LG	43	36	35	28	508	341	247	200
SK	24	23	21	18	466	335	227	200
Top four	178	173	160	128				
Daewoo	43	60	62	63	474	527	588	n.a.[d]

Source: Kwai, Lieberman, and Mako, "Assessing Corporate Restructuring in Asia."

a. Excludes asset revaluations.
b. First half year.
c. Includes Kia debt of 7.5 trillion won.
d. Not available.

supervise the Capital Structure Improvement Plans (CSIPs) of the top five chaebols, so the task fell to the FSS and through the FSS directly to the president's office.[28]

Corporate Workouts: Chaebols Six to Sixty-Four and Other Large Firms

In July 1998, with encouragement from the Financial Supervisory Commission, 210 local financial institutions embarked on a contractual approach to out-of-court workouts as an alternative to unsupervised "bankruptcy avoidance loans" (bailouts) and court-supervised insolvency.[29] These institutions signed a Corporate Restructuring Agreement (CRA) on June 25, 1998, that provided for a one-to-three-month standstill (subject to due diligence requirements) and could be extended for one month; a creditors' committee led by a lead creditor, typically the chaebol's lead bank; a 75 percent threshold for creditor approval of a workout agreement to avoid a "cram down" by small creditors; a seven-person Corporate Restructuring Coordination Committee (CRCC), selected by signatories, to provide workout guidelines and arbitrate intercreditor differences in cases where creditors could not approve a workout plan after three votes; and CRCC imposition of fines (up to 30 percent of a credit or 50 percent of the amount of noncompliance) for noncompliance with an arbitration decision.[30]

The Korean government, under the auspices of the FSS, encouraged lead banks to first focus on voluntary (that is, out of court) workout of the mid-tier chaebols (six to sixty-four, ranked by asset size). These chaebols tended to be in deepest distress, generally lacking the financial resources and clout to restructure on their own. A large number of insolvencies in this group could have created an upsurge in unemployment, putting severe social distress and political pressure on the government to abandon its reform program. Moreover, a series of major defaults could have provoked a secondary financial crisis, leading to pressure on the currency and interest rates. The six to sixty-four chaebols tended to be less complex and therefore potentially easier to restructure than the top five chaebols. In the FSS's view, experience gained by restructuring chaebols from among the mid-tier group would prepare lead banks (and their professional advisers) to take on the top five chaebols, whose size and complexity placed them in a league of their own.

The CRA provided expedited procedures and tight deadlines. The time frame, though aggressive, encouraged an initial emphasis on balance sheet restructuring before asset sales and new equity investment that tended to be more time-consuming. It took some three to six months on average to reach agreement on a workout plan. Under the pressure of tough deadlines, the initial due diligence before a workout agreement tended to focus on financial viability and financial projections and place little emphasis on sensitivity analysis and alternative restructuring scenarios. Moreover, inadequate emphasis was placed on deeper restructuring, replacement of management, and an analysis of the fundamental viability of the business in the longer term.

By the end of 1999 virtually all of the corporate workouts had been completed (see Tables 12-7 and 12-8). Given the leverage of these companies, the initial emphasis was on debt rescheduling, capitalization of interest in arrears, unwinding guarantees, and some debt equity swaps. There was relatively little new money on offer. Initially, there was little real restructuring. However, a number of companies (estimated at 15–20 percent of the initial group) underwent a second round of restructuring with greater emphasis on real restructuring, including changes of management, asset disposals, and injection of fresh capital. Finally, if a firm needed to go through a third round of restructuring, that generally led to initiation of liquidation proceedings. The ability to use the bankruptcy system in exceptional cases or when a debtor was unwilling to come to the table was critical to the success of the workout program. The CRC also played an important role in resolving disputes over workouts.

Daewoo—Too Big to Fail

On July 9, 1999, Daewoo, the second largest chaebol by assets, under severe financial distress due to its exceedingly high leverage and little progress under its CSIP in raising equity or selling assets, petitioned its domestic creditor financial institutions to

TABLE 12-7.   Korea: Workout Cases under the Corporate
Restructuring Agreement Framework

				Outcome thereof	
Groups	Applications	Dropout	Graduation	Workout plan agreed	Workout plan yet to be agreed
Top five chaebols	12 (by Daewoo)	0	0	12	
Firms six to sixty-four	47 (of 17 chaebols)	5	0	42 (of 16 chaebols)	
Other large and medium-sized firms	43	3	1	38	1
Leasing companies	2	1	0	1	
Total	104	9	1	93	1

Source: Corporate Restructuring Coordination Committee (CRCC), as of December 2, 1999; Kawai, Lieberman, and Mako, "Assessing Corporate Restructuring in Asia."

supply 4 trillion won in new financing in order to allow Daewoo to repay extremely short-term overnight debts. The chairman of Daewoo, Kim Woo-jung, committed to provide 10 trillion won (US$7.1 billion) in collateral from affiliates and his own personal assets. Creditor banks and investment trust companies (ITCs) with government suasion agreed to Daewoo's request and also agreed to reschedule some 12 trillion won (US$8.6 billion) in debts due to creditors by year-end.[31]

Daewoo's financial problems threatened a secondary financial crisis with significant debt due to a large number of ITCs and large banks. There were concerns over an investor run on ITCs. The Daewoo situation also threatened to derail the successful reform program and to undermine investor confidence in the Korean economy, which was growing strongly in 1999. In the days following the bailout the Korean stock market fell 11 percent.[32]

Because of its numerous and complex overseas holdings and large number of listed and unlisted holdings in Korea, it was difficult for the government and the creditor institutions to know the exact amount of Daewoo's debt and its maturity structure. According to FSC and Federal Trade Commission (FTC) data as of the end of 1998, Daewoo's debt was 59.9 trillion won (US$42.9 billion), of which 52 percent was short term, due within one year. However, these figures substantially understated the total group debt because Daewoo failed to consolidate the offshore liabilities of its 396 overseas subsidiaries and 134 branches at the end of 1998. Overseas, foreign currency debts were estimated at US$9.9 billion as of June 1999, of which US$5.48 billion

TABLE 12-8.   Korea: Summary of Corporate Restructuring
Agreement Workouts

Workout type	Agreed amounts (billions of won)	Actual implementation as of September 30, 1999 (percent)
Self-help		
Real estate sales	3,956	23
Affiliate sales	1,047	7
Other asset sales	995	46
Foreign capital	1,650	58
Rights issues	433	53
Cost reductions/capital contributions	1,262	44
	9,343	34
Debt restructuring		
Rate reduction and deferral	23,302	96
Deferral	4,857	93
Conversion to equity or convertible bonds	4,329	78
Other[a]	2,412	105
	34,900	94
Total	44,243	81
New money	2,025	

Source: Financial Supervisory Service; Kawai, Lieberman, and Mako, "Assessing Corporate Restructuring in Asia."

a. Includes repayment and writeoffs.

(over 50 percent) was short term. This figure excludes trade finance, commercial liabilities, and accounts payable. ITCs held some 21.9 trillion won of this debt—commercial paper and bonds (US$15.6 billion) and banks 14.5 trillion won (US$10.35 billion)—loans, commercial paper, and bonds plus guarantees extended by banks on Daewoo's behalf of 23.5 trillion won (US$16.8 billion).[33]

Government reaction was swift. Unlike the other top five chaebols, it was clear that Daewoo could not be trusted to control its own restructuring program. On July 25 the senior economic team consisting of the minister of finance and economy, the chairman of the FSC, the president's secretary for economic affairs, and the governor of the Bank of Korea met and announced the following measures: (i) the government would provide liquidity as necessary to the ITCs; (ii) the government would use public funds as necessary to maintain the stability of the banking system; (iii) the Bank of Korea would maintain its present low interest rate policy; (iv) creditor financial institutions would be given collateral of 1.5 times their obligations to Daewoo.[34]

The restructuring/workout of Daewoo was to follow the workout process approved in law for the six to sixty-four group of chaebols, with the major creditor banks leading the restructuring and financial advisers and major international auditing firms retained to provide maximum speed, expertise, and transparency. On July 27 four major banks were appointed to lead the workout process. In Daewoo's case the group would be split into five or six small groups which, following due diligence, would be disposed of through sale or merger. Complicating the process was the existence of foreign creditors who had declined to participate in the previous workout and also declined in this case to participate in the Daewoo workout. Foreign creditors secured by inventory for Daewoo Motors began to seize inventories of cars in Belgium and Amsterdam to protect themselves.[35] On August 16, 1999, the government announced the detailed basis for restructuring Daewoo under a special memorandum of understanding (MOU) that indicated how the major group companies and assets would be disposed of, the composition of the six groups for due diligence and workout with the bank, and the audit company assigned to each group.[36] On September 5, 1999, the government announced Daewoo's final restructuring plan, subject to due diligence[37] (see table 12-9).

Given the vulnerability of Daewoo's diverse business lines to market and financial uncertainty and the rigid and lengthy procedures in bankruptcy, preliminary due diligence provided an estimate of recoveries in liquidation through the formal bankruptcy process—37 percent for electronics, 29 percent for motors, 25 percent for corporate's construction business, and 18 percent for corporate's trading business. This would have represented enormous losses for the financial system, which in turn would have required a further injection of government capital to support the system. The workout process, though imperfect, was designed to maintain the various lines of business, to the extent possible, as going concerns that could in time attract acquirers or merger partners.[38]

On November 24 and 25, CRA signatories agreed on a general approach to workouts for Daewoo. The focus of the workouts was on the restructuring of debts. Of the proposed 57 trillion won (US$40.7 billion) in debt restructuring, 51 percent would be derived from interest rate reductions and grace periods on repayment, 9 percent would be debt-equity conversions, and 36 percent would be the conversion of debt into convertible bonds at 0.1 percent interest rate. Commitment of new money, 6.6 trillion won (US$4.7 billion), largely from the Korean banks, would be for trade finance and working capital requirements to allow the businesses to continue operating. The present value calculation of losses was greater than 50 percent for each of

TABLE 12-9. Daewoo: Overview of Proposed Workouts

Billions of won

Daewoo division	Debt deferral		Debt conversion				
	Reduced rate	Normal rate	Equity	Convertible bonds	Other	Total	New money
Corporate	6,044	n.a.[a]	2,000	16,700	251	24,995	1,909
Heavy	7,556	n.a.	1,349	n.a.	n.a.	8,905	148
Motors	6,751	n.a.	1,470	1,878	n.a.	10,099	2,154
Ssangyong Motors	1,587	n.a.	130	n.a.	19	1,736	264
Telecommunications	1,054	n.a.	200	1,145	18	2,417	318
Motor sales	n.a.	539	n.a.	n.a.	n.a.	539	n.a.
Electronics	3,689	n.a.	395	1,065	1,144	6,293	n.a.
Electronic Components	117	36	n.a.	n.a.	n.a.	153	5
Orion Electronics	1,230	121	n.a.	n.a.	n.a.	1,351	38
Kyungnam Enterprises	92	85	134	n.a.	218	529	10
Capital	4,757	n.a.	40	138	n.a.	4,935	n.a.
Diners Club	1,238	n.a.	n.a.	n.a.	n.a.	1,238	n.a.
Total	34,115	781	5,718	20,926	1,650	63,190	4,846

Source: FSS; Kawai, Lieberman and Mako, "Assessing Corporate Restructuring in Asia."
a. Not applicable.

the workout cases. The only reasonable solution was to let the workouts take place. In several cases this meant recalibration of the workouts in a second or third pass, as reliable cash flow projections for the various business lines and entities were very difficult to make under the time pressure of reaching an initial solution for Daewoo. This process played out over a number of years, buying time for the financial institutions, the government, and the economy to fully recover.[39] The banks and ITCs eventually sold a large proportion of their Daewoo loans to KAMCO. As of the end of 2002, KAMCO held 32.3 trillion won (US$22.9 billion) of Daewoo debt, some 70 percent of KAMCO's assets at that point in time.[40]

Daewoo was at the extreme, but the workout process overall often represented second-best solutions to restructuring the company in distress, when there was not time in the middle of the crisis to achieve a first-best solution—a full restructuring. The workout process allowed the stakeholders—the government, the financial institutions, and the corporate sector—to buy time until the immediate crisis was over. This was also true with respect to injecting liquidity into the small-business sector to prevent thousands of small businesses from going to the wall.

"Big Deals"

Toward the end of 1998 the government and big industry—the top five chaebols—announced a framework for reducing overcapacity in several basic sectors of the economy. The program, which became known as "Big Deals," was to involve mergers and asset swaps among the largest chaebols in sectors such as semiconductors, petrochemicals, automobiles, aerospace, heavy equipment manufacturing, and oil refining.[41] In general, the program did not work. Only the semiconductor deal was concluded by the end of 1999, with Hyundai acquiring LG's operations. It seemed clear to me as a close observer of this process that the large groups, normally intense competitors, were fighting over valuations, and this would prevent any such program from operating beyond the immediate crisis period. The asset swap program was not viewed as a success by outside observers such as the IMF, the World Bank, and the rating agencies.

Land Reform

Foreign ownership of land was liberalized in June 1998. To stimulate real estate divestiture as a way of reducing corporate leverage, a legal framework for asset-backed securities was created in September 1998. The government also provided tax incentives and information services to foreigners to boost real estate sales. In addition, the Korean Land Corporation negotiated the purchase of 3 trillion won (US$2.2 billion) of real estate by September 1998.[42]

It was understood that the companies that agreed to sell real estate holdings would have a call on the real estate within five years and would be able to repurchase based on a pricing formula agreed at the time of sale.

Credit Guarantee Facilities and Export Finance for SMEs

The government operated a very successful program of partial risk guarantees for SME financing through risk guarantee agencies (a form of insurance fund) with credit offered and partially guaranteed though the banks. In 1998 these agencies provided some 41 trillion won (US$2.9 billion) in credit guarantees (not clear that this was all for SMEs) with government fiscal resources of some 2.6 trillion won in the first half of 1998 and another 1.8 trillion won allocated for the second half of 1998 (US$3.14 billion in total).[43] In addition, export financing of US$5.3 billion was provided by the banks, while the Korea Export Insurance Corporation's capital was expanded by the government from 20 trillion to 31 trillion won (from US$14.3 billion to US$22 billion) to try and sustain Korean exports, at the heart of Korea's economic success.

Corporate Governance

A major weakness of the Korean corporate structure was its governance. Family groups controlled the chaebols, even the largest ones with listed companies as part of the group. The chairman's position was typically hereditary or passed through to the logical heir in the immediate family that controlled the company. Control was absolute, though the controlling family usually controlled a small minority of the shares and the extended family a larger percentage of the shares, but still a minority. There were no independent members on the board, contrary to what was considered good practice in the West. That is, a small group of families had tight control over an important group of companies that were widely viewed as too big to fail. As these firms grew and expanded their scope of activity, to maintain control of the companies these families assumed more and more debt. In the years leading up to the crisis the chaebols became more and more risk laden and susceptible to an economic downturn.[44]

Policy Measures and Increased Transparency

The government sought to improve transparency and accountability through a series of policy measures before the end of 1998; these included: (i) requiring consolidated financial statements for the groups from 1999 forward; (ii) adoption of international accounting standards (timing not stated); (iii) elimination of restrictions on voting rights for institutional investors from June 1998; (iv) amendment of bankruptcy laws in February 1998 to facilitate the exit of insolvent firms (at the end of March 1998, cross-debt guarantees were unwound in an amount of 10 trillion won (US$7.14 billion), some 30 percent of total guarantees among the thirty largest chaebols (the rest were dissolved in the process of corporate workouts during 1999); (v) elimination of the requirement of cross guarantees by financial institutions as of April 1, 1998.[45]

Social Safety Net

In order to reduce labor opposition to crisis measures such as reducing the work force and other corporate reforms, the government, corporate leadership, and labor signed a tripartite accord in February 1998.[46] Based on the accord, the government moved to expand the social safety net at a projected cost of some 10 trillion won (US$7.1 billion) for new job creation, job training, job security support measures, and income compensation for laid-off workers. The government estimated that some 2.9 million recipients would benefit from these measures.

TABLE 12-10.   Size of Korea's Corporate Restructuring Program

Indicator	Amount (trillions of won)
Bankruptcies by end of 1997	28
Top five chaebols' asset sales and recapitalization	47
Corporate workouts	44
Daewoo restructuring workout	63
Small-business liquidity support	24
Total	206[a]

Source: Analysis of data provided by the Korean Financial Supervisory Agency; Michael Pomerleano and William Shaw, eds., Corporate Restructuring: Lessons from Experience (Washington: World Bank, 2005), p. 68.

a. Approximately $171.6 billion at 1,200 won to the U.S. dollar. Excludes KAMCO's asset purchases. KAMCO purchases had a nominal value of 101 trillion won.

Conclusions

Korea climbed out of its crisis with almost 10 percent GDP growth in 1999. Over the course of 1998 and 1999, the government mounted a massive program of financial and corporate restructuring (see table 12-10), significant policy reforms, and a broad liberalization of the economy in areas such as capital markets and restriction of FDI. Efforts to improve corporate governance and reduce the power of the families that owned the largest chaebols was an important step in the effort to democratize capitalism in Korea. If the expression "a crisis is a terrible thing to waste" has any meaning, then the Korean response was the embodiment of this expression.

THIRTEEN

The Turkish Crisis

2001–05

The Turkish financial/economic crisis began in the first quarter of 2001. It capped a series of crises that began in 1994; in 1999 two earthquakes caused severe economic disruption and loss of life. In the first quarter of 2001 Turkey experienced its deepest crisis since World War II. This chapter discusses that crisis and the recovery through 2005.[1]

Turkey was hardly new to sovereign crises. Turkey faced a series of external sovereign debt restructurings in the late 1970s and early 1980s. The latter was viewed as one of the precursors to the debt crises of the early 1980s discussed in Part II of this book. The Turkish debt renegotiations in 1979, 1980, and 1981 involved protracted efforts to arrive at a complex set of agreements with commercial banks and other trade creditors. Included in the June 1979 agreement was new bank financing for trade-related purposes and rescheduling of bank credit. In August 1979 commercial banks agreed to reschedule convertible Turkish lira deposits in a principal amount of $2.27 billion.[2] In July 1980 Turkey also restructured its official loans and suppliers' credits in an amount of $1.5 billion, representing a consolidation of three years of debt service arrears from 1978 through 1980.[3] As a study by the International Monetary Fund (IMF) observed, "Turkey faced a highly critical debt situation that required massive debt rescheduling by official creditors and commercial banks, emergency aid by OECD countries and successive adjustment programs."[4]

Turkey, unlike Mexico and Argentina, did not undertake extensive structural reforms after the 1980s debt crisis or before the 2001 crisis. In fact, Turkey was a lagging case relative to these countries and a number of other countries, including the Central and Eastern European countries, which were focused on accession to the European Union (EU) after the mid-1990s. Its macroeconomic situation was also unstable. Turkey started its major reforms in response to the crisis in 2001 and continued strongly through 2005.

Following the crisis, the electorate sharply rejected the coalition of parties that had ruled Turkey during the previous decade. The post-crisis government was run by a party with a parliamentary majority, committed to an orthodox macroeconomic policy, under the guidance of an IMF stand-by program, and with a vision of reforms focused on EU accession. EU accession did not happen, but during this period the government worked hard to meet EU standards on both economic and legal reforms; these new policies provided confidence to the corporate sector as well as consumers, and the economy grew strongly from the initial recovery year 2002 through 2005.

Overview of the Crisis

Companies and business associations had little confidence in Turkey's political establishment. This, together with the collapse of domestic markets in 2001, translated into a lack of business confidence. Many businesspeople believed in the government's stabilization program, which was established in early 2000 in conjunction with the IMF. When the program failed in February 2001, over what was perceived as political infighting, businesses across the country were hurt—many were on the brink of insolvency—and business activity was paralyzed for several months.[5]

The spark that ignited the conflict was the infighting between the president and prime minister on addressing corruption within the government. Markets already sensitized by the East Asian and Russian crises reacted swiftly and overshot—overnight rates jumped to an unprecedented level of 6,200 percent. The exchange rate collapsed, and Turkey announced that it was moving to a floating rate system. The deeper-seated cause of the crisis was an unstable macroeconomic environment: high inflation, high real interest rates, a large budget deficit, substantial public sector borrowing requirements, and the perceived fragility of the banking system following the intervention of Demir Bank and its takeover by the State Deposit and Insurance Fund (SDIF).

The Government's Economic Growth Program and Developments in 2001

The government's economic growth program in agreement with the IMF, as a modification of the 2000 Stand-by Agreement, aimed to sharply reduce inflation by the end of 2002, stabilize the currency, lower real interest rates, and ease public sector borrowing requirements and the associated crowding out of financial markets.[6] The program originally anticipated that GNP growth would turn positive by the fourth quarter of 2001 and reach 5 percent in 2002. In addition, the government committed to a series of structural reforms, including restructuring and privatizing state banks, divesting previously intervened banks, resuming the privatization program, and attracting foreign direct investment (FDI). These reforms were inevitably slowed, however, by the deep recession in the domestic economy and the worsening external environment, especially after the September 11, 2001, terror attacks in the United States. Increasing FDI by restarting the privatization program and attracting FDI and portfolio investment to distressed corporations and banks was made especially difficult with the flight to quality that occurred in international capital markets. It was also exceedingly difficult for the government to raise funds in global capital markets—funds that it desperately needed to service debt.

In addition, worker remittances dropped by a third in the first half of 2001, and tourism revenues—robust through August and one of the few bright spots in the economy—were of deep concern in light of September 11.With these developments, Turkey became far more reliant on official capital flows from the IMF and World Bank, and on bilateral arrangements through the G-7.

To implement this program, the dysfunctional coalition government appointed Kemal Derviş as state minister for the economy (effectively the sultan in charge of steering the economy through the crisis). Derviş, a vice president at the World Bank, had been closely involved in directing the Bank's efforts in support of the transition economies. Derviş was also a highly respected economist and an insider who would be immediately acceptable to the IMF, the World Bank, and presumably bilateral funders.

The government enacted important reforms in support of its economic program, and by the end of 2001 it was apparent that the macroeconomic stabilization effort had taken hold—with inflation falling, lower interest rates, and the generation of a primary surplus. In addition, the government managed its debt servicing requirements and debt rollovers with agility. In 2002 the expectations were that inflation would continue to fall, interest rates would decline, and the government would hold

TABLE 13-1.   Turkey: Macroeconomic Projections, 2001 and 2002

Percent unless otherwise indicated

	2001		2002	
	Government projection: original program	*IMF projection: 10th stand-by review*[a]	*Government projection: original program*	*IMF projection: new stand-by agreement*[a]
GNP growth	−3	−9.4	5	3
Nominal interest rate	81	100	41	69.1
CPI inflation (December to December)	53	65	20	35
Current account balance (billions of US$)	−0.6	1.2	−0.9	−1.4
Depreciation (December to December)	79	139	17	22
Primary balance/GNP	5.5	5.5	6.5	6.5
Net public debt/GNP	78.5	93.5	70.4	81.3
Domestic debt/GNP	44.3	53.9	42.1	45.5
Auction debt	23.2	24.1	28.3	27.2
Auction debt (billions of US$)	35	28	49	33
Domestic debt amortization/GNP	21.8	20.9	16.6	22.8

Source: IMF and World Bank estimates.

a. Revised IMF baseline is preliminary.

to its target of creating a substantial primary surplus. There was an emphasis on achieving growth in the program as GNP declined by 9.4 percent in 2001, far more than the original forecast of −3.0 percent and a revised forecast −5.5 percent (see table 13-1). Moreover, Turkey remained highly indebted and therefore vulnerable to external shocks, political or economic. Interest rates were bound to remain high because of the government's sustained need to continue financing itself through the capital markets.

A Deeper Crisis

Economic indicators pointed to the steep decline in business when the crisis began in February 2001. The crisis was deeper and potentially more adverse to industry than any since World War II.[7] Instead of a V-shaped recovery led by an export surge due to the sharp devaluation of the Turkish lira that had occurred in 1994, it appeared that Turkey was experiencing a U-shaped recovery, potentially extending over a long period, with only modest growth in 2002. Private consumption fell 2.6 percent in 1999, but was projected to fall 9.4 percent in 2001 (see table 13-2).

Exports and Imports

Turkey's trade deficit declined in line with government expectations, with exports increasing 12.3 percent and imports falling 25.7 percent for 2001 relative to 2000 (see table 13-3).[8]

Unemployment

Formal unemployment rose to 10.6 in the fourth quarter, 884,000 more unemployed workers than in 2000. Interviews and surveys suggest that unemployment was much higher among small and medium-sized enterprises (SMEs) than among large-scale manufacturers. Small companies lost an average of 19 percent of jobs in the first half of 2000. This experience was similar to Korea's crisis experience discussed in chapter 12. In medium-sized companies, job losses ranged from 10 to 22 percent. In larger companies the real issue was underemployment. Employers were reluctant to lay off workers and therefore used every means possible of cutting their hours: accelerating vacation schedules, eliminating overtime, introducing earlier closings for plant maintenance, and informally furloughing workers with the promise of rehiring them when conditions improved. The number of production-related manufacturing workers in the private sector fell 11.9 percent and hours worked fell 13.8 percent in the third quarter of 2001 from the same period in 2000 (see table 13-4).

TABLE 13-2.   Turkey: Change in GNP by Sector, January–December 2001

Percent

Sector	2001			
	Q1	Q2	Q3	(9 months)
Agriculture	6.7	−3.2	−4.5	−3.2
Industry	−1.3	−8.5	−9.2	−6.7
Construction	−5.2	−7.7	−8.8	−7.5
Trade	−4	−1.3	−7.3	−7.8
Transportation and communication	−3.7	−8.2	−4.5	−5.5
Financial institutions	−5.3	−10	−9.2	−8.2
Home ownership	2.2	2.1	2.1	2.1
Miscellaneous services	−1.9	−8.9	−7.6	−6.5
Public services	3.3	3.2	2.3	−2.9
Private non–profit organizations	1.7	−0.3	−0.3	0.3
Import tax	−10.4	−32.1	27.9	23.9
GNP	−4.4	−11.4	−8.5	−8.3

Source: State Institute of Statistics, February 2002.

TABLE 13-3.   Turkey: Exports, Imports, and the Trade Deficit, December and
January–December, 2000–2001

Millions of US$ unless otherwise indicated

Indicator	December			January–December		
	2000	2001	Change (percent)	2000	2001	Change (percent)
Exports	2,489	2,536	1.9	27,774	31,186	12.3
Imports	4,437	3,473	−21.7	54,502	40,506	−25.7
Trade deficit	−1,948	−936	−51.9	−26,727	−9320	−65.1
Sufficiency ratio (percent)	56.1	73		51	77	

Source: State Institute of Statistics, Foreign Trade Statistics, February 2002.

Company Openings and Closings

According to the State Institute of Statistics, the crisis slowed the rate of company openings and sped up closings. For 2001 company openings fell 10.5 percent, while firm openings (small businesses and sole proprietorships) fell 24.4 percent and company closings increased 30.5 percent and firm closings some 13.7 percent relative to 2000 (see table 13-5).[9]

TABLE 13-4.   Turkey: Production-Related Labor in Manufacturing,
Quarter 3, 2000–01

Percentage change

Sector	Number of workers	Number of hours worked
Public	−10.4	−8.9
Private	−11.9	−13.8
Average	−11.7	−13.2

Source: State Institute of Statistics, February 2002.

TABLE 13-5.   Turkey: Number of Companies Opened and Closed,
December and January–December, 2000–01

Category[a]	2000		2001		Change (percent)	
	December	January–December	December	January–December	December	January–December
Newly established companies and cooperatives	3,472	33,161	2,410	29,665	−30.6	−10.5
Closed companies and cooperatives	225	1,887	298	2,464	32.4	30.5
Newly established firms	1,863	21,404	1,415	16,171	−24.05	−24.4
Closed firms	1,135	12,055	866	13,707	−23.7	13.7

Source: State Institute of Statistics, Enterprise Creation and Closure Statistics, December 2001.

a. Companies are enterprises that have a corporate form, while firms are most often sole proprietorships.

The Informal Economy

The informal economy consisted of income-generating activities that were unregulated or concealed from the government. In Turkey these activities involved tax evasion, off-the-books employment, self-employment, and illegal activities such as drug trafficking. The informal economy was quite large and undoubtedly grew because of the crisis.[10]

The so-called suitcase trade was a unique feature of Turkey's informal economy. The suitcase trade got its name from the luggage used by traders from Commonwealth of Independent States (CIS) countries and the Balkans who transported Turkish goods to CIS and Eastern European markets. The suitcase trade, which was largely unrecorded and untaxed, was a major source of hard currency for Turkey and was expected to increase as a result of the economic crisis.

Inspections by Ministry of Finance auditors indicate that the rate of tax evasion was 25 percent in 1997, 28 percent in 1998, 45 percent in 1999, and 35 percent in 2000. The central bank estimated that the informal economy accounted for 20–26 percent of the economy. In 2001 the Association of Tax Controllers estimated that unregistered transactions represented 45 percent of economic activities and that tax evasion and tax losses equaled $15 billion a year.[11]

Poverty

Per capita income was projected to fall to $2,261 in 2001, the lowest level since 1994 and 25 percent lower than in 2000.[12] The crisis had an especially adverse effect on industry, above all on SMEs, in poorer areas such as the southeast and the Black Sea coast. These firms were largely family owned and managed, and most of the work was done by the family members. Sometimes such firms are called lifestyle firms because the family unit depends on the business for its subsistence. The crisis clearly worsened Turkey's income distribution and increased inflation, and hit poor people especially hard.

Fragility in the Banking Sector

In response to the crisis, nineteen banks, mostly smaller and mid-sized banks, were "intervened" by the Banking Regulation and Supervision Agency (BRSA), and their assets assumed by the State Deposit Insurance Fund (SDIF). The SDIF became in effect a public asset management agency. Some of these banks were subsequently resold, and others were consolidated into holding company banks.[13] In addition, one of the larger group-owned commercial banks, Pamukbank, was intervened, and its sister bank, Yapi Kredi Bank (YKB), was also sold as a result of the restructuring of the Çukurova Group (see box 13-1 in this chapter on the workout of the Çukurova Group, which had borrowed heavily from its own banks and lacked the liquidity to repay the loans). The large private commercial banks, owned by large groups, were subject to double audits and intense review by the banking supervisor in the wake of the crisis.

The state banks, acting largely as fiscal agents of the state in absorbing large "duty losses," had to be recapitalized at great expense and restructured. Duty losses were essentially politically directed credits to support agriculture, small and micro-business, and other sectors of the economy at subsidized rates. Invariably, directed credits lead to corruption because they are often directed to political and business connections and friends and family. They have been a major source of corruption in developing and emerging market countries. One of these banks, Vakif Bank, was privatized via an initial public offering (IPO) in December 2005. Emlak Bank was partly liquidated and partly merged with Ziraat Bank. Both Halk Bank and Ziraat Bank were restructured, but neither was privatized through 2005, contrary to government commitments. These changes led to substantial consolidation in the banking sector, large-scale entry by foreign banks through mergers and acquisitions, and a substantial reduction of the state's role in the banking sector.

To reinforce the competitive position of their banks, large Turkish groups opened up to investment by international banks. At the start of the crisis foreign penetration of the banking system was low, as it was in the East Asian countries, Mexico, and Argentina before their crises. The existing banks were small by international standards, so strengthening their capital base and partnering with major money center banks was important. Consolidation was expected to continue over time. At the end of 2005 there were some forty-seven banks in Turkey, down from some eighty banks in 1999–2000, the years preceding the crisis. There were thirty-four deposit and fourteen nondeposit-taking banks, but 96.5 percent of assets were held by the deposit banks. Because of the restructuring of the state banks and intervention of smaller banks, as well as aggressive expansion since the crisis, banking in Turkey grew significantly more concentrated. The top ten banks owned 69 percent of assets, 72 percent of deposits, and 71 percent of loans in 2000, and 84 percent of assets, 89 percent of deposits, and 78 percent of loans as of 2005.

The sector experienced deep losses in 2001, forcing the state banks and the government to recognize long "hidden" losses that effectively wiped out their capital. The government was forced to inject capital into the state banks to make up for their "duty losses." In the private banks, capital adequacy exceeded Basel standards (through June 2005). Shareholders' equity in the sector rose from $15 billion in 2002 to $35 billion in 2005 (June 30). The market capitalization of the banks (whose shares were traded on the Istanbul Stock Exchange, or ISE) rose from $7.5 billion in 2002, following writeoffs and provisioning of nonperforming loans from the crisis, to some $35 billion in June 2005. The new banking law of February 2002 was designed to bring Turkish banking regulations and supervision into closer harmony with EU standards.

Impact on the Corporate Sector

Data for 1997–2001 for nonfinancial companies listed on the Istanbul Stock Exchange suggest that net profitability declined steadily between late 1997 and late 2000—and turned sharply negative in the first quarter of 2001 for a broad range of sectors and companies These losses continued in the second quarter, leaving many listed companies in a fragile condition; domestic demand grew modestly in the third quarter, so companies saw lower losses, were able to break even, or even showed a small profit. Overall, the recovery in the third quarter was far too modest to relieve corporate distress.[14]

The fourth quarter was a setback during which industry experienced the worst operating losses, due partially to seasonal factors and partially to events surrounding September 11. But poor operating results were obscured by the fact that reported corporate net profits were positive for the quarter. The Turkish lira appreciated during the last quarter and reduced financial charges and foreign exchange losses, thereby allowing firms to show positive results.

Overall in 2001, for ISE-listed companies (industry and services), sales declined by 19 percent; exports increased by 31 percent (serving as a mitigating factor); cash flow from operations declined some 12.5 percent; financial charges and foreign exchange losses increased by 240 percent; net earnings (industrial and service companies) declined by $504 million from 2000. The thirty ISE companies that were more leveraged than the average ISE company lost more than a billion dollars, in part as a consequence of rising interest rates and higher financial costs.[15]

During 2001 losses were broad and deep in virtually all sectors of the economy. Even sectors such as textiles, which reoriented themselves primarily to exports, generated losses throughout the year. However, sectors that were largely dependent on domestic demand—autos, consumer durables, retailing, and communications, as examples, absorbed large losses. The ability of companies to service their debts declined markedly during 2001. Some sectors and companies (especially large companies) started to see leverage rise above 2:1 at the end of the first quarter of 2001.[16] Having steered their way through a series of crises in the 1990s, the large Turkish groups were much less leveraged than the Korean chaebols and therefore much less vulnerable to the devaluation and spike in interest rates at the beginning of the crisis.

The crisis affected mid-cap companies and SMEs most deeply. In several of these companies interest coverage dropped below a ratio of one in the fourth quarter of 2000 and stayed there in the first and second quarters of 2001—meaning that cash flows did not cover interest expenses. In contrast, interest coverage appears to have been acceptable in 1998 and 1999. Debt was predominantly short term—up to 85 percent for many listed companies—which increased financial vulnerability because loans were repriced quarterly. The spike in interest rates during the early part of the crisis and prevailing high real interest rates thereafter made it difficult for firms to service debt. By the end of March the losses of small listed companies were $126 million (in comparison with profits of $38 million in the same period in 2000), and by the end of June losses had reached $284 million (down from profits of $48 million). Medium-sized stand-alone companies also suffered losses in sectors such as textiles, food and beverages, retailing, marketing, and distribution.

Turkish companies were vulnerable to drops in operating cash flows (such as those arising from contractions in demand) and spikes in interest expenses. As the crisis progressed the debt burden for most listed companies rose to unsustainable levels, with the average ratio of net debt to equity (weighted by market capitalization) jumping from 13 percent at the end of 2000 to 53 percent in the first quarter of 2001—and then to 95 percent in the second quarter. By comparison, during the 1994 crisis this ratio peaked at 68 percent.

Export-Led Growth

The government's economic program anticipated that, as in past crises, recovery would be led by a surge in exports. During the first quarter of 2001 the textiles sector and the machinery and equipment sector were able to export a significantly larger portion of their sales than they were able to in the first quarter or full year of 2000. Still, all sectors except cement and glass suffered major losses in the first half of 2001.[17]

In commodity sectors such as steel and chemicals, the ability to export at given times during the year served to reduce losses in the sector. Even the main exporting sectors derived more than half of their revenues from the domestic market. The health of the domestic market determined when and how quickly the real sector would recover. Companies in virtually all sectors generated losses—exporters and non-exporters. Some large exporting companies, such as auto companies and white goods producers, were far more dependent on the domestic market than they were on exports. Traditional exporting sectors such as textiles remained mired in financial difficulty. Thus a restoration of business confidence and an increase in domestic demand were essential to economic recovery.

High Reliance on Bank Borrowing in Some Sectors

Most of the major export sectors increased their bank borrowing as a percentage of both long- and short-term liabilities.[18] Textiles, machinery and equipment, and food, beverages, and tobacco not only had the largest shares of short-term liabilities, they also had high shares of bank debt in those liabilities Short-term liabilities proved to be a problem in all of the emerging market crises I examine in this part of the book. Also, dependence on bank financing poses difficulties in a crisis when banks freeze

TABLE 13-6.   Turkey: Number of Distressed Companies, 1998–2001

Status[a]	1998	1999	2000	2001 Q1
Sustainable	73	59	70	30
Operationally distressed	5	5	4	6
Financially distressed	13	22	11	40
Technically insolvent	9	14	15	24

Source: World Bank, "Turkey: Corporate Sector Impact Assessment" Report No. 23153-TU (Washington: March 1983).

a. A company in financial distress is operating at a loss after all financial charges. A company in operational distress has losses from operations prior to financial charges.

new credits to all but the most creditworthy companies. Access to bank financing presented a serious problem for SMEs and mid-cap companies during and in the immediate aftermath of all of the crises; Turkey was no exception. Most of the large corporate groups also owned banks, so access to credit was less of a problem for group companies. However, the banking supervisor began to tighten rules on affiliated lending as the crisis progressed. The same issue, intragroup lending, arose in Mexico, and in East Asia.

Companies Damaged by the Crisis

During the first quarter, seventy listed firms were in distress: twenty-four had negative equity and were technically insolvent, forty were financially distressed, and six were operationally distressed.[19] Some 210 companies were listed on the Istanbul Stock Exchange, but that number included financial companies, group holding companies, and state enterprises, all of which were excluded from this analysis. The crisis greatly increased corporate distress in the private sector. During 1999, a year of crisis due to earthquakes, corporate distress peaked in the fourth quarter at forty-one firms in distress among 213 listed companies (see table 13-6).

Not surprisingly, bank nonperforming loans (NPLs) continued to rise during 2001, and most banking analysts regarded stated NPLs as significantly understated based on the experience with SDIF-intervened banks. After intervention, it was clear that these banks had significantly understated their NPLs. Moreover, as the year progressed many of the commercial banks reduced their provisions for bad loans, a move that was inconsistent with rising NPLs. It became clear that a workout program styled after those designed and implemented during the East Asian crisis, specifically the Korean program discussed in chapter 12, was required. A World Bank team worked with the Association of Bankers and a committee of leading commercial banks to implement this program, which quickly became known as the Istanbul Approach.[20]

Corporate Resolution: The Istanbul Approach

Although most corporations were not overly leveraged before the crisis, the substantial devaluation of the Turkish lira left many corporate groups unable to service their debt. Banking Law 4743 introduced a quasi-formal workout procedure in June 2002 known as the Istanbul Approach (IA) to assist companies in restructuring their bank debt.[21] In addition, the BRSA established clear provisioning rules to support workouts and coordinate workouts with intervened banks.[22]

At the heart of the IA was a framework agreement (intercreditor agreement) approved by the BRSA and signed in June 2002 by thirty-four commercial banks and nonbank financial intermediaries, as well as intervened and state banks. Foreign-owned banks, state-owned banks, and the SDIF responsible for intervened banks tried their best to avoid the Istanbul workout process. This became a problem, particularly for state and SDIF banks, because they held a sizable share of NPLs. The reason they abstained was that the Turkish parliament refused to offer the civil servants that managed these institutions indemnity against legal action if they accepted writeoffs as part of the workout agreements. The large commercial banks objected to their unwillingness to participate in the process as workouts largely became concentrated in the major commercial banks.

By statute, the IA was in effect for three years, from June 2002 to June 2005, during which time over $6 billion of debt was restructured for a total of 322 companies. Of the total, $5.374 billion in total debt was restructured for 221 large-scale companies (some $3 billion was to one risk group, the Çukurova Group), while $647 million was restructured for 110 small-scale companies. Loans restructured under the IA by the end of 2002 constituted 16 percent of the total gross loan volume.[23] Some 91.5 percent of debt restructured under the Istanbul Approach was completed within the first eighteen months of operation (see table 13-7).

As an incentive for banks and debtors to engage in restructuring, the IA was supported by tax exemptions and incentive certificates: it exempted transactions under the IA from stamp duties and fees, banking and insurance transactions taxes, and vehicle purchase taxes; it also exempted new credits from similar taxes, duties, fees, and fund levies.[24]

TABLE 13-7.   Istanbul Approach Results, 2002–05

Sector (number of companies)	2002	2003	2004	2005	Total
Textiles and textile goods	26	12	4	0	42
Food and animal products	27	11	2	0	40
Tourism and entertainment	10	15	0	0	25
Transportation, storage, and communication	19	3	0	2	24
Metal products and works	18	4	0	0	22
Construction	11	8	2	0	21
Financial, leasing, intermediation, and financial services	17	1	0	0	18
Other sectors	69	15	2	2	88
Other manufacturing and administrative activities	14	31	6	0	51
Total	211	100	16	4	331
Size of companies					
Number of employees	30,679	15,892	1,507	342	48,420
Total export volume (millions of US$)	656	110	20	12	798
Total current volume (millions of TL)	2,271	702	116	5	3,094
Total value of assets (millions of TL)	6,574	1,004	187	53	7,818
Contracted companies					
Number of corporate groups	5	19	2	4	30
Large-scale companies	68	116	21	16	221
Small-scale companies	16	56	29	0	101
Total companies	84	172	50	16	322
Aggregate restructured debt					
Large scale	3,113	1,832	117	311	5,374
Small scale	227	337	83	0	647
Total	3,340	2,169	201	311	6,021

Source: Bankers Association of Turkey.

Highly Effective in the Early Years

The Istanbul Approach was particularly instrumental in helping to facilitate a resolution of corporate distress, especially in the first eighteen to twenty-four months following its adoption, when most banks lacked adequate internal risk management and restructuring teams to address the problems of corporate distress. It was even effective in the absence of a viable bankruptcy system, serving as a stick to reluctant debtors to participate in the process. In contrast, in Korea a number of large and mid-sized groups and companies were put into bankruptcy, lending credibility or implicit enforcement powers to the "voluntary" workout program. (See chapter 12 in this volume.)

It is difficult to evaluate the success of the restructurings under the IA since most debt was rescheduled with long-term maturity, most for fifteen years. Although no formal assessments were conducted to determine the status and success of enterprises that went through the process, some banks estimated that 55–60 percent of the loans were recovered or were performing. Most restructurings were debt reschedulings rather than operational restructurings; this approach is a common one in crisis-affected markets where workout frameworks have been adopted. Such restructurings often lead to a second or third round of operational restructuring, as took place in Korea.

A Lack of Liquidity in the System and Access to New Money

The World Bank conducted a corporate sector impact assessment in 2001 and 2002 to determine the extent to which the corporate sector was affected by the crisis.[25] The assessment recommended strategies to promote corporate renewal. In the middle of a liquidity crisis, the assessment team found that a key obstacle to restructuring was the lack of access to refinancing, new financing, or recapitalization either through banks or the equity markets. This is not unusual in a crisis, since banks typically are constrained by their own distressed assets and in no position to provide new money to risky credits. Therefore a credit squeeze ensues during the crisis, particularly as NPLs rise. Similarly, during crises, equity markets tend to be in decline and market participants are unwilling to buy newly issued stock. As difficult as it is for large companies to get access to new finance, small and medium-sized enterprises have an even more difficult challenge. Efforts were made to establish a fund that would provide new financing to companies willing to go through the IA, but these efforts did not materialize. The IA could have been stronger if the state banks, intervened banks under the SDIF, and foreign banks in Turkey had joined the workout process, but they abstained from doing so.

Large Corporate Groups at the Core of Turkey's Private Sector-Led Growth

Like Korea, Turkey's economy was also controlled by large corporate groups that were conglomerates and family owned. Also like Korea, many of these groups' companies were publicly listed.[26] In addition, several of the large groups owned large commercial banks. During the crisis, several of the large groups generated large losses; for

BOX 13-1. Workout of Çukurova Group, a Large Corporate Banking Group

On June 18, 2002, the Banking Regulation and Supervision Agency (BRSA) decided to intervene in Pamukbank T.A.S. and to pass its management and control to the State Deposit and Insurance Fund (SDIF). The intervention also had a significant potential impact on Yapi Kredi Bankasi (YKB) because Pamukbank was a significant shareholder of YKB (13.1 percent). Intervention was largely due to some $5 billion owed by the Çukurova Group to its two group banks and the inability of the Çukurova Group to service those loans. Together these banks represented about 20 percent of the assets of the banking system.

A temporary injunction against this action by the General Assembly of Turkey's Council of State created uncertainty about the status of the banks and protection for their shareholders and depositors, and on January 24, 2003, the SDIF decided to return ownership rights to Çukurova. On January 27, 2003, the parties announced an agreement under which SDIF would manage the ownership rights of Pamukbank and the ownership rights in YKB, less dividends paid out, and that the Çukurova Group would be subject to a workout under the Istanbul Agreement.

YKB was to be sold by the group in two years; if this did not occur, an investment bank would be retained to handle this assignment. In the meantime, YKB was to be professionally managed by a team chosen by an advisory group. The Çukurova Group agreed to drop a lawsuit it had initiated against BRSA. BRSA sought a comprehensive solution to this problem in order to remove further uncertainty from the financial system and the capital markets, to protect the franchise value of YKB, and to provide ample opportunity for the Çukurova Group to repay the debts due. Included in the agreement was the sale of Turkcell's shares held by Pamukbank back to Çukurova (Turkcell was a major cellular phone company in Turkey).

The workout was for nine years, with three years of grace in an amount of $2.301.9 billion at the London Interbank Offered Rate (LIBOR) plus 3.5 percent, and including a debt-equity swap of $268.9 million. The workout involved some thirty Çukurova Group companies. As part of the sales and purchase agreement, Koc Financial Services (KFH) agreed to write off $303.8 million from the total debt owned by Çukurova. Çukurova also received a substantial reduction in its debt to SDIF (which acquired the debt through its takeover of

(continued)

BOX 13-1.   Workout of Çukurova Group, a Large Corporate Banking Group (continued)

Pamukbank) by utilizing a prepayment option installed in the rescheduling agreement executed earlier.

Note: Ira W. Lieberman and Zekeriya Yildirim, "Turkey: Corporate Sector Assessment 2002-2005" (Washington: World Bank, 2006), p. 58. The information for this case discussion is based on a series of detailed press releases issued by the BRSA from December 2002 to January 2003. The agreement between the Çukurova Group and the BRSA was signed on January 31, 2003, including a $2.3 billion workout under the Istanbul Approach.

example, Sabanci Holding lost $210 million, Koc Holding $359 million, Is Bank, $639 million, and Dogus Holding $1.3 billion.[27] Smaller and mid-sized groups experienced distress, and many had their banks intervened, which meant they lost their core source of funding. These groups, some thirteen of them, made up the core of the Istanbul Approach workout program. Two groups were forced either to restructure (the Çukurova Group) or to liquidate (the Uzan Group) after major lawsuits alleging fraud by the group and its owners. The Çukurova Group's Pamukbank was intervened, and it was forced to sell its other bank, Yapi Kredi Bankasi. Çukurova was overextended to its own banks (see box 13-1). The Uzan Group had a number of its assets— cement plants, GSM operations, and a TV station—auctioned off by the SDIF and its utilities taken over by the government.

The Role of State-Owned Enterprises in Turkey's Crisis

At its birth in 1923, Turkey was largely an agricultural country, with most commerce and services in the hands of foreign minorities, many of whom left Turkey during the years of conflict and leading up to the establishment of the state.[28]

The Origin and Growth of SOEs in Turkey

As Turkey sought to modernize during the ensuing years, state-owned enterprises were established in virtually every basic industry needed to support an economy in both tradable and nontradable sectors (primarily infrastructure) and banking.[29]

Ataturk actually founded one of Turkey's most important banks, Is Bank, and it became one of the country's largest and also one of Turkey's largest corporate groups.[30] SOEs dominated sectors such as steel, cement, oil refining, distribution and retailing, petrochemicals, energy and electricity, telecom, mining, forestry, sea ports, airports, aviation, railways, tobacco, alcohol, and more. Many utilities such as water and sewage and inner-city transport were owned or controlled by the municipalities.

By the mid-1980s, when Prime Minister Turgut Ozal initiated Turkey's first privatization program, the state owned and monopolized virtually every basic or commodity sector of the economy and all of the utilities.[31] Competitiveness in downstream sectors was largely driven by the performance of these SOEs in these sectors. By 1985, SOEs employed some 650,000 workers, representing 7.8 percent of all nonagricultural employment and some 11.5 percent of GDP, some 30.4 percent of fixed investment, and 80.4 percent of public indebtedness.[32] Many of these SOEs were politicized and chronically overstaffed. Losses were substantial, yet SOEs had a number of conferred advantages over the private sector, including ready access to Treasury financing, no requirement to pay taxes, and few benchmarks measuring their performance. In this respect Turkey's development path was little different from that of emerging market economies such as Argentina and Mexico. Although Mexico and Argentina largely nationalized many of their SOEs in basic sectors after World War II, the basic model focused on import substitution.

By the mid-1990s, following a succession of start-and-stop privatization programs, Turkey lagged behind most comparable emerging market economies and virtually all of the transition economies in privatization of SOEs.[33] Losses from SOEs were substantial. Eight SOEs accounted for 95 percent of the losses of SOEs, 85 percent of borrowing requirements, 75 percent of direct budgetary transfers, and almost 60 percent of accumulated debt. The performance of these enterprises such as SEKER (sugar beet refineries), TEKEL (tobacco and spirits), TEAS and TEDAS (electricity generation, transmission, and distribution), TCDD (railways), TDCI (iron and steel), and TTK (hard coal) was very costly to the state.[34] But most problematic of all was the utilization of the state-owned banks as off-balance-sheet vehicles for hiding or "tucking away" large fiscal deficits. These so-called duty losses of the state banks were guaranteed by the state and mushroomed out of control during a series of crises in the 1990s that led up to the crisis of 2001, when the government was forced to face up to the duty losses and restructure the state banks. By 2001 the state banks represented 40 percent of banking assets.

Privatization of SOEs to Raise Capital

Over the course of the 1980s and 1990s, many of the larger SOEs were partially privatized through IPOs on the Istanbul Stock Exchange in order to raise capital to support their operations. Normally this occurred when an SOE came into the portfolio of the Privatization Agency (PA) and the firm was corporatized (converted from an SOE to a joint stock company or state-owned enterprise) pursuant to privatization. These flotations were normally for a small percentage of the firm's shares because of the limited capacity of the market to absorb a very large issue. These flotations did little to resolve the fundamental problems of the SOEs, such as improving quality of management and governance, but in fact stalled the inevitable need to reprivatize many of these firms to real private owners who could manage them efficiently. By the mid-1990s firms such as TUPRAS (oil refining), PETKIM (petrochemicals), THY (airlines), and ERDEMIR (steel) became some of the largest companies quoted on the ISE, but were controlled by the state and only partially privatized.

Despite tariff and price adjustments and the advantage of negative effective protection for producers of commodities such as petrochemicals and steel, some of the SOEs scheduled for privatization experienced large losses in the first half of 2001.[35] By the end of the first quarter the leverage of Turkish Airlines had increased substantially, to 687 percent. Similarly, ERDEMIR (steel) experienced much lower sales, much higher inventory accumulation (228 days of sales were held in inventory), and a substantial increase in debt (measured in Turkish lira) that eroded the country's financial position.[36]

Ongoing losses of SOEs required either the Treasury or the Privatization Administration to recapitalize these firms before divestiture. This was a major problem for the privatization process because two-thirds of revenues generated from privatization were used to cover the losses of other SOEs, instead of allowing Turkey to pay down debt. The cumulative after-tax loss of SOEs of $21 billion in the 1985–2004 period (excluding the recapitalization of the state banks) (Turkish Treasury figures)[37] created a huge burden both on public finances and on the entire economy. Therefore it was anticipated that a projected surge in privatization revenues postcrisis (based on 2005 commitments) would be used to lower the public sector budget deficit, reduce the debt overhang, and allow the Treasury to borrow much less from both internal and external capital markets.

Perhaps the greatest concern for privatizing state enterprises in the aftermath of the crisis was the potentially substantial erosion in value of the energy system. During the crisis TEDAS (distribution) was unable to keep its payments current with TEAS (generation and transmission) and TEAS was not paying BOTAS (gas transmission and trade). The substantial accumulation of affiliated enterprise arrears, especially in the electricity distribution companies, had to be cleared before any of these companies could be privatized. Large nontechnical losses, largely due to pilferage, inevitably lowered the value of some distribution companies and potentially left some not saleable.[38]

Postcrisis Recovery

The twin anchors of business confidence negotiations were over Turkey's accession to the European Union and adherence to the IMF program. The European Union had agreed with Turkey to accession negotiations that were expected to last for some time. This was an important anchor for stability for ongoing political and economic reforms and the attraction of FDI, as it was for the earlier accession countries in Central and Eastern Europe and the Baltic countries, and as it was proving to be for next-in-line countries Bulgaria, Croatia, and Romania, the latter a historically reluctant reformer. The possibility of convergence with EU economic performance benchmarks by 2008–10 received wide analytic coverage from the investment banks that followed Turkey.[39] The government also adhered to an IMF stand-by program and achieved remarkable macroeconomic stability during this period, as well as a noticeable reduction in its problems managing the public debt stock. The IMF Stand-by Arrangement was the second important anchor for economic growth and long-term economic stability.

Dynamics of the Recovery

In fact, it was not just macroeconomic stability that was so important, but the overwhelming positive dynamics of the change. Macroeconomic factors included strong economic growth in GDP averaging some 7 percent from 2002 to 2004 and 5 to 6 percent for 2005 and 2006; a dramatic reduction in consumer inflation from 54.4 percent (CPI) in 2001 to 8.2 percent in 2005; or 62 percent wholesale price inflation (WPI) in 2001 to 6 percent for 2005; a stabilization of the exchange rate and reduction of volatility; a strong primary surplus of some 5.5 percent since the crisis; and well-managed debt dynamics in which the debt-to-GDP ratio came down from a high of 107.5 percent in 2001 to 70 percent in 2005 (see table 13-8). Improvements in microeconomic factors included a substantial turnaround in consumer confidence and a dramatic increase in consumer demand, in part fueled by availability of con-

TABLE 13-8.   Macroeconomic Indicators 2001, 2004–2005E

	2001	2004	2005E
Real GDP growth (%)	−7.4	8.9	5.3
CPI (average)	54.4	10.6	8.2[a]
WPI (average)	61.6	11.1	5.9[a]
Current account/GDP (%)	2.3	−5.1	−6.3
Treasury bill (3 month average)	71.0	21.5	17.0
Real interest rate (average)	30.0	15.1	9.1
Exports (US$ billion)	31.3	63.0	73.5
Imports (US$ billion)	41.4	97.5	115.0
Budget deficit (% of GDP)	11.1	7.2	2.8
Total external debt (US$ billion)	113.6	161.9	165.3[b]
% GDP	78.3	54.0	44.4
%Exports, goods and services	213.7	174.6	155.3
Reserves (excludes gold) (US$ billion)	18.7	36.0	48.5[a]

Source: World Bank, IMF, and The Koc Group.

a. Actual.

b. As of 3Q 2005.

sumer finance; dynamic export-led growth; a renewal of domestic investment; robust privatization and merger and acquisition activity; greater access to capital in external markets by Turkish corporate groups and banks, with terms increasingly more favorable to Turkey; and a substantial increase in FDI, portfolio investment, and long-term financing from abroad, combined with a remarkable switch in bank deposits from foreign-exchange-denominated to Turkish lira–denominated deposits.[40] The few years after the crisis year witnessed changes that were both dynamic and remarkable.

Significant structural reforms that began with World Bank support remained critical issues going forward to maintain growth, development, and business confidence. The government undertook structural changes in privatization, banking, and capital markets, systemic corporate restructuring during the crisis, bankruptcy reform, accounting and auditing standards, and social security reforms. It also liberalized, restructured, and regulated key infrastructure sectors pursuant to privatization or the granting of operating concessions, such as in energy and electricity, ports, and airport facilities. Most of these structural reforms were still ongoing several years after the crisis—for example, accounting and auditing standards, corporate governance, privatization of the Privatization Administration's (PA's) portfolio, restructuring of SOEs, liberalization, and private sector entry into infrastructure. Some of these efforts were inadequate, such as the reform of the bankruptcy system. Several needed to be modified to adhere to EU standards. But all supported Turkey's long-term economic growth, its ongoing ability to attract capital, and Turkey's competitiveness.

The Economic and Political Economy Bottom Line

These reforms created business confidence both within Turkey and abroad that will continue to accrue to Turkey's benefit, assuming that the key anchors of stability—political stability, macro-economic stability, and structural reforms—remain in place and continue to progress. Since this chapter was written in July 2016, Turkey has continued to grow moderately, and macroeconomic stability has remained in place, but much has changed to increase the perceived risks in Turkey. These factors are: (i) deteriorating political and economic conditions and ongoing conflict on Turkey's borders—Syria and Iraq and the migration of over a million refugees into Turkey; (ii) the failure of the EU and Turkey to agree on accession; (iii) the relatively low growth in Europe, an important export market for Turkey; and (iv) the erosion of democracy within Turkey, such as the decline in freedom of the press and the coup attempt on July 15, 2016, and emergency decrees that the ruling party has used to run the country and also to jail many of its opponents.

FOURTEEN

The Argentine Crisis

2001–04

The 2001 financial and economic crisis in Argentina had been brewing for some time. The crisis arose despite macroreforms early in the decade that addressed hyperinflation and exchange rate instability. Argentina also implemented structural adjustments or reforms focused on the privatization of the large loss-making state-owned enterprise sector, deregulation, and trade liberalization through the MERCOSUR (Southern Cone Common Market) agreements in 1991 among Argentina, Brazil, Uruguay, and Paraguay. All of these measures were intended to reverse the long-term trend of slow growth, low labor productivity, excessive state intervention in the economy, a low domestic savings rate, weak investment (in particular, lack of foreign direct investment [FDI] to revitalize the economy), and twenty-five years of chronic inflation. When hyperinflation broke out in 1989, the rate of poverty in the country had reached some 40 percent.[1]

From 1991 to 1999 the Argentine economy grew steadily at an average rate of 4.8 percent, despite being hit by two economic shocks—the Tequila Crisis in Mexico (1994–96) and the collapse of the Real Plan in Brazil (the large devaluation of the Brazilian real in 1999). During 1995 and 1996, as a result of the Tequila Crisis in Mexico, Argentina experienced a short but intense banking crisis. The government reacted quickly by liberalizing its financial sector and allowing entry of a number of international banks that acquired or took investment stakes in Argentine banks. Some foreign banks that had been in Argentina for some time, such as Citicorp and Bank Boston, deepened their capital base and expanded their operations. Weak provincial banks were liquidated, merged into other banks, or acquired.

The peso was overvalued owing to the combination of the appreciation of the U.S. dollar, which the Argentine peso was pegged to through a currency board, and the collapse of the Real Plan. The overvaluation of the peso adversely affected Argentine competitiveness with Brazil, its major trading partner in MERCOSUR. Argentina's inflation remained low during this period. Argentina's fiscal deficit receded from 6 to 8 percent of GDP for much of the 1980s to 1.4 percent in 1998, but then began to grow again in 1999 and 2000.[2]

By 1998, Argentina's economic miracle began to unwind. The country entered a recession that lasted through 2000. Fiscal discipline eroded, especially the always troublesome arrangements between the federal government and the provinces. The consolidated fiscal deficit (including the provinces) was largely financed by large external debt issues at reasonable spreads over U.S. Treasuries—foreign denominated (dollars and euros), and external indebtedness grew. With a narrow export base, and declining competitiveness, external debt represented more than four times the export base, and debt service increased from 64 percent in 1997 to 92 percent of exports in 2000, leaving the economy more vulnerable to external shocks.[3]

Both the Argentine government and the private sector borrowed substantially, primarily in the bond market, starting in the early 1990s. Its reform program made Argentina the poster child for the IMF and the darling of emerging market investors. Argentina even took advantage of the euro and issued some of the earliest Eurobonds. Both the government and the private sector became deeply indebted in dollar terms. Government debt grew increasingly short-term, a sign in other crises of trouble to come. The economy was largely dollarized.

The East Asian crisis (1997–99) and the Russian crisis (1998) led to global contagion and a "flight to quality" among emerging of market investors. The 1999 massive devaluation of the real by Brazil was perhaps the decisive blow. By 2000 it was virtually inevitable that Argentina would fall into crisis. If the East Asian crisis was the least anticipated of recent crises, the Argentine crisis, like the Russian crisis, was expected. The real question was timing: just when would the crisis hit, and how deep and how extensive would it be?[4]

The Financial and Economic Crisis of 2001

During 2001 the crisis that had been simmering exploded into the open, and throughout 2001 and 2002 Argentina sank into a deep financial and economic crisis and an extended political crisis.

Political Turmoil and Erratic Policy Decisions

There were five changes of president, five ministers of the economy (equivalent to the finance minister in other countries), and two changes of central bank governor during this time. Ricardo Lopez Murphy, a distinguished Chicago-trained macroeconomist, lasted just a week as minister of the economy after President Fernando de la Rua refused to back tough fiscal adjustment measures he proposed.[5] Barry Eichengreen compared the crisis in Argentina and Turkey as follows:

> In these circumstances, a domestic political disturbance that casts a shadow over the prospects for fiscal adjustment and economic adjustment generally could upset the apple cart. . . . In Argentina it was the disintegration of support for the fiscal cuts demanded by [Economy Minister] Jose Luis Machinea and his politically short-lived successor, Ricardo Lopez Murphy. As the future grew clouded, interest rates shot up, damaging the prospects for growth and creating doubts about debt sustainability.[6]

After the departure of Lopez Murphy, President de la Rua next called on Domingo Cavallo, in March 2001, to be minister of economy. Cavallo was famous as the original architect of the stabilization and reform program in the early 1990s, including the peg to the dollar, and the currency board, under President Carlos Menem. Cavallo insisted on broad authority to take policy initiatives to stem the crisis by decree, rather than seek approval from a fractious Congress.[7]

Unfortunately, Cavallo's policy initiatives were too late to restore external confidence in Argentina. Moreover, the government faced a larger budgetary deficit than projected, exacerbated by higher demands from the provinces than anticipated. The government was also unable to float additional bond issues in private markets or to borrow from banks abroad. Finally, the government was unable to borrow a sufficient amount from official creditors, primarily the IMF, to cover the private market shortfall. Cavallo's position became increasingly precarious: "Continued redesign of the budget draft eroded Cavallo's political capital and prompted new confrontations with governors and congressmen over distributional issues. . . . Cavallo's credibility is suffering domestically."[8]

In November 2001 the cash position of the government was precarious, there were large withdrawals from the banks, and the country's foreign reserves were being drawn down rapidly. By the end of November the run on the banks reached some $1 billion a day. The government was forced to close the banks and announce that when they reopened cash withdrawals would be limited to $250 per week. This was presented as a temporary measure. The so-called *corralito* (deposit freeze) went into effect.[9]

The situation was socially explosive. After three years of recession, with unemployment approaching 20 percent and deprived of normal access to banks accounts, the citizenry rebelled, looting shops and ransacking bank branches. Some lost their lives before order was restored. Minister Cavallo resigned, as did President de la Rua soon thereafter. Three new presidents followed in short order over a period of ten days before President Eduardo Duhalde was appointed by the Congress. He confirmed the end of the Convertibility Plan and a default of Argentina's sovereign debt estimated at some $150 billion.[10] The Convertibility Plan was put in place by Cavallo as minister of finance under President Carlos Menem, during his first term in the early 1990s. The plan pegged the Argentine peso to the U.S. dollar and also established a currency board to provide oversight over the plan. Its purpose was to contain inflation, but the plan fell apart when the crisis hit. Michael Mussa wrote:

> Argentina's decade long experiment with hard money and orthodox policies has ended in tragedy—the depths of which are not fully known. The economy is well into its fourth year of recessions and rapidly spiralling downward. Most of the banking system has effectively been closed since the beginning of December 2001. . . . The exchange rate peg is gone, and the peso is trading at substantially depreciated exchange rates against the dollar. Economic and financial chaos banished from Argentina since the hyperinflation of 1990, have returned. . . . With formal default on its sovereign external debt, Argentina has been transformed within barely two years from the darling of emerging market finance to the world's leading deadbeat.[11]

One observer described the arrival of an external group of experts to sort out Argentina's differences with the IMF this way: "When you arrive in Argentina on July 22 [2002,] you will find a sick country: its government has defaulted; its politicians are discredited; its money is despised; and its financial system is frozen."[12]

What Issues Led to Such a Deep-Seated Crisis?

As is usually the case, no one factor led to the crisis. In Argentina a series of factors contributed to the initial crisis and thereafter its deepening. These included, among others: (i) persistent budget deficits, in particular the consolidated budget deficit (when the provincial deficits were included with the federal deficit); (ii) excessive borrowing, even though the government generated large privatization revenues for several years preceding the crisis; (iii) turmoil and erratic or desperate policy decisions by government, especially as the crisis loomed; (iv) a decision to prolong pegging the exchange rate to the dollar and retain the Convertibility Plan, including the currency board, when more exchange rate flexibility was necessary; (v) the "corralito," which bottled up the public's savings and also the working capital of thousands of small family businesses dependent on their businesses for their livelihood; (vi) the government's decision to raid the newly privatized pension funds and stuff them full of public debt; (vii) the decision to devalue the peso and to arbitrarily force a dual rate mechanism on the banks, which together with rising NPLs and losses on government loans, totally decapitalized the banking system; (viii) deep corporate distress as demand declined; revenues, particularly for recently privatized utilities, were now generated in pesos, while debts were largely external in dollars or euros; and, (ix) a convergence of several exogenous shocks leading to contagion—the East Asian crisis, the Russian crisis, the devaluation of the Brazilian real after the collapse of Brazil's Stability Plan, and the Turkish crisis, which made it increasingly difficult for Argentina to roll over its debts and tap the bond market for new funds. To the extent that the government could borrow, it was at wider and wider spreads. These factors are discussed below in more detail. Comparing Argentina to the earlier crises, an ING Barings analyst noted, "The situation in Argentina has rapidly deteriorated to be worse than other worst-case scenario emerging market crises, notably Indonesia in 1997–98 and Russia 1998–99."[13]

During the period 1993–98, when the Argentine economy was performing well and the government received substantial revenues from privatization, which in principle should have been used to retire debt, the public sector debt-to-GDP ratio rose by 12 percent.[14] This reflected the lack of fiscal discipline. It also reflected Argentina's easy access to the bond markets. "Indeed with the collapse into the financial crisis of many previously successful Asian emerging market economies in 1997–1998 and the developing difficulties in Russia and Brazil, Argentina stood out as the one success story."[15]

At the end of 1999, the external debt was estimated at $148 billion, or some 52 percent of GDP, larger than the debt of other middle-income countries at the time.

The size of debt relative to exports of goods and services and remittances was very high, at some 436 percent. The ratio was over four times that of Mexico; nearly ten times larger than Brazil's; larger than Turkey's, which experienced a crisis in parallel with that in Argentina; and the largest of any emerging market borrower. Short-term debt was estimated at $31.5 billion according to World Bank estimates. and at $22.1 billion according to IMF staff estimates. Although the absolute amount of short-term debt was moderate, the amount of short-term debt plus longer-term debt maturing in one year was large, at 176 percent of reserves (at the end of 1999) and as such presented a significant problem for the government.[16] Eichengreen noted that, "Countries should pay careful attention to the maturity structure of their obligations, both because excessive short-term debt is a leading indicator of problems and because short maturities can aggravate the difficulty of coping with other sources of instability."[17] I have observed earlier in this book that increases in short-term external debt, in earlier periods sometimes referred to as floating debt, untied to trade transactions and exceeding hard currency reserves, were a signal that a crisis was potentially at hand.

Concerns about Argentina's fiscal sustainability affected access to external markets, and secondary market spreads on Argentine debt issues rose accordingly. The spread on Argentine bonds was 750 basis points higher than that of Mexican bonds in November 1999 and was about 500 basis points higher in January 2001.[18]

The Banking Crisis

From a banking perspective, the crisis started much earlier than the deposit freeze of December 1, 2000, and the rapid 30 percent devaluation of the currency. The Argentine banks lost over $19 billion in deposits throughout 2000. Banks did not have a maturity mismatch before the devaluation. Most banks were long on dollars and were, for the most part, well capitalized. The crisis was not due to poorly managed and weakly supervised banks, as it was in Mexico, Turkey, or Indonesia, as examples. Some 40 percent of the assets of the system were in the hands of first-tier international banks. However, banks' clients were exposed to foreign exchange risks because they carried dollar-denominated loans, while their revenue base was in pesos after the devaluation. The banking crisis was induced primarily by inconsistent and poor government policy decisions that were largely populist in nature. Finally, the banking system was highly dollarized, with over 70 percent of loans and deposits in dollars.[19]

However, the banking system as a whole had its problems—25 percent of its assets were in the hands of public banks, including the two major state-owned banks, Banco de la Nacion and Banco de la Provincia de Buenos Aires; there were too many

TABLE 14-1. Structure of the Argentine Banking System, mid-2001

	Public banks	Private domestic banks	Foreign banks	Nonbank financial institutions	System
Number of institutions	13	35	39	23	110
Assets (percent of system)	27.54	18.80	52.26	1.40	100.00
Loans (percent of system)	29.48	20.28	48.12	2.12	100.00
Loans (percent of total) in:					
Pesos	23.27	36.70	27.20	40.36	28.25
Dollars (billions)	76.73	63.30	72.80	59.64	71.75
Liabilities (percent of system)	28.12	17.20	53.54	1.14	100.00
Deposits (percent of system) in:	32.94	17.88	48.76	0.42	100.00
Pesos	37.91	34.06	29.24	23.23	
Dollars (billions)	62.09	65.94	70.76	76.77	67.07
Net worth in US$ billion					16.24
Percent of system	23.89	30.46	42.26	3.40	100.00

Source: World Bank, "Argentina's Financial Crisis," Briefing Note (Washington: World Bank, March 2002), p. 2.

small banks in the system, and the banking system still needed to be consolidated; loan quality was most likely overstated after four years of recession; and perhaps most important were the efforts by the government to weaken the independence of the central bank (BCRA) and also weaken banking supervision (see table 14-1).

Depositors took a series of measures in reaction to the distress of the economy and turmoil in the political leadership: they withdrew deposits and capital flight ensued; they shifted savings to sight deposits and moved funds from banks perceived as weaker to stronger banks, in particular out of domestic banks such as Banco Galicia and the state banks into banks owned by international investors.[20] The deposit freeze, known as the "corralito," beginning in December 2000, was largely a reaction to these moves: "The deposit freeze is a desperate measure to prevent a complete meltdown of the banking system, since it is impossible to return all deposits at the same time, given the illiquid nature of a large portion of bank assets."[21]

The "pesification" effectively wiped out a significant portion of the capital of the banks, and the question was whether foreign banks, many of which had invested in Argentina only in 1995 and 1996, would eventually rescue their banks and inject more equity into the banks: "The 'pesification' of part of the assets, while keeping most of the banks' liabilities in dollars, created an explosive currency mismatch and enormous losses for the banks."[22]

The immediate problem facing the government and the central bank was how to restore confidence in the financial system and how best to inject liquidity into the banking system to eventually restore both consumer and corporate lending, which was effectively frozen as a result of the crisis. Additional losses, still to be realized, were due to an increased recognition of nonperforming loans (NPLs) in the system after the earlier recession and to deepening corporate distress as a result of the crisis. Finally, the banks had significant exposure to government loans, which were effectively in default. The question arose, to what extent would the government provide "compensating bonds" to stabilize the system? However, "banks over lent to the Argentine government, perhaps thinking that a scenario in which things could go wrong was remote. . . . They never suspected, as they should have, that they might be dragged into the country's bankruptcy, nor did they think that the government would design policies to harm them, as it did."[23]

Estimates of the losses generated from (i) the foreign exchange mismatch caused by the asymmetric devaluation of the peso; (ii) the expected increases in NPLs; (iii) the losses of the banks; and (iv) exposure to government debt were projected to reach $48.6 billion, representing 2.9 times the banks' net worth. The residual net worth of the banking system was projected at negative −$32.2 billion (see table 14-2).[24]

Argentina allowed a strong, well-capitalized, largely privately owned banking system, with the exception of two large state-owned banks, to collapse. World Bank financial specialists would note, "We would say that this is the first crisis of a globalized, and well integrated, national financial system. . . . To a large extent we are facing a financial manifestation of a fiscal crisis."[25]

The central bank, Banco de la Republica Central de Argentina (BRCA), stepped in and injected liquidity into the banking system and also established a special fund as a 5 percent reserve on deposits. The effect was to redistribute liquidity in the system to the weaker national banks, especially Galicia and the two large public banks. Finally, a 75 percent incremental reserve was established on bank deposits to try and stem the flow of deposits from weaker to stronger banks.[26] These measures implicitly discriminated against the foreign banks. There was no effort initially to intervene weaker or illiquid banks; the initial move was to prop up the banking system.

Major international banks J. P. Morgan, HSBC, Citicorp, Banco Santander, Banco Viscayo-Bilbao, and others took major hits from the Argentine crisis. At least two major international banks withdrew from Argentina during the crisis—Bank of Nova Scotia and Credit Agricole. The others had to decide whether or not to inject additional liquidity into their individual banks.[27]

TABLE 14-2.   Argentina: Estimated Bank Losses

	Estimated losses		
Impact	*US$ millions*	*Percent*	*Number of times banks' net worth*
Foreign exchange losses (using an exchange ratio @ $1.0 to pesos 2.0)	17,725	36	1.0
Unrecognized losses in public sector exposures	14,873	31	0.9
Subtotal: estimated losses resulting from public policies	32,598	67	1.9
Potential losses in loans to private sector	16,041	33	0.9
Total potential loss	48,639	100	2.9
Negative net worth	32,197		

Source: World Bank, "Argentina's Bank Losses," p. 8.

Privatized Pension Funds

As part of its reform program before the crisis, the government privatized the social security pension system by setting up a number of privately managed or administered pension funds. The privatized system was modeled after the successful reforms in Chile. The social security reforms were another factor affecting Argentina's fiscal stability, as budgetary revenues were diverted to the private funds. Social security revenues declined from some 5.8 percent of GDP in 1993 to 3.8 percent by 2000. This reflected a change in the allocation of funds of some $20.3 billion. At the same time, payments for social security during this period rose from 5.3 to 6.1 percent of GDP, reflecting a cumulative budgetary deficit from 1995 to 2000 of $30.9 billion.[28]

During the crisis the government sought to stay afloat and, at Cavallo's initiative, forced the newly appointed fund managers to accept government debt in exchange for the funds' liquidity. The government effectively debased the newly established private pension system, guaranteeing lower returns, losses on government debt paper, and potentially lower pension payouts in the future.[29]

Corporate Sector Distress

A lack of demand and an inability to secure working capital financing led a large number of small and medium-sized enterprises (SMEs) to fail. Large companies were also badly affected, particularly those that had borrowed in dollars and did not export substantially. In a note to the government on the impact of the crisis on Argentina's corporate sector and potential resolution strategies, a World Bank team observed:[30]

1. Businesses were paralyzed by deep uncertainty over the rules of the game, a sharp downturn in domestic demand, and the inability of the payment system to operate.[31]

2. Salient obstacles to economic recovery were primarily the following: (a) Argentina's sovereign default made it difficult for businesses to raise capital abroad; (b) frequent changes in regulation, capital flows, exchange, and financial sector controls such as the corralito effectively derailed the payment system; (c) the flotation of the peso posed uneven risks. For example, exporters would largely benefit if adequate export financing was available; however, the economic slowdown in the rest of the world made export expansion difficult, and export margins were bound to be lower than domestic margins. On the other hand, privatized utilities with large external debts faced large difficulties unless their tariffs were adjusted to keep pace with inflation, devaluation, and debt service; (d) the crisis brought a large downturn in domestic demand, which meant that businesses dependent on domestic demand—autos, construction, consumer durables, and retailing, for example—were all suffering. Many nonexporting businesses failed. The government needed to put in place a resolution strategy; (e) SOEs, many of which operated at the margin, were failing in large numbers, exacerbating existing social and political problems. This was also the experience in Korea, Thailand, and Turkey; (f) the government decision on corporate debt conversion at 1:1 against the conversion of bank liabilities at 1.4 pesos to the dollar effectively wiped out bank capital. Even with compensating bonds, the banks would not be entirely whole. The banks were highly risk-averse following "pesification," which brought with it a credit freeze for all but the most creditworthy borrowers and a terrible credit crunch. Resolution strategies should have been aimed at restoring the creditworthiness of firms but were never put in place; and, (g) intercompany receivables and payables were stretched to the point that business was increasingly conducted in cash or by barter. The informal or gray economy flourished and tax receipts declined. Restaurants and small retail establishments of all kinds accepted different forms of paper money species in lieu of pesos as payments.

3. The government's decision to weaken the bankruptcy system and the failure to veto key aspects of new bankruptcy legislation removed incentives for debtors to settle their debts with their creditors.

TABLE 14-3. Argentina: Direct Foreign Debt by Nonbank Private
Corporations, as of June 30, 2001

Billions of US$

	Amount	Percent	Average amount
YPF	3.31	7.2	
Telecom Argentina	2.18	4.7	
Telefonica de Argentina	2.09	4.5	
Perez Companc	1.74	3.8	
Transportadora Gas del Sur	0.94	2	
Subtotal, 5 largest debtors	10.26	22.3	2.05
CTI–Telefonos	0.81	1.8	
Minera Alumbrera	0.79	1.7	
Cablevision	0.77	1.7	
Monsanto Argentina	0.74	1.6	
Shell Argentina	0.71	1.5	
Subtotal, next 5 largest debtors	3.81	8.3	0.76
Next 10 largest debtors (11–20)	5.86	12.7	0.59
Next 10 largest debtors (21–30)	4.37	9.5	0.44
Next 10 largest debtors (31–40)	3.33	7.2	0.33
Next 11 largest debtors (41–51)	3.01	6.5	0.27
51 largest debtors (>US$250 million each)	30.64	66.6	0.6
Next 52 largest debtors (52–103) (<US$250 million and >US$100 million)	8.88	19.3	0.17
253 other debtors (<US$100 million each)	6.48	14.1	0.03
All (356) debtors (>US$0.1 million each)		100.0	0.03

Source: Argentine Secretary of Finance Faustino Garza, "Argentina Corporate Debt," Briefing Note (Washington: World Bank, March 30, 2002), p. 4.

Corporate debt was estimated at $45 billion as of June 30, 2001, with foreign debt held by some 356 different companies. Of these, 103 companies owed over $100 million each.[32] Particularly hard hit were the privatized utilities—power, water, and gas producers and distributors, as well as public transportation and telephone service providers (see table 14-3). Their owners held substantial external debts related to loans acquired in purchasing the large utilities during privatization, but their revenue base was now entirely in devalued pesos (as of June 30, 2001, the peso was at Ar$3.0 to US$1, a 67 percent devaluation).

Also, government contractual commitments to allow utility rates to rise were not honored during this period.[33] The government feared popular resistance to utility

TABLE 14-4.   Argentina: Estimated Impact of the Financial Crisis on
Twenty Large Debtors

Billions of US$

	Five largest debtors		Two steel companies		Thirteen other debtors	
	Precrisis	Postcrisis	Precrisis	Postcrisis	Precrisis	Postcrisis
EBITDA[a]	7.9	4.5	0.3	0.6	1.8	0.5
Increase (decline)[b]		−0.43		0.91		−0.74
Debt	14.1	14.0	2.5	2.4	7.1	6.8
Equity	20.3	6.2	4.6	10.7	5.6	−3.3
Total capital		20.2	7.0	13.1	12.7	3.5
Increase (decline)[b]		−0.41		0.86		−0.72
Debt/EBITDA	1.8	3.1	7.6	4.0	3.9	14.3
EBITDA/interest	5.6	2.2	1.3	1.7	2.6	0.5
EBITDA/capital	0.23	0.22	0.05	0.05	0.14	0.14

Source: Faustino Garza, "Argentina Corporate Debt," p. 4.

a. Earnings before interest, taxes, depreciation, and amortization.

b. Percent.

price increases, especially during the recession and with the corralito in effect. "Electricity and gas concerns, which have sunk millions into Argentina over the past decade have been battered by government decrees that switched their contracts from dollars to less valuable pesos—and then froze utility rates to protect consumers."[34] In any event, many Argentines would have found it difficult to pay for these increases in the middle of the crisis (see table 14-4).

Other crisis countries such as Mexico and Turkey, as well as in East Asia, were able to develop and implement corporate workout programs, but this proved not to be possible in Argentina owing to lack of macrostability, lack of a resolution program preceding corporate resolution for the banks, a decision by the government to effectively abrogate the bankruptcy law,[35] and most important, a lack of viable counterparts in government with whom it could work to develop and implement appropriate resolution policies. In other words, the government lacked the capacity—the human capital in authority in government—to implement a crisis resolution program.[36] Many of the larger firms hired financial advisers to negotiate workouts with their creditors in order to demonstrate good faith, recognizing that they would need to return to the capital markets in the future.[37]

Confluence of Exogenous Shocks and Crisis Contagion

Argentina was adversely affected by a series of exogenous shocks that made it increasingly difficult to hold off the looming crisis. These included the Mexican crisis in 1994, which affected GDP growth, created a banking crisis, and forced Argentina to open its banking system to foreign banks—all in all a good outcome. The East Asian crisis (1997–98) and the Russian crisis (1998) made it increasingly difficult for emerging market countries to borrow; or if they were able to, as was Argentina, they were forced to borrow at higher and higher spreads. Finally, Brazil's devaluation of the real made Argentina's exports less competitive, especially within the framework of MERCOSUR. Ricardo Hausmann and Andres Velasco observed:

> Argentina obviously had a streak of bad luck. The terms of trade were negatively impacted after the East Asian crisis in the second semester of 1997. Financial markets dried up after the Russian default in August 1998. Brazil abandoned its crawling band and massively depreciated its currency in January 1999. The euro sank by over 20 percent in 2000, further weakening Argentina's competitiveness vis-à-vis the important European market. The world entered into recession in 2001.[38]

The Argentine Debt Default

Argentina defaulted on its sovereign debt and World Bank loans and in a face-saving gesture for both the IMF and Argentina agreed to a rescheduling of its IMF loans at the very last moment. Negotiations with the private bondholders to restructure Argentina's external debts were extended and difficult. On February 20, 2003, the government retained an economic adviser, the firm Lazard Freres, for the negotiations with external creditors to restructure some $81.8 billion of defaulted debt at face value plus $20.8 billion in defaulted interest on the debt. The negotiations were long and difficult and ultimately unsuccessful.

An IMF Support Package

With all other funding options unavailable, Cavallo leaked to the press that the Fund would accelerate its funding to the government, and without prior consultation with the Fund or even other government ministries Cavallo implied that the Fund had agreed to a large support package. Cavallo sought to "trap" the Fund in a fait accompli, a tactic unlikely to work given the highly structured process of review and approval needed to have any such program approved in the institution. The large support package approved in January 2001 by the executive board of the Fund was already a large increase in a prior Fund program, and another augmentation was highly unlikely without well-understood agreement on conditions for the loan and, more than likely, implementation of prior actions.[39]

With great pressure from President George W. Bush expressing support from the U.S. government, a personal visit by Prime Minister Tony Blair of the United Kingdom, concerns voiced by Chancellor Gerhard Schroeder of Germany, and the desire of the Fund's management not to be seen as the cause of Argentina's collapse, the IMF provided the government with a large tranche of its existing commitment in September 2001, which postponed the inevitable by just three months.[40]

Other Sources of Support

The IMF maintained support for the Argentine government throughout the early 1990s reform period under Menem and Cavallo, continuing through the impact of the peso crisis (1995–96) and the recession beginning in 1998. In a highly detailed policy paper of March 25, 2002, Michael Mussa, former chief economist of the IMF, elaborated on the relationship between the Fund and the government of Argentina in this period leading to the 2001 crisis and the Fund's decision to continue supporting the government in a substantial way in 2000.[41]

Mussa argued that the Fund made two important, perhaps critical (my word) mistakes: (i) not pressing the Argentine authorities to have a more responsible fiscal policy, particularly in the three high-growth years following the Tequila Crisis of 1995; and (ii) extending substantial additional support to Argentina during the summer of 2001, after it became clear the government's economic program had little chance of success.[42]

"By 2000, there was clear recognition in the Fund that Argentina was vulnerable to a crisis. Some recognized that there was significant risk of sovereign default, collapse of the Convertibility Plan and financial chaos, while others merely shuddered at such possibilities."[43]

Rather than halt the support program and risk plunging Argentina into a crisis and inevitable debt default, the IMF decided to provide a package of support in 2001 that was substantially larger than standard support programs, augmenting a three-year Stand-by Arrangement in place as of 2000. Conditionality emphasized constraint on spending and fiscal sustainability. Official financing would be sizable enough to meet virtually all of Argentina's external financing needs for 2001. The package was announced at $40 billion, with $14 billion available from the IMF, $5 billion from the World Bank and Inter-American Development Bank, and $1 billion from the government of Spain. The package also sought some $20 billion from the private sector as a voluntary market-based support. The private sector funding was not assured and only likely to occur if the program held (according to a Fund press release in January 2001).[44] This was seen by Fund officials as offering Argentina one last chance to avoid catastrophe.

Mussa notes, "I shall argue below that one of the most important costs of the (in my view, misguided) decision to augment the Fund support for Argentina in the summer of 2001 was precisely that this support was wasted in what clearly was a lost cause."[45] In fact, Mussa notes the cause may have been lost as early as 2000, but there was still some basis for supporting Argentina at that point.

In August 2001 the Fund announced a disbursement of over $6 billion, which was formally approved in September, with $3 billion more in support of a yet-to-be-defined debt restructuring. Both the amount of the September disbursement and the procedure were highly unusual from the Fund's perspective because there existed no government program that the Fund could certify as sustainable. This additional large tranche called for a new assessment of the entire Argentine program, which clearly would not have passed muster.[46] "By August 2001, however, prospects for a favourable outcome were pure fantasy."[47] Here there was a failure of intellectual courage to face up to the realities of the situation in Argentina, and a failure of moral courage "to take the difficult decision to decline substantial additional support to policies that no longer had any reasonable chance of success."[48]

An external observer of the Argentine crisis, writing a detailed journalistic account of the crisis and Argentina's interaction with the Fund, observes:

> The long and the short of the matter is that another sorry chapter was about to unfold in Argentina's relations with the international community, compounding errors that had already been committed. Despite all of the thought given to challenging the Argentines aggressively on the need to consider an entirely new economic policy framework, the IMF would essentially adopt a passive stance during the last few months of 2001 as the country hurtled toward regime change.[49]

External Debt Default and Protracted Negotiations with Bondholders

Following the failed debt negotiations in 2003, in 2005 the government made a uni-lateral offer with terms unfavorable to its bondholders to try and settle the default. Of $81.8 billion in principal in default, $62.3 billion of principal was to be exchanged for $35.2 billion of new bonds. Past-due interest was not addressed. Some $18.6 billion of bonds together with accrued interest were not tendered. Also not addressed was $6.3 billion in Paris Club debt and $9.5 billion owed to the IMF. The proposed re-structuring was unprecedented in size at $102.6 billion, length of time to resolve (over three years), and its low recovery (27–30 percent).[50] The forced settlement was closer to repudiation than any other settlement with bondholders during this period or, for that matter, than the settlements and debt forgiveness on the 1980s debt de-faults discussed in Part II of this book.

A diverse group of "holdouts" did not agree to the debt swap or exchange. A small number of bondholders chose to litigate, seeking repayment in full. This group pri-marily consisted of hedge funds (commonly known as "vulture funds"); they had pur-chased Argentine debt at a deep discount and sought to recover those bonds, issued under New York law, through litigation. Bonds issued in euros or in pesos were not subject to protracted litigation since the European and Argentine courts rejected bondholder claims. The principal amount under litigation was some $1.4 billion plus interest in arrears. The litigation extended through 2015 in a series of trials and ap-peals that has left the government unable to raise long-term sovereign debt in inter-national capital markets.[51] The rule of excluding a sovereign debtor from the bond markets until their debt was renegotiated held.

In 2005 the government announced that it would pay its debt due to the IMF in full. The government had reduced this debt from $15.5 billion in 2003 to $10.5 billion at the time of the announcement. On January 3, 2006, the government paid most of the debt due, $9.5 billion, canceling debt installments due in 2006, 2007, and 2008. President Nestor Kirchner said that "with this payment we bury an ignominious past of eternal infinite indebtment."[52]

In 2010, seeking to resolve its sovereign debt issues and gain access to the capital markets, Argentina offered a second settlement to bondholders. Bondholder arrears were approximately $29 billion, and Paris Club debt due was $6.3 billion. A formal offer was made on April 30, 2010. The bond exchange closed on June 22, 2010, and a second stage on December 31, 2010. Some $12.4 billion of $18.4 billion in bonds in default were tendered, leaving untendered $6.0 billion from the two exchanges. This meant that 91.3 percent of the original bonds due had been tendered in the two exchanges, a level normally commensurate for admission to the capital markets.

However, Argentina was still tied up in litigation with the holdouts and unable to enter the markets. As of December 31, 2010, Argentina was in arrears with holdouts and the Paris Club in an amount of $11.2 billion, $6.8 billion in principal and $4.4 billion in interest.[53] The Paris Club debt was eventually settled for $9 billion, including penalties and interest[54] (see table 14-5).

Of all of the crisis countries in the 1990s, Argentina best fits the thesis advanced in this book governing sovereign debt and the fine line between the sanctity of contracts, *pacta sunt servanda*, the basis of all contract law, and the vital interests of states under changing or stressful conditions, *clausula rebus sic stantibus*. In cases where debt service is perceived as a threat to their stability, states saw it in their self-interest to default. Keynes among others spoke of the "will" of the debtor or lack thereof to pay under adversity.[55]

As a result of the Argentine and some smaller cases, financial markets have acted to prevent minority creditors from holding out and holding up debt service. Collective action clauses have become the "market standard" in U.S. bond issues, as they are under British law. They can compel minority holdouts by clamping down on them to agree to a negotiated solution by a supermajority of creditors.[56]

The Beginnings of a Recovery in 2003

The crisis deeply affected Argentina's economy. After more than three years of recession, GDP was a negative −4.4 percent in 2001 and a negative −10.9 percent in 2002. Poverty affected some 57 percent of the population at the end of 2002, with extreme poverty at 28 percent and the official unemployment rate at 18 percent.

By the first quarter of 2003, economic recovery had begun, largely supported by expansion of industrial output and construction, with 16.4 percent and 37 percent increases in January on a year-on-year percent. The exchange rate stabilized, actually appreciated slightly, against the dollar, from 3.40 pesos to the dollar to 3.20 pesos to the dollar. The fiscal accounts were in surplus, at 1.5 billion pesos for the first quarter. These results reflected improved tax collections and strong expenditure discipline. The consolidated fiscal accounts were in balance, in large part the result of improved fiscal discipline at the provincial level.[57]

In 2003, GDP growth of 8.8 percent reflected a sharp reversal of 2002 results. Buoyed from 2004 through 2008 by strong commodity prices in world markets, growth averaged 8.4 percent during this period. Foreign exchange reserves grew from a low of $10.4 billion in 2002 to $52.2 billion by 2010, and real wages were 63 percent over 2003 levels. Argentina ran a primary fiscal balance of 2.8 percent in 2003, rose to

TABLE 14-5.   Argentina: Debt Tables and Debt Restructuring, Selected Years 1995–2010

Millions of US$ unless otherwise indicated

	1995	2000	2005	2006	2007	2008	2009	2010
Summary external debt data								
External debt stocks	98,465	140,914	124,939	115,863	117,317	118,902	120,283	127,849
Long-term external debt	70,979	107,543	80,586	87,564	98,058	98,925	100,651	92,844
Public and publicly guaranteed debt	54,913	81,633	54,225	60,754	68,029	68,627	72,927	67,331
Private nonguaranteed debt	16,066	25,909	26,361	26,811	30,028	30,298	27,723	25,514
Use of IMF credit	6,131	5,056	9,513	0	0	0	0	0
Short-term external debt	21,355	28,315	34,841	28,299	19,260	19,977	19,637	35,005
Interest arrears on long-term debt	0	0	7,735	7,452	9,452	10,003	10,760	5,457
Memorandum items								
Principal arrears on long-term debt	0	0	11,193	12,125	16,157	18,466	19,637	9,156
Long-term public sector debt	54,891	81,582	54,205	60,655	67,935	68,539	72,866	67,283
Long-term private sector debt	16,088	25,961	26,381	26,909	30,123	30,386	27,785	25,561
Public and publicly guaranteed commitments	8,381	11,985	2,462	5,747	7,522	4,969	3,375	1,156
Ratios								
External debt stocks to exports (percent)	335.4	364.1	243.4	192.3	160.8	135.4	171.2	152.1

External debt stocks to gross national income (percent)	38.9	50.9	70.8	55.5	45.9	37.2	40.4	36.1
Debt service to exports (percent)	30.2	69.4	19.4	36.2	12.3	8.8	17.3	16.7
Short-term to external debt stocks (percent)	21.7	20.1	27.9	24.4	16.4	16.8	16.3	27.4
Multilateral to external debt stocks (percent)	9.5	11.5	12.5	12.9	12.7	12.4	13.4	13.2
Reserves to external debt stocks (percent)	16.2	17.8	22.5	27.6	39.3	39.0	39.9	40.8
Reserves to imports (months)	5.5	6.3	7.2	7.3	8.4	6.9	9.3	7.8
Debt restructurings								
Total amount rescheduled	248	0	20,136	2,096	983	0	0	8,115
Total amount forgiven	863	689	40,333	3	0	0	10	9,347
Debt buyback	0	2,745	0	0	0	0	0	0

Source: World Bank, *Global Development Finance 2012* (Washington: World Bank).

TABLE 14-6. Argentina: Selected Economic Data, 2000–10

	2000	2001	2002	2003	2004	2005	2006	2007	2008	2009	2010
GDP growth (percent)	−0.8	−4.4	−10.9	8.8	9.0	9.2	8.5	8.7	6.8	0.9	9.2
Overall fiscal balance (percent)	−3.6	−6.8	−2.0	0.9	3.7	2.1	1.9	0.6	0.7	−0.8	−0.1
Primary fiscal balance (percent)	0.4	−1.3	0.7	2.8	5.3	4.4	4.0	2.7	2.8	1.4	1.5
Current account balance (percent of GDP)	−3.1	−1.4	8.5	6.3	2.1	2.9	3.6	2.8	1.5	2.1	0.8
Public debt (percent of GDP)	45.7	53.7	166.3	138.2	126.4	72.8	63.6	55.7	48.5	48.5	45.1
Inflation rate according to INDEC (percent)[a]	−0.7	−1.5	41.0	3.7	6.1	12.3	9.8	8.5	7.2	7.7	10.9
Inflation rate according to others (percent)								15.0	25.0	15.8	10.9
Real wages (index 2005 = 100)				85.2	93.1	100.0	108.9	118.8	129.2	144.3	163.0
Terms of trade (index 2005 = 100)				100.3	102.2	100.0	106.0	110.0	124.6	118.9	118.4
International reserves (billions of US$)	32.5	5.3	10.4	13.8	19.3	27.3	31.2	45.7	46.2	48.0	52.2
International bond issues (millions of US$)	13,468	2,711	0	100	200	540	1,896	3,256	65	500	3,146

Source: United Nations Economic Commission on Latin America and the Caribbean (ECLAC), Preliminary Overview of the Economies of Latin America and the Caribbean, December 2012; International Monetary Fund online statistics; J. F. Hornbeck, "Argentina's Defaulted Sovereign Debt: Dealing with the 'Holdouts,'" CRS Report to Congress 7-5700 (Washington: Congressional Research Service, February 6, 2013), p. 14.

a. These figures are from the Instituto Nacional de Estadística y Censos (INDEC), Argentina's official government statistical office, which has come under criticism for understating inflation rates since 2007. Adjusted inflation rates are added on the line below to reflect an estimate of private sector analyses of annual inflation rates since 2007.

5.3 percent in 2004, and remained at over 4 percent through 2006. Terms of trade were highly favorable beginning in 2006 through 2012. Inflation at 41 percent in 2002 ranged between 6 and 11 percent during this period (2004–12). Not able to tap the debt markets and having settled its sovereign debt on highly favorable terms, public debt to GDP declined from 166.3 percent in 2002 to 41.2 percent in 2011[58] (see table 14-6).

Postscript on the Sovereign Debt Settlement

As of the end of 2015, Argentina was still in dispute with and entangled in the U.S. courts with a minority group of creditors. These were primarily U.S. hedge funds that had purchased Argentine debt in secondary markets at deep discount and took Argentina to court over its refusal to pay minority creditors that remained and were unwilling to settle at levels dictated by the government.[59] Finally, in the first quarter of 2016 the newly elected president of Argentina, Mauricio Macri, agreed to settle the litigation and pay the minority creditors some $4.65 billion, subject to approval by the Argentine Congress.[60] In order to repay the creditors and meet financing needs, the government of Argentina was expected to go to the capital markets to raise some $15 billion in 2016, the first time Argentina was able to approach the capital markets in almost fifteen years. The principle established in the nineteenth century that debtors in default cannot approach the bond market until they have composed their debts prevailed in the Argentine case.[61]

Part IV

THE GREAT RECESSION AND CRISES IN THE ADVANCED ECONOMIES, 2007–15

FIFTEEN

The Japanese Crisis as a Precursor to Crises in the Advanced Economies

Starting in 2007 the United States and the eurozone went into a deep financial crisis, which morphed thereafter into an economic crisis. The eurozone and the United States faced different sets of problems. In fact, we could call them nonidentical-twin crises, yet they were joined at the hip, as was much of the world's economy. The political economy of these crises was complex and critical to their resolution. Policymakers at times found themselves unable by law or statute, and often unwilling, to make policy decisions that would lead to crisis resolution. This was particularly so in the eurozone. The United Kingdom, a member of the European Union but not of the eurozone, also experienced its own crisis at or around the time of the eurozone crisis, but like the United States the U.K. emerged earlier and more robustly than the eurozone countries. Iceland, also not a eurozone member, experienced a severe banking, currency, and economic crisis at roughly the same time as the eurozone countries. Japan experienced its crisis much earlier than the other advanced economies, starting in 1991, and as such was a precursor to the crises in the United States and Europe. Growth in Japan's economy has remained low or negative, with a deflationary cycle that makes it extremely difficult for Japan to break out.

A number of these crises started as banking and financial sector crises, in large part tied to real estate bubbles. Japan, the United States, Spain, and Ireland are examples. Eventually, virtually all of the crisis countries experienced deep banking and financial sector crises. These crises were similar to the crises in the emerging market countries in the 1990s and early 2000s in Mexico, East Asia, and Turkey. However, the crisis economies in the eurozone countries were not able to use monetary policy to de-peg or float their currencies and allow their currencies to devalue, as the emerging market countries were able to do to stimulate exports and compress imports as part of the process of crisis resolution. Similar to the earlier emerging market crises, the crises in a number of the advanced economies morphed into sovereign debt crises as governments and the European Central Bank (ECB) were forced to become lenders of last resort to first assist in resolving their banking crises and then assist those countries that needed bailouts—Greece, Portugal, Ireland, and eventually Cyprus. These bailouts were supported by the troika of the ECB, the European Commission (EC), and the International Monetary Fund (IMF). Iceland was on its own, and its central bank lacked the capacity to operate as a lender of last resort. A package was put together to assist Iceland that looked more like the packages for the East Asian emerging market countries such as Korea and for Mexico and Turkey. In Iceland's case, the IMF was at the center of the assistance program as the international lender of last resort, with the Nordic countries and the European Union also providing assistance.

The IMF played an active role in the crises in the advanced countries as an international lender of last resort, just as it had in the developing country sovereign debt crises in the 1980s (as discussed in Part II of this book), and the emerging market crises in the 1990s and early 2000s (as discussed in Part III). As part of the troika with the EC and the ECB this was the first occasion in which the IMF had played such an extensive role in crisis resolution in the advanced economies.

A large part of the world's economy therefore, primarily the advanced economies, experienced financial and economic crisis starting in 2007, followed by low or intermittent negative growth when the immediate crisis was over. These crises were characterized by low aggregate demand, low inflation bordering on deflation, low to near-zero interest rates, and high unemployment, making exit from the current low-growth cycle very difficult for many of the countries. (Japan was an exception with respect to unemployment, though Japanese industry did move to using contract workers extensively as its low to negative growth has continued over the two decades from 1991 to the present.) Several of these economies have also emerged from their crisis highly indebted. The United States and Japan, two of the major creditor countries, have become substantial sovereign debtors with decreasing room for maneuver should another crisis occur. They have been joined more recently by China, which has a large public debt but overall remains a net creditor to the rest of the world.

Others, above all Greece, have remained highly fragile. Approaches to crisis resolution have varied greatly by region and country.

By the beginning of 2016 there was little optimism that robust growth would emerge again soon, especially as China and some of the other large emerging market and oil-exporting countries—Russia, Brazil, Venezuela, Nigeria, and Saudi Arabia, as examples—also struggled to deal with the fall in oil and other commodity prices. Most important, the decline in growth and demand from China for oil and other commodities—metals and agricultural products from developing and emerging countries in Africa and Latin America—adversely affected growth in those economies and also led to a flight of capital out of emerging markets.

The crisis in the advanced economies does little to change our historical view of sovereign crises. It is another, albeit important, chapter on sovereign debt and related financial crises. In the years leading up to the crisis in the advanced economies there was a strong sense that a crisis such as that experienced during the Great Depression was unlikely to occur again, particularly in the advanced economies, which had sophisticated macroeconomic tools and the ability to shape monetary policy. Bubbles and resulting crises, to the extent that they occurred in these countries in the years following the Great Depression, were promptly addressed. Most crises were V-shaped; that is, the affected country went into and out of the crisis relatively rapidly. The crisis of 2007–10 in the United States and 2008–15 in the eurozone was anything but V-shaped and is the closest crisis in the post–World War II economic era to the Great Depression. That is why many analysts have called it the Great Recession.

This chapter first also explores the crisis in Japan that began in the early 1990s and continues into the present. Part IV then moves on to the U.S. crisis of the early 2000s, the trigger for the world crisis. The first U.S. chapter, chapter 16, addresses the causes of the crisis; chapter 17 is on the financial crisis and the ad hoc approach to crisis resolution up to Lehman's collapse; chapter 18 deals with the systemic approach to crisis resolution post-Lehman; and chapter 19 discusses the impact of the financial crisis and related real estate bust on the U.S. economy, including the impact of the crisis resolution strategy on U.S. sovereign debt and debt sustainability. Part IV concludes with two chapters on the eurozone crisis—chapter 20 on the overall crisis and chapter 21 on specific crisis countries that required bailouts and the approach to crisis resolution in those countries.

Not discussed in the chapters that follow is the financial and banking crisis in the Nordic countries that started in 1987 in Norway (1987–93) and at about the time of the Japanese crisis in 1991 in Sweden (1991–94) and Finland (1991–94). In each of these countries the banking crisis was severe, and their respective central banks and governments were forced to intervene in several banks. In Norway some of the banking difficulties emerged from bad real estate loans. But none of the Nordic country crises amounted to a sovereign debt crisis and did not cause contagion in other parts of the world; they were reasonably isolated. These crises extended for several years and as such did not resemble the V-shaped crises and crisis recoveries of the post–World War II era in most of the advanced industrial countries before the Great Recession.[1] I also do not discuss the crises in the Baltic countries—Latvia, Estonia, and Lithuania—that began in 2008 because these crises occurred in very small open economies that had recently transitioned from political and economic control by the Soviet Union to open market economies and as such were somewhat sui generis.[2]

The Japanese Crisis as a Precursor to the Crisis in the Advanced Economies

Japan was the earliest advanced economy to be hit by crisis, a real estate bubble that deeply affected the Japanese banks. The Japanese crisis began in February 1991 and lasted two decades—what have come to be known as the "lost decades" in Japan. The crisis, or better, the crises, can be viewed in three phases: from 1991 to 1997, the negative wealth effects of the real estate and stock market bust; from 1997 to 2000, a banking crisis that deepened in response to the East Asian crisis from 1997 to 2001; and from 2007 to the present owing to the impact of the Great Recession. The crisis in Japan continued with little respite to the end of 2016 despite the efforts by Prime Minister Shinzo Abe to stimulate the economy and bring inflation above 2 percent. It has left Japan in a deflationary spiral that it has had great difficulty escaping. These crises have also left Japan deeply in debt, the most indebted country in the world relative to GDP, though virtually all of that debt is held by Japanese households and institutions. The debt is not viewed as threatening a sovereign crisis. However, the sheer magnitude of the debt is narrowing Japan's fiscal options and has locked Japan into a debt-deflation trap that has proven very difficult for Japan to exit. Also, Japan's debt and fiscal situation may prove unsustainable in the longer term, particularly as the population ages.

Three Phases of the Financial/Economic Crisis

The first phase or crisis began in February 1991 and was followed by a deep and long economic contraction. Stock and real estate prices, which had risen steadily during Japan's boom years in the 1980s, plunged in value. This led to weaker aggregate demand and a sharp reduction in financial intermediation, since business loans were normally collateralized by land. Banks also held real estate and stocks as investments, and their capital base was adversely affected by the deterioration in value of these investments.[3]

Phase two, the second crisis, began in 1997 with the default of Sanyo Securities in November 1997. This was followed initially by the failure of smaller cooperative banks, then by the failure of regional banks, and thereafter by large banks and securities firms. Most of these institutions had failed to address nonperforming loans (NPLs) and a deterioration in their balance sheets after the erosion of their capital base caused by their excessive investments in land and publicly traded equities.[4] The problems of the banks were exacerbated by the East Asian crisis and loans outstanding by Japanese banks to both banks and nonbank private sector borrowers in East Asia—Thailand, Korea, Indonesia, and Malaysia—in the midst of the East Asian crisis. The banking crisis continued until the Bank of Japan (BoJ) took a more systemic approach to the crisis beginning in 2000.[5]

Phase three, or crisis three, resulted from the spillover of the global recession, the Great Recession. Though the U.S. and European crises were most visible in the banking and financial sector, the impact in Japan was on trade. The annual GDP rate in Japan fell 5.5 percent in 2009 because of the decline in demand in the United States and Europe. Japanese exports also declined by 26.2 percent in 2009.[6] Immediately after the crisis, Japanese growth (GDP, interest rates, and inflation) hovered at or near zero as Japan remained in a deflationary cycle.

Japan's Financial/Banking Crisis

The banking crisis that began in 1997 evolved over the course of a few years as larger institutions began to fail and the system appeared to be increasingly at risk.[7] By March 2001, 110 deposit-taking institutions had been dissolved under the deposit insurance system. The cost of addressing the banking crisis was some 86 trillion yen, or 17 percent of GDP, to address: (i) nonperforming loans in the banking system, including writeoffs and provisions for bad debts by the banks; (ii) transfers by Japan's Deposit Insurance Corporation (DIC) to cover losses in failed institutions; and (iii) capital injections into the banks. As the crisis evolved, the Bank of Japan and other relevant authorities had to move from ad hoc, case-by-case intervention in problematic banks to a systemic approach to the crisis. This involved, as in other countries such as Korea, building institutional capacity to address failing bank and nonbank financial institutions and also drafting laws and regulations granting authority to these institutions to intervene and fund crisis resolution. Like the crisis itself, the approach to crisis resolution evolved over time, just as it did in the United States and the eurozone, as we will see in subsequent chapters.[8]

The Early Stages, 1991–94

Japan had experienced no major banking crises in the post–World War II era. The Ministry of Finance (MoF) regulated banks tightly, and the banks were overseen by the central bank (BoJ). It was understood that weak banks would be intervened in by the MoF as necessary and folded into stronger banks. The banks in turn were expected to be safe depository institutions for household savings. The propensity to save was extremely high in Japan post–World War II, and the banks were reliable intermediaries for Japanese industry as Japan built a formidable, highly competitive, export-based industrial sector in the 1970s and 1980s. There was little financial product innovation and also little interest rate competition among the financial institutions. In fact, the banks were tied closely to the major industrial groups in Japan as so-called house banks. While the economy continued to grow, the system worked well.

The government began to deregulate the financial system in the 1970s, but slowly and cautiously, step by step. In 1971 the government established a deposit insurance system and modified that system in 1986 by creating the Deposit Insurance Corporation (DIC), which emulated the system in the United States. By 1987 the DIC insurance fund was large enough to support intervention in relatively small, weak banks, but inadequate to deal with larger institutions or a systemic crisis. Japan began experiencing failures of financial institutions after the bubble burst in 1991, but these were relatively small institutions and considered to be isolated cases. There was optimism in Japan that the economy would return to health and authorities could afford to wait and see and refrain from proactive intervention in the financial system.[9]

By mid-1994 the economy had failed to recover sufficiently, and pressures mounted on the BoJ to take more decisive action in dealing with problematic financial institutions. However, lacking a comprehensive safety net for the banks and other financial institutions, the BoJ was forced to intervene on a case-by-case basis. This was also the approach taken by the U.S. Treasury and Federal Reserve Bank (the Fed) in 2007 and early 2008 up to the bankruptcy of Lehman Brothers. Neither the MoF and BoJ in Japan nor the U.S. Treasury regarded the initial banking and other nonbank financial failures as the beginning of a major crisis, and neither pushed for a systemic approach early in the crisis.

On December 9, 1994, two urban credit cooperatives, Tokyo Kyowa and Anzen, failed. Their failure tested the limits of the case-by-case approach to intervention that had been used up to that point. First, there were no financial institutions willing to absorb them, and there were limits to the payout the DIC could make to any individual institution. However, the government recognized the need to resolve these cases and avoid depositor losses, fearing a potential run on the system. To overcome these obstacles to bank resolution, the government announced a resolution package on December 9 that incorporated the following measures: (i) the BoJ and private financial institutions established a new bank, Tokyo Kyoudou Bank (TKB), to assume the business of the two failed banks; (ii) the BoJ subscribed 20 billion yen in capital to TKB under article 25 of the Bank of Japan Law that allowed the BoJ to act as a lender of last resort. This was the first time in thirty years that the BoJ had been forced to act as a lender of last resort. The private financial institutions added another 20 billion yen; (iii) the DIC assisted TKB up to its payout limit. To protect the depositors, private financial institutions also provided TKB with low-interest loans to ensure that the bank was profitable.[10]

The provision of collective institutional support by private financial institutions was one of the alternative approaches that U.S. Secretary of the Treasury Henry Paulson tried with respect to rescuing Lehman Brothers, which ultimately failed.

Failure of Larger Institutions, 1995 and 1996

When other banking institutions failed in 1995 and 1996, the government followed a similar approach. However, in one institution, Kizu Credit Cooperative, the anticipated losses were so large, in excess of 1,000 billion yen (some US$9.9 billion at 101 yen to the dollar), the authorities decided that "bailing in" private financial institutions would no longer be feasible. The approach no longer seemed sustainable because it was anticipated that additional institutions would need to be supported. The government sought to amend the deposit insurance system law to eliminate the payout limit on intervened cases, signaling that the government, through the BoJ and the DIC and possibly other institutions, would now assume the burden of crisis resolution. In addition, in September 1995, Daiwa Bank, which was active in major international markets as well as Japan, announced a loss of $1.1 billion due to a fraud committed by one of its employees in New York. On November 3 the bank was ordered by U.S. regulators to close all of its U.S. operations. What had been a strictly domestic banking problem now had international implications.[11]

Failure of the Jusen

In 1995–96 the financial system was also adversely affected by nonbank financial institutions such as the *jusen,* housing loan institutions that were owned by the major banks but operated outside the formal banking system. In the 1980s the jusen began lending to real estate developers. With little experience in commercial lending and caught by the bust in real estate, the collective losses of the seven jusen amounted to 6,410 billion yen ($63.5 billion), as determined by MoF inspectors in the summer of 1995. The banks as owners of these institutions were unable to cover their losses, and after a fierce debate in the Diet (Japan's parliament) a package was approved to support the jusen with taxpayers' funds. The losses were allocated among the founder banks, the lenders (banks other than the parents), and agricultural financial institutions. A residual amount of 680 billion yen ($6.7 billion) was covered by taxpayers' funds. The BoJ was also involved, providing 100 billion yen toward the capital of the Housing Loan Administration, which was newly established to assume the NPLs of the jusen. The Housing Loan Administration was also financed in the amount of 900 billion yen by private financial institutions. The jusen problem produced a strong political backlash from the public, and the use of public funds to finance banking bailouts was largely off the table until 1997, when several of the large banks failed.[12]

The Financial Crisis Erupts, 1997 and 1998

The increasing number of NPLs began to affect some of Japan's largest financial institutions. Initially, Nippon Credit Bank (NCB), an international bank with assets of 15 trillion yen ($129 billion), and Hokkaido Takushoki Bank (HTB), an important regional bank, were perceived as vulnerable. It was soon clear that the DIC, even with no payout limits, was too small to deal with the larger banks. Also, there was no framework for direct capital injections into the banks. This was also the case for the major U.S. banks following the Lehman crash. Treasury Secretary Paulson, Fed Chairman Ben Bernanke, and President of the Federal Reserve Bank of New York Timothy Geithner had to persuade the George W. Bush administration and a reluctant U.S. Congress to approve the Troubled Asset Relief Program (TARP) with $700 billion in funding in the second half of 2008.

After an initial restructuring and capital injection by a consortium of banks and the BoJ, NCB continued to perform poorly, and in December 1998, seventeen months after the restructuring, NCB failed and was nationalized. Hokkaido Bank found a merger partner, but that merger failed and HTB eventually collapsed.[13]

By the fall of 1997 the BoJ began to anticipate more bank failures but failed to foresee the contagion effects of bank failures on the rest of the financial system. When securities firms such as Yamaichi began to fail toward the end of 1997, the BoJ needed to step in in an unprecedented way to support several nonbank financial institutions and also prop up the interbank market. The BoJ moved from being the lender of last resort to also being the market maker of last resort. The BoJ injected massive liquidity into the interbank market through the purchase of eligible bills, repos, and bilateral lending to banks, with support reaching some 22 trillion yen ($190 billion) at its peak.[14]

In this respect the Japanese banking crisis resembled the U.S. crisis in 2008 when the shadow banking system began to fail. The U.S. Treasury and Fed supported several major investment banks; AIG (one of the largest insurance companies in the world); the government-sponsored enterprises (GSEs) Fannie Mae (the Federal National Mortgage Association) and Freddie Mac (the Federal Home Loan Mortgage Corporation), which represented a large proportion of mortgage financing; the commercial paper market; and the repo market as the U.S. Fed also went from the lender of last resort to market maker of last resort. The effort to rescue Yamaichi, one of Japan's largest securities and brokerage firms, involved a BoJ intervention under article 25, with the BoJ acting as a lender of last resort to a nonbanking financial institution. At its peak the intervention involved some 1,200 billion yen ($11.1 billion). However, by June 1999, after its financial condition steadily deteriorated, Yamaichi was declared bankrupt, with net losses of some 160 billion yen ($1.5 billion).[15]

A New Law on Restructuring Financial Institutions

The failure of the Long-Term Credit Bank of Japan (LTCB) in March 1998, the largest failure yet with an exposure to derivatives of 50 trillion yen ($240 billion), led to significant new legislation. The Diet approved the Law Concerning Emergency Measures for the Reconstruction of the Functions of the Financial System under which LTCB was nationalized in October 1998 and new capital provided to allow the bank to operate as a going concern. Subsequently the bank was put up for bid in 2000 and the U.S. investment fund Ripplewood and other international investors acquired the bank. Highly unusual for Japan, almost without precedent, foreign investors were allowed to acquire a major Japanese bank.[16]

A Financial Reconstruction Commission

The newly formed Financial Reconstruction Commission reported to the prime minister's office and had the authority to inspect and supervise financial institutions through the new Financial Supervisory Agency (FSA), which was now separate from the Bank of Japan. These institutional changes were similar in scope to those adopted by Korea during the crisis in 1997–99, where the head of the Korean FSA was responsible for both bank and corporate restructuring and reported to the president's office. Financial resources for financial intervention in Japan were doubled to 60 trillion yen. Under the new framework the Japanese authorities were no longer required to find an assuming bank first and moved quickly to systematically clean up the financial system. The aggregate amount injected into the banks during 1999 to deal with NPLs on the books plus anticipated provisions was 7.5 trillion yen ($65 billion); of this amount 6.2 trillion yen was to inject tier-one capital into the banks.[17] Capital injections were supported by a mandate that the banks submit plans to restructure their banks—so-called management improvement plans. In many ways the management improvement plans were similar to the approach taken by the Korean government in restructuring the largest chaebols (conglomerate structures). It was also similar to the decision by Timothy Geithner as secretary of the Treasury in the Obama administration to conduct stress tests of the banks, once capital had been injected into these banks through the TARP.

The option to convert preferred shares to common-share ownership potentially allowed the government of Japan to take a direct ownership stake in a bank if the government was unhappy with progress under the management improvement plan. In addition to direct capital injection, the government created the Resolution and Collection Corporation, a merger of two older institutions to serve as an asset management agency, with the authority to acquire bad assets from both insolvent banks and banks that simply wanted to clean up their balance sheets. Through stricter provisioning requirements, direct capital injection into the banks, and the removal of bad assets from the banks' balance sheets, tier-one capital in Japanese banks rose to 11 percent by the end of 1999 and the banking crisis was largely over.[18]

Effects of The Japanese Crisis on the Real Economy

Although the banking and financial sector crisis had a strong negative effect on the Japanese economy, perhaps of greater importance was the negative wealth effect when the asset bubble burst in 1991. Land prices declined to their 1975 value and the stock market declined to 25 percent of its peak before the bubble burst. From 2000 to the end of 2015, GDP growth averaged less than 1 percent, and inflation hovered at near zero and negative levels. Debt, almost exclusively held by Japanese families and institutions, ballooned to 242 percent of GDP by 2013 and was projected by the IMF to reach close to 250 percent by the end of 2016.[19]

Export-Led Growth until the Mid-1980s

Japan relied on an export-led model to fuel growth until the mid-1980s. Japanese multinationals such as Toyota, Honda, Sony, Panasonic, and Mitsubishi in autos, electronics, and heavy industry such as shipbuilding, with high productivity tied to management practices such as just-in-time delivery and extensive use of automation and robotics, made Japanese producers some of the most competitive companies in the world. By the mid-1980s the appreciation of the yen and competition from other East Asian newly industrialized countries—Korea, Singapore, Hong Kong, and Taiwan, all focused on export-led growth—had an adverse impact on the Japanese economy. One outcome of the decline in the export-led model in Japan has been that industrial workers who were typically guaranteed lifetime employment and benefits have seen job security erode; Japanese firms now employ many more contract workers as a part of their work force.[20] In 1999 the BoJ cut short-term interest rates to near zero. The government has relied since then on a combination of stimulus and quantitative easing to reignite the economy. Japan is caught in a trap. It has repeatedly utilized stimulus measures to try and ignite growth; but the debt from past stimulus measures threatens growth. "The lessons are clear. Low interest rates and large budget deficits, the basic ingredients of a stimulus, have limits and can be self-defeating."[21]

Commenting on the role of the Bank of Japan, Jerald Schiff, former mission chief for the IMF in Japan, observed first that the Japanese central bank's stimulus was insufficient in the early stages of the crisis; second that the BoJ was inconsistent, starting and stopping in its extended effort to contain the banking crisis; and third that the BoJ was reactive and instead should have stated its inflation target from the start.[22]

Causes of the Crisis, according to Richard Koo

In examining the causes of the long-term recession in Japan, Richard Koo, a highly respected Japanese economist, accepts that Japan has a series of structural impediments that slow Japan's growth, which several economists view as the root of the recession. These issues, among others, are: (i) a low birth rate and an aging population whose lower demand for goods and services from the private sector, increasing demand for government support for health care and social services, and fewer active workers per total population have reduced the tax base;[23] (ii) the more limited role of women in the work force than in the United States and Europe; and (iii) resistance to immigrants and guest workers from poorer East Asian economies to supplement the work force.[24] However important these structural impediments may be to more dynamic growth, Koo does not believe that these were or remain fundamental causes of Japan's long-term recession. He sees structural problems signaling supply-side problems, while Japan's problems were largely weak demand: "Japan's economy was characterized by ample supply but insufficient demand. Japanese products were in high demand everywhere but in their home market."[25]

Koo also does not accept that the recession was caused by the banking/financial crisis. The interest rates charged by Japanese banks fell steadily for fifteen years to the lowest levels in Japan's modern economic history. Koo maintains that had loan demand been unsatisfied, interest rates would have risen rather than declined, foreign banks would have increased their market share, and the corporate bond market would have been robust. However, Koo notes that just the opposite occurred.[26]

Japan, asserts Koo, experienced a balance sheet recession. Japan's corporate sector had vibrant cash flow from exports, but when the bubble burst highly leveraged Japanese firms found that they had substantial debt collateralized by real estate, whose price had collapsed and as a result "put a hole in their balance sheets" that led to negative net worth. So rather than borrow with interest rates near zero in order to invest, Japanese firms paid down debt and deleveraged over a twelve-year period starting in the early 1990s. "Yet many of these firms had negative net worth because of the huge hole left in their balance sheets by the plunge in domestic asset prices. Thousands—perhaps even tens of thousands—of firms fell into this category. The urgency of debt repayment was heightened by the fact that Japanese firms in the 1980s were much more highly leveraged than their U.S. or European counterparts."[27]

In comparison with other East Asian countries, only Korean corporations dominated by the chaebols were more leveraged than the Japanese corporations.[28] Koo therefore views the decline in corporate wealth due to the bursting of the asset bubble as the prime cause of the recession and associated deflation. He terms it a balance sheet recession. He believes that his view on causation also explains the Great Depression in the 1930s. In this he differs from Keynes, who Koo believes viewed recession through the prism of the loan cycle and the need for government stimulus to replace the diminished role of the private sector in the economy. Koo views Irving Fischer's debt deflation theory of recessions, also derived from the experience of the Great Depression, as aligned with his view of a balance sheet recession, except as to causation.[29] Interestingly, Atif Mian and Amir Sufi align with Koo and view as mistaken the widespread perception that the Great Recession in the United States was largely caused by a financial/banking crisis. Their view is that the asset bubble in housing and real estate that burst in the in 2007, and its adverse wealth effect, was the primary cause of the recession. The financial and subprime mortgage crisis largely deepened a crisis that, in their view, would have occurred in any event. (I discuss Mian and Sufi's views in chapter 16.)[30]

Attempt at Fiscal Consolidation

In 1997, after several years of fiscal stimulus and corresponding fiscal deficits, the administration of President Kazuhito Hashimoto was the first in Japan to begin a program of fiscal consolidation in order to reduce the fiscal deficit. The government enacted a number of tax increases and abandoned a supplementary budget. This resulted in the financial crisis, falling tax receipts, and an explosion of the deficit from 26 trillion yen in 1996 to 38 trillion yen in 1999. Koo notes: "Fiscal consolidation at a time like this sparks a vicious cycle of economic deterioration, falling tax receipts and rising budget deficits."[31] In 2003 the administration of Junichiro Koizumi abandoned yet another effort at fiscal reform and allowed the government stabilizer to kick in.[32] Economic growth ensued, albeit at a low level, largely driven by a weak yen and exports: "The longest period of growth (2002–2007) depended heavily on a cheap yen that revived the export model."[33]

Effects of the Great Recession of 2008

The crisis that radiated out from the United States to Japan starting in 2008 again pushed Japan into recession with continued low growth, deflation, and an inability to escape the debt deflation trap. Over the two decades from 1995 to 2014 the GDP growth rate was an anemic 0.72 percent per year; its ratio of gross debt to GDP, now the highest in the world, is close to 250 percent of GDP; and inflation was at deflationary levels throughout almost all of this period.[34]

The Abe Plan

On entering office, Prime Minister Shinzo Abe tabled a plan in late 2012 and early 2013 to bring Japanese inflation above 2 percent per year and to restore growth. The plan was supported by the BoJ's large-scale purchase of assets through its quantitative easing framework QE.[35] An IMF team analyzing the potential for the Abe plan to work notes the challenge: "At the heart of Japan's economic challenge lie four closely related intertemporal problems: ending deflation, raising growth, securing fiscal sustainability, and maintaining financial stability. These objectives need to be achieved against the background of Japan's rapidly aging society, entrenched deflationary expectations, and a global economy that remained mired in subdued growth."[36]

The initial impact of Abenomics was successful, but progress became uneven in the course of 2013 as consumer confidence declined. Growth slowed strongly by the third quarter of 2014 after the introduction of an 8 percent consumption tax in April 2014 that effectively offset the stimulus measures: "The effects of the April consumption tax increase to 8 percent were stronger and longer lasting than anticipated, halting the recovery in its tracks by Q3:2014." This led the BoJ to increase its stimulus program in the last quarter of 2014 and the government to postpone the next installment of the consumption tax increase to 10 percent.[37] Growth rates have been low since the consumption tax was introduced, and the rate of inflation has remained near or at deflationary levels.

Japan's Sovereign Debt: Fiscal Risks

The crisis caused Japan's debt to grow substantially. Most of the debt was held by Japanese citizens and institutions and as such did not threaten a debt crisis. In the long term, however, the level of debt relative to GDP is not sustainable and will make it more difficult for Japan to address a future crisis.

Japan's fiscal deficits and its rapidly growing debt over the last two decades are attributable to a series of factors: (i) the 1993 bubble bursting and the rapid decline in the stock market and real estate prices. Tied to this shock was the decline in growth and in the tax base from 19 percent of GDP to 16 percent; (ii) the fiscal costs of the financial crisis that began in 1994 and reached its height in 1997 and 1998; (iii) the spillover effects of the East Asian crisis from 1997 to 1999; (iv) the Great Recession, which started in the United States in 2007, rapidly moved to Europe, and adversely affected Japan largely because of the decline in demand for Japanese exports; (v) the large earthquake and tsunami that hit Japan in 2011; and (vi) the increasing costs of a rapidly aging society. Social security spending accounted for 37 percent of the increase in debt between 1990 and 2012, including pension spending, which more than doubled from 5.2 percent of GDP to 10.9 percent of GDP; likewise, health and long-term care for seniors increased from 4.1 percent of GDP to 8.3 percent of GDP. In this respect, aging may have contributed more to debt than the economic slowdowns did. However, efforts by various governments at fiscal consolidation were frustrated by low growth and a number of external shocks.[38]

Is the Debt Sustainable?

Although though Japanese households and domestic institutions hold over 90 percent of Japanese debt, Japanese debt has offered lower and lower yields. The fiscal situation is not without downside risks. Particularly as the population ages it is anticipated that their savings rate and the absolute amount saved will decline. While gross debt is expected to range from 240 to 245 percent of GDP in the next few years,[39] projections are that by the mid-2020s Japan will increasingly need to reach to foreigners to absorb Japanese government bonds. Moreover, debt projections are subject to macro-economic shocks such as the need to pay higher interest rates to attract bond purchasers, and other shocks such as another massive earthquake. Also, Japan's dependency ratio is expected to continue to rise, and the costs of providing services to Japan's aging population will continue to have a major fiscal impact on government budgets and in the absence of external shocks will be a primary driver of greater indebtedness. Under present policies Japan's debt appears to be unsustainable in the medium term.[40]

A Lesson for the Other Advanced Economies

The crisis in Japan should have been a warning to the other advanced economies. One example was the initial ad hoc, case-by-case manner in which Japanese authorities addressed difficulties in bank and nonbank financial institutions, rather than waiting until several years into the crisis to take a systemic approach. The failure of the ad hoc approach in Japan should have informed former Treasury Secretary Paulson, Treasury Secretary Geithner, and Fed Chairman Bernanke as they initially took on financial sector resolution one emergency case at a time. Only after the failure of Lehman Brothers did they begin to address failures in the sector systemically through a $700 billion crisis appropriation from Congress, managed by the Treasury, known as the Troubled Asset Relief Program (TARP).[41] The eurozone countries should have learned the lessons of the debt deflation trap faced by Japan in the 1990s and as formulated in theory by Irving Fisher after the Great Depression.[42] Also, both the United States and Europe should have learned the lesson about the higher fiscal costs of servicing an aging population. However, Japan's problems at the time were viewed as unique by the other advanced economies. In hindsight that turns out to have been wrong.

Finally, The United States and Japan went from being two of the world's primary creditor countries to becoming two of the world's largest sovereign debtors. For a variety of reasons it is doubtful that either will face a sovereign debt crisis in the near future; however, their long-term debt position appears to be unsustainable. It should also be clear that both countries have less room to address the next serious economic downturn or crisis. The chapters that follow focus on the crisis in the United States from 2007 to 2012 and the crisis in the eurozone from 2009 to 2015, collectively known as the Great Recession.

SIXTEEN

Causes of the U.S. Crisis

2007–10

In 2008 the United States became the epicenter of the global financial/economic crisis with a housing and real estate bust and associated collateralized debt obligations (CDOs). The crisis was often referred to as the subprime mortgage crisis. As the crisis developed, mortgage-backed securities rose from $87 billion in 2001 to $465 billion in 2005, and Alt-A mortgages (variable-rate mortgages) grew from $11 billion to $332 billion during this same period.[1] The collapse of the subprime mortgage and related CDO market forced the George W. Bush administration, against its ideological convictions, to rescue the financial system through the Troubled Asset Relief Program (TARP) and provide capital to most of the largest banks and investment banks, the latter opting to become banks to become eligible for the capital infusion. TARP funds also rescued American International Group (AIG), one of the world's largest insurance companies, which had provided risk insurance to many of the banks and investment banks for the CDOs. Finally, the government exercised its "implicit" guarantee of the obligations of the Federal National Mortgage Association (Fannie Mae) and the Federal Home Loan Mortgage Corporation (Freddie Mac) by placing these two government-sponsored enterprises (GSEs) into "conservatorship" (September 7, 2008), akin to nationalization. No companies were as exposed as these two, which owned or guaranteed trillions of dollars in mortgages. The Federal Reserve

317

Bank (the Fed) initially injected $100 billion of capital into these two agencies plus generous credit lines, and was subsequently required to inject billions more.[2]

The rescue of the global investment bank Bear Stearns was the signal to markets, and to the Treasury and the Fed, that the markets and institutions were fragile. The failure of the financial services firm Lehman Brothers, and the inability of the Treasury and Fed to rescue Lehman, as it had Bear Stearns, was the trigger event that plunged the world into crisis by creating a crisis of confidence in U.S. and world financial markets.

A Complex Set of Interconnected Causes

In general, finance played a much larger role in the U.S. and world economies in the 1990s and 2000s leading up to the crisis than it had after World War II. It represented a larger proportion of corporate profits and was larger relative to the real economy than it had been historically. In 1980, financial sector profits were some 15 percent of overall corporate profits; in 2003 they reached 33 percent of corporate profits; and in 2006 profitability declined to 27 percent of profits as the crisis approached.[3] There was ample liquidity in the system; one might term it a financial tsunami. Stock market turnover increased dramatically. Foreign exchange trading grew much more rapidly than real trade in goods and services, capital flows grew much more rapidly than long-term real investment, and financial innovation, in particular securitization, led to a dramatic growth in derivative contracts. By 2008 there were some $400 trillion in derivative contracts outstanding.[4]

The list that follows is not meant to prioritize one cause over another. The causes for the most part overlapped and were interlinked. The list seeks to outline the complexity and magnitude of the financial crisis in the United States, which was by far the largest and deepest crisis since the Great Depression.

The Housing Bubble

Both the residential housing market and the commercial real estate market were overheated by 2006, and the complex set of financial instruments and derivatives that supported the financing of home mortgages had stoked the flames of the expansion. In 2000, largely owing to low interest rates and readily available mortgage financing, home sales began to increase rapidly, as did the prices of new homes. Average home prices increased 67 percent in the eight years that followed, 2000 to 2007. Housing starts nationwide increased 53 percent from 1.4 million in 1995 to more than 2 million in 2005. Refinancing of homes increased from $460 billion in 2000 to $2.8 trillion by 2003, allowing families to withdraw equity from their homes to finance other needs or consumption items. Americans extracted $2.0 trillion in equity from their homes between 2000 and 2007. Speculation was active, particularly in a select set of markets, such as in the Sun Belt—Phoenix, San Diego, Los Angeles, West Palm Beach, Miami, and Fort Lauderdale, among others. By 2005, one in ten homes sold was to an investor, speculator, or second-home buyer.[5] Eventually the bubble had to burst, as it had in other crises and other countries such as Japan in the early 1990s, Thailand in 1997, and Ireland and Spain in the eurozone crisis.

Atif Mian and Amir Sufi offer two primary observations with respect to the housing bubble and the crisis: (i) that the housing bubble would have caused a crisis whether or not there had been a related financial crisis; and (ii) the housing bubble had a disproportionate impact on the poor and as such exacerbated the problem of income inequality in the United States. With respect to crises the authors write:

> The most severe recessions in history were preceded by a sharp rise in household debt and a collapse in asset prices. Both the Great Recession and the Great Depression in the United States followed this script. . . . The key problem is debt. Debt amplifies the decline in asset prices due to foreclosures and by concentrating losses on the indebted, who are almost always households with the lowest net worth in the economy. This is the fundamental feature of debt: it forces the debtor to bear the shock. This is especially dangerous because the spending of indebted households is extremely sensitive to shocks to their net worth—when their net worth is decimated, they sharply pull back on spending. The demand shock overwhelms the economy, and the result is economic catastrophe.[6]

With respect to lending to families with low credit scores (a proxy for poorer families), Mian and Sufi write: "Throughout American cities credit was pumped into low credit score zip codes that were experiencing declining income growth. . . . The direction of the credit flow was particularly dysfunctional during the early years of the mortgage boom. . . . The behavior of lenders from 2002 to 2005 produced a very unusual statistical pattern: mortgage credit growth and income became negatively correlated."[7]

When the bubble did burst the impact was virulent in the housing sector, threatening some of the country's most important and largest financial institutions. On "Main Street," millions of households faced eviction and loss of their homes because they were unable to service their mortgages. During the post–World War II era the default rate had never risen above 6.5 percent. By 2009 the default rate was over 10 percent. Mian and Sufi note: "It is pretty safe to say that in the Great American Recession the household default rate reached its highest level since the Great Depression."[8]

Many of these same families, using the equity in their house as collateral, borrowed from home improvement lines to finance other needs; some were also overextended in other areas—with credit card debts, school loans, and auto loans, as examples. Cumulatively there was a large-scale deleveraging of the economy; lenders froze the credit of all but the most creditworthy of large businesses and households. Of course the housing and related sectors were a huge source of employment—in construction, architecture and design, the furniture industry, home appliances, and services (mortgage brokers, lawyers, and so on). The crisis soon led to large-scale unemployment and failures in the housing sector and other important segments of the economy.

Excessive Liquidity, Growing Indebtedness, and the Subprime Mortgage Problem

There was excessive liquidity in the system, and indebtedness grew in all sectors of the economy for an extended period of time. From 1960 to 1974 the leverage ratio of banks in the United States increased by some 50 percent and rose more quickly during the 1980s and 1990s. In 1981 private sector debt was equal to 123 percent of GDP, but by the end of 2008 it had risen to 290 percent. The nonfinancial corporate sector was largely prudent with respect to its debt ratios. Corporate sector debt increased from 53 percent to 76 percent of GDP during this same period. Household debt, in contrast, grew from 48 percent of GDP in 1981 to 100 percent by 2007. Much of this was due to increasing leverage in the housing sector, where it was possible to obtain a subprime mortgage with a very small or no down payment. Overall mortgage indebtedness in the United States rose from $5.3 trillion in 2001 to $10.5 trillion in 2006. The mortgage debt of American households rose in just six years almost as much as it had risen in the 200 years since the founding of the country.[9] In 1994 subprime mortgages were some 5 percent of new mortgages, but by 2005 that number had risen to 20 percent. By far the worst of the subprime mortgages were those financed by the shadow banking system in 2006 and 2007.[10]

Many of the subprime mortgages were packaged and collateralized. These collateralized debt obligations grew dramatically from 2004 and then explosively in the two years leading to the crisis, 2006 and 2007. The investment banks and banks that bought the mortgage assets and then collateralized the mortgages most often structured them in special-purpose vehicles (SPVs); the original mortgages were then sliced into tranches, with different layers of risk and a precise "waterfall" based on cash proceeds from the cash receipts of the underlying securities that were collateralized.[11] These tranches were then issued as bonds and sold as securities or packaged in SPVs. Many of the securities, which were eventually marked down substantially, were initially given triple-A credit ratings by the major credit rating agencies. Investors purchased these securities based on their risk tolerance.

Although the credit rating agencies deserve significant blame for the debacle that followed, the investment banks and hedge funds that originated, marketed, and distributed these securities throughout the world were the primary actors in this market and deserve the lion's share of the blame: "Between 2003 and 2007, as house prices rose 27% nationally and $4 trillion in mortgage backed securities were created, Wall Street issued nearly $700 billion in CDOs that included mortgage backed securities as collateral. In effect, the CDO became the engine that powered the mortgage supply chain."[12] CDOs were responsible for $542 billion in losses of the nearly trillion dollars in losses suffered by the financial sector in 2007 and 2008. The relative importance of various CDO properties in contributing to the collapse of this market were as follows, based on a study of 735 CDOs between 2004 and 2007: (i) the asset classes and year of issue (vintage) were the most important contributor to failure; (ii) the identity of the underwriter was a significant predictor of CDO performance; J. P. Morgan's CDOs consistently underperformed, and those issued by Goldman Sachs were among the top performers; (ii) the original credit ratings, especially those in the triple-A class, were grossly inflated.[13] Based on her empirical study of 735 asset-backed CDOs, Anna Katherine Barnett-Hart observes:

> CDOs were flawed from the outset, used too often as a junkyard for risky and substandard assets. CDOs survived because of changes in the credit markets that produced an excess quantity of these assets and herds of investors hungry for higher yields. . . . The marriage of the CDO and subprime was thus consummated and Wall Street became inextricably linked with the riskiest homebuyers in America. In 2006 Merrill Lynch, Citigroup, and Bear Stearns plunged headfirst into the CDO business, loading up on the steady supply of questionable mortgages coming from a *milieu* of mortgage brokers. . . . The best predictors of banks' write-downs was not the quality of CDOs, but instead the amount of CDOs they issued in 2007, for very few of these CDOs would ever leave the balance sheet of their creators.[14]

The hedge against losses in CDOs was credit default swaps (CDS), derivative instruments that served as insurance against default. Unlike the numerous market makers in CDOs, the credit default market was highly concentrated in AIG and a few other "monoline" insurance companies. A subsidiary of AIG, one of the largest insurers in the world, AIG Financial Products (AIGFP) was created in 1987. In 2000 it began to insure against collateralized loan products such as credit card debt, auto loans, student loans, aircraft loans, and prime mortgage loans. By the end of 2004 the products being insured were increasingly concentrated in subprime mortgage loans that were securitized and uniquely packaged as CDOs. From just 2 percent in 2000, by 2004 95 percent of AIGFP's credit default swaps were insuring subprime loans, or some $50 billion of insured bonds. This concentrated risk put the parent firm at risk, but no one seemed to notice. The business was so profitable and dynamic that it apparently received little scrutiny from AIG management or its board of directors.[15]

While debt increased in the nonfinancial private sector and in the household sector during this period, the financial sector debt soared; between 1981 and 2008 financial sector debt grew from 22 percent of GDP to 117 percent of GDP.[16] Leverage, especially in the shadow banking sector, reached unprecedented levels by 2007. At the end of 2007, capital levels at the five largest Wall Street investment banks—Bear Sterns, Lehman Brothers, Merrill Lynch, Morgan Stanley, and Goldman Sachs—were just 3 percent of assets; it was even lower at the GREs—Fannie Mae and Freddie Mac—at 1 percent of assets in their portfolio.[17] The national commission investigating the causes of the economic crisis concluded:

> There was untrammeled growth in risky mortgages. Unsustainable, toxic loans polluted the financial system and fueled the housing bubble. . . . Subprime lending was supported in significant ways by major financial institutions. Some firms such as Citigroup, Lehman Brothers, and Morgan Stanley acquired subprime lenders. In addition, major financial institutions facilitated the growth in subprime mortgages—lending companies with lines of credit, securitization, purchase guarantees and other mechanisms.[18]

Low Interest Rates

Because interest rates were kept too low for too long they encouraged excessive leverage: "From early 2001 through the middle of 2003, Greenspan [Alan Greenspan, chairman of the Federal Reserve Board] cut the Fed funds rate by some 5.5 percent (or in banking parlance, by 550 basis points). He then kept rates too low for too long a time, an easy-money policy that would help foster the unsustainable credit and housing boom."[19] When the Fed raised the rates from 2004 to 2006, long-term interest and mortgage rates hardly moved. Liquidity tightening had little effect at that point in the cycle as money poured into the markets from the large exporting countries with significant savings, such as China, Japan, and Germany.

Bank Deregulation and the Repeal of Glass-Steagall

It is arguable that deregulating the banks allowed them to diversify their product mix and grow so large that they became "too big to fail."[20] As the major U.S. banks grew they pressed their regulators, state legislatures, and Congress to repeal restrictive banking laws. They had a great deal of success in their lobbying efforts. In 1994 Congress authorized nationwide banking through the Riegle-Neal Interstate Banking and Branching Efficiency Act. The new law allowed bank holding companies to acquire banks in every state and removed most state restrictions on multiple branch openings in a given state. Removing regulatory barriers removed barriers to consolidation, and between 1990 and 2005 seventy-four large-scale mergers occurred among larger banks. The ten largest banks went from controlling 25 percent of the sector's assets to 55 percent. From 1998 to 2007 the combined assets of the five largest U.S. banks more than tripled. Investment banks also grew substantially when most of the larger investment banks converted from private partnerships to publicly traded companies and also acquired or merged with smaller investment banks.[21]

One could further argue that the financial tsunami began with the repeal of the Glass-Steagall Act in 1999. The Glass-Steagall Act was a Depression-era law enacted in 1933 that prohibited banks from investment banking activity and speculative financing activity such as proprietary trading. It was repealed by the Gramm-Leach-Bliley Act of 1999.[22] The end of Glass-Steagall opened the doors for banks such as Citibank to become complex financial supermarkets and engage in investment banking, trading activity, mortgage finance, and a wide variety of other financial services, in addition to their more traditional financial activities in corporate and consumer finance, especially credit card lending. The large banking groups such as Citigroup became too large and complex to manage and too large to fail. When the crisis was full blown, each of these large institutions needed to be saved. That is, the Fed and the Treasury felt compelled to support or rescue these institutions to ensure that the crisis could be contained and that the U.S. financial system would not collapse. As Joseph Stiglitz notes: "The most important consequence of the repeal of Glass-Steagall was indirect. When the repeal brought investment and commercial banks together, the investment banking culture came out on top. There was the demand for the kind of high returns that could be obtained only through high leverage and big risk taking. There was another consequence: a less competitive and more concentrated banking system dominated by ever larger banks."[23]

U.S. Capital Markets and the Growth of the Shadow Banking Institutions

U.S. capital markets were complex, agile, and robust. In addition to the traditional stock and bond markets, the U.S. financial sector, mostly Wall Street institutions, supported a variety of capital markets that intermediated a very diverse set of financing instruments, such as money market funds, which had accumulated some $3 trillion in assets by 2007; the commercial paper market at $1.2 trillion; and the tri-party repo market, which was also a significant market with some $2.75 trillion outstanding.[24]

In addition to the regulated banking sector, the so-called shadow banking system, which had no deposit base, grew enormously during this period by tapping into these markets, often through short-term financing. The shadow banking market, at best lightly regulated, included investment banks, private equity funds, hedge funds, government-sponsored enterprises such as Fannie Mae and Freddie Mac, corporate financial vehicles such as General Electric Capital Corporation (GE Capital), and other diverse institutions such as housing finance intermediaries—for example, Countrywide Financial Corporation.

AIG, one of the largest insurance carriers in the world, provided counterpart insurance in the form of derivative hedges for the CDOs, which were held in increasingly large amounts by many of the shadow banking institutions. AIG's counterpart insurance gave the rating agencies comfort so that the CDOs could be highly rated and make it appear to investors that these instruments were largely risk free.

The investment banks were enormously leveraged and had large-scale and concentrated risks in CDOs. The investment banks were not subject to the same capital requirements as the commercial banks. The commercial banks mobilized deposits from the public and were required to have adequate capital to protect depositors, though that later proved to be an illusion. The investment banks were given a wide berth to determine their capital requirements according to their own risk management systems. By 2007 Goldman Sachs had a leverage ratio of 32:1 (1 dollar of equity for every 32 dollars of debt); Morgan Stanley and Lehman Brothers reached 40:1 in 2007.[25] Their business models had changed during this period from relying on traditional financial advisory fees such as supporting initial public offerings, assisting firms to raise capital in the capital markets, and merger and acquisition assignments. They increasingly relied on asset management and trading activities. With no deposit base and much of their borrowing short term, they simply were not structured to face a large shock. Also, because they lacked a deposit base the investment banks financed a great deal of their activity with short-term instruments that led to critical maturity mismatches for these institutions, when the CDO market froze and the value of these instruments began to decline rapidly. Mark-to-market valuation of their portfolio holdings led to very large quarterly losses during 2008, which in turn led to rapid and large declines in their stock prices. The investment banks as publicly listed companies were primarily regulated by the U.S. Securities and Exchange Commission (SEC), and as such they were weakly regulated from a financial perspective. Again, the commission investigating the economic crisis concluded:

> The shadow banking system was permitted to grow to rival the commercial banking system with inadequate supervision and regulation. That system was very fragile due to high leverage, short-term funding, risky assets, inadequate liquidity, and the lack of a federal backstop. When the mortgage market collapsed and financial firms began to abandon the commercial paper and repo lending market, some institutions depending on them for funding their operations failed or, later in the crisis, had to be rescued. These markets and other interconnections created contagion, as the crisis spread even to markets and firms that had little to no direct exposure to the mortgage market.[26]

The GSEs—Fannie Mae and Freddie Mac

At the heart of the country's mortgage markets, GSEs were able to raise funds, both equity and bonds, in both the United States and from international institutions. The GSEs had implicit U.S. government guarantees, they were triple-A rated, and they were able to raise capital at costs just above those of U.S. Treasuries. Virtually every money market fund, pension fund, insurance company, and central bank around the world held positions in the GSEs. In 2008, China alone held some $700 billion in GSE mortgage-backed securities, a bit more than China held in U.S. Treasuries.[27] During the height of the crisis, Henry M. Paulson Jr., Treasury secretary, who had close ties to the Chinese government from his days as CEO of Goldman Sachs, made sure that his Chinese counterpart was holding firm on China's large-scale positions in the GSEs, and the Chinese in turn wanted assurance from Paulson that the U.S. government would support the GSEs if required to do so.[28]

These institutions were weakly regulated, but had enormous political support in Congress. The GREs were also very thinly capitalized, operated with very high leverage, and held large portfolios of subprime mortgages. During the growth of the housing market in the 1990s and 2000s up to the beginning of the crisis in 2007, the GSEs began to lose market share to the shadow banks, particularly the investment banks, several of which acquired mortgage brokers and operated throughout the supply chain from mortgage origination to packaging into CDOs and distribution throughout the world, principally in the advanced economies. The investment banks also created special-purpose investment vehicles of CDOs to which they attracted investors. To maintain market share and profitability, the GSEs began to participate in the financing of subprime mortgages with the result that they lowered their underwriting standards and had enormous exposure to subprime assets when the financial crisis ensued.

Some analysts of the crisis claimed that the GSEs were pushed to finance subprime mortgages in order to meet their quota in servicing disadvantaged populations. That does not seem to be accurate, according to the commission investigating the causes of the financial crisis. By September 2005, Fannie Mae began to acquire riskier loans. By the end of 2005, its Alt-A loans were $181 billion, its loans without full documentation were $278 billion, and its interest-only mortgages were $75 billion. To cover the potential losses for all of its portfolio, Fannie Mae had just $41 billion in capital. Freddie Mac also dropped its underwriting standards and was at least as thinly capitalized.[29] By dropping their underwriting standards, the GSEs clearly contributed to the crisis. Their governance model contributed to this problem: they were public-private vehicles, with support from the Treasury and an implicit loan guarantee from the government, but management had been privatized and they had private investors as equity holders. The same greed that drove the privately owned commercial banks and shadow banks to increase their leverage and drop lending standards also prevailed at the GSEs (see table 16-1). In this case the GSEs were socializing the potential losses and privatizing the gains.

Unregulated Hedge Funds

The hedge funds managed huge pools of capital, were free of regulation (except corporate regulation by the SEC), and were able to move agilely and swiftly. A number of hedge funds became a source of instability during the crisis by systematically attacking and shorting the stock of the investment banks. The Lehman failure, the spark that ignited the worldwide financial crisis, was in part due to large-scale and systematic shorting of Lehman Brothers' stock by hedge funds and other investors.

TABLE 16-1.   United States: Bank versus Market-Funded Financial Institutions,
1990, 2007, and 2012

Institution type	Trillions of US$	Percent
1990	7.1	
Depository institutions	4.5	63
Asset-backed securities	0.3	4
Finance companies	0.6	8
Broker dealers	0.3	4
Government-sponsored enterprises	1.5	21
2007	29.5	
Depository institutions	12.4	42
Asset-backed securities	4.5	15
Finance companies	1.9	6
Broker dealers	3.1	10
Government-sponsored enterprises	7.6	26
2012	28.1	
Depository institutions	15.1	54
Asset-backed securities	2.1	7
Finance companies	1.5	5
Broker dealers	1.8	6
Government-sponsored depositories	7.2	27

Source: Timothy Geithner, *Stress Test: Reflections on Financial Crises* (New York: Broadway Books, 2014), pp. 506–07.

Note: Percentages may not add to 100 because of rounding.

Following Lehman Brothers' collapse, these institutions put other financial institutions with large exposure to CDOs' toxic assets under pressure, such as Merrill Lynch, Morgan Stanley, and Wachovia Bank: "The bankers complained bitterly about hedge funds, which they felt were shorting their stocks and manipulating credit default swaps and in the CEOs' minds, all but trying to force some institutions under. Almost every one of them wanted to regulate the funds."[30] Although the hedge funds did little to cause the crisis (except those that were significant investors in subprime mortgage assets and CDOs), the pressure they put on financial institutions, including Lehman and post-Lehman, left the Fed and the Treasury little alternative but to rescue them as quickly as possible following the Lehman debacle. Criticism by Stiglitz and others that there should have been orderly workouts of the financial institutions under Chapter 11 of the U.S. bankruptcy code does not take into account the reality of the situation and the pressure brought by the hedge funds on these institutions.[31]

Weak Governance, Distorted Compensation Incentives, and Excessive Risks

Large complex institutions that were too big to fail also turned out to be too big and complex to manage or govern well. In a review of Citigroup's role in the crisis, the national commission reviewing the causes of the crisis determined that Citicorp's senior management—including CEO Chuck Prince, and Robert Rubin, former chairman and CEO of Goldman Sachs, former secretary of the Treasury, and chairman of the Executive Committee at Citigroup—were completely unaware of the potential large-scale losses in CDOs, including direct guarantees, and liquidity puts, made by Citibank anchoring some of this business, until very late in the game. Moreover, the commission found that some divisions of the group were selling their positions while others were increasing their positions in subprime mortgages and CDOs. The commission observed:

> The liquidity put was yet another highly leveraged bet, a contingent liability that would be triggered in some circumstances. Citigroup did not have to hold any capital against such contingencies. Rather, it was permitted to use its own risk models to determine the appropriate capital charge. . . . The events of 2007 would reveal the fallacy of those assumptions and catapult the entire $25 billion in commercial paper straight on to the bank's balance sheet, requiring it to come up with $25 billion in cash, as well as more capital to satisfy bank regulators.[32]

Ultimately, Citigroup's losses from subprime exposure were $55 billion. CEO Charles Prince was forced to resign just five days after Merrill Lynch's CEO Stanley O'Neal.[33]

Above all, distorted compensation incentives provided to management of these financial institutions encouraged them to take extraordinary risks. Senior management in investment banks, hedge funds, and AIG's finance unit focused on derivatives; they were generating enormous profits for their firms and in turn were being paid very large bonuses and stock options. This resulted in concentrated risks and the failure of risk management systems to stem the tide as losses accumulated. Even when large losses were realized, some firms such as Merrill Lynch paid out large separation packages to their CEOs. With $55 billion in gross retained CDO positions and billions of dollars in losses, Merrill paid its CEO a package worth $161.5 million, on top of his 2006 salary of $91.5 million, a year in which the firm was beginning to accumulate CDO positions that led to these large losses.[34]

In the case of AIG, the firm paid out contractually agreed bonuses to retain their teams as markets became volatile and firms needed these staff to liquidate their positions. The payment by AIG of some $165 million in contractually agreed bonuses to its small financial unit, despite enormous losses and a bailout by the U.S. government that was in excess of $110 billion, had significant political fallout for the newly elected Obama administration. The Treasury, under Timothy Geithner's leadership, felt that it was not in a position to force AIG to cancel contractual commitments and as such was unable to prevent the political hit to the administration.[35] "The AIG bonus scandal would take the media frenzy to and the public anger to new levels, and I knew it would be another devastating blow to confidence and our crisis response."[36]

Concentrated risks were often ignored until it was far too late for many financial firms to avoid deep losses. Management put their own institutions at risk, put the U.S. and international financial system at risk, and caused great damage to the U.S. economy and ordinary citizens but were paid appalling sums of money, even when forced to leave their firms as part of contractually agreed exit packages. Nouriel Roubini notes, "The biggest issue is the bonus culture on Wall Street, in which employees are compensated when their best bets pay off, but are not penalized when those bets cost the firm money. This system encourages risk taking that generates oversize 'alpha' returns in the short-term, with little consideration of long-term consequences."[37] Also, their boards failed to exercise their fiduciary responsibility to protect their institutions from concentrated and excessive risks.

Highly Interconnected Markets and Institutions

The interconnectedness of the financial system implied that if a major firm such as Lehman was at risk of failing, it was highly probable that other firms would be dragged down with it. The investment banks without a deposit base needed to reach into short-term capital markets to raise funds, or they borrowed from one another with appropriate collateral. They traded with each other actively. With the market value of the CDOs declining rapidly, the investment banks needed to mark to market daily. When Lehman Brothers was suspected of not doing so, other institutions stopped trading with them, accelerating their decline; others such as Goldman Sachs sought more collateral to protect its position. AIG provided insurance cover for much of the financial industry dealing in CDOs. As AIG's ratings began to decline, they were forced to provide more collateral to the counterparties they had insured. The great fear of Paulson, Geithner, and Bernanke was that the interconnectedness of both institutions and markets would lead to massive losses in the financial sector as a whole, unless they could provide a comprehensive approach to resolving, or at least calming, the crisis in the financial sector. Ad hoc approaches to saving institutions that had worked at the beginning of the crisis with Bear Stearns, the GSEs, and AIG were simply not workable once Lehman Brothers failed.

A "Balkanized" Supervisory System That Lagged Market and Product Developments

The weak and fragmented supervisory system in the United States allowed firms to operate at significant leverage ratios, undercapitalized, and assuming concentrated risks. In his memoir, Alan Greenspan, chairman of the Federal Reserve from 1987 to 2006 and an ardent supporter of free markets, wrote that he had favored the repeal of Glass-Steagall and admitted that one of his concerns was excessive regulation. He believed that regulators could not keep pace with financial product innovation. "Fortunately, Gramm-Leach-Bliley, which restored financial flexibility to the financial industries, is no aberration. Awareness of the detrimental effects of excessive regulation and the need for adaptability has advanced substantially in recent years. We dare not go back."[38] Greenspan's reputation as one of the most astute Fed chairs was largely in tatters as a result of his support for deregulation under Glass-Steagall and, more important, the failure of the Fed under his watch to contain the housing bubble and to adequately supervise the large complex commercial bank groups, which became too big to fail, overextended, and overleveraged on his watch.[39]

The Fed was the regulator for the largest federally chartered bank holding companies. The Federal Deposit Insurance Corporation (FDIC), the Office of the Comptroller of the Currency, and state regulators were each responsible for different groups of banks. The Office of Thrift Supervision supervised the "thrifts," which were largely financial institutions focused on mortgage markets; and the Commodity Futures Trading Commission supervised commodities trading and had oversight over the institutions that actively traded commodities. The fragmentation in the regulatory and supervisory system over the banking system led to regulatory arbitrage. In addition, there were large gaps in the regulatory and supervisory system for nonbank financial institutions: the shadow banking system such as the investment banks and hedge funds GE Capital and General Motors Acceptance Corporation, which were supervised by the Securities and Exchange Commission as public corporations but not as important financial institutions. Finally, the GSEs were supervised by yet another regulator, the Federal Housing Finance Agency (FHFA).

On March 31, 2008, Paulson introduced a detailed strategy for reorganizing the regulatory structure, the Blueprint for a Modernized Financial Regulatory System: "The regulatory structure organized around traditional business lines had not begun to keep up with the evolution of the markets. As a result, the country had a patchwork system of state and federal supervisors dating back 75 years. This might have been fine for the world of the Great Depression, but it led to counterproductive competition among regulators, wasteful duplication in some areas, and gaping holes in others."[40] However, it was clear to all of the major players, above all Paulson, that this reorganization could not happen while the crisis was in progress.[41] Geithner notes that "a big part of the problem was America's balkanized regulatory system. It was riddled with gaps and turf battles. It was full of real and perceived sources of capture. And nobody was responsible for the stability of the entire system."[42]

With the exception of the FDIC, the regulators had no capacity to provide direct capital injection or to provide guarantees to banking institutions. The FDIC could also intervene and wind up banks under its supervision but could not do so for the largest, too-big-to-fail, commercial banks under the Fed's supervision. The investment banks were under SEC supervision, and neither the Fed nor the FDIC could assist them. The Fed simply lacked the tools to address the crisis: it lacked the authority to intervene and wind up the largest financial institutions or to provide financial guarantees to nonbank financial institutions, even if they were systemically critical, such as the large investment banks or AIG.

By exception, the Fed did have the authority under section 13(3) of the Federal Reserve Act to intervene in bank or nonbank financial institutions, but that power had not been exercised since the Great Depression and was limited to use in only the most extreme cases. The institution had to be viewed as systemically important, be deemed solvent, and have collateral to support the Fed loans.[43] Given the limits of these emergency powers, eventually Paulson, Bernanke, Geithner, and Sheila Bair (chair of the FDIC) had to petition President Bush, his advisers, and Congress for policy approval, funding, and broad, flexible authority to address the cascading failure of both institutions and markets during the crisis. The delays in getting congressional approval and the ideological resistance to interventions in markets and bailouts, particularly among Republican members of the president's own party, exacerbated the crisis and brought the financial system to the brink. The commission investigating the causes of the crisis concluded:

> The Securities and Exchange Commission failed to adequately enforce its disclosure requirements governing mortgage securities, exempted some sales of them, and preempted states from applying state laws to them, thereby failing

in its core mission to protect investors. The Federal Reserve failed to recognize the cataclysmic danger posed by the housing bubble to the financial system and refused to take timely action to constrain its growth, believing that it could contain the damage from the bubble's collapse.[44]

An additional conclusion noted that "the Securities and Exchange Commission's poor oversight over the five largest investment banks failed to restrict their risky activities and did not require them to hold adequate capital and liquidity for their activities, contributing to the failure or need for government bailouts of all five of the supervised investment banks during the financial crisis.[45]

Stiglitz observed that self-regulation cannot work with respect to systemic risks and protecting the economy as a whole:

> The crisis has made it clear that self-regulation, which the financial industry promoted [and was largely successful in achieving], doesn't work. But even if a given bank was managing its own risks well, that doesn't address systemic risk. Systemic risk can exist without there being a single systemically important bank, if all of the banks behave similarly—as they did, given their herd mentality. This is an especially important point as much of the current discussion focuses on regulating large, systemically important institutions. That is necessary, but not sufficient.[46]

The Rating Agencies

Finally, the rating agencies—Fitch, Moody's, and Standard and Poor's—could have prevented the excesses of the crisis by properly rating the securitized CDOs and the underlying financial institutions that originated them. The rating agencies were retained by the financial institutions to prepare the ratings. They generated huge fees from rating CDOs. Consequently, they were in conflict vis-à-vis the institutions and their product they were rating and these same institutions as their clients who were paying them enormous fees. The rating agencies bear significant responsibility for the crisis, and it is a wonder that they still play an important role in rating countries and financial institutions, given the extent that the lead-up to the crisis appeared to have compromised their independence and integrity.[47] The commission investigating the causes of the crisis concluded that "the high ratings erroneously given CDOs by credit rating agencies encouraged investors and financial institutions to purchase them and enabled the continued securitization of nonprime mortgages. There was a clear failure of governance at Moody's, which did not ensure the quality of its ratings on tens of thousands of mortgage-backed securities and CDOs."[48]

The commission also wrote that ratings of structured finance deals overall were not stable. From 1983 through 2006, only 56 percent of triple-A rated securities retained their original ratings over a five-year period. In 2007, 20 percent of CDOs would be downgraded, but by 2008, 91 percent of CDOs had been downgraded, signaling the complete collapse of the market and the failure of the rating agencies to see the risks.[49]

Observations of Leading Participants and Analysts about the Causes of the Crisis

Nouriel Roubini is an economist and professor at New York University and a former staff member of the International Monetary Fund. He was one of the earliest analysts to cry wolf and inform the economic world that the crisis was looming and inevitable. Roubini and his coauthor Stephen Mihm reject the thesis that the crisis was primarily a subprime mortgage problem. They write:

> While the housing bubble rested in part on subprime mortgages, the problem was more pervasive and widespread. Nor were these problems of recent origin; they were rooted in deep structural changes in the economy that date back many years. In other words, the securitization of bad loans was but the beginning; long-standing changes in corporate governance and compensation schemes played a role too. Government also shoulders some of the blame, most obviously policies pursued by Alan Greenspan. In the end the significance of government intervention was dwarfed by the significance of government inaction. For years, federal regulators turned a blind eye to the rise of a new shadow banking system that made the entire financial system dangerously fragile and prone to collapse. . . . This fact underscores a cardinal principle of crisis economics: the biggest and most destructive financial disasters are not produced by something so inconsequential as subprime mortgages. . . . Nor are they merely produced by a speculative bubble. Rather, much as with earthquakes, the pressures build for many years and when the shock finally comes it can be staggering.[50]

Henry Paulson, secretary of the Treasury during the height of the crisis and with a long career on Wall Street, including as CEO of Goldman Sachs, observes:

In retrospect, the crisis that struck in August 2007 had been building for years. Structural differences in the economics of the world had led to what analysts call "imbalances" that created massive and destabilizing cross-border flows. In short, we were living beyond our means—on borrowed money and on borrowed time. The dangers for the U.S. economy had been obscured by an unprecedented housing boom, fed in part by low interest rates. The housing bubble was driven by an increase in loans to less creditworthy or subprime borrowers that lifted home ownership rates to historic levels. . . . Regulators failed to see, or stop, the worst excesses. All bubbles involve speculation, excessive borrowing and risk taking, negligence, a lack of transparency, and outright fraud, but few bubbles ever burst as spectacularly as this one would.[51]

Timothy F. Geithner spent years working in the U.S. Treasury with oversight responsibility for the emerging market crisis in the 1990s; he was president of the New York Fed at the time the crisis emerged and subsequently secretary of the Treasury during the first term of the Obama administration, following Paulson into office. He had this to say about the crisis and its causes:

The fundamental causes of this crisis were familiar and straightforward. It began with a mania—the widespread belief that devastating financial crises were a thing of the past, that future recessions would be mild, that gravity-defying home prices would never crash to earth. . . . This mania of overconfidence fueled an explosion of credit in the economy and leverage in the financial system. And much of the leverage was financed by uninsured short-term liabilities that could run at any time. This combination of a long rise in borrowing fueled by leverage in runnable form is the foundation of all financial crises, and it would have been dangerous in any system. But it was much more dangerous for us, because many of the overleveraged major firms that were borrowing short and lending long were outside our traditional banking system . . . what made our storm into a perfect storm was nonbanks behaving like banks without bank supervision or bank protections, leaving by some measures more than half the nation's financial activity vulnerable to a run. When the panic hit, and the run gained momentum, we did not have the ability to protect the economy until conditions were scary enough to provoke actions by Congress.[52]

Ben S. Bernanke, chairman of the Federal Reserve Bank throughout the crisis and an academic expert on the Great Depression,[53] notes:

For me as a student of monetary and financial history, the crisis of 2007–2009 was best understood as a descendent of the classical financial panics of the nineteenth and early twentieth centuries. Of course, the recent crisis emerged in a global financial system that had become much more complex and integrated, and our regulatory system, for the most part, had not kept up with the changes. That made the analogies to history harder to discern and effective responses more difficult to devise. . . . Based on the historical parallels, I believed then and believe now that the severity of the panic itself—as much as or more so than its immediate triggers (most prominently sub-prime mortgage lending abuses and the house price bubble)—was responsible for the enormous financial and economic costs of the crisis.[54]

Alan Blinder, a distinguished professor of economics and social affairs at Princeton University, former deputy governor of the Federal Reserve Board from 1994 to 1996, and a member of President Bill Clinton's Council of Economic Advisers, summarized the causes of the crisis as follows:

The U.S. financial system, which had grown far too complex and far too fragile for its own good—and had too little regulation for the public good—experienced a perfect storm during the years 2007–2009. Things started unraveling when the much-chronicled housing bubble burst, but the ensuing implosion of what I call the "bond bubble" was probably larger and more devastating. The stock market also collapsed under the strain. . . . Ruin spread to every part of the bloated financial sector. Few institutions were spared. . . . We came perilously close to what Federal Reserve Chairman Ben Bernanke called "a global meltdown."[55]

An objective review of the crisis and its causes is presented in the "Financial Crisis Inquiry Report" by the National Commission on the Causes of the Financial and Economic Crisis in the United States (final report, January 2011). These are the commission's conclusions about the causes of the crisis:[56]

- We conclude dramatic failure of corporate governance and risk management at many systemically important institutions were a key cause of the crisis;

- We conclude a combination of excessive borrowing, risky investments, and lack of transparency put the financial system on a collision course with the crisis;

- We conclude the government was ill prepared for the crisis and its inconsistent response added to the uncertainty and panic in financial markets;

- We conclude there was a systematic breakdown in accountability and ethics;

- We conclude that collapsing mortgage-lending standards and the mortgage securitization pipeline lit and spread the flame of contagion and crisis;

- We conclude that over-the-counter derivatives contributed significantly to this crisis;

- We conclude the failures of credit rating agencies were essential cogs in the wheel of financial destruction.

SEVENTEEN

Ad Hoc Interventions before the Lehman Brothers Collapse

During the last quarter of 2006 the U.S. housing market had begun to decline, with a drop of 4 percent in 2007 from the peak in 2006.[1] On February 7, HSBC, one of the largest international banks based in London, announced that it was setting aside reserves of $10.6 billion to cover potential bad debt losses from U.S. subprime losses. On that same day New Century Financial Corporation, the second largest subprime lender in the United States, announced that it expected to generate losses in the fourth quarter of 2006. By April 2, 2007, New Century was bankrupt. Two weeks later Washington Mutual, the biggest savings and loan bank in the United States, announced that 9.5 percent of its $217 billion portfolio was in subprime mortgages and that its profits had fallen 21 percent in the first quarter of 2007.[2]

A Signal of the Crisis—The Decline of Mortgage Markets and Failure of Key Institutions

In the summer of 2007, Bear Stearns, the fifth largest U.S. investment bank, signaled the beginning of the financial crisis when two of its hedge funds failed, costing its investors $1.6 billion.[3] The term "toxic assets," referring to subprime housing loans packaged as complex collateralized financial instruments (collateralized debt obligations, or CDOs), quickly emerged as the focus of the crisis. The subprime mortgage market began to fall apart in August 2007, resulting in global contagion, and financial institutions began to fail thereafter.[4]

The mortgage problem was not confined to the United States. In addition to HSBC's problems, on August 9, 2007, the large French bank BNP Paribas stopped redemptions in three of its investment funds. Their value had plunged 20 percent in just a couple of weeks. The funds had $2.2 billion in assets, of which some 20 percent were mortgage-backed bonds: "In retrospect, many investors regarded the suspension of the French funds as the beginning of the 2007 liquidity crisis."[5] These instruments became difficult to value, and even more so to divest, as the market for CDOs spiraled downward. The European interbank market began to tighten, and the European Central Bank (ECB) announced that it would open a window to allow the banks to draw on as much funding as they needed. Within hours of the announcement, the ECB would later reveal, some forty-nine banks had drawn €94.8 billion (US$130 billion).[6]

In the summer of 2007, Mervyn King, the governor of the Bank of England, had spoken in strong opposition to market intervention by the Federal Reserve (the Fed) and the ECB. He explained that the provision of such liquidity encourages excessive risk taking and sows the seeds of future financial crises. In other words, he worried about moral hazard. By mid-September he was singing another tune and announced the injection of 10 billion British pounds (approximately US$17.5 billion) at three-month intervals into the market. Governor King's conversion was due to the arrival of the financial crisis on Britain's High Street. On September 14 the Bank of England had to stop a depositor run in Northern Rock, one of Britain's largest mortgage banks. It was the first such bank run in Great Britain since 1866, which led to Bagehot's famous work on the role of the central bank as a lender of last resort in a crisis. Britain lacked mortgage insurance, and with the run the Bank of England felt compelled to lend to Northern Rock, subsequently to guarantee all of its depositors, and in February 2008 to assume public ownership of Northern Rock.[7]

Finally, on August 15, Countrywide Financial Corporation, the largest mortgage originator and the largest U.S. subprime originator, was in trouble.[8] During 2006, Countrywide had originated a half-trillion dollars in mortgage loans.[9] Countrywide was financing itself in the commercial paper and repurchase (repo) market and in short-term financing markets. It soon had difficulty accessing the market and was forced to draw down on $11.5 billion in backstop lines of credit it had with several banks. A week later Bank of America (B of A) purchased preferred shares in Countrywide for $2 billion and in January 2008 purchased Countrywide outright.[10] Geithner would observe: "Most of the action was in the unsupervised non-bank affiliates on the wild frontier of the mortgage markets. It was a case study in regulatory balkanization: big enough to matter but without a regulator responsible for overseeing the institution as a whole. Countrywide had helped lead the erosion in lending standards across the country, selling exotic mortgages to families with dubious credit."[11]

A Series of Ad Hoc Rescues

The rout in the housing and real estate and related subprime mortgage market was on and would quickly envelop a number of the most important financial institutions in the United States.

The Bear Stearns Bailout

Bear Stearns (Bear), the fifth largest Wall Street investment bank, was the first to go, in March 2008. Bear had been an important player on Wall Street since 1923. After the stock market crash of 1929, it had survived without having to lay off a single employee. Bear was known for taking risks. Bear purchased the deeply discounted debt of the railway companies during World War II when President Franklin Roosevelt took control of the railways. Bear made a fortune on railway bonds after the war, when the railways were restored to private ownership.[12] Bear was a significant player in the creation of CDOs; like other firms, it not only securitized and marketed these instruments to third parties but also kept a large portfolio of these collateralized mortgages in its portfolio to enhance its profits.

Following the failure of its hedge funds in 2007, Bear brought $1.6 billion in subprime assets onto its books from its High Grade Fund; these contributed to $1.9 billion in writedowns in mortgage-related assets in November 2007. Mortgage securitization was the largest profit contributor to Bear's most profitable business division, the fixed-income business, which generated some 45 percent of the company's total revenues. Bear, the smallest of the five large investment banks, remained among the three largest underwriters of private-label mortgage-backed securities from 2000 to 2007. In 2006 it underwrote $36 billion in collateralized debt obligations—more than double the amount underwritten in 2005. Bear funded much of its operations short term in the repo market, borrowing $50–70 billion from that market throughout 2007.[13] Alan Blinder notes, "One way in which Bear Stearns set its own course during the bubble was by becoming a huge player in the mortgage business, especially in the subprime mortgage business. . . . For example, even though it was much smaller than its Wall Street rivals, Bear ranked in the top three in underwriting private-label mortgage-backed securities, from 2000–2007."[14]

Bear's losses mounted in the third and fourth quarters of 2007. Other institutions understood that Bear was in trouble and stopped trading or pulled their funds out of the firm.[15] On March 13, Bear reported that it had lost 88 percent of its liquid assets, the result of creditors refusing to roll over short-term credit. Both the Treasury and the Fed were very concerned about the spillover effects of a Bear failure. Bear's activities were interconnected with virtually every other financial institution on Wall Street. It had 400 subsidiaries, 5,000 trading counterparties, and 750,000 open derivative contracts.[16]

Over a frantic weekend the collective action of Treasury Secretary Henry M. Paulson, Federal Reserve Chairman Ben Bernanke, and New York Fed President Timothy Geithner intervened heavily to prevent Bear from failing. Paulson induced J. P. Morgan to acquire Bear, initially at a price of $2 a share; this was later increased to $10 a share when Bear's board resisted. The N.Y. Fed agreed to provide a $30 billion facility to J. P. Morgan, secured by Bear's collateralized mortgage portfolio, with J. P. Morgan agreeing to take the first loss on these assets of up to $1 billion. The Bear case was not a full bailout: although the shareholders of Bear were largely wiped out, the creditors and counterparties were effectively bailed out.

Soon thereafter, in a dramatic break with precedent, the Fed opened a Primary Dealer Credit Facility to the remaining large investment banks, operating as a lender of last resort to nonbank financial institutions for the first time since the Great Depression to ensure that the investment banks had access to necessary liquidity as markets seized up. The Fed also opened the liquidity window further for commercial banks, increasing the maximum maturity from thirty to ninety days. In addition, the Fed cut the discount rate for the window by ¼ percent to 3¼ percent, just ¼ percent above the target for the Fed funds rate.[17]

The National Commission on the Causes of the Financial and Economic Crisis would conclude that "the failure of Bear Stearns and its resulting government assisted rescue was caused by exposure to risky mortgage assets, its reliance on short-term funding, and its high leverage. These were a result of weak corporate governance and risk management. Its executive and employee compensation system was based on return on equity, creating incentives to use excessive leverage and to focus on short-term gains such as annual growth goals."[18]

Even with large losses in 2007, Bear paid out 58 percent of its revenue in compensation. From 2000 through 2008, Bear's top five executives took home $325 million in direct cash compensation, primarily bonuses based on performance, and also generated some $1.1 billion in stock sales based on stock awards.[19]

Conservatorship for the GSEs—Fannie Mae and Freddie Mac

Soon after the Bear intervention, the crisis intervention troika—Paulson, Bernanke, and Geithner—and their staff working nights and weekends, developed a strategy to intervene in the GSEs—the Federal National Mortgage Association and the Federal Home Loan Mortgage Corporation, commonly known as Fannie Mae and Freddie Mac. Congress had created Fannie and Freddie to support home ownership in the United States. Both started as government agencies. Fannie was started in the Great Depression in 1938, Freddie in 1970 to bring competition in mortgage markets to Fannie. Fannie was converted to a shareholder-owned corporation by Congress in 1968 and Freddie in 1989. They were regarded as quasi-private/quasi-public institutions, and from a risk perspective they were rated just above U.S. Treasury bonds by investors. Therefore, they were able to borrow at rates lower than triple-A corporations, making it difficult for the private sector to compete in mortgage financing. Though private, Fannie and Freddie were regulated by the federal government and had lines of credit from the Treasury. Also, they were exempt from Securities and Exchange Commission (SEC) regulation and from taxes. The risks associated with Fannie and Freddie came from their ambiguous status: Congress did not explicitly recognize a guarantee to support the GSEs in the event they were in difficulty, yet investors relied on an implicit guarantee and fully expected the government to support them if they got into trouble.[20]

With the failure of major institutions that were deeply involved in the mortgage markets such as the Independent National Mortgage Corporation (Indy Mac), Fannie and Freddie remained at the heart of the mortgage market in the United States, and that market was in deep difficulty. Their share of the market rose from 46 percent to 76 percent as other sources of credit to the market dried up.[21] It was important to the market and the economy overall that they continue to finance the market with reasonably priced mortgage credit. The two GSEs held or guaranteed some $5 trillion in mortgage debt. They were funding three of every four new mortgages in the United States, clearly propping up the system.[22] These institutions had a thinner capital base than the investment banks and were leveraged even higher at forty to one; perhaps of greater significance, their portfolios were loaded with subprime mortgages and subprime securities.[23] Risky loans were overwhelming their capital. By the end of 2007, guaranteed and portfolio mortgages with FICO (credit rating) scores below 660 exceeded Fannie Mae's reported capital by seven to one; Alt-A loans and securities by more than six to one; and loans with incomplete documentation by more than ten times reported capital.[24]

An additional problem was that by their charters the GSEs could not diversify their portfolios, hence their risk. Mortgages, mortgage securities, and mortgage guarantees essentially constituted 100 percent of the assets, other than liquid assets, of Fannie and Freddie. So when the housing market turned down precipitously, they were in a death spiral, given their thin capital base.[25]

Geithner had been wary of Freddie and Fannie since his days at the Treasury watching the Clinton administration and Greenspan try to rein in these institutions: "Closely entwined with the government since birth, they were the most dangerous example of moral hazard in the financial system. Fannie and Freddie borrowed at artificially low rates, because markets assumed that the government would never let them default."[26]

The intervention strategy had to be readied in deep secrecy, since Fannie and Freddie, though government sponsored (at best an ambiguous term), had private shareholders and relied on capital markets and institutions all over the world for funding, not the government. They were not supervised by the Fed or report to the Treasury in any formal way, and they had always been highly protected politically by Congress. Over the years, Fannie and Freddie had assiduously lobbied and courted congressional representatives in both the House of Representatives and the Senate. On July 11 and 12, Paulson sought permission first from President George W. Bush to seek extraordinary powers from Congress to deal with the GSEs and then made the rounds of key congressional leaders to ask for legislation granting those powers. Paulson sought authority through 2009 to increase the Treasury's line of $2.25 billion to the GSEs, to be allowed to buy equity in the GSEs if needed, and to have the Fed serve as the consultative regulator to the GSEs. This meant that Fed examiners could examine their books. On July 13, Bernanke and the Fed's board agreed to provide temporary backup to the GSEs through the New York Fed.[27]

This was a delicate operation. If Paulson formally asked for the powers and was denied them and the process became overtly politicized and publicized, the risks were high that the markets would blow up and the GSEs would sink into a deeper crisis. A report from Lehman Brothers in the spring had suggested that the GSEs required up to $75 billion in additional capital. By July 11, when Paulson was seeking permission to deal with the GSEs, they had lost half of their market value.[28] As Paulson noted, "the stakes were enormous: more than $5 trillion in debt either guaranteed or issued by Fannie and Freddie. Every time spreads grew—that is the yields of these securities increased relative to Treasuries—investors lost billions of dollars. . . . A collapse of the GSEs would have drastic consequences for the economy and the financial system."[29]

With a generally hostile or skeptical Congress, but with significant support from the president and his advisers, negotiations over whether to grant the powers and the details of what those powers would entail continued for several days with congressional leaders. Meanwhile, the situation of the GSEs became more and more precarious. On July 23, 2008, the Housing and Economic Recovery Act (HERA) passed the House, and three days later the Senate. Paulson had been granted his authority until December 31, 2009. The legislation granted Treasury-wide discretion to provide financial support to the GSEs on terms and conditions to be set by the Treasury.[30] However, it left oversight authority with Fannie and Freddie's newly appointed regulator, the Federal Housing Finance Agency (FHFA, previously the Office of Federal Housing Enterprise Oversight, OFHEO), as Congress's way of protecting these agencies. Paulson had to reach agreement with the FHFA in order to intervene in Fannie and Freddie.[31]

With HERA in place, the Treasury and the Fed launched an immediate analysis of Fannie and Freddie—the Fed and Office of the Comptroller of the Currency (OCC) sent in examiners and Treasury hired a financial adviser, Morgan Stanley, when Morgan Stanley's CEO offered to send in a team for free. The situation was clearly urgent. On August 6, Freddie reported that it had lost $821 million and Fannie $2.3 billion in the prior quarter. When news of Fannie and Freddie's problems became public, international investors from Japan, China, and Russia began to pressure the Treasury to make sure that the government would do the right thing and not let the GSEs fail. They wanted assurances that the government would stand behind its implicit guarantee; an even larger issue was the government's guarantee of other U.S. obligations, such as U.S. Treasury bonds.[32]

Analysis of Fannie and Freddie by the Fed and OCC examiners, the Morgan Stanley team, and Black Rock, one of the largest asset managers, concluded that the GSEs were significantly undercapitalized, that the quality of their capital was suspect, and that guarantees provided by borrowers had not been carefully evaluated to reflect the decline in market conditions. In short, they projected that by November 2009 Fannie and Freddie would eat though all of their capital and the government would be forced to inject some $110 billion into the two entities.[33]

The best approach to intervening in Fannie and Freddie was discussed with external counsel. The initial view that they should be put into receivership pursuant to Chapter 11 bankruptcy was rejected as having adverse consequences as bad as the ones Treasury was trying to avoid. It was agreed that the GSEs would be put into conservatorship and left in their present legal form. It was a race against time, since other large financial institutions were also in difficulty. Paulson had hoped to act by the end of the summer, by Labor Day, but the process was delayed by the need to prepare the legal case to intervene and to devise a legal agreement that would work in these unique circumstances. The advisers and Treasury designed a "keepwell" agreement, a Preferred Stock Purchase Agreement, which allowed Treasury to maintain a positive net worth in the GSEs no matter how much they lost in the foreseeable future. The investment also addressed the problem of the nine-month expiration of Treasury's powers as long as the investment was made before December 31, 2009.[34]

Now it was necessary to prepare the groundwork for the intervention and above all get the FHFA examiners to agree with the Fed and OCC examiners and the financial advisers that there was a significant capital gap in each of the GSEs. As the official regulatory agency for the GSEs, the FHFA had to agree and come on board. Incredibly, the FHFA had recently advised the GSEs that their capital met capital adequacy standards. After a few days of persuasion, the FHFA finally agreed to the intervention with the understanding that the Treasury would invest $100 billion in each GSE—Fannie and Freddie—under the "keepwell" arrangement, and significant lines of credit would also be made available. (The amount was later raised to $200 billion each by the Obama administration as each institution continued to lose money for some time thereafter.) On Friday, September 5, an intervention led by Paulson and including Fed Chairman Bernanke and FHFA Chairman James B. Lockhart met with the management to inform them of the transaction. On Saturday, September 6, they met with the board of directors of each institution to have the boards approve the deal. On Sunday, September 7, it was announced that Fannie Mae and Freddie Mac had been placed in conservatorship. At that time new CEOs were appointed for each entity to begin at the start of business on Monday.[35]

The national commission investigating the crisis would conclude that "the business model of Fannie Mae and Freddie Mac (the GSEs), as private sector, publicly traded, profit-making companies with implicit government backing and a public mission, was fundamentally flawed."[36]

Lehman Brothers: The Spark That Ignited the Crisis

Soon after the Bear Stearns transaction was completed, Lehman Brothers, a venerable Wall Street institution, came under fire. Its stock was being hammered, and short sellers, in particular several hedge funds, were focused on Lehman as the next financial institution expected to fail. David Einhorn, managing director of Greenlight Capital, with $6 billion of assets under management, had openly questioned Lehman's valuation of its portfolio and the adequacy and timeliness of marking these assets to market in a rapidly declining market. At an investor's forum with several of the leading hedge fund managers in attendance, Einhorn ended his speech as follows: "My hope is that Mr. Cox [chairman of the SEC Christopher Cox], Mr. Bernanke, and Mr. Paulson will pay heed to the risks to the financial system that Lehman is creating and that they will guide Lehman towards a recapitalization and recognition of its losses—hopefully before federal taxpayer assistance is required."[37]

Einhorn was not the only one worried about Lehman. On March 27, 2008, soon after he had completed his efforts to save Bear, Secretary Paulson called Richard Fuld, longtime CEO of Lehman, to check in with him on the status of the markets and Lehman's own situation. Fuld and Paulson had long been rivals as CEOs, respectively, of Lehman Brothers and Goldman Sachs. Now in his position as secretary of the Treasury, Paulson was deeply concerned about the turbulence and volatility in the financial markets and Lehman's ability to withstand market pressures on the company. Paulson also wanted to be briefed on Fuld's plans to raise capital, presumably to save his firm.[38]

Fuld, reluctant to find a purchaser and give up the control he had exercised over Lehman for many years, pursued a series of opportunities to raise capital, none of which was successful, as his firm's position continued to deteriorate. Fuld had brief talks with Warren Buffett, negotiations with the Korean Development Bank, and brief discussions with Morgan Stanley and Merrill Lynch on merging.[39]

Finally, it was clear that Lehman was going to have to sell to a bank with significant assets and a deeper capital base, though Fuld still held out hope that he could sell a minority share to a bank and, in addition, receive substantial support in the form of longer-term debt than the short-term debt Lehman was drawing on from the financial markets. In the end it came down to Bank of America (B of A) and Barclays Bank. B of A's CEO, Ken Lewis, had been induced to come to the table by Paulson and the president of Barclays, Bob Diamond, who envisioned Barclays having a major presence on Wall Street through the acquisition of Lehman. Lehman also had a large presence in London that could be merged into Barclays.

Paulson and Geithner also called an emergency meeting of a selected list of the major investment banks and large commercial banks (excluding Barclays and B of A) over the weekend of September 12 to 14 to consider a private sector rescue or a possible enhancement of a deal with Barclays or B of A. Bernanke stayed in Washington, but remained plugged in to the negotiations with B of A and Barclays and the work of the investment banks, all of which were occurring simultaneously. The potential rescue by a group of banks would be a replay of the rescue of the hedge fund Long-Term Capital Management in 1998, when a group of fourteen Wall Street banks had collectively put together a $3.8 billion package for 90 percent of the equity in the hedge fund, which they then liquidated over time.[40]

The collective rescue was also similar to the Argentine default in 1890 on *cedulas* (asset-backed land titles) that threatened Baring Brothers, one of the largest merchant banks in London. Lord Rothschild and the Bank of England put together a group of merchant banks and country banks, which had both deposits and a larger capital base than the merchant banks, to save Barings. This was one of the earliest examples of a collective lender of last resort acting internationally.[41]

The Lehman case would require much more capital than Long-Term Capital Management or Bear Stearns at a time when all of the financial institutions were under stress. They also knew that if Lehman failed the pressure they were under would increase substantially and relentlessly. Lehman was even bigger than Bear (with some $600 billion in assets) and even more interconnected than Bear. On September 10, Lehman announced a $3.9 billion loss. Hedge funds and other financial institutions were withdrawing funds from Lehman or refusing to trade with Lehman. According to Paulson, "The market smelled a corpse."[42]

Paulson had come under unrelenting criticism for the rescue of Bear and the GSEs Fannie and Freddie, and he was determined that government money would not support a rescue of Lehman. Also, without a banking partner the Fed would have had to use its emergency powers again, and Paulson, Bernanke, and Geithner were reluctant to use Fed money to save Lehman without a clear understanding of how the Fed would be repaid. Bernanke explains the difficulty of rescuing Lehman:

> As Saturday [September 13] wore on, [the weekend of negotiations with B of A and Barclays and the investment bank rescue discussions], it became evident that Lehman was deeply insolvent, even allowing for the likelihood that fire sales and illiquid markets had pushed the values of its assets to artificially low levels. . . . Lehman's insolvency made it impossible to save with Fed lending alone. Even when invoking our 13(3) emergency authority, we were required to lend against adequate collateral. The Fed had no authority to inject capital or . . . make a loan that we were not reasonably sure could be fully repaid.[43]

Both B of A and Barclays found significant holes in Lehman's capital due to the overvaluation of Lehman's portfolio assets, especially its collateralized mortgages. B of A sought federal government or Federal Reserve Bank support to do a deal with Lehman. Its bad assets, initially estimated at $40 billion and soon thereafter estimated at $65–70 billion, would likely wipe out Lehman's equity of $28.4 billion.[44] Barclays found similar bad assets that it estimated at some $52 billion. It was clear that with teams doing due diligence, under great pressure, the banks could at best estimate the potential portfolio losses, and as experienced bankers they would err on the conservative side of the ledger.

B of A proposed a complex deal in which the government would bear most of the risk. When it became obvious that that would not work, B of A used the weekend in New York to meet and agree in principle to a deal to acquire Merrill Lynch, its preferred target all along and clearly under great stress due to Lehman's problems. On Sunday, September 14, B of A agreed to purchase Merrill Lynch at $29 a share for $50 billion, one bit of good news in an otherwise highly distressed situation; but this left only one player bidding for Lehman—not a good situation.[45]

Barclays was potentially prepared to do a deal for Lehman, which had a significant presence and assets in London in addition to those in the United States, but the U.K. banking regulator, Callum McCarthy, informed Geithner that he would not approve the deal, a decision supported by Alistair Darling, chancellor of the Exchequer (the U.K. finance minister), during a call with Paulson. Also, under U.K. securities law an acquisition such as the Lehman transaction required shareholder approval, which would have taken up to ninety days to complete. Meanwhile, Barclays presumably would have needed to finance or guarantee Lehman's trades, a risk it was not prepared to assume. Without the B of A and Barclays deal, there was no way to implement the collective bank rescue being discussed. Lehman was simply going to be allowed to fail. Lehman filed for bankruptcy at 1:45 a.m. on Monday, September 15, 2008.[46]

In his memoir Bernanke is clear that he, his colleagues at the Fed, and Paulson and his staff at Treasury considered Lehman's failure a major problem both in the United States and internationally: "We had little doubt a Lehman failure would massively disrupt financial markets, and impose heavy costs on many parties other than Lehman's shareholders, managers and creditors, including millions of people around the world who would be hurt by the economic shock waves."[47]

Virtually every analyst of the crisis agrees that the failure of Lehman Brothers was the event that sparked the global financial crisis that we now know as the Great Recession. Alan Blinder perhaps puts it best: "There is close to universal agreement that the demise of Lehman Brothers was the watershed event of the entire financial crisis and that the decision to allow it to fail was the watershed decision. Virtually every discussion of the financial crisis divides history into two epochs: 'before Lehman' and 'after Lehman.' . . . the whole economy seemed to fall off the table immediately after September 15."[48]

Markets Begin to Collapse, AIG Is Rescued, and Other Interventions

In a reaction to the Lehman failure, markets began to collapse and were in, according to Bernanke, "the grip of a full-blown panic of an intensity not seen since the Depression."[49] The Dow Jones lost over 500 points on Monday, the day Lehman filed for bankruptcy, the biggest one-day loss since the tragedy of September 11, 2001. The selloff spread to markets worldwide.[50]

The AIG Rescue

AIG was the world's largest insurance company by the mid-1990s. Founded in 1919 by C. V. Starr, who initially sold insurance in Shanghai, it had a legendary history. The company fled China in 1949 when the Communist Revolution led by Mao Tse-tung took control of the country. AIG's headquarters were in New York, but its Asian and international roots remained deep. As one of the few triple-A-rated companies in the United States, it was allowed to borrow at highly competitive rates and to borrow a great deal. The triple-A rating made AIG an accredited seller of credit default swaps (CDS). The swaps were classified as derivatives rather than the insurance products that they really were. Derivatives were left unregulated by the Commodity Futures Modernization Act. And AIG's insurance regulator did not require AIG to reserve against the CDS as it did for routine insurance products. By the time AIG stopped selling CDS in 2006, the market was at a point of collapse.[51]

Paulson, Geithner, and Bernanke knew that AIG was in deep trouble, but needed to focus on resolving Lehman's problems first. On the Monday of Lehman's bankruptcy filing, the credit rating agencies downgraded AIG, forcing it to post more collateral to support its huge derivatives portfolio. AIG's management estimated that they would need $85 billion to resolve their problems.[52] Paulson and Bernanke found themselves having to go back to Washington to brief the president and subsequently Congress to explain the urgency of the AIG rescue. The politics were terrible. It was an election year, and the president's own Republican Party opposed bailouts in its convention platform. With more than $1 trillion in assets, AIG was 50 percent larger than Lehman; and as the world's largest insurance company it operated in 130 countries and had over 74 million customers. AIG provided commercial insurance to 180,000 small businesses and other corporations. AIG's insurance products covered pension funds, municipalities, and 401(k) retirement plans for millions of people.

Most directly relevant to the crisis, a small financial subsidiary of AIG's had utilized exotic derivative instruments, credit default swaps, to insure collateralized subprime mortgages for virtually all of the financial institutions in the collateralized subprime debt market. AIG's insurance cover was the basis for the high ratings provided by the rating agencies so that these instruments could be sold to institutions throughout the world as essentially risk free. The decline in the value of the mortgages required AIG to increase its collateral in support of its insurance products, and the company was simply being rapidly drained of its liquidity. If the Fed did not act swiftly AIG would fail and bring down many connected institutions. The Fed believed that it could lend to AIG if the company's many subsidiary insurance companies retained sufficient value to serve as collateral for the loan.[53] Unlike Lehman when it was close to collapse, AIG had a very valuable, profitable, and even liquid insurance operation that had significant collateral value. Much of that collateral backed its insurance policies throughout the world and was carefully supervised in the United States by a state-level supervisor, as well as by other supervisors throughout the world. It was not available to AIG's financial subsidiary to provide collateral against subprime mortgage contracts.[54] As Paulson observed, "If any company defined systemic risk, it was AIG, with its $1 trillion balance sheet and massive derivatives business connecting to hundreds of financial institutions, governments, and companies throughout the world."[55]

On Tuesday, September 16, the Fed announced that it was providing a two-year $85 billion loan to AIG that would be collateralized by AIG's assets, including stock in its regulated subsidiaries. The Fed would take a 79.9 percent equity interest in AIG with the right to veto dividend payments.[56] Bernanke would note with respect to the risks: "Without doubt the risks we would be taking would be huge. Though $85 billion was an enormous sum, much more was at stake than money. If AIG failed even with the loan, the financial panic would intensify and market confidence in the Fed's ability to control the crisis could be destroyed. Moreover, the future of the Fed could be at risk."[57] AIG continued to bleed cash during the months ahead, and the Fed was forced to inject $40 billion in additional capital for a total of $112.8 billion and restructure this capital into two special-purpose vehicles called Maiden Lane.[58] AIG continued to bleed, and eventually the Fed committed some $182 billion to its rescue.[59] The commission investigating the causes of the crisis concluded:

> AIG failed and was rescued by the government primarily because its enormous sales of credit default swaps were made without putting up initial collateral, setting aside capital reserves, or hedging its exposure—a profound failure in corporate governance, particularly risk management practices. AIG's failure was possible because of the sweeping deregulation of over-the-counter (OTC) derivatives, including credit default swaps, which effectively eliminated state and federal regulation of these products, including capital

and margin requirements that would have lessened the likelihood of AIG's failure. . . . AIG engaged in regulatory arbitrage by setting up a major business in this unregulated product, locating much of the business in London, and selecting a weak federal regulator, the Office of Thrift Supervision (OTS). . . . AIG was so interconnected with so many large commercial banks, investment banks, and other financial institutions through counterparty credit relationships on credit default swaps and other activities such as securities lending that its potential failure created systemic risk. The government concluded that AIG was too big to fail and committed more than $180 billion to its rescue. Without the bailout AIG's default and collapse would have brought down its counterparties, causing cascading losses and collapses throughout the financial system.[60] (See table 17-1 on payments to AIG counterparties.)

Washington Mutual (WaMu), the Country's Largest Thrift

Another major player in mortgage markets, Washington Mutual, was yet another domino to fall. Soon after the Lehman failure, depositors pulled $17 billion out of WaMu in just ten days, its stock fell 90 percent, and WaMu had reported and accumulated losses since the beginning of the crisis in 2007. The FDIC intervened in the bank, which had some $300 billion in assets, over 2,000 branch offices, and banking operations in fifteen states.[61] WaMu was just smaller than Bear Stearns but was the largest FDIC-insured bank ever to fail. Sheila Bair, president of the FDIC, quickly agreed to sell WaMu to J. P. Morgan Chase, which would assume its insured and uninsured deposits but gain its extensive branch network in Florida and on the West Coast. J. P. Morgan was not required by the FDIC to stand behind WaMu's other obligations, so not only were shareholders wiped out, but so were subordinated debt holders and senior creditors. In Geithner's view, the FDIC should have used its systemic risk exception to protect the creditors in the middle of the crisis. Wiping out the creditors significantly raised the perceived risk of investing in and lending to U.S. banks.[62] Blinder agrees: "Bair's decision was intended to teach a moral hazard lesson and thereby to restore some semblance of 'market discipline.' She had not been happy with either the rescue of Bear Stearns or the decision to make all of AIG's creditors whole. . . . The decision to impose losses on WaMu's creditors was immediately controversial—and immediately disastrous."[63]

TABLE 17-1. U.S. Crisis: Payments to AIG Counterparties

Billions of US$

Payments to AIG securities lending counterparties		Payments to AIG credit default swap counterparties	Maiden Lane III	Collateral payments by AIG
September–December 2008		As of November 17, 2008		
Barclays	7.0			
Deutsche Bank	6.4	Société Générale	6.9	9.6
BNP Paribas	4.9	Goldman Sachs	5.6	8.4
Goldman Sachs	4.8	Merrill Lynch	3.1	3.1
Bank of America	4.5	Deutsche Bank	2.8	5.7
HSBC	3.3	UBS	2.5	1.3
Citigroup	2.3	Calyon	1.2	3.1
Dresdner Kleinwort	2.2	Deutsche Zentral-Genossenschaftsbank (DZG)	1.0	0.8
Merrill Lynch	1.9	Bank of Montreal	0.9	0.5
UBS	1.7	Wachovia	0.8	0.2
ING	1.5	Barclays	0.6	0.9
Morgan Stanley	1	Bank of America	0.5	0.3
Société Générale	0.9	Royal Bank of Scotland	0.5	0.6
AIG International	0.6	Dresdner Bank AG	0.4	0.0
Credit Suisse	0.4	Rabobank	0.3	0.3
Paloma Securities	0.2	Landesbank Baden Wuerttemberg	0.1	0.0
Citadel	0.2	HSBC USA	0.0	0.2
Total	43.7		27.1	35.0

Source: "The Financial Crisis Inquiry Report," Final Report of the National Commission on the Causes of the Financial and Economic Crisis in the United States (Washington: 2011), p. 377.

Note: Of these amounts, $19.5 billion came from Maiden Lane II, $17.2 billion from the Federal Reserve Bank of New York, and $7.0 billion from AIG. Amounts may not total because of rounding.

Wachovia Bank

Wachovia was twice as big as WaMu, with a funding base of 27 million depositors and $800 billion in assets. It had lost substantial funds through the activities of its mortgage financing subsidiary Golden West Financial, the large California thrift, which it had acquired in 2006 as the mortgage markets were turning down.[64]

Wachovia, the nation's fourth largest commercial bank, experienced a silent run as depositors and creditors began to withdraw funds. On Friday, September 26, the bank lost $5.7 billion of deposits and $1.1 billion in commercial paper and repos. In one day its ten-year bonds fell from 73 cents to 29 cents on the dollar. Wachovia's stock fell 27 percent, wiping out $8 billion in market value in one day. Worried long-term creditors sought repayment of half of its $50–60 billion in long-term debt. As a consequence, Treasury officials, the Fed, and the FDIC were not prepared to allow Wachovia to reopen on Monday, September 29, without a buyer.[65]

Wachovia had two bidders—Citigroup, which was not in great shape itself, and Wells Fargo Bank, not as big as Citigroup but also without Citi's major risks. Neither bank would bid without FDIC support. With Bair highly resistant to any form of bailout, Ben Bernanke and Don Cohn of the Fed had to convince Bair and the FDIC to use its systemic risk exception for the first time in the crisis, recognizing that the "haircuts" imposed on creditors by the WaMu sale had increased stress in the financial system as a whole. The FDIC initially accepted a Citigroup offer over the Wachovia bid, both of which required substantial FDIC support. In a sudden reversal after the government had committed in principle to Citi, Wells Fargo offered $7 a share for Wachovia with no FDIC support, seven times the value of Citigroup's offer. Bair accepted the Wells Fargo offer and another bailout was avoided, despite Geithner's strong objections to the FDIC reversing itself after the Citi deal had been announced.[66]

After the failure of Lehman Brothers and a series of ad hoc interventions, it was clear to Bernanke (who convinced Paulson) that the Treasury, the Fed, and the FDIC could no longer continue to address crisis resolution on a case-by-case ad hoc basis. Chapter 18 discusses a more systemic approach to crisis resolution post-Lehman.

EIGHTEEN

A Systemic Approach to Crisis Resolution after the Lehman Brothers Collapse

Once it had become clear to Federal Reserve Chairman Ben Bernanke and Treasury Secretary Henry Paulson that the ad hoc approach to crisis resolution needed to be supplanted by a more systemic approach, they needed to convince the Bush administration and a reluctant Congress, both conservative Republicans and liberal Democrats.

Support for the Capital Markets

After the failure of Lehman Brothers and the rescue of AIG, Paulson, Bernanke, and Timothy Geithner recognized that the Treasury and the Federal Reserve (the Fed) needed to move swiftly to provide more comprehensive support for important financial institutions besieged by the crisis. Even those economists and analysts favorably disposed to the Fed criticized Bernanke for the inconsistent treatment of Lehman and AIG. If AIG could be bailed out, why not Lehman? The rationale for propping up an insolvent and illiquid Lehman versus a solvent but illiquid AIG was simply lost on most critics.[1]

The interconnectedness of institutions and markets soon manifested itself. The Reserve Primary Fund, one of the oldest money market funds, had invested heavily in

Lehman in order to boost returns. By September 2008 it had $785 million invested in Lehman, or 1.2 percent of the fund's assets. Within days of Lehman's announced bankruptcy, the Reserve Primary Fund was overwhelmed with redemption requests, amounting to about half of the fund's account balances. On September 16 the fund's management announced that Lehman's paper was without value and was forced to "break the buck." This meant that it would return 97 cents for each dollar placed in the fund, a 3 percent loss. This was previously unheard of; money market managers in corporations and other institutions regarded money market funds as equivalent to bank accounts, with better yields but no deposit insurance. Yields came from investing beyond short-term Treasury bills to the GSEs and other commercial paper regarded as safe. By September 2008 money market funds had $3.4 trillion in balances. Breaking the buck was viewed as one of the signal events of the crisis; in just a week $350 billion fled from money market funds and tried to crowd in to U.S. Treasury bills. In addition, fund managers had to liquidate their holdings of commercial paper, in effect bringing that market to a screeching halt.[2]

Paulson, a highly experienced investment banker, immediately recognized the systemic threat to the market and decided to use the Treasury's Exchange Stabilization Fund (ESF) to guarantee the money market funds. Again he needed to go to President George W. Bush for approval. He decided to use $50 billion from the ESF to set up an insurance fund to guarantee the safety of funds deposited in the money market funds. The ESF had rarely been used over the years. A major and controversial intervention occurred during the Mexican crisis of 1994, when the United States extended $20 billion to Mexico from the ESF.[3] The fund managers had to pay a fee to use the insurance cover.

Very quickly Sheila Bair, head of the Federal Deposit Insurance Corporation (FDIC), recognized that a blanket guarantee would threaten the banking system since the FDIC covered only $100,000 (later changed to $250,000) per account, and all of the incentives would be in favor of money managers moving their balances to the money market funds. Paulson and his team quickly amended the program to protect balances in money market funds until September 19, but not deposits thereafter. The Fed also supported this effort by establishing the Asset-Backed Money Market Mutual Fund Liquidity Facility (AMLF) to extend nonrecourse loans at low interest to banks willing to purchase high-quality, asset-backed commercial paper. The Fed announced the facility three days after the Reserve Primary Fund broke the buck and made it operational just three days later.[4] The Treasury and the Fed acted with amazing speed and agility given the nature of the two institutions, and in doing so protected the two most important U.S. money markets from a meltdown.

Stanley Fischer, former deputy managing director of the International Monetary Fund, former governor of the Bank of Israel, and thereafter deputy governor of the Fed, notes, "There is the approach that the Fed unsuccessfully tried to name 'credit easing' actions directed at reviving particular markets whose difficulties were creating serious problems in the financial system. For instance, when the commercial paper market in the United States was collapsing, the Fed entered on a major scale as a purchaser, and succeeded in reviving the market. Similarly it played a significant role in keeping the mortgage market alive. In this regard the Fed became the *market-maker of last resort*."[5]

Interestingly, the three financial firms that drew the most from the AMLF were foreign financial institutions with operations in the United States: UBS (a Swiss bank) borrowed $72 billion over time; Dexia (a French-Belgian financial conglomerate) $53 billion; and Barclays (a British bank) $38 billion. Nonbank financial firm borrowers included GE Capital ($16 billion), Prudential Funding ($2.4 billion), and Toyota Credit Corporation ($3.6 billion). Finally, a number of nonfinancial corporations also drew on the facility—Verizon, Harley-Davidson, McDonald's, and Georgia Transmission—generally in smaller amounts than the financial institutions.[6]

In addition to its support for the commercial paper market, recognizing the threat to global markets after the Lehman debacle and the rescue of AIG, Bernanke conferred with his counterparts in central banks throughout the world. They were all in agreement that the U.S. Fed could not risk allowing another major financial institution such as AIG to fail. The Fed announced a substantial increase of $180 billion in its swap lines to other central banks around the world for lending to their commercial banks.[7]

From Ad Hoc Intervention to a Systemic Approach

Following the back-to-back-to-back resolution of AIG, WaMu, and Wachovia Bank, and the support for the money market and commercial paper market, the troika of Paulson, Bernanke, and Geithner sought support from the president and Congress for funding to support a more systemic intervention in order to resolve, or at worst mitigate, the crisis's impact on the economy. Bernanke had pressed Paulson to seek congressional support: "I was growing weary of putting out fires one by one. We needed a more comprehensive solution to the crisis and that meant asking Congress for taxpayer dollars. . . . The Fed couldn't do it alone. . . . To secure the necessary authority, fiscal firepower, and the democratic legitimacy needed to stop the crisis and avoid unthinkable outcomes, we had to go to Congress."[8]

Paulson realized that this would not be easy. The president and many Republicans in Congress were strongly against bailouts and continuous government intervention in the crisis. Many felt that the market should run its course. Market failure was not a concept they readily recognized. The Democrats, on the other hand, sought support for Main Street with much more emphasis on stemming job losses and repossession of homes. They were against supporting the big banks and investment banks, which they viewed as the cause of the crisis. The Democrats sought a large Keynesian stimulus package and an active role in regulating the banks, other financial institutions, and markets so that in the future institutions that were "too big to fail" and unfettered markets would not be able to do such damage to the economy and the American public. Moreover, the country was in an election year, and Paulson was concerned that the candidates would politicize the crisis, the bailouts, and any proposed large-scale intervention to prop up the banks. Paulson devoted time to briefing both Senator John McCain and Senator Barack Obama, the two presidential candidates.[9] As Paulson noted:

> We had been dealing with these crises one at a time, on an ad hoc basis. But we now needed to take a more systematic approach before we bled to death. We all knew that the root cause lay in the housing market collapse that had clogged bank balance sheets with toxic mortgage assets that made them unwilling to lend. We were going to need to buy those bad assets where necessary, actions that required new powers from Congress and a massive appropriation of funds. In asking for this we would be bailing out Wall Street. And that would look just plain bad to everyone from free-market devotees to populist demagogues. But not doing this would be disastrous for Main Street and ordinary citizens.[10]

Paulson and Bernanke briefed the president, who promised that he and his team would put their weight behind their effort to secure support from Congress. Paulson and Bernanke then briefed the congressional leadership in both the House of Representatives and the Senate. Bernanke warned of the severity of the crisis and its potential impact both in the United States and globally. He stressed the urgency of the situation: "There is a matter of days before there is a meltdown in the global financial system." Paulson's pitch was based on buying toxic assets from the banks; as had been done in Mexico and East Asia, a distressed asset management company or companies would need to be established. This would require a very large and somewhat unknown pool of capital since the banks were loaded with toxic assets but no one knew quite how much.

Bernanke was in favor of injecting capital into the banks, rather than making bad asset purchases: "With more and more assets coming under suspicion, spending every penny of the $700 billion of new capital in TARP money on toxic assets might not be enough to stabilize the system. Providing $700 billion of new capital, on the other hand, would increase the capital of the banking system by half or more, reassuring creditors and customers and bolstering banks' confidence to lend."[11] During the process of negotiating the Troubled Asset Relief Program (TARP) with Congress, Paulson came around to Bernanke's viewpoint, but held out hope for a subsequent asset purchase program.[12]

Several members of Congress pushed for compensation restrictions; others wanted the government to receive warrants for funding the banks; and yet others wanted to impose a financial transaction tax—all of which would have made the recapitalization more complex. Paulson resisted these ideas in order to get as many financial institutions as possible to accept the program as quickly as possible, but eventually needed to relent and give way to congressional pressures, on some of these issues, to get his proposed program through.[13]

After a series of congressional hearings, most of which were highly contentious, Paulson settled on and proposed to Congress the Troubled Assets Relief Program of $700 billion to, in principle, buy nonperforming (toxic) assets from the banks but giving the Treasury full flexibility to do what it needed to do to stem the crisis. It soon became clear to Paulson, Bernanke, and Geithner that setting up an asset management fund or a series of funds, getting the banks committed to the process (which meant they would need to recognize large losses from the sale of these assets at a discount, in the event the assets were not already marked down), valuing the assets, and purchasing the assets would be a lengthy process even under the best of conditions.[14] They then turned to Plan B, to convert the investment banks to bank holding companies and invest a large chunk of capital into the major banks and investment banks. They also realized that they needed to provide loan guarantees in order to encourage the banks to make loans to these and other institutions. Capital injections were by themselves insufficient. Capital injection could prevent a solvency problem, but loans were needed to stem the liquidity crisis.[15]

Perhaps the best or most relevant U.S. example was the asset management agency established during the savings and loan (S&L) crisis in the early 1980s. However, during the crisis, as savings and loan banks were intervened in, their bad assets automatically moved into the asset management fund. Valuation was not an issue. But it was a substantial issue for the TARP as banks would be reluctant to sell assets at a deep discount, requiring that they increase reserves for their remaining portfolio and also incur deeper losses. The better analogy is the various emerging market crises in the 1990s and early 2000s (as discussed in Part III of this book). In several of these crises—Mexico, East Asia, and Turkey—asset management companies were established to take bad assets from the books of banks that had been intervened in (and sometimes banks that had not been intervened in). Most of these vehicles took time to organize, were very costly to administer, and generated large losses for their governments. KAMCO in Korea is the best example of an asset management company that worked well by complementing other intervention measures.[16]

The Major Investment Banks

After the failure of Lehman, the rescue of AIG, and the purchase of Wachovia by Wells Fargo, Goldman Sachs and Morgan Stanley were the next to draw the attention of market analysts and short sellers. Both had much stronger balance sheets than Lehman, but both depended on raising capital in the market on a short-term basis, while lending on a longer-term basis. They were also highly leveraged. When subjected to the stress of the crisis, this model had largely fallen apart. Both of these historically important investment banks now aggressively sought to find major investors. They also made the critical decision to become bank holding companies, which in effect would end the tradition on Wall Street of independent, nonregulated investment banks. On Sunday, September 21, at 9:30 p.m., the Federal Reserve announced that it had approved Goldman Sachs and Morgan Stanley's applications to become bank holding companies. In addition, both investment banks found large investors to boost their capital: Goldman found the most respected investor in the United States, Warren Buffett, who committed to invest $5 billion in 10 percent preferred shares. Mitsubishi UFJ announced its intentions of purchasing shares in Morgan Stanley. After support for the deal was conveyed from the U.S. Treasury through the Japanese Ministry of Finance for the deal, Mitsubishi invested $9 billion in Morgan Stanley on October 13, 2008, in convertible preferred and preferred shares, giving it 21.5 percent of the voting rights in the company.[17]

The TARP Transactions

On Saturday, September 27, Paulson and his team hammered out a deal in principle on TARP with representatives from the House and Senate. They incorporated the following principles: (i) $700 billion in funding, but in tranches; (ii) compensation restrictions on financial institutions receiving TARP funds, limiting tax deductions to

$500,000 in salary; also not allowing "golden parachutes" (large retirement or redundancy payments) to senior executives of institutions that drew on TARP; (iii) various levels of congressional oversight, but allowing Treasury to manage the program flexibly; (iv) a provision for the government to receive warrants that would convert to equity in the companies drawing on TARP; (v) a vague concept of recovering costs through some form of transaction tax.

On Monday, September 29, the House voted TARP down, 228 to 205; two-thirds of Republicans and 40 percent of Democrats had voted against the bill. When the news hit the markets, the Dow Jones suffered its worst single-day loss: 778 points, or 7 percent of its value. Some $1 trillion in stock market value was wiped out, hitting both the wealthy and millions of average citizens' retirement savings.[18]

To get TARP approval the administration needed to align it with some deal enhancements such as mark-to-market accounting regulations, the minimum alternative tax, and other measures. In turn the administration pushed for and received the authority to increase deposit insurance to $250,000 per account from the earlier limit of $100,000. Reacting to growing market distress in the United States and globally, and to calls from their constituents who had been hit hard by the market, on Wednesday, October 1, the Senate approved the "tweaked TARP" with a vote of 74 to 25, and on Friday, October 3, the House passed the Emergency Economic Stabilization Act of 2008, 263 votes to 171. More Republicans and more Democrats had come on board.[19] Discussing the politics of the situation right before the presidential election, Geithner remarked, "A month before a high-stakes election, a Democratic-controlled Congress helped a Republican President with a 27 percent approval rating pass a wildly unpopular but desperately needed bill."[20]

In the week of October 6, after TARP was announced, markets deteriorated further. The U.S. stock markets experienced their worst week since the 1933 Depression. The "fear" or volatility index, the VOX Index, hit an all-time high, and the spread for interbank loans also reached a new high. The week previously, General Electric—perhaps the premier U.S. industrial company but with a large financial group representing a substantial part of its profits—had to raise $3 billion in capital from Warren Buffett before lenders would roll over its commercial paper. Interest rates on corporate bonds and the costs of insuring against corporate default increased substantially—a clear signal that market analysts and traders were expecting corporate failures.[21]

The Treasury would need to move quickly on TARP, but that alone would be insufficient. Paulson, Bernanke, and Geithner also sought a way to guarantee loans, much as Ireland and the U.K. had already, and to restore liquidity to the commercial paper market. The Treasury's plan to inject capital into financial institutions was essentially ready by October 11, a week after approval by Congress. The Capital Purchase Program (CPP), with a first tranche of $250 billion, was designed to inject equity into the banks—both profitable and loss-making banks. The Fed, assisted by the OCC, developed the criteria for selecting the first, second, and third tier of banks. The first tier represented systemically important banks representing 50 percent of U.S. deposits. The Treasury abstained from any involvement. The program was voluntary, but it soon became clear that the Treasury, the Fed, and the New York Fed, with oversight over the largest institutions, would apply suasion to the largest institutions to secure their participation. The plan was to inject up to 3 percent of the banks' risk-weighted assets, with a limit of $25 billion for the biggest banks. To generate income from the investment and give the banks an incentive to raise their own capital in time, the initial dividend was set at 5 percent; it would rise to 9 percent in year three. The program was designed for the banks to apply through their own regulators, who in turn would pass on a reviewed and approved application to the Fed. This approach was fine for the second- and third-tier banks, but in order to ensure real impact for the TARP in stabilizing markets, Paulson had the CEOs of the largest banks visit the Treasury together, much as had been done for a potential collective rescue of Lehman at the Fed's offices. These included the four largest commercial banks—J. P. Morgan, Wells Fargo, Citigroup, and Bank of America; the three former investment banks—Goldman Sachs, Morgan Stanley, and Merrill Lynch; and also State Street Corporation and New York Mellon, two major clearing and settlement banks vital to the markets' infrastructure. Paulson sought maximum market impact and wanted to quickly announce that the banks had agreed to accept $125 billion of capital, or one-half of the Capital Purchase Program.[22]

At a meeting at the Treasury on October 13, Paulson explained the reason for the capital injection and sought the support from the CEOs so that news of the capital injection could be announced the next day. Bernanke explained the importance of this operation to stabilize markets and to prevent a deeper recession. Geithner announced the amounts allocated to each institution: $25 billion to Citigroup, Wells Fargo, and J. P. Morgan; $15 billion to Bank of America; $10 billion to Merrill Lynch, Goldman Sachs, and Morgan Stanley; $3 billion to Bank of New York Mellon; and $2 billion to State Street Corporation. After extended discussion, some limited negotiation, and some suasion by Paulson, all of the CEOs committed to accept the capital. The terms of the deal placed limits on dividends to common shareholders for three years, established that warrants up to the value of 15 percent of the preferred stock invested would be part of the transaction, and that executive pay would be affected with respect to tax deductibility of salaries at and above $500,000 and golden parachutes for departing senior executives would not be acceptable for institutions

TABLE 18-1.   United States: Troubled Asset Debt Relief Program

Billions of US$

Programs	Originally committed	Actual cost
Financial system bailout	450	−5[a]
Capital purchase plan	250	−16
Systemically important institutions	115	15
Federal Reserve (TALF)[b]	55	−1
Public-Private Investment Program (PPIP)[c]	30	−3
Auto bailout	84	17
General Motors	64	14
Chrysler	15	3
Auto suppliers	5	0
Small business aid	15	0
SBA loan purchase	15	0
Community Development Capital Initiative	N/A	0
Housing bailout	52	28
Homeowner Affordability and Stability Pact	52	28
FHA Short Refinance Program	N/A	0
Total	600	40

Source: Alan S. Blinder and Mark Zandi, "The Financial Crisis: Lessons for the Next One" (Washington: Center on Budget and Policy Priorities, October 15, 2015).

a. A negative number means that the Treasury made a profit on the program after disposition of shares or assets held.
b. Term Asset-Backed Securities Loan Facility.
c. Public-Private Investment Program.

taking TARP money.[23] By the end of the program Treasury had invested $205 billion in 707 financial institutions.[24]

In addition, after some effort by Paulson, Bernanke, and Geithner to persuade Sheila Bair to use FDIC's guarantee authority, she agreed, and a loan guarantee program, the Temporary Liquidity Guarantee Program (TLGP), became an integral part of the capital program in support of the banks. Sheila Bair explained to the CEOs that this program was tied to their taking TARP capital, and she then presented terms—pricing and eligible instruments. The FDIC would guarantee new unsecured senior debt made on or before January 30, 2009, when the program would then expire.[25] This program was used broadly, particularly by the nonbank financial institutions—among the large banks, Goldman Sachs took $26 billion, Morgan Stanley $16 billion, and GE Capital $35 billion. Citigroup drew $32 billion and J. P. Morgan Chase $21 billion at the end of 2008. All of these institutions substantially increased their level of debt guaranteed by the FDIC as of the end of 2009 (see table 18-1).[26]

Too Big to Fail—Citigroup and Bank of America

Despite the capital injections into the largest financial institutions, during the period following the presidential election on November 2, 2008, until the new administration took office on January 20, 2009, markets remained volatile. Citigroup, which had raised substantial capital on its own and also received an injection of $25 billion from the TARP, was in deep distress. In the period leading up to the crisis, Citi was constructed along the lines of a financial supermarket by the vision of its former chairman Sandy Weil. The bank group operated throughout the world in some 100 countries and with some $2 trillion in assets. Citi operated many lines of business, and its regulators were concerned about its inability to measure risks on a company-wide basis. It was the classic case of an institution that was both too big to manage and too big to fail. Citi's banking subsidiary, Citibank, relied on a large deposit base, some $500 billion, from its worldwide banking operations, which were not insured by the FDIC. It also relied on wholesale funding. Both had the potential to take flight with the institution under distress. Citi calculated that a 7.2 percent withdrawal in deposits would wipe out its capital surplus.[27] During the crisis Citi became increasingly vulnerable as some of the special-purpose vehicles it had established to manage collateralized mortgages lost their external funding and Citi was forced to bring these assets, some $17.4 billion, on to its balance sheet. On November 19, Citi's share price plunged 23 percent; since the beginning of the crisis it had fallen by 88 percent. Its credit spreads also started to increase dramatically. With its accumulated losses, Citi became the most leveraged major bank in the country, with liabilities at sixty times top-flight or first-tier capital.[28]

Citi's various regulators were worried about the risks of Citi's failure. On Friday, November 21, 2008, the U.K.'s Financial Services Authority imposed a $6.4 billion cash lock-up on Citi to protect its broker dealers based in London. On that weekend the FDIC, supported by other Citigroup regulators, the Fed, and the Treasury, decided to inject more comprehensive liquidity into Citi.[29] Citigroup was systemically important, and the Treasury, Fed, and FDIC operating in concert had vowed, after the Lehman collapse, not to allow a systemically important institution to fail. On November 23, the Fed, the Treasury, and the FDIC announced the package to stabilize Citigroup. An additional $20 billion would be provided through TARP capital in the form of preferred shares with an 8 percent dividend. In addition, the agreement called for backstopping or ring-fencing a $306 billion portfolio of troubled assets. Citi would bear the first $37 billion in losses and the government 90 percent of any additional losses. The TARP would take the next $5 billion of losses, the FDIC the next

$10 billion, and the Fed any losses beyond those guaranteed by the TARP and FDIC, taking all of the assets as collateral. For its guarantees the Treasury and FDIC would receive $7 billion in preferred stock plus warrants. Citi also faced restrictions on compensation and dividend payments, and it pledged to work with a government program on mortgage modifications.[30]

Bank of America quickly followed Citigroup. Although B of A had acquired Merrill Lynch for $50 billion at the time Lehman Brothers was failing, Merrill's losses were growing. B of A now threatened to unwind the transaction by using an escape clause, which stipulated that there could be no material adverse change (MAC) from the time of the accepted bid to the closing of the transaction. John Lewis, the CEO of B of A, informed Paulson that Merrill's losses for the third quarter of 2008 were approaching $18 billion, later revised to $22 billion, and that his board wanted to unwind the deal, even though the shareholders of both companies had approved it. Clearly B of A was reaching out to Treasury for government support. Paulson recognized that unwinding the deal would leave Merrill, the largest brokerage company in the country, in bankruptcy, but would also have a strongly adverse effect on B of A. In a meeting with Lewis, Paulson and Bernanke pushed back at the notion that the deal could be unwound and refused to provide support. They made it clear, however, that the Treasury and the Fed would not allow a systemically important bank to fail and would work on a support package with Merrill after the closing of the transaction, if needed. B of A and Merrill were highly connected to the capital markets—67 percent of B of A's securities funding and repos, some $384 billion, were rolled over every night. And Merrill also rolled over $144 billion overnight. Like Citigroup, the two institutions were systemically important and "too big to fail."[31]

The B of A deal closely resembled the Citigroup transaction. On January 15, in the waning days of the Bush administration, the government invested $20 billion of TARP funds into B of A in preferred stock paying an 8 percent dividend; B of A would absorb the first $10 billion of losses of a pool of troubled assets amounting to $118 billion; losses beyond that would be split 90/10 between the government and B of A, similar to the proportions between the Treasury, FDIC, and the Fed in the Citigroup transaction. Like Citi, B of A agreed to constraints on executive pay and agreed to provide assistance on mortgage modifications. The deal was announced in the early morning of Paulson's last day in office as Treasury secretary.[32]

Summing Up

The unique role played by Paulson, Bernanke, and Geithner, and supported by Sheila Bair at FDIC, prevented the collapse of the U.S. financial system. The Fed also provided support in the form of swap lines to central banks in Europe, Japan, and selected emerging markets.

Human Capital and Institutional Capacity

This group was bold, inventive, and highly knowledgeable, and they needed all of their skills to prevent a global financial system meltdown. Serving jointly as the collective lender of last resort to the U.S. banks and financial markets, they undertook the following: (i) they reduced the target interest rate from 5.5 percent in September 2007 to near zero by December 2008; (ii) the Fed initiated a quantitative easing program to buy bonds to inject liquidity into the economy; (iii) the Fed expanded its balance sheet from $870 billion to $2.2 trillion, extending financing far beyond the traditional commercial banking system; (iv) the Fed restored confidence in and provided liquidity to the repo and commercial paper markets, while the Treasury guaranteed money market funds; (v) the Fed became a lender of last resort to international markets, providing unlimited foreign exchange swaps to central banks throughout the world, including to emerging markets such as Brazil, Mexico, Korea, and Singapore; and (vi) the three institutions—the Fed, Treasury, and FDIC—and their leaders used their capital, authority, knowledge of markets and institutions, and a great deal of suasion to prevent the failure of a diverse set of critical institutions such as Bear Stearns, Fannie Mae and Freddie Mac, AIG, Wachovia Bank, Merrill Lynch, Goldman Sachs, Morgan Stanley, and Citigroup. These transactions were very large and complex and required the financial capacity under law of the three major institutions. Paulson's years of experience at Goldman Sachs putting complex transactions together was clearly of great value. When institutions had to be intervened, such as WaMu, the FDIC did so, prepared it for sale, and quickly resold the institution, preventing depositor losses.[33]

Moreover, Paulson, Bernanke, and Geithner had to deal with a very difficult political process: persuading a president with highly conservative, free market roots and a Congress in which ideologues on both sides of the aisle were deeply opposed to bailouts in any shape or form, to act together. In addition, since it was an election year, they needed to continuously brief the presidential candidates John McCain and Barack Obama to keep them from politicizing the process. They brought all of these constituencies on board to support their interventions at the same time that the markets were rapidly deteriorating and heading toward the worst collapse since the 1930s Great Depression.

What is clear from their memoirs and my own experience advising governments on emerging market crises is that, in the middle of a crisis, policymakers receive and make all sorts of projections and assumptions, but information and data lag behind events. Often policymakers in the midst of a crisis are forced to make critical decisions with little real knowledge about what is happening. Uncertainty surrounds all policy decisions during a crisis, comparable to what has been described during combat as the "fog of war." In that respect, the experience and capacity of leading policymakers and their willingness to make decisions quickly and with less-than-perfect information proved decisive in avoiding a much deeper crisis. As Bernanke noted, "Despite the feeling at times that we were working with chewing gum and baling wire, our policies (and the Treasury's and the FDIC's) drew heavily on classic prescriptions for fighting financial panics, and they ultimately eased the crisis. If they hadn't, historical experience suggests that the nation would have experienced an economic collapse far worse than the very severe slump we endured."[34]

If there was a critical failure in the process, it was not managing to save Lehman. That was the critical event that signaled the Great Recession, and once it had failed there was no going back. Anatole Kaletsky, an editor for the *Times* of London and formerly an economics and financial journalist with the *Financial Times*, took the most extreme view of Paulson's policy decisions at Treasury and his failure to have a Plan B to save both Lehman and the U.S. financial system more broadly:

> Lehman precipitated a complete "collapse of confidence" among the creditors and depositors of every financial institution. Only when the financial system suffered this unprecedented breakdown did the real economy of consumption, global trade, and industrial orders "fall off the cliff." . . . The corollary is that the world economy would not have suffered a serious recession had the Lehman bankruptcy not been allowed to trigger the world's greatest financial panic . . . to bankrupt Lehman but to do nothing to prepare for the consequences was a case of reckless negligence.[35]

Stress Tests

Soon after being appointed secretary of the Treasury, Geithner proposed to a recently elected President Obama that stress tests be conducted on nineteen systemically important financial institutions—fifteen banks and four nonbank financial intermediaries (Met Life, Goldman Sachs, Morgan Stanley, and General Motors Acceptance

Corporation (GMAC).[36] The stress tests were to be undertaken by the Fed; if required, the banks would be backed up by the Treasury and the Fed to shore up their capital in the event they were unable to raise the necessary funds in the capital markets. Geithner proposed these tests because financial markets were still volatile and there was uncertainty whether the capital of the major banks was impaired by still-hidden nonperforming loans (NPLs) on their balance sheets. The objective of the stress tests was to reduce uncertainty and ultimately volatility. The earlier decision by Paulson to use the TARP to recapitalize the banks rather than purchase their bad loans through an asset management fund meant that the NPLs had not been flushed out of the system.[37]

The idea of the stress tests was initially resisted by prominent members of Obama's new economic team such as Larry Summers, former secretary of the Treasury, who was serving as the senior economic adviser to the president. His concerns were essentially that doing the stress tests was risky: on one hand the markets would view the tests as a whitewash, and volatility would increase; on the other hand the stress tests could identify huge capital holes in the banks that the administration lacked the funding through TARP to support. There was great reluctance to go back to the Congress for additional funding for bank bailouts at the beginning of the new administration.[38]

When the decision was made to proceed, the tests were designed to assess the capital adequacy of the banks in the event that two years of economic downturn were to occur. In other words, the tests were to be done assuming conditions of financial market and economic distress, which in fact the banks were just emerging from.[39] One of the problems associated with implementing the stress tests was the amount of time required to complete and analyze the results. During that time markets became increasingly volatile.[40]

The results of the tests proved fortunate for the administration, which decided to be fully transparent in sharing the results, a move that carried its own risks. First, the market accepted the results. And second, it was determined that the capital needed to fill the capital gap was achievable without seeking additional funding from Congress. Of the nineteen financial institutions, nine did not require additional capital, and five were considered negative outliers who would potentially need capital support. Bank of America faced the largest capital shortfall among the major commercial banks, $33.9 billion; Wells Fargo was next with $13.9 billion; and GMAC, one of the nonbank financial institutions, required $11.5 billion, almost twice its capital. As of January 1, 2009, the banks required some $185 billion in new equity, according to the results of the stress tests, but by then they had already raised

$110 billion. Treasury assumed that the banks could raise much of the shortfall in the market, although GMAC was a major exception.[41]

Blinder observed, "The bank-by-bank detail created a whole new level of transparency. And, importantly the numbers were judged to be credible. Yes, the regulators got it just right, and confidence began to come back. In fact, most bank stocks rose after the test results were announced."[42]

Following the stress tests, the pressure on financial markets effectively eased and the acute phase of the crisis was essentially over.

NINETEEN

The Great Recession

From Financial Crisis to Economic Crisis

$\mathbf{G}$ross domestic product in the United States fell 4.5 percent for all of 2008, but at a much deeper 8.5 percent during the last quarter of 2008 as the panic set-in—the country experienced the worst performance in fifty years. Falling stock market prices, falling home prices, and the lowest reading in consumer confidence in over thirty years all led to the deepening of the crisis in the real economy. As the economy declined, employers soon began shedding employees in virtually all sectors of the economy, particularly in construction and related sectors.[1]

Over an extended period of time starting in the 1970s and 1980s and continuing throughout the 1990s, the U.S. consumer had become the major taker of the world's goods and services, the "consumer of last resort" to the world economy. This supported the export orientation of Japan and the East Asian newly industrialized economies (NICs) in the 1970s and 1980s, and then migrating to China as the largest exporter in the world. Using the increasing wealth in their homes, the U.S. consumer piled up massive credit card debt, auto loans, student and college loans—and defaulted on many of them in alarming numbers. These defaults were also linked to the mortgage crisis and high levels of default on mortgages. The economic crisis morphed from a financial crisis to a demand crisis that first and foremost adversely affected the U.S. economy but also radiated out to the rest of the world. The U.S. consumer was forced to deleverage and could no longer play the role of consumer of last resort to the rest of the world. Atif Mian and Amir Sufi write: "Economic disasters are almost always preceded by a large increase in household debt. Large increases in household debt and economic disasters seem to be linked by a collapse in spending."[2]

Bernanke believes the financial panic in the last quarter of 2008 is what led to such a deep economic crisis. "Based on the historical parallels, I believed then and believe now that the severity of the panic itself—as much as or more so than its immediate triggers (most prominently subprime mortgage lending abuses and the housing bubble)—was responsible for the enormous financial and economic costs of the crisis."[3]

By June 2009 the country was officially out of recession, but growth was slow and unemployment remained high. At its peak, unemployment reached 10.3 percent in October 2009. This recession was L-shaped and not V-shaped as it had been in most previous crises after World War II. Although the country was officially out of the recession in the latter part of 2009, recovery was sluggish, and growth and employment did not rebound fully until the end of 2015. Moreover, economic inequality worsened, leaving much of the population angry over the bailout of Wall Street and lack of attention to the economic problems faced by "main street," average citizen or the middle class.

Declining Home Prices and Rising Foreclosure Rates

The price of housing fell throughout the country, but much more sharply in markets such as Arizona and Florida, where speculation was rampant. Almost a quarter of homeowners would owe more on their mortgages than their homes were worth. Lenders initiated foreclosure on 1.7 million homeowners in 2008, 2.1 million additional foreclosures in 2009, and 1.8 million in 2010.[4] Millions of Americans lost their homes through default on their mortgage or simply walked away from their homes and the mortgage payments when the value of the house sank well below the mortgage obligation. Housing price declines adversely affected new housing starts and construction, as well as the furniture and home furnishings, architecture and design, and related sectors such as brokerages, insurance, and legal services.

Both the Bush and Obama administrations tried to prop up the mortgage market and reduce the level of housing foreclosures. Perhaps the most important initiative was to rescue and recapitalize the Government National Mortgage Association (Ginnie Mae) and the Federal Home Loan Mortgage Corporation (Freddie Mac), the major sources of funding for new mortgages. A variety of other initiatives to prevent mortgage foreclosures were introduced but were too modest in scope or too complex to make a difference. Ideologically, most Republicans were against bailing out people who could not pay their mortgages, while most progressives and liberals favored mortgage relief and opposed the large Wall Street bailouts. For example, one scheme favored by the Federal Deposit Insurance Corporation (FDIC) that was adopted after the failure of the Independent National Mortgage Corporation (Indy Mac), one of the large thrifts, capped mortgages for homeowners either by extending maturities or by lowering interest rates. Sheila Bair at the FDIC pushed Henry Paulson and the Treasury Department to provide Troubled Asset Relief Program (TARP) funds to significantly broaden the scheme, but Paulson resisted, and more than half of the loans modified in the first quarter of 2008 went back into default. Families that were in default on their mortgage were often in default or had problems managing other debts as well, such as credit cards and auto and school loans.[5]

With the arrival of the Obama administration in January 2009, pressure mounted to support the housing market and mortgage relief for beleaguered families. Liberals and most of the Democratic members of Congress favored funding to support homeowners and criticized the Bush administration and the Republicans for bailing out Wall Street but not Main Street. Over the course of a few years, from 2009 to 2011, the Obama administration introduced a series of measures to reduce foreclosures; they had acronyms such as HAMP (the Home Affordable Modification Program), HARP (Home Affordable Refinancing Program), and HAUP (the Home Affordable Unemployment Program). Alan Blinder notes, "The multifaceted Obama anti-foreclosure efforts failed to stop the tsunami. . . . Yet new waves of foreclosures, plus a large unsold inventory of foreclosed homes, continued to depress house prices, which continued to depress homebuilding, which continued to depress the whole economy."[6]

According to Timothy Geithner, the housing program had a few key objectives: (i) to stabilize housing prices, which it did largely by rescuing Freddie Mac and Ginnie Mae and by providing continuous resources to these two institutions so that the mortgage market could function; (ii) to maintain low mortgage rates for families seeking to purchase a new home, which it did through the Federal Reserve program of quantitative easing (QE); (iii) to maintain low mortgage rates for families who wanted to refinance their mortgages and make them more affordable through the HARP program and through QE; and (iv) to provide mortgage owners in difficulty with mortgage relief through the HAMP program. This last proved more difficult to achieve.

Geithner asserts that by the fall of 2009, 2 million homes were in the process of foreclosure and another 7 million were at risk of foreclosure. About 11 million home-owners were underwater with some $700 billion in negative equity. The impact on families, particularly low- and middle-class families, was enormous; their homes were their major asset, often the asset families considered the base of their retirement nest egg. By 2013, HAMP had provided support for some 1.3 million homeowners, sav-ing the median homeowner more than $500 per month in mortgage payments, but far short of the 4 million homeowners that had been targeted by HAMP in 2009. The banking and home finance industry modified some 3 million mortgages on their own (without government support) to prevent costly defaults and nonpayments.[7]

Alan Blinder's analysis of the foreclosure issues and efforts by the Bush and Obama administrations to address the problem acknowledges that the issues were complex, particularly because mortgages had been chopped, sliced and diced, and then pack-aged in bundles so they could be securitized and sold to financial intermediaries.[8] However, when compared with the Roosevelt administration program during the Great Depression, the efforts by the Bush and Obama administrations were simply too timid or lacked the necessary resources—both human capital and financial re-sources—to address the problem adequately. Blinder specifically notes the Home Owners Loan Corporation (HOLC), which provided support for mortgage relief dur-ing the Great Depression in an amount of $3.5 billion, or some 5 percent of GDP at the time; the equivalent during the 2007–08 crisis would have been $800 billion.[9] He admits that his proposal to re-create a HOLC-like institution gained little traction in Washington. Following the large-scale losses and bailout of Freddie Mac and Ginnie Mae, there was little appetite in Congress or either administration to re-create a pub-lic institution to deal with mortgage relief.

Deep Social and Distributive Impact

Unemployment rose to just over 10 percent at the height of the crisis, and underem-ployment increased the employment problem. There were some 15 million unem-ployed workers, and unemployment and underemployment was estimated as high as 18 percent. By the end of 2010 some 4 million workers had been unemployed for more than a year. Unemployment fell disproportionately on noncollege graduates, re-cent college graduates, and minorities. African Americans and Latinos were dispro-portionately affected by the loss of both their jobs and their homes. Real wages had stagnated for the middle class, and social mobility had slowed; real wages had been stagnant for some twenty-five years, and the disparity in income and asset ownership between the wealthiest 10 percent of the population and the poorest 10 percent had widened dramatically. The United States had become one of the least equitable countries among the advanced economies. And that wealth gap widened as the recession progressed.

The poverty numbers rose, according to the Census Bureau's revised report on poverty. At the end of 2010 there were some 49 million people in the United States living below the poverty line—16 percent of the population, or one out of every six Americans. Poverty increased for four consecutive years. At the end of 2010 the poverty rate for children was 22 percent. In 2010, 27.5 percent of African Americans, 28.2 percent of Hispanics, and 14.3 percent of whites lived in poverty. Among seniors sixty-five and older the poverty rate was 15.9 percent, a figure that was revised substantially upward from earlier estimates. Some 49 million Americans were not covered by health insurance. The Gini coefficient, which measures income inequality, was 0.469 (zero is perfect equality and 1.0 is perfect inequality), signaling that the United States was among the most unequal societies in income and wealth among the advanced countries.[10]

A number of highly respected economists saw this growing inequality and the enrichment of the top 1 percent of the population as the most serious long-term issue both before and after the crisis. The crisis deeply exacerbated the problem.[11]

Branko Milanovic, a highly respected former senior economist at the World Bank, produced a wonderful small book in 2011, *The Haves and the Have Nots*. In it he notes:

> To understand the origins of the crisis, one needs to go to income inequality within practically all countries in the world, and the United States, in particular, over the past thirty years. In the United States the top 1 percent of the population doubled its share in national income from around 8% in the mid-70s to 16% in the 2000s. That eerily duplicated the situation just prior to the crash in 1929. The real median wages in the United States have been stagnant for the last 25 years. About one half of all real income gains between 1976 and 2006 accrued to the richest 5 percent of households. . . .

With broader and easier credit, he goes on to say, "people began to live by acquiring ever-rising debts on their credit cards, taking on more car debts and larger mortgages. . . . Thus was born the Great American consumption binge that saw household debt increase from 48 percent of GDP in the early '80s to 100 percent of GDP before the crisis."[12]

Restructuring and "Bailing Out" General Motors and Chrysler

In addition to bailing out the major financial institutions and the financial sector more broadly, and attempts to stem the tide on housing foreclosures, the Obama administration stepped in to assist the real economy. Its major initiative was the rescue of two of the big-three U.S. automakers. After an effort by Congress to push through $14 billion in support for Chrysler and General Motors (GM), which was opposed by Republican senators, the Bush administration, on one of its last days in office, decided to use the TARP to assist the automakers. The Treasury, still under Paulson's direction, agreed to provide loans of $4 billion for Chrysler and $13.4 billion for General Motors through TARP, with the last $4 billion for GM-dependent suppliers, contingent on approval by Congress to release the second tranche of the TARP. These loans were just enough to "kick the can down the road" so that the Obama administration would have to deal with the problem after the election. To receive the loans the companies had to agree to restructure, including making wage and benefit concessions, and their creditors had to make concessions as well.[13]

In the Obama administration Geithner took over as Treasury secretary, and "team auto" was led by an experienced investment banker, Steve Rattner. Both General Motors and Chrysler underwent extensive restructurings and a prepackaged bankruptcy. A prepackaged bankruptcy is an out-of-court workout, such as those discussed in Part III of this book on the East Asian crisis. The auto industry workouts were an improvement on the East Asian workouts since they were "prepackaged" outside the court system and then approved by a bankruptcy court; thus the agreements could not easily be challenged by minority creditors and shareholders.[14] The auto restructuring was a courageous act, but it is unlikely that any new president would have willingly watched two of the three major national automakers slide into bankruptcy, with a potential loss of several hundred thousand jobs, in the midst of a crisis. They were simply too big to fail. In total, the Treasury injected $84 billion, largely through TARP, into the auto sector: $64 billion into General Motors, $15 billion into Chrysler, and another $5 billion into auto parts suppliers.[15] In addition, the Treasury provided financing to General Motors Acceptance Corporation and Chrysler Finance through TARP.

The Stimulus

The administration also got Congress to pass an $800 million stimulus package, the American Reinvestment and Recovery Act (ARRA), to inject liquidity into the economy through a mix of infrastructure spending, support for states and municipalities,

TABLE 19-1. Fiscal Stimulus during the U.S. Crisis

Billions of US$

Programs	Amount spent
Total fiscal stimulus	1,484
Economic Stimulus Act of 2008	170
American Recovery and Reinvestment Act	832
Infrastructure and other spending	147
Transfers to state and local government	188
Transfers to persons	307
Tax cuts	190
Cash for Clunkers	3
HIRE Act (job credits)	17
Worker, Home Ownership, and Business Assistance Act of 2009	91
Department of Defense Appropriations Act of 2010	2
Education, Jobs, and Medical Assistance Act	26
Tax Relief, Unemployment Insurance Reauthorization, and Job Creation Act of 2010	189
Temporary Payroll Tax Cut Continuation Act of 2011	29
Middle Class Tax Relief and Job Creation Act of 2012	125

Source: Alan S. Blinder and Mark Zandi, "The Financial Crisis: Lessons for the Next One" (Washington: Center on Budget and Policy Priorities, October 15, 2015), pp. 11–12, table 4.

extension of unemployment benefits to the unemployed, and reduction of the payroll tax, which probably saved a couple of million jobs; but it is hard to prove a counterfactual—that is, what would have occurred without the stimulus.[16] The administration also agreed with Congress to extend the Bush tax cuts. The stimulus appears to have worked well. However, unemployment continued to rise during this period, so Republican critics conflated the rise in unemployment with the stimulus in their criticism of the new administration, and the public was easily convinced that the stimulus was ineffective. It turns out that the stimulus package was seriously undersized, since the actual downturn in GDP was much worse than initially anticipated. As Paul Krugman, the Nobel Prize–winning liberal economist, consistently argued, the package should have been on the order of $1.5 trillion or more to better match the economic decline and the size of the U.S. economy ($15 trillion). Also, the two years of the stimulus probably should have been extended to three or four years in tranches so that more necessary infrastructure investments could have been included (see table 19-1).[17]

Attempts by the Obama administration to introduce a large-scale infrastructure program that would have augmented the stimulus program, added millions of jobs (particularly for workers with construction skills), and increased the growth rate were consistently rejected by the leadership in Congress, who cited budgetary and debt concerns.

Quantitative Easing

The Federal Reserve (the Fed) used quantitative easing (QE) in a variety of ways.[18] The term was derived from the practices of the Bank of Japan during Japan's financial crisis in the 1990s.[19] QE was used as an alternative monetary tool by the Fed when the Fed interest rate was at or near zero. The Fed initially used QE (before it was called that) to inject liquidity into the market by selling Treasury bills and purchasing less liquid obligations, such as loans to banks. Another objective of QE was to bend the yield curve on long-term interest rates. The Fed purchased commercial paper (CP) in 2008 in order to breathe life into the commercial paper market, an essential short-term market, to fund working capital for the corporate sector. The objective was to reduce the spreads in the CP market over Treasuries. Under QE1 the Fed purchased massive amounts of Fannie Mae and Freddie Mac mortgage bonds and mortgage-backed securities in order to support the mortgage market (at the time, Fannie Mae and Freddie Mac represented up to 80 percent of market activity). Again, an objective of QE1 was to reduce the market spread over Treasuries. QE2 was announced in December 2010 and lasted until June 2011; it was used to purchase medium-term Treasuries to reduce long-term interest rates.[20] In the runup to the presidential election, QE2 brought a furious response from conservative Republicans, such as vice-presidential candidate Sarah Palin, who seemed to have just discovered that central banks purchased Treasury bills. QE in different forms continued until September 2015, while the Fed rate remained near zero.

In discussing lessons for central banks from the crisis, Stanley Fischer opined that the crisis taught central bank staff throughout the world that there is much that central banks can do when interest rates approach zero:

> In the first instance there is the policy of *quantitative easing*—the continuation of purchases of assets by the central bank even when central bank interest rate is zero. Although these purchases do not reduce the short-term interest rate, they do increase liquidity. Further, by operating in long-term assets, as in QE2, the central bank can affect longer term interest rates, which may

have an additional impact on the private sector's demand for longer term assets, including mortgages and corporate investment.[21]

Cumulatively, QE in its various forms reached some $2 trillion in economic stimulus. Seven years to the day after the Fed took its interest rates to zero, Janet Yellen, the new Fed chair, announced that the Fed would reverse course and begin to increase rates, though cautiously, starting with a quarter of a percent rise.[22] The Fed increased the size of its balance sheet substantially through QE, and the risks were perceived as eventually contributing to inflation, which was considered to be of little risk given the slow and extended recovery and near-zero inflation levels that persisted; potential losses to the Fed were also exaggerated by its critics.[23]

The Budget Deficit

The federal budget deficit was extraordinarily high as a result of the crisis and several other factors, reaching over 10 percent of GDP in 2008. Factors contributing to the deficit were:

(i) *A decline in tax receipts.* The downturn caused tax revenues to fall and the Bush administration had cut taxes across the board before the crisis, despite fighting two wars. The tax cuts were then renewed by the Obama administration in the midst of the crisis.

(ii) *Fiscal and trade deficits.* The U.S. economy ran persistent trade and fiscal deficits for many years before and during the crisis (excluding a brief period during the Clinton administration when the economy experienced a fiscal surplus).

(iii) *Wars and high military expenditures.* During the Bush years the administration chose to fight two wars—in Afghanistan and in Iraq—essentially off budget, while enacting tax cuts that disproportionately benefited the wealthiest. The estimated direct costs of the two wars, including the cost of debt service attributed to military expenditures, was $1.6 trillion. A long-term moderate projection of these costs is as high as $3 trillion if the costs of long-term medical care and other benefits are included for war veterans.[24] In 2012 the United States spent $682 billion on defense, more on defense annually than the next ten countries cumulatively. And in 2014, after several years of cuts due to the "sequester" (discussed below), the United States spent $610 billion, or more than the next seven countries cumulatively, expenditures that contributed significantly to recurring deficits and the national debt and constrained funding for the stimulus.[25]

(iv) *The stimulus package.* The Obama administration added to the fiscal deficit through the stimulus package and other measures to prop up the economy, and by agreeing to the extension of the Bush tax cuts. The stimulus was in fact a small contributor to the overall deficit. The fiscal deficits rose from 3.2 percent of GDP in fiscal year 2008, an acceptable number, to 10.1 percent of GDP in 2009, a very worrisome number and the largest deficit since World War II. The stimulus, though temporary, added $183 billion to the deficit in 2009, $405 billion in 2010 (equal to approximately one month's trade deficit), and $145 billion in 2011, a relatively small amount in a $16 trillion economy.

(v) *The sequester.* With the budget deficit still very high in 2010 and 2011 (some $1.3 billion, or 9 percent of GDP), in the lead-up to the 2012 election deficit hawks in the Republican Party tried to force the administration's hand by refusing to pass the budget, threatening a shutdown of the government, and refusing to approve an increase in the debt ceiling, which would in time have led the nation to default on its obligations. Other deficit hawks pushed for a constitutional amendment requiring a balanced budget, which would have pushed the economy into a deep recession again. Yet there were many advocates for the amendment.[26] The fight on the budget and the debt cap in 2011 leading up to the election undermined confidence in the government.

This ultimately led to a budget cut known as the sequester, which cut government programs across the board, including defense spending. Conservatives, primarily Republicans, were deeply unhappy with the defense cuts, and liberals, primarily Democrats, were unhappy with cuts in education and other government social programs. Policymakers were also unable to agree on necessary tax reforms. The parties were very far apart. The conservatives wanted to largely dismantle or significantly reduce most federal government programs, significantly reduce entitlement programs, and maintain a large defense budget, while cutting taxes largely in favor of the wealthy—their constituency. Liberals wanted to maintain government programs, expand entitlement programs, and reduce inequality by increasing the minimum wage and reducing or providing free tuition to community colleges, while taxing the wealthy so they at least paid their "fair" share of taxes (the so-called Buffett rule).[27]

The biggest danger to the U.S. economy was neither the deficit nor the national debt, but rather the inability of policymakers to agree on necessary medium- and longer-term policy reforms—to come to agreement on a budget that made sense, reform of entitlement programs and necessary tax reform, a reduction in the federal debt, and a commitment to infrastructure spending both to increase employment and to modernize the country's infrastructure (for example, the seriously outdated rail, bridge, and highway system).

Evaluating the Impact of the Crisis Resolution Process

The measures taken by the Treasury and the Fed, supported by the FDIC, to stem the crisis were criticized by economists and politicians on both the left and the right. Joseph Stiglitz, the Nobel Prize–winning economist, former chairman of the Council of Economic Advisers, and former chief economist at the World Bank, had a litany of complaints: (i) the failure of both Alan Greenspan and Ben Bernanke at the Fed to raise interest rates and to prick or contain the real estate bubble leading up to the crisis; (ii) the failure of the Fed to properly forecast the depth of the crisis; (iii) the failure of the Fed and other regulators to stop subprime lending; (iv) the failure by the Treasury and the Fed to save or restructure Lehman Brothers; (v) the subsequent decision to throw massive amounts of money at large loss-making financial institutions, at taxpayers' expense, without punishing their shareholders or management; (vi) the failure to address problem banks through proper workouts in Chapter 11 bankruptcy proceedings; (vii) the failure to save millions of homeowners when they were forced to default on their mortgages; (viii) the failure to support community financial institutions as well as small and medium-sized business owners and homeowners in favor of the large banks; and (ix) the inadequacy of the stimulus to lift the economy.[28]

More broadly, both Stiglitz and Krugman attacked the economic assumptions and policies pursued by several economists and policymakers that markets were efficient and self-correcting and would not lead to crises such as the Great Depression. These policymakers and economists believed that the real problem was government intervention and overregulation. Bernanke, among others, believed that severe recessions had largely been tamed and termed the 1990s the Great Moderation. Stiglitz and Krugman criticized the failure of policymakers to learn the lessons of the Great Depression: the important role of government in moderating or regulating markets and intervening in markets during a crisis, and a need for a Keynesian stimulus when the crisis emerged. Stiglitz observed:

I believe that markets are at the heart of every successful economy but that markets do not work well on their own. In this sense I'm in the tradition of the celebrated British economist John Maynard Keynes whose influence towers over the study of modern economics. . . . Economies need a balance between the role of markets and the role of government—with important contributions by non-market and non-governmental institutions. In the last twenty-five years America lost that perspective, and it pushed its unbalanced perspective on countries around the world . . . managing the crisis is only my first concern. I am also concerned about the world that will emerge after the crisis. We won't and can't go back to the world as it was before.[29]

In discussing Depression economics, Krugman simply observed: "We understand—or would understand, if so many weren't refusing to listen, how these things happen. Keynes provided much of the analytical framework needed to make sense of depressions . . . the central message of all of this work is that it doesn't have to be happening."[30]

As discussed in chapter 18, crisis intervention by the Treasury, Fed, and FDIC was massive and applied to a number of systemically important institutions and financial markets. What was the cost versus the benefit of these interventions to the U.S. economy? A simple measure of cost is how much these interventions ultimately cost the taxpayer. Table 19-2 indicates that anticipated taxpayer returns from the crisis were a positive $166 billion as of 2013, after recouping the initial injection of some $2 trillion.

A sophisticated analysis by Alan Blinder and Mark Zandi, of Moody's Analytics, tests the counterfactual: What would have happened to GDP, employment, inflation, and all the rest if there had been no crisis intervention or if specific interventions such as the stimulus package—the American Reinvestment and Recovery Act—had not been employed. The authors use a highly sophisticated econometric model developed by Moody's Analytics, similar to models used by the Fed, the Congressional Budget Office, and the Office of Management and Budget to analyze the U. S. economy.[31] Their findings can be summarized as follows: (i) without the policy responses, including the stimulus in late 2008 and 2009, the peak-to-trough decline in GDP would have been close to 14 percent (instead it was just over 4 percent); (ii) the economy would have contracted for twice as long as it did; (iii) more than 17 million jobs would have been lost, about twice the number actually lost; (iv) the unemployment rate would have peaked at 16 percent (it actually peaked at 10 percent); (v) the budget deficit would have reached 20 percent of GDP (instead of 10 percent), or $2.8 trillion in fiscal year 2011; the economy (as of the second quarter of 2015) would have been

TABLE 19-2. United States: Taxpayer Returns from Crisis Intervention: Projected Returns and Losses, End 2013

Billions of US$

Fannie Mae/ Freddie Mac conservatorship	88
Treasury purchases of mortgage-backed securities	25
Bank investments in the Troubled Asset Relief Program (TARP)	24
AIG commitments	23
Federal Reserve liquidity program	20
Federal Deposit Insurance Corporation (FDIC) programs	13
TARP credit market programs	3
Bear Stearns commitments	2
Money market fund guarantees	1
State and local HFA initiative	−2
TARP auto program	−15
TARP housing program	−16
Total projected return	$166 billion

Source: Timothy Geithner, *Stress Test: Reflections on Financial Crises* (New York: Broadway Books, 2014), p. 497.

TABLE 19-3. Outcomes of U.S. Policy Responses to the Great Recession, 2009–12

Category	Year	Boost to real GDP (cumulative percent)	Number of jobs added (cumulative millions)	Change in unemployment (cumulative percent)
Total policy response	2009	6.0	3.6	−2.0
	2010	13.5	8.5	−5.4
	2011	16.3	10.1	−6.8
	2012	16.0	9.9	−6.7
Fiscal Stimulus and	2009	1.6	0.8	−0.3
Recovery Act	2010	3.6	2.7	−1.2
	2011	3.3	2.7	−1.7
	2012	2.9	2.2	−1.4
Financial response	2009	2.8	2.1	−1.0
	2010	5.6	4.5	−2.7
	2011	5.6	4.9	−2.9
	2012	6.4	4.9	−2.8

Source: Blinder and Zandi, "Financial Crisis," p. 3, table 1.

far weaker (roughly $800 billion lower), there would have been 3.6 million fewer jobs, and unemployment would have been 7.6 percent (instead of the 5 percent it reached in 2015).[32]

The authors provide a series of analytical tables in the text and in annexes that display the results of their model by type of stimulus and areas of the economy affected. Learned economists will dispute or challenge these numbers since it is exceedingly difficult to prove a counterfactual. But as an indication of what would have occurred without the various policy initiatives, the Blinder and Zandi analysis is a valuable analytical contribution to the debate on effective crisis resolution measures (see table 19-3).

The United States as a Large Sovereign Debtor

One legacy of the crisis and the years leading up to it is the increase in the sovereign (national) debt of the United States. Historically, the national debt has peaked during major crises (such as the Great Depression) and wars. It was at its highest during and immediately after World War II—over 120 percent of GDP. The same was true during the recent crisis: national debt was 56 percent of GDP in 2001 and reached 70 percent at the height of the crisis in 2008, and was projected at 102 percent of GDP as a legacy of the crisis in ensuing years.[33] One might therefore assume that debt as a percentage of GDP will decline steadily now that the crisis is over, or is this time different?

Defining the national debt is complex. Most comparative analyses refer to the gross debt, and to the (gross) debt-to-GDP ratio in comparisons with other countries. The gross debt is divided into two subparts: (i) the net debt, debt held in Treasury securities by the public or investors such as individuals, corporations, pension institutions, the Federal Reserve, and foreign, state, and local governments; and (ii) debt held in government accounts or intragovernmental debt, nonmarketable securities, such as the Social Security Trust Fund account, the Federal Housing Administration, the Federal Savings and Loan Corporation Resolution Trust Fund, and the Federal Hospital Insurance Trust Fund (Medicare).[34]

Excluded from the national debt are guarantees, until the guarantees are called upon. If the guarantees provided during the crisis had been called upon, they would have increased the debt substantially, but all of those guarantees expired in 2012 without impact. Future obligations to the various trust funds, such as Social Security, are not included in the national debt. Nor are implicit obligations to agencies such as the government-sponsored enterprises (GSEs)—Fannie Mae and Freddie Mac.

When the GSEs were taken into conservatorship the decision was made by the White House budget director to exclude their debts from the federal budget because the conservatorship was temporary. This represented an off-balance-sheet obligation of the government of some $5 trillion at the time they were intervened in. Fortunately, the investment through TARP and Treasury loans to the GSEs was returned with a profit, and these agencies are operating profitably; but because they are still under conservatorship and no decision has yet been made on ownership resolution, the U.S. government remains a contingent guarantor of the debts of these agencies.[35]

Certain spending, such as "extraordinary appropriations," is offline or not included in the budget but does add to the national debt. The wars in Iraq and Afghanistan were off-budget appropriations, and the costs of funding these wars, combined with the Bush tax cuts, substantially increased the debt. It was irresponsible of the Bush administration and Congress, to say the least, not to include these items in the federal budget. Direct funding mechanisms such as the TARP were included in the budget, but much of that money was returned to the Treasury and the Treasury actually generated a profit from most TARP operations.[36]

Since 1980 the national debt has risen substantially. As of June 30, 2015, debt held by the public in the form of marketable securities—Treasury bills, notes, and bonds— was $13.08 trillion, or 74 percent of GDP; and intragovernmental holdings, which are nonmarketable, stood at $5.07 trillion, giving a combined gross national debt of $18.15 trillion, or about 102 percent of GDP. Some $6.2 trillion of this debt, or one-third, was held by foreign investors, including foreign governments such as China and Japan ($1.3 trillion and $1.2 trillion, respectively) and some 47 percent by the public. Foreign ownership of the national debt leaves the U.S. economy subject to changes in sentiment by other countries. For the longer term it is not a comfortable position for U.S. policymakers. The national debt was projected to reach $19.3 trillion by year-end 2016.[37]

During the crisis there was frequently expressed concern that China, for example, would sell off its holdings of U.S. Treasuries to mitigate its risks, and also because interest rates were near zero. In fact, the opposite occurred. There was a "flight to safety" by investors broadly into Treasury instruments, and the dollar appreciated significantly after the crisis, particularly against the euro. A strong dollar is ultimately not good for U.S. exporters, but it does demonstrate the perception of investors about the strength of the U.S. economy and the dollar relative to other economies and currencies (see table 9-4).[38]

The increase in our sovereign debt is not good news. First, the gross debt at 102 percent of GDP is high by any comparative measure. If another crisis emerges the government will have less leeway to fight the crisis. Second, the trend line is for

TABLE 19-4.   Public Debt of the United States, Selected Years

Fiscal year	Total debt (billions of $)	Percent of GDP
2000	5,659	55.8
2008	10,001	67.9
2010	13,551	91.6
2015	18,138	101.3

Source: Wikipedia, "National Debt of the United States" (http//en.wikipedia.org/wiki./National-debt-of-the-United-States).

increasing deficits and debt, particularly if Congress and a future administration cannot agree on the necessary policy reforms to address the growing obligations under entitlement programs—Social Security, Medicare, Medicaid, and the Affordable Care Act. The U.S. government is obligated under current law to make mandatory payments for programs such as Medicare, Medicaid, and Social Security. The Government Accountability Office (GAO) has projected that as the population ages tax revenues will be insufficient to cover the costs of those programs. The present value of these unfunded mandates is estimated at $45.8 billion, and the unfunded gap is expected to grow substantially by 2035. The trend line according to the Congressional Budget Office is unsustainable. Third, as interest rates rise from their current levels, the cost of debt service will rise and add to the government's fiscal deficit.[39] A rise in interest rates is perhaps the most immediate threat to the sustainability of debt at current levels.

In 2010, Federal Reserve Chairman Ben Bernanke stated, "Neither experience nor economic theory clearly indicates the threshold when government debt begins to endanger prosperity and economic stability. But given the significant costs and risks associated with a rapidly rising federal debt, our nation should soon put in place a credible plan for reducing deficits to sustainable levels over time."[40]

Crisis Prevention and Mitigation in the Future

The damage caused by the Great Recession has led to a number of steps to reform the financial system, in particular to significantly improve regulation that protects the consumer. Stanley Fischer has set forth these priorities based on deliberations of the Basel Committee on Banking Supervision, the Financial Stability Board, and the Group of Thirty. Importantly, these are not just U.S. goals or objectives but also those of the global financial oversight community:

1. To strengthen the stability and robustness of financial firms, with particular emphasis on standards for governance, risk management, capital and liquidity;

2. To strengthen the quality and effectiveness of prudential regulation and supervision with higher standards for systemically important firms;

3. To build the capacity for undertaking effective macroprudential regulation and supervision;

4. To develop suitable resolution regimes for financial institutions;

5. To strengthen the infrastructure of financial markets, including markets for derivative transactions;

6. To improve compensation practices for financial institutions;

7. To strengthen international coordination of regulation and supervision, particularly with regard to the regulation and resolution of global systemically important institutions;

8. To better monitor risks within the shadow banking system, and find ways of dealing with them; and,

9. To improve the performance of the credit rating agencies, which were deeply involved in the collapse of markets for collateralized and securitized lending instruments, especially those based on mortgage finance.[41]

From a U.S. perspective the major initiative to regulate the financial sector was the passage of the Dodd-Frank Act on July 21, 2010. This long and complex piece of regulation goes part of the way toward restoring the prudential regulation and supervision that was previously in place under the Glass-Steagall Act, though it does not force commercial banks to exit the investment banking business. Some of its main contributions are to require banks to have more tier-one capital. There has been discussion to require the banks to carry "bail-able" long-term capital; it established a consumer protection agency to prevent the kinds of abuses that occurred in the mortgage industry in the lead-up to the crisis; it restricts banks from trading with their own capital, and creates a mechanism for developing a "workout" for large, systemically important financial institutions in a crisis, presumably to prevent the need for large-scale bailouts at taxpayer expense. Regular stress testing is also an important innovation that emerged from the U.S. crisis, and it is also used by the European

Central Bank for the European banks.[42] On the negative side of the ledger, Dodd-Frank limited the Fed's ability to intervene specific firms, as occurred with AIG, Citigroup, and Bank of America. Also, it takes away the FDIC's guarantee authority. Both are valuable tools in addressing a crisis.[43]

The reforms, in particular Dodd-Frank, have been meaningful. But basic questions go unanswered: Do any of these measures actually prevent crises from emerging? Probably not. Can macroprudential standards be set such that a Fed chairman will be willing in the future to prick the bubble or contain a budding financial crisis? This is extremely difficult to do and extremely difficult to time, and central banks do not have much of a track record in pricking a bubble before it bursts on its own. The banking and financial sectors are more concentrated than before the crisis. Financial firms such as Citi, Bank of America, and J. P. Morgan are still too big to fail. Is there the political will in the country to break up the large banks? Almost certainly not. Is it credible that a future administration will seek to work out or resolve these institutions during a financial crisis rather than bailing them out? Doubtful. In future crises will policymakers—the Treasury, the Fed, and Congress—be prepared to do more for the real sector, for consumers and small and medium-sized enterprises (SMEs), to mitigate the crisis impact on Main Street? Probably not. All of the crisis mechanisms globally are focused on addressing the problems of the banking and financial sectors; little thought has been given to systemic measures for resolving the problems of corporate groups, SMEs in distress, or households.

At present, the greatest constraint on crisis intervention is likely to be the politics of crisis intervention. Populist politicians and the population at large on both the right and the left have whipped up the population to believe that all evil begins and ends on Wall Street. Indeed, the public has witnessed irresponsible and reckless behavior by management and the boards of directors responsible for overseeing the banks, and they have also seen unmitigated greed in the compensation demands of both management and boards, as well as corruption. Some transgressions brought large fines but few criminal or civil charges against bank staff, especially senior management, at these institutions. They have also seen far too much money thrown at problematic banks and far too little support for homeowners or SMEs. The greatest constraint on crisis resolution in the United States in the foreseeable future is likely to be the popular anger that would erupt from any such intervention. That would in turn restrict policymakers' willingness to support such interventions and their ability to agree on appropriate policy interventions during a crisis.

I started this book by stating that it is critical in good times to prepare for crisis. It seems to me that the United States is far from prepared to address the next large crisis.

Postscript on the Crisis

As this book is readied for publication, it would be remiss of me not to note some changes in some fundamental factors that are likely to affect the prospects for another crisis in the United States in the foreseeable future. Since the beginning of the recovery in 2010, the U.S. economy has grown at a slow but steady pace, with GDP averaging a little over 2.0 percent per annum. Employment increased every year from 2010 to 2017, and unemployment rests at a postrecession low of 4.0 percent as of the end of 2017. Inflation has also remained low but has begun to heat up. The U.S. Fed has stopped its program of quantitative easing in recognition that there has been a full recovery and has begun to increase interest rates to try and dampen emerging inflation.

On the negative side of the ledger, both trade and fiscal deficits have remained stubbornly in place. In addition, there has been no effort by either the Obama or Trump administrations or Congress to reform entitlements. Without such reforms, fiscal deficits will continue to increase, and our public debt will become unsustainable. If those were our only problems, however significant they are, there would be no need for this postscript as these are well-known issues and need not be reviewed here.

In the course of 2017, the Trump administration and Congress came together and passed a tax reform bill and approved a budget that threaten the stability of the U.S. economy and in particular will potentially lead to increasingly higher interest rates, which will have an adverse impact on economic performance, induce high fiscal deficits, and lead to higher and increasingly unsustainable public debt. Both the tax reforms and the budget accord bring us closer to a potential crisis or, at a minimum, will make it extremely difficult for us to address the next crisis when it does arrive.

A few facts are required to support these assertions. The Congressional Budget Office has projected that from 2019 to 2028, the federal government will run cumulative annual deficits of $12.4 trillion, or some 5 percent of GDP. Our deficits have reached such a level in only six years since 1950 and mostly as a result of a crisis (1983, 1985, and 2009–12). The debt will exceed 100 percent of GDP, a level reached previously after World War II. Balancing the budget would require up to a trillion dollars a year in tax increases or spending cuts, or one-fifth of federal spending, which is now being borrowed, adding to the debt.[44] Neither of the major parties has shown the will to address the deficit and the tax reform, which largely benefits the wealthy, will only exacerbate the problem for the foreseeable future. Tax revenues are expected to be some $700 billion dollars less than anticipated before the tax cut in 2019 and are likely to be as low as 17.5 percent of GDP in 2025, with mandatory spending rising substantially. Mandatory spending, or entitlements, will increase by some $2 trillion over the next decade, largely to meet the claims of the baby boomers. In addition, the interest needed to service the debt is likely to cost some $915 billion in 2028 or 3.2 percent of GDP—larger than the defense budget.[45]

The title of this book is *In Good Times Prepare for Crisis*. We have just seen the U.S. government do exactly the opposite. It has increased the likelihood of a crisis.

TWENTY

The Eurozone Crisis

2008–15

This chapter primarily addresses the eurozone crisis. However, other crises were occurring in Europe at roughly the same time as or in parallel to the eurozone crisis—in Iceland, Great Britain, and a few of the countries in Eastern and Central Europe.

There were early signals of a crisis in Europe and in the eurozone. On February 7, 2007, HSBC, one of the largest international banks, based in London, announced that it was setting aside reserves of $10.6 billion to cover potential bad debt losses from U.S. subprime losses.[1] On August 9, 2007, BNP Paribas, one of the largest French banks, stopped redemptions in three of its investment funds. The funds had $2.2 billion in assets, of which some 20 percent were mortgage-backed bonds; but their value had plunged 20 percent in just a couple of weeks: The U.S. national commission investigating the causes of the crisis noted that "in retrospect, many investors regarded the suspension of the French funds as the beginning of the 2007 liquidity crisis."[2] These instruments became difficult to value as the market for collateralized debt obligations (CDOs) spiraled downward, and even more difficult to divest. European interbank markets began to tighten, and the European Central Bank (ECB) announced that it would open a window to allow the banks to draw on as much funding as they needed. Within hours of the announcement, the ECB would later reveal, some forty-nine banks had drawn €94.8 billion ($130 billion).[3]

In the summer of 2007, Mervyn King, the governor of the Bank of England, had spoken in strong opposition to market intervention by the U.S. Federal Reserve (the Fed) and the ECB. He explained that the provision of such liquidity encourages excessive risk taking and sows the seeds of future financial crises; in other words, he worried about moral hazard. By mid-September he was singing another tune and announced the injection of £10 billion (approximately $17.5 billion) into the market at three-month intervals. Governor King's conversion was due to the arrival of the financial crisis on Britain's High Street. On September 14 the Bank of England had to stop a depositor run on Northern Rock, one of Britain's largest mortgage banks. It was the first such bank run in Great Britain since 1866, leading to Bagehot's famous work on the role of the central bank as a lender of last resort in a crisis.[4] Britain lacked mortgage insurance, and after the run the Bank of England felt compelled to lend to Northern Rock, subsequently to guarantee all of its depositors and in February 2008 to assume public ownership of, and effectively nationalize, Northern Rock.[5]

Initially, Europe viewed the crisis that emerged as one transmitted from the United States to the rest of the world. The real estate bubble and related toxic mortgage problem that led to the collapse of Lehman Brothers on September 15, 2008, was seen by European policymakers as the event that sparked the global crisis. Europe, especially the eurozone, had stored up many of its own problems since the creation of the euro in 1999, and these problems were now coming home to roost. The focus at the inception was on banking problems in the eurozone and two non-eurozone countries, Iceland and Great Britain. The eurozone banks not only had their own nonperforming loans (NPLs) to address, but were also deeply invested in the bonds of the various eurozone countries, particularly those that were later seen as bearing greater risk. They invested throughout the eurozone because they were not required by their banking regulators to provision against these investments and because other countries offered a higher return than, for example, German bonds offered. Their perception was that bonds issued by a eurozone member country were essentially without risk.

In at least two countries in the eurozone—Ireland and Spain—there was also a real estate bust, which led to the banking crisis and eventually a deeper economic crisis. In other countries, such as Portugal and Greece, the problems were transmitted initially through their banks. But these countries had borrowed heavily to prop up social systems that were largely unsustainable within economies that were not particularly competitive and relied primarily on small business and tourism. Their banking crises also morphed into deeper economic crises.

For countries in the region that had borrowed heavily at rates not much above the rate Germany borrowed at, and were also running large budget deficits, problems of sovereign debt sustainability soon emerged. Spreads quickly rose for what became known as the peripheral eurozone countries—namely Italy, Ireland, Spain, Portugal, and Greece. Others referred to the split in the eurozone as the southern versus the northern tier, though Ireland did not fit the geographic split. By 2010 a series of country crises had emerged—first Iceland (not in the eurozone), then Greece, Ireland, Portugal, and subsequently Cyprus, all of which needed to be bailed out. Spain was not bailed out in the same way as the others but needed external support to prop up its banking system. By 2010 the eurozone crisis was full blown, and it could no longer be attributed to the U.S. crisis.

Birth of the Euro and the Eurozone

The euro was born out of a desire by members of the European Union (EU) to continue the process of political and economic integration in Europe. Economics were important but played only a secondary role in the process. The euro was also a grand political bargain, agreed to by the Germans and the French, the two primary promoters of European integration, and tied to German unification.[6] Another reason for adopting the euro, both political and economic, was the desire of European leaders to see their currency become one of the primary reserve currencies able to rival the U.S. dollar. If the euro emerged as an important reserve currency, world trade between Europe, one of the largest trading blocs in the world, and the rest of the world would increasingly be denominated in euros. Also, European countries and private financial and corporate nonfinancial institutions would be able to raise capital in European capital markets denominated in euros.

The need for the euro evolved over time with the global shift to floating exchange rates in the 1990s and raised concerns among European policymakers; a purely market-driven exchange rate was not acceptable to European leaders. There was concern in Germany, for example, that freely floating rates would lead to substantial devaluation of other European currencies against the deutsche mark, eroding Germany's export competitiveness. As tensions persisted in European currency markets, European leaders adopted a number of systems such as the "currency snake," and eventually in 1979 the European Exchange Rate Mechanism (ERM), with the goal of reducing exchange rate volatility. Neither mechanism was particularly effective. It was against this background that the idea of a common currency was promoted.

In 1989 the European Commission president, Jacques Delors, issued a report that outlined a three-stage plan for building an economic and monetary union within ten years.[7]

The Maastricht Treaty of 1999

The idea of a common currency languished for several years. But when West Germany's chancellor Helmut Kohl announced a ten-point plan to unify East and West Germany, François Mitterrand, France's president, pushed Germany to give up the deutsche mark and accept European currency unification in return for support from EU countries for the unification of Germany. In 1991, European leaders signed the Maastricht Treaty and formalized the process for adopting the euro. European leaders expected that, in time, all of the EU members would adopt the euro.

But that was not to be the case. The United Kingdom and the northern European countries, which had strong attachments to their currencies and long democratic traditions, did not want to give up their currencies. Many analysts in the U.K. and political leaders had objections to the euro; perhaps the most important of which was Prime Minister Margaret Thatcher's. With London as the most important financial center in Europe, and equally important to the U.K. economy, the British government analyzed the risks and benefits and opted out, as did the Swedes. The British decision put a dent in the idea of European capital markets as an important source of capital for Europe and a world denominated in euros. This was especially true as a eurobond, backed by the full faith and credit of each member of the eurozone, failed to materialize. Instead, each country raised its own bonds, based on its own creditworthiness. This became a significant problem as the crisis emerged. Most Germans during the 1990s objected to giving up the deutsche mark, but no referendum was held and Kohl held up his end of the bargain with France. The southern European countries largely supported the euro.[8]

Launch of the Euro

During 1997 and 1998 the predecessor to the ECB, the European Monetary Institute, screened euro applicants according to five eligibility criteria: low inflation, low government budget deficits, moderate government debt, a stable exchange rate, and long-term interest rates that were close to the average of rates prevailing in other candidate countries. These so-called Maastricht criteria were overlooked for a number of countries. Greece was the only applicant that failed all five criteria and was not allowed to join the eurozone in 1999. But Greece was allowed to join in 2001, after a delay of just two years, and it is doubtful that it met the Maastricht criteria by that time. In total, eleven countries joined the eurozone at the start, and by the beginning of the crisis in 2008 there were seventeen eurozone members. Membership in the eurozone was intended to increase convergence among the members, and initially that is what occurred as financial resources flowed from the strongest economies in the eurozone to the weaker economies. Strong growth was not uniform. Italy experienced only an initial boost after adopting the euro, and thereafter its growth averaged 1 percent per year for several years. Germany's economic performance was shaped largely by the cost and impact of unification.[9]

As one analyst noted in discussing the crisis, "The more basic problem is with the euro itself. After decades of experimentation, what Europeans are discovering is how difficult it is for countries with widely varying income levels, widely varying productivity growth, and closed labor markets to all share the same currency."[10] Instead of convergence, which the eurozone countries experienced in the early years, after the euro's launch the eurozone experienced divergence as the crisis ensued.[11]

Joseph Stiglitz, a sharp critic of the eurozone as it is structured, felt that the convergence criteria for eurozone membership were inappropriate to promote full employment and growth, the ultimate objective of such a currency union. "The founders of the euro seemed to believe that satisfying the convergence criteria was key to ensuring the viability of the euro. They were obviously wrong."[12]

The euro was launched on January 1, 1999. Initially it was a hybrid system, with the euro used for electronic transactions but the coins and notes of the eleven adopting countries remaining in use for cash transactions. Retail prices were quoted in euros and in the old currency. However, the exchange rate was fixed to the euro. The euro was initially set at €1 to US$1.18 and in its first year floated between parity with the U.S. dollar and $1.20.

With a common currency came a common monetary policy. The European Central Bank, a new institution, was modeled after the Bundesbank, the German central bank. Its exclusive role was to contain inflation. Each member of the region named a member to the governing council, which together with the president of the ECB set interest rates for the entire eurozone. Notably, each country retained its own central bank as well. After an initial three-year transition period, the euro replaced the older currencies for cash purposes and the euro was fully launched.[13] Another of Stiglitz's criticisms of the euro's structure is that the ECB was restricted to fighting inflation and was not mandated to support full employment, growth, and stability.[14]

Economic and Institutional Weaknesses of the Euro

The eurozone had no institutional capacity other than the ECB. There was little thought given to what would occur if there was a financial or economic crisis in one or more member countries. There was no emergency fund set up to address a potential crisis. Also, there were no common financial instruments beyond the euro itself, such as Eurobonds backed by all of the member nations. Faith in the euro was based on an implicit guarantee that its members, particularly Germany, the powerhouse of the region, would never allow the euro or any of its members to fail.

This implicit guarantee was similar in some respects to the U.S. Treasury's support for the government-sponsored enterprises (GSEs)—Fannie Mae and Freddie Mac. The GSEs borrowed at very low interest rates from the U.S. capital markets and in world markets. Although the GSEs were very thinly capitalized and operated with very high leverage, there was an implicit understanding that the U.S. government stood behind them. That implicit guarantee was severely tested in the financial crisis from 2007 to 2008 when the U.S. government was forced to step in with a massive amount of capital to save these institutions and to acquire most of their equity.

The implicit sovereign guarantee in the eurozone allowed the various eurozone countries to borrow at very thin spreads over German bonds, and borrow they did in very substantial amounts from 1999 to 2008 when the crisis hit.[15]

Perhaps the critical institutional and policy weaknesses were: (i) the currency union came without a banking union, and each national banking regulator/supervisor was left to oversee its banks; and (ii) there was no fiscal union, so each country controlled its own budget and fiscal deficits. The Maastricht guidelines were clear, but there was no one in place to enforce them, and often the guidelines were ignored even by the stronger economies in the region.

From an individual country perspective, the euro deprived each country of the ability to use monetary policy to set interest rates or print money in addressing its economy. At the time of the crisis, the emerging market countries—Mexico, the East Asian countries, and Turkey—could devalue their currencies as part of the crisis resolution process, but the eurozone countries had no such remedy. That constraint reduced their ability to escape the crisis and the low-growth deflationary trap several of the countries experienced. The euro did not function as a national currency for its member states; instead it functioned like a foreign or external currency.

Stiglitz observes that "the Eurozone created a new situation. Countries and firms and households within countries borrowed in euros. But though they were borrowing in the currency they used, it was a currency they did not control. Europe unwittingly created the familiar problem faced by highly indebted developing countries and emerging markets."[16]

The sovereign debt of several eurozone countries—Greece, Portugal, Spain, and Italy, as examples—seemed unsustainable as borrowing spreads rose during the crisis. Greece's debt remains unsustainable despite three bailouts from 2010 to 2015 and will need to be largely written off at some point. The large overhang of debt leaves these countries potentially vulnerable to the next crisis.

George Soros noted, "The euro was an incomplete currency to start with. The Maastricht Treaty established a monetary union without a political union. The euro boasted a common central bank but it lacked a common treasury. It is exactly this sovereign backing that financial markets started questioning that was missing from the design."[17]

Banking/Financial Sector Crises

Banks in the eurozone were quick to invest in the public or sovereign bonds of the various member countries. They did so to gain yield by investing in Italian, Greek, or Spanish bonds instead of German bonds and because of their perception that bonds of the member countries were essentially without risk.

Cross-Border Holdings of Sovereign Debt

With the launch of the euro, the sovereign bond holdings of banks in the region grew dramatically. One reason was the incentive offered by the ECB of regulatory forbearance. That is, banks were not required to hold reserves against investments in bonds of eurozone member states. From a regulatory perspective, German government bonds and Italian government bonds were treated identically, so banks reached for the additional yields and ignored the differences in risk. Lending from German and French banks to the so-called peripheral countries in the region (Portugal, Ireland, Greece, and Spain) grew rapidly in the 1990s up to the crisis, and their exposure to these countries reached well over a trillion euros by 2007.[18]

The interconnectedness between financial institutions and institutions and markets with respect to the U.S. financial crisis also existed in the eurozone. The cross-border holdings by banks in the eurozone and in the region more broadly can be viewed through a *New York Times* analysis and related graphic illustration.[19] For example, total exposure of European banks to the five most distressed economies in Europe as of June 2011 is shown in table 20-1.

TABLE 20-1.   European Bank Exposure to Most-Distressed European Debtors

Country	Billions of US$	GDP (percent)
Italy	837.5	41
Spain	643.2	46
Ireland	380.1	184
Portugal	196.7	86
Greece	120.8	40
Total	$2.178 trillion	

Source: Bill Marsh and others, "It's All Connected: A Spectator's Guide to the Euro Crisis," *New York Times,* October 23, 2011.

The exposure of individual countries was as follows: (i) German banks' exposure to Italian borrowers was $161.8 billion, though Germans owed Italian banks more than Italians owed to Germany; (ii) British and Irish banks owed each other a roughly equivalent amount, but the exposure of British banks (England was not a eurozone member) to a distressed Ireland was $140.8 billion; (iii) the exposure of German banks to Ireland was $110.5 billion; (iv) Italians owed French banks $416.4 billion, or one-fifth of Italian GDP; and (v) U.S. banking risk to Europe was $68.8 billion to Spain, $53.6 billion to Ireland, and $46.9 billion to Italy.[20]

Too Big to Fail—Systemically Important Banks

If we look at large, systemically important banks and their national and cross-border holdings of sovereign debt, the concern of policymakers with respect to the European banking system becomes abundantly clear. For example, a July 2011 report by the Bank for International Settlements (BIS) on European bank exposure notes that the National Bank of Greece held €18 billion in Greek bonds; a 50 percent writedown would have wiped out the bank's capital; BNP Paribas (France) and Commerzbank (Germany) held €5 billion and €3 billion respectively in Greek bonds; however, it was Italy that had the greatest exposure: BNP Paribas, for example, owned €28 billion in Italian bonds, some 50 percent of its core capital; Commerzbank €11 billion; Crédit Agricole (France) €10.7 billion; and Unicredit Bank, one of the largest Italian banks, held €49 billion in Italian bonds, 140 percent of its core capital.[21]

In general, European large banks were undercapitalized and highly leveraged. Also, regional or municipal banks in various countries, such as the *Landesbanken* in Germany, the *cajas* in Spain, and the *caixas* in Portugal, fared poorly during the crisis, with rising NPLs due to their holdings of loans to small businesses and households. Banking supervision was uneven throughout the eurozone and Europe more broadly, and individual countries were forced to bail out large banks considered too big to fail (now often referred to as "systemically important banks").

In addition to rescuing Northern Rock, the Bank of England also rescued the Royal Bank of Scotland, one of Europe's largest banks, and injected capital into Lloyds Bank, one of England's largest retail banks. The Dutch were forced to support ING Bank, one of Europe's largest bank and insurance groups,[22] and France and Belgium were forced to intervene in the Franco-Belgium bank Dexia, which ultimately had to be rescued with a balance sheet of €700 billion, roughly equal to Lehman's before Lehman Brothers failed. After the crisis had seemed to pass, Portugal had to intervene in the restructuring of one of its largest corporate financial groups, Banco Espiritu Santo and its parent holding group. The most spectacular broad-scale banking failures were in Iceland (not a eurozone member); Ireland because of a massive real estate bust; Cyprus late in the crisis; and Spain (which was forced to provide large-scale capital to its banks also largely because of a real estate bust). The bailouts for Iceland, Ireland, and Cyprus and the support to the Spanish banks are discussed in chapter 21, along with a broader discussion of bailouts to Greece and Portugal.

Sovereign Indebtedness and the Rescue of the Banks

During the initial crisis years 2008 and 2009, without a broader crisis mechanism in the eurozone and without the ECB playing the role of lender of last resort, each of the eurozone countries was on its own to save its banks. During the annual meetings of the International Monetary Fund (IMF) and World Bank in Washington in October 2008, the G-7 countries pledged to do whatever was necessary to save systemically important financial institutions.[23] The Bank of England estimated that the initial costs of supporting these financial institutions as of mid- to late 2009 was, respectively, 18 percent of eurozone GDP, 73 percent of U.S. GDP, 74 percent of U.K. GDP, and globally 25 percent of world GDP.[24]

Saving these institutions in the eurozone countries was a double-edged sword. National banks in these countries already held large positions in the sovereign debt of their respective countries, and the countries had to substantially increase their indebtedness to save their banking systems. Through the bailout, contagion passed from the heavily indebted banking system to the individual countries and their sovereign debt, and back to the banks as the market discounted their holdings of sovereign bonds. Alan Blinder notes:

> The tight link between European banks and their governments opens up new lines of contagion. . . . Another line of contagion also opened in 2010 from

TABLE 20-2.   Total Bank Bailouts Approved, 2008–September 2012

Country	Billions of €	GDP (percent)
Britain	873	50.0
Germany	646	25.1
Spain	575	53.6
Ireland	571	365.2
France	371	18.6
Belgium	359	97.4
Netherlands	313	52.0
Sweden	162	41.8
Italy	130	8.2
Greece	129	59.9
Portugal	77	45.0
Latvia	9	46.0
Total European Union	5,086	40.3

Source: Jack Ewing, "In Germany, Little Appetite to Change Troubled Banks," *New York Times*, August 10, 2013, p. B3.

Greek government debt to its banks (which own a lot of Greek government bonds) and then to banks in other European countries (which have important counterparty relations to Greek banks) and from there to the whole world financial system. The contagion goes the other way, too. In 2012 a European bailout of Spanish banks cast further doubt on Spanish sovereign debt because it initially took the form of new loans to the Spanish government.[25]

Bank bailouts in the eurozone and in the European Union were very large in absolute amounts and as a percentage of individual countries' GDP (see table 20-2).

Continuing Capital Support for the Banks

It was clear in 2011 following the individual country bailouts that eurozone banks needed ongoing support. The *Financial Times* observed, "Whatever mechanism European politicians come up with for the forced re-capitalization of the continent's banks it will need to be sizable. If analysts are right, Euros 200 billion or more will be needed to boost banks' capital reserves." The article goes on to say that J. P. Morgan analysts projected the banks' capital needs at €150 billion, and as much as €230 billion under more bearish conditions. Nomura analysts projected a €200 billion shortfall; and Morgan Stanley a €190 billion capital shortfall. For specific distressed countries analysts were assuming a 60 percent haircut for Greek debt, 40 percent for

Portugal, and 20 percent each for Italy and Spain. The concern was that markets would close to some banks and distressed sovereigns, and Europe would find itself in an enormous credit crunch. In fact, the interbank market had largely closed.[26]

The other major concern was a Greek default with unknown consequences. With a eurozone fund mechanism, the European Financial Stability Facility, lacking adequate powers to resolve the banking problem, European finance ministers sought a concerted effort by each country acting on its own. Olli Rehn, EU finance minister, was quoted in the *Financial Times* as follows: "Capital positions of European banks must be reinforced to provide additional safety margins and thus reduce uncertainty. . . . This should be regarded as an integral part of the EU's comprehensive strategy to restore confidence and overcome the crisis."[27] Also reacting to the possibility of a Greek default and its potential spillover effects to other distressed sovereign debtors, Chancellor Angela Merkel of Germany backed aid for European banks in dire need in consultation with European Commission President José Manuel Barroso. In support of this view, the IMF reported that banks in the region faced potential losses of $300 billion due to their holdings of distressed country debt.[28]

Stress Testing the Banks

Even as late as 2014 a stress test of the capital and capital adequacy ratio of the eurozone banks made it clear that the Italian banks in general and some specific banks in Italy in particular were undercapitalized and had not adequately addressed their writeoffs of NPLs. The recapitalization requirements of individual Italian banks such as Monte dei Paschi di Siena were estimated at over €4 billion. Italian banks also had the largest adjustment to make with respect to NPLs to risk-weighted assets; at 12 percent of risk-weighted assets, as compared to just over 6 percent for German banks, 1 percent for Spanish banks, and less than 1 percent for Irish banks.[29]

Role of the ECB in the Banking Crisis

At its creation the European Central Bank was modeled after the Bundesbank, Germany's central bank, and located in Germany's financial capital, Frankfurt. Given Germany's experience with hyperinflation during the interwar years, Germany insisted that the primary mandate for the ECB was to control inflation within the eurozone. The ECB was specifically prohibited from participating in bailouts and as such could not serve as a lender of last resort to the sovereign states in difficulty in the eurozone. It was far from clear that it could even play that role for the banking system in the eurozone. In fact, Jean-Claude Trichet, the president of the bank, raised interest rates twice during the crisis, in April and July 2011.[30] He was opposed to a role for the ECB in bank restructuring. Nevertheless, the ECB had a large exposure to banks in the distressed economies: Irish banks €121 billion, Greek banks €95 billion, Portuguese banks €50 billion, Spanish banks €68 billion, and Italian banks €32 billion as of the end of 2010.[31]

The approach of the next ECB president, Mario Draghi, who was appointed on November 1, 2011, was very different. Draghi was quoted in a speech delivered in London on July 26, 2012, as saying, "Within our mandate, the ECB is ready to do whatever it takes to preserve the Euro. And believe me it will be enough."[32] That gave a great boost of confidence to financial markets. He followed up his words with decisive action.[33] The ECB cut its benchmark interest rate two months in a row. It also injected some €1 trillion into the European banking system, in two tranches, in the form of three-year loans, known as longer-term refinancing operations (LTROs), to avert a liquidity crisis; some €700 million needed to be refinanced by eurozone banks in 2012.[34] Most of this capital was redeposited into the ECB by the banks but served as a hedge in the event the banks were unable to meet their short-term liquidity needs.[35] On another issue, however, Draghi dashed market expectations when he refused to assist in direct support for eurozone countries in distress by buying their bonds. Doing so was clearly outside the mandate of the ECB, and Draghi indicated that the problem was for eurozone politicians to address.[36]

While markets applauded and the banking sector praised Draghi's intervention to contain the banking crisis, highly conservative German members of the ECB council from the Bundesbank, and the president of the Bundesbank, Jens Weidmann, warned in a letter that was leaked of the dangers of ECB support for the eurozone banks. This was followed by a statement from Jürgen Stark, a German and a former ECB executive board member, on the shocking quality of the ECB's portfolio. Draghi objected to the Bundesbank's airing of its concerns in public and noted that the Bundesbank had not objected when the LTROs were proposed. Draghi also objected strongly to the possibility of disturbing the consensus that had been achieved on taking aggressive action to contain the immediate crisis. He called the LTROs an overwhelming success.[37]

Crisis Resolution Measures Proposed and Taken

After months of stalling that left them behind the crisis curve repeatedly, policymakers from the eurozone countries agreed to a series of crisis intervention measures.

The first measure was the Greek restructuring and continued bailout (discussed in chapter 21). The second measure was to augment the capital of the other

European banks to cover their potential losses on sovereign loans. The third measure was to augment the capital of the European Financial Stability Facility (EFSF). To support crisis resolution, eurozone governments set up an emergency liquidity fund, the EFSF, in an amount of some €440 billion, with some €200–250 billion pledged to support the initial workouts in Greece, Ireland, and Portugal. There was some €250 billion left to "ring-fence" other exposed countries such as Spain and Italy, an amount that was completely inadequate given the size of the Spanish and Italian economies, the Spanish banking problems, and Italy's sovereign indebtedness and banking problems. No second or third bailout for Greece was contemplated or discussed at that time.

Markets quickly recognized that the fund was inadequate to deal with the problems of Spain and Italy should the crisis spread. Before the seventeen eurozone countries could even approve the initial fund, member governments were forced back to the drawing board to approve a larger fund. How the fund would work and what its powers would be remained to be defined.[38] But Germany strongly resisted a French proposal to have the fund leverage itself by borrowing from the ECB. Another proposal by European Commission President Barroso suggested that Eurobonds be floated, backed, or cross guaranteed by the eurozone countries. This idea was also quickly rejected by the Germans and others. These two potential solutions—to have the ECB act as an effective lender of last resort and to issue Eurobonds—were ways to resolve liquidity issues in fighting the crisis and would have assured markets that a crisis solution was in hand.

The eurozone governments agreed to augment the EFSF to as much as €1.0 trillion, or approximately $1.3 trillion. They wanted the fund to be large enough that it did not have to be called on. Since the eurozone governments did not want to put up more funds for the facility, the idea was to attract sovereign wealth funds or wealthy governments such as China. The fund would serve as a partial risk guarantee facility—for example, guaranteeing a first loss on Italian or Spanish bonds of 20 percent. But at the end of 2011 the risks were perceived as real, so the market seemed to be looking to a 30 percent first risk guarantee that would potentially push the fund size up.[39]

At the G-20 conference on November 4, 2011, the non-eurozone countries politely told the eurozone countries to dig deeper into their own resources. Another idea floated at the G-20 summit was to have the IMF augment the European stability fund. There was strong resistance from non-European countries, and even from the U.K., to allowing the IMF to place its funds directly into the stability facility. The Obama administration resisted expansion of the IMF's capital because of the U.S.'s own financial situation and assuredly strong resistance from a Republican-controlled House of Representatives in an election year.[40] In my view, placing IMF resources at the disposal of an emergency fund would have created a poorly conceived precedent and was simply not in the cards. The German government resisted enhancing the EFSF from eurozone member resources, as Germany would have been the largest payer. The eurozone left open the risk that it would not be able to ring-fence a speculative attack against Italy or Spain or both should one occur.[41]

The Eurozone's Continuing Economic Problems

The European economies were deeply affected when their real estate and sovereign bubbles burst. The Great Recession had clearly arrived. Between the third quarter of 2008 and the first quarter of 2009, GDP fell sharply in all of the major advanced economies: 6.4 percent in France, 7 percent in the U.K., 7.1 percent in the United States, 10.2 percent in Italy, 11.7 percent in Germany, and 13.8 percent in Japan.[42] In the second quarter of 2009 the world economy began to turn around, particularly the U.S. economy, and avoided the more extended downturn of the Great Depression. But the recession was far from over in the eurozone as it turned out. Blinder writes:

> When the housing and bond bubbles burst, recession quickly descended upon Europe, just as it had here [in the United States]. And if homegrown real estate and bond bubbles were not enough, virulent infection from the United States after Lehman Day sealed the deal. Virtually every nation in Europe experienced a slump; some were devastatingly long and deep. Greece, Ireland and Iceland spring to mind as particular horror stories, with the UK and Spain also hard hit. Even mighty Germany, a stable and conservative country, that had no real estate bubble, saw its GDP contract 6.8 percent between 2008:1 and 2009:1. That is substantially larger than the 4.7 percent contraction in the United States—and we're the ones that started the mess.[43]

Following the initial crisis shock and the 2010–11 sovereign crises, the eurozone headed back into recession. The European Union downgraded what were already anemic growth forecasts for the eurozone, predicting just 0.5 percent growth in 2012. Earlier projections were for 1.8 percent growth. All seventeen countries in the eurozone bloc had their growth prospects downgraded. Interestingly, the projections for the core countries, the stronger economies, downgraded most severely: Germany from 1.9 to 0.8 percent, France from 2 to 0.6 percent, and the Netherlands from 1.7 to 0.5 percent. The EC did not rule out a recession in 2012.[44] (See tables 20-3 and 20-4.)

TABLE 20-3. Macroeconomic Data, Advanced Economies, 2011–12

Percent of GDP unless otherwise noted

Country	Trade balance 12 months (billions of $)	Current account 2011	Budget balance 2011	Budget balance 2012[a]
United States	($707)	−3.3	−9.1	−8.0
Japan	32	2.4	−8.3	−10.2
China	175	4.0	−1.8	−2.0
Britain	(160)	−2.0	−8.8	−4.4
Euro area	(33)	−0.5	−4.2	−3.4
France	(93)	−2.5	−5.8	−4.8
Germany	194	5.1	−1.7	−70.0
Greece	(37)	−8.2	−10.0	n.a.[b]
Italy	(49)	−3.7	−3.7	−2.8
Spain	(65)	−4.4	−6.5	−6.8

Source: The Economist, October, 8, 2011.

a. International Monetary Fund, Global Financial Stability Report (Washington, January 2012).

b. Not available.

TABLE 20-4. Data on Public Debt, Advanced Economies, 2011–12

Percent of 2011 GDP

Country	Gross govt. debt	Net govt. debt	Financing need in 2012	Financing need in 2013	External funding
United States	100	73	30	29	30
Japan	233	131	59	54	15
China	n.a.[b]	n.a.	n.a.	n.a.	n.a.
Britain	81	74	15	13	19
France	87	81	21	20	50
Germany	83	57	11	8	41
Greece[a]	166	n.a.	17	15	91
Italy	121	100	24	19	51
Spain	67	56	21	19	28
Ireland	109	99	14	15	61

Source: International Monetary Fund, Global Financial Stability Report (Washington, September 2011).

a. Greece assumes debt reduction is completed.

b. Not available.

Austerity pushed the eurozone into a debt deflation trap that it found itself unable to easily escape. There was also a crisis of both investor and consumer confidence, and in that the twin crises in the United States and the eurozone had much in common. A longer-term problem for several of the eurozone countries was how they would address their lack of competitiveness. Their inability to devalue their currency exacerbated their competitiveness problems.

With many of the European countries adopting austerity measures, several of the eurozone members remained in recession over the seven years from 2009 to 2015, as did the eurozone as a whole. A prolonged recession with accompanying low inflation hovering at deflationary levels did great damage to the European economy and to its population, above all the system of social protection. Unemployment remained high in the euro area at 10–11 percent throughout the crisis, and higher in several European countries. Unemployment in Ireland reached 14 percent, in Spain 25 percent, and in Greece more than 20 percent at the beginning of 2012. Most dramatically, youth unemployment remained over 50 percent for much of the crisis in Spain. We know from experience that unemployment and underemployment always add up to a larger number than official unemployment numbers; a major exception might be Spain, where rigid labor laws made contract employment the norm. There were violent protests and work stoppages in Greece when austerity measures were adopted and welfare support was reduced. If the major outcome in the United States was the increase in inequality, the concern of many Europeans was excessive liberalization of highly protective labor laws and the weakening of what had been a very strong social safety net.

In effect, a two-tier eurozone emerged, and the divergence continued to grow. The peripheral or southern countries—Greece, Portugal, Spain, and Italy plus Ireland—constituted one tier, and countries such as Germany, France, the Netherlands, and Austria were in the second. France's economy was on the border between the two and performed poorly, with unemployment over 10 percent. Many analysts held the view that Europe, like Japan over the previous two decades, would fall into a period of prolonged deflation and fail to grow. By the first quarter of 2016, however, the eurozone appeared to be emerging from the crisis, albeit from a low base, and growth was projected at 1.5 percent for 2016. Some of the crisis countries, such as Spain and Ireland, seemed to be growing strongly. Nevertheless, unemployment remained high in the region—20.5 percent in Spain (though youth unemployment was still 45 percent), 24 percent in Greece, 11.5 percent in Italy, and 10.3 percent in the euro area. Inflation remained very low at near zero.[45] No longer-term solutions have been adopted to fix the fundamental flaws in the euro.

Eurozone Crisis Politics

The eurozone operates under the same principles as the EU. All decisions have to be made unanimously, which inevitably slows the pace of decisionmaking to a crawl and results in kicking the can down the road when it comes to solving problems.

Sclerosis in Decisionmaking Deepens the Crisis

Crisis decisions were being made by finance ministers and often even prime ministers meeting in a series of crisis summits.[46] This process created inevitable delays at a time when decisions needed to be made quickly. The great flaw in the eurozone's approach to resolving the crisis, beyond its basic structural flaws, was its lack of an institutional mechanism to deal with a crisis in a member country or a systemic crisis in several countries across the region. Crisis resolution requires strong leadership, the institutional capacity to make good policy decisions, a mandate from the political leaders, adequate financial resources from a lender of last resort, as well as speed, agility, and decisiveness to provide confidence to markets. The U.S. crisis resolution effort had all of that, especially after the failure of Lehman Brothers. The U.K. also had this capacity. Korea, an emerging market economy that had not experienced an economic downturn in twenty years, also had the capacity and the will to make the necessary policy decisions to address its crisis in the period 1997–99. The eurozone possessed almost none of the essential ingredients. The troika of the ECB, the EC, and the IMF tried to serve as a substitute for such capacity, but it had little political backing or clout. Their contributions were primarily technocratic mechanisms for overseeing the bailouts and bailout conditionality. In the end, Chancellor Merkel was the go-to person during the crisis, and she maintained a steady opposition to large fiscal support measures from the eurozone members acting in concert and instead focused on austerity measures. Paul Krugman notes: "The inherent problem of the euro has been aggravated by bad policy. European leaders insisted and continue to insist, in the teeth of the evidence, that the crisis is all about fiscal irresponsibility, and have imposed savage austerity that makes a terrible situation worse."[47]

Smaller countries such as Finland were able to hold up the Greek bailout by demanding collateral for their funds, and when the Greeks agreed, Austria and the Netherlands piled on, which led to another round of extended negotiations. The same occurred with the bailout facility when the Slovaks held up approval of the facility after realizing how much they would need to contribute. Merkel and Nicolas Sarkozy, president of France, clearly led the process, but their own disagreements and the differing views of the governors of the ECB also caused delays.

The crisis and political process of approving the crisis resolution measures and austerity plans led to several changes of government in Portugal, Spain, Greece, and Italy, and eventually in France in 2012. The move to technocrat-led governments in Greece and Italy seemed like a very good idea; with Lucas Papademos as prime minister of Greece and Mario Monti as prime minister of Italy, both were presumably governments of unity. But they were soon replaced by politicians and a new wave of political parties. The German parliament, the Bundestag, required Chancellor Merkel to come to parliament for approval of all crisis-related agreements, though she remained popular in Germany and was one of the few leaders to remain in power throughout the crisis. Parliament's demands were supported by rulings by Germany's constitutional court.[48]

Moreover, a public opinion poll found an increasing majority of Europeans in eurozone countries with the view that the euro was doing more harm than good.[49] In short, we could call this a crisis of confidence in the leadership of the eurozone. As the crisis progressed, political parties on both the right and the left—Syriza in Greece, Podemos in Spain, the National Front in France, and right-wing governments in Hungary and Poland, as well as a rising right-wing party in Austria, gained greater traction with the voters.[50] Several European leaders in alignment with the ECB began to resist Germany's insistence on austerity, but lacked the clout to effect a change in policy.[51]

Germany as the Leader of the Eurozone

As the largest economy in the eurozone, with large external trade surpluses and the only economy able to lead a collective financing effort and provide guarantees that the region would not experience a series of sovereign failures due to market contagion, Germany soon became the stand-alone leader of the eurozone. And in the effort to resolve the crisis, Chancellor Merkel became the most powerful leader in Europe. She resisted all efforts that would entangle Germany in collective solutions to the crisis and in further financial integration, such as a fiscal union or Eurobonds. Merkel in fact was constrained by Germany's Federal Constitutional Court, which ruled, based on complaints brought to the court against the European Stability Mechanism (ESM) and the European Fiscal Compact (EFC), that all such collective support measures on behalf of the eurozone would need to be approved by the German parliament and also be specifically quantified as to their budget impact up to a set limit. This effectively ruled out Eurobonds and collective bailouts without clearly defined limits to Germany's exposure.[52]

Merkel insisted that the peripheral countries would need to swallow "bitter medicine" and adopt austerity measures, just as Germany did after unification. Germany was against bailing out what many Germans regarded as the undisciplined and profligate Greeks, Spaniards, and Italians, forgetting how the United States had supported the reconstruction of Europe after World War II through the Marshall Plan. Germany also defaulted on both private market loans to the German banks and municipalities from New York and London and failed to pay reparations during the Great Depression.

George Soros noted in a series of articles in the *Financial Times* that even if the eurozone managed to escape a Greek exit or a banking collapse in one or more of the crisis countries, the lack of collective support would still leave the region in significant difficulty due to the split between debtors and creditors: "The euro crisis had its origin in German Chancellor Angela Merkel's decision, taken in the aftermath of the Lehman Brothers default in September 2008, that the guarantee against further defaults should come not from the European Union, but from each country separately. And it was Germany's procrastination that aggravated the Greek crisis and caused the contagion that turned into an existential crisis in Europe."[53] Later he wrote:

> Even if a fatal accident can be avoided, the division between creditor and debtor will be reinforced and the "periphery" countries will have no chance to regain competitiveness because the playing field is tilted against them. This may serve Germany's narrow self-interest but it will create a very different Europe from the open society that fired people's imaginations. It will make Germany the centre of an empire and put the periphery into a permanently subordinated position. That is not what Mrs. Merkel or the majority of Germans stand for.[54]

Martin Wolf, reinforcing Soros's view, notes:

> Germany wants to minimize the financing and continue to run huge external surpluses. This cannot work. Some will argue that Germany adjusted into surplus in the 2000s. Why can't its partners do so now? Germany moved into surplus with partners who willingly ran deficits. But Germany does not want to run deficits. Given that its partners cannot run surpluses, unless they do so with the world, this would be possible only with a huge weakening of the Euro or depression in weaker countries. The latter would ensure waves of sovereign and bank defaults and the end of the eurozone. Such one-sided adjustment will surely fail.[55]

The Euro Falls Apart

There was increasing sentiment in Europe that Greece might have to leave or would be better off out of the eurozone, the so-called Grexit option. There was also growing sentiment in Europe against the euro. If Germans did not have the history of the Weimar Republic and all that followed thereafter, I believe they would have been tempted to pull out of the euro and readopt the deutsche mark and the Bundesbank in a heartbeat. Many astute analysts believed there was a real possibility that the euro would fall apart. But in the short term, such an event would be very messy and would initially have had an adverse impact on Europe's economies, as well as Europe's and the world's capital markets. Politically it would have severely damaged the case for European integration.

In the long term, dissolving the eurozone might be a good thing unless the eurozone undertakes significant reforms such as moving toward a banking union, a fiscal union, and a common financial instrument, Eurobonds, guaranteed jointly and severally by the eurozone countries. These reforms would in principle move the euro toward both a reserve currency status, which is of major importance in world trade, and would deepen European financial markets, lessening country dependence on borrowing from their banks. The eurozone countries have in principle moved, albeit slowly, toward a banking union in which the ECB supervises systemically important banks.[56]

Martin Wolf of the *Financial Times* writes, "Will the Euro survive? The leaders of Germany and France have now raised this question, for the cause of Greece. If policymakers understood two decades ago what they understand now, they would never have launched the single currency. Only fear of the consequences of a breakup is now keeping it together. The question is whether that will be enough. I suspect the answer is, no."[57]

With the immediate debt crisis fading, the initial cries seemingly contained in the individual crisis countries, and the leaders of the eurozone apparently determined to remain in the eurozone, the presidents of the various European political institutions (the European Council, the European Commission, the Eurogroup, and the ECB) were asked by the European Council to provide unified policy recommendations for resolving the structural deficiencies in the eurozone. They proposed four measures, known as the four unions: (i) a fiscal union; (ii) a banking union; (iii) an economic union; and a (iv) political union.[58] To date, only the banking union has gained any traction, and even that has progressed slowly now that the immediate crisis has faded from sight. On this topic, Kemal Derviş and Jacques Mistral write:

The fading away of the acute debt crisis and the welcome signs of recovery in the eurozone do not imply the path ahead is clear of dangers or that the deeper issues surrounding the successful functioning of the monetary union have been resolved—far from it. Europe and the eurozone are going through an "existential" crisis with huge social problems in the southern countries, a steep decline in public support for the European institutions, and difficult unanswered questions as to how the wider EU can relate to the smaller eurozone.[59]

Stiglitz, a strong critic of the euro and the eurozone as structured, accepts that there would be great costs to the Eurogroup (the member countries of the eurozone), the EU, and the world economy were the euro to fail. He also believes that the current situation is untenable and will lead to years of low growth and potentially more crises in the eurozone. His major criticism is that the economic integration moved ahead of the will for political integration. He suggests that there are three possible ways forward: (i) continue kicking the can down the road and do little to reform the system—the current path; (ii) adopt a flexible euro; or (iii) divorce (break up) at great cost. For example, Germany or the northern-tier countries might leave or set up their own fiscal union to resolve the great divergences among the eurozone economies. Stiglitz observes: "Three messages emerge clearly from my analysis. A common currency is threatening the future of Europe. Muddling through will not work. And the European project is too important to be sacrificed on the cross of the euro. Europe—the world—deserves better. I have shown that there are alternatives to the current system."[60]

With the rise of populist and nationalist parties in Europe; the resignation of Prime Minister Renzi of Italy; the 2017 elections in the Netherlands, France, Germany, and Austria; the turn right in Hungary, Poland, and Austria; Brexit; the pressures created by immigration from the Middle East and Africa into Europe; and pressures on the EU from Russia and Turkey, as examples, there appears to be little will to move forward on the necessary political and economic reforms that would potentially make the euro and the eurozone viable for the long term. Muddling through appears to be the only alternative for the moment. That reality seems to portend low growth, high sovereign debt, and a need to resolve problems in the banking systems in several eurozone countries. It also leaves the eurozone vulnerable to the next crisis.

TWENTY-ONE

The Eurozone Crisis

From Banking Crises to Sovereign Debt Crises to Bailouts

Between 2008 and 2015 a series of European sovereign crises emerged—in Greece, Portugal, Ireland, the United Kingdom, and Iceland (the latter two are non-eurozone countries) between 2009 and 2011, in Spain and Cyprus in 2012 and 2013, respectively. Most of these began as a banking crisis that morphed into an economic crisis and in some cases a sovereign debt crisis. In Ireland, Spain, and Great Britain (the latter to a lesser extent), the immediate trigger or spark for the crises was a real estate bust. George Soros commented on the crisis as follows: "The 'euro crisis' is generally seen as a currency crisis, but it is also a sovereign debt and, even more, a banking crisis. The situation is complex. The complexity has bred confusion, and this has political consequences. Europe's various member states have formed widely different views and their policies reflect their views rather than their national interests. The clash of perceptions carries the seeds of serious political conflict."[1]

The brief discussions of the crises that follow clearly illustrate Soros's views, including those that happened outside the eurozone.

Iceland

In 2008 Iceland was the first of the European countries to enter into a deep financial/currency crisis that then morphed into a deep economic and eventually an external sovereign debt crisis. The trigger was the collapse of Lehman Brothers in September 2008, which brought to an abrupt end the large-scale capital flows, entirely out of proportion to the size of its economy or financial system to handle, that had entered Iceland during the years leading up to the crisis. As a small single-currency economy, Iceland lacked the capacity to resolve its own crisis. Like the emerging market countries discussed in Part III of this book and the eurozone countries discussed in this chapter, Iceland had to be rescued or bailed out by the International Monetary Fund (IMF) and the Nordic countries serving as lenders of last resort.

Collapse of the Currency and the Banking System

In the dramatic financial/currency crisis that began in 2008 the Icelandic krona (ISK) collapsed, and so did the banking system. The crisis led to the collapse of the asset bubble in housing and in the stock market, high unemployment, and a collapse in consumer spending. As the smallest single-currency area in the world, Iceland's central bank was unable to print money and act as a lender of last resort. As such, Iceland's crisis embodied many of the features of the U.S. and eurozone crises, although unlike the eurozone countries in crisis, the ISK's sharp devaluation allowed the country to compress imports and increase exports and emerge from the crisis relatively quickly, albeit with an extremely high ratio of gross debt to GDP. Iceland required IMF support and also that of several of the Nordic countries, the European Union, and Poland to resolve its crisis.[2]

The road to the crisis began with the collapse of the cod stocks and the decision of the Icelandic government to undertake a series of "Thatcherite" reforms, including liberalization of the economy and structural adjustment measures such as privatization of the banking system. They undertook them in this order: (i) in 1991 the government lowered the corporate income tax to 15 percent, the tax on financial income to 10 percent, and the personal income tax to 35 percent; (ii) in 1993 it sold state assets, including the banks; (iii) also in 1993 Iceland became an associate member of the European Common Market (with Norway) through the European Economic Area (EEA) Treaty allowing for free flow of goods, labor, services, and capital; and (iv) in 1994 the capital account was opened. These reforms brought with them upgrades by the rating agencies, and in 2002 Moody's rated Iceland AAA. Iceland's banks were in turn able to borrow and attract massive deposits from abroad relative to the initial capital base of the three largest banks.[3]

The banks were state owned until 1993. In virtually all countries state ownership leads to politically directed and subsidized credits and often corruption. Iceland was no exception. In this case, loans were subsidized or soft credits directed to the fishing industry and agriculture. Leading politicians also benefited from board positions and their ability to arrange connected lending. Privatization apparently lacked transparency, and sales were made to insiders with little or no prior banking experience. With weak financial supervision, the banks went on a borrowing and lending spree that increased banking leverage and assets from approximately 100 percent of GDP in 2000 to 1,000 percent of GDP by mid-2008, the highest level among the advanced economies. Average annual growth of bank assets in the period 2003–07 was 60 percent, also the highest level among the advanced economies. The explosion in lending led to asset bubbles similar to those experienced in Japan, Thailand, the United States, Spain, and the U.K.; Iceland's stock market rose 519 percent from January 2002 to July 2007, and housing prices increased 67 percent. These bubbles were fed by easy access to global liquidity and very low interest rates.[4]

During 2005 the three Icelandic banks issued €14 billion in foreign debt securities, a little over the size of Iceland's GDP that year. One of the banks, Landsbanki, created branches in the U.K. and the Netherlands offering high returns on deposits, and eventually attracted more than 150,000 depositors from the U.K. and the Netherlands, largely utilizing these offshore branches. As branches rather than subsidiaries of the bank, they were outside the supervisory purview of their host countries. From the end of the third quarter of 2006 until mid-2007 deposits in Landsbanki's foreign branches increased by €9 billion.

Once the liquidity crisis began in the United States and Europe in 2007, foreign depositors and short-term securitized funding became the main source of funding for the banks. This short-term funding was sensitive to market conditions and an eventual run. The banks raised equity to support their rapid growth by allowing their investors (owners) to borrow against their stock holdings, a dubious practice at best. There was a significant level of tied lending and investment between the banks and the investment holding groups of their owners. The three banks, representing 85 percent of banking assets in Iceland, financed ISK300 billion of their own shares by mid-2008, which a special investigation commission on the crisis termed "weak equity." Weak equity represented some 25 percent of the banks' core capital, and when cross lending was included approximately 70 percent of core capital.[5] The banking system was overleveraged, overextended, inadequately capitalized, inadequately

---

BOX 21-1.   Timeline of the Crisis in Iceland

- September 15, 2008: Lehman Brothers defaults, followed by a money market meltdown on both sides of the Atlantic.
- September 24: The U.S. Federal Reserve grants all Nordic countries, except Iceland, an overdraft facility. The Icelandic currency market collapses.
- September 28: The Icelandic government moves to intervene in Glitnir, one of Iceland's three major banks.
- September 29: The Icelandic government and the banks are downgraded, and a run begins on Landsbanki's Icesave Internet accounts.
- October 3: Landsbanki is drained of liquidity and a run begins on Kaupthing Edge Internet accounts.
- October 6: The Icelandic government passes an emergency law and the Financial Supervisory Agency (FSA) takes control of Landsbanki.
- October 7: The FSA takes control of Glitnir.

---

supervised, and subject to the crisis that arrived full force in 2008 when liquidity dried up (see Box 21-1).

When the banks collapsed in 2008 there was an inevitable significant reduction in the value of their assets. The commission investigating the financial crisis was of the opinion that the value of assets had begun to erode at least twelve months before the collapse, without disclosure or provisioning by the banks. The value of these assets was adjusted in November 2008 from IKR11,764 billion to IKR4,427 billion, a writedown of almost 60 percent. The GDP of Iceland for 2008 was IKR1,476 billion; so the banking writedown equaled five years of GDP, an astonishing statistic.[6]

The three major banks that the Financial Supervisory Agency (FSA) intervened in represented 85 percent of banking assets in Iceland. The nationalization of the banks continued in 2009 and 2010 with Straumur Investment Bank, the investment bank for Internet savings funds, and Spron, the largest savings bank, each nationalized in March 2009. Other smaller banks and savings funds were nationalized during the first half of 2010.[7]

Resolution of the banking crisis was complicated by international politics. First, the central bank of Iceland had not secured lines of credit with the U.S. Federal Reserve, the European Central Bank (ECB), or the Bank of England, and it lacked the capacity to resolve the crisis as a lender of last resort. Second, it clearly needed assistance from the IMF and G-7 or others. Third, the governments of the U.K. and the Netherlands held the Icelandic Republic responsible for making good on the losses of its depositors through Internet savings and branch deposits with the Icelandic banks. Though there were no deposit insurance or guarantees protecting these deposits, and the banks were private, in virtually all of the crises governments have moved to protect and guarantee the depositors, largely to prevent a run on the banks. Iceland had made it clear that it would meet its international obligations even though there were no guarantees; however, the Dutch and British governments were able to block IMF support for bank restructuring until there was clear agreement on restitution to the deposit holders in the U.K. and the Netherlands. Fourth, eventually a support package was put in place with the IMF at its center, as the international lender of last resort, with additional support from the Nordic countries, the EU, and the government of Poland.[8]

Economic Impact of the Crisis

The crisis started with a collapse of the ISK and a devaluation of almost 60 percent in early 2008. This was followed in turn by a decline in housing prices by 50 percent, a stock market crash of almost 100 percent, and the collapse of the banking system. By 2009 core inflation had risen to 19 percent and unemployment rose to just shy of 10 percent. There was a large contraction in consumption: −8 percent in 2008 and −15 percent in 2009. The decline in GDP was −9 percent in the first quarter of 2010. The crisis led to an enormous fiscal account turnaround, from a fiscal surplus in 2007 of +4 percent of GDP to a negative −13 percent of GDP in 2008. Gross debt increased from 30 percent of GDP in 2007 to 96 percent in 2009. The current account balance was −25 percent in 2006, −16 percent in 2007, and −14 percent in 2008. With the large devaluation, there was a sharp compression of imports and an expansion of exports as Icelandic products became more competitive; a substantial inflow of tourism brought hard currency with it, so by 2009 the current account balance was a positive 8 percent and Iceland was on the road to recovery.[9] As in the emerging market crisis countries but not the eurozone crisis countries, the currency crisis led to a large devaluation of the ISK, which supported a relatively quick recovery. Having no ability to affect monetary policy, the eurocurrency countries had no opportunity to recover quickly, and their prolonged crises led to low growth and near deflationary conditions from 2009 to 2015.

Policy Response to the Crisis

The government adopted a conventional monetary policy by moving interest rates to 18 percent and seeking to stabilize the currency; it also adopted a more unconventional policy of imposing capital controls to prevent capital flight. Chile imposed capital controls after its debt crisis in the early 1980s, and Malaysia did so during the East Asian crisis in late 1997 to much criticism internationally but eventual acknowledgment by the IMF and others that it had been a prudent thing to do. The ISK exchange rate stabilized and strengthened substantially against the euro from 2009 to 2010, and the credit default swap (CDS) spread declined from 1,600 basis points in September 2008 to 200 basis points in March 2010. The government also imposed expenditure cuts and increased taxes to reduce the fiscal deficit and to move Iceland to a sustainable debt path. By the first quarter of 2012 unemployment had fallen to 6 percent, and by the first quarter of 2013 to 5 percent, substantially better than the eurozone on average or the eurozone crisis countries more specifically. Inflation declined from 17 percent in the first quarter of 2009 to 2 percent in the first quarter of 2012.[10]

The government adopted an economic stabilization program as a condition for receiving IMF support. The government also applied to join the EU, which has its own conditions for accession. Iceland also cleaned up its banking system by setting up new banks (so-called good banks) with clean assets owned by the foreign creditors and "bad banks" with the written-down nonperforming loans (NPLs). By 2010 Iceland was on its way to recovery, with the weak currency supporting exports and growth.[11] Iceland was one of the top economic performers in Europe from 2010 to 2015. It has repaid its loans from the Nordic countries and Poland, as well as much of its IMF debt, while maintaining adequate reserves. Inflation and unemployment rates are low and its exchange rate is stable. Problems remain, specifically its debt hangover, though its external sovereign debt declined after 2010. Its crisis resolution process and recovery was successful; it more closely resembled the resolution process of the East Asian countries such as Korea and Malaysia than it did the policies and programs adopted by the eurozone countries in crisis. An IMF survey of Iceland published in March 2015 stated:

> Iceland's recovery can also be explained by sound policies. The quick restoration of the domestic banking system and early steps to facilitate domestic debt restructuring were important. Steady fiscal adjustment while preserving its Nordic welfare model, has made Iceland one of just a handful of European countries running a budget surplus. Central bank policies have helped steer inflation close to target, while capital controls provide breathing room to address remaining vulnerabilities.[12]

Greece

The first crisis in Greece started in October 2009 when the Greek Socialist Party won the general election and formed the government. In one of its first steps the government of Prime Minister George Papandreou restated, or corrected, the economic figures produced by its predecessor government led by the Conservative Party. The prime minister announced a very large public sector deficit of 10 percent of GDP; the markets had been anticipating 6–8 percent, and the European Union guidelines called for a maximum of 3 percent. Greece's debt was much higher than previously disclosed. In fact, the actual deficit turned out to be closer to 15 percent. Greece's government not only spent more than it could afford, but its revenue collection rate was among the lowest in the eurozone.[13] Tax evasion was a sport in Greece, for everyone from cash business operators in the service sector that supports Greece's important tourist industry to wealthy Greek shipping magnates. The rating agencies moved quickly to downgrade Greece's credit, and institutional investors began to unload Greece's government bonds.[14]

Because Greece relied so heavily on two export or foreign-exchange-earning industries, tourism and shipping, the worldwide recession hit Greece very hard. Between late 2008 and 2009 world trade largely collapsed, and many people affected by the crisis postponed vacations. Between the third quarter of 2008, when Lehman Brothers collapsed, and the end of 2010, real GDP in Greece contracted by 10 percent, and it continued to fall. By the end of 2011 it was some 16 percent below its 2008 peak.[15]

The investment world had considered the sovereign bonds of the advanced economies totally safe. Not since World War II had markets experienced a default by one of the advanced economies. The eurozone was viewed as safe because investors perceived that there was an implicit mutual guarantee in support of the euro and eurozone members, especially given the strength of its leading economy, Germany. Now that confidence had been shaken and the markets experienced greater volatility and widening spreads for the bonds of what were now viewed as the weaker economies in the eurozone: "The shock to confidence in eurozone financial markets was tremendous."[16] European leaders convened an emergency conference in May 2010 to address Greece's problem and to prevent a disorderly default by Greece and potential contagion to the rest of the eurozone. This conference was to be one of many on the topic convened during 2010 and 2011 and attended by its finance ministers and prime ministers. The eurozone had no bailout institution or mechanism, and its regulations specifically prohibited the ECB from participating in a bailout.

The Initial Greek Bailout

On April 23, 2010, Prime Minister Papandreou formally requested an international rescue (bailout) for Greece. On May 2, 2010, the Greek government and other eurozone leaders agreed to a €110 billion support package from the EU with additional support from the IMF; it was backed by parliamentary approval of a series of austerity measures and pension reforms, the latter a key condition of the EU and IMF. Austerity measures included a pension freeze, an increase in the value-added tax (VAT), increases in consumption taxes on fuel, cigarettes, and alcohol, and a cap on wages in state-owned companies. These measures were protested by work stoppages and violent protests.[17]

On October 27, 2011, investors in Greek bonds accepted a haircut consisting of €100 billion in debt reduction and a 50 percent "voluntary" reduction in Greek bonds held by private banks, hedge funds, and other investors (the final agreement ended up requiring a haircut that was closer to 77 percent), including Greece's own banks. The haircut in Greece resembled the haircut negotiated by Argentina in 2003 and again in 2010; but the Greek case threatened the other eurozone countries, above all those in the periphery. Austerity measures, improvements in the tax system, and structural measures such as bank restructuring and privatization of state-owned enterprises were overseen by the troika—the ECB, the EC, and the IMF. Since it took so long to carve out an acceptable deal for Greece, there was little movement on structural reforms that were meant to support economic recovery. For example, the original bailout plan called for Greece to generate some €50 billion from privatization over a three- to- five-year period. That target number steadily declined.[18] There was some sentiment, expressed openly by Chancellor Merkel of Germany and President Sarkozy of France, that Greece would have to leave the eurozone.

The Second Greek Bailout

The second bailout that was agreed to on February 21, 2012, avoided an uncontrolled default by Greece. The total support for Greece from eurozone countries and the IMF rose to €246 billion by 2016, 135 percent of GDP. The costs of the crisis to the Greek economy—with unemployment over 20 percent and sharp austerity measures biting into minimum wages and pension payouts—were very steep.[19]

On May 6, 2012, PASOK and New Democracy, two mainstream parties, took a beating in the election: the radical left-wing parties Syriza, KKE, and Dimar and the right-wing parties ANEL and XA won the election. No coalition emerged, and new elections were held on June 17, 2012. A coalition was formed with Antonio Samaras as the new prime minister.

The Third Greek Bailout

After considerable political turmoil and instability, on January 25, 2015, Syriza won a historic victory, and Syriza and the New Greeks formed a coalition government. The leader of Syriza was a young, aggressive, and inexperienced politician, Alexis Tsipras; he was named prime minister, and the even more aggressive Yanis Varoufakis was named his finance minister.[20] Their primary objective was to renegotiate the second bailout, which had been approved just two months before the election. They sought to renegotiate and substantially reduce both austerity conditionality and the level of debt that Greece was forced to service. This led to confrontation with other members of the eurozone, in particular Germany and its Finance Minister Wolfgang Schäuble, and to discussion of a Greek exit known popularly as Grexit: "This debate hit the mainstream media and was plastered all over the global press. The break-up of the Euro had moved from being an esoteric theoretical idea to being a topic of dinner room conversation across Europe and the world."[21]

Eventually, after much brinksmanship the Greek banks were closed on June 28, 2015, and opened only to allow pensioners to withdraw €120 a week. (This is reminiscent of the Argentine crisis and the so-called *corralito* when the banks were closed and only opened to allow limited withdrawals each week.) Greece also missed a payment to the IMF; it was not considered a default, but it was an event that rarely occurs in world financial circles. On July 20, 2015, the banks reopened and Greece paid back loans to the IMF and ECB. A referendum by Greece on the terms of the bailout—a revision to the terms of the second bailout—was agreed to by Greece and other eurozone countries; it provided an additional €86 billion in support over three years on July 13, 2015, though it still needed to be approved by all of the eurozone members and the Greek parliament. On August 14, 2015, the Greek parliament approved measures in support of a third bailout. Alan Blinder would note:

> Greece's difficulties went beyond mere arithmetic, however. Greece was a poor patient with unmanageable politics. A succession of Greek governments had made deals with its citizens that the state could no longer afford. Suddenly Greeks were asked to pay higher taxes, do without public services, earn lower wages, and live less well. And why? To placate foreign bondholders? It's no wonder Greeks protested vehemently and the government failed to deliver on its promises time and time again.[22]

Each of the bailouts simply postponed the inevitable and left Greece with sovereign debt of €323 billion, or 177 percent of GDP and the Greek economy in deep difficulty, with little possibility that it would be able to substantially reduce its sovereign debt, which is clearly unsustainable.[23] The unavoidable conclusion is that Greece will remain with a large debt overhang that will be written down to a more sustainable level, more than likely during the next crisis.

The assumption was that the Greek case was sui generis; that was clearly not the case.[24] The Greek case was not even sui generis to the Greeks, as Greece was in default on its sovereign debts for more than half of its early history as a modern republic, starting in the 1830s, during the Great Depression, and through World War II.[25] There was little reason to believe that Greece had the capacity or the will to service its sovereign debt after emerging from the eurozone crisis and the ill-conceived bailouts.

Eventually the IMF grew tired of supporting a program that was not viable, and the IMF and Greece began squabbling over what might constitute the terms of a fourth bailout, which presumably would include a large debt reduction. Under the proposed program, Greece was supposed to cut spending and raise taxes to the point where it maintains a primary surplus of 3.2 percent a year of GDP over the next ten or twenty or more years. The IMF realized that this has not been accomplished by any country emerging from a crisis and began, in June 2016, pushing Greece to adopt a realistic program. Greece, however, was pushing a program that did not impose a burden on its poor and lead to a debt writedown, with the view that in the future benchmarks and programs would come and go. The European Commission (read Germany), as part of the troika, wanted to achieve yet other objectives through the negotiations: to write down as little debt as possible, to get Greece to achieve the largest possible surpluses so the debt could be serviced, and also to protect the most vulnerable.[26] As Martin Wolf observes, "Greece was the Eurozone's Lehman. While the worst of the post-Lehman crisis was both severe and relatively brief, the aftermath of the Greek crisis was less severe and longer lasting. It triggered what turned out to be a long-running crisis, as fundamental weaknesses in the Eurozone's economies and institutional structure were laid bare."[27] Kemal Derviş and Jacques Mistral ask a fundamental question:

> How did the (mis)management of a crisis in a marginal economy, Greece (whose GDP is 2 percent of that of the eurozone), become a continental and then a global risk? . . . What made the Greek crisis so special is that Greece belongs to a monetary union. Greece cannot devalue its currency, and there was no Treasury in Brussels, no EU institution (like the IMF) in charge of dealing with a financial crisis.[28]

Ireland

The view that the eurocrisis was limited to Greece unraveled less than six months after the first Greek bailout, when other countries were viewed by the markets to be in difficulty.

The second wave of crises hit the region in late 2010 and hit Ireland the hardest. While other countries experienced housing/real estate bubbles, the Irish case was the most extreme. By 2011 the cumulative decline in housing prices had reached 50 percent. Banks were then hit as defaults rose steeply. Irish banks had also financed properties in the United Kingdom and the United States. When the global crisis emerged in 2008, the Irish government had acted boldly, perhaps far too boldly, and guaranteed all banking deposits and debts: "The Irish government guaranteed all of the money in the Irish banks on the morning of 30 September 2008—a decision that turned out to be ruinous for Irish taxpayers and the Irish economy, but also triggered interventions elsewhere."[29] Donal Donovan and Antoin Murphy, writing about the crisis, observe:

> Seldom in the economic and financial history of a country has one single action proved as controversial as the decision on the night of 29 September 2008 to provide a comprehensive government guarantee in respect of nearly all the financial liabilities of the domestic Irish banking system. This decision, despite receiving broad domestic support at the time, later came to represent for many the source of much of the enormous financial difficulties the State has faced in the four and a half years since that fateful night.[30]

The Irish Bailout

The total government guarantee in turn adversely affected the yields on Irish government bonds. The yields rose sharply in the last quarter of 2010 owing to the contingent liability of the government in favor of supporting the banking system. The projected cost of the bank bailouts was $571 billion, or 365 percent of GDP. In fact, guarantees were called near the end of 2010 and by early 2013 cost the government €64 billion ($83.20 billion at US$1.30 to the euro), or 40 percent of Irish GDP—not as large as the estimate but still a very big number. A bailout package was negotiated for Ireland and announced in November 2010. The bailout amounted to €68 billion in loans from the eurozone bailout fund and from the IMF; it was projected to cover Irish funding needs for a three-year period. The government of Ireland also received bilateral loans from the U.K., Sweden, and Denmark.[31] One analyst has observed that, "In practice, Ireland's rash actions turned a banking crisis into a sovereign debt crisis. Ireland's annual government deficit in 2010 was a shocking 32 percent of GDP, likely setting a modern day record."[32]

The Irish collapse was particularly shocking as Ireland used EU and eurozone entry to become an open economy. With English as its primary language, its proximity to London as a financial market, a low tax rate, a highly educated population, and its integration into Europe, Ireland began to attract direct foreign investment, mainly U.S. technology firms that set up their European headquarters and manufacturing facilities in Ireland. In January 1988 *The Economist* had termed Ireland the poorest of the rich, with GDP per capita at 64 percent of the European Community average. Ireland soon became the poster child for advertising the benefits of EU integration and support. By 1997 *The Economist* reported that Ireland was as prosperous as the European average and getting richer all the time.[33] Increasingly it was called the Celtic tiger, after the newly industrialized Asian tigers such as Hong Kong, Korea, Malaysia, and Indonesia. From 1994 to 2007, GDP growth ranged from 4.2 percent to 10.9 percent. Public (sovereign) debt was 109 percent of GDP in 1988, fell as low as 24.8 percent in 2007 just before the crisis, and reached over 100 percent again in 2011. In 2008 growth was a negative −3.0 percent and in 2009 a negative −7.0 percent, with unemployment reaching 14 percent; and net emigration, which had been considered over and done forever, picked up again on a sizable scale, a shocking reversal.[34]

The United Kingdom

Partially as a consequence of the Irish banking crisis and the decision of the Irish government to guarantee all of the liabilities of its banks, the U.K. government felt compelled to take action. On October 8, 2010, Chancellor of the Exchequer Alistair Darling and Prime Minister Gordon Brown announced a £500 billion rescue package for the banks, with up to £50 million for equity injections into the banks to increase their capital, an increase in the Bank of England's "special liquidity" scheme from £100 billion to £200 billion, and £250 billion in guarantees. The equity went to the Royal Bank of Scotland, the largest rescue (the government owned some 80 percent of the bank's equity), and to Lloyds Bank, where the government owned some 43 percent. The government gave the banks little choice but to accept ownership dilution and government ownership.[35] The United States took a similar position through the Troubled Asset Relief Program (TARP). Treasury Secretary Henry Paulson insisted that their major banks and investment banks (the latter converted to bank holding companies) accept government capital.

The economic crisis that followed the real estate and banking crisis, though as steep as that in several of the eurozone countries, with a large budgetary deficit and even a double dip recession, ended in the U.K. much before that of the eurozone countries. Also, there was no sovereign debt crisis; spreads and interest rates remained low. The usual explanation was that the U.K. had its own currency and could adjust to the crisis through its own monetary policy. The U.K. also had the Bank of England, which could operate as a true lender of last resort if required. In short, the U.K. had the institutional capacity, above all the human capital—highly experienced technocrats in the Treasury and the Bank of England as well as strong leadership from the chancellor of the Exchequer and the governor of the Bank of England—to address the crisis and was not restricted by the euro.[36]

Portugal

In May 2011, the markets turned to Portugal, which had suffered from low growth, poor fiscal performance, and high debts since the crisis emerged in 2008. Portugal, unlike Ireland or Spain, did not suffer from a housing/real estate bubble, but from low growth and a lack of competitiveness, in addition to its immediate fiscal and balance of payments problems.[37] The Portuguese economy depended on small and medium-sized businesses (SMEs) and tourism. When the crisis hit, many SMEs were unable to borrow from the banks and had lines of credit frozen or not renewed. As late as 2013, thousands of SMEs had defaulted on their bank debts and NPLs were continuing to rise in the Portuguese banking system. The banks and the government lacked the capacity to address SME defaults, and many defaults were ending up in the bankruptcy system and in subsequent liquidation.[38] Portugal also received bailout assistance from the European bailout facility and the IMF: €78 billion from Europe, €22.5 billion for three years from the IMF.[39] In 2014, with NPLs continuing to rise in the banking system and the failure of one of Portugal's largest corporate banking groups, Espiritu Santo International SA (the corporate holding company) and Espiritu Santo Financial Group, which owned one of the largest banks in Portugal, Banco Espirito Santo, Portugal experienced a secondary banking crisis that led to additional restructuring of its banking system but little change in addressing NPLs and liquidations of SMEs.[40]

The Role of the Troika

By now a pattern of assistance had emerged. The bailouts were provided by the European bailout fund and the IMF with payout tranches contingent on macroeconomic and structural reforms. The reform packages were overseen by the so-called troika of the European Commission (EC), the European Central Bank, and the International Monetary Fund. The conditionality set by the troika was similar to the approach taken by the IMF during the emerging market crises or similar to the conditionality set by the IMF when addressing balance of payments problems of developing countries. The unique aspect of the eurozone crisis was that—for the first time since the Bretton Woods institutions were established after World War II—the IMF was called on to systemically address the needs of advanced economies.[41]

Spain and Italy

In 2011, following the Portuguese bailout, the capital markets turned their attention to two much larger economies, Spain and Italy. Both fell into financial difficulty, and spreads on their bonds rose significantly.[42] Greece, Ireland, and Portugal were relatively small economies representing cumulatively just 5.7 percent of eurozone GDP, and they were readily accommodated by the eurozone's bailout facilities. That was not the case for Spain and Italy. Spain on its own represented some 10.8 percent and Italy 16.5 percent of eurozone GDP, and neither could be handled on a stand-alone basis by any of the support mechanisms contemplated by eurozone policymakers. That was particularly true because the ECB was still precluded from acting as a lender of last resort for any of the individual eurozone countries. Italy was a member of the G-7 and had the third largest public debt in the world at that time, after Japan and the United States.

Spain's Crisis

For a decade before the eurozone crisis, Spain was viewed as the ideal example of economic development and growth in the eurozone. Between 1997 and 2008, the Spanish economy grew on average at 2.5 percent per year, well over that for the euro area as a whole. Much of it was based on private consumption, with imports increasing from some 25 percent of GDP to 41 percent of GDP. During this period the current account moved from a small surplus to a deficit of 10.0 percent. The growth model was rapidly becoming unsustainable, but Spain was able to postpone adjustment because of its accession to the EU, its membership in the euro, and low interest rates. Spain attracted significant foreign direct investment and was able to borrow at spreads only slightly higher than German bonds.[43]

By 2007, Spain's economy was becoming increasingly susceptible to a crisis. The reasons included a high and unsustainable current account deficit, dependence on foreign financing, high levels of private debt, and diminishing competitiveness. The exposure of European banks to Spain was very large, the highest of the five major eurozone debtor countries except Italy, at $643.2 billion as of mid-2011, or some 46 percent of Spain's GDP.[44] Available financing and low interest rates led to an asset bubble in the housing sector. When the recession hit in 2008, a banking crisis ensued, with loans to nonfinancial companies and individuals at some 170 percent of GDP in 2008, and rapidly rising NPLs. The government stepped in to offset the adverse effects of the credit crunch, and as a result the public deficit remained high; and public debt, relatively modest at the start of the recession, rose rapidly. Total debt (household, corporate, financial institution, and public sector) was 342 percent of GDP in 2008. External debt (public and private) was 168 percent of GDP by 2008.[45] Spain also experienced serious deficits in its independent regions; Catalonia, with Barcelona at its center, had a serious budget shortfall that had to be covered by the federal budget.[46]

Spain experienced two recessions starting in 2009 with five consecutive years of negative growth by 2013. Unemployment averaged some 25 percent a year and youth unemployment some 50 percent a year. By 2013, public debt had risen rapidly from 37 percent of GDP to 93 percent of GDP.[47]

In the end Spain did not have to be bailed out, nor did it undergo surveillance by the troika. Spain did ask for and receive a loan of €100 billion to support its banks.[48] The total banking bailout was €575 billion, or 53.6 percent of GDP, among the highest in the European Union next to the bailouts of Ireland, Greece, and Belgium.[49]

By 2013, Spain was showing signs of emerging from the crisis. Still, it had a number of structural problems to be addressed in the longer term: (i) high chronic unemployment, especially youth unemployment, which was above 50 percent throughout the crisis; (ii) high public and private indebtedness; (iii) lack of competitiveness in several nontradable sectors; and (iv) an inefficient tax system, among other issues.[50]

The Italian Crisis

While most of the advanced economies grew strongly in the 1990s, Italy's economy did not, and it saw its competitiveness erode, as measured by total factor productivity and low GDP growth relative to its peers in the EU and the eurozone. In addition, since World War II, Italy has had chronically unstable governance, including frequent changes of government. As this chapter was being finalized, the Italian electorate defeated a referendum to streamline the Italian constitution, which would have made it easier to address structural reforms. As a result, Prime Minister Matteo Renzi resigned, leaving a struggling economy in limbo.[51]

The Great Recession exposed many of Italy's structural problems, and as such Italy experienced one of the slowest recoveries within the eurozone. Italy entered the recession with an aggregate debt of 100 percent of GDP. A contraction of −5.5 percent of GDP, and continued declines from 2008 to 2009 and from 2012 to 2013, led to a substantial increase in the debt-to-GDP ratio, which reached 130 percent of GDP in 2014. As in other eurozone countries, fiscal austerity appears to have extended the recession in Italy. Italy's growth rate remained sluggish. The low growth rate arises from a host of structural problems and a lack of competitiveness in important areas of the economy, specifically labor market efficiency, financial sector performance, and a decline in competitiveness among SMEs. Despite these problems, Italy, particularly northern Italy, retained a strong export base throughout the recession.[52]

Much of Italy's fiscal adjustment during the crisis focused on raising taxes on an already heavy tax burden rather than cutting expenditures. It is likely that the increases in taxation have led to lower demand and investment and increases in the unemployment rate. Italy's social protection expenditures remain among the highest in the EU. Pension reforms implemented in 2011 should have a favorable impact on GDP, but only in the medium term, starting in 2020.[53]

Italy's banking system has remained vulnerable. As of mid-2011 the exposure of European banks to Italy was $837.5 billion, 41 percent of Italy's GDP, the highest in the southern-tier or crisis countries.[54] Relatively little government capital went into bailing out the Italian banks: €162 billion, or just 8.1 percent of GDP, the lowest among the EU countries. Major Italian banks continue to be highly exposed, and at least one important bank fragile and its recapitalization unresolved. After the stress tests of the European banks, it was clear that Italian banks were undercapitalized and would require the largest adjustment relative to risk-weighted assets. Monte dei Paschi di Siena, an important regional bank, was estimated to require a capital injection of some €4 billion. The bank has remained fragile and a problem that the government may have to address sooner rather than later.[55]

The bond market seems to have shrugged off Italy's latest political crisis, but a financial/economic crisis in Italy could not be easily addressed by the eurozone's crisis mechanism without a greater commitment from Germany and without agreement to allow the ECB to play the traditional central bank role as a lender of last resort.

Cyprus

On May 15, 2013, a bailout package was arranged to rescue Cyprus's oversized banks, after a bitter debate on its terms. It was a difficult and at times chaotic bailout process that shut down the entire banking system for a week.[56] Cyprus's banks had been badly hit by the Greek crisis. In this case the bailout also involved a haircut for depositors, 100 percent for deposits over €100,000 in Laki Bank and 60 percent for deposits over €100,000 in the Bank of Cyprus. The haircut for depositors was the first of its kind in the region. It was well known that substantial flight capital had landed in Cyprus from Russia. The eurozone countries were determined to avoid using their scarce capital to support Russian oligarchs. The IMF provided €1 billion under its extended fund facility, with the rest coming from the European Stability Mechanism.[57]

The eurozone crisis was unprecedented in the advanced economies since the interwar debt crises triggered by the Great Depression, debts of succession, war debts, and reparations. Since the Marshall Plan assisted in restoring war-torn Europe after World War II, no advanced economy had required a bailout and support from a lender of last resort. The eurozone countries emerged from the crisis in 2016 and have continued to grow since then, albeit at a low level, with near deflationary levels of inflation and high levels of sovereign debt in several member countries. Institutional reforms such as the banking union, to potentially shelter the eurozone from the next crisis, have been partial at best. If in good times it is wise to prepare for crisis, the eurozone is simply not there yet.

TWENTY-TWO

Conclusion

Are We Prepared for the Next One?

In broad terms, the major conclusion derived from my analysis is that the defaults and restructurings resulting from the Great Recession of the early 2000s are not unique. Rather, debt crises are recurring; hence the title of this book: *In Good Times Prepare for Crisis.* Relatively few peripheral or developing states, and more recently emerging market countries, have been able to absorb high levels of external sovereign debt; therefore sovereign debt crises have occurred in repeating cycles, with debt service disruptions and defaults relatively common occurrences. In the recent crisis the advanced economies were deeply affected, starting with Japan in 1991 and moving on to the United States in 2007 and the eurozone in 2008–09. Moreover, in some cases a crisis in one country led to contagion in other countries, such as the East Asian crisis that began in 1997 in Thailand and moved rapidly to Korea, Indonesia, and Malaysia.

Crises have frequently been triggered by a mania or bubble and a subsequent collapse, such as a stock market crash or the bursting of a real estate bubble. Examples include the New York Stock Exchange crash in 1929, the bursting of the real estate and stock market bubbles in Japan in 1991, and the real estate crises in Thailand in 1997, in the United States in 2007 and in Ireland and Spain during the eurozone crisis.

Crises can be complex, and sovereign debt crises have often emerged from a sequence of crises, such as a currency crisis with a steep devaluation that leads to a financial or banking crisis, followed by an overall economic crisis, and finally to a sovereign debt crisis. The sequencing may differ, and not all crises are so complex. However, this complexity was present in several of the emerging market crises in the 1990s—Mexico, Indonesia, Turkey, and Argentina as examples. It was present as well in several eurozone countries—Greece, Ireland, Portugal, and Cyprus—as well as Iceland (not a eurozone member), all of which needed to be bailed out during the Great Recession.

Crisis resolution has often proven difficult for states to handle on their own. Crisis resolution requires an infrastructure of sorts: very strong leadership, qualified institutional capacity to make good policy decisions, a mandate from the political leadership, adequate financial resources from a lender of last resort, speed, agility and decisiveness in decisionmaking to address the crisis and to provide confidence to markets. The U.S. effort to resolve the recent crisis, the Great Recession, had all of that, especially after the failure of Lehman Brothers. The United Kingdom also had this capacity. Korea, an emerging market economy that had not experienced an economic downturn in twenty years, also had the capacity and the will, if not the experience, to make the necessary policy decisions to address its crisis, which began in late 1997 and was mostly resolved by the end of 1999. But some individual countries, such as Argentina and Greece, lacked the institutional capacity and the will to resolve their crises over the years.

Despite the sophistication and capacity of individual member states, the eurozone has offered almost none of the essential ingredients during the recent crisis. Its decisionmaking was slow because it relied on the leadership of the seventeen eurozone countries to make decisions collectively. Those leaders frequently postponed or delayed making crucial decisions. At the start of the crisis there were no institutional mechanisms and no eurozone funds to address it. The European Central Bank (ECB) was precluded by statute from acting as a lender of last resort, but in the end, under Mario Draghi, who was appointed governor in 2011, it was the one institution that performed well during the crisis. The troika of the European Commission, the ECB, and the International Monetary Fund (IMF) provided a second-best institutional approach to managing the crisis. Because the stability funds were inadequately capitalized, the eurozone sought capital from other sources—including China, the G-20, and the IMF—to top off their funds. This generally proved unsuccessful. Germany resisted collective solutions such as Eurobonds or a fiscal union. The reaction of German leaders to such initiatives was that Germany had joined a currency union and not a transfer union. Eurozone countries were initially on their own to recapitalize their banks and to deal with an economic and/or sovereign debt crisis. Policy decisions, such as the decision to focus on austerity to resolve the crisis, were inappropriate and inadequate.

Moreover, the structure of the eurozone as a currency union but not a fiscal union prevented the individual countries in distress from using monetary policy to support crisis resolution. In other crises, such as the East Asian crisis, devaluations allowed the countries to restore export competitiveness, compress imports, and return to growth relatively quickly. In contrast, the crisis in the eurozone countries has been prolonged.

Crisis resolution has invariably required a lender of last resort. The function of a central bank in a national economy is well defined as a lender of last resort to the banking system and to the financial system. Analysts such as Charles Kindleberger have stressed the importance of this function for the international financial system as well. In the nineteenth century the classically cited example is the role of the Bank of England and a consortium of banks in their support for Barings during the Argentine *cedula* (land-backed securities) crisis of 1890. This support also included a debt restructuring plan and a subsequent funding loan for the Argentine government.

During the interwar period, the Bank for International Settlements (BIS) was established in part to serve this function after the defaults during the Great Depression. However, the BIS's failure to supply timely support for Credit Anstalt contributed to the banking crisis in Austria and Germany and ultimately led to the standstill agreements. There was no effective international lender of last resort during the Great Depression, particularly as international economic cooperation deteriorated following the World Economic Conference of 1933.

The IMF has played an important role as a lender of last resort in most of the major crises since World War II. It has generally not played a role in the crises in the advanced economies such as the Japanese crisis and the crises in the Nordic countries in the early 1990s or in the U.S. crisis from 2008 to 2010. The major exception has been the eurozone crisis, where the IMF has formed part of a troika with the European Commission and the European Central Bank to provide both financial and technical assistance in the various bailouts.

During the 1980s debt crisis, debtors were required to reach agreement with the IMF as a prerequisite to entering into restructuring agreements with the syndicates of bank creditors. The lessons of the 1930s seemed to have been well learned: bridging loans were provided to countries such as Hungary, Yugoslavia, Mexico, and Argentina while the debt restructurings were being negotiated. The IMF's role was supported by the U.S. Treasury through the Baker and Brady Plans as the U.S. and European governments sought to preserve their large international banks, which were severely overcommitted to Eastern European, Latin American, and other develop-ing country debtors. Official restructurings through the Paris Club after World War II also required the IMF to provide its seal of approval on the debtors' economic program.

During the emerging market crises, starting with Mexico in 1994 and ending with Argentina in 2004, the IMF was effectively the international lender of last resort, supported by the World Bank, regional development banks, and, where appropriate, guarantees or credits from the G-7 countries. The idea was to make the support packages sufficiently large so that they were credible. G-7 funds were only to be drawn upon at penalty rates in the event of absolute need. IMF and World Bank support packages came with policy conditionalities that sought economic reforms. IMF and World Bank staff also provided advisory support in areas such as bank restructuring, corporate workouts, bankruptcy systems, and policy measures. Where in-country expertise was lacking technical assistance funding from these two insti-tutions convened worldwide experts to assist countries in crisis.

During the eurozone crisis the IMF was part of the troika that also included the ECB and European Commission, which assisted countries that were bailed out. This was the first time the IMF was called on to form part of an international lender of last resort for one of the advanced countries.

Debt service disruptions, or defaults on contractual debt service, have been fre-quent, and renegotiation or resolution of defaults has traditionally followed pre-scribed practices based on a case-by-case approach, with a debtor state restructuring with its creditors. Since the initial defaults in the nineteenth century, there has al-ways been a fine line between the sanctity of contracts, *pacta sunt servanda*, the basis of all contract law, and the vital interests of states under changing conditions, *clausula rebus sic stantibus*. In extreme crisis, states have seen fit to default. In the four crisis periods examined herein, analysts warned of the dangers of external loans for sovereign states. Keynes perhaps expressed it most clearly: "The investor has no remedy at all . . . none whatsoever against default. There is, on the part of most for-eign countries, a strong tendency to default on the occasions of wars, revolutions and whenever the expectation of further loans no longer exceeds in amount the interest payable on the old ones. Defaults are worldwide and frequent."[1]

Keynes, as well as other analysts such as Dragoslav Avramovic, spoke of the "will" of the debtor to repay its loans under adversity. The issue that comprehensive debt statistics cannot address is whether a sovereign debtor has the economic and political will to repay its loans. I would add to this the institutional capacity to work its way out of a crisis. Some countries, such as Greece, Turkey, Mexico, and Argentina, have often lacked the will to continue servicing their debts; and during their most recent crises Argentina (in 2001) and Greece (in 2009) lacked the institutional capacity to resolve their crises.

Debt restructurings following an initial crisis were generally recurring, and the debt overhang of one period often contributed to the crisis in the next period. My conclusion is that debt crises have normally been long-term problems that have not usually been resolved in any decisive way until a major event, such as war or the next crisis, has compelled a solution. Although relatively few repudiations have taken place, debtors have often failed to pay their external sovereign debts in full, and creditor losses have been substantial. Carmen Reinhart and Kenneth Rogoff write: "The problem is that crisis-prone countries, particularly serial defaulters, tend to overborrow in good times, leaving them vulnerable during the inevitable downturns. The pervasive view that 'this time is different' is precisely why this time usually is *not* different and why catastrophe eventually strikes again."[2]

Case-by-case negotiations between a debtor and its creditors have remained the customary way to resolve defaults. Despite the prevailing practice in international law that states will no longer intervene directly on behalf of their citizens or financial institutions as private creditors, creditor states and their financial institutions do not remain powerless against long-standing defaults or repudiation. Most of the numerous defaults during the nineteenth century, the interwar period, and the most recent debt crisis have been resolved through case-by-case negotiations between a sovereign debtor and its creditors. For the most part, debtors in default have been denied access to credit markets until they composed their debts, a practice still in effect in the international bond markets. Argentina, for example, was only allowed access to the international bond market in 2016, after it settled its debts with a small minority group of dissident creditors, some thirteen years after the initial settlement proposal.

The Bolshevik debt repudiation in the interwar period led to a denial of loans to Russia during that era and after World War II on both economic and ideological grounds. During the post–World War II period, prolonged defaults by states such as Cuba, Vietnam, and Nicaragua—defaults that were ideologically as well as economically based—left these states largely cut off from major credit markets, as well as from loans from multilateral sources such as the IMF and the World Bank.

The willingness to extend additional credit as part of the renegotiation or restructuring of external sovereign debt has proved the most effective way of terminating the debt service disruption by sovereign debtors. During the Great Depression, when the capital markets failed to open, the process of negotiation ultimately broke down. During the 1980s sovereign debt crises, the provision of involuntary lending by commercial banks under the auspices of the Brady Plan was an essential feature of restructuring efforts.

Despite the existence of a variety of ways to prolong debt service moratoriums, most sovereign debtors have perceived that it is in their self-interest to negotiate.

There remain serious weaknesses in the case-by-case approach to negotiating a resolution and restructuring debts in default. The weakness inherent in the present system of debt restructuring is that it is normally a protracted solution that fails to address underlying economic issues. It often results in a large "overhang" of external sovereign debt that is subject to disruption in the next economic or political crisis. The appeal of one-time solutions to the sovereign debt problem suggested by many analysts during the 1980s crisis was very strong. However, the external sovereign debt requirements of many advanced and developing countries is a continuous theme. Capital, if unregulated or unconstrained, will always flow to perceived areas of economic opportunity or high return. No comprehensive solution has adequately addressed the issue of moral hazard. There is, at present, no global central bank or monetary institution to monitor the appropriateness of global credit levels or potential asset bubbles; nor is it certain that this approach would be effective, largely because creditors would likely resist. There is also no one institution that is charged with restructuring debts due to a default. The problem of external sovereign debt has to be viewed, therefore, as a historical continuum, with debt service disruption and renegotiation leading to debt restructuring as an essential feature. The major exception has been the HIPC (Heavily Indebted Poor Countries) Initiative in which the World Bank and IMF partially forgive the debts of some of the poorest debtor countries in Africa and elsewhere if the debtor adopts an economic reform program acceptable to these institutions. But this debt forgiveness has been primarily on debt due to official multilateral agencies and not to private market lenders from the capital markets or international banks.

Even though the manner in which defaults are resolved remains consistent from crisis to crisis, the institutional arrangements for debt negotiations have varied greatly. During the nineteenth century, individual country committees were established to represent bond holders in each of the creditor countries for each of the debtor countries in default. These creditor committees cooperated with one another in renegotiating defaults. During the interwar years, commissions were established to deal with war debts, reparations, debts of succession, the League of Nations Loans, and private market loans. After World War II, defaults on trade loans guaranteed by bilateral export credit and insurance agencies were renegotiated through the Paris Club, with the IMF certifying the debtor's economic program. The resolution of the 1980s debt crisis through frequent debt reschedulings and restructurings between a sovereign debtor and its banks, at times hundreds of banks, was under the auspices of the London Club and committees of leading bankers to an individual country; again the country's economic program was certified by the IMF. Finally, in the recent eurozone crisis, the troika negotiated the workout, which needed the approval of all seventeen eurozone countries, less the debtor. Despite the difference in institutional mechanism, the principle remained the same—debts in default were negotiated on a case-by-case basis between the debtor and its creditors.

As such, there is always an overriding international issue in cases involving a sovereign debtor and its creditors: the fine line between the sanctity of contracts, *pacta sunt servanda*, and the vital interests of states under changing conditions, *clausula rebus sic stantibus*. In extreme cases where debt service is perceived as a threat to a state's political, social, or economic existence, it is in the state's clear self-interest to default. Thus generally accepted practices for reaching an agreement on the resumption of debt service once disruption has occurred are needed.

The impact of crises on the populations of the crisis countries is often deep and extends well beyond the crisis itself. High unemployment and rising levels of poverty in the United States and throughout much of the world during the Great Depression have been well documented.

During the Argentine crisis, with the banking system in deep distress, the government imposed the *corralito* (a corral, or ring-fence) on bank depositors to prevent bank runs. The *corralito* allowed individuals to withdraw only a particular amount each day to cover day-to-day living expenses. I vividly remember walking to a meeting at the central bank of Argentina and seeing masses of protestors, many of them old people, beating on pots and pans to demand access to their deposits.

Joseph Stiglitz discusses how crises affects poverty using the East Asian crisis as an example. Indonesia, which was most deeply affected, wiped out some twenty years of economic gains for its population. In the mid-1970s six of every ten people in the East Asian region lived on less than US$1 a day. Over a period of twenty years, per capita income growth averaged 5.5 percent a year. By the mid-1990s, growth had led to faster and larger reduction of poverty in East Asia than in any other region.[3]

Reversing the trends of rising prosperity prior to the crisis, unemployment grew rapidly in the crisis countries, from some 5.3 million people in 1996 to an estimated 18 million people at the end of 1998. In Thailand and Indonesia, which have large rural, agricultural populations, the impact of the crisis was exacerbated by drought. In Thailand at the end of 1997, 70 percent of the unemployed were poor rural workers in the northeast. World Bank estimates for 1998 using US$1 a day as the poverty level in Indonesia and the Philippines and US$2 a day for Malaysia and Thailand, indicated that poverty was projected to increase by some 17 million more people in Indonesia, bringing the total number of poor to 56.5 million people.[4]

When I was working on crisis resolution policy and corporate workouts in Korea from late 1997 through 2001, thousands of small-business owners were unable to sustain their businesses, which supported their workers and the family unit. The Korean press reported that many men were living in public parks or disappearing into the woods, ashamed at not being able to provide for their families. Thousands of small businesses were forced to close from 1998 through 2001 and possibly beyond, despite government efforts to provide liquidity to the sector. The failure of small businesses because they lack access to liquidity is a theme that has played out repeatedly in countries in crisis, including Mexico, Turkey, Greece, and Portugal. The same thing happened in the United States in the early 2000s.

The eurozone crisis has brought similar issues of high unemployment to the eurozone overall. At the end of 2015, some seven years after the crisis began, unemployment was still at 10 percent. Unemployment was as high as 25 percent in Spain for much of the crisis period, and youth unemployment exceeded 50 percent. In Greece unemployment remained above 20 percent, and poverty deepened, particularly for those living on fixed incomes, such as pensioners. The Greek public faced its own version of the *corralito*, when bank withdrawals were limited for a time in order to prevent a bank run.

During the U.S. crisis, GDP fell 4.5 percent for all of 2008, but at a much deeper 8.5 percent during the last quarter of 2008 as the panic set in—the worst performance in fifty years. Falling stock market prices, falling home prices, and the lowest reading in consumer confidence in over thirty years all led to the deepening of the crisis in the real economy. As the economy declined, employers soon began shedding employees in virtually all sectors of the economy, particularly in the construction and related sectors.[5] There were some 15 million unemployed workers, and unemployment and underemployment were estimated to be as high as 18 percent. By year-end 2010, some 4 million workers had been unemployed for more than a year. Unemployment fell disproportionately on non–college graduates, recent college graduates, and minorities. African Americans and Latinos were disproportionately affected by job and home losses.

The United States became one of the least equal countries among the advanced economies. And that wealth gap widened as the recession progressed. The poverty numbers rose, according to the Census Bureau's revised report on poverty; as of the end of 2010 there were some 49 million people in the United States living below the poverty line, 16 percent of the population, or one out of every six Americans. Poverty increased for four consecutive years. At the end of 2010 the poverty rate for children was 22 percent. In 2010, 27.5 percent of African Americans and 28.2 percent of Hispanics lived in poverty, as did 14.3 percent of whites. Among seniors sixty-five and older the poverty rate was 15.9 percent. Some 49 million Americans were not covered by health insurance. The Gini coefficient, which measures income inequality, was

0.469 (zero is perfect equality and 1.0 is perfect inequality), and signaled that in income and wealth, U.S. society is more unequal than that of many other advanced countries.[6]

So, crises often have a deep impact on the population of the crisis countries that carries on well after the formal declaration by economists that the crisis has come to an end. The impact by far outlives the immediate crisis period.

In good times prepare for crisis. What have we learned, and where are we on the spectrum of preparedness? The views of leading economists in the 1990s, and even now, that markets should be allowed to operate freely with a minimum of regulation and supervision and that the potential for crises has been moderated by advances in macroeconomic management, seem to ignore the lessons of past crises and the analytical work of John Maynard Keynes. Both Joseph Stiglitz and Paul Krugman have criticized the views of free market economists and their failure to anticipate and address the recent crises in the United States and Europe. Large financial institutions free to operate throughout the world without adequate regulation and supervision are simply dangerous, they say, and the benefits of unfettered banking, shadow banking, and global financial flows are dubious. The same is true of unregulated derivative contracts and trading of derivatives.

I believe that even with improved macroprudential regulation, banking supervision and regulations, and institutional mechanisms to address crises we are still vulnerable to crises such as those catalyzed by real estate and stock market bubbles. Recognizing a bubble, choosing the right time to prick the bubble, and avoiding the negative outcomes of doing so still seems to be elusive for central bankers.

Moreover, both the United States and Europe have a very long way to go to address the issues of systemically important institutions, previously known as "too big to fail," such as large international money center banks, nonbank financial institutions, and the shadow banking system—the major investment banks, large equity and hedge funds, and corporate financial institutions that are either lightly regulated or not regulated. These systemically important banks and nonbank financial institutions are still too big to fail. Also, banking has grown more concentrated. Many of these financial institutions, especially in the advanced economies, such as Citigroup, Bank of America, J. P. Morgan Chase, BNP Paribas, Barclays Bank, and Deutsche Bank, operate throughout the world as giant financial supermarkets and have proven too complex to manage effectively.

Policy and reform issues emerged from the last crisis with respect to banks that are systemically important. Among those that still need to be addressed: (i) increasing capital and liquidity requirements; (ii) limiting leverage and having "bail-in" capital; (iii) having consolidated supervision in both Europe and the United States—in the United States eliminating regulatory shopping and in the EU finalizing the banking union; (iv) reducing or eliminating trading activity; (v) putting in place a "living will"; (vi) defining the scope of and intervals between regular stress tests and clearly identifying a resolution authority. Could the impact of crises be mitigated if these policy measures were implemented? I believe so. But the administration of President Donald Trump is bent on rolling back some of the Dodd-Frank bill and has little appetite for regulation of any kind. Now that the eurozone countries are growing again, there is little impetus to complete a banking union or, perhaps more important, move to a fiscal union. There is still no formal institutional mechanism in the eurozone to assist countries in crisis or to respond to contagion from country to country.

The idea that bailouts are a thing of the past just because the Dodd-Frank bill legislates against them does not reflect economic or political reality. If Citigroup or J. P. Morgan Chase in the United States or Barclays Bank in the United Kingdom or Deutsche Bank in Germany or BNP Paribas in France were in distress, it is virtually certain that their central banks and Treasury equivalents would quickly feel pressure to rescue them as interest rate spreads increased and the "fear" index, stock markets, and other financial markets began to register their reactions to this distress. Clearly, given the lessons of the recent crisis, our preparedness for crisis is far less than it should be.

Emerging market countries face similar issues, especially those with financial-industrial groups (FIGs)—large corporate groups that have banks as part of or at the center of their groups. Historically, these are prevalent in Mexico, Turkey, Thailand, and Russia. In addition, state-owned banks and state capitalism as they have emerged in China, Vietnam, Russia, and several other countries are far from a proven model for the longer term. State-owned banks have been at the heart of financial crises in Turkey, Indonesia, and Russia. China was forced to set up four asset management agencies during the East Asian crisis to clean up its banking system. State-owned banks are invariably corrupted through directed credits and often operate as allocators of capital, rather than as independent banks able to make informed judgments about the creditworthiness of their customers.

As a result of the recent crisis or the desire to maintain growth during the crisis, the United States, Japan, and China, the three largest economies in the world, are now highly indebted. So are some countries in the eurozone and among the emerging market countries, which also sought to maintain growth during the crisis. When the next economic downturn occurs, or the next crisis, these countries will have far less capacity to act and as a result are more likely to experience a prolonged or deep downturn. Because of policies of quantitative easing, the central banks of the United States, the United Kingdom, and Japan have large balance sheets that need to be addressed. At low rates of interest and with highly indebted balance sheets, they also have less capacity to fight the next downturn or crisis.

Perhaps my greatest concern, given the pressure on the EU and eurozone and the deep political divide in the United States, is that it is difficult to envision policymakers making the right decisions about the policies and institutions that should be in place to address the next crisis. In the United States the tax reform plan that was passed in late 2017 moves in the diametrically opposite direction from what is needed to address continuous fiscal deficits and the country's unsustainable public debt.

My final words, then, are: in good times prepare for crisis, and hope that it is not too late.

A Comparative Overview of Debt-Crisis Regimes:
From the Great Depression through the Great Recession

Basis of comparison	1919–39	1946–90	1990–2005	2007–15
1. Major creditors	United States, Great Britain, France, Sweden, Switzerland, Netherlands, Belgium, Japan	United States, Great Britain, France, Germany, Japan, Netherlands, Switzerland, other OECD states, Gulf states, multilateral and regional financial institutions	United States, Great Britain, France, Switzerland, Netherlands, Belgium, Japan, Gulf States, multilateral and regional financial institutions, convenience centers	United States, Europe, Singapore, China, Japan, Hong Kong, multilateral and regional financial institutions, convenience centers—Luxembourg, Cayman Islands, others
2. Major debtors	Germany, Central and Eastern Europe, Latin American states, Canada, Australia, New Zealand	Latin America, Eastern Europe, African countries, Turkey	Latin America, East Asia, Turkey, Russia	Japan, United States, eurozone periphery—Italy, Spain, Ireland, Portugal, Greece, Cyprus, non-eurozone debtor Iceland, China, and Japan
3. Sovereign default restructuring	Russia (1917 repudiation), Latin American states (except Argentina), Germany, Central and Eastern Europe (successor and cessionary states of the Austro-Hungarian and Ottoman Empires), China	Latin America, Central and Eastern Europe, African countries, Morocco, Philippines, Turkey	Mexico (1994–97), East Asia: Thailand, Indonesia, Korea, Malaysia (1997–2003), Russia (1998), Turkey (2001–02), Argentina (2001–16)	• Japan: stock and real estate bust 1991; financial crisis 1993–97; debt-deflation low growth 1990s and 2000s, becomes major sovereign debtor • Nordics: early 1990s financial crises • United States: 2007 real estate crisis, morphs into financial crisis, economic crisis, and growth of sovereign debt • Eurozone countries: banking and financial crisis for countries on the periphery, bailouts under the auspices of the troika (European Commission [EC], European Central Bank [ECB], and International Monetary Fund [IMF])

4. Principles of debt reorganization	• Interim negotiated arrangements 1931–33, Depression (e.g., standstills) • Prolonged defaults attributable to closure of the capital markets • Exchange controls, capital market repurchase of debt, blocked currency accounts, clearing agreements, unilateral termination of the "Gold Clause" • Negotiated settlements of debts at a fraction of their value 1946–55	Debt restructurings: • Official debt primarily via Paris Club negotiations • Commercial bank restructurings via steering or bank advisory committees • IMF, BIS, central banks as international lenders of last resort	Currency crises, morphed into financial crisis; Argentina only major sovereign default	• Japan: major effort to restructure and reform the banking system; Bank of Japan quantitative easing • United States: bailouts under the TARP; capital injections into financial institutions ("too big to fail"; nonbank financial companies such as GE Capital, GM Acceptance Corp., AIG); intervention into Fannie Mae and Freddie Mac under custodianship; mortgage banks intervened in and sold by FDIC; support for money markets; TARP $700 billion support vehicle primarily used to inject capital into the failing financial institutions, guarantees provided to support markets; Fed quantitative easing; eurozone bailouts under auspices of the troika; two funds created to provide liquidity to the banking system and to augment the bailouts; principle of austerity governs workouts; ECB provides liquidity to the banking system
5. Creditor institutions in debt negotiations/ lender of last resort	• Extension of the pre–World War I approach; U.S. Foreign Bond-holders Protective Council formed in 1933	Creditor clubs: Paris, Hague, and London Club merged into Paris Club for official restructurings	IMF, World Bank, and regional development banks as lenders of last resort, supported as needed by G-7	• United States: U.S. Federal Reserve (Fed), U.S. Treasury, Federal Deposit Insurance Corporation, and TARP; Fed extends lines to some fourteen central banks throughout the world

(continued)

Appendix Table A (continued)

Basis of comparison	1919–39	1946–90	1990–2005	2007–15
	• Control commissions for successor and cessionary states largely ineffective • League of Nations Control Commission • Reparations Commission	• OECD Consortium (Turkey) • World Bank Aid Consortium (Pakistan and India) • Bank advisory: creditor committees, governed by money center banks • Baker and Brady Plans supported by G-7, led by U.S. Treasury		• Bank of England provides support of U.K. banks in trouble and to prevent a run at Northern Rock • Eurozone: troika serves as lender of last resort to crisis countries and ECB to the banking system
6. Debt instruments	Bonds, trade finance acceptances	Eurocurrency syndicated loans, Eurobonds, trade finance, interbank lines, multilateral institutional loans, official loans and credits	Primarily Eurobonds	U.S. money center banks, investment banks, GSEs, international banks securitized subprime real estate loans
7. Monetary institutions and debt crisis	New York Federal Reserve Bank, Bank of England, Bank of France, Bank for International Settlements (BIS) 1930 (first use of BIS as an international lender of last resort)	Bretton Woods institutions (IMF and World Bank), OECD central banks, BIS serve as ad hoc international lenders of last resort	IMF supported by World Bank, regional development banks, and G-7 as needed	U.S. Fed, Bank of England, ECB, Bank of Japan; U.S. Fed extends lines to central banks of some fourteen different countries

Compiled by author.

APPENDIX TABLE B

Commercial Bank Debt Restructurings with Sovereign Debtors, 1980–89[a]

Country	*Type of credit*[b]	*Principal amount*[c] *(millions of US$)*	*Amortization /Grace period (years)*	*Average interest rate 0/0 (over LIBOR)*
Number of restructurings 1980: 5				
Peru[d]	Refinancing: public and publicly quoted debt, new loan	340	5/2	1 ¼
				Principal: 1,101
Number of restructurings 1981: 6				
Romania[d]	Rescheduling: arrears of 1981 obligations	1,598	6.5/3	1 ¾
				Principal: 1,210
Number of restructurings 1982: 7				
Poland	Rescheduling	4,600	7/4	1 ¾
				Principal: 6,386
Number of restructurings 1983: 21				
Argentina[e]	Refinancing: arrears, new medium-term loans, trade credit lines	23,322	3/7	2 ⅛
Brazil[d]	Refinancing: four part plan, range of credits	40,245	8/2.5	2.125–2.50
Chile	Refinancing: short- or medium- term debt	6,400	8/4	2 ⅛
Mexico[d]	Rescheduling: short- or medium-term, private arrears	25,000	8/4	1 ⅞–2 ¼
Yugoslavia	Refinancing: short- or medium-term loans, new credits	2,350	6/3	1 ⅝
				Principal: 105,578
Number of Restructurings 1984: 28				
Argentina	Due in 1984 and 1985: 100% of principal	16,522	12/3	1 ⅜
	Trade credit maintenance and deposit facilities	1,700	–	

	New financing	3,700		
	Standby money market facility	1,400	10/3	1 3/8–1 1/4
	Principal	23,322	–	
Brazil[d]	Rescheduling of medium- and long-term debt due in 1984, 100% of principal	5,213	9/5	2–1 3/4
	Short-term debt—trade related	9,800		
	New loan	6,500		
	Principal	21,513		
Ecuador	Refinancing of 1985–89 public debt: 100% and a deposit facility	4,360	12/3	1 3/8
	Rescheduling of 1983 loan	431	10/2	
	Extension of trade finance	700	–	1 5/8–1 1/4
Chile	Short-term nontrade debt converted to medium-term financing (100% of principal)		8/4	2 1/8
	New loan	1,200	9/5	1 3/4–1 1/2
	Rollover of trade lines	780		
	Moratoria on public and private debt due Jan.–April 1985	1,700	6 months	Original rates
	Principal	280		
Mozambique		1,400	–	–
Mexico[d]	New financing	3,800	10/5 1/2	1 1/2–1 1/8
	Rescheduling of public medium- and long-term debt previously rescheduled 1987–90: 100%		14	7/8–1 1/4
	Rescheduling of 1983 syndicated loan: 100%	23,600	10/5	
	Principal	5,000	10/5	1 1/2–1 1/8
Poland[e]	Medium- and long-term debt due 1984–87		10/5	1 7/8

(continued)

Appendix Table B (continued)

Country	*Type of credit*[b]	*Principal amount*[c] *(millions of US$)*	*Amortization /Grace period (years)*	*Average interest rate 0/0 (over LIBOR)*
	New trade credits	1,615		
	Rollover of short-term credit facility	235	5	1 ¾
	Principal	465	–	1 ¾
Peru	Medium- and long-term debt 1984–85: 100%		9/5	1 ⅝–1 ¼
	Short-term working capital outstanding: 100%	460		
	New financing: loan covering undisbursed portion of 1983 loan	965	9/5	1 ⅝–1 ¼
	Short-term trade credit	200		
	Principal	800	8/ ¼	Rollover 1 ⅝–1 ¼
Philippines	Rescheduling of public sector debt Oct. 1983–Dec. 1985, due in 1986: 100%	1,492	10/5	1 ⅝
	Restructuring of private financial sector debt medium- and long-term 1983–86	722	10/5	1 ⅝
	Restructuring of corporate medium- and long-term debt	760		
	1983–86 and short-term debt	925	9/5	
	New medium-term loan	2,975		1 ¾
	Revolving of short-term trade facility	6,874		1 ¼
Yugoslavia	Refinancing of medium- and long-term public sector debt, 100% due in 1984	1,200	7/4	1 ⅝–1 ½
	In-process public sector debt due between 1985 and 1989	3,500	11/5	?
Venezuela	Rescheduling of medium- and long-term debt due 1983–88	21,203	12/ ½	1 ⅛
				Principal: 138,842

Restructurings 1985: 15				
Argentina	Bridge loan to be repaid with IMF disbursement	483		
	Term credit facility			
	Short-term credit and deposit facility	3,700	10/3	1 ⅝
	Public and private 1982–85 principal	500	4	1 ⅝
	Maintenance of short-term trade lines	14,200		
	Maintenance of money market lines	1,200	?	?
	Principal	1,400		
Cuba[e]	Rescheduling of 1985 debt due	90	10/6	1 ½
	Maintenance of trade lines	373		
	Maintenance of COMECON lines 1985–86	117		
Ivory Coast	Rescheduling tranche A, Dec. 1983–Dec. 1984: 100% of principal	240	7/2	1 ⅞
	Tranche B, 1/85–12/85: 90% of principal	220		
	Suppliers debt 12/83–12/85	105	8/3	1 ⅞
	Principal	565	8/3	
Mexico	Amendment of 1983 credit agreement to conform to 1984 pricing; $1,200 to be repaid in 1985	5,000	10/5	1 ½
	Debts due between 1/85 and 12/90 to be spread from 1988 to 98			
	Six-month extension of prepayment due Oct. 1985	23,600	14/–	Rate graduates up over time
	Principal	950		⅞ to 1 ¼
Philippines	New money	925	9/5	1 ⅝
	Public debt 10/83–12/86	1,270	10/5	1 ⅝
	Private financial sector short-term debt convertible to convertible bond obligations	2,210	10/5	1 ⅝
	Private financial sector medium-term debt	2,276	10/5	1 ⅝

(continued)

Appendix Table B   (continued)

Country	Type of credit[b]	Principal amount[c] (millions of US$)	Amortization /Grace period (years)	Average interest rate 0/0 (over LIBOR)
	Private corporate medium-term debt	1,100		1 ⅜
	Maintenance of ST trade lines to June 1991	2,975		1 ¼
	Principal			**Principal: 77,471**
Restructurings 1986: 11				
Argentina	180-day rollover of principal due in 1986	7,500	–	–
	Extension of short-term credit line	2,500	–	–
	Principal	10,000		
Brazil	1985 principal to be repaid in 5 equal installments starting 3/15/91	6,100	7/5	1 ⅛
	1986 principal to be postponed for a year	9,500		
	Trade debt outstanding to be maintained for 1 year			
	Interbank debt owed by foreign branches of Brazilian banks to be maintained for 1 year	9,500		1 ⅛
	Principal	5,250		
Ecuador	Maintenance of ST trade lines	700	12/3	1 ⅜
	Rescheduling of 1983 agreement, plus new money	431		
	Private debt 1/85–12/89	200	10/2	1 ⅞
	Oil export prefinancing agreements	1,356		
	Principal	220	12/3	1 ⅜

Country	Description	Amount	Date	Rate
Venezuela	Rescheduling of public debts 11/82–12/88	20,944	12/1	1 ⅛
	Down payment of $750 million, quarterly repayments thereafter starting in 1987; currency switch option limited to $3 billion, limit to 45–50% of each bank's claims			
Nigeria	In negotiations since 11/86	2,800	8/3	1 ¼
	Restructuring medium-term loans 4/86–12/87	2,100		
	Refinancing letters of credit			
	New money with 3 drawings linked to World Bank trade policy loan	320		1 ¼
	Principal	5,200		1 ¼
Poland	95% of 1986 principal	860	8/4	1 ⅜
	80% of 1987 principal	1,200	8/4	1 ⅜
	15% of private trade revolving trade facility			
	95% of 1986–87 principal previously rescheduled in 1981–82	1,540	8/4	1 ⅜
	Total principal	3,600		

Principal: 80,791

Restructurings 1987: 15

Country	Description	Amount	Date	Rate
Argentina	Refinancing of 1982–85 maturities and 1986 maturities	30,500	19/7	13/16
	New funding with refinancing above			
	Term credit agreement for investment projects, public and private sector borrowers	1,550	12/5	13/16
	Trade credit maintenance	350	2.0	13/16
	Trade credit facility	400	2.0	13/16
	Standby money market facility	1,000		¾

(continued)

Appendix Table B   (continued)

Country	Type of credit[b]	Principal amount[c] (millions of US$)	Amortization /Grace period (years)	Average interest rate 0/0 (over LIBOR)
Brazil	-Suspension of interest payments, medium and long-term debt	68,000		
	-Request for a 60-day standstill on short-term debt and trade credit lines (followed by a request for a 90-day extension)	15,000		
	- Rescheduling debts			
	- 1986–89 consolidation of all payments due including interest, capitalization of interest in arrears, new financing, debt conversion, and a contingency facility			
	1987: 100% due, 1988: 60% due, 1989: 60% due (request to creditors)	10,400		LIBOR+0
	-Refinancing interest payments due 4th qtr. 1987	1,000		
	-Refinancing of interest payments 2/87–9/87	1,000		⅞
Chile	-Restructuring of public sector debt due 1988–91	1,533	15/6	1.0
	-Restructuring and repricing of previously restructured debt 1983–87	7,706	15/6	1.0
	-Repricing of 1983–85 new money facilities and consolidation of interest payments into one annual payment	3,200		1 ⅛
	-Short-term trade facility extended until 12/89	1,700		1 ⅜

Country		Amount		
Ecuador	-Rescheduling	4,000	19/7	15/16
	-New funding, including 150 million World Bank loan agreement allows debt/equity conversions	350	8/2	15/16
	-Rescheduling of 1983–85 new money facilities	651	10/3	15/16
Mexico	-Parallel sectoral financing with World Bank	5,000	12/5	13/16
	-Transport sector cofinancing with World Bank	1,000		
	-Contingent investment financing	1,200	15/9	13/16
	-Growth contingency refinancing	500		
	-Amendments to maturity schedules of the 52 restructuring agreements	23,600	8/4	13/16
	-Amendments to the maturity schedule of 35 restructuring agreements	20,100	12/7	13/16
	-Amendment of 1983 credit agreements	8,800	20/7	13/16
	-Rescheduling of private sector debt	9,700	20/7	13/16
Nigeria	Request: Rescheduling of $3.7 billion of validated promissory notes, capitalization of interest due, unmatched trade claims to be cancelled est. $2.6 billion		22/2	5.0% fixed (?)
Zambia	10% export ceiling of funds devoted to debt repayment			
Poland[e]	-MYRA 95% of principal due rescheduled for 1987–93, tied to successful IMF program	8,000	15	15/16
	-Maintenance of short-term credit lines	1,000		

Principal: 259,946

(continued)

Appendix Table B   (continued)

Country	Type of credit[b]	Principal amount[c] (millions of US$)	Amortization /Grace period (years)	Average interest rate 0/0 (over LIBOR)
Restructurings 1988: 15				
Poland	-Rescheduling	8,310	15/0	15/16
	-Short-term credit maintenance	1,000		
Restructurings 1989: 4				**Principal: 10,869**

Sources: E. Brau, R. C. Williams, P. M. Keller, M. Nowak, "Recent Multilateral Debt Restructurings with Official and Bank Creditors," Occasional Paper 25 (Washington: 1983), pp. 35–42, p. 23, table 9. Maxwell Watson, Peter Keller, Donald Mathieson, "International Capital Markets, Developments and Prospects," Occasional Paper 31 (Washington: 1984), pp. 64–76. IMF, "Recent Developments in External Debt Restructuring," Occasional Paper 40 (Washington: October 1985), pp. 48–62. Commonwealth Group of Experts, *The Debt Crisis and the World Economy* (London: Commonwealth Secretariat, 1984), pp. 86–96. World Bank Debt Management and Financial Advisory Services, "Commercial Banks' Debt Restructuring and New Money Facilities" (Washington, November 13, 1987). World Bank, *Global Development Finance* (Washington: 1998), table A 3.9, pp. 93–102)

Note: At times the diverse sources on restructurings have not been in agreement on the terms or timing of a restructuring. Where available, IMF data are used, and they are based on Agreed Minutes of Reschedulings. The differences, however, do not appear to be material to the overall magnitude of restructuring efforts in the years analyzed. Because this table draws on a variety of sources, there is no certainty that it represents 100 percent of the cases. However, since it captures the major restructurings, principally of the Latin American debtors during this period, any missing cases are unlikely to be material. Excluded from the restructuring count are requests to restructure not concluded in the year, and unilateral moves by countries to impose debt payment ceilings or payment moratorium while debt negotiations were in progress.

a. Selected list of large, complex cases. Total number of commercial bank restructurings 1980–89: 116. Principal amount restructured: US$697 billion.

b. Rescheduling/refinancing—complex restructurings Mexico, Argentina, Brazil, Poland, and Yugoslavia, as examples, contain elements of both. If new funds were provided, restructuring has been classified as a refinancing.

c. Does not include principal of bridging loans or credits from official bilateral and multilateral sources—including BIS, IMF, and various central banks.

d. Completed official Paris Club restructuring as well during the 1980–89 period.

e. Not an IMF member.

Notes

Introduction

1. Charles P. Kindleberger, *Manias, Panics, and Crashes: A History of Financial Crises*, 6th ed. (London: Macmillan Press, 2011), p. 4.

2. Kenneth S. Rogoff and Carmen M. Reinhart, *This Time Is Different: Eight Centuries of Financial Folly* (Princeton University Press, 2009), p. xxv.

3. I consider any disruption of debt service to be a default, including a debt restructuring, debt bailout, a moratorium, or standstill on payments, and of course a repudiation. Rogoff and Reinhart, *This Time Is Different*, use a similarly broad definition.

4. The eurozone crisis was the first one in which the IMF was called upon to intervene in the advanced economies.

5. Transition economies were countries that were part of the Soviet Union or Yugoslavia. When these blocs fell apart, most of the individual countries in the bloc moved away from socialism, in transition, toward an open market economy. Many of these countries joined the European Union (EU) starting in 1995 through a process known as accession. China and Vietnam were also transition economies that followed their own economic reform process and currently operate under state capitalism.

6. Walter Bagehot, *Lombard Street*, 7th ed. (London: C. Kegan, 1978).

7. Kindleberger, *Mania, Panics, and Crashes*, p. 4.

8. Ibid.

9. In the case of the ECB there was significant resistance from the Bundestag and the German representatives on the ECB's advisory council to allowing the ECB to play its role as lender of last resort.

10. Henry M. Paulson, *On the Brink: Inside the Race to Stop the Collapse of the Global Financial System* (New York: Hachette Book Group, 2010), writes about his extensive discussions with members of Congress before various House and Senate committees on proposals

by the Treasury, the Federal Reserve Bank, and the FDIC to provide support for banks, shadow banks, and financial markets during the crisis. The bailouts were opposed by both sides of the aisle and by conservatives and liberals, making Paulson's job in getting congressional support for the bailouts particularly difficult.

11. Notable examples of books that discuss the history of crises include Susan Strange, "Debt and Default in the International Political Economy," in *Debt and the Less Developed Countries,* edited by Johnathan David Aronson (Boulder, Colo.: Westview Press, 1970), pp. 7–26; George Albert C. Cizuskas, "International Debt Renegotiations: Lessons from the Past," *World Development* 7 (February 1979): 199–210; and Albert Fishlow, "Lessons from the Past: Capital Markets during the 19th Century and the Interwar Period," *International Organization* 39 (Summer 1985): 383–439. Recent works include Nouriel Roubini and Stephen Mihm, *Crisis Economics* (New York: Penguin Books, 2010).

12. Edwin Borchard and William H. Wynne, *State Insolvency and Foreign Bondholders,* Vols. 1 and 2 (Yale University Press, 1951).

13. Borchard, "Section XIX Readjustment of Governmental Defaults," in Borchard and Wynne, *State Insolvency and Foreign Bondholders*, Vol. 1, p. 307.

14. Council of Foreign Bondholders (CFBH), Annual Report, 1873 (London: Council of the Corporation of Foreign Bondholders, 1874), pp. 18, 24.

15. Kindleberger, *Manias, Panics, and Crashes*, presents a history of debt-related financial crises.

16. CFBH, Annual Report, 1982–1983, pp. 48–64. The British Council of Foreign Bondholders, incorporated in 1873, has prepared annual reports every year since 1874 to the present that detail all defaults on foreign bonds involving British creditors.

17. Thomas Piketty, *Capital in the Twenty-First Century* (Belknap Press of Harvard University Press, 2014), pp. 120–21.

18. Joseph E. Stiglitz, *Globalization and Its Discontents* (New York: W. W. Norton, 2002), pp. 91–92; see also World Bank, *Global Economic Prospects, beyond Financial Crisis 1998/1999,* pp. 102–05.

19. E. H. Carr, *The Twenty Years' Crisis 1919–1939,* 2nd ed. (London: Macmillan Press, 1946), pp. 187–90; Borchard and Wynne, *State Insolvency and Foreign Bondholders*, pp. 127, 235–36.

20. J. M. Keynes, "Foreign Investment and National Advantage," reprinted from *The Nation* and *Athenaeum* (August 1924) in *The Collected Writings of J. M. Keynes,* Vol. 19, edited by Donald Moggridge (London: Macmillan Press for the Royal Economic Society, 1978), p. 277.

See the chapters herein on the Argentine crisis and the chapters on the eurozone crisis for the discussion, as well as Dragoslav Avramovic and others, *Economic Growth and External Debts* (Johns Hopkins University Press, 1964), p. 7.

Chapter One

1. The term "export of capital" is employed because the statistics from this period often do not distinguish between share investments and loans. However, the majority of investments were the long-term portfolio type aimed at a fixed return on capital. See Michael Edelstein, *Overseas Investment in the Age of High Imperialism: The United Kingdom 1850–1914* (London: Methuen, 1982), pp. 18–19.

2. Albert H. Imlah, *Economic Elements in the Pax Britannica* (New York: Russel & Russel, 1969), pp. 2–4; Herbert Feis, *Europe, the World's Banker, 1870–1914* (London: Frank Cass, 1936), p. xv.

3. Royal Institute of International Affairs, *The Problems of International Investment* (Oxford University Press, 1937), p. 128.

4. The discussion of nineteenth-century sovereign debt and debt service disruption is largely a summary of four chapters from my doctoral thesis at Oxford University: Ira W. Lieberman, "The History of External Sovereign Debt: The Reaction of Creditors and Debtors to Disruption of Debt Service—An International Relations Perspective," 1989, part 1, chaps. 1–4.

5. Consols and *rentes* were securities issued by the British and French governments to the public for fixed income returns; they were the benchmarks against which interest and dividend returns from external loans and investments were measured. They were the equivalent of U.S. Treasury bills or notes.

6. A. R. Hall, *The London Capital Market and Australia, 1870–1914* (Australian National University Press, 1963), pp. 71–74.

7. Karl Erich Born, *International Banking in the 19th and 20th Centuries* (Warwickshire, England: Berg, 1983), provides a comprehensive treatment of the interrelated role of the banks and capital markets; originally published as *Geld und Banken im 19. und 20. Jahrhundert* (Stuttgart: Alfred Kroner Verlag, 1977).

8. Edwin M. Borchard and William S. Wynne, *State Insolvency and Foreign Bondholders,* Vols. 1 and 2 (Yale University Press, 1951), pp. 102–05, cite some instances of guarantees by creditor governments during this period.

9. P. L. Cottrell, *British Overseas Investment in the Nineteenth Century* (London: Macmillan Press, 1975), pp. 17–18.

10. Report of a Study Group of the Royal Institute of International Affairs, "The Problem of International Investment" (Oxford University Press, 1937), p. 128, quoting Robert W. Dunn, *American Foreign Investments* (New York: Viking Press, 1926), p. 3.

11. Berlin is the exception because of its political status and the shift from Berlin to Frankfurt as Germany's principal financial center.

12. Rondo E. Cameron, *France and the Economic Development of Europe, 1800–1914: Conquests of Peace and Seeds of War* (New York: Octagon Press, 1975), p. 195; see also J. Riesser, *The German Great Banks and Their Concentration in Connection with the Economic Development of Germany* (Washington: U.S. Government Printing Office, 1911), p. 45; see also pp. 386–87 and 423–33.

13. Both China's and Japan's sovereign or public debts are domestic in nature and as such do not risk the threat of an external sovereign crisis. China is also a large creditor to the rest of the world. The United States depends in part on investors from other countries to take up its bonds.

14. Leland H. Jenks, *The Migration of British Capital to 1875* (New York: Knopf, 1927), p. 207. For details on capital export to Australia and Canada, see Hall, *The London Capital Market and Australia,* p. 10; and Jacob Viner, *Canada's Balance of International Indebtedness 1900–1913* (Harvard University Press, 1924), pp. 138, 303–04, table LXI.

15. Fred Rippy, *British Investments in Latin America, 1822–1914* (University of Minnesota Press, 1959), pp. 20–21; see also Jenks, *The Migration of British Capital,* pp. 421–22. The

appendixes provide a detailed listing of loans by year and country, giving the issue house and the price, interest rate, principal amount, and amortization.

16. For statistics on the volume and location of lending for railways and public works in this period, see Feis, *Europe, the World's Banker*, p. 27; and Matthew Simon, "New British Portfolio Investment, 1865–1914," in *Capital Movements and Economic Development*, edited by J. H. Adler (London: Macmillan Press, 1967), pp. 55–59.

17. Albert Fishlow, "Lessons from the Past: Capital Markets during the 19th Century and the Interwar Period," *International Organization* 39 (Summer 1985): 383–439, esp. 403–08, distinguishes between developmental borrowers (for example, Australia, Canada, Brazil, and Argentina) and revenue borrowers (for example, Russia, Egypt, and Turkey), noting that the former were prone to default based on a decline in export revenues, while the latter eventually defaulted when government revenues could no longer meet the debt service.

18. C. K. Hobson, *The Export of Capital* (London: Constable, 1914), p. 101. The author provides a detailed listing of the early loans from 1818 to 1825, as well as the interest rates and discounts; see also D. C. M. Platt, "Foreign Finance in Argentina for the First Half-Century of Independence," *Journal of Latin American Studies* 15 (May 1983): 28.

19. David S. Landes, *Bankers and Pashas* (London: William Heinemann, 1958), p. 84. The full title of this work, *Bankers and Pashas: International Finance and Economic Imperialism in Egypt, Based on Letters of Alfred Andrew (haute banque) and Edward Dervieu, Private Bankers to Viceroy of Egypt, 1860–1868*, is indicative of the situation that prevailed. See also Council of Foreign Bondholders (CFBH), Annual Report, 1884 (London: Council of the Corporation of Foreign Bondholders, 1884), pp. 46–47, on the Egyptian floating debt.

20. J. M. Keynes, "Foreign Investment and National Advantage," reprinted from *The Nation and Athenaeum* (August 9, 1924) in *The Collected Writings of J. M. Keynes,* Vol. 19, edited by Donald Moggridge (London: Macmillan Press, for the Royal Economic Society, 1978), pp. 277–78.

21. See the chapters herein on the Argentine crisis and the chapters on the eurozone crisis for a discussion of the Greek default and subsequent bailouts.

22. Max Winkler, *Foreign Bonds: An Autopsy—A Study of Defaults and Repudiations of Government Obligations* (Philadelphia: Roland Swain, 1933), p. 10.

23. CFBH, First Annual Report, 1873, p. 18, reviews the refusal of the London, Amsterdam, Brussels, and Antwerp exchanges to quote loans for Greece, long in default; and see p. 24 on the cooperation of the New York Stock Exchange with London in excluding bonds of the state of Virginia.

24. Ben S. Bernanke, *The Courage to Act* (New York: W. W. Norton, 2015), pp. 363–64.

25. CFBH, Annual Report, 1901–1902, pp. 305, 307–08, on acceptance by the French, German, British, Dutch, and Belgian bondholder committees; pp. 315–18, on the Paris Treaty of June 3, 1902, noting the terms of conversion on Portugal's debt. See also Feis, *Europe: The World's Banker*, pp. 251–53. Feis maintained that Portugal repaid its loans thereafter under threat of a British-German Convention of 1898 to divide its colonies of Angola and Mozambique in the event of future default. Winkler, *Foreign Bonds*, pp. 35–37, notes the defaults of Austria in 1802, 1805, 1811, 1816, and 1868. In 1868 the Hapsburgs initiated a coupon tax of 16 percent on external bonds. London and Amsterdam thereafter ordered the removal of Austrian bonds

from active trading on their stock exchanges. Spain, Russia, and Italy emulated Austria's practice.

26. William R. Cline, *International Debt Reexamined* (Washington: Institute for International Economics), pp. 208–09 on the Baker Plan; pp. 215–45 on the Brady Plan.

27. Thomas Piketty, *Capital in the Twenty-First Century* (Belknap Press of Harvard University Press, 2014), p. 121.

28. E. H. Carr, *The Twenty Years' Crisis, 1919–1939,* 2nd ed. (London: Macmillan Press, 1946), p. 125.

29. See J. A. Hobson, *Imperialism: A Study*, 3rd ed. (1902; repr. London: George Allen & Unwin, 1938); Rudolph Hilferding, in *Finance Capital*, edited by T. Bottomore (London: Routledge & Kegan Paul, 1981); first published as *Finanz Kapital*, 1910); V. I. Lenin, *Imperialism—The Highest Stage of Capitalism,* 2nd ed. (1917; repr. London: Martin Lawrence, 1934).

30. See Joseph E. Stiglitz, *Globalization and Its Discontents* (New York: W. W. Norton, 2002); Joseph Stiglitz, *Freefall: America, Free Markets, and the Sinking of the World Economy* (New York: W. W. Norton, 2010), pp. 220–21.

31. Lieberman, "The History of External Sovereign Debt," pp. 116–24 (on loans to the Ottoman Empire, Egypt, and North Africa) and pp. 125–27 (on intervention in China); see also Stiglitz, *Freefall,* pp. 219–20 (on China).

32. Lieberman, "Debt Allocations to the Successor and Cessionary States," in "The History of External Sovereign Debt," pp. 266–69.

33. Cline, *International Debt Reexamined,* p. 26.

34. Raymond Aron, *Peace and War: A Theory of International Relations* (London: Weidenfeld, 1966).

35. As reported in vivid detail in David S. Landes, *Bankers and Pashas.*

Chapter Two

1. United Nations, *International Capital Movements during the Inter-War Period* (Lake Success, N.Y.: United Nations Department of Economic Affairs, 1984), p. 4.

2. Royal Institute of International Affairs (RIIA), *The Problem of International Investment* (Oxford University Press, 1937), pp. 130–31.

3. United Nations, *International Capital Movements,* p. 5.

4. Ibid.

5. Cleona Lewis, *The United States and Foreign Investment Problems* (Brookings, 1948), p. 3.

6. United Nations, *International Capital Movements ,* pp. 12–15.

7. Ilse Mintz, *Deterioration in the Quality of Foreign Bonds Issued in the United States, 1920–1930* (New York: National Bureau of Economic Research, 1951), p. 52.

8. Ibid., p. 386.

9. Harvey E. Fisk, *Inter-Ally Debts: An Analysis of their Post-War Finance, 1914–1923* (New York: Bankers Trust Company, 1924), p. 309.

10. Ibid., p. 311.

11. C. P. Kindleberger, *The World in Depression, 1929–1939* (London: Allen Lane Penguin, 1973), p. 34.

12. Ibid., p. 38.

13. Vincent Carosso, *Investment Banking in America* (Harvard University Press, 1970), pp. 38–39.

14. Ibid., pp. 256–67.

15. Karl Erich Born, *International Banking in the 19th and 20th Centuries* (Warwickshire, England: Berg, 1983); originally published as *Geld und Banken im 19. und 20. Jahrhundert* (Stuttgart: Alfred Kroner Verlag, 1977), pp. 202–03.

16. C. P. Kindleberger, *Comparative Studies in Trade, Finance, and Growth* (Harvard University Press, 1978), p. 74; Paul Einzig, *The Fight for Financial Supremacy* (London: Macmillan, 1931), pp. 49–57.

17. Mintz, *Deterioration in the Quality of Foreign Bonds*, pp. 12–13.

18. Charles C. Abbott, *The New York Bond Market, 1920–30* (Harvard University Press, 1937), pp. 198–202.

19. RIIA, *The Problems of International Investment*, p. 171.

20. Hal B. Lary, *The United States in the World Economy: The International Transactions of the United States during the Inter-War Period* (Washington: U.S. Government Printing Office, 1943), p. 99.

21. Mintz, *Deterioration in the Quality of Foreign Bonds*, p. 70; see also pp. 63–68.

22. Carosso, *Investment Banking in America*, pp. 263–64.

23. Lary, *The U.S. in the World Economy*, p. 4.

24. Mintz, *Deterioration in the Quality of Foreign Bonds*, pp. 70–72.

25. Lary, *The U.S. in the World Economy*, pp. 97–98.

26. RIIA, *The Problem of International Investment*, p. 170.

27. Lewis, *The United States and Foreign Investment Problems*, p. 26.

28. RIIA, *The Problem of International Investment*, p. 175.

29. United Nations, *International Capital Movements during the Inter-War Period*, pp. 9–10.

30. Ibid., pp. 32, 35.

31. C. R. S. Harris, *Germany's Foreign Indebtedness* (Oxford University Press, 1935), p. 117 and appendix XIV.

32. Sir Robert Kindersley, "British Foreign Investments in 1929," *Economic Journal* 41 (1931): 381–83.

33. Sir Robert Kindersley, "British Overseas Investments in 1931," *Economic Journal* 43 (1933): 199.

34. Ibid., p. 201.

35. Ibid., p. 180, table II.

36. David Williams, "London and the 1931 Financial Crisis," *Economic History Review* 15 (1962–1963): 521.

37. J. M. Keynes, "Foreign Investment and National Advantage," reprinted from *The Nation and Athenaeum* (August 1924), in *The Collected Writings of J. M. Keynes,* Vol. 19, edited by Donald Moggridge (London: Macmillan Press, for the Royal Economic Society, 1978), p. 278.

38. Keynes, "Some Tests for Loans to Foreign and Colonial Government," reprinted from *The Nation and Athenaeum* (January 17, 1925) in ibid., pp. 329–30.

39. Ibid., p. 329.

40. Keynes, "Foreign Investment and National Advantage," in *The Collected Writings of J. M. Keynes,* edited by Moggridge, pp. 277–83.

41. RIIA, *The Problem of International Investment*, p. 141.

42. Einzig, *The Fight for Financial Supremacy,* p. 4.

43. Ibid., pp. 2–3.

44. Born, *International Banking in the 19th and 20th Centuries,* p. 234.

45. United Nations, *International Capital Movements during the Inter-War Period*, p. 4.

46. Keynes, "Foreign Investment and National Advantage," p. 277.

47. Harold C. Moulton and Cleona Lewis, *The French Debt Problem* (London: George Allen & Unwin, 1925), pp. 27–28.

48. Ibid., p. 30.

49. RIIA, *The Problem of International Investment*, p. 203.

50. United Nations, *International Capital Movements during the Inter-War Period,* pp. 9–10.

51. RIIA, *The Problem of International Investment,* p. 203.

52. Charles P. Kindleberger, *Manias, Panics, and Crashes: A History of Financial Crises* (London: The Macmillan Press, 1978), p. 193; Einzig, *The Fight for Financial Supremacy,* p. 85.

53. Kindleberger, *The World in Depression,* pp. 49–50; Kindleberger, *Manias, Panics, and Crashes,* p. 193.

54. RIIA, *The Problem of International Investment*, p. 204.

55. Einzig, *The Fight for Financial Supremacy*, p. 84.

56. Ibid., p. 59; see also Anthony Tihamer Komjathy, *The Crisis of France's East Central European Diplomacy, 1933–1938* (Boulder, Colo.: East European Quarterly, 1976).

57. Einzig, "The Fight for Financial Supremacy," pp. 58–67.

58. Born, *International Banking in the 19th and 20th Centuries*, p. 167; Margaret S. Myers, *Paris as a Financial Centre* (London: P. S. King & Sons, 1936), p. 112.

59. Myers, *Paris as a Financial Centre,* p. 85.

60. Ibid., pp. 85–87, where Myers cites *Bulletin de Statistique et de Legislation Comparte* 1 (April 16, 1930): 725.

61. RIIA, *The Problem of International Investment,* p. 219.

62. United Nations, *International Capital Movements during the Inter-War Period,* pp. 9–10.

63. RIIA, *The Problem of International Investment,* p. 131; Fisk, *Inter-Ally Debts,* pp. 313–15.

64. United Nations, *International Capital Movements during the Inter-War Period*, pp. 13–14.

65. "Reparations and War Debts," *The Economist—Supplement*, January 23, 1932, p. 9; Harris, *Germany's Foreign Indebtedness*, p. 3.

66. Born, *International Banking in the 19th and 20th Centuries*, pp. 214–23.

67. Derek Aldcroft, *From Versailles to Wall Street, 1919 to 1929* (London: Allen Lane–Penguin Books, 1977), p. 225. The author notes that foreigners also invested some 6 to 7 billion marks in German domestic securities, real property mortgages, and other instruments (n44).

68. "The Credit Situation of Germany," *The Economist—Supplement* (Text of the Report of the Committee appointed on the recommendation of the London Conference 1931), August 21, 1931, p. 2. The Wiggins Committee consisted of financial experts appointed by the BIS to evaluate Germany's financial situation. Albert Wiggins, chairman of the board of Chase National Bank of New York, was its chairman.

69. Harris, *Germany's Foreign Indebtedness*, p. 10.

70. "Reparations and War Debts," *The Economist—Supplement*, January 23, 1932, p. 11.

71. J. M. Keynes, "The German Transfer Problem," *Economic Journal* 39 (March 1929): 1–7; Bertil Ohlin, "The Reparation Problem: A Discussion: Transfer Difficulties Real and Imagined," *Economic Journal* 39 (June 1929): 172–78; Jacques Rueff, "Mr. Keynes' Views on the Transfer Problem—A Criticism," *Economic Journal* 39 (September 1929): 388–99.

72. Aldcroft, *From Versailles to Wall Street*, p. 256; Harris, *Germany's Foreign Indebtedness*, pp. 6–9.

73. Harris, *Germany's Foreign Indebtedness*, pp. 11–12, and appendix XIV, pp. 116–17, which provides details of the capital issues from the United States and Great Britain to Germany from 1924 to 1931. It illustrates the diversity of borrowing by Germany.

74. Born, *International Banking in the 19th and 20th Centuries*, pp. 241–45.

75. H. W. V. Temperley, ed., *A History of the Peace Conference of Paris*, Vol. 5 (London: Henry Frowde and Hodder & Stroughton, 1921), pp. 2, 14–15, 21–32. Temperley's volumes provide a detailed analysis of the complex calculations leading to the apportionment of the prewar sovereign debts of the Austro-Hungarian and Ottoman Empires to the successor states.

76. Aldcroft, *From Versailles to Wall Street*, p. 252.

77. V. N. Bandera, *Foreign Capital as an Instrument of National Economic Policy: A Study Based on the Experience of East European Countries between the World Wars* (The Hague: Martins, Nijhoff, 1964), p. 27.

78. "League Loans," *The Economist*, November 19, 1932, pp. 938–39; see Edwin Borchard, *State Insolvency and Foreign Bondholders*, Vol. 1 (Yale University Press, 1951), p. 108, for a discussion of the guarantee mechanism, and pp. 296–99 for a discussion of the League Loans and their supervision.

79. RIIA, *The Problem of International Investment*, pp. 232–33.

80. Bandera, *Foreign Capital as an Instrument of National Economic Policy*, p. 25.

81. Ibid., pp. 35–40.

82. Ibid., p. 112.

83. Ibid., pp. 113–14, 173; tables XVIII and XIX summarize the debt service payments, interest, dividends, and amortization on foreign capital for Czechoslovakia, Hungary, Poland, Estonia, Latvia, and Lithuania from 1923 to 1937. The first table shows out-payments only, the second table net payments.

84. United Nations, *International Capital Movements during the Inter-War Period*, pp. 11–12, table 1. Net inward (+) or outward (–) capital movements are measured by estimating the deficits or surplus on account of goods, services, and gold. Figures are reported for the period 1919–38 for Czechoslovakia, Estonia, Finland, Latvia, Bulgaria, Lithuania, Romania, Yugoslavia, and Poland.

85. Samuel Flagg Bemis, *The Latin American Policy of the United States: An Historical Interpretation* (New York: Harcourt Brace, 1943), p. 187.

86. Aldcroft, *From Versailles to Wall Street*, p. 248.

87. Ibid., pp. 250–51; Carlos F. Diaz Alejandro, "Stories of the 1930's for the 1980's," in *Financial Policies and the World Capital Market: The Problem of Latin American Countries*, edited by Pedro Aspe Armella, Rudiger Dornbusch, and Maurice Obstfeld (University of Chicago Press, 1983), pp. 26–28.

88. "Coffee Loans," *The Economist*, December 31, 1932, pp. 1251–52.

89. Kindleberger, *The World in Depression,* pp. 83–96.

90. RIIA, *The Problem of International Investment,* pp. 268–70. As of 1930, tin accounted for 73 percent of Bolivia's exports; coffee 71 percent of Brazil's and 61 percent of Colombia's; nitrate and copper 84 percent of Chile's; petroleum and copper 58 percent of Peru's; and petroleum 76 percent of Venezuela's.

91. Ibid., p. 303, on British loans and investments in Latin America, and p. 187, on U.S. loans to Latin America.

92. Saburo Okita and Takeo Miki, "Treatment of Foreign Capital—A Case Study of Japan," in *Capital Movement and Economic Development,* edited by J. H. Adler with Paul Kuzmets (London: Macmillan Press, 1967), p. 151.

93. Okita and Miki, "Treatment of Foreign Capital," pp. 151–52.

94. Ibid., p. 153.

95. Feis, *The Diplomacy of the Dollar, 1919–1932* (1950; repr. New York: W. W. Norton, 1966), pp. 33–35.

96. RIIA, *The Problem of International Investment,* p. 266; United Nations, *Public Debt 1914–1916* (Lake Success, N.Y.: Department of Economic Affairs, 1948), pp. 92–93.

97. C. F. Remer, *Foreign Investments in China* (New York: Macmillan, 1933), p. 133.

98. Ibid.

99. Immanuel C. Y. Hsu, *The Rise of Modern China,* 2nd ed. (Oxford University Press, 1975).

100. Remer, *Foreign Investment in China,* p. 161.

101. E. H. Carr, *The Twenty Years' Crisis, 1919–1939,* 2nd ed. (London: Macmillan Press, 1946), p. 162.

102. Feis, *The Diplomacy of the Dollar,* pp. 30–32.

103. M. E. Falkus, "United States Economic Policy and the 'Dollar Gap' of the 1920s," *Economic History Review* 24 (1971): 599.

Chapter Three

1. Council of Foreign Bond Holders (CFBH), Annual Report 1886 (London: Council of the Corporation of Foreign Bondholders), pp. 81–87.

2. CFBH, Annual Report 1914, pp. 214–19.

3. Ibid., p. 14.

4. CFBH, Annual Report 1922, pp. 21–23; pp. 233–38, text of debt settlement, June 16, 1922, approved by presidential decree, September 29, 1922; and pp. 239–46, which provides details on the debt subject to settlement, including Mexico's $509 million of total debt, of which $244 million was external railway debt.

5. CFBH, Annual Report 1923, p. 28; Annual Report 1924, p. 12.

6. CFBH, Annual Report 1925, pp. 25–26, agreement between the Mexican government (June 16, 1922) and the International Committee of Bankers on Mexico (October 23, 1925); see also pp. 279–87 for details of the agreement.

7. CFBH, Annual Report 1926, p. 12; Annual Report 1927, p. 14.

8. CFBH, Annual Report 1927, p. 306.

9. CFBH, Annual Report 1928, p. 13.

10. CFBH, Annual Report 1930, pp. 29–30; pp. 264–69 on the agreement between Mexican Finance Minister Ochoa and T. W. Lamont, International Committee of Bankers, Mexico (July 25, 1930); and pp. 269–76 on the details of the agreement on external debt.

11. Ibid., p. 277.

12. CFBH, Annual Report 1931, p. 34.

13. CFBH, Annual Report 1933, pp. 39–40.

14. Ibid., p. 317.

15. CFBH, Annual Report 1934, p. 12; CFBH, Annual Report 1942, pp. 40–45, on the agreement presented to bondholders by Thomas Lamont, chairman, International Committee of Bankers on Mexico (December 19, 1942) and ratified by the Mexican Congress (December 24, 1945).

16. CFBH, Annual Report 1948, pp. 52–55, on the plan offered to holders of railway debt pursuant to the terms of an agreement between the United Mexican States, the administration of the National Railways of Mexico and the International Committee of Bankers on Mexico (April 7, 1948).

17. CFBH, Annual Report 1948, pp. 56–59.

18. Harold G. Moulton and Leo Pasvolsky, *World War Debt Settlements* (London: George Allen & Unwin, 1927), p. 60.

19. Harvey E. Fisk, *Inter-Ally Debts: An Analysis of War and Post-War Finance* (New York: Bankers Trust Publications, 1924), p. 302, with percentages calculated by me and rounded to the nearest percent.

20. Moulton and Pasvolsky, *World War Debt Settlements*, p. 61; Fisk, *Inter-Ally Debts*, p. 111, 132–33.

21. See V. I. Lenin, *Imperialism, the Highest Stage of Capitalism*, 2nd ed. (1917; repr. London: Martin Lawrence, 1934);Nikolai Bukharin, *Imperialism and World Economy* (London: Martin Lawrence, 1917); and Rosa Luxemburg, *The Accumulation of Capital* (1913; repr. London: Routledge & Kegan Paul, 1951). See also J. A. Hobson, *Imperialism—A Study*, 3rd ed. (1902; repr. London: George Allen & Unwin, 1938); and Rudolf Hilferding, *Finance Capital*, edited by Tom Bottomore (London: Routledge & Kegan Paul, 1981); first published as *Finanz Kapital*, 1910). Lenin drew extensively on the works of Hobson and Hilferding, among others, in the preparation of his work on imperialism.

22. E. H. Carr, *The Bolshevik Revolution, 1917–1923,* Vol. 2 (London: Macmillan, 1952), pp. 131–32.

23. Ibid., p. 138.

24. J. L. Talmon, *The Myth of the Nation and the Vision of Revolution* (London: Secker & Warburg, 1980), pp. 390–95.

25. James Joll, *Europe since 1920—An International History,* 2nd ed. (Middlesex, England: Penguin Books, 1976), p. 197, quoting Lenin from "Letters from Afar," *Collected Works,* Vol. 20 (New York: 1932), p. 28.

26. Talmon, *The Myth of the Nation,* p. 434.

27. Carr, *The Bolshevik Revolution,* Vol. 2, pp. 138–39.

28. See United States Department of State, *Foreign Relations of the United States,* 1918, Russia, Vol. 3 (Washington, D.C.: U.S. Government Printing Office, 1918), p. 33 (http://digital.library.wisc.edu/1711.dl/FRUS.FRUS1918Russia), for the text of the diplomatic pro-

test by diplomatic representatives at meetings of the diplomatic corps in Petrograd (February 12, 1918); telegram from Ambassador Francis to the secretary of state.

29. Carr, *The Bolshevik Revolution,* Vol. 2, p. 132.

30. Ibid., p. 133.

31. Moulton and Pasvolsky, *World War Debt Settlements*, p. 62; Harold G. Moulton and Leo Pasvolsky, *Russian Debts and Russian Reconstruction* (New York: McGraw Hill, 1924), p. 4.

32. Moulton and Pasvolsky, *Russian Debts and Russian Reconstruction,* p. 5.

33. Irving Fisher, "The Debt Deflation Theory of Great Depressions," *Econometrica* 4 (1933): 341, 346.

34. Charles P. Kindleberger, *The World in Depression, 1929–1939* (London: Allen Lane & Penguin Press, 1973), p. 145.

35. Fisher, "The Debt Deflation Theory of Great Depressions," pp. 337–57; Nouriel Roubini and Stephen Mihm, *Crisis Economics* (New York: Penguin Books, 2011), discuss extensively how Fisher's theory applies to the crisis beginning in 2008–14, pp. 52–53, 139–40.

36. Robert H. Ferrell, *American Diplomacy in the Great Depression: Hoover-Stimson Foreign Policy, 1927–1933* (Yale University Press, 1957), p. 18.

37. A. J. P. Taylor, *The Origins of the Second World War* (1962; repr. London: Book Club Associates, 1972), p. 61.

38. Derek H. Aldcroft, *From Versailles to Wall Street, 1919–1929* (London: Allen Lane & Penguin Books, 1977), p. 262.

39. Charles Cortez Abbott, *The New York Bond Market, 1920–1930* (Harvard University Press, 1937), Appendix L, pp. 220–23.

40. Kindleberger, *The World in Depression*, p. 71.

41. United Nations, *International Capital Movements during the Inter-War Period* (Lake Success, N.Y.: Department of Economic Affairs, 1949), p. 39.

42. CFBH, Annual Report 1923, p. 12.

43. Ibid., pp. 80–83, for a synopsis of the Austro-Hungarian proposed agreement that established the Caisse de la Dette (debt fund office) in Paris. The Caisse was to receive quotas on debt service payable by various states and arrange their distribution among bondholders; CFBH, Annual Report 1925, pp. 84–92, on the Prague Agreement (November 4, 1925), which modifies and amends the Innsbruck protocol.

44. CFBH, Annual Report 1923, pp. 33–34; see also pp. 376–85. CFBH, Annual Report 1924, pp. 34–38. The debts before October 17, 1912, were apportioned to Turkey (62.13 percent), Greece (10.49 percent), Syria (8.33 percent), Yugoslavia (5.23 percent), Iraq (3.95 percent), Palestine (2.45 percent), Transjordan (0.65 percent), and other (6.77 percent).

45. CFBH, Annual Report 1930, pp. 26–28, 33–35, 383–91.

46. CFBH, Annual Report 1928, pp. 16–19; CFBH, Annual Report 1930, pp. 102–05.

47. CFBH, Annual Report 1926, pp. 11–12.

48. CFBH, Annual Report 1928, p. 11, Agreement (June 13, 1928).

49. League of Nations, *World Economic Survey, 1931–1932* (Geneva: Intelligence Service of the League, 1932), pp. 319–22, table VI.

50. Max Winkler, *Foreign Bonds: An Autopsy—A Study of Defaults and Repudiation of Government Obligations* (Philadelphia: Roland Swain, 1933), p. 204; see also pp. 183–204 for details on specific bonds in default in all sovereign entities.

51. Royal Institute of International Affairs, *The Problem of International Investment* (Oxford University Press, 1937), pp. 305–08, cites Bulletin no. 85, Internal Institute of Finance (April 6, 1936); see also Foreign Bondholders Protective Council (FBHPC), Annual Report 1934, Appendix.

52. R. M. Kindersley, "British Overseas Investments in 1935 and 1936," *Economic Journal* 47 (1937): 646; Royal Institute of International Affairs, *The Problem of International Investment*, pp. 300–02.

53. Cleona Lewis, *The United States and Foreign Investment Problems* (Brookings, 1948), p. 42.

54. Bank for International Settlements (BIS), Sixth Annual Report, 1935/1936 (Basel, 1936), pp. 7–8.

55. United Nations, *International Capital Movements during the Inter-War Period,* pp. 61–62.

56. Anatole Kaletsky, "Lessons of the 1930s—When the Debtors Said No," *Financial Times*, December 28, 1983.

57. Lewis, *The United States and Foreign Investment Problems,* pp. 42–43.

58. Ibid., p. 43.

59. "League Loans," *The Economist*, November 19, 1932, p. 939.

60. Lewis, *The United States and Foreign Investment Problems*, p. 43.

61. FBHPC, Annual Report 1940–41, Appendix.

62. "South American Bonds," *The Economist*, January 24, 1931, p. 3.

63. "The Credit Situation of Germany—Report of the Committee Appointed on the Recommendation of the London Conference, 1931," *The Economist—Supplement*, August 21, 1931, p. 3.

64. Karl Erich Born, *International Banking in the 19th and 20th Centuries* (Warwickshire, England: Berg 1983), p. 258; first published as *Geld und Banken im 19. and 20. Jahrhundert* (Stuttgart: Alfred Kroner Verlag, 1977).

65. Bank for International Settlements (BIS), Second Annual Report, 1931–32 (Basel: 1932), p. 5.

66. Kindleberger, *The World in Depression,* pp. 148–51.

67. C. R. S. Harris, *Germany's Foreign Indebtedness* (Oxford University Press, 1935), p. 16.

68. Born, *International Banking in the 19th and 20th Centuries,* pp. 260–61.

69. Ferrell, *American Diplomacy in the Great Depression*, p. 116.

70. Harris, *Germany's Foreign Indebtedness,* p. 16; Kindleberger, *The World in Depression*, pp. 154–55.

71. Born, *International Banking in the 19th and 20th Centuries*, pp. 262–63.

72. Ibid., p. 263.

73. Kindleberger, *The World in Depression,* p. 156.

74. "The Credit Situation of Germany," *The Economist—Supplement*, August 21, 1931, p. 3.

75. Harris, *Germany's Foreign Indebtedness*, p. 17.

76. Hal B. Lary, *The United States in the World Economy* (Washington: U.S. Government Printing Office, 1943), p. 118.

77. E. H. Carr, *The Twenty Years' Crisis, 1919–1939*, 2nd ed. (London: Macmillan Press, 1946), p. 62 (the author addresses this issue in some depth throughout his work, in particular

in chapters 5, 8, and 9); H. W. Arndt, *The Economic Lessons of the Nineteen Thirties* (Oxford University Press, 1944), p. 12.

78. Aldcroft, *From Versailles to Wall Street,* p. 256; BIS, Second Annual Report, 1931–32, p. 11.

79. Harris, *Germany's Foreign Indebtedness,* pp. 25–31. The 1931 standstill agreement was renegotiated in the beginning of 1932 for another twelve months; a third standstill began in 1933. The agreements effectively channeled short-term creditors into swapping their foreign-currency-denominated credits into mark-denominated assets, as the National Socialists made it more and more difficult for creditors to obtain foreign exchange.

80. League of Nations, "World Economic Survey 1932/33," various issues 1931/32 through 1938/39 (Geneva: League Intelligence Service), p. 274. A second standstill was nego-tiated on January 20, 1932, between the Austrian banks and their creditors; a third standstill (May 12, 1933) was agreed to by the Credit Anstalt and foreign creditors, backed by the Aus-trian government. The Hungarian standstill agreements (November 8, 1932, and February 1, 1933) were reached with British, American, and Swiss creditors.

81. Harris, *Germany's Foreign Indebtedness*, p. 88; see also Ferrell, *American Diplomacy in the Great Depression,* p. 110.

82. David Lloyd George, *The Truth about Reparations and War Debts* (London: William Heinemann, 1932), pp. 16, 124; "Mr. Hoover and the War Debts," *The Economist,* Novem-ber 26, 1932, p. 968; Elizabeth Johnson, ed., *The Collected Writings of John Maynard Keynes,* Vol. 18 (London: Macmillan Press, 1978), p. 384.

83. Edwin M. Borchard and William S. Wynne, *State Insolvency and Foreign Bondhold-ers,* Vols. 1 and 2 (Yale University Press, 1951), p. 143.

84. Harris, *Germany's Foreign Indebtedness*, pp. 36–38; see also Arndt, *The Economic Les-sons of the Nineteen Thirties*, pp. 183–84.

85. United Nations, *International Capital Movements during the Inter-War Period,* p. 45.

86. Ibid., p. 46; see also BIS, Fifth Annual Report 1934–35, pp. 19–40.

87. BIS, Fifth Annual Report 1934–35.

88. Harris, *Germany's Foreign Indebtedness,* p. 60.

89. Royal Institute of International Affairs, *The Problem of International Investment,* pp. 318–20.

90. Borchard and Wynne, *State Insolvency and Foreign Bondholders*, p. 135.

91. H. C. Wallich, "The Future of Latin American Dollar Bonds," *American Economic Review* 33 (June 1943): 332–33.

92. Arndt, *The Economic Lessons of the Nineteen Thirties*, p. 189. See also pp. 187–98 for a full discussion of the German clearing arrangements.

93. Ibid., p. 116.

94. "War Debts," *The Economist—Supplement,* November 12, 1932, pp. 5–7; Herbert Feis, *The Diplomacy of the Dollar, 1919–1932* (1950; repr. New York: W. W. Norton, 1966), pp. 21–24; Moulton and Pasvolsky, *World War Debt Settlements*, pp. 119–23.

95. See "Reparations and War Debts," *The Economist—Supplement,* January 23, 1932, pp. 2–4; see also essays by J. M. Keynes, *A Revision of the Treaty* (London: Macmillan Press, 1922), p. 71; Keynes, "A Breathing Space—The Dawes Plan," pp. 323–28; "Search for a Final

Settlement the Young Plan 1928–30," pp. 329–36; and "How It Ended," p. 351, all in Johnson, *The Collected Writings of John Maynard Keynes,* Vol. 18; Hjalmar Schacht, *The End of Reparations,* edited by George Glasgow (London: Jonathan Cape, 1931), pp. 38–39.

96. Ferrell, *American Diplomacy in the Great Depression,* pp. 18–19.

97. Borchard and Wynne, *State Insolvency and Foreign Bondholders,* p. 215. As of 1933 the League Loan Committee issued a series of annual reports to monitor progress on negotiating and servicing the League Loans similar to the CFBH's annual reports; CFBH, Annual Report 1933, pp. 242–44, on the negotiation of the League Committee with Greece, and pp. 375–78, on negotiations with Romania, League Committee, and bondholder councils.

98. V. N. Bandera, *Foreign Capital as an Instrument of National Economic Policy* (Netherlands: Springer, 1964), pp. 120–21.

99. CFBH, Annual Report 1933, pp. 26–27; on the Brazilian funding scheme (March 14, 1932), see pp. 120–21.

100. CFBH, Annual Report 1934, p. 18, on Romania's three-year settlement, July 24, 1934; p. 25, on Bulgaria, which rolled its arrangement forward three years; pp. 27–29, Chile, bill for the partial resumption of the external debt; and pp. 234–36, on Greece, which announced its ability to pay only a maximum of 35 percent of the debt service.

101. CFBH, Annual Report 1935, p. 15, on the Colombia funding agreement, which ended in 1934 and was not renewed; p. 18, on Romania, which went into full default in the last quarter of 1935; and pp. 47–48, on El Salvador, which went into full default after negotiations broke down.

102. CFBH, Annual Report 1936, pp. 39–40.

103. Ibid., p. 19.

104. CFBH, Annual Report 1937, pp. 18, 29–30, 144–45.

105. CFBH, Annual Report 1943, pp. 12–16, on the Brazilian loan settlement; Annual Report 1948, p. 9, on the settlement with Chile and Italy; Annual Report 1949, pp. 9–10, notes the lack of agreement with China, Germany, Japan, Bulgaria, Poland, and several Latin American states (Costa Rica, Ecuador, and Peru); p. 63, which refers to the USSR and former Baltic states, which were in total default.

106. CFBH, Annual Report 1951, pp. 28–31, on the settlement of German federal debt, May 26, 1951; Annual Report 1952, pp. 92–97, reviews the memorandum of agreement on the Japanese prewar external bonded debts; Annual Report 1953, pp. 13–16, on the Austrian referendum agreement based on the Rome Conference, November 25–December 6, 1952.

107. CFBH, Annual Report 1950, p. 11, quotes the World Bank Annual Report, 1949–50; see also Lewis, *The United States and Foreign Investment Problems,* pp. 80–81.

108. CFBH, Annual Report 1983, pp. 48–53, on loans with adjusted service under debt settlement; pp. 54–57, on loans redeemed July 15, 1972–December 31, 1983; and pp. 60–66, on loans in default.

Chapter Four

1. Harvey E. Fisk, *The Inter-Ally Debts: An Analysis of War and Post-War Public Finance, 1914–1923* (New York: Bankers Trust Publications, 1924), pp. 1–2.

2. Ibid., pp. 92, 101–02; Vincent P. Carosso, *Investment Banking in America—A History* (Harvard University Press, 1970), pp. 204–07.

3. Karl Erich Born, *International Banking in the 19th and 20th Centuries* (Warwickshire, England: Berg Publishers Ltd., 1983); first published as *Geld und Banken im 19. and 20. Jahrhundert* (Stuttgart: Alfred Kroner Verlag, 1977), pp. 189–92.

4. Fisk, *Inter-Ally Debts*, pp. 188, 241.

5. "War Debts," *The Economist—Supplement*, November 12, 1932, p. 2.

6. Derek H. Aldcroft, *From Versailles to Wall Street, 1919–1929* (London: Allen Lane & Penguin Books, 1977), p. 93.

7. "Reparations and War Debts," *The Economist—Supplement*, January 23, 1932, p. 4; Fisk, *Inter-Ally Debts*, p. 214.

8. Aldcroft, *From Versailles to Wall Street*, p. 5.

9. J. M. Keynes, *The Economic Consequences of the Peace* (London: Macmillan, 1920), p. 253; see also pp. 267–68.

10. "War Debts," *The Economist—Supplement*, November 12, 1932, p. 4; "Reparations and War Debts," *The Economist—Supplement*, January 23, 1932, p. 5.

11. David Lloyd George, *The Truth about Reparations and War Debts* (London: William Heinemann, 1932), p. 116.

12. Harold C. Moulton and Leo Pasvolsky, *World War Debt Settlements* (London: George Allen & Unwin, 1927), p. 27; "Reparations and War Debts," *The Economist—Supplement*, January 23, 1932, p. 6.

13. Parliamentary Papers (PP), CMD 1737, "Dispatch to the Representatives of France, Italy, Serb-Croat Slovene State, Rumania, Portugal and Greece London Respecting War Debt," 1922, Vol. 23.

14. Herbert Feis, *The Diplomacy of the Dollar, 1919–1932* (1950; New York: W.W. Norton, 1966), p. 78.

15. Ibid., p. 20.

16. "War Debts," *The Economist—Supplement*, November 12, 1932, p. 5.

17. Aldcroft, *From Versailles to Wall Street*, p. 95.

18. John Maynard Keynes, *The Collected Writings of John Maynard Keyes*, Vol. 18: *Activities 1922–1932, The End of Reparations*, edited by Elizabeth Johnson (London: Macmillan Press, for the Royal Economic Society, 1978), p. 194.

19. Feis, *The Diplomacy of the Dollar*, pp. 21–23. Ivar Kreuger arranged loans for sovereign states based on the creditworthiness of his industrial empire in return for a monopoly on matches. During the Depression the economic empire fell apart when sovereign loans went into default. See "The Kreuger Group," *The Economist*, March 19, 1932, pp. 615–16, 637–38.

20. Moulton and Pasvolsky, *World War Debt Settlements*, pp. 119–23.

21. The Kellogg-Briand Pact, 1928, officially the General Treaty on Renunciation of War, was signed on August 27, 1928 (https://en.wikipedia.org/wk/Kellogg-Briand_Pact).

22. Feis, *The Diplomacy of the Dollar*, p. 24.

23. "War Debts," *The Economist—Supplement*, November 12, 1932, p. 7.

24. John Maynard Keynes, *A Revision of the Treaty* (London: Macmillan, 1922), pp. 160–61.

25. Moulton and Pasvolsky, *World War Debt Settlements*, p. 131.

26. Robert H. Ferrell, *American Diplomacy in the Great Depression* (Yale University Press, 1957), p. 107.

27. C. R. S. Harris, *Germany's Foreign Indebtedness* (published under the auspices of the Royal Institute of International Affairs by Oxford University Press, 1935), p. 21.

28. Ferrell, *American Diplomacy in the Great Depression*, p. 113.

29. Charles P. Kindleberger, *The World in Depression, 1929–1939* (London: Allen Lane & Penguin Press, 1973), pp. 154–55.

30. "Reparations and War Debts Supplement," *The Economist*, January 23, 1932, p. 7.

31. Ferrell, *American Diplomacy in the Great Depression*, pp. 18–19.

32. Kindleberger, *The World in Depression,* pp. 159–60, for a discussion on the impact of the sterling devaluation; p. 172 on trade protectionism; p. 177 on German deflation.

33. Ferrell, *American Diplomacy in the Great Depression*, chap. 14.

34. Keynes, *The Collected Writings of John Maynard Keynes*, Vol. 18, p. 384.

35. "Mr. Hoover and the Debts," *The Economist*, November 26, 1932, p. 968.

36. Ferrell, *American Diplomacy in the Great Depression,* p. 21.

37. Keynes, *The Collected Writings of John Maynard Keynes*, Vol. 18, p. 390.

38. Royal Institute of International Affairs, *The Problem of International Investment* (Oxford University Press, 1937), p. 82.

39. "War Debts and Reparations," *The Economist—Supplement*, p. 12, statistical appendix III.

40. Keynes, *The Economic Consequences of the Peace*, pp. 15, 32–33, 52–53. See also John Maynard Keynes, *A Revision of the Treaty* (London: Macmillan, 1922), p. 99; and H. W. V. Temperley, ed., *A History of the Peace Conference of Paris*, Vols. 2 and 5 (Oxford University Press, Henry Frowde and Hodder & Stoughton, 1920) (Vol. 2), 1921 (Vol. 5).

41. Keynes, *The Economic Consequences of the Peace*, pp. 51, 173.

42. Hjalmar Schacht, *The End of Reparations,* edited by George Glasgow (London: Jonathan Cape, 1931), p. 46.

43. Keynes, *A Revision of the Treaty*, pp. 72–95; Keynes, "The Transfer Problem," *Economic Journal* 39 (March 1929): 17.

44. Bertil Ohlin, "The Reparation Problem: A Discussion: Transfer Difficulties Real and Imagined," *Economic Journal* 39 (June 1929): 172–78; Jacques Rueff, "Mr. Keynes' Views on the Transfer Problem—A Criticism," *Economic Journal* 39 (September 1929): 388–99.

45. Etienne Mantoux, *The Carthaginian Peace or the Economic Consequences of Mr. Keynes* (Oxford University Press, 1946), p. 10.

46. Ibid., p. 15.

47. Aldcroft, *From Versailles to Wall Street*, pp. 86–91; see also Fritz Machlup, *International Monetary Economics* (London: George Allen & Unwin, 1966), pp. 394–95.

48. Keynes, *The Collected Writings of John Maynard Keynes*, Vol. 18, chap. 6.

49. John Maynard Keynes, *The Nation and Athenaeum,* June 15, 1929, 329–36.

50. Bank for International Settlements (BIS), Second Annual Report (Basel, 1931), p. 22.

51. National Industrial Conference Board, *The International Financial Position of the United States* (New York, 1929), pp. 183–84.

52. Royal Institute of International Affairs, *The Problem of International Investment*, p. 305.

53. Jackson E. Reynolds, "The Bank for International Settlements as the Focal Point of the Settlement," in *The Young Plan in Operation,* Vols. 5 and 14, edited by Parker Thomas Moon (New York: Proceedings of the American Academy of Political Science, 1931), pp. 17–24.

54. BIS, First through Seventh Annual Reports (Basel, March 31, 1931, to March 31, 1938).

55. Keynes, "Foreign Investment and National Advantage," reprinted from *The Nation and Athenaeum* (August 9, 1924): 277.

56. Kindleberger, *The World in Depression*, pp. 27–28.

57. A. J. P. Taylor, *The Origins of the Second World War* (1962; London: Book Club Associates, 1972), p. 28.

58. Temperley, *A History of the Peace Conference of Paris*, Vol. 5, p. 2.

59. E. H. Carr, *International Relations since the Peace Treaties* (London: Macmillan, 1945), pp. 16–17.

60. Temperley, *A History of the Peace Conference of Paris*, Vol. 5, p. 40.

61. Ibid., pp. 14–15.

62. Ibid., p. 21.

63. Ibid., pp. 21–32. The reparations and financial clauses of the Austrian, Hungarian, and Bulgarian treaties are presented in detail on pp. 30–50, 219–61 and 327–35, respectively.

64. Ibid., p. 446.

65. "Reparations and War Debts," *The Economist—Supplement,* p. 2.

66. "Turkish Debt Negotiation," *The Economist*, September 17, 1932, p. 516.

67. Edwin M. Borchard and William S. Wynne, *State Insolvency and Foreign Bondholders*, Vols. 1 and 2 (Yale University Press, 1951), p. 285.

68. J. L. Talmon, *The Myth of the National and the Vision of Revolution* (London: Secker & Warburg, 1981), pp. 433–40.

69. The Treaty of Brest-Litovsk was a peace treaty signed by the Bolshevik government with the Central Powers (Germany, Austria-Hungary, Bulgaria, and the Ottoman Empire) on March 3, 1918 (https://en.wikipedia/wk/Treaty_of_Brest-Litovsk).

70. James Joll, *Europe since 1870: An International History* (Middlesex, England: Pelican Books, 1976), p. 246.

71. Lionel Kochan, *Russia and the Weimar Republic* (Cambridge, England: Bowes & Bowes, 1954), p. 25. The author cites Georgy Chicherin, "Foreign Policy of Soviet Russia, Report of Narkomindel to Russian Congress of Soviets," English translation (London: 1920), pp. 5–6.

72. E. H. Carr, chap. 17, "War Communism," deals with the economic aspects of this period in Russia in *The Bolshevik Revolution*, Vol. 2 (London: Macmillan, 1952), pp. 147–268.

73. Ibid., p. 348.

74. Leo Pasvolsky and Harold G. Moulton. *Russian Debts and Russian Reconstruction* (New York: McGraw Hill, 1924), p. 6.

75. Council of Foreign Bondholders (CFBH), Annual Report 1924 (London: Council of the Corporation of Foreign Bondholders), pp. 32–33.

76. Ibid., p. 32.

77. Feis, *The Diplomacy of the Dollar,* p. 46, cites Secretary of State Hughes, March 21, 1943.

78. Moulton and Pasvolsky, *Russian Debts and Russian Reconstruction*, p. 241.

79. Feis, *The Diplomacy of the Dollar*, pp. 46–47.

80. Great Britain, Parliamentary Papers (PP), CMD/667, *Papers Relating to International Economic Conference, Genoa, April–May, 1922*, Vol. 23 (1922), Memorandum Sent to the Russian Genoa Delegation, May 3, 1922, pp. 30–31.

81. Ibid.

82. Ibid., pp. 38–42, Reply of the Russian Delegation to the Memorandum (No. 5), May 3, 1922.

83. Lionel Kochan, *Russia and the Weimar Republic* (Cambridge, England: Bowes & Bowes), pp. vii–viii.

84. A. Ulam, *Expansion and Coexistence: The History of Soviet Foreign Policy, 1917–1967* (London: Secker & Warburg, 1968), p. 166.

85. The Roosevelt Corollary was an addition to the Monroe Doctrine by President Theodore Roosevelt in his State of the Union Address in 1904 after the Venezuelan crisis of 1902–03; it sought to justify U.S. intervention in Latin America (https//:en.wikipedia.org/wk/Roosevelt_Corollary).

86. United States, *Papers Related to the Foreign Relations of the United States* (U.S. Department of State, Office of the Historian, various years 1918 to 1935): *1922*, p. 824, on El Salvador; *1915*, pp. 431–33, on the Haitian financial treaty with the United States; *1916*, pp. 328–32, on the Haitian customs control; and *1917*, p. 1014, on the veto of loans to Mexico.

87. Samuel Flagg Bemis, *The Latin American Policy of the United States: An Historical Interpretation* (New York: Harcourt Brace, 1943), p. 186, Bryant to President Wilson, August 6, 1913.

88. Feis, *The Diplomacy of the Dollar*, pp. 27–28.

89. Ibid., pp. 25–26; see also Bemis, *Latin American Policy of the United States*, p. 209. J. Reuben Clark Jr., under secretary of state, prepared a memorandum on the Monroe Doctrine, issued on December 17, 1928, that detailed the faults and apparent illegality of the Roosevelt Corollary.

90. Cleona Lewis, *The United States and Foreign Investment Problems* (Brookings, 1948), p. 151.

91. Feis, *The Diplomacy of the Dollar*, p. 27.

92. Donald R. Shea, *The Calvo Clause* (Minneapolis, Minn.: Lund Press, 1955), p. 20.

93. Shea, *The Calvo Clause*, p. 36.

94. Bemis, *The Latin American Policy of the United States*, p. 338.

95. Shea, *The Calvo Clause*, pp. 56–58.

96. Bemis, *The Latin American Policy of the United States*, pp. 291–93; see also chap. 16.

97. Feis, *The Diplomacy of the Dollar*, p. 33; see also United States, *Papers Related to the Foreign Relations of the United States, 1918*, p. 155, Charge in China (MacMinnay) to Sec. of State, Peking (September 9, 1918), noting the influence of Japanese banks through Nishihara; the U.S. government was involved in a request for loans to China, as the Allies sought to offset the power of Japan in China during the war; pp. 167–68, U.S. Minister in China Reinsch to Secretary of State (April 12, 1918); pp. 172–73, certain American banks to the secretary of state, N.Y. (June 8, 1918), expressing concern over the open door basis for reviewing loans to China.

98. Feis, *The Diplomacy of the Dollar*, p. 38.

99. C. F. Remer, *Foreign Investments in China* (New York: Macmillan, 1933), p. 138, table 16.

100. Remer, *Foreign Investment in China*, pp. 546–48.

101. Benjamin Williams, *Foreign Loan Policy of the United States since 1933*, Twelfth Session of the International Studies Conference, Bergen, Norway, August 27–September 2, 1939 (New York: American Coordinating Committee for International Study), pp. 38–39.

102. United States Department of Commerce, *World Economic Review, 1933* (Washington: U.S. Government Printing Office, 1934), p. 15.

103. Kindleberger, *The World in Depression*, p. 198.

104. Born, *International Banking in the 19th and 20th Centuries*, pp. 274–76.

105. Kindleberger, *The World in Depression*, p. 200.

106. "Report of the World Economic Conference," *The Economist—Supplement*, July 22, 1933.

107. Ibid.; see the text of Roosevelt's messages issued on July 3 and July 5, where he reiterates his objection to temporary exchange stabilization measures.

108. Ferrell, chap. 15, "The World Economic Conference," in *American Diplomacy in the Great Depression*.

109. "Report of the World Economic Conference," *The Economist—Supplement*, p. 11. The five points are paraphrased.

110. H. W. Arndt, *The Economic Lessons of the Nineteen Thirties*, issued under the auspices of the Royal Institute of International Affairs (Oxford University Press, 1944). The Tripartite Monetary Agreement of 1936 was clearly an exception to this point. See BIS, Seventh Annual Report, 1936/1937, Annex VII.

111. League of Nations, "The Evolution of Autarky," *World Economic Survey, 1936/37*, p. 193.

112. BIS, Fourth Annual Report, 1933/34, p. 15.

113. Ibid., p. 13.

114. Joll, *Europe since 1870*, pp. 324–61; Arndt, *The Economic Lessons of the Nineteen Thirties*, p. 242.

115. Ibid., pp. 357–58.

116. Ibid., pp. 326–27.

117. Ibid., pp. 352–53. Russia joined the League of Nations in 1934, supported the Popular Front in France in 1935, and gave support to the Popular Front in Spain during its civil war.

118. Carr, *The Twenty Years' Crisis*, pp. 124, 121.

119. Ibid., p. 125; see also pp. 125–26, for a comparison between nineteenth-century lending by France to Russia and France's support for the Little Entente and Poland in the interwar period.

120. Williams, *Foreign Loan Policy of the United States since 1933*, p. 9.

121. Ibid., p. 10, cites U.S. Congress, Senate Special Committee on the Investigation of the Munitions Industry, U.S. Senate Report, 1944, p. 9.

122. Ibid., cites U.S. Statutes at Large, Vol. 49, p. 1153.

123. Royal Institute of International Affairs, *The Problem of International Investment*, pp. 88–94.

124. Williams, *Foreign Loan Policy of the United States since 1933*, pp. 43–45.

125. Ibid., p. 25.

126. Bemis, *The Latin American Policy of the United States*, p. 352; Lewis, *The United States and Foreign Investment Problems*, pp. 225–26.

127. Ibid., p. 352.

128. Ibid., pp. 353–54.

Chapter Five

1. United Nations, *The International Flow of Private Capital 1946–52,* E.2531/ST/ECA/2 (New York: United Nations, Department of Economic Affairs, 1954), p. 40.

2. Charles R. Frank Jr., *Debt and Terms of Aid,* Monograph 1 (Washington: Overseas Development Council, 1970), p. 12; Nathaniel McKitterick and B. Jenkins Middleton, *The Bankers of the Rich and the Bankers of the Poor: The Role of Export Credit in Development Finance* (Washington: Overseas Development Council, 1972), pp. 29–30.

3. Robert Solomon, *The International Monetary System 1945–1981* (New York: Harper & Row, 1982), pp. 9–13.

4. Richard N. Gardner, *Sterling Dollar Diplomacy in Current Perspective* (Columbia University Press, 1980), pp. 348–80.

5. George F. Kennan, *Memoirs 1925–1950* (London: Hutchinson, 1968), pp. 331–41. The Marshall Plan was formally passed by the U.S. Congress as the European Recovery Act (July 2, 1947) but is usually referred to as the Marshall Plan, after Secretary of State George Marshall.

6. Ibid., pp. 320–22. The Truman Doctrine was initially applied to provide U.S. economic and military support to Greece and Turkey in 1947, but it soon took on a universal character to contain subversion by economic and military support to third world countries perceived as threatened.

7. United States Senate, Committee on Finance, Subcommittee on International Finance and Resources, 93rd Cong., 1st sess., *Foreign Indebtedness to the United States* (Washington: U.S. Government Printing Office, 1973), p. 10, for a summary of overseas loans and grants for all countries.

8. W. M. Scammell, *The International Economy since 1945* (London: Macmillan Press, 1980), p. 148, table 10.1, puts U.S. direct foreign investment in 1950 at a book value of $10.3 billion and in 1970 at $53.2 billion, of which investment in developing countries was $4.4 billion and $21.3 billion, respectively.

9. M. Stefan Mendelsohn, *Money on the Move: The Modern International Capital Market* (New York: McGraw-Hill, 1980), pp. 32–34.

10. Lester B. Pearson, *Partners in Development*, Report of the Commission on International Development (London: Pall Mall Press, 1969), p. 5; see also Hedley Bull, "The Revolt against the West," in *The Expansion of International Society,* edited by H. Bull and Adam Watson (Oxford: Clarendon Press, 1984), p. 227.

11. United Nations, *The Capital Development Needs of the Less Developed Countries*, A/AC.102 5 (New York: United Nations, Department of Economics and Social Affairs, 1962), p. 15.

12. Pearson, *Partners in Development*, p. 69.

13. United Nations, *International Flow of Long-Term Capital and Official Donations, 1951–59,* H 4906/Rev 1 ST ECA 70 (New York: United Nations, Department of Economics and Social Affairs, 1961), p. iii; United Nations, *The Capital Development Needs of the Less Developed Countries*, pp. 9–11.

14. Chandra S. Hardy, *Rescheduling Developing Country Debt, 1956–1981: Lessons and Recommendations*, Monograph 15 (Washington: Overseas Development Council, 1982).

15. The Paris Club comprises some twenty financial officials from the world's biggest economies. It is an informal group that meets from time to time on an ad hoc basis. Under the auspices of the French Ministry of Finance, the Paris Club dealt with the rescheduling and restructuring of official credits, including export financing from the export finance institutions of the major creditor countries.

16. United Nations, *The International Flow of Private Capital, 1946–52*, pp. iii, 77–78.

17. Ibid., pp. 40–42, 57.

18. United Nations, *The International Flow of Private Capital, 1956–58* (New York: United Nations, Department of Economic and Social Affairs, 1959), p. 54.

19. United Nations, *The International Flow of Private Capital, 1946–52*, pp. 10–11; United Nations, *The External Financing of Economic Development, 1963–67* (New York: United Nations, Report of the Secretary General, 1970), p. 9.

20. United Nations, *The External Financing of Economic Development, 1963–67*, pp. 5, 23–24; see also United Nations, *The International Flow of Private Capital, 1956–58*, pp. 58–60, 65.

21. United Nations, *The External Financing of Economic Development, 1963–67*, pp. 69–72.

22. Ibid., p. 74.

23. Dragoslav Avramovic, *Debt Servicing Problems of Low-Income Countries, 1956–1958* (Johns Hopkins University Press, 1960), p. 4; Frank, *Debt and Terms of Aid*, pp. 5–6. The Development Assistance Committee (DAC) of the Organization for Economic Cooperation and Development (OECD) measures the degree of concessionality of a loan, or its grant element, by discounting the value of loan payments over the life of the loan to the present value, using an arbitrary interest rate of 10 percent as a hypothetical standard, expressed as the concessional value as a proportion of the face value of the loan.

24. Frank, *Debt and Terms of Aid*, p. 12.

25. McKitterick and Middleton, *The Bankers of the Rich*, p. 36.

26. Pearson, *Partners in Development*, p. 16.

27. OECD, *Financial Market Trends,* no. 27 (Paris: OECD, March 1984), pp. 149–51, International Capital Markets Historical Series, table 1.31, International Medium and Long-Term Bank Loans.

28. Ibid.

29. United Nations, *The International Flow of Long-Term Capital and Official Donations, 1961–65* (New York: United Nations, Department of Economic and Social Affairs, 1966), p. 35.

30. United Nations, *The Capital Development Needs of the Less Developed Countries*, A/AC.102/5 (New York: United Nations, Report of the Secretary General, Department of Social and Economic Affairs), pp. 9–12, table 3, a summary of the global estimate of the foreign capital required by underdeveloped countries.

31. Helen Hughes, "Debt and Development: The Role of Foreign Capital in Economic Growth," *World Development* 7 (February 1979): 103.

32. M. Ayub and S. Hegstad, *Public Industrial Enterprises* (Washington: World Bank, 1986), p. 11.

33. Dragoslav Avramovic, assisted by Ravi Gulhati, *Debt Servicing Capacity and Post-War Growth in International Indebtedness* (Johns Hopkins University Press, 1958).

34. United Nations, *International Flow of Long-Term Capital*, pp. 43–45; *United Nations, The External Financing of Economic Development, 1963–67*, pp. 108–17; UNCTAD, *Debt*

Problems of Developing Countries, TD/118/Supp 6, Rev. 1 (New York: United Nations, UNC-TAD Secretariat, 1972); UNCTAD, *Debt Problems in the Context of Development*, TD/B/C3/109, Rev. 1 (Geneva: UNCTAD, 1974), p. 34; Pearson, *Partners in Development*, pp. 153–64.

35. Pearson, *Partners in Development*, pp. 383–84, table 20; Hardy, *Rescheduling Developing Country Debt*, pp. 4–9, table 2.

36. Pearson, *Partners in Development*, p. 158; UNCTAD, *Debt Problems in the Context of Development*, pp. 21–22; George G. Abbott, "Aid and Indebtedness—A Proposal," *National Westminster Bank Review* (May 1972): 55–67.

37. Frank, *Debt and Terms of Aid*, pp. 17–23; UNCTAD, *Debt Problems in the Context of Development 1974*, pp. 7–17; Avramovic and Gulhati, *Debt Servicing Problems of Low-Income Countries, 1956–1958*, pp. 47–51.

38. Pearson, *Partners in Development*, pp. 157–58; UNCTAD, *Debt Problems in the Context of Development*, pp. 18–22.

39. Avramovic and Gulhati, *Debt Servicing Capacity and Post-War Growth in International Indebtedness*, pp. 31–34.

40. Avramovic and Gulhati, *Debt Servicing Problems of Low-Income Countries, 1956–1958*, p. 49.

41. Ibid., p. 4; Dragoslav Avramovic, *Economic Growth and External Debt* (Johns Hopkins University Press, 1964), p. 34.

42. Avramovic and Gulhati, *Debt Servicing Capacity and Post-War Growth in International Indebtedness*, p. 35.

43. Pearson, *Partners in Development*, pp. 72–73.

44. United Nations, *The External Financing of Economic Development, 1963–67*, p. 108.

45. Ibid., pp. 111–17; UNCTAD, *Debt Problems in the Context of Development*, TD/B/C3/109/Rev. 1, p. 15, reported the external debt of eighty-one developing countries at $79.2 billion in 1971 and $88 billion in 1972 based on World Bank data.

46. Robert Solomon, *The International Monetary System, 1945–1982* (New York: Harper & Row, 1982), pp. 186–87.

47. Solomon, *The International Monetary System*, pp. 209–11; Brian Tew, *The Evolution of the International Monetary System, 1945–81*, 2nd ed. (London: Hutchinson, 1982), pp. 181–86.

48. Graham Bird, *The International Monetary System and the Less Developed Countries*, 2nd ed. (London: Macmillan Press, 1982), pp. 288–91, table 12.1.

49. The G-10 is made up of eleven advanced economies that cooperate on economic, monetary, and financial matters (http://www.bus.org//list/G-10publications/).

50. Solomon, *The International Monetary System*, pp. 235–66.

51. Robert A. Pastor, *Congress and the Politics of U.S. Foreign Policy* (University of California Press, 1982), pp. 117–23.

52. W. M. Scammell, *The International Economy since 1945* (London: Macmillan Press, 1982), pp. 166–68.

53. World Bank, *World Development Report, 1984* (Oxford University Press, 1984), pp. 17–19; Neil McMullen, *The Newly Industrializing Countries: Adjusting to Success* (Washington: British-North American Committees, 1982), pp. 90–96.

54. "A Thing of Rags and Feathers," *The Economist*, December 25, 1982, p. 81; Bela Balassa, *The New Industrializing Countries in the World Economy* (Oxford: Pergamon Press, 1981), pp. 127–48.

55. Joel Darmstadter and Hans H. Landsberg, "The Economic Background in the Oil Crisis in Perspective," *Daedalus* 104 (Fall 1975): 21, table 9.1.

56. Peter R. Odell, *Oil and World Power,* 7th ed. (Middlesex, England: Penguin Books, 1983), pp. 212–30.

57. United States Senate, *Multinational Corporations and United States Foreign Policy*, Hearings before the Subcommittee on Multinational Corporations of the Committee on Foreign Relations, 93rd Cong., 1st and 2nd sess. (Washington: U.S. Government Printing Office, 1975), p. 288, figure 9.1. The average price of oil for all OPEC countries was $1.35 per barrel in 1971, $1.56 in 1972, $2.26 in 1973, and $9.07 in 1974.

58. The term petrodollar is used because crude oil has consistently been reference-priced and traded in world markets on a U.S. dollar basis.

Chapter Six

1. Joel Darmstadter and Hans H. Landsberg, "The Oil Crisis in Perspective," *Daedalus* 104 (Fall 1975): 21. Western Europe and Japan were particularly dependent on Mideast and North African oil. As of 1972, 80.4 percent and 78.9 percent, respectively, of the crude oil came from this area, representing 59.6 percent and 73 percent of their total energy consumption, respectively.

2. International Monetary Fund (IMF), Annual Report, 1974, p. 25.

3. Geoffrey Maynard, "The Recycling of Oil Revenues," *The Banker* (January 1975): 39; J. Nicholas Robinson, "The Role of Oil Funds Recycling in International Payments and Adjustment Problems," *OPEC Review* 4 (Summer 1980): 98–103.

4. Leslie de Quillacq, "OPEC High Absorbers—Low Absorbers," *International Herald Tribune*, November 30, 1982. The high absorbers were Venezuela, Algeria, Nigeria, Indonesia, Ecuador, and Gabon, and eventually Iraq and Iran because of their war of attrition after 1980. The low absorbers were the Arab Gulf states, Saudi Arabia, Qatar, Kuwait, and the United Arab Emirates. IMF, Annual Report, 1974, p. 29.

5. Organization for Economic Cooperation and Development (OECD), *Financial Market Trends* (Paris: March 1984), p. 142, table 5.2. Funds raised in the Euromarket by oil exporters, chiefly "high absorbers," were as follows: 1975 $3.3 billion, 1976 $3.8 billion, 1977 $6.9 billion, and 1978 $12.0 billion.

6. "Oil and Money in the Middle East," *The Banker* (March 1975): 277–329; Institute of Strategic Studies, "The Military Balance 1977/78" (London: 1977), p. 72. The "front-line" states were those actively confronting Israel.

7. Bank for International Settlements (BIS), Forty-eighth Annual Report, 1977/78 (Basel, 1978), pp. 82–83.

8. M. Stefan Mendelsohn, *Money on the Move: The Modern International Capital Market* (New York: McGraw-Hill, 1980), pp. 18–20. Hard currencies are the key currencies, such as U.S. dollars, sterling, deutsche marks, Swiss francs, and more recently, yen.

9. George W. McKenzie, *The Economics of the Eurocurrency System* (London: Macmillan Press, 1976), pp. 88–101; and George W. McKenzie, *The Economics of the Euro-Currency System* (London: Palgrave, 1976), pp. 103–26.

10. BIS, *The International Interbank Market* (Basel: BIS, 1983), p. 11.

11. Charles P. Kindleberger, *International Money—A Collection of Essays* (London: George Allen & Unwin, 1981), pp. 100–10.

12. David I. Lomax and P. T. G. Gutmann, *The Euromarket and International Financial Policies* (London: Macmillan Press, 1981), p. 5; BIS, *The International Interbank Market*, p. 18. The study indicates that the market was 70 percent interbank by the end of 1981, so these end-of-1978 figures might exaggerate the net market size.

13. Anthony Angelini, Maximo Eng, and Francis A. Lees, *International Lending, Risk and the Euromarkets* (London: Macmillan Press, 1979), p. 19.

14. Paul Mentre, "The Fund, Commercial Banks and Member Countries," Occasional Paper 26 (Washington: IMF, 1984), p. 5.

15. Ibid., p. 5.

16. Ibid., p. 6n9.

17. Paul A. Volcker, Chairman, Board of Governors of the U.S. Federal Reserve System, "Statement before the Committee in Banking Finance and Urban Affairs, U.S. House of Representatives," February 2, 1983, *Federal Reserve Bulletin* 69 (January–June 1983): 83.

18. Angelini, Eng, and Lees, *International Lending, Risk and the Euromarket*, p. 86.

19. Mendelsohn, *Money on the Move*, p. 18.

20. Ibid., pp. 71–76. LIBOR is the money rate offered to the most creditworthy money center banks in the interbank market. In practice, the cost of funds to any individual bank reflects its mix of deposits in the eurocurrency market. For banks lending euros and deutsche marks, the Luxembourg interbank rate, LUXIBOR, was quoted; the Paris interbank rate was used for sterling loans. In all cases the principle remained the same.

21. Irving S. Friedman, *The World Debt Dilemma: Managing Country Risk* (Washington: Council for International Banking Studies, and Philadelphia: Robert Morris Associates, 1983), p. 3.

22. OECD, *Financial Market Trends* (March 1980): 149–51, table 1.31.

23. Graham Bird, *The International Monetary System and the Less Developed Countries*, 2nd ed. (London: Macmillan Press, 1982), p. 219.

24. Mendelsohn, *Money on the Move*, p. 139.

25. Ibid., p. 137.

26. OECD, *Financial Market Trends* (March 1984): 144–45, table I.11.

27. IMF, Annual Report, 1978, p. 48.

28. Ibid., p. 48.

29. OECD, *Financial Market Trends*, 150–51, table 1.31.

30. Ibid., p. 149.

31. Ibid., p. 151. The OECD statistics include Yugoslavia as a developing, not Eastern European, country.

32. OECD, *External Debt of Developing Countries, 1983 Survey* (Paris: 1984), table D.

33. World Bank, *World Debt Tables, 1983/84 Edition*, p. 2.

34. Ibid., p. 3. The ratio of total debt to exports rose from 84.7 percent to 103.8 percent and total debt to GNP from 14.3 percent to 19.6 percent. Debt service ratios ran from 10.3 percent to 14.5 percent for all developing countries.

35. OECD, *External Debt of Developing Countries, 1983 Survey*, p. 12; Robert Solomon, "A Perspective on the Debt of Developing Countries," *Brookings Papers on Economic Activity* 2 (1977): 479–501; Harold Van B. Cleveland and W. H. Brittain, "Are the LDCs in over Their Heads?," *Foreign Affairs* 55 (July 1977): 732–50.

36. World Bank, *World Debt Tables, 1983/84 Edition*, p. 3.

37. World Bank, *World Development Report, 1983* (Oxford University Press, 1983), p. 3, table 1.1.

38. Bahran Nowzad and Richard C. Williams, "External Indebtedness of Developing Countries," Occasional Paper 3 (IMF, 1981), p. 13, table 9.

39. Benjamin J. Cohen in collaboration with Fabio Basagni, *Banks and the Balance of Payments: Private Lending in the International Adjustment Process* (Montclair, N.J.: Allanheld, Osmun, 1981), p. 96.

40. Robert Solomon, "The Debt of Developing Countries: Another Look," *Brookings Papers on Economic Activity* 2 (1981): 604.

41. Cohen and Basagni, *Banks and the Balance of Payments*, pp. 133–39, appendix. Ten country studies assess the adjustment process following its postponement because of the acquisition of commercial bank loans.

42. World Bank, *World Development Report, 1983*, p. 3, table 1.1. GDP growth, 1974–78, for non-oil-producing less-developed countries was 5.3, 4.0, 5.3, 5.6, 6.6 percent (p. 7). The growth of GDP, 1960–73, averaged 6.0 percent.

43. IMF, Annual Report, 1978, pp. 48–49.

44. Benjamin J. Cohen, "Balance of Payments Financing: Evolution of a Regime," *International Organization* 36 (Spring 1982): 470–71; Bird, *The International Monetary System and the Less Developed Countries*, pp. 160–68.

45. Cheryl Payer, *The Debt Trap: The IMF and the Third World* (Harmondsworth, Middlesex, England: Penguin Books, 1974).

46. Cohen and Basagni, *Banks and the Balance of Payments*, p. 144.

47. IDA is the World Bank's soft loan window; it provides long-term development loans to the poorest countries on subsidized terms. IDA's capital is subscribed to every three years by the advanced economies in the form of grants.

48. World Bank, Annual Report, 1984 (Washington, 1984), p. 11.

49. Bird, *The International Monetary System and the Less Developed Countries*, p. 5; World Bank, *World Development Report, 1983*, p. 4.

50. IMF, Annual Report, 1975, p. 22.

51. Tim Anderson, "In the Year of the Rescheduling," *Euromoney*, August 1982, p. 21.

52. World Bank, *World Development Report, 1983*, p. 22.

53. Cohen and Basagni, *Banks and the Balance of Payments*, pp. 93–94.

54. Daniel Badger and Robert Belgrave, "Oil Supply and Price; What Went Right in 1980?," Energy Paper 2 (London: Royal Institute of International Affairs, 1982), pp. 95–98, 113–19. The spot oil market, centered in Rotterdam, reflected the current or immediate price at which

crude oil was traded, primarily on a physical basis; the "marker" crude, Saudi Arabian light crude, served as a benchmark for pricing other crude oils in the market.

55. Edwin A. Deagle Jr., *The Future of the International Oil Market* (New York: Group of Thirty, 1983), p. 11.

56. World Bank, *World Development Report, 1984*, p. 30.

57. Deagle, *The Future of the International Oil Market*, p. 7, table 1; Joan Pearce, ed., *The Third Oil Shock: The Effects of Lower Prices* (London: Routledge & Kegan Paul for the Royal Institute of International Affairs, 1983), p. 1.

58. Pearce, *The Third Oil Shock*, p. 10.

59. "Bob Cratchit's Turn," *The Economist*, December 25, 1982, p. 9; Pearce, *The Third Oil Shock*, p. 15, table 1.1.

60. Badger and Belgrave, "Oil Supply and Price," pp. 119–26.

61. Pearce, *The Third Oil Shock*, p. 16; OECD, *External Debts of Developing Countries, 1983 Survey*, p. 12; World Bank, *World Development Report, 1984*, p. 27, box 2.4.

62. BIS, Fifty Third Annual Report, 1982/1983 (Basel, 1983), p. 123.

63. BIS, Fifty-Fourth Annual Report, 1983/84 (Basel, 1984), p. 6; IMF, Annual Report, 1984, p. 11.

64. BIS, Fifty-Fourth Annual Report, 1983/84; IMF, p. 1; BIS, Fifty-Third Annual Report, 1982/83, p. 124.

65. World Bank, *World Debt Tables, 1983/84 Edition*, p. 3.

66. P. A. Volcker, "Statement to the Committee on Foreign Affairs, House of Representatives," August 8, 1984, *Federal Reserve Bulletin* 70 (July–December 1984): 638.

67. "Turning Red," *The Economist*, May 4, 1985, p. 68.

68. World Bank, *World Development Report, 1983*, p. 11; IMF, Annual Report, 1984, p. 16.

69. The World Bank, Annual Report, 1984, Statistical Annex, pp. 57–59, table 4.

70. Susan Strange, "Protectionism and World Politics," a paper presented to the Australian National University Research School of Pacific Studies, April 19, 1984, p. 21. The author takes the position that despite fears about protectionism, trade was still flourishing, and the effects of the "new protectionism" on trade were not the major issue. Her concern focused on the international monetary system.

71. William R. Cline, *International Debt Reexamined* (Washington: Institute for International Economics, 1995), p. 13, table 1.4.

72. For a discussion of external debt and domestic economic-policy-related issues from 1946 to 1973, see Dragoslav Avramovic and others, *Economic Growth and External Debt* (Johns Hopkins University Press, 1964); UNCTAD, Ad Hoc Group of Experts, *Debt Problems of Developing Countries: The External Debt Experience of Developing Countries following Multilateral Renegotiations in Selected Countries*, TD/B.C.3/AC89 (Geneva, 1974); and Chandra S. Hardy, *Rescheduling Developing Country Debt, 1956–81: Lessons and Recommendations*, Monograph 15 (Washington: Overseas Development Council, 1982).

73. Mentre, "The Fund, Commercial Banks and Member Countries," p. 26.

74. World Bank, *World Development Report, 1984*, pp. 26–28.

75. Jungsoo Lee, "The External Debt-Servicing Capacity of Asian Developing Countries," *Asian Development Review* 1, no. 2 (1983): 69, table 3.

76. Ibid., p. 68, table 1; Seij Naya, D. H. Kim, and W. James, "External Shocks and Policy Response: The Asian Experience," *Asian Development Review* 2, no. 1 (1984): 2, table 1.

77. OECD, *External Debt of Developing Countries, 1983 Survey*, p. 31; World Bank, *World Development Report 1984*, p. 29, box 2.5.

78. IMF, *World Economic Outlook 1983* (Washington), p. 144.

79. Stockholm International Peace Research Institute, *SIPRI Year Book 1984* (Stockholm, 1984), p. 97.

80. OECD, *External Debt of Developing Countries, 1983 Survey*, p. 46. The estimated gross exposure of commercial banks to all non-oil-producing developing countries (non-OPEC and non-OECD) at the end of 1983 was estimated at $312 billion, excluding short-term debt, with net exposure of $192 billion, representing 40 percent average growth per year from 1977 to 1983. Of this amount, Argentina, Brazil, South Korea, and Mexico represented 62 percent of the gross exposure.

81. Great Britain House of Commons, *International Monetary Arrangements, International Lending by Banks, Fourth Report from the Treasury Service Committee Session 1982–83,* Vol. 1 (March 15, 1983).

82. OECD, *External Debt of Developing Countries, 1983 Survey,* p. 46. The stock of short-term bank credits in 1977 was $31 billion and in 1982 $104 billion.

83. House of Commons, *International Monetary Arrangements,* Vol. I.

84. "Japanese Banking—The International Retreat," *Euromoney,* March 1983, pp. 122–23; Volcker, "Statement before Committee on Banking, Finance and Urban Affairs, p. 83. In the 1970s, U.S. banking represented 35 percent of the loans to developing countries; by 1979–81, the proportion was under one-third.

85. "The Crash of 198?," *The Economist,* October 16, 1982, pp. 21–24; "Behind the Banking Turmoil: Bad Loans at Home—Not in the Third World—Are Shaking the System," *Business Week,* October 29, 1984, pp. 56–62.

86. Leo Goodstadt, "How the Banks Are Riding Out Hong Kong's Property Crisis," *Euromoney,* January 1983, pp. 89–92; "Alfa of Mexico Seeks to Suspend Debt Payment 90 Days," *Wall Street Journal,* May 3, 1982.

87. "Bankers Aweigh," *The Economist,* January 19, 1985, p. 65.

88. Cline, *International Debt,* p. 22, table 2.1.

89. Volcker, "Statement to Committee on Banking and Urban Affairs," p. 84.

90. House of Commons, *International Monetary Arrangements,* Vol. 1, pp. xix, xx.

91. Paul A. Volcker, "Statement before the Joint Economic Committee of the U.S. Congress," July 27, 1983, *Federal Reserve Bulletin* 69 (January–June 1983): 78.

Chapter Seven

1. Paul Volcker, "Statement before the Committee on Banking, Finance and Urban Affairs, U.S. House of Representatives," February 2, 1983, *Federal Reserve Bulletin* 69 (January–June 1983): 81.

2. E. Brau and others, "Recent Multilateral Debt Restructurings with Official and Bank Creditors 1983," Occasional Paper 25 (Washington: IMF, 1983), p. 22, table 8.

3. M. Stefan Mendelsohn, *The Debt of Nations* (New York: Priority Press, 1984), p. 33.

4. Ibid., p. 61, table 2.

5. Susan Strange, "Debt and Default in the International Political Economy," in *Debt and the Less Developed Countries,* edited by Jonathan David Aronson (Boulder, Colo.: Westview Press, 1979), p. 19. The author cites three crises in 1966—in Ghana, Indonesia, and the United Arab Republic—that heightened discussion of this issue.

6. United Nations Conference on Trade and Development (UNCTAD), *Debt Problems of Developing Countries*, TD/118/Supp. 6/Rev.1, p. 26.

7. Ibid., p. 22; Lester B. Pearson, *Partners in Development, Report of the Commission on International Development* (London: Pall Mall Press, 1969), p. 157.

8. Albert C. Cizauskas, "International Debt Renegotiations: Lessons from the Past," *World Development* 7 (February 1979): 201.

9. UNCTAD, *Debt Problems of Developing Countries*, p. 22.

10. Ibid.

11. Ibid., p. 6–7.

12. Pearson, *Partners in Development*, pp. 157–62; UNCTAD, *Debt Problems of Developing Countries*, pp. 24–26; UNCTAD, *Debt Problems in the Context of Development*, TD/B/G3/109/Rev. 1, pp. 9–10; UNCTAD, *Ad Hoc Group of Governmental Experts on Debt Problems of Developing Countries, Present Institutional Arrangement for Debt Renegotiations*, TDB/C.3 AC.B 13 (Geneva: UNCTAD, 1975).

13. P. T. Bauer, "Debt Cancellation for Development?" *National Westminster Bank Review* (November 1974): 40–51.

14. Cizauskas, "International Debt Renegotiations," p. 203; Chandra S. Hardy, *Rescheduling Developing Country Debt, 1956–1981: Lessons and Recommendations*, Monograph 15 (Washington: Overseas Development Council, 1982), pp. 65–67, Annex I.

15. Hardy, *Rescheduling Developing Country Debt*, pp. 59–60, Annex I, Indonesia, 1965–1970.

16. Cheryl Payer, *The Debt Trap: The IMF and the Third World* (Harmondsworth, Middlesex, England: Penguin Books, 1974), provides a somewhat radical condemnation of the entire process of aid, debt, rescheduling, and IMF involvement in this period.

17. Tim Anderson, "In the Year of Rescheduling," *Euromoney*, August 1982, p. 21; see also Hardy, *Rescheduling Developing Country Debt*, pp. 4–9, table 2.

18. Darrell Delamide, *Debt Shock* (London: George Weidenfeld and Nicholson, 1984), pp. 56–57.

19. Maxwell Watson, Peter Keller, Donald Mathieson, "International Capital Markets: Development and Prospects, 1984," Occasional Paper 31 (Washington: IMF, 1984), pp. 73–74. Convertible Turkish lira deposits were created by the government to attract external funds. They were short-term liabilities, primarily bank deposits, guaranteed against currency risks, and they paid a high interest return. Turkey defaulted on these liabilities, too, and rescheduled them together with the other external debts.

20. Hardy, *Rescheduling Developing Country Debt*, p. 8, table 2.

21. Paul Mentre, "The Fund, Commercial Banks, and Member Countries," Occasional Paper 26 (Washington: IMF, 1984), p. 17.

22. Watson, Keller, and Mathieson, "International Capital Markets: 1984," pp. 74–75; World Bank, "World Development Report, 1983," p. 22.

23. Commonwealth Group of Experts, *The Debt Crisis and the World Economy* (London: Commonwealth Secretariat, 1984), p. 104, appendix 3.1.

24. Watson, Keller, and Mathieson, "International Capital Markets: 1984," p. 71.

25. Hardy, *Rescheduling Development Country Debt*, p. 6.

26. Delamide, *Debt Shock*, p. 73

27. Richard Portes, "East Europe's Debt to the West: Interdependence Is a Two Way Street," *Foreign Affairs* (July 1977): 751, 757.

28. Watson, Keller, and Mathieson, "International Capital Markets: 1984," p. 87, table 28; Bank for International Settlements (BIS), Fifty-Third Annual Report, 1982/83 (Basel: 1983), p. 119, puts the total at $61 billion, up from $10 billion in 1973.

29. "Debt of Soviet Bloc Grew during 1981, Member Economies Slowed, Panel Says," *Wall Street Journal,* March 17, 1982, cites the United Nations Economic Commission for Europe; "The Issue in Poland," *Wall Street Journal,* January 8, 1982, estimates the debt service ratios for East Germany at 43, Hungary 57, Poland 87, and Romania 32.

30. "East European Debt: To Many a Bullish Western Banker, the Issue Is Rescheduling," *International Herald Tribune,* November 29, 1982.

31. "USSR Finds Borrowing Costly," *Euromoney,* December 1982, p. 7; "Add the Soviet Union to the List of Those with Cash Problems," *Wall Street Journal*, March 18, 1982.

32. OECD, *Financial Market Trends* 27 (March 1984): 162, table 1.31.

33. "Debtor Leverage," *Wall Street Journal,* March 5, 1982; Richard Portes, "Declaring Default on the Polish Debt Is Irrelevant," *Wall Street Journal*, May 26, 1982.

34. Donald Putnam Henry, *How Lending to Eastern Nations Affects the Developing World* (Santa Monica, Calif.: RAND Corporation, 1983), pp. v–vii.

35. Commonwealth Group of Experts, *The Debt Crisis*, p. 104, appendix 3.1.

36. Watson, Keller, and Mathieson, "International Capital Markets: 1984," p. 76.

37. "Bankers Meet Today on Polish Debt amid Uncertainty over Interest Payments," *Wall Street Journal*, January 7, 1982.

38. "Signed: The First COMECON Rescheduling," *Euromoney,* May 1982.

39. "Debt Relief, Poland's Case a Landmark," *International Herald Tribune,* November 29, 1982.

40. Watson, Keller, and Mathieson, "International Capital Markets: 1984, p. 76.

41. "Poland Asks Creditors for 'Realistic Attitude,'" *International Herald Tribune,* December 30, 1982.

42. Delamide, *Debt Shock*, pp. 83–85.

43. "Roumania Bid to Reschedule Debt to Commercial Banks," *Wall Street Journal,* March 3, 1982.

44. Watson, Keller, and Mathieson, "International Capital Markets: 1984," p. 72.

45. Commonwealth Group of Experts, *The Debt Crisis*, p. 104.

46. Delamide, *Debt Shock*, pp. 87–90; BIS, Fifty-Third Annual Report, 1982/83, pp. 126, 164–65. The BIS provided $100 million in March 1982, and in May 1982 a group of central banks supported an additional $110 million facility through the Bank for International Settlements (BIS). These initial loans were repaid before the end of BIS's fiscal year. By September 1982, with market conditions still unfavorable, the BIS provided a new bridging facility of $300 million that was also promptly repaid.

47. Mentre, "The Fund, Commercial Banks, and Member Countries," p. 19.

48. Delamide, *Debt Shock*, pp. 90–91; "Yugoslavia Loan Slow," *Wall Street Journal*, October 11, 1982.

49. "The Yugoslav Debt and Socialist 'Self-Management,'" *Wall Street Journal*, October 13, 1982; Mentre, "The Fund, Commercial Banks, and Member Countries," p. 20.

50. "Yugoslavia Aid of $1.3 billion in '83 Is Set by 15 Nations," *Wall Street Journal*, January 20, 1983.

51. "Panel of Bankers to Aid Yugoslavia in Financial Crisis," *Wall Street Journal*, January 19, 1983; Delamide, *Debt Shock*, pp. 92–93.

52. Commonwealth Group of Experts, *The Debt Crisis*, p. 96; Watson, Keller, and Mathieson, "International Capital Markets: 1984," p. 74.

53. Susan Kaufman Purcell, "War and Debt in South America," *Foreign Affairs* 61 (1982): 660–61.

54. BIS, Fifty-Third Annual Report, 1982/83, p. 126.

55. "Mexico's Debt Load Trouble Banks," *Wall Street Journal*, April 21, 1982.

56. "Pemex Has Oil Customers Back Its Debts," *Wall Street Journal*, July 20, 1982.

57. Joseph Kraft, *The Mexican Rescue* (New York: Group of Thirty, 1984), pp. 27–28; "Mexico's Debt Load Troubles Banks," *Wall Street Journal*, April 21, 1982.

58. "Mexico Seeks to Stop Paying Debt Principal," *Wall Street Journal*, August 20, 1982; William R. Cline, *International Debt Reexamined* (Washington: Institute for International Economics, 1995), p. 17; "The Ripples from Mexico Are Crossing the Rio Grande, *The Economist*, November 20, 1982, pp. 69–70; "The Debt Bomb," *Time Magazine*, January 10, 1983, pp. 4–10.

59. BIS, Fifty-Third Annual Report, 1982–83, p. 128.

60. Kraft, *The Mexican Rescue*, pp. 19–22.

61. Ibid., pp. 5–17.

62. M. Stefan Mendelsohn, *Commercial Banks and the Restructuring of Cross-Border Debt* (New York: Group of Thirty, 1983), pp. 23–25.

63. E. Brau and others, "Recent Multilateral Debt Restructurings, p. 37; Kraft, *The Mexican Rescue*, pp. 25–27, 43, 51.

64. Watson, Keller, and Mathieson, "International Capital Markets: 1984," p. 70.

65. William R. Rhodes, "The Role of the Steering Committee: How It Can Be Improved," in *Rescheduling Techniques: An International Conference on Sovereign Debt* (London: Group of Thirty, 1983), p. 31.

66. BIS, Fifty-Third Annual Report, 1982/83, p. 128; Kraft, *The Mexican Rescue*, pp. 48–51; IMF, "Annual Report, 1984," p. 94, appendix III, Schedule 4, Status of Standby and Extended Arrangements.

67. OECD, "External Debt of Developing Countries, 1983 Survey," p. 8; House of Commons, *International Monetary Arrangement, International Lending by Banks*, Vol. I, p. xxxii; Paul A. Volcker, "Statement before a Joint Economic Committee of the U.S. Congress, January 27, 1983," *Federal Reserve Bulletin* 69 (January–June 1983): 78–79.

68. IMF, *World Economic Outlook, 1983* (Washington, 1983), p. 16.

69. "Brazil Battles Problems of Inflation, Trade Deficit, but Local Politics and Global Slump Hurt Effort," *Wall Street Journal*, August 13, 1982; "Brazil Debates Renegotiating Its Huge Debt," *Wall Street Journal*, August 25, 1982.

70. "Risks World Trade Bust Brazilian Says," *Wall Street Journal*, September 28, 1982; "Brazil Will Seek Loans from IMF of up to $6 Billion," *International Herald Tribune*, November 29, 1982; "Reagan Unveils Credit to Brazil of $1.23 Billion," *Wall Street Journal*, December 2, 1982.

71. "Brazil's Foreign Debt the Largest in World, Total $83.8 Billion at End Last Year," *Wall Street Journal*, February 3, 1983.

72. Delamide, *Debt Shock*, p. 122.

73. "Brazil to Receive $1.2 Billion Loan under 815 Accord," *International Herald Tribune*, December 24, 1982.

74. "Brazil Invents the Sambatorium," *The Economist*, January 8, 1983, p. 69.

75. Mendelsohn, *Commercial Banks and the Restructuring of Cross-Border Debt*, p. 29.

76. Watson, Keller, and Mathieson, "International Capital Markets: 1984," pp. 64–65.

77. "Brazil Is Driving Them Nuts in Manhattan," *The Guardian*, May 18, 1983; "Brazil Attempts to Delay Payments on Bridging Loans," *Financial Times*, March 1, 1983.

78. Watson, Keller, and Mathieson, "International Capital Markets: 1984," p. 65.

79. "Banks Report Slowdown in Argentine Repayments," *Wall Street Journal*, May 29, 1982; "IMF Group Expected to Doubt Argentina's Ability to Pay Debt," *Wall Street Journal*, July 30, 1982.

80. Delamide, *Debt Shock*, p. 114; Anthony Sampson, "A Lady's Journey and a Banker's Nightmare," *International Herald Tribune*, December 27, 1982.

81. "Argentina Says It Won't Default on Its Debt—Top Officials Are Seeking Ways to Pay Short-Term Loans Coming Due in 1982," *Wall Street Journal*, September 20, 1982.

82. Commonwealth Group of Experts, *The Debt Crisis*, p. 86, appendix 2.1; Watson, Keller, and Mathieson, "International Capital Markets: 1984," p. 64.

83. "Argentina Junta Attempts to End Debt Deadlock," *Financial Times*, September 16, 1983; "New Argentine Government Calls for Debt Moratorium," *The Times* (London), December 16, 1983.

84. "Pressure for Early Agreement on Argentine Debts," *Financial Times*, April 2, 1984.

85. "U.S. Steps in with Short-Term Solution for Argentina," *Financial Times*, April 2, 1984; Commonwealth Group of Experts, *The Debt Crisis*, p. 86, appendix 2.1. The $500 million to clear the interest arrears was provided as follows: (1) $300 million from Mexico, Brazil, Colombia, and Venezuela, guaranteed by the U.S. government; (2) $100 million from the banks; and (3) $100 million from Argentine reserves.

86. "Now Cry for Argentina," *The Times* (London), September 24, 1984.

87. "Argentine Debt—Now for the Sales Pitch," *The Economist*, December 8, 1984, pp. 89–90.

88. "Latin American Debt Nearly Shutters Market," *International Herald Tribune*, November 29, 1982.

89. Watson, Keller, and Mathieson, "International Capital Markets: 1984," pp. 36–37.

90. Inter-American Development Bank, "Economic and Social Progress in Latin America: 1984 Report" (Washington: Inter-American Development Bank, 1984), p. 186.

91. "Lost Horizon," *Euromoney*, March 1983, p. 20.

92. "What Happens to the IMF if a Whole Continent Calls on It?" *The Economist*, December 11, 1982, pp. 19–25; IMF, Annual Report, 1984, pp. 91, 94.

93. "Ecuador Says It Must Reschedule Debts," *Wall Street Journal*, October 11, 1982; "Peru Asks to Pay Debt of $1 Billion over Eight Years," *International Herald Tribune*, July 29, 1983; "Chile Intervention into Banking System May Signal Renegotiations of Foreign Debt," *Wall Street Journal*, January 17, 1983; Commonwealth Group of Experts, *The Debt Crisis*, p. 88, appendix 2.1, notes that Chile received $350 million in bridging support from the BIS and $180 million from creditor banks.

94. "Honduras Seeks Rescheduling of Foreign Debt," *Wall Street Journal*, November 4, 1982; "Costa Rica Reaches an Accord with Banks on Restructuring Debt," *Wall Street Journal*, December 16, 1982; "Uruguay Seeks 90 Days Delay in Paying Debt," *Wall Street Journal*, March 11, 1983; "Dominican Republic Banks to Renegotiate Debt of $820 Million," *Wall Street Journal*, August 9, 1983.

95. "Venezuela to Try to Refinance Debt of $15.8 Billion," *International Herald Tribune*, June 9, 1983; "Caracas to Ask Payment Delay on $35 Billion," *International Herald Tribune*, January 5, 1984.

96. "Cuba Said to Reschedule Almost Half of Its Debt," *International Herald Tribune*, December 27, 1983.

97. Commonwealth Group of Experts, *The Debt Crisis*, pp. 104–06.

98. "Debt Problem Becoming a Serious Burden across Sub-Saharan Africa," *International Herald Tribune*, November 28, 1983; World Bank, Annual Report, 1984, p. 86.

99. World Bank, Annual Report, 1984, p. 154.

100. World Bank, "World Development Report, 1984," p. 31.

101. Commonwealth Group of Experts, *The Debt Crisis*, pp. 41–42.

102. Jessee Wright, "Financial Relief with Strings Attached," *African Business* (May 1984): 49; "Major Western Nations Agree to Reschedule Malawi's Official Debt, Extend New Credit," *Wall Street Journal*, September 24, 1982; "Smaller Problem Borrower Lost in Flurry over Debts of South America, East Europe," *Wall Street Journal*, December 10, 1982, which notes Kenya, Zambia, and Senegal; "Ghana Hopes for $100 Million from Paris Conference," *The Times* (London), November 23, 1982.

103. World Bank, "World Development Report, 1984," p. 31.

104. "Zaire Wins More Time to Repay Debt, Clearing Way for IMF Aid Package," *International Herald Tribune*, December 22, 1983; Commonwealth Group of Experts, *The Debt Crisis*, p. 106.

105. Commonwealth Group of Experts, *The Debt Crisis*, p. 93; "Exporters Agree on Nigeria Debt Terms," *Financial Times*, January 30, 1984.

106. World Bank, Annual Report, 1984, pp. 3, 15, 23; Wright, "Financial Relief with Strings Attached," *African Business* (May 1984): 51.

107. IMF, Annual Report, 1984, p. 91, table 24, Drawings under Supplementary Financing Facilities; and p. 94, Status of Stand-by and Extended Arrangements; "Why the IMF Is the Big Baas in Southern Africa," *The Economist*, January 22, 1983, pp. 59–61.

108. "Going It Alone—Austerity Puts Nation to Test," *International Herald Tribune*, Nigeria, a Special Economic Report, March 12, 1985.

109. "Moroccan Central Bank Supports Debt Package," *Financial Times*, December 12, 1984; Watson, Keller, and Mathieson, "International Capital Markets: 1984," p. 70.

110. "Philippine Economy Worries Banks," *Wall Street Journal*, September 17, 1982; "Philippines May Be Forced to Stretch Out Payments to Banks, Wharton Study Says," *Wall Street Journal*, November 1, 1982.

111. "Far East Financial Survey," *The Economist*, November 13, 1982, p. 6; "Growing Economic Crisis Seen as Threat to Marcos," *International Herald Tribune*, December 7, 1983.

112. Watson, Keller, and Mathieson, "International Capital Markets: 1984," p. 72.

113. Commonwealth Group of Experts, *The Debt Crisis*, p. 94.

114. Cline, *International Debt Reexamined*, pp. 208–15. The Baker Plan was named for U.S. Treasury Secretary James Baker; the plan shifted the restructurings from short-term balance of payments support to longer-term structural reforms for a targeted set of fifteen highly indebted countries.

115. Ibid., p. 8.

116. John H. Makin, "How to Defuse the Mexican Debt Crisis," *Financial Times*, May 14, 1986; and Cline, *International Debt Reexamined,* p. 208; see also A. W. Clausen, "World Bank Response to the Baker Initiative," address delivered in Buenos Aires, Argentina, December 9, 1985, p. 8.

117. World Bank, "The Mexican Debt Negotiation," Washington, October 28, 1986, unpublished memo, p. 2.

118. During the latter part of 1985 and all of 1986, I worked for the World Bank on industrial restructuring programs in Mexico and was directly involved in the policy discussions on restructuring the fertilizer monopoly, Fertilizantes Mexicanos, and was the mission leader for subsector restructurings. I also served as a member of the team that prepared the agricultural sector loan and led a team that prepared a study on the restructuring of CONA-SUPO, the agro-industrial SOE.

119. See World Bank, "The Mexican Debt Negotiation," p. 1.

120. William R. Cline, *International Debt Reexamined* (Washington: International Institute for Economics, 1995), p. 210.

121. Ibid., pp. 212–13.

122. I remember vividly being asked to join a large World Bank mission to Mexico following the oil collapse to prepare in thirty days a $1.5 billion support facility for Mexico in three tranches of $500 million each, linked to deregulation measures that the Mexicans had already implemented in sectors such as autos, pharmaceuticals, and agribusiness.

123. Cline, *International Debt Reexamined*, pp. 214–15.

124. Ibid., pp. 215–45 provides a detailed examination of the Brady Plan.

125. Ibid., pp. 218–19.

126. Ibid., pp. 221–22.

127. Ruben Lamdany, "The Market-Based Menu Approach in Action: The 1988 Brazilian Financing Package," in *Dealing with the Debt Crisis*, edited by Ishrat Husain and Ishac Diwan (Washington: World Bank, 1989), pp. 163–73, for a comprehensive view of the Brazilian deal.

128. Cline, *International Debt Reexamined*, pp. 231–33; see p. 237 for Cline's description of the IDA and the financial engineering for these transactions.

129. Michel H. Bouchet and Jonathan Hay, "The Rise of the Market-Based 'Menu' Approach and Its Limitations," in *Dealing with the Debt Crisis*, edited by Husain and Diwan, pp. 146–59.

130. Cline, *International Debt Reexamined*, pp. 236–37 and 238–40.

131. Ibid., pp. 248–49.

132. Hardy, *Rescheduling Developing Country Debt*, p. 23; Brau and others, "Recent Multilateral Debt Restructurings," p. 21.

133. Brau and others, "Recent Multilateral Debt Restructurings," p. 11.

134. Hardy, *Rescheduling Developing Country Debt*, p. 23.

135. IMF, "External Indebtedness of Developing Countries," Occasional Paper 3 (Washington: 1981), p. 22.

136. Friedman, *The World Debt Dilemma*, pp. 115, 108.

137. Brau and others, "Recent Multilateral Debt Restructurings," p. 9.

138. Jean-Claude Trichet, "The Paris Club: 25 Years of Rescheduling Experience," International Conference on Sovereign Debt Rescheduling Techniques, London, November 3–4, 1983. Trichet was joint chairman of the Paris Club.

139. Hardy, *Rescheduling Developing Country Debt*, p. 23.

140. Trichet, "The Paris Club"; Brau and others, "Recent Multilateral Debt Restructurings," p. 17.

141. Brau and others, "Recent Multilateral Debt Restructurings," p. 10; Irving S. Friedman, *The World Debt Dilemma—Managing Country Risk* (Washington and Philadelphia: Council for International Banking Studies and Robert Morris Associates, 1983), pp. 111–13.

142. IMF, "External Indebtedness of Developing Countries," p. 22.

143. Brau and others, "Recent Multilateral Debt Restructurings," p. 10.

144. Friedman, *The World Debt Dilemma*, p. 114.

145. IMF, "External Indebtedness of Developing Countries," p. 30.

146. Alfred Mudge, "Sovereign Debt Restructurings, A Current Perspective," in *Default and Rescheduling Corporate and Sovereign Borrowers*, edited by David Suratgar (London: Euromoney Publications, 1984), p. 89.

147. Mendelsohn, *The Debt of Nations*, p. 41.

148. Rhodes, "The Role of the Steering Committee," pp. 26–27.

149. Ibid., p. 30.

150. IMF, "External Indebtedness of Developing Countries," pp. 34–35.

151. Cline, *International Debt*, p. 30; Erik Ipsen, "After Mexico, the Regionals Are in Retreat," *Euromoney,* January 1983, pp. 58–65.

152. Friedman, *The World Debt Dilemma*, p. 133.

153. Ibid., p. 134.

154. Brau and others, "Recent Multilateral Debt Restructurings," p. 24.

155. Ibid., pp. 24–25.

156. Ibid., pp. 24–25, 30–32, table 11.

157. Mendelsohn, *The Debt of Nations*, p. 45.

158. Rhodes, "The Role of the Steering Committee," p. 29.

159. Mendelsohn, *The Debt of Nations*, p. 46.

160. Watson, Keller, and Mathieson, "International Capital Markets: 1984," pp. 73–74; Mentre, "The Fund, Commercial Banks, and Member Countries," p. 30.

161. Friedman, *The World Debt Dilemma*, p. 133; Brau and others, "Recent Multilateral Debt Restructurings," p. 13.

162. Commonwealth Group of Experts, *The Debt Crisis*, p. 86.

163. Brau and others, "Recent Multilateral Debt Restructurings," pp. 30–32, table 11.

164. Hardy, *Rescheduling Developing Country Debt*, p. 38.

165. Commonwealth Group of Experts, *The Debt Crisis*, pp. 88, 92, 93.

166. Watson, Keller, and Mathieson, "International Capital Markets: 1984," p. 88, table 29.

167. IMF, "External Indebtedness of Developing Countries," p. 35.

168. Brau and others, "Recent Multilateral Debt Restructurings," pp. 30–32, table 11.

169. Volcker, "Statement before the House Committee on Banking and Urban Affairs," pp. 84–87.

170. Hardy, *Rescheduling Developing Country Debt*, p. 38.

171. Peter Field, David Shirneff, and William Ollard, "The IMF and Central Banks Flex Their Muscles," *Euromoney,* January 1983, pp. 35–44.

172. Mentre, "The Fund, Commercial Banks, and Member Countries," p. 14.

173. Ibid., p. 26.

Chapter Eight

1. Albert C. Cizauskas, "International Debt Renegotiation Lessons from the Past," *World Development* 7 (February 1979): 203–05; Chandra S. Hardy, *Rescheduling Developing Country Debt, 1956–81: Lessons and Recommendations*, Monograph 15 (Washington: Overseas Development Council, 1982), pp. 52–56; J. Daniel O'Flaherty, "Finding Jamaica's Way," in *Developing Country Debt,* edited by Lawrence C. Franks and Marilyn J. Seiber (Oxford: Pergamon Press, 1979), pp. 126–40; Jennifer Sharpley, "Jamaica 1972–80," in *The IMF and Stabilization: Developing Country Experiences,* edited by Tony Killick (London: Heinemann Educational Books, 1984), pp. 154–55.

2. Richard Williams and others, "Recent Multilateral Debt Restructurings with Official and Bank Creditors, 1983," Occasional Paper 25 (Washington: IMF, 1983), p. 17, table 7; Hardy, *Rescheduling Developing Country Debt*, p. 2, table 1.

3. Commonwealth Group of Experts, *The Debt Crisis and the World Economy* (London: Commonwealth Secretariat, 1984), p. 46.

4. Joel Metais, "Less Developed Countries' Rising Indebtedness and the Lender of Last Resort in an International Context," in *Financial Crises: Theory, History, and Policy,* edited by Charles P. Kindleberger and Jean Pierre Laffargue (Cambridge University Press, 1982), p. 231.

5. Hardy, *Rescheduling Developing Country Debt*, pp. 26–29, table 13.

6. World Bank, *World Development Report, 1984* (Oxford University Press, 1984), p. 252, table 18.

7. "Fund's Chief Took on Big Role in Attacking World's Financial Ills," *Wall Street Journal,* March 14, 1983.

8. Charles P. Kindleberger, *Manias, Panics, and Crashes: A History of Financial Crises* (London: Macmillan Press, 1978), p. 215.

9. Group of Thirty, *Bank Supervision around the World* (New York, 1982), p. 4.

10. Stephany Griffith-Jones and Michael Lipton, *International Lenders of Last Resort: Are Changes Required?* (London: Midland Bank International Trade and Finance, 1984), p. 15.

11. Metais, "Less Developed Countries," p. 232.

12. Jack Guttentag and Richard Herring, "The Lender-of-Last-Resort in an International Context," Princeton University Essay in International Finance 151 (1983), pp. 10–11; Robert M. Solow, "On the Lender of Last Resort," in *Financial Crises*, edited by Kindleberger and Laffargue, pp. 242–46.

13. Solow, "On the Lender of Last Resort," p. 242.

14. Great Britain, House of Commons, *International Monetary Arrangements: International Lending by Banks*, Vol. 1, p. xli; Warren D. McClan, "Financial Fragility and Instability: Monetary Authorities as Borrowers of Last Resort," in *Financial Crises,* edited by Kindleberger and Laffargue, p. 286; Guttentag and Herring, "The-Lender-of-Last-Resort in an International Context," p. 12.

15. "New Crisis Has Begun in International Debt Banking, Experts Warn," *Wall Street Journal*, June 8, 1983.

16. Albert Fishlow, "The Debt Crisis: Round Two Ahead?" in *Adjustment Crisis in the Third World*, edited by Richard Feinberg and Valeriana Kallab (New Brunswick, N.J.: Transaction Books, 1984), pp. 32–33; William E. Simon, "Cut off the International Loan Lushes," *Wall Street Journal*, April 6, 1983; Donald T. Regan, "The United States and the World's Debt Problem," *Wall Street Journal*, February 8, 1983.

17. IMF, Annual Report, 1984, p. 92.

18. Ibid., p. 74, table 18; "The IMF and Latin America: What Happens to the IMF If a Whole Continent Calls on It?" *The Economist*, December 11, 1982, pp. 19–25. Special Drawing Rights (SDRs) is a currency created by the IMF as the "Central Bank" of central banks primarily focused on assisting developing countries. The SDRs are backed by the capital of the IMF subscribed by the advanced industrial economies—the United States, Germany, United Kingdom., etc.

19. IMF, Annual Report, 1984, p. 94, Appendix VIII. Annual limits of 125 percent, three-year limits of 375 percent, and cumulative limits of 500 percent of the quota were established.

20. Commonwealth Study Group, *Towards a New Bretton Woods: Challenges for the World Financial and Trading System* (London: Commonwealth Secretariat, 1983), p. 47.

21. "Even the IMF Has a Few Bad Debts," *The Economist*, June 8, 1985, pp. 63–64; "Vietnam Loans Ended by IMP," *The Times* (London), April 12, 1985.

22. "A Dramatic Change at the IMF," *New York Times*, September 1, 1983); Benjamin J. Cohen in collaboration with Fabio Basagni, *Banks and the Balance of Payments: Private Lending in the International Adjustment Process* (Montclair, N.J.: Allanheld, Osmun., 1981), p. 144.

23. These issues are discussed in depth in Tony Killick, ed., *The Quest for Economic Stabilization* (London: Heinemann Educational Books, 1984); and Killick, ed., *The IMF and Stabilization*. See also John Williamson, ed., *IMF Conditionality* (Washington: Institute for International Economics, 1983).

24. Cohen and Basagni, *Banks and the Balance of Payments*, pp. 134–35, table 4.6.

25. Tony Killick and Jennifer Sharpley, "Extent, Causes and Consequences of Disequilibria in Developing Countries," in *The Quest for Economic Stabilization,* edited by Killick, p. 49. See also Joan M. Nelson, "The Politics of Stabilization," in *Adjustment Crisis in the Third World,* edited by Feinberg and Kallab; Williamson, *IMF Conditionality*, pp. 99–118, 231–563. A radical view of these experiences is presented in Payer, *The Debt Trap*.

26. "IMF Grants $1.4 Billion for Standby Loan to Buenos Aires," *The Times* (London), September 27, 1984.

27. Sarah Hogg, "Lenders under Fire from All Sides," *The Times* (London), September 24, 1984; "Focus on the Fund," *The Times* (London), June 12, 1984.

28. "Brazil, IMF Set Talks on Reform to Permit Loan," *International Herald Tribune*, May 13, 1985.

29. Anatole Kaletsky, *The Costs of Default* (New York: Priority Press, 1985), p. 4; "High Finance, High Politics," in *Uncertain Future*, edited by Feinberg and Kallab, pp. 117–22.

30. Pedro Pablo Kuczynski, "The Outlook for Latin American Debt," *Foreign Affairs* (Fall 1987): 135.

31. Deborah M. R. Coyne, *Monetary and Financial Reform: The North-South Controversy* (Ottawa, Canada: North-South Institute, 1984), p. 43; also Commonwealth Study Group, *Towards A New Bretton Woods*, pp. 80–81.

32. In November 1988 I completed negotiations of a $250 million credit for Mexico on behalf of the World Bank. One major issue in the negotiations was the rise in the cost of World Bank funds.

33. IDA's funds are lent for fifty years interest-free with up to seven years' grace. The borrower pays a commitment fee for these funds.

34. Coyne, *Monetary and Financial Reform*, pp. 4, 48; World Bank, Annual Report, 1984, pp. 11, 20; "World Bank to Try to Tap Fresh Source of Money," *International Herald Tribune*, November 28, 1983.

35. Stanley Please, "The World Bank Lending for Structural Adjustment," in *Adjustment Crisis in the Third World*, edited by Feinberg and Kallab, pp. 85–86.

36. Commonwealth Group of Experts, *The Debt Crisis*, p. 61.

37. World Bank, "Memo to Operational Vice Presidents," March 14, 1986.

38. World Bank, *Operational Strategy in the Heavily Indebted Middle Income Countries* (Washington, 1988), p. 4.

39. Latin American debtors, for example, reduced imports from $100 billion in 1981 to approximately $60 billion in 1986. "The Impact of the Latin American Debt Crisis on the U.S. Economy," Joint Economic Committee, Congress of the United States, Staff Study, May 10, 1986, p. 3.

40. Richard Feinberg, "The Adjustment Imperative and U.S. Policy," in *Adjustment Crisis in the Third World*, edited by Feinberg and Kallab, p. 12; W. W. Rostow, "Terms of a North-South Economic Partnership," London School of Economics, Suntory/Toyota Lecture, March 13, 1984, p. 6; William H. Bliss and Jorge Del Canto, "LDC Debt beyond Crisis Management," *Foreign Affairs* (Summer 1983): 1106.

41. Benjamin J. Cohen, "International Debt and Linkage Strategies: Some Foreign Policy Implications for the United States," *International Organization* 39 (Autumn 1985): 703–04.

42. Harold Lever and Christopher Huhne, *Debt and Danger* (Boston: Atlantic Monthly Press, 1985), p. 83.

43. Cizauskas, "International Debt Renegotiations," p. 203; Ali Likaraosmanoglu, "Turkey's Security and the Middle East," *Foreign Affairs* (Fall 1983): 160–61.

44. Queh Peck Lim, "LBI Gets Caught in Cross Fire," *Euromoney*, February 1983, pp. 29–35.

45. Ian Davidson, "Mexico: A Long-Haul Ahead," *Financial Times*, May 24, 1983.

46. Robert A. Manning, "The Philippines in Crisis," *Foreign Affairs* (Winter 1984–85), pp. 392–410.

47. Donald Putnam Henry, *How Lending to Eastern Nations Affects the Developing World* (Santa Monica, Calif.: Rand Corporation, 1983), p. v; "Debtor Leverage," *Wall Street Journal*, March 5, 1982.

48. "General Jaruzelski's Cupboard Is Bare," *The Economist*, February 12, 1983, pp. 71–75; "The Issue in Poland," *Wall Street Journal*, January 8, 1982; "Polish Access to Credits at Issue, Experts Say," *International Herald Tribune*, June 18–19, 1983.

49. "Yugoslav Economy—Balkan Blues," *The Economist*, January 22, 1983, p. 64; "6 Billion Yugoslav Credit Set," *International Herald Tribune*, January 24, 1983.

50. Bradley Graham, "East Bloc Tug-of-War: Desire for Autonomy vs. Need for Moscow Aid," *International Herald Tribune*, June 17, 1985.

51. "Banks Rush to Sign Up for East German Credit," *International Herald Tribune*, February 25, 1985; "East Bloc Nations Widen Trade Surplus with West," *International Herald Tribune*, November 29, 1983.

52. Bradley Graham, "In the Soviet Shadow—Autonomy Is Dependency: Russia Driving Harder Trade Bargains with Allies," *International Herald Tribune*, June 18, 1985.

53. World Bank, *World Development Report, 1984*, p. 228, table 6, records the growing aid in cereals and food, the decline in the value added in agriculture in 1970 and 1982, cereal imports in 1974 and 1982, and the average index of food production (1969–71 base) in 1980–82 for lower- and lower-middle-income countries, trends that demonstrate Africa's agricultural dilemma; see also the Brandt Commission, *Common Crisis: North-South Cooperation for World Recovery* (London: Pan Books, 1983), pp. 119–32.

54. Jesse Wright, "Financial Relief with Strings Attached," *African Business* (May 1984): 53; "Can They Manage without the IMF?," *Euromoney*, May 1982, p. 156; Jonathan Power, "Two Aspects of Nigeria: A Land with Snap in the Air," *International Herald Tribune*, May 19, 1983; and Jean Herskowitz, "In Trouble That Needs U.S. Aid," *International Herald Tribune*, May 19, 1983.

55. Hedley Bull, "The Third World in International Society," *Year Book of World Affairs*, Vol. 33 (London: Steven & Sons, under the Auspices of the Institute of World Affairs, 1979).

56. "External Debt Position of Sub-Saharan Africa Has Worsened Considerably," *IMF Survey* (June 1988): 178–79, 187, Exhibit 7.

57. Ibid., p. 178.

58. Ibid., p. 179.

59. World Bank, *Financing Adjustment with Growth in Sub-Saharan Africa, 1986–1990* (Washington, 1986), p. 11.

60. "External Debt Position of Sub-Saharan Africa," *IMF Survey*, p. 180; see also World Bank, *Financing Adjustment with Growth in Sub-Saharan Africa, p. 50,* for a reiteration of this view.

61. Kathie L. Krumm, "The External Debt of Sub-Saharan Africa," World Bank Staff Working Paper 741 (Washington, 1985), p. 27; "Summit Adopts Debt Relief Plan to Help Poorest Countries," *IMF Survey* (June 1988): 219–22, for a list of specific steps to promote debt relief.

62. Kaletsky, *The Costs of Default*, pp. 13–20; Thomas I. Enders and Richard P. Mattione, *Latin America: The Crisis of Debt and Growth* (Brookings, 1984); see also Lever and Huhne, *Debt and Danger*, p. 30.

63. Ariel Buira, "The Exchange Crisis and the Adjustment Programme in Mexico," in *Prospects for Adjustment in Argentina, Brazil and Mexico,* edited by John Williamson (Washington: Institute for International Economics, 1983), p. 59; Miguel de la Madrid, "Mexico: The New Challenges," *Foreign Affairs* (Fall 1984): 2–26; Pedro Pablo Kuczynski, "Latin American Debt: Act Two," *Foreign Affairs* (Fall 1983): 23, 28.

64. Riordan Roett, "Democracy and Debt in South America: A Continent's Dilemma," *Foreign Affairs* (America and the World, 1983): 695.

65. "Don't Forgive the Debtors," *The Economist*, May 14, 1988, p. 13.

66. Jonathan Eaton and Mark Gersovitz, "Debt with Potential Repudiation, Theoretical and Empirical Analysis," *Review of Economic Studies* 48 (April 1981): 290; Jeffrey Sachs, *Theoretical Issues in International Borrowing*, Studies in International Finance 54, (Princeton University, Department of Economics, 1984), pp. 4–5; Lever and Huhne, *Debt and Danger*, pp. 91–107, for an extensive discussion of this issue.

67. World Bank, "Commercial Banks' Debt Restructuring and New Money Facilities Agreements," Debt Management and Financial Advisory Services 9 (Washington, November 13, 1987), pp. 4, 4a, 19.

68. Lever and Huhne, *Debt and Danger*, p. 91.

69. C. Fred Bergsten, William R. Cline, and John Williamson, *Bank Lending to Developing Countries: The Policy Alternatives* (Washington: Institute for International Economics, 1985), p. 59.

70. Ibid., pp. 55–58; Bill Bradley, "Debtor Countries That Need a Break," *Washington Post*, September 28, 1987. Senator Bradley was a strong advocate of debt relief as a means of resolving the crisis.

71. Lever and Huhne, *Debt and Danger*, pp. 124–25.

72. The Chapter 11 bankruptcy process in the United States and the Concordat proceedings on the European continent normally offer some form of debt relief. This analogy assumes that debtor states can be compared to companies facing the threat of bankruptcy.[

73. "Don't Forgive the Debtors," *The Economist*, p. 13.

74. Morgan Guaranty Trust, "Strengthening the LDC Debt Strategy," *World Financial Markets* (September/October 1985): 2.

75. Ibid., p. 1.

76. "Don't Forgive the Debtors," *The Economist*, p. 13.

77. Krumm, "The External Debt of Sub-Saharan Africa," p. 37. For 1985 to 1987, multilateral servicing amounted to 14 percent of public debt service.

78. "Summit Adopts Debt Relief Plan to Help Poorest Countries," *IMF Survey* (June 27, 1988): 222.

79. World Bank, "Commercial Banks' Debt Restructuring and New Money Facilities Agreements," pp. 2, 15–16, and 22 for the Argentina, Mexico, and Philippine 1987 restructurings.

80. Developing country debt trades in a relatively thin secondary market at discounts ranging from 20 percent to 90 percent, depending on the debtor country and the status of the

debt service payments at any point. See Richard J. Bentley, "Debt Conversion in Latin America," *Columbia Journal of World Business* (Fall 1986): 38.

81. Kuczynski, "The Outlook for Latin American Debt," p. 134.

82. Shearson Lehman Brothers, "A Guide to Debt Equity Swaps," *Institutional Investor* (Special Sponsored Section) (December 1987): 2. Mexico suspended its program at the end of 1986 because of inflationary concerns and the adoption of an austerity program. See also Carl Ludvik, "Chile's Foreign Debt Conversion Schemes" (Washington: World Bank, July 24, 1986), Annex 3; and Felipe Larrain, "Market-Based Debt-Reduction Schemes in Chile: A Macro Economic Perspective," CPD Discussion Paper 1987–2 (Washington: World Bank, 1987).

83. World Bank, "Commercial Banks' Debt Restructuring and New Money Facilities Agreements," p. 3.

84. Barry Eichengreen and Richard Portes, "Dealing with Debt: The 1930s and the 1980s," Working Papers in Debt and International Finance (Washington: World Bank, August 1989).

85. H. C. Wallich, "The Future of Latin America Dollar Bonds," *American Economic Review* 33 (June 1943): 321–35.

86. Michael P. Dooley, "Market Valuation of External Debt," *Finance and Development* 24 (March 1987): 7.

87. Kuczynski, "The Outlook for Latin American Debt," p. 143. See also Mohsin S. Kahn and Nadeem Ul Haque, "Capital Flight from Developing Countries," *Finance and Development* 24 (March 1987): 4–5; they estimate capital flight from major debtors as a percentage of total external debt at approximately 35 percent for Mexico, Argentina, and Venezuela using one methodology and higher using a different methodology.

88. Kuczynski, "The Outlook for Latin American Debt," pp. 144–45.

89. Morgan Guaranty Trust, "Strengthening the LDC Debt Strategy," p. 8.

90. Ibid., pp. 8–9.

91. Ibid., p. 12.

92. Bergsten, Cline, and Williamson, *Bank Lending to Developing Countries*, pp. 53–54.

93. Ibid., pp. 133–59. The authors examine the costs and benefits of a range of smoothing alternatives.

94. World Bank, "Commercial Banks' Debt Restructuring and New Money Facilities Agreements."

95. "Japan Proposes Debt Plan for Third World," *The News* (Mexico City), September 28, 1988.

96. "Debtors Call for Dialogue," *The Times* (London), February 11, 1985.

97. John Maynard Keynes, *The Economic Consequences of the Peace* (London: Macmillan Press, 1920), p. 134.

Chapter Nine

1. Many authors of this period use developing countries and emerging market countries interchangeably. For purposes of this part of the book I use "developing countries" for lower-income countries; "emerging markets" for middle-income countries as well as some East Asian countries such as Korea that are moving beyond middle-income status; and "transition econ-

omies" for a new category of country that refers to Central and Eastern Europe (CEE), the former Soviet Union (FSU), China, and Vietnam.

2. William R. Cline, *International Debt Reexamined* (Washington: Institute for International Economics, 1995), pp. 218–49, has an extensive discussion of the Baker Plan focused on debt restructuring and new lending by the banks in the immediate aftermath of the crisis to 1986–87, and the Brady Plan focused on debt reduction and forgiveness from 1998 to 2004.

3. Eugenio Cerutti, Galina Hale, and Camelia Minoiu, "Financial Crises and the Composition of Cross-Border Lending," Working Paper 14/185 (Washington: International Monetary Fund, October 2014). The paper covers the period from 1995 to 2012, but in the early 1990s after the debt crisis and restructurings of the late 1980s, syndicated lending was quite muted and only rose as the era progressed.

4. Dipak Dasgupta and others, "Short-Term Debt and Financial Crises," in *Managing Financial and Corporate Distress*, edited by Charles Adams, Robert E. Litan, and Michael Pomerleano (Brookings, 2000), p. 32.

5. Ira W. Lieberman and Christopher D. Kirkness, eds., *Privatization and Emerging Equity Markets* (Washington: World Bank and Flemings, 1998). During this period I worked in a number of Latin American countries for the World Bank on industrial restructuring, including Fertilizantes Mexicanas (FERTIMEX) and CONASUPO in Mexico; the Instituto de Fomento Industrial (Industrial Development Bank) of Colombia, which owned several large loss-making SOEs; and Sociedad Mixta Siderurgia Argentina (SOMISA, the state-owned integrated steel maker in Argentina).

6. For a discussion of reforms in the CEE and the FSU, see World Bank, *Transition: The First Ten Years* (Washington, 2002) and World Bank, *World Development Report 1996: From Plan to Market* (Washington, 1996). For a comprehensive review of structural reforms, see Ira W. Lieberman and Daniel J. Kopf, eds., *Privatization in Transition Economies: The Ongoing Story* (New York: Elsevier, 2007).

7. World Bank, *World Development Report 1996*, p. 135, discusses association and accession agreements; for a more extensive treatment of this subject see Katalin Fabian, ed., *Globalization: Perspectives from Central and Eastern Europe* (Oxford: Elsevier, 2007).

8. BBC, "On This Day," December 31, 1999; for a discussion of the oligarchs, see Chrystia Freeland, *Sale of the Century: Russia's Wild Ride from Communism to Capitalism* (New York: Crown Books, 2000). For a discussion of Russian reforms and their collapse, see Ira Lieberman and Rogi Veimetra, "The Rush for Shares in the 'Klondyke' of Wild East Capitalism: Loans-for-Shares Transactions in Russia," *George Washington Journal of International Law and Economics* 29, no. 3 (1996): 737–68; Ira Lieberman and John Nellis, eds., *Russia: Creating Private Enterprises and Efficient Markets* (Washington: World Bank, 1994). See also Maxim Boycko, Andrei Shleifer, and Robert Vishny, *Privatizing Russia* (MIT Press, 1995); and Andrei Shleifer and Daniel Triesman, *Without a Map: Political Tactics and Economic Reform in Russia* (MIT Press, 2000).

9. William Mako and Chunlin Zhang, "Why Is China So Different from Other Transition Economies?," in *Privatization in Transition Economies*, edited by Lieberman and Kopf.

10. World Bank, *World Development Report 1996*, p. 136.

11. Phumchai Kambhato, "American Depository Receipts, Global Depository Receipts, and Other Financing Instruments," in *Privatization and Emerging Equity Markets*, edited by Lieberman and Kirkness.

12. World Bank, *World Development Report 1996*, p. 136.

13. Ira Lieberman, "Privatization: The Development Theme of the 1990s," *Columbia Journal of World Business* (Spring 1993): 28, 1.

14. This section on privatization is largely taken from Ira Lieberman and Robert Fergusson, "Introduction," in *Privatization in Transition Economies*, edited by Lieberman and Kopf. I have also used variants on this theme in other published works in Ira Lieberman and Robert Fergusson, "Overview of Privatization and Emerging Equity Markets," in *Privatization and Emerging Equity Markets,* edited by Lieberman and Kirkness.

15. Nancy M. Birdsall and others, *The East Asian Miracle: Economic Growth and Public Policy* (Oxford University Press, 1993); James A. Roumasset and Susan Barr, eds., *The Economics of Cooperation: East Asian Development and the Case for Pro-Market Intervention* (Boulder, Colo.: Westview Press, 1992).

16. Ira W. Lieberman, "Introduction," in *Privatization in Transition Economies,* edited by Lieberman and Kopf, p. 4.

17. Ibid.

18. I was on the staff of the World Bank from 1985 to 1987 and worked in an industrial restructuring unit focused on assisting governments to restructure SOEs. My initial work was on large SOEs in Mexico such as FERTIMEX, the state-owned fertilizer monopoly, and CONASUPO, the large agribusiness conglomerate owned by the state. From 1987 to 1990, as a consultant for the World Bank, I worked in Colombia on the restructuring of the Instituto de Fomento Industrial (the state-owned development bank), which owned several loss-making SOEs, and in Argentina advising the government on privatization at the Ministry of Defense on the restructuring pursuant to privatization of SOMISA, the integrated steel producer. Most of these large SOEs, except CONASUPO, were large loss makers, heavily indebted, overstaffed, and poorly managed. It became clear that the governments lacked the political will and the capability to restructure these firms. See Ira Lieberman, *Industrial Restructuring: Policy and Practice* (Washington: World Bank, 1989).

19. Lieberman, "Introduction," in *Privatization in Transition Economies*, edited by Lieberman and Kopf, p. 5; World Bank, *World Development Report 1996*, p. 50.

20. The Washington Consensus refers to a set of broadly free market economic ideas, supported by prominent economists and international organizations such as the IMF, the World Bank, the European Union, and the United States. The Washington Consensus advocated free trade, floating exchange rates, free markets, and macroeconomic stability. The ten principles were originally laid out by John Williamson in 1989 and include ten sets of relatively specific policy recommendations.

21. I rejoined the staff of the World Bank in February 1993, having advised the government of Argentina and the Polish government on privatization and having prepared SOEs in Mexico and Colombia for privatization, to comanage the World Bank's privatization program. I joined this discussion and intellectual ferment and advised several governments in

the CEE and FSU—Poland, Russia, Ukraine, Albania, Uzbekistan, and eventually Serbia, as well as the Turkish government—on their privatization programs.

22. Lieberman and Fergusson, "Overview of Privatization and Emerging Equity Markets," in *Privatization and Emerging Equity Markets,* edited by Lieberman and Kirkness, pp. 4–5, tables on pp. 12–14.

23. Most of the transition economies in the CEE and FSU operated under the Napoleonic Code. Laws drafted by lawyers were often from legal firms in the United States or the United Kingdom, which drafted laws in line with U.S. or U.K. case law. Needless to say, a major effort after the initial reforms in these countries included programs to support and fund harmonization of these laws, modernize the court systems, and train judges, bankruptcy administrators, and others to implement the laws.

24. Lieberman and Fergusson, "Introduction," *Privatization and Emerging Capital Markets,* edited by Lieberman and Kopf, pp. 8–9.

25. Gary J. Fine and Enna Karlova, "Privatization and the New Securities Markets in the Czech Republic, Poland and Russia," in *Privatization and Emerging Equity Markets,* edited by Lieberman and Kirkness, pp. 25, 27.

26. Ibid., pp. 22–23, 29.

27. Phumchai Kambhato, "The Flagship Role of Telecom Privatizations," in *Privatization and Emerging Equity Markets,* edited by Lieberman and Kirkness, p. 88.

28. Ibid.

29. This section is primarily based on Lieberman, "The Role of Emerging Market Equity Funds," in *Privatization and Emerging Equity Markets,* edited by Lieberman and Kirkness, pp. 124–27.

30. Ibid., pp. 124–25.

31. Ibid., p. 124.

32. Phumchai Kambhato, "American Depository Receipts, Global Depository Receipts, and Other New Financing Instruments," in *Privatization and Emerging Equity Markets,* edited by Lieberman and Kirkness, pp. 116–17.

33. Ibid.

34. Steven Radelet and Jeffrey Sachs, "The Onset of the East Asian Financial Crisis," National Bureau of Economic Research (NBER) Currency Crises Conference, February 6–7, 1998, p. 9.

35. Ibid.

36. Joseph Stiglitz, *Globalization and Its Discontents* (New York: W. W. Norton, 2002), pp. 67–68. Stiglitz also gives his views on the downsides of FDI, when larger multinational corporations and banks crowd out domestic companies.

37. World Bank, *Global Economic Prospects and the Developing Countries, 1998/1999: Beyond Financial Crisis* (Washington, 1999), pp. 60–64; Joseph E. Stiglitz, "Reforming the Global Reserve System," in *Making Globalization Work* (New York: W.W. Norton, 2007).

38. Radelet and Sachs, "The Onset of the East Asian Financial Crisis," pp. 16–17 and table III.

39. World Bank, "Global Economic Prospects and the Developing Countries, 1998/1999," p. xii.

40. For a discussion of debt relief that is beyond the scope of this book, see Nancy Birdsall and John Williamson, with Brian Deese, *Delivering on Debt Relief* (Washington: Center for Global Development and Institute for International Economics, 2002); and Carlos A. Primo Braga and Dorte Domeland, eds., *Debt Relief and Beyond* (Washington: World Bank, 2009).

Chapter Ten

1. For a detailed discussion of the Mexican crisis, see William R. Cline, *International Debt Reexamined* (Washington: Institute for International Economics, 1995); U.S. Treasury, "Monthly Report by the Secretary of the Treasury Pursuant to the Mexican Debt Disclosure Act of 1995," November 1996; and World Bank, "Mexico Financial Sector Strategy" (Washington, July 22, 1996); among others.

2. Cline, *International Debt Reexamined*, p. 495.

3. Ibid., pp. 294–96.

4. I worked for the World Bank in Mexico from 1985 following the earthquake through 1987 on structural adjustment programs and was very much aware of support provided by the bank to the government on trade and price liberalization though a series of policy and structural adjustment projects/loans.

5. Cline, *International Debt Reexamined*, pp. 292–93, 298–302.

6. Thayer Watkins, "The Mexican Peso Crisis of 1994–1995" (San Jose State University, Economics Department) (www.sjsu.edufaculty/Watkins/mexico95.htm), p. 1.

7. Steven Radelet and Jeffrey Sachs, "The Onset of the East Asian Financial Crisis" (Cambridge, Mass.: Harvard Institute for International Development, March 30, 1998), table 3 (percentages calculated by the author).

8. The PRI, *Partido Revolucinario Institucional*, had dominated Mexican politics for over 60 years since the Mexican Revolution, but the election of 1994 was hotly contested.

9. Watkins, "The Mexican Peso Crisis," p. 1; Sri-Ram Aiyer, "Anatomy of Mexico's Banking System following the Peso Crisis," Latin American and Caribbean Technical Department Report 45 (Washington: World Bank, December 1996), p. 4.

10. U.S. Treasury, "Monthly Report by the Secretary of the Treasury Pursuant to the Mexican Debt Disclosure Act of 1995" (Washington, November 1996), pp. 501–05.

11. World Bank, "Mexico Financial Sector Strategy" (draft), July 22, 1996, p. 2.

12. Ibid., p. 66.

13. Aiyer, "Anatomy of Mexico's Banking System," p. 2.

14. World Bank, "Mexico Financial Sector Strategy," p. 2.

15. World Bank, "Mexico: Strengthening Enterprise Finance," Report 1773ME (Washington, 1998), p. iii.

16. Roy A. Karaoglan and Michael Lubrano, "Mexico's Banks after the December 1994 Devaluation—A Chronology of Government Response" (draft) (Washington: International Finance Corporation, December 1995), pp. 60–63.

17. World Bank, "Mexico Financial Sector Strategy," p. 2.

18. U.S. Treasury, "Monthly Report by the Secretary of the Treasury Pursuant to the Mexican Debt Disclosure Act of 1995," p. 1.

19. Ibid., p. 7.

20. Ibid., pp. 4–5.

21. World Bank, "Country Assistance Strategy for the United Mexican States" (Washington, November 25, 1996), p. 3 of 32. *Maquilas* were conversion facilities owned by U.S. investors taking advantage of low-cost Mexican labor. The U.S. operator would ship products such as blue jeans across the border, usually from Texas; the jeans would be sewn together in Mexico and shipped back to the U.S. operator.

22. World Bank, "Mexico Financial Sector Strategy," pp. 2, 12.

23. Cline, *International Debt Reexamined*, p. 495. Cline discusses the prospective macro-adjustment program in some detail on pp. 495–500.

24. U.S. Treasury, "Monthly Report by the Secretary of the Treasury Pursuant to the Mexican Debt Disclosure Act of 1995," p. 85.

25. Cline, *International Debt Reexamined*, p. 499.

26. U.S. Treasury, "Monthly Report by the Secretary of the Treasury Pursuant to the Mexican Debt Disclosure Act of 1995," pp. 500–501.

27. World Bank, "Mexico Financial Sector Strategy," p. 3.

28. Ibid.

29. Ibid.

30. Ibid.; Karaoglan, "Developments and Performance of the Mexican Commercial Banking System in the First Quarter of 1996" (Washington: International Finance Corporation, June 1996), pp. 7–13.

31. World Bank, "Mexico Financial Sector Strategy," p. 7; Karaoglan, "Developments and Performance of the Mexican Commercial Banking System," pp. 4–6.

32. World Bank, "Mexico Financial Sector Strategy," pp. 8–12.

33. Ibid., pp. 4–5.

34. Ibid., pp. 29–30.

35. Ibid., p. 75, quotes a Mexican expert on the bankruptcy law: "In summary, we know of no one who believes that [the bankruptcy law] is a good law, not even a mediocre [law]."

36. Raymond Davies, "Overview of Post-Peso Crisis Mexican Corporate Restructurings and Lessons Learned," Conference on Corporate Restructuring (Seoul, Korea: May 7–8, 1998), p. 113.

37. World Bank, "Mexico Financial Sector Strategy," p. 4.

38. Ibid., p. 115.

39. Peter Jones, "UCABE: A Troubled Debt Restructuring Unit," draft consultant's report to the World Bank, February 1996.

40. Jones, "UCABE," pp. 2–3, 12.

Chapter Eleven

1. Jason Furman and Joseph Stiglitz, "Economic Crises: Evidence and Insights from East Asia," *Brookings Papers on Economic Activity* (September 3–4, 1998): 10.

2. Paul Krugman, "What Happened to Asia?," p. 1 (http//web.mit.edukrugman/www/DISINTER.html).

3. Steven Radelet and Jeffrey Sachs, "The Onset of the East Asian Financial Crisis" (Cambridge Mass: Harvard Institute for International Development, March 30, 1998.) p. 1.

4. Stiglitz and Furman, "Economic Crises," pp. 3–4.

5. I worked for the World Bank throughout the crisis, with oversight over corporate workouts in the various crisis countries, but specifically on the corporate workout program in Korea. I was well aware of the support programs provided by the IMF and World Bank to the crisis countries as well as the extent of the support packages from the G-7. I was deeply involved with the technical and financial assistance provided by the World Bank to Korea.

6. I have added "in excess of trade requirements." Sachs and Radelet, Stiglitz and Furman, and Krugman do not make this distinction, but it is essential. As open export-oriented economies, much of the financing needs of industry were for trade finance to cover imports and the conversion of goods for re-export. In the normal course of events, trade finance is self-liquidating—that is when the goods are exported, the exporter normally gets paid, mostly through letters of credit, and the financing needed in support of the trade is reduced. It is when such financing is used to expand plants and equipment, or more problematically, when it is used for speculation in real estate as in Thailand, that the maturity mismatches become a problem for the banks and the companies. This is especially true when a speculative asset bubble arises: when the bubble deflates, it is hard to sell the assets except at distressed prices, which will then often not cover the debt. Short-term external debt, with maturity under one year, is not reported in official debt statistics by the IMF because it is generally assumed to be trade finance.

7. Radelet and Sachs, "The Onset of the East Asian Crisis," p. 9.

8. Ibid.

9. Ibid., citing IMF board discussions in July 1996, appendix, p. 33.

10. Furman and Stiglitz, "Economic Crises," pp. 15–17; see also exchange rate discussion on pp. 21–24.

11. Ibid., p. 20.

12. Ibid., p. 21.

13. Krugman, "What Happened to Asia?," p. 2.

14. See Masahiro Kawai, Ira Lieberman, and William Mako, "Financial Stabilization and Initial Restructuring of East Asian Corporations: Approaches, Results and Lessons" in *Emerging Markets in the New Financial System: Managing Financial and Corporate Distress* (Brookings 2005), for a discussion of these issues.

15. Joseph E. Stiglitz, *Globalization and Its Discontents* (New York: W. W. Norton, 2002), p. 95.

16. Barry Eichengreen, *Toward a New International Financial Architecture: A Practical Post-Asia Agenda* (Washington: Institute for International Economics, 1999), writes extensively about such reforms and the need for international standards in support of a more globalized and open economy as a reflection on the observed weaknesses in the crisis economies.

17. This issue arises again in Part IV of the book in a discussion of bank bailouts, shadow banking institutions, and capital markets during the U.S. crisis, when both conservatives and liberals in Congress were against bailouts, for different reasons. Also, during the eurozone crisis the European Central Bank was restricted by statute from participating in bailouts.

18. For extensive discussions of financial sector restructuring in Asia, see Gregory Root and others, "Financial Sector Restructuring in East Asia," in *Managing Financial and Corporate Distress: Lessons from Asia*, edited by Charles Adams, Robert E. Litan, and Michael Po-

merleano (Brookings, 2000); David Scott, "Governments as Managers of Systemic Financial Crises: Controlling Costs by Integrating Bank and Corporate Restructuring," in idem.

19. For an extensive discussion of bankruptcy and the resolution of financial distress, see Stijn Claessens, Simeon Djankov, and Ashoka Mody, *Resolution of Financial Distress: An International Perspective on the Design of Bankruptcy Laws* (Washington: World Bank Institute, 2001).

20. David Woo, "Resolution of Nonperforming Assets during Financial Crises: The Role of Asset Management Companies and Out-of-Court Centralized Debt Workout Frameworks," IMF Working Paper (Washington, January 2000), pp. 12, 3.

21. Woo, "Resolution of Nonperforming Assets," p. 13.

22. Daniela Klingebiel, "The Rise of Asset Management Companies in the Resolution of Banking Crises: Cross Country Experience" (draft) (Washington: World Bank, 1999).

23. For a more extensive discussion of the London Rules and corporate workouts in East Asia, see Ira Lieberman and others, "Recent International Experience in the Use of Voluntary Workouts under Distressed Conditions," in *Corporate Restructuring: Lessons from Experience*, edited by Michael Pomerleano and William Shaw (Washington: World Bank, 2005); and Kawai, Lieberman, and Mako, "Financial Stabilization and Initial Restructuring of East Asian Corporations," in *Emerging Markets in the New Financial System*.

24. World Bank, *Global Economic Prospects 2000* (Washington, 2000), pp. 38–39.

25. Stiglitz, *Globalization and Its Discontents*, pp. 91–92.

26. World Bank, *Global Economic Prospects and the Developing Countries: Beyond Financial Crisis 1989/1999* (Washington, 1999), pp. 102–03.

27. Ibid., pp. 104–05.

28. Ibid., p. 102.

Chapter Twelve

1. *Korea's Economy 2003,* Vol. 19 (Washington: Korean Economic Institute and Korean Institute for International Economic Policy, 2003).

2. The war between the Democratic People's Republic of Korea (North Korea) and the Republic of Korea (South Korea) began on June 25, 1950, when the North invaded the South. The United States supported the South and the Chinese the North, resulting in a stalemate. A ceasefire between North Korea and the United States was signed in 1953. Since the split between North and South into two countries, South Korea, the focus of this discussion, has evolved into a democracy. Its first democratically elected president, Kim Dae Jung, took office in the middle of the economic crisis. See also Wonhyuk Lim, "The Emergence of the Chaebol and the Origins of the 'Chaebol Problem'" (draft) (Seoul: Korea Development Institute, October 2000), p. 1.

3. *Korea's Economy 2003.*

4. World Bank, "Korea: Financial and Corporate Sector Restructuring Nexus" (draft) (Washington, September 18, 1998), p. 1.

5. Tight monetary policy encouraged by the IMF led to the sharp rise in interest rates and left all of the chaebols and other large corporations in Korea technically bankrupt. Joseph Stiglitz, the World Bank's senior economist at the time, sharply criticized the IMF's policy

prescriptions for Korea and other East Asian economies. He has also criticized the troika's crisis policies in the eurozone.

6. World Bank, "Korea: Financial and Corporate Sector Restructuring Nexus," p. 1.

7. Ibid., pp. 1–2; *Korea's Economy 2003*.

8. *Korea's Economy 2003*, pp. 8–12; I led the World Bank's support to Korea on corporate restructuring/workouts and had supervisory oversight over a $2 billion balance of payments loan and a $33 million Technical Assistance Facility backed by the government to adopt and implement a corporate workout plan. I was therefore well aware of the details of the funding packages and relative responsibilities of the different funders.

9. I led the advisory work on corporate restructuring and workouts for the World Bank and was responsible for assisting the FSC in retaining international workout groups.

10. Government of Korea, "Korean Economy under New Leadership" (Seoul, December 1998), p. 1.

11. Ibid., p. 5.

12. For convenience, I am using 1,400 won to US$1 as the exchange rate to show the order of magnitude of the bailout program. This was a rate at which the won stabilized against the dollar. The actual rate during this period may have varied.

13. Government of Korea, "Korean Economy under New Leadership," pp. 6–13.

14. Ibid., pp. 14–18.

15. All of these countries had registered foreign banks representing a small percentage of banking assets. They were largely wholesale banks with corresponding relationships to the larger domestic financial institutions. Most were not deposit-taking institutions. In this case, the crisis allowed foreign investors to make substantial inroads into the domestic financial sector.

16. Government of Korea, "Korean Economy under New Leadership," pp. 19–24.

17. Ibid., pp. 24–25.

18. The discussion that follows is drawn from published and unpublished sources. I led the World Bank's corporate advisory team for Korea from late 1997 through 1999. This section is based on my direct knowledge of the corporate workout experience in Korea, from extensive mission reports of February 2, 2008; April 13, 1998; August 17, 1998; October 5, 1998; December 1, 1998; December 16, 1998; January 7, 1999; January 29, 1999; and February 9, 1999. These mission reports are confidential and therefore not quoted directly. There are also published sources, several of which were written by me and my colleague William Mako.

19. Ira Lieberman and William Mako, "Korea—Corporate Restructuring Strategy" (Washington: World Bank, August 17, 1998); Ira Lieberman and others, "Korea's Corporate Crisis—Its Origins and a Strategy for Corporate Restructuring" (Washington: World Bank, October 13, 1998).

20. The debt coverage ratio is a measure of EBITDA—earnings before interest, taxes, depreciation, and amortization—which is a measure of corporate cash flow over debt service; interest payments, which are known from financial statements, and principal can usually be postponed. If the ratio is below 2 or 1.5, the corporation is in distress. Below 1, the company is viewed as unable to meet its commitments. This turned out to be the single best measure among many financial ratios we evaluated for measuring corporate distress.

21. The Korean government and analysts in Korea typically used the following classification to segment the structure of the enterprise sector in Korea: the top five chaebols are the largest groups and considered "too big to fail"; chaebols six to sixty-four are other large conglomerates, large independent firms, and SOEs. Korea had a few very large SOEs, most of which were managed well and were not at the heart of the problem; many SMEs were satellites of the chaebols.

22. Masahiro Kawai, Ira W. Lieberman, and William Mako, "Assessing Corporate Restructuring in Asia: Korea's Corporate Restructuring Program" (mimeo) (Conference on Emerging Markets and Financial Development, Seattle, March 30–April 1, 2000), p. 4.

23. Lieberman and others, "Korea's Corporate Crisis," p. 7.

24. Kawai, Lieberman, and Mako, "Assessing Corporate Restructuring in Asia," p. 5.

25. Government of Korea, "Korean Economy under New Leadership," pp. 25–32.

26. Lim, "The Emergence of the Chaebol."

27. Notes from meetings with the chairmen of Samsung and Daewoo during a World Bank mission, February 6–21, 1998.

28. FSC presentation material for a meeting of April 17, 1999, presided over by the president of Korea.

29. Ira Lieberman and others, "Recent International Experience in the Use of Voluntary Workouts under Distressed Conditions," in *Corporate Restructuring: Lessons from Experience*, edited by Michael Pomerleano and William Shaw (Washington: World Bank, 2005), pp. 69–74.

30. Financial Supervisory Commission, "Corporate Restructuring Agreement," July 1998.

31. Young-Seok Jung, consultant to the World Bank Corporate Advisory Group, "Daewoo Situation and Related Issues" (mimeo) (Seoul, July 28, 1999), p. 1.

32. Goldman Sachs Investment Research, "Korean Investment Strategy, Market Reaction to Daewoo Situation Overdone" (July 26, 1999); "Ailing Daewoo Gets Cash Injection: $5 Billion Package; $50 Billion Debt a Major Risk to Banking System," *Financial Times*, July 27, 1999; "Seoul SE Braced for Another Nervous Week over Daewoo," *Financial Times*, August 2, 1999.

33. Jung, "Daewoo Situation and Related Issues," pp. 2–3.

34. Ibid., p. 4.

35. Ibid., pp. 5–6

36. Masahiro Kwai, Ira Lieberman, and William Mako, presentation at Conference on Emerging Markets and Financial Development, Brookings Institution, World Bank, and IMF, March 30-April 1, 2000.

37. Ibid.

38. William P. Mako and Y. S. Yung, "Daewoo Recent Developments" (Washington: World Bank, November 30, 1999), p. 7.

39. Ibid., pp. 8–12.

40. World Bank, "East Asia Update: Progress in Financial and Corporate Restructuring" (Washington: World Bank, November 2003), p. 6.

41. Government of Korea, "Korean Economy under New Leadership," pp. 29–31.

42. Ibid. I have never seen anything that spelled out conditions or the framework for purchases by the Korean Land Corporation. My understanding on the call arrangement was from discussions with FSC staff. I do know that the Korean government was very concerned about

an asset collapse similar to that experienced by Japan and wanted to shore up the price for commercial real estate.

43. Government of Korea, "Korean Economy under New Leadership," p. 32.

44. For an extensive discussion of chaebol ownership and governance, see Lim, "The Emergence of the Chaebol"; and Jeanne Gobat, "Corporate Restructuring and Corporate Governance" (Washington: IMF, May 14, 1998).

45. Government of Korea, "Korean Economy under New Leadership," p. 33.

46. Ibid., p. 39.

Chapter Thirteen

1. I led a World Bank team focused on privatization and other structural reforms in Turkey during 1993–94 until the crisis made it difficult to pursue privatization at that time. I also worked on Turkey for the World Bank during the financial and economic crisis in 2001 through 2003, and assisted the government and the major commercial banks, through the Bankers Association, in developing a workout program for the corporate sector through the banking system, based on my experience in Korea (as discussed in chapter 12).

2. Maxwell Watson, Peter Keller, and Donald Mathieson, "International Capital Market: Development and Prospects, 1984," Occasional Paper 31 (Washington: IMF, 1984), pp. 73–74. Convertible Turkish lira deposits were created by the government to attract external funds. They were short-term liabilities, primarily bank deposits, guaranteed against currency risks, and they paid a high interest return. Turkey defaulted on these liabilities too, and rescheduled them together with the other external debts.

3. Chandra S. Hardy, *Rescheduling Developing Country Debt, 1956–81: Lessons and Recommendations*, Monograph 15 (Washington: Overseas Development Council, 1982), p. 8, table 2.

4. IMF, "The Fund, Commercial Banks and Member Countries," Occasional Paper 26 (Washington, 1984), p. 17.

5. World Bank, "Turkey: Corporate Sector Impact Assessment," Report 23153-TU (Washington: World Bank, March 2003), pp. 3–4. I was the principal author and task manager for this report with a World Bank team from Washington, D.C., and the Bank's Ankara office.

6. This section is based on Ibid., pp. 3–12.

7. Ibid., pp. 4–5.

8. Ibid., pp. 5–6.

9. Sources of information include the State Institute of Statistics website: www.die.gov.tr /Turkish/sonist/sirket/temmuz2001.

10. World Bank, "Turkey: Corporate Sector Impact Assessment," p. 10.

11. *Turkish Daily News*, October 30, 2000.

12. *Executive Digest*, October 15, 2001.

13. This section is based on Ekrem Keskin, "Recent Developments in the Turkish Economy and the Banking Sector," in Ira W. Lieberman and Zekeriya Yildirim, "Turkey: Corporate Sector Assessment 2002–2005" (mimeo) (Washington: World Bank, 2006), pp. 45–52.

14. This section of the chapter is drawn from Ira W. Lieberman and Zekeriya Yildrim, "Turkey: Corporate Sector Assessment, 2002–2005" (draft) (Washington: World Bank, 2006), pp. 30–43.

15. Ibid., pp. 30–32.

16. Ibid., p. 32.

17. Ibid., pp. 35–39.

18. Ibid., pp. 39–40.

19. Ibid., pp. 40–43.

20. I led the team that worked with the Bankers Association in assisting the banks, supported by the BRSA, to implement this program. The Istanbul Approach was negotiated through the Bankers Association with a committee of ten leading private banks.

21. World Bank, "The Republic of Turkey: An Assessment of the Corporate Restructuring Framework Including the Effectiveness of the Bankruptcy Act, Background Note" (draft) (Washington: World Bank, June 2010), pp. 6–8.

22. Ira W. Lieberman and others, "Recent International Experience in the Use of Voluntary Workouts under Distressed Conditions," in *Corporate Restructuring: Lessons From Experience*, edited by Michael Pomerleano and William Shaw (Washington: World Bank, 2005); World Bank, "Turkey: Corporate Sector Impact Assessment," pp. 55–60, for a detailed description of the IA.

23. Lieberman and others, "Recent International Experience in the Use of Voluntary Workouts under Distressed Conditions."

24. Banking Law 4743, art. 3. The IA was enacted in Banking Law 4743 and in a circular issued by the Banking Regulation and Supervision Agency (BRSA) in February 2002.

25. I led the team that prepared this report. It was based on a series of notes our team prepared each quarter, which we presented to the World Bank director for Turkey and also to the Turkish Treasury, which had oversight over the crisis.

26. This section is drawn from Lieberman and Yildirim, "Turkey: Corporate Sector Assessment," pp. 57–61.

27. Ibid., Annex 1. See spread sheets on a selected number of large groups.

28. Andrew Mango, *Ataturk: The Biography of the Founder of Modern Turkey* (New York: Overlook Press, 1999).

29. In Turkey, SOEs were called state economic enterprises (SEEs). For consistency with other chapters of this book, I am calling them state-owned enterprises (SOEs); Nilgun Gokgur, "Turkish Privatization Proceeds Apace" (Boston Institute for Development Economics, January 9, 2006), mimeo, p. 2.

30. Mango, *Ataturk*.

31. This section is based on Lieberman and Yildirim, "Turkey: Corporate Sector Assessment," pp. 21–27.

32. Gokgur, "Turkish Privatization Proceeds Apace," p. 2.

33. See Ira Lieberman and William Fergusson, "Overview of Privatization and Emerging Equity Markets," in *Privatization and Capital Market Development*, edited by Ira Lieberman and Christopher D. Kirkness (Washington: World Bank, 1998), for a comparative analysis of privatization by regions and key countries; and Ira Lieberman, "Privatization and Capital Market Development in Turkey and Egypt," in idem.

34. Lieberman, "Privatization and Capital Market Development in Turkey and Egypt," p. 80.

35. Lieberman and Yildirim, "Turkey: Corporate Sector Assessment," pp. 23–24.

36. World Bank, "Turkey: Corporate Impact Assessment," pp. 74–75.

37. Serhan Cevik, "On Privatization" (New York: Morgan Stanley, September 19, 2005).

38. Ibid.; see also Lieberman and Yildirim, "Turkey: Corporate Sector Assessment," pp. 27–30.

39. It became clear after a few years of negotiation with the EU that some of the EU member states were prepared to block Turkey's membership. They were simply unprepared to allow a large Muslim country to integrate into predominantly Christian Europe. This has remained an issue between the Erdogan-led government and the EU in recent years.

40. World Bank, "Unlocking Turkey's Potential for Growth and Preparing for EU Accession," in *Turkey: A Country Economic Memorandum, Promoting Sustained Growth and Convergence with the European Union* (Washington, November 18, 2005), draft; Institute of International Finance (IIF), "Summary Appraisal of Turkey" (Washington, July 22, 2005).

Chapter Fourteen

1. World Bank, "Argentina Contingency Plan Outline" (Washington: World Bank, July 13, 2001), p. 1.

2. Ibid.

3. Ibid.; see also Michael Mussa, "Argentina and the Fund: From Triumph to Tragedy" (Washington: Institute for International Economics, March 25, 2002), p. 2.

4. For an extensive discussion of the Argentine crisis, see Mussa, "Argentina and the Fund"; and Paul Blustein, *And the Money Kept Rolling In (and Out): Wall Street, the IMF, and the Bankrupting of Argentina* (New York: Public Affairs, 2005).

5. Mussa, "Argentina and the Fund," p. 2.

6. Barry Eichengreen, "Crisis Prevention and Management: Any New Lessons from Argentina and Turkey?," Background Paper for the World Bank's Global Development Finance 2002 (Washington: October 2001), p. 6.

7. Mussa, "Argentina and the Fund," p. 2.

8. J. P. Morgan, "Data Watch: Argentina" (New York: J. P. Morgan Economic Research, December 14, 2001), p. 25.

9. Ibid., pp. 10–11.

10. Ibid., p. 12.

11. Mussa, "Argentina and the Fund," p. 2; for additional views on the crisis see J. P. Morgan, "Argentina: More Fallout to Come" (Buenos Aires: J. P. Morgan Economic Research, January 7, 2002); J. P. Morgan, "Argentina: Latest Pesification Measures Help Banking Sector, but at What Price?" (Buenos Aires: J. P. Morgan Economic Research, January 23, 2002).

12. Martin Wolf, "Finding Cures for an Ailing Argentina," *Financial Times*, July 15, 2002, p. 9.

13. ING Barings, "More Tears for Argentina" (New York: ING Barings, January 23, 2002), p. 2.

14. Mussa, "Argentina and the Fund," p. 10.

15. Ibid., p. 12.

16. World Bank, "Argentina Contingency Plan Outline," pp. 16–17.

17. Eichengreen, "Crisis Prevention and Management," p. 18.

18. Ibid., pp. 17–18.

19. World Bank, "Argentina's Financial Crisis," Briefing Note (Washington: World Bank, March 2002), p. 1.

20. Ibid., p. 3.

21. Ibid., p. 3.

22. Ibid., p. 5.

23. Standard and Poor's, "The Argentine Banking Crisis: No Turnaround in Sight" (Buenos Aires: May 15, 2002), p. 4.

24. World Bank, "Argentina's Financial Crisis," p. 7.

25. Ibid., p. 1–2.

26. Ibid., p. 3–4.

27. See Standard and Poor's, "The Argentine Banking Crisis," for a discussion on the overall problems of the banking system and the situation of some individual banks; Salomon Smith Barney, "Argentine Financial System" (New York: Salomon Smith Barney, Equity Research: Latin America, February 13, 2002), pp. 9–10, on whether foreign banks should inject more liquidity into their banks.

28. Ricardo Hausmann and Andres Velasco, "The Argentine Collapse: Hard Money's Soft Underbelly" (Harvard Kennedy School of Business, 2002), p. 11.

29. World Bank, "Argentina's Financial Crisis," p. 15.

30. World Bank, "Briefing Note on the Impact of the Crisis on Argentina's Corporate Sector and Potential Resolution Strategies," to Lic. Lisandro Barry, Secretary of Finance, Ministry of Economy (World Bank, February 18, 2002), pp. 1–2. I led this mission with an experienced team of former World Bank Group staff and external consultants.

31. Salomon Smith Barney, "Argentine Financial System," page 3 notes that it is impossible for us [Salomon Smith Barney's analysts] to conceive of the recovery of economic activity in the country without a functioning payment system.

32. Faustino Garza, "Argentina Corporate Debt," Briefing Note (Washington: World Bank, March 30, 2002), p. 2. Garza was a consultant to the World Bank who worked with my team on the possibilities for corporate workouts in Argentina.

33. Ibid., p. 2.

34. "Argentine Crisis Deepens as Peso Tumbles—U.S. Utilities Lobby Washington, Buenos Aires on Behalf of Latin Units," *Wall Street Journal,* March 26, 2002.

35. World Bank, "Argentine Corporate Restructuring: Policy Note" (Washington: World Bank, March 14, 2003), p. 1. Argentine Social Credit and Emergency Law 25.563 suspended executions in bankruptcy proceedings, nearly all individual executions; it also derogated article 48 of the bankruptcy law (on cramdowns) preventing successful out-of-court resolutions between creditors and debtors. This policy note spelled out the necessary conditions for a corporate workout program and for an effective bankruptcy program.

36. I led several missions to Argentina in the first half of 2002 to try and advise the government on a corporate workout program, as I had in Korea (1998–2001) and Turkey (2001–03), where these governments, with World Bank technical advisory assistance, developed and implemented effective workout programs. In Argentina there was effectively "no one home" in government at that time with whom to engage in dialogue.

37. Garza, "Argentina Corporate Debt," p. 3.

38. Hausmann and Velasco, "The Argentine Collapse," p. 4. Hausmann and Velasco offer a highly articulate and sophisticated analysis of the causes of the Argentine crisis that often differs from that of other observers such as Mussa and World Bank and IMG analysis. In my view, they fail to give adequate credit to the chaos in government and frequent turnover of presidents and economy ministers in the period leading up to and during the crisis. Also, Cavallo and others made erratic policy decisions as they tried to stave off the crisis, rather than design and implement a robust resolution strategy with IMF, World Bank, Inter-American Development Bank, and potentially the G-7 and others such as the Spanish government.

39. Mussa, "Argentina and the Fund," pp. 6–9: Mussa discusses the Fund's actions and decisionmaking process leading up to the default and collapse of the Argentine economy. It is a detailed account and provides the best insights among many such documents I have read of an unfolding sovereign crisis and the action of the Fund in support of a sovereign client.

40. Ibid., p. 9.

41. Ibid.

42. Ibid., pp. 3–4.

43. Ibid., p. 19.

44. Ibid.

45. Ibid., p. 20.

46. Ibid., p. 7.

47. Ibid., p. 8.

48. Ibid., p. 9.

49. Blustein, *And the Money Kept Rolling In*, p. 157.

50. J. F. Hornbeck, "Argentina's Defaulted Sovereign Debt: Dealing with the 'Holdouts,'" CRS Report for Congress 7-5700 (Washington: Congressional Research Service, February 6, 2013), pp. 4–6.

51. Hornbeck, "Argentina's Defaulted Sovereign Debt," pp. 8–10; this paper has an extensive discussion of the litigation and various appeals and its impact on Argentina's ability to service the debt under the debt settlements and its inability to raise funds in the capital markets. An additional source is Wikipedia, "Argentine debt restructuring," 2015 (http://wikipedia.org/wiki/Argentine_debt_restructuring).

52. Wikipedia, "Argentine Debt Restructuring," 2015 (http://wikipedia.org/wiki/Argentine_debt_restructuring).

53. Hornbeck, "Argentina's Defaulted Sovereign Debt," pp. 6–7.

54. Wikipedia, Argentine debt restructuring," 2015 (http://wikipedia.org/wiki/Argentine_debt_restructuring).

55. This issue is discussed in the introduction to this book, citing E. H. Carr, *The Twenty Years' Crisis, 1919–1939,* 2nd ed. (London: Macmillan Press, 1946), pp. 187–90; Edwin M. Borchard and William S. Wynne, *State Insolvency and Foreign Bondholders*, Vols. 1 and 2 (Yale University Press, 1951), pp. 127, 235–36; and J. M. Keynes, "Foreign Investment and National Advantage," reprinted from *The Nation and Athenaeum* (August 1924) in *The Collected Writings of J.M. Keynes,* Vol. 19, edited by Donald Moggridge (London: Macmillan Press, for the Royal Economic Society, 1978), p. 277.

56. Hornbeck, "Argentina's Defaulted Sovereign Debt," p. 13.

57. World Bank, "Argentina-Uruguay Technical Briefing Recent Developments," Board Briefing (Washington: World Bank, March 5, 2003), p. 1.

58. Hornbeck, "Argentina's Defaulted Sovereign Debt," p. 14.

59. Floyd Norris, "Argentina Debt Case Has No Victors, Many Losers," *New York Times,* November 21, 2014.

60. The Argentine Congress approved the settlement at the end of March 2016.

61. Julie Wernau and Taos Turner, "Argentina Settles Fund Claims," *Wall Street Journal,* March 1, 2016.

Chapter Fifteen

1. Carmen M. Reinhart and Kenneth S. Rogoff, *This Time Is Different: Eight Centuries of Financial Folly* (Princeton University Press, 2011); Finland is discussed on p. 362, Norway on p. 376, and Sweden on pp. 383–84.

2. Martin Wolf, *The Shifts and the Shocks* (London: Allen Lane, 2014), pp. 299–301.

3. Naohisa Hirakata and others, "Japan's Financial Crises and Lost Decades," Working Paper 220 (Federal Reserve Bank of Dallas, Globalization and Monetary Policy Institute, December 2001), p. 2.

4. Hirakata and others, "Japan's Financial Crises and Lost Decades," p. 2.

5. Hiroshi Nakaso, "The Financial Crisis in Japan during the 1990s: How the Bank of Japan Responded and the Lessons Learnt" (Basel: Bank for International Settlements, October 2001), p. 2.

6. Hirakata and others, "Japan's Financial Crises and Lost Decades," p. 2.

7. This section of the chapter relies extensively on Nakaso's discussion of the banking and financial crisis in Japan from 1997 to 2000 in Nakaso, "The Financial Crisis in Japan during the 1990s."

8. Ibid., p. 2.

9. Ibid., pp. 2–3.

10. Ibid., pp. 4–5.

11. Ibid., pp. 5–6.

12. Ibid., pp. 6–7.

13. Ibid., pp. 7–8.

14. Ibid., pp. 9–10.

15. Ibid., pp. 10–11.

16. Ibid., pp. 12–14.

17. Ibid., pp. 12–15.

18. Ibid., pp. 13–16, 20.

19. IMF, *World Development Report 2015* (Washington).

20. On labor reform, see Che Aoyagi and Giovanni Ganelli, "Labor Market Reform: Vital to the Success of Abenomics," in *Can Abenomics Succeed? Overcoming the Legacy of Japan's Lost Decade,* edited by Dennis Botman, Stephen Danninger, and Jerald Schiff (Washington: International Monetary Fund, 2015).

21. Robert J. Samuelson, "Japan's Stimulus Trap," *Washington Post*, February 4, 2013.

22. Jerald Schiff, "Japan: Number One or Numbered Days?," Comments on a presentation by Millard Long to the 1818 H Society (Retirees) at the World Bank, April 29, 2015. Mr. Schiff was IMF deputy director for Asia and IMF mission chief in Japan; he is coeditor of *Can Abenomics Succeed?*

23. On Japan's aging problem, see Dennis Botman, "Can Abenomics Overcome the Head-winds from Population Aging?," in *Can Abenomics Succeed?,* edited by Botman, Danninger, and Schiff.

24. See Aoyagi and Ganelli, "Labor Market Reform," in *Can Abenomics Succeed?*, edited by Botman, Danninger, and Schiff.

25. Richard S. Koo, *The Holy Grail of Macroeconomics: Lessons from Japan's Great Reces-sion* (New York: John Wiley & Sons, Asia, 2008), pp. 3–5.

26. Ibid., pp. 6–9.

27. Ibid., p. 15.

28. Dominique Dwor-Frecaut, Francis Colaco, and Mary Hallward-Driemeier, eds., *Asian Corporate Recovery: Findings from Firm-Level Surveys in Five Countries* (Washington: World Bank, 2000), p. 103, table 7.7.

29. Koo, *The Holy Grail of Macroeconomics*, pp. 171–74.

30. Atif Mian and Amir Sufi, *House of Debt* (University of Chicago Press, 2014).

31. Koo, *The Holy Grail of Macroeconomics*, p. 52.

32. Ibid.

33. Samuelson, "Japan's Stimulus Trap."

34. Millard Long, "Japan: Number One or Numbered Days?," Presentation to the 1818 H Society at the World Bank, April 29, 2015. Mr. Long was a former director for finan-cial sector operations at the World Bank.

35. Dennis Botman, "Abenomics: Lessons from Two Decades of Conventional and Un-conventional Monetary Policy," in *Can Abenomics Succeed?,* edited by Botman, Danninger, and Schiff, pp. 24–26.

36. Dennis Botman, Stephen Danninger, and Jerald Schiff, "Foreword," in *Can Aben-omics Succeed?*, edited by Botman, Danninger, and Schiff.

37. Dennis Botman, "Can Abenomics Overcome the Headwinds from Population Aging?," in ibid., p. 30.

38. Ikuo Saito, "Japan's Fiscal Risks," in *Can Abenomics Succeed?*, edited by Botman, Dan-ninger, and Schiff, pp. 54–57.

39. IMF, "World Economic Outlook Data Base" (Washington, October 15).

40. Saito, "Japan's Fiscal Risks," in *Can Abenomics Succeed?,* edited by Botman, Danninger, and Schiff, pp. 52–58.

41. Chapter 18 in this volume discusses the rescue of the financial institutions and the TARP in some detail, and chapter 19 examines the impact of the TARP and other rescue measures on the economy.

42. Irving Fisher, "The Debt Deflation Theory of Great Depressions," *Econometrica* (Oc-tober 1933): 337–57.

Chapter Sixteen

1. "The Financial Crisis Inquiry Report," Final Report of the National Commission on the Causes of the Financial and Economic Crisis in the United States (Washington: 2011), p. 123.

2. Henry M. Paulson Jr., *On the Brink: Inside the Race to Stop the Collapse of the Global Financial System* (New York: Hachette Book Group, 2010), p. 170; see pp. 145–70 for the story of the GRE workout; Michael Lewis, *The Big Short* (New York: W. W. Norton, 2011); Andrew Ross Sorkin, *Too Big to Fail* (New York: Penguin Books, 2010).

3. "The Financial Crisis Inquiry Report," pp. 64–65.

4. Adair Turner, *Between Debt and the Devil: Money, Credit, and Fixing Global Finance* (Princeton University Press, 2016), p. 1.

5. Lewis, *The Big Short*; Sorkin, *Too Big to Fail*; "The Financial Crisis Inquiry Report," p. 5.

6. Atif Mian and Amir Sufi, *House of Debt* (University of Chicago Press, 2015), pp. 70–71.

7. Ibid., p. 79.

8. Ibid., p. 104.

9. "The Financial Crisis Inquiry Report," p. 7.

10. Ben S. Bernanke, *The Courage to Act: A Memoir of a Crisis and Its Aftermath* (New York: W. W. Norton, 2015), p. 93.

11. A "waterfall" in this case defines how (expressed as a percentage return) the different layers or tranches of risk were to be compensated and in what sequence.

12. "The Financial Crisis Inquiry Report," p. 129.

13. Anna Katherine Barnett-Hart, "The Story of the CDO Market Meltdown: An Empirical Analysis" (Honors Thesis, Harvard College, 2009), pp. 2–7.

14. Ibid., pp. 94–96.

15. Lewis, *The Big Short*, pp. 70–71.

16. Stephen Mihm and Nouriel Roubini, *Crisis Economics: A Crash Course in the Future of Finance* (New York: Penguin Books, 2015), p. 83.

17. Timothy F. Geithner, *Stress Test: Reflections on Financial Crises* (New York: Broadway Books, 2014), p. 96.

18. "The Financial Crisis Inquiry Report," p. 101.

19. Mihm and Roubini, *Crisis Economics*, p. 33.

20. The term "too big to fail" means that in the event of a financial crisis or banking run the FDIC, the Fed, and/or the Treasury would need to find a way to step in and save these institutions. The commonly used term was "bailout," as opposed to workout or restructuring.

21. "The Financial Crisis Inquiry Report," pp. 52–53.

22. Sorkin, *Too Big to Fail*, p. 175.

23. Joseph E. Stiglitz, *Free Fall: America, Free Markets, and the Sinking of the World Economy* (New York: W. W. Norton, 2010), p. 163; see also pp. 162–64 for a more extensive discussion of the Glass-Steagall Act, the Great Depression, and the consequences of repealing Glass-Steagall.

24. Paulson, *On the Brink*, p. 99; see also Geithner, *Stress Test*, pp. 124–27.

25. "The Financial Crisis Inquiry Report," p. 66.

26. Ibid., p. 255.

27. Bernanke, *The Courage to Act*, p. 231.

28. Paulson, *On the Brink*, p. 18.

29. "The Financial Crisis Inquiry Report," pp. 178–87.

30. Paulson, *On the Brink,* p. 130.

31. Stiglitz, *Free Fall*, pp. 121–27.

32. "The Financial Crisis Inquiry Report," pp. 138–39.

33. Ibid., pp. 260–65.

34. Ibid., p. 259.

35. Geithner, *Stress Test*, pp. 315–18.

36. Ibid., p. 317.

37. Mihm and Roubini, *Crisis Economics*, p. 187.

38. Alan Greenspan, *Age of Turbulence* (New York: Penguin Press, 2007), p. 376.

39. Mihm and Roubini, *Crisis Economics*, p. 33.

40. Paulson, *On the Brink*, p. 125.

41. Ibid., pp. 125–27; a major exception to reorganization of supervisory institutions was a bill passed by the Senate Banking Committee on May 20, 2008, that established a stronger regulator for the GSEs: the FHFA, with the authority to set minimum capital requirements and sound portfolio management standards for the GSEs (p. 135).

42. Geithner, *Stress Test,* p. 96.

43. Ibid., p. 82.

44. "The Financial Crisis Inquiry Report," p. 187.

45. Ibid., p. 155.

46. Stiglitz, *Free Fall*, p. 149.

47. Mihm and Roubini, *Crisis Economics*, p. 33.

48. "The Financial Crisis Inquiry Report," p. 155.

49. Ibid., pp. 146–50. Moody's was a particular test case for the commission, but the three major rating agencies all performed poorly.

50. Mihm and Roubini, *Crisis Economics*, pp. 61–62.

51. Paulson, *On the Brink*, pp. 64–65.

52. Geithner, *Stress Test*, pp. 389–90.

53. Ben S. Bernanke, *Essays on the Great Depression* (Princeton University Press, 2000).

54. Bernanke, *The Courage to Act,* p. 398.

55. Alan S. Blinder, *After the Music Stopped: The Financial Crisis, the Response, and the Work Ahead* (New York: Penguin Press, 2013), p. 5.

56. "The Financial Crisis Inquiry Report," pp. xvii–xv.

Chapter Seventeen

1. "The Financial Crisis Inquiry Report," Final Report of the National Commission on the Causes of the Financial and Economic Crisis in the United States (Washington: 2011), p. 233.

2. Henry M. Paulson, *On the Brink: Inside the Race to Stop the Collapse of the Global Financial System* (New York: Hachette Book Group, 2010), p. 65.

3. Timothy F. Geithner, *Stress Test: Reflections on Financial Crises* (New York: Broadway Books, 2014), p. 148; Andrew Ross Sorkin, *Too Big to Fail* (New York: Penguin Books, 2010), p. 67.

4. Sorkin, *Too Big to Fail*, 5.

5. "The Financial Crisis Inquiry Report," pp. 250–51.

6. Paulson, *On the Brink*, pp. 61–62; Geithner, *Stress Test*, p. 117.

7. Ben S. Bernanke, *The Courage to Act: A Memoir of a Crisis and Its Aftermath* (New York: W. W. Norton, 2015), pp. 164–65.

8. See "The Financial Crisis Inquiry Report," pp. 248–50, on Countrywide's crisis.

9. Geithner, *Stress Test*, p. 122.

10. Paulson, *On the Brink*, p. 72; Geithner, *Stress Test*, pp. 123–27.

11. Geithner, *Stress Test*, p. 122.

12. Bernanke, *The Courage to Act*, p. 210.

13. "The Financial Crisis Inquiry Report," pp. 280–81; see pp. 280–91 for a detailed account of Bear Stearns's problems and ultimate collapse.

14. Alan S. Blinder, *After the Music Stopped: The Financial Crisis, the Response, and the Work Ahead* (New York: Penguin Press, 2013), p. 101.

15. Bernanke, *The Courage to Act*, p. 212.

16. Ibid., p. 215.

17. Stephen Mihm and Nouriel Roubini, *Crisis Economics: A Crash Course in the Future of Finance* (New York: Penguin Books, 2010), p. 105; Paulson, *On the Brink*, pp. 97–121, for a detailed blow-by-blow description of the Bear rescue; see also Bernanke, *The Courage to Act*, pp. 215–22.

18. "The Financial Crisis Inquiry Report," p. 291.

19. Ibid., p. 285.

20. Bernanke, *The Courage to Act*, pp. 226–47; see also Sorkin, *Too Big to Fail*, pp. 185–86. Sorkin discusses Fannie's historical importance dating to the presidency of Franklin Roosevelt as one of the measures used to counter the Great Depression.

21. Bernanke, *The Courage to Act*, p. 232; the intervention by the FDIC in Indy Mac cost some $13 billion; see pp. 241–242 on Washington Mutual (WaMu); Geithner, *Stress Test*, p. 215, discusses the FDIC intervention in September 2008 after the Lehman Brothers failure. WaMu, largely wiped out its shareholders and subordinated debt holders, but also inflicted heavy losses on senior creditors, in effect putting increasing pressure on the other banks such as Wachovia, which was viewed as next in line to fail.

22. Geithner, *Stress Test*, p. 169.

23. Mihm and Roubini, *Crisis Economics*, p. 108.

24. "The Financial Crisis Inquiry Report," p. 312; see pp. 309–23 for a detailed account of the conservatorship of the GSEs.

25. Blinder, *After the Music Stopped*, p. 116; see also pp. 114–19 for another version of Fannie and Freddie's move toward conservatorship and Treasury support.

26. Geithner, *Stress Test*, p. 169.

27. Paulson, *On the Brink*, p. 147.

28. Sorkin, *Too Big to Fail*, pp. 191–92.

29. Paulson, *On the Brink*, p. 147.

30. Ibid., p. 155.

31. Geithner, *Stress Test*, pp. 170–71.

32. Paulson, *On the Brink*, pp. 157–59.

33. Ibid., p. 162.

34. Ibid., pp. 164–67.

35. Ibid., pp. 168–70.

36. "The Financial Crisis Inquiry Report," p. 323.

37. Sorkin, *Too Big to Fail*, p. 108; for the full story on Einhorn and Lehman see pp. 100–108.

38. Ibid., p. 53.

39. Ibid., pp. 54–57; Buffett discussions pp. 109–16; Korea discussions pp. 211, 216–18.

40. Paulson, *On the Brink*, p. 178.

41. Council of Foreign Bondholders (CFBH), Annual Report 1892, pp. 16–17.

42. Paulson, *On the Brink*, pp. 180–81; also see pp. 182–93 on the runup to the Lehman bankruptcy.

43. Bernanke, *The Courage to Act*, p. 264.

44. Paulson, *On the Brink*, p. 199.

45. Geithner, *Stress Test,* p. 188.

46. Ibid., pp. 185–87; Bernanke, *The Courage to Act*, pp. 266–67.

47. Bernanke, *The Courage to Act*, p. 262.

48. Blinder, *After the Music Stopped*, p. 128.

49. Bernanke, *The Courage to Act*, p. x.

50. Ibid.

51. Blinder, *After the Music Stopped*, pp. 130–32.

52. Paulson, *On the Brink*, p. 229.

53. Paulson, *On the Brink*, p. 229.

54. Bernanke, *The Courage to Act*, pp. x–xi.

55. Paulson, *On the Brink*, p. 204–205.

56. Ibid., p. 241.

57. Bernanke, *The Courage to Act*, p. xiii.

58. Geithner, *Stress Test*, pp. 245–46.

59. Ibid., p. 329.

60. "The Financial Crisis Inquiry Report," p. 352.

61. Blinder, *After the Music Stopped*, p. 155.

62. Geithner, *Stress Test*, pp. 213–16.

63. Blinder, *After the Music Stopped,* p. 156.

64. Ibid., p. 157.

65. "The Financial Crisis Inquiry Report," p. 367; see pp. 366–71 for a detailed discussion of Wachovia.

66. Geithner, *Stress Test*, pp. 217, 222–23; see also Blinder, *After the Music Stopped*, pp. 157–61.

Chapter Eighteen

1. Ben S. Bernanke, *The Courage to Act: A Memoir of a Crisis and Its Aftermath* (New York: W. W. Norton, 2015), pp. 292–93.

2. Alan S. Blinder, *After the Music Stopped: The Financial Crisis, the Response, and the Work Ahead* (New York: Penguin Press, 2013), pp. 143–45.

3. Henry M. Paulson, *On the Brink: Inside the Race to Stop the Collapse of the Global Financial System* (New York: Hachette Book Group, 2010), p. 253.

4. Blinder, *After the Music Stopped,* pp. 146–49.

5. Stanley Fischer, "Introduction," in *The Great Recession, Lessons from Central Bankers,* edited by Jacob Braude and others (MIT Press, 2013), p. 2.

6. "The Financial Crisis Inquiry Report," Final Report of the National Commission on the Causes of the Financial and Economic Crisis in the United States (Washington: 2011), p. 373.

7. Bernanke, *The Courage to Act,* p. xx; Paulson, *On the Brink,* p. 252.

8. Bernanke, *The Courage to Act,* p. 299.

9. Paulson, *On the Brink,* pp. 278–80.

10. Ibid., p. 256.

11. Bernanke, *The Courage to Act,* p. 339.

12. Paulson, *On the Brink,* pp. 323–24, 337.

13. Ibid., pp. 256–61; see also pp. 293–300 on the discussions with Congress and the political by-play; and pp. 304–14 for details on the negotiations with Congress on the specifics of the program.

14. This was the process pursued by each of the East Asian crisis countries, as discussed in Part III of this book. The asset management companies and agencies usually took some time to be established, acquire bad assets from the banks, and process those assets for resale. The East Asian economies had mixed results with their asset management companies and agencies. But among the lessons learned from East Asia was that purchasing bad assets from U.S. banks was not a measure likely to stem pressure on the banks and financial markets in the short term.

15. Timothy F. Geithner, *Stress Test: Reflections on Financial Crises* (New York: Broadway Books, 2014), pp. 224–27.

16. See chapter 12 in this volume on the crisis resolution in Korea.

17. Paulson, *On the Brink,* pp. 278–84; Bernanke, *The Courage to Act,* pp. 295–98; see pp. 359–60 on the Mitsubishi transaction.

18. Paulson, *On the Brink,* pp. 319–21.

19. Geithner, *Stress Test,* p. 221; Paulson, *On the Brink,* p. 328.

20. Geithner, *Stress Test,* p. 222.

21. Ibid., pp. 227–28.

22. Paulson, *On the Brink,* pp. 358–59.

23. Ibid., pp. 364–68.

24. "The Financial Crisis Inquiry Report," p. 375.

25. Paulson, *On the Brink,* pp. 363–64; see also Geithner, *Stress Test,* pp. 230–40, for a discussion of the FDIC guarantee program and the capital injection program through TARP.

26. "The Financial Crisis Inquiry Report," p. 374; see also pp. 371–76.

27. Ibid., p. 380.

28. Bernanke, *The Courage to Act,* p. 369; Paulson, *On the Brink*, pp. 402–03; Geithner, *Stress Test,* p. 306.

29. "The Financial Crisis Inquiry Report," p. 381; see also pp. 379–382.

30. Bernanke, *The Courage to Act*, pp. 370–71; Paulson, *On the Brink,* pp. 404–14.

31. "The Financial Crisis Inquiry Report," p. 385.

32. Paulson, *On the Brink*, pp. 425–32; Bernanke, *The Courage to Act*, pp. 373–76.

33. Geithner, *Stress Test*, pp. 254–55.

34. Bernanke, *The Courage to Act*, p. 398.

35. See Anatole Kaletsky, *Capitalism 4.0: The Birth of a New Economy in the Aftermath of Crisis* (New York: Public Affairs, 2010), p. 136, for an expanded discussion of his views of the direct causes of the crisis; see also pp. 128–55 on Mr. Paulson.

36. Blinder, *After the Music Stopped*, p. 257.

37. Geithner, *Stress Test*, pp. 286–87, 291–93.

38. Ibid., p. 288; see Blinder, *After the Music Stopped*, pp. 258–59, for a discussion of the risks.

39. Geithner, *Stress Test*, pp. 311–12.

40. Ibid., pp. 345–47.

41. Ibid., pp. 345–50.

42. Blinder, *After the Music Stopped*, p. 259.

Chapter Nineteen

1. Ben S. Bernanke, *The Courage to Act: A Memoir of a Crisis and Its Aftermath* (New York: W. W. Norton, 2015), p. 163.

2. Atif Mian and Amir Sufi, *House of Debt* (University of Chicago Press, 2015), p. 9.

3. Bernanke, *The Courage to Act,* p. 398; see pp. 401–07 for a more extended discussion of the U.S. crisis.

4. Ibid., p. 411.

5. Henry M. Paulson, *On the Brink: Inside the Race to Stop the Collapse of the Global Financial System* (New York: Hachette Book Group, 2010), pp. 376–81; see also Alan S. Blinder, *After the Music Stopped: The Financial Crisis, the Response, and the Work Ahead* (New York: Penguin Press, 2013), pp. 330–32 for a discussion of Bair vs. Paulson on mortgage relief.

6. Blinder, *After the Music Stopped*, pp. 333–34.

7. Timothy F. Geithner, *Stress Test: Reflections on Financial Crises* (New York: Broadway Books, 2014), pp. 378–79; see also pp. 379–84 for an extensive discussion of efforts to implement the HAMP program.

8. Blinder, *After the Music Stopped*, pp. 320–42, for a detailed discussion of foreclosure issues and efforts by the Bush and Obama administrations to address them.

9. Blinder, *After the Music Stopped*, pp. 324–27.

10. Carol Morales, "About 44 Million in U.S. Lived Below the Poverty Line in 2009 Census Data Show," *Washington Post,* September 16, 2010.

11. Paul Krugman, *End This Depression Now* (New York: W. W. Norton, 2012), pp. 71–90, esp. 82–90; also see Joseph E. Stiglitz, *Re-writing the Rules of the American Economy: An Agenda for Growth and Shared Prosperity* (New York: W. W. Norton, 2015).

12. Branko Milanovic, *The Haves and the Have-Nots—A Brief and Idiosyncratic History of Global Inequality* (New York: Basic Books, 2011), pp. 193–95.

13. Paulson, *On the Brink*, pp. 418–25, 428.

14. Geithner, *Stress Test*, pp. 337–38.

15. Alan S. Blinder and Mark Zandi, "The Financial Crisis: Lessons for the Next One" (Washington: Center on Budget and Policy Priorities, October 15, 2015), p. 9.

16. Blinder, *After the Music Stopped*, pp. 232–34.

17. Krugman, *End This Depression Now*, pp. 116–26.

18. Blinder, *After the Music Stopped,* pp. 248–56.

19. Ibid., p. 250.

20. Ibid., pp. 251–52.

21. Stanley Fischer, "Introduction: Central Bank Lessons from the Global Crisis," in *The Great Recession: Lessons from Central Bankers*, edited by Jacob Braude and others (MIT Press, 2013), p. 2.

22. Ylan Q. Mui, "What If Saving the Economy was the Easy Part?," *Washington Post,* December 26, 2015.

23. Blinder, *After the Music Stopped*, pp. 253–56.

24. Congressional Research Service, "The Cost of Iraq, Afghanistan, and Other Costs of the Global War on Terror Since 9/11" (Washington, December 8, 2014), p. 1; Joseph Stiglitz and Linda Blimes, *The Three Trillion Dollar War: The True Costs of the Iraq Conflict* (New York: W. W. Norton, 2008).

25. Mark Koba, "U.S. Spends $682 Billion on Defense, 10 Next Countries $652 Billion," *NBC News*, February 24, 2014 (2012 figures); in its "2015 Fact Sheet for 2014," the Stockholm International Peace Research Institute estimates the defense costs as US$610 billion, or 3.5 percent of GDP.

26. Blinder, *After the Music Stopped,* pp. 234–35.

27. The Buffett rule is based on an often quoted observation by the very wealthy investor Warren Buffett that his income tax rate should not be lower than his secretary's.

28. Joseph E. Stiglitz, *Free Fall: America, Free Markets, and the Sinking of the World Economy* (New York: W. W. Norton, 2010), p. xx.

29. Stiglitz, *Free Fall,* pp. xii–xiii.

30. Krugman, *End This Depression Now*, p. 22.

31. Blinder and Zandi, "The Financial Crisis."

32. Ibid., p. 2.

33. See "Federal Debt" (http://www.usgovernmentspending.com/federal_debt).

34. Ibid.; see also Wikipedia, "National Debt of the United States" (https://en.wikipedia .org/wiki/National_debt_of_the_United_States).

35. Ibid.

36. Ibid.

37. Ibid.

38. See Francis E. Warnock, "How Dangerous Is U.S. Debt?" (Washington: Council on Foreign Relations, June 2010), for a balanced discussion of foreign holdings of U.S. Treasuries (debt), the recent moves into Treasuries by foreign investors in response to the crisis, and potential risks to fiscal stability in the event of an interest rate rise.

39. See Wikipedia, "National Debt of the United States" (https://en.wikipedia.org /wiki/National_debt_of_the_United_States); see also Terence B. Jeffrey, "CBO: Debt Headed to 103% of GDP; Level Seen Only in WWII; 'No Way to Predict Whether or When a Fiscal Crisis Might Occur Here,'" (http://cnsnews.com/news/article/terence-p-jeffrey/cbo-debt -headed-103-gdp-level-seen-only-wwii-no-way-predict-whether).

40. Ben S. Bernanke, Speech before the National Commission on Fiscal Responsibility and Reform, "Achieving Fiscal Responsibility," April 27, 2010.

41. Stanley Fischer, "The Great Recession: Moving Ahead," Board of Governors of the Federal Reserve Bank, Paper presented at a conference sponsored by the Swedish Ministry of Finance, Stockholm, Sweden, August 11, 2014, p. 3.

42. Fischer, "The Great Recession," p. 3.

43. Geithner, *Stress Test*, p. 516.

44. Robert J. Samuelson, "The Consensus on the Debt Crisis: Do Nothing," *Washington Post*, April 16, 2018, p. A15.

45. Glenn Kessler, "Ryan's Remarks on the Budget Complicate an Already Mind-Boggling Subject," *Washington Post,* April 29, 2018, p. A6.

Chapter Twenty

1. Henry M. Paulson, *On the Brink: Inside the Race to Stop the Collapse of the Global Financial System* (New York: Hachette Book Group, 2010), p. 65.

2. "The Financial Crisis Inquiry Report," Final Report of the National Commission on the Causes of the Financial and Economic Crisis in the United States (Washington: 2011), pp. 250–51.

3. Paulson, *On the Brink,* pp. 61–62; Timothy F. Geithner, *Stress Test: Reflections on Financial Crises* (New York: Broadway Books, 2014), p. 117.

4. Walter Bagehot, *Lombard Street,* 7th ed. (London: C. Kegan, 1978).

5. Martin Wolf, *The Shifts and the Shocks* (London: Allen Lane, 2014), pp. 19–20; Ben S. Bernanke, *The Courage to Act: A Memoir of a Crisis and Its Aftermath* (New York: W. W. Norton, 2015), pp. 164–65.

6. Jens Nordvig, *The Fall of the Euro: Reinventing the Eurozone and the Future of Global Investing* (New York: McGraw-Hill Education, 2014), p. 1.

7. Ibid., pp. 20–22.

8. Ibid., pp. 24–31.

9. Ibid.

10. Steven Pearlstein, "Europe's Symptoms Can Be Found Closer to Home," *Washington Post*, May 19, 2010.

11. George Soros, "Europe Should Rescue Banks before States," *Financial Times*, December 15, 2010, p. 2.

12. Joseph E. Stiglitz, *The Euro: How a Common Currency Threatens the Future of Europe* (New York: W. W. Norton, 2016), p. 89.

13. Nordvig, *The Fall of the Euro*, pp. 33–34.

14. Stiglitz, *The Euro*, p. 8.

15. Nordvig, *The Fall of the Euro*, p. 47.

16. Stiglitz, *The Euro*, p. 116.

17. George Soros, "The Future of the Euro and Germany's Role," Speech at Humboldt University, Berlin (George Soros.com, Newsletter, June 23, 2010), p. 2.

18. Nordvig, *The Fall of the Euro*, pp. 41, 47; Soros, "Europe Should Rescue Banks before States."

19. Bill Marsh and others, "It's All Connected: A Spectator's Guide to the Euro Crisis," *New York Times*, October 23, 2011, p. SR7; the data in the *New York Times* graphic on euro-zone debt are based on BIS data as of June 2011 representing bank holdings of debt and do not include debt holdings of nonbanks—for example, a German corporation lending to a Spanish corporation.

20. Marsh and others, "It's All Connected."

21. Landon Thomas Jr., "Pain Building in Europe's Sovereign Debt Risk," *New York Times*, July 18, 2011, pp. 1–2.

22. Chad Bray, "ING to Repay Netherlands Early for Big Bank Bailout," *International New York Times*, November 6, 2014; ING repaid €10 billion in principal and €3.5 billion in interest and premiums for the loan that was provided in 2008.

23. Wolf, *The Shifts and the Shocks*, pp. 27–28.

24. Ibid., p. 28.

25. Alan S. Blinder, *After the Music Stopped: The Financial Crisis, the Response, and the Work Ahead* (New York: Penguin Press, 2013), p. 420.

26. Patrick Jenkins and Gerrit Wisemann, "How to Recapitalize a Continent's Banks," *Financial Times*, October 7, 2011; "UK Banks Cut Periphery Eurozone Lending," *Financial Times*, November 17, 2011. The articles discuss the wholesale withdrawal of London-based banks from the eurozone interbank market.

27. Peter Spiegel and Alex Barker, "EU Examines Bank Rescue Plan," *Financial Times*, October 5, 2011.

28. Michael Birnbaum and Howard Schneider, "Merkel Backs Aid for European Banks in Dire Need," *Washington Post*, October 6, 2011.

29. "Bank Stress Tests Fail to Tackle Deflation Spectre," *Financial Times*, Companies section.

30. Jack Ewing, "ECB Moves to Head Off Credit Crunch," *New York Times*, December 10, 2012, Global Business section.

31. "Vote for Trichet," *Financial Times*, November 17, 2010.

32. Wolf, *The Shifts and the Shocks*, p. 56.

33. Martin Wolf, "Be Bold Mario, Put Out the Fire," *Financial Times*, October 25, 2011, pp. 1–2, encourages Draghi to be bold to address the eurozone problems as a lender of last resort to both the banks and the sovereigns in difficulty.

34. Tracy Alloway, "Strong Take-up of ECB Loans Expected," *Financial Times*, December 20, 2011.

35. Mary Watkins and James Wilson, in "Banks Turn to ECB for €530 billion," *Financial Times*, February 29, 2012, discuss the drawdown by various European banks of the LTRO three-year facility set up by the ECB.

36. Jack Ewing, "ECB Moves to Head Off Credit Crunch," *New York Times*, December 10, 2011, Global Business section.

37. Ralph Atkins and Claire Jones, "Draghi Takes on German Critics," *Financial Times,* March 8, 2012.

38. Jacob Funk Kirkegaard, "What Europe Must Accomplish at Its Next Summit," Petersen Institute for International Economics, October 7, 2011; Kirkegaard discusses the role of the president of the European Council, Herman van Rumpoy, in trying to get agreement on the EFSF and other collective action to mitigate the crisis.

39. "Market Volatility Limits EFSF Firepower," *Financial Times,* November 11, 2011.

40. Alana Beattie and Peter Spiegel, "IMF Requests $500bn for Bail-out Loans," *FT .com,* January 19, 2012.

41. Landon Thomas Jr., "Europe's Fear: Spain and Greece Sink Together," *New York Times,* May 22, 2012.

42. Wolf, *The Shifts and the Shocks,* pp. 32–34.

43. Blinder, *After the Music Stopped,* pp. 410–11.

44. "European Commission Downgrades Eurozone's Growth Prospects," *Financial Times,* November 11, 2011.

45. "Economic and Financial Indicators," *The Economist,* March 26–April 1, 2016, p. 104.

46. Michael Slackman, "Europe's Financial Crisis Flares before Summit Meeting," *Washington Post*, December 16, 2010.

47. Paul Krugman, "Crisis of the Eurocrats," *New York Times*, May 22, 2014, Editorial Section.

48. Friedrich Heinemann, "Germany's Constraints in the Crisis," in *Europe's Crisis, Europe's Future,* edited by Kemal Derviş and Jacques Mistral (Brookings, 2014), p. 110.

49. Quentin Peel, "European Voters Threaten Crisis Backlash," *FT.com*, November 3, 2011.

50. Harold Meyerson, "The Rise of the Euro-Right," *Washington Post*, May 29, 2014.

51. Jim Yardley and Jack Ewing, "Bloc in Europe Starts to Balk over Austerity," *New York Times*, October 17, 2014; Raphael Minder, "Austerity Backlash Shifts Political Winds in Southern Europe," *New York Times International*, December 22, 2015.

52. Heinemann, "Germany's Constraints in the Crisis," pp. 111–13.

53. George Soros, "Three Steps to Resolving the Eurozone Crisis," *Financial Times*, August 14, 2011.

54. George Soros, "How to Shift Germany out of Its Can't Do Mode," *Financial Times*, June 26, 2012; also note Soros's series of interviews with *Der Spiegel* on these same themes, compiled now in a small book: George Soros with Peter Schmitz, *The Tragedy of the European Union: Disintegration or Revival* (New York: Public Affairs, 2014).

55. Martin Wolf, "Creditors Can Huff but They Need Debtors," *Financial Times*, November 1, 2011; also see Martin Wolf, "Germany Is a Weight on the World," *Financial Times*, November 6, 2013, p. 9.

56. Douglas J. Elliott, "The Financial Sector: Key Issues for the European Banking Union," in *Europe's Crisis, Europe's Future*, edited by Derviş and Mistral, pp. 133–47; the authors discuss the policy decisions that will need to be made to finalize agreement on a Banking Union. Given the recent crisis experience, a key decision is how future bank resolution will be handled, and by whom.

57. Martin Wolf, "Will the Euro Survive?," *Financial Times,* November 8, 2011.

58. Kemal Derviş and Jacques Mistral, "Europe's Crisis, Europe's Future: An Overview," in *Europe's Crisis, Europe's Future,* edited by Derviş and Mistral, p. 6.

59. Ibid., p. 7.

60. Stiglitz, *The Euro,* p. 326; see also pp. 239–305.

Chapter Twenty-One

1. George Soros, "How Germany Can Avoid a Two-Speed Europe," *Financial Times,* March 22, 2011.

2. Asgeir Jonsson, "Why Iceland?," Presentation to the Martindale Program students and faculty of Lehigh University (Reykjavik, April 2010); Thorvaldur Gylfason, "Iceland after the Fall," *Milken Institute Review* (First Quarter 2010); Thorarinn G. Petursson, "Iceland from Boom to Bust and Back Again," Presentation to Martindale Program students and faculty of Lehigh University (Central Bank of Iceland, May 14, 2010).

3. Jonsson, "Why Iceland?," p. 5.

4. Gylfason, "Iceland after the Fall," pp. 44–47; Petursson, "Iceland from Boom to Bust and Back Again."

5. Presentation of the Special Investigation Commission Report, Main Results as Presented by the Icelandic Parliament.

6. Ibid.

7. PriceWaterhouseCoopers, "The Icelandic Crisis," Presentation to the Martindale Center Program at Lehigh University (Reykjavik, April 2010), pp. 27–28.

8. Jonsson, "Why Iceland?," pp. 24–25.

9. Petursson, "Iceland from Boom to Bust and Back Again."

10. Ibid.

11. Jonsson, "Why Iceland?," pp. 24–25.

12. Karin Hammer, "IMF Survey: Iceland Makes Strong Recovery from 2008 Financial Crisis" (Washington: IMF, March 12, 2015), p. 2.

13. Martin Wolf, *The Shifts and the Shocks* (London: Allen Lane, 2014), pp. 45–46.

14. Jens Nordvig, *The Fall of the Euro: Reinventing the Eurozone and the Future of Global Investing* (New York: McGraw-Hill Education, 2014), pp. 50–51.

15. Alan S. Blinder, *After the Music Stopped: The Financial Crisis, the Response, and the Work Ahead* (New York: Penguin Press, 2013), p. 414.

16. Nordvig, *The Fall of the Euro,* p. 53.

17. See Wikipedia, "Greek Government-Debt Crisis Timeline."

18. I was in touch with a senior member of Greece's privatization team and an adviser to two of Greece's finance ministers during the crisis about eventually advising the government on their privatization program. The first bailout took so long to finalize that the assignment never materialized.

19. See Wikipedia, "Greek Government-Debt Crisis Timeline"; also see Ira W. Lieberman, "A Tale of Two Crises: Europe and the United States of America—A Global Perspective" (San Antonio, Tex.: H. J. Simms 2012 Late Winter Conference for Non-Profit and Proprietary Senior Living Providers), p. 16.

20. See Wikipedia, "Greek Government-Debt Crisis Timeline."

21. Nordvig, *The Fall of the Euro*, p. 65; also see an extensive discussion of Greece, Grexit, and the potential breakup of the eurozone, pp. 64–66.

22. Blinder, *After the Music Stopped*, p. 416.

23. See "Government Debt GDP," *Trading Economics* (www.tradingeconomics.com /greece/government-debt-gdp).

24. Nordvig, *The Fall of the Euro*, pp. 53–54.

25. Blinder, *After the Music Stopped*, p. 413, citing Reinhart and Rogoff, "This Time Is Different"; Ira W. Lieberman, "The History of External Sovereign Debt: The Reaction of Creditors and Debtors to Disruption of Debt Service—An International Relations Perspective" (PhD thesis, Oxford University, 1989), pp. 31–32; Greece was in default for fifty years on its initial loans from the London market and agreed to pay interest on these loans only to regain access to that market.

26. Matt O'Brien, "Three Sides to Greece's Bailout Talks, and Three Totally Different Sets of Priorities," *Washington Post*, April 26, 2016.

27. Wolf, *The Shifts and the Shocks*, p. 45.

28. Kemal Derviş and Jacques Mistral, "Europe's Crisis, Europe's Future: Overview," in *Europe's Crisis, Europe's Future,* edited by Kemal Derviş and Jacques Mistral (Brookings, 2014), p. 3.

29. Wolf, *The Shifts and the Shocks*, p. 26.

30. Donal Donovan and Antoin E. Murphy, *The Fall of the Celtic Tiger: Ireland and the Euro Debt Crisis* (Oxford University Press, 2013), p. 197.

31. Nordvig, *The Fall of the Euro*, pp. 54–56; Wolf, *The Shifts and the Shocks*, p. 49, has the bailout at €85 billion, of which €22.5 billion came from the IMF standby facility and the rest from the European Financial Stabilization Mechanism (EFSM) and the European Financial Stability Facility (EFSF).

32. Blinder, *After the Music Stopped*, p. 412.

33. Donovan and Murphy, *The Fall of the Celtic Tiger*, p. 14; see also pp. 14–30.

34. Ibid., pp. 2, 16.

35. Wolf, *The Shifts and the Shocks*, p. 26.

36. Blinder, *After the Music Stops*, p. 419.

37. Wolf, *The Shifts and the Shocks*, p. 49, quoting the acting IMF director for Portugal on Portugal's economic problems.

38. Constant Verkoren and others, "Portugal: Corporate Restructuring," (Washington: IMF, January 2014).

39. Wolf, *The Shifts and the Shocks*, p. 49.

40. Ambrose Evans-Pritchard, "Portugal Banking Crisis Sends Tremors through Europe," *The Telegraph*, July 10, 2014; and Tim Worstall, "Portugal's Banking Crisis Isn't So Much a Banking Crisis as a Corporate One," *Forbes*, July 10, 2014. I visited Portugal twice during the crisis—the first time in 2013 with the troika and the second time in 2015 with just the IMF to evaluate Portugal's approach to out-of-court workouts for the corporate sector, specifically for the thousands of SMEs in default and unable to resolve their defaults and secure new financing. The government's approach to corporate/SME resolution was institutionally weak and offered little capacity to resolve the problem on a systemic basis, forcing many SMEs, as a consequence, into liquidation.

41. I participated with the troika on missions to Portugal in 2013 and 2015 tied to the Portuguese bailout, the problems of NPLs in the banking system, and the government's approach to workouts.

42. Nordvig, *The Fall of the Euro*, pp. 57–59, for a discussion on Italian bond holdings and investors' concerns.

43. Angel Pascual-Ramsay, "Spain: A New Quest for Growth," in *Europe's Crisis, Europe's Future*, edited by Derviş and Mistral, pp. 45–46.

44. Bill Marsh and others, "It's All Connected—A Spectator's Guide to the Euro Crisis," *New York Times*, October 23, 2011.

45. Pascual-Ramsay, "Spain," in *Europe's Crisis, Europe's Future*, edited by Derviş and Mistral, pp. 46–47.

46. Nordvig, *The Fall of the Euro*, pp. 66–69.

47. Pascual-Ramsay, "Spain," in *Europe's Crisis, Europe's Future*, edited by Derviş and Mistral, p. 48.

48. Wolf, *The Shifts and the Shocks*, pp. 50–51; also see Blinder, *After the Music Stopped*, pp. 417–19.

49. Jack Ewing, "In Germany, Little Appetite to Change Troubled Banks," *New York Times*, August 10, 2013, p. B3.

50. Pascual-Ramsay, "Spain," in *Europe's Crisis, Europe's Future*, edited by Derviş and Mistral, pp. 48–63.

51. "Italy Referendum: Prime Minister Renzi Quits as Voters Deliver Stinging Rebuke," *Wall Street Journal*, December 5, 2016.

52. Domenico Lombardi and Luigi Paganetto, "Italy: Strategies for Moving from Crisis to Growth," in *Europe's Crisis, Europe's Future*, edited by Derviş and Mistral, pp. 64–79.

53. Ibid., pp. 72–75.

54. Marsh and others, "It's All Connected."

55. "Bank Stress Tests Fail to Tackle the Deflation Spectre," *Financial Times*, October 27, 2014, Companies section; Paul J. Davies, "Italian Dilemma: To Bend the Rules or Break the Banks," December 5, 2016, discusses the problem faced by the government in providing state aid to Monte dei Paschi under EU regulations.

56. Nordvig, *The Fall of the Euro*, p. 70.

57. Wolf, *The Shifts and the Shocks*, pp. 49–50. Wolf asserts that many of the affected depositors were not in fact Russian and that this bailout discriminated between countries and banks in the eurozone.

Chapter Twenty-Two

1. J. M. Keynes, "Foreign Investment and National Advantage," from *The Nation and Athenaeum* (August 1924), in *The Collected Writings of J. M. Keynes*, Vol. 19, edited by Donald Moggridge (London: Macmillan Press, 1978), p. 277.

2. Carmen M. Reinhart and Kenneth S. Rogoff, *This Time Is Different: Eight Centuries of Financial Folly* (Princeton University Press, 2009), p. 80; the authors provide schedules of serial defaulters on pp. 90–97.

3. World Bank, *Global Economic Prospects, Beyond Financial Crisis 1988/1989* (Washington, 1989), pp. 102–03.

4. Ibid., pp. 104–05.

5. Ben S. Bernanke, *The Courage to Act: A Memoir of a Crisis and Its Aftermath* (New York: W. W. Norton, 2015), p. 163.

6. Carol Morales, "About 44 Million in U.S. Lived Below the Poverty Line in 2009 Census Data Show," *Washington Post,* September 16, 2010.

Index